The
New
Father

—

A Dad's Guide
to the First Year

The
New
Father

A Dad's Guide
to the First Year

Armin A. Brott

Abbeville Press • Publishers
New York • London • Paris

To Tirzah and Talya,
without whom being a dad just wouldn't be the same

EDITOR: Jacqueline Decter
DESIGNER: Celia Fuller
PRODUCTION EDITOR: Leslie Bockol
PRODUCTION MANAGER: Lou Bilka

First edition
10 9 8 7 6 5

For cartoon credits, see page 239.

Library of Congress Cataloging-in-Publication Data
Brott, Armin A.
    The new father : a dad's guide to the first year / Armin A. Brott.
        p.   cm.
    Includes bibliographical references and index.
    ISBN 0-7892-0275-1
    1. Infants.   2. Infants—Care.   3. Father and infant.   I. Title.
HQ774.B777   1997
649′.122—dc21   96-47489

Contents

Acknowledgments 7

Introduction 9

1 WEEK
Coming Home 13

1 MONTH
Getting to Know You 31

2 MONTHS
First Smiles 49

3 MONTHS
Let the Games Begin 67

4 MONTHS
Born to Be... 83

5 MONTHS
Work and Family 102

6 MONTHS
Gaining Confidence 115

7 MONTHS
A Whole New Kind of Love . . 130

8 MONTHS
Perpetual Motion 142

9 MONTHS
The Building Blocks of
Development 153

10 MONTHS
Forming an Identity 172

11 MONTHS
Planes, Trains, and
Automobiles 182

12 MONTHS
There Now, That Wasn't
So Bad, Was It? 197

Selected Bibliography 217

Resources 224

Index 232

Acknowledgments

I'd like to thank the following people (in alphabetical order), whose help has made this book far better—and far more accurate—than it otherwise might have been:

Jim Cameron and the folks at Temperament Talk, whose work on temperament changed my life; Phil and Carolyn Cowan and Ross Parke for their comments, suggestions, and inspiration; Jackie Decter, for her wisdom, insight, patience, sense of humor, and, above all, her sharp eye; Bruce Drobeck, Bruce Linton, and Glen Palm, who, completely independently of each other, have made major contributions to the literature on fatherhood and freely shared their research with me; Celia Fuller, for making me look good with yet another inspired design; Ken Guilmartin and Edward Gordon for their distinct but equally valuable contributions to the sections on music; Amy Handy, for her constructive criticism and for smoothing out the rough edges; Seth Himmelhoch, who more than once magically pulled out from his files precisely what I needed; Pam Jordan, for her wisdom, guts, and encouragement; Jim Levine, for getting everyone together with a minimum of bloodshed; the wonderful, compassionate, and completely selfless folks at the SIDS Alliance; Dawn Swanson, the incredible children's librarian at the Berkeley Public Library, for helping me select—and arrange developmentally—the best kids' books; Eric Tyson, for reviewing, commenting on, and adding to the sections on money and insurance; and finally, Andrea, who put our disagreements aside for the greater good and once again read every word; and my parents, for their hospitality, careful editing, and for not getting too upset when I griped about their parenting techniques—thirty years too late for them to do anything about it.

Introduction

Nobody really knows how or when it started, but one of the most widespread—
and most cherished—myths about childrearing is that women are naturally
more nurturing than men, that they are instinctively better at the parenting
thing, and that men are nearly incompetent.

The facts, however, tell a very different story. A significant amount of research
has proven that men are inherently just as nurturing and responsive to their children's needs as women. What too many men (and women) don't realize is that to
the extent that women are "better" parents, it's simply because they've had more
practice. In fact, the single most important factor in determining the depth of
long-term father-child relationships is opportunity. Basically, it comes down to
this: "Having children makes you no more a parent than having a piano makes
you a pianist," writes author Michael Levine in *Lessons at the Halfway Point*.

"In almost all of their interactions with children, fathers do things a little
differently from mothers," writes researcher David Popenoe. "What fathers do—
their special parenting style—is not only highly complementary to what mothers
do, but by all indications important in its own right for optimum childrearing."

Not surprisingly, then, fathers have very different needs from mothers when
it comes to parenting information and resources. But nearly every book, video,
seminar, and magazine article on raising kids has been geared specifically to
women and to helping them acquire the skills they need to be better parents.
Fathers have been essentially ignored—until now.

How This Book Is Different

Because babies develop so quickly, most books aimed at parents of infants
(babies from birth through twelve months) are broken down by month. The

same goes here. But while the majority of parenting books focus on how babies develop during this period, the primary focus of *The New Father: A Dad's Guide to the First Year* is on how *fathers* develop. This is an approach that has rarely, if ever, been tried. Each of the chapters is divided into three major sections:

What's Going On with the Baby

This section is designed to give you an overview of the four major areas of your baby's development: physical, intellectual, verbal, and emotional/social. A lot of what a man experiences as a father is directly related to, or in response to, his children. So knowing the basics of their growth will help put your own growth into better perspective. Please remember, however, that all babies develop at different rates and that the range of "normal" behavior is very wide. If your baby isn't doing the things covered in the predicted month, don't worry. But if he is six months behind, check with your pediatrician.

What You're Going Through

Because the experience of fatherhood has largely been ignored in parenting books, many men think the feelings they are having are abnormal. In this section we examine at length what new fathers go through and the ways they grow and develop—emotionally and psychologically—over the course of their fatherhood. You're a lot more normal than you think.

You and Your Baby

This section gives you all the tools you need to understand and create the deepest, closest possible relationship with your child—even if you have only half an hour a day to spend with her. In this section we cover topics as diverse as play, music, reading, discipline, and temperament.

Family Matters

A number of the chapters feature a "Family Matters" section in which we discuss a variety of issues that will have a major impact not only on you but also on your family as a whole. Topics include dealing with crying, postpartum depression (which men get too!), childproofing, family finances, and finding appropriate child care.

Why Get Involved?

First, because it's good for your kids. "Everything we know shows that when men are involved with their children, the children's IQ increases by the time they are six or seven," says pediatrician T. Berry Brazelton. Brazelton adds that with the father's involvement "the child is also more likely to have a sense of humor, to develop a sort of inner excitement, to believe in himself or herself, to be more motivated to learn."

In contrast, a father's emotional distance can have a profound negative impact. "Research clearly documents the direct correlation between father absence and higher rates of aggressive behavior in sons, sexually precocious behavior in daughters and more rigid sex stereotypes in children of both sexes," writes Dr. Louise B. Silverstein of New York University.

Second, it's good for you. A mountain of research has shown that fathers who are actively involved with their children are more likely to be happily married and are more likely to advance in their careers. "Being a father can change the ways that men think about themselves," writes Ross Parke, one of the major fatherhood researchers. "Fathering often helps men to clarify their values and to set priorities. It may enhance their self-esteem if they manage its demands and responsibilities well, or alternatively, it may be unsettling and depressing by revealing their limitations and weaknesses. Fathers can learn from their children and be matured by them."

Third, being an involved father is good for your partner and for your marriage. Division of labor issues are the number one marital stressor, and the more support mothers get from their husbands, the happier they are in their marriages and the better they perform their parenting duties. Men whose partners are happy in their marriages tend to be happier themselves. And men who are happy in their marriages are generally more involved in their fathering role. It just never ends; and there's no reason why it should.

A Note on Terminology

He, She, It

In the not so distant past (the present, too, really) parenting books, in which the parent is assumed to be the mother, almost always referred to the baby as "he." While there's an argument to be made that in English the male pronoun is sort of a generic term, I'm pretty sensitive to issues of gender neutrality. And as the father of two girls, I wanted to see at least an occasional "she," just to let me know that what was being said might actually apply to my children. But as a writer, I find that phrases like "his or her," "he or she," and especially "s/he" make for cumbersome reading and awkward sentences. The solution? I decided simply to alternate between "he" and "she" as often as possible. Except in a few specific cases (circumcision, for example), the terms are interchangeable.

Your Partner in Parenting

In the same way that calling all babies "he" discounts the experience of all the "shes" out there, calling all mothers "wives" essentially denies the existence of the many, many other women who have children: girlfriends, lovers, live-in companions, fiancées, and so on. So, to keep from making any kind of statement about the importance (or lack of importance, depending on how you feel) of marriage, I refer to the mother of your child as your "partner," as we did in *The Expectant Father: Facts, Tips, and Advice for Dads-to-Be.*

If Some of This Sounds a Little Familiar . . .

If you read *The Expectant Father* (and if you didn't, it's not too late), you may notice that there's some overlap between the end of that book and the early part of this book. I assure you that this repetition of material is less the result of laziness on my part than of the necessity born of having to cover several of the same important topics in both books.

What This Book Isn't

While there's no doubt that this book is filled with information you can't get anywhere else, it is not intended to take the place of your pediatrician, financial planner, or lawyer. Naturally, I wouldn't suggest that you do anything I wouldn't do (or haven't done already). Still, before blindly following my advice, please check with an appropriate professional.

WEEK

Coming Home

What's Going On with the Baby

Physically

♦ Although most of your newborn's physical capabilities are run by a series of reflexes (see pages 38–43), she does have some control over her tiny body.

♦ She can focus her eyes—for a few seconds, at least—on an object held 8 to 10 inches from her face, and she may be able to move her head from side to side.

♦ She probably won't eat much for the first 24 hours, but after that, she'll want 7 to 8 feedings each day.

♦ She seems to be doing everything at an accelerated pace: at 33 breaths and 120 heartbeats/minute, her metabolism is moving about twice as fast as yours.

♦ Her intestines are moving even faster: she'll urinate as many as 18 times and move those brand-new bowels 4 to 7 times every 24 hours.

♦ Needing to recover from all that activity, it's no surprise that she spends 80 percent of her time asleep, taking as many as 7 to 8 naps a day.

Intellectually

♦ Right from birth, your baby is capable of making a number of intellectual decisions.

♦ If she hears a sound, she can tell whether it's coming from the right, left, or straight ahead.

♦ She can distinguish between sweet and sour (preferring sweet, like most of us).

♦ She also has a highly developed sense of smell. At seven days, she'll be able to tell the difference between a pad sprinkled with her own mother's milk and one from another mother.

♦ She prefers simple patterns to complex ones and the borders of objects (such as your jaw or hairline) to the inner details (mouth and nose).

♦ She can't, however, differentiate herself from the other objects in her world. When she grasps your hand, for example, her little brain doesn't know whether she's holding her own hand or yours.

Verbally

♦ At this point, most of the vocal sounds your baby produces will be cries or animal-like grunts and squeaks.

Emotionally/Socially

♦ Although she's alert and comfortable for only 30 or so minutes out of every 4 hours, your baby is already trying to make contact with you.

♦ When she hears a voice or other noise, she'll become quiet and try to focus.

♦ She's capable of showing excitement and distress, and will probably be quiet when you pick her up.

What You're Going Through

Comparing How You Imagined the Birth Would Go with How It Went

Let's face it: every expecting couple secretly (or not so secretly) hopes for a pain-free, twenty-minute labor, and nobody ever really plans for a horrible birth experience. Even in childbirth education classes, if the instructor talks at all about the unpleasant things that can happen, she usually refers to them as "contingencies"—a word that makes it seem as though everything is still under control.

If your partner's labor and delivery went according to plan, chances are you're delighted with the way things turned out and you're oohing and ahhing over your baby. But if there were any problems—induced labor, an emergency C-section, a threat to your partner's or your baby's life—your whole impression of the birth process may have changed. It's not unusual in these cases to blame the baby for causing your partner so much physical pain and you so much psychological agony. It can happen easily, without your really being aware of it.

So pay close attention during the first few weeks to how you're feeling about your baby. And if you find yourself being angry or resentful of her, or thinking or saying things—even in jest—such as "All the pain is the baby's fault," or (as I did) "The baby had jammed herself in there sideways and refused to come out," try to remember that no matter how brilliant and talented you think your baby is, she was a completely passive player in the entire process. Giving in to the temptation to blame your baby for *anything* at this point can seriously interfere with your future relationship together.

The Brief "Is This Really My Baby?" Phase

The first thing I did after both my daughters were born was make sure they had two arms and legs, and ten fingers and toes. Once all limbs and extremities were accounted for, I quickly looked over both my daughters to see whether they had "my" nose or chin.

Later on, I felt a little guilty about that—after all, shouldn't I have been hugging and kissing my daughters instead of giving them a full-body inspection? Maybe, but as it turns out, that's what almost all new fathers do within the first few minutes after the birth of their babies. "They immediately look for physical similarities to validate that the child was theirs," says researcher Pamela Jordan. And this happens for a reason: for almost all new fathers—regardless of how many of their partner's prenatal doctor appointments they went to, how many times they heard the baby's heartbeat or saw him squirm around on an ultrasound, and how many times they felt him kick—the baby isn't "real" until *after* the birth, when father and baby have a chance to meet each other face to face. "Seeing the infant emerge from his mate's body through vaginal or cesarean birth is a powerful experience for each father," writes Jordan. "Birth proved that this infant had been the growth within the mother's abdomen."

As it turns out, only one of my daughters has "my" chin, and it's looking like both of them will go through life without my nose (and, hopefully, the accompanying sinus problems). But what I really found disheartening at the time was that neither of them shared the Brott family webbed toes (it isn't all that noticeable, but it helps my swimming immeasurably).

Babies hardly ever look exactly as you imagined they would before they were born. And being disappointed about a nose, a chin, or even some toes is something you'll get over soon enough—especially when you discover in a few weeks that the baby does have something of yours (they always do).

But what if the baby has a penis or a vagina when you were expecting the opposite? Getting a boy when you expected a girl, or vice versa, can be a real shock. "When one's fantasy is not fulfilled, there is a period of regret for what might have been," writes Ellen Galinsky, head of the Work and Family Institute. "And this unhappiness can stand in the way of the parents' reaching out, accepting the baby."

Fortunately, things don't have to be this way. The conflict between fantasy and reality, says Galinsky, "can also be the trigger point for growth—one can either stay still, hang onto the old feeling, or one can change."

At Long Last, Reality

At some point not long after the baby is born, just about every new father gets hit with a sharp jolt of reality: he's a father, with new responsibilities, new pressures, new expectations to live up to. For some new fathers, this seemingly basic epiphany comes early, before they leave the hospital. For others, reality may not hit for a few days. But whenever it happens, a new father's realization that his life has changed forever can have some interesting results.

Only a day after the birth of his daughter, Hannah, Ken Canfield pulled into his driveway. "I . . . stared out through the windshield at the wooden steps leading up into our house," he writes in *The Heart of a Father*. "The steps were rickety. One board was a little rotten on one end, and the rusty nails had gouged their way to the surface. Another board had warped up off the supports. I had never given any thought to those steps before . . . but the thought occurred to me that in less than 48 hours, a new mother carrying a new baby would be climbing those rickety stairs. So, exhausted as I was, with blood-shot eyes and the aroma of my sleepless hospital visit about me, I got out the power saw, some wood, a handful of nails, a square, and a hammer. For the next three hours I built steps."

You and Your Baby

Getting to Know Each Other

"Most people make babies out to be very complicated," says comedian Dave Barry, "but the truth is they have only three moods: Mood One: Just about to cry. Mood Two: Crying. Mood Three: Just finished crying. Your job, as a parent, is to keep the baby in Mood Three as much as possible." With just a few days of fatherhood under your belt you may be inclined to go along with Barry's summary. But the real truth is that babies' moods are a bit more subtle.

In the previous book in this series, *The Expectant Father: Facts, Tips, and Advice for Dads-to-Be,* I discussed the six clearly defined behavioral states that are evident within moments of every baby's birth. "By recognizing them and realizing when they occur and what the expected responses are in each," write Marshall and Phyllis Klaus, authors of *The Amazing Newborn,* "parents not only can get to know their infants but also can provide most sensitively for their needs."

In my first few weeks of fatherhood, I found that learning about these six states was absolutely critical to my getting to know my babies. So I thought it would be worthwhile to go over them again. Here, then, is a summary of the six states, based on the Klauses' wonderful book.

QUIET ALERT

Babies in the quiet alert state rarely move—all their energy is channeled into seeing and hearing. They can (and do) follow objects with their eyes and will even imitate your facial expressions.

Within the first hour of life, most infants have a period of quiet alertness that lasts an average of forty minutes. During his or her first week, the normal baby spends only about 10 percent of any twenty-four-hour period in this state. It is in this state, however, that your baby is most curious and is absorbing information about his or her new world. And while the baby is in this state, you will first become highly aware that there's a real person inside that tiny body.

ACTIVE ALERT

In the active alert state, the baby will make small sounds and move his or her arms, head, body, face, and eyes frequently and actively.

The baby's movements usually come in short bursts—a few seconds of activity every minute or two. Some researchers say these movements are designed to give parents subtle clues about what the baby wants and needs. Others say these movements are just interesting to watch, and therefore promote parent–infant interaction.

CRYING

Crying is a perfectly natural—and for some, frequent—state (for more on this, see pages 39, 42–45). The infant's eyes may be open or closed, the face red, and the arms and legs moving vigorously.

Often just picking up the baby and walking around with him or her will stop the crying. Interestingly, researchers used to think that babies were soothed by being held or rocked in the upright position. It turns out, though, that what makes them stop crying is not *being* upright, but the movement that gets them there.

Keep in mind, too, that crying is not a bad thing—it not only allows the baby to communicate but also provides valuable exercise. So if your efforts to calm aren't immediately successful (and the baby isn't hungry or stewing in a dirty diaper), don't worry; chances are the tears will stop by themselves in a few minutes.

DROWSINESS

Drowsiness is a transition state that occurs as the baby is waking up or falling asleep. There may still be some movement, and the eyes will often look dull or unfocused. Leave the baby alone to drift off to sleep or move into one of the alert stages.

QUIET SLEEP

During quiet sleep the baby's face is relaxed and the eyelids are closed and still. There are no body movements and only tiny, almost imperceptible mouth movements.

When your baby is in this state, you may be alarmed at the lack of movement and be afraid she has stopped breathing. If so, lean as close as you can and listen for the baby's breath. Otherwise, gently put a hand on the baby's stomach (if she's sleeping on her back) or back (if she's sleeping on her stomach) and feel it rise and fall. (For information on back versus stomach sleeping, see page 69.) Try to resist the urge to wake the baby up—most newborns spend up to 90 percent of their first few weeks sleeping.

ACTIVE SLEEP

Eyes are usually closed, but may occasionally flicker open. The baby may also smile or frown, make sucking or chewing movements, and even whimper or twitch—just as adults do in their active sleep state.

Half of a baby's sleep time is spent in quiet sleep, the other half in active sleep, with the two states alternating in thirty-minute shifts. So, if your sleeping baby starts to stir, whimper, or seems to be waking up unhappy, wait a few seconds before you pick him up to feed, change, or hold. Left alone, he may well slip back into the quiet sleep state.

Newborn babies are capable of a lot more than crying, sleeping, filling their diapers, and looking around. Just a few hours out of the womb, they are already trying to communicate with those around them. They can imitate facial expressions, have some control over their bodies, can express preferences (such as for simple patterns over more complex ones), and have remarkable memories.

Marshall Klaus describes playing a game with an eight-hour-old girl in which he asked one colleague (who was a stranger to the baby) to stick out her tongue slowly while holding the baby. After a few seconds, the baby imitated the woman. Then Dr. Klaus took the baby and passed her around to twelve other doctors and nurses who were participating in the game, all of whom were told not to stick their tongues out. When the baby finally came back to the first doctor, the baby—without any prompting—immediately stuck out her tongue again. Even at just a few hours old, she had apparently remembered her "friend."

Interacting with the Baby

Although it may be tempting just to sit and stare at your baby, marveling at every little thing she does, you'll need to do a lot more than that if you're really going to get to know her. Here are some of the best ways to get to know your child:

♦ **Hold her.** Newborns love to be carried around, whether held in your arms or in a pack.

♦ **Talk to her.** No, she can't understand a word you're saying. In fact, she barely even knows you exist. But talk to her anyway—explain everything you're doing as you're doing it, tell her what's happening in the news, and so forth—it will help her get to know the rhythm of the language.

♦ **Change his diapers.** It doesn't sound like much fun, but it's a great time to interact with the baby one on one, to rub his soft belly, tickle his knees, kiss his tiny fingers. For at least the first month or so, he needs to be changed every two hours—a baby's super-sensitive skin shouldn't stew in human waste—so there are plenty of opportunities. And don't worry: changing diapers is an acquired skill; in just a few days you'll be able to do it with your eyes closed (although you probably shouldn't). In the mean-time, even if you don't do it right, baby stool washes right off your hands and won't stain your clothes. One hint, though: immediately after undoing the diaper, put something (such as a towel or cloth diaper) over baby for a few seconds. The sudden rush of fresh air on the baby's crotch can result in your getting sprayed.

A Note on Diapers and Wipers

It seems as though you can hardly do anything anymore without having to make choices—do you want the Tastes Great kind of beer or the Less Filling kind? do you want toothpaste with tartar control or with peroxide and baking soda? Fortunately, most of the choices we make are pretty easy. But some come with their very own built-in political controversy: Death penalty or life in prison? Smoking or non-smoking? Paper or plastic? Well, now that you're a parent, you can add "Disposable diapers or cloth?" to your list.

Americans throw away some eighteen billion disposable diapers a year, enough to constitute more than 1 percent of the nation's landfill. Disposables are made of plastic and will stay in their present form for about five hundred years. "Biodegradable" disposables are available in some places, but some environmentalists have complained that they use *more* plastic than the regular kind and take just as long to break down.

Cloth diapers, in contrast, are all natural. The problem is that they're made of cotton, which is taxing on farmland. And in order to sterilize cloth diapers properly, diaper services wash them seven times in near-boiling water, con-suming huge amounts of power, water, and chemical detergents. The diapers are then delivered all over town in trucks that fill the air with toxic pollutants. One study concluded that "use of a diaper service appears to consume three times as much fuel and cause nine times as much air pollution as use of disposable diapers."

Tough choice, and it's all yours.

And let's not forget the cost factor:

♦ **Disposable diapers:** $8 to $9 for a package of forty-four newborn size. As your baby and his diapers get bigger, the number of diapers per package goes down, but the cost per package stays about the same. Since you'll be using 5 to 8 diapers a day, this option can get pretty pricey. But if you keep your eyes out for coupons (most parenting magazines have a bunch of them in every issue), you can save a lot. In addition, places like Toys "Я" Us have generic or house brands that are a lot cheaper and usually just as good.

Some people say that kids who grow up with disposable diapers tend to become potty trained later than those who use cloth. Apparently, the disposable kind keep so much moisture away from the baby's bottom that the baby stays comfortable for a longer time.

♦ **Cloth diapers:** about $12 for a package of six. The availability and cost of diaper cleaning services vary greatly around the country. If you sign up with a diaper service, you'll probably start with about eighty diapers per week. If you're doing your own laundry, you should buy about forty.

Even if you decide against using cloth diapers for the baby, buy a dozen anyway—they're great for drying baby bottoms on changing tables and for draping over your shoulder to protect your clothes when your baby spits up.

Whichever you choose, make sure you stay away from commercial baby wipes for the first few weeks; they contain too many chemicals for brand-new skin. Use warm, wet washcloths instead. If you're taking the baby out during this period, bring along some moistened disposable washcloths in a resealable plastic bag. Finally, skip the lotions for a few weeks (again, too many chemicals and potential allergens) and never, never use powders (besides being a carcinogen, powder can cause pneumonia if inhaled).

If you happen to have been raised in a family that doesn't think a baby is properly changed unless her bottom is covered in white powder, try using cornstarch. Some people find that corn starch (which doesn't have the same health hazards as traditional baby powder) absorbs moisture and reduces diaper rash. But remember, you're not baking a cake here: a little goes a long way.

What about Play?

During the first few weeks, forget about football and chess. But try to spend at least twenty minutes a day (in five-minute installments) doing something with the baby one on one. Chatting, reading aloud, rocking, making faces,

Different Isn't Bad, It's Just Different

From the moment their children are born, men and women have very different ways of handling them. Men tend to stress the physical and high-energy more, women the social and emotional. Your baby will catch on to these differences within days, and she'll begin to react to you and your partner very differently. When she's hungry, she'll be more easily soothed by your partner (if she's breastfeeding), but she'll be happier to see you if she wants some physical stimulation. Don't let anyone tell you that the "guy things" you do are somehow not as important as the "girl things" your partner may do (or want *you* to do). Ultimately your baby needs both kinds of interactions, and it's a waste of time to try to compare or rate them. Just be gentle.

experimenting with the baby's reflexes (see pages 38–43) or even simply catching her gaze and looking into her eyes are great activities. Here are a couple of things to remember:

♦ **Take your cues from the baby.** If she cries or seems bored, stop what you're doing. Too much playing can make your child fussy or irritable, so limit play sessions to five minutes or so.

♦ **Schedule your fun.** The best time for physical play is when the baby is in the active alert state; playing with toys or books is fine during the quiet alert state (see page 17). Also, choose a time when your full attention can be devoted to the baby—no phone calls or other distractions.

♦ **Be encouraging.** Use lots of smiles and laughter as well as verbal encouragement. Although the baby can't understand the words, she definitely understands the feelings. Even at only a few days old, she'll want to please you, and lots of reinforcement will help build her self-confidence.

♦ **Be gentle.** Because babies' heads are relatively large (one-quarter of their body size at birth versus one-seventh by the time they're adults) and their neck muscles are not yet well developed, their heads tend to be pretty floppy for the first few months. Be sure to support the head from behind at all times, and avoid sudden or jerky motions. *Never* shake your child. This can make their little brains rattle around inside their skulls, causing bruises or permanent injuries. Never throw the baby up in the air. Yes, your father may have done it to you, but he shouldn't have. It looks like fun but can be extremely dangerous.

Family Matters

Coming Home

Boy, has your life changed. You're still your partner's lover and friend, just as you were a few weeks ago, but now, of course, you're also a father. You may be worried about how you're going to juggle all your various roles, but for a few days the most important thing you can do is to be a solid support person to your partner. Besides her physical recovery (which we'll talk more about below), she's going to need time to get to know the baby and to learn (if she chooses to) how to breastfeed.

Your first days as a father will be awfully busy—mine sure were: cooking, shopping, doing laundry, fixing up the baby's room, getting the word out, screening phone calls and visitors, and making sure my partner got plenty of rest.

Recovery

As far as the baby is concerned, there's not much to do in the beginning besides feeding, changing, and admiring. But your partner is a different story. Despite whatever you've heard about women giving birth in the fields and returning to work a few minutes later, that's not the way things usually happen. Having a baby is a major shock—physically and emotionally—to a woman's system. And, contrary to popular belief, the recovery period after a vaginal birth is not necessarily any shorter or easier than the recovery period after a C-section. In fact, my wife—who has delivered both ways—says recovering from the C-section was a lot easier.

Physically, whatever kind of delivery your partner has, she'll need some time—probably more than either of you think—to recover fully. Fatigue, breast soreness, and lingering uterine contractions may not disappear for months, and vaginal discomfort, hemorrhoids, poor appetite, constipation, increased perspiration, acne, hand numbness or tingling, dizziness, and hot flashes may continue for weeks after delivery. In addition, between 10 and 40 percent of women feel pain during sexual intercourse (which they won't get around to for a few months anyway, so don't bother thinking about it), have respiratory infections, and lose hair for three to six months.

Emotionally, your partner isn't much better off. She's likely to be a little impatient at her lack of mobility, and while she's undoubtedly excited to be a mother and relieved that the pregnancy is finally over, she may well experience at least some postpartum depression (see pages 45–47). Now that the baby

Pets

Don't expect your pet to be as excited as you are about the birth of your baby; many dogs and cats do not appreciate their new (lower) status in your house. To minimize the trauma for your pet (and to minimize the chance your pet will do something to harm the baby), try to get your pet used to the baby as early as possible.

You can do this even before the baby comes home by putting a blanket in the baby's bassinet in the hospital, then rushing the blanket home to your pet. It'll give Rover or Fluffy a few days (or hours, at least) to get used to the interloper's smell.

"Homewrecker!"

is really here, she may feel a lot of pressure to assume her new role as mother and to breastfeed properly. Fortunately, as she and the baby get to know each other, her confidence will grow and a lot of her anxieties should disappear.

Here are some things you can do to make the recovery process as easy as possible and to start parenting off on the right foot:

♦ Help your partner resist the urge to do too much too soon.
♦ Take over the household chores or ask someone else to help. And if the house is a mess, don't blame each other.

Parents, In-Laws, Siblings, and Other "Helpers"

One of the most common questions you'll hear from people is whether they can help out in any way. Some people are serious; others are just being polite. You can tell one group from the other by keeping a list of chores that need to be done and asking them to take their pick.

Be particularly careful about accepting offers of help from people—especially parents (yours or hers)—who arrive on your doorstep with suit-cases and open-ended travel arrangements. New grandparents may have more traditional attitudes toward parenting and may not be supportive of your involvement with your child. They may also have very different ideas about how babies should be fed, dressed, carried, played with, and so on.

The same can be said for just about anyone else who offers to move in with you for a few days, weeks, or months to "help out," especially people who have their own kids. With all your other responsibilities, the last thing you want to do is play host to a bunch of relatives. If someone does stay with you to help out after the birth, make sure he or she understands that although you appreciate their help and their suggestions, you and your partner are the baby's parents and what the two of you say ultimately goes.

♦ Be flexible. Expecting to maintain your normal, prefatherhood schedule is unrealistic, especially for the first six weeks after the birth.
♦ Be patient with yourself, your partner, and the baby. You're all new at this.
♦ Be sensitive to your partner's emotions. Her emotional recovery can take just as long as her physical one.
♦ Make sure to get some time alone with the baby. You can do this while your partner is sleeping or, if you have to, while you send her out for a walk.
♦ Control the visiting hours and the number of people who can come at any given time. Dealing with visitors takes a lot more energy than you might think. And being poked, prodded, and passed around won't make the baby very happy. Also, for the first month or so, ask anyone who wants to touch the baby to wash his or her hands first.
♦ Keep your sense of humor.

Feeding the Baby: Breast versus Bottle

At the time most of the people reading this book were born, breastfeeding was out of style and most women our mothers' age were given a wide variety of reasons (by their doctors, of course) not to breastfeed. But in the nineties you'd be hard-pressed to find anyone in the medical community who doesn't agree that breast-feeding is just about the best thing you can do for your child. Here's why:

FOR THE BABY

♦ Breast milk provides exactly the right balance of nutrients needed by your newborn. In addition, breast milk contains several essential fatty acids that are not found in baby formula.

♦ Breast milk adapts, as if by magic, to your baby's changing nutritional needs. Neither of our children had a single sip of anything but breast milk for the first seven or eight months of life, and they're both wonderfully healthy kids.

Just Because You Don't Have Breasts Doesn't Mean You Can't Help Breastfeed

Sounds strange, but *you* play a major role in determining how long—and how well—your partner will breastfeed. Several studies have shown that women breastfeed longer when their partners learn about breastfeeding (which you'll do as you read these pages). And English breastfeeding expert Sheila Kitzinger has found that besides learning, the father's support and confidence in his partner are decisive factors in the mother's desire and ability to breastfeed.

- Breastfeeding greatly reduces the chance that your baby will develop food allergies. If either of your families has a history of food allergies, you should withhold solid foods for at least six months.
- Breastfed babies are less prone to obesity in adulthood than formula-fed babies. This may be because with the breast it's the baby—not the parent—who decides when to quit eating.
- Breastfed babies have a greatly reduced risk of developing respiratory and gastrointestinal illness.
- Breastfeeding is thought to transmit to the infant the mother's immunity to certain diseases.

Just Because Your Partner Has Breasts Doesn't Mean She Knows How to Use Them

As natural as breastfeeding appears to be, your partner and the baby may need anywhere from a few days to a few weeks to get the hang of it. The baby won't immediately know how to latch on to the breast properly, and your partner—never having done this before—won't know exactly what to do either. This initial period, in which cracked and even bloody nipples are not uncommon, may be quite painful for your partner. And with the baby feeding six or seven times a day, it may take as long as two weeks for your partner's nipples to get sufficiently toughened up.

Surprisingly, your partner won't begin producing any real milk until two to five days after the baby is born. But there's no need to worry that the baby isn't getting enough food. Babies don't eat much the first 24–48 hours, and any sucking they do is almost purely for practice. Whatever nutritional needs your baby has will be fully satisfied by the tiny amounts of colostrum your partner produces. (Colostrum is a kind of premilk that helps the baby's immature digestive system get warmed up for the task of digesting real milk later.)

Overall, the first few weeks of breastfeeding can be very stressful for your partner. If this is the case, do not be tempted to suggest switching to bottles. Instead, be supportive, praise her for the great job she's doing, bring her something to eat or drink while she's feeding, and encourage her to keep trying. You also might ask your pediatrician for the name of a local lactation consultant (what a job!).

♦ It's convenient—no preparation, no heating, no bottles or dishes to wash . . .

♦ It's free. Formula can cost a lot of money.

♦ It gives your partner a wonderful opportunity to bond with the baby. In addition, breastfeeding will help get your partner's uterus back into shape and may reduce her risk of both ovarian and breast cancer.

♦ In most cases, there's always as much as you need, and never any waste.

♦ Your baby's diapers won't stink. It's true. Breastfed babies produce stool that—especially when compared to formula stools—doesn't smell half bad.

What If Your Partner Doesn't Breastfeed

JUICE

If you and your partner decide not to breastfeed or decide to supplement breastfeeding with a bottle, don't fill it with juice. A recent study found that children who drink large quantities of fruit juice—especially apple juice— suffer from frequent diarrhea and, in the worst cases, may fail to grow and develop normally. The problem is that babies love juice so much that, if you give them all they want, they'll fill up their tiny stomachs with it, leaving no room for the more nutritious foods they need. The American Dietetic Association recommends that parents refrain from giving their babies juice until they're at least six months old, and then restrict juice intake until age two.

FORMULA

Prices vary. You can use powdered, full-strength liquid, or liquid concentrate. But when you start checking formula prices, your partner may decide to keep breastfeeding a while longer. When we weaned our older daughter, we put her on the powdered formula; I made a pitcher of it every morning and kept it in the refrigerator.

A Few Cosmetic Details

SKIN

Before my first daughter was born, I'm pretty sure that I believed that she— even right after her birth—would look radiant and have clear, glowing skin. Well, chalk up another victory for the ad execs. The fact is that in most cases, babies' skin isn't radiant or clear. But before you panic and call a dermatologist, here are some of the more common, and perfectly normal, newborn skin conditions you should know about:

♦ **Acne.** These cute little pimples are usually confined to the baby's face and are either the result of your partner's hormones continuing to swim through the baby's system or of his underdeveloped pores. Either way, don't squeeze, poke, pick at, or scrub these pimples. Just wash them with water a few times a day, pat them dry, and they'll go away in a few months.

♦ **Blisters.** Pictures taken of babies in utero have shown that long before birth, they frequently suck their thumbs—or any other part of their body they can reach. Sometimes they suck so hard they raise blisters.

♦ **Jaundice.** If your baby's skin and/or the whites of his eyes seem a little yellow, he may have jaundice. This condition is the result of the baby's liver being unable adequately to process bilirubin, a yellowish by-product of red blood cells. It affects about 25 percent of newborns (and a higher percentage of preemies), appears within the first five days of life, and is usually gone a few days later.

♦ **Splotches, blotches, birthmarks.** They can be white, purple, brown, or even yellow with white bumps in the center, and they can appear on the face, legs, arms, back. In most cases, they'll go away on their own if you just leave them alone. But if you're really worried, check with your pediatrician.

♦ **Cradle cap.** Also called seborrheic dermatitis, cradle cap looks like flaky, yellowish, sometimes greasy dandruff. It usually shows up on the head, but can also work its way into baby's eyebrows. It isn't a serious condition and will bother you much more than it does the baby. Frequent shampooing with a baby shampoo will help it go away.

CLEANING

Your baby's umbilical cord stump will drop off anywhere from one to three weeks after she's born. Until then, limit your baby-washing efforts to sponge baths. Keep the stump as dry as possible and clean it with rubbing alcohol on a cotton swab every time you change her diaper. Folding down the front of the diaper exposes the stump to more air and speeds up the falling-off process.

Until your baby starts moving around by herself, don't bathe her any more often than three times a week. (You may take a shower every day, but until she starts crawling, she's unlikely to do anything that would get her terribly dirty.) Any more than that could unnecessarily dry her skin. A few exceptions: it's okay to clean the baby's face every day, and be sure to carefully clean everything covered up by her diapers every time you change one.

For Boys Only

I'm assuming that by now, you and your partner have already made your decision about whether or not to circumcise your son. Whatever your choice, your son's penis requires some special care.

THE CIRCUMCISED PENIS

The penis will be red and sore for a few days after the circumcision. Until it's fully healed, you'll need to protect the newly exposed tip and keep it from sticking to the inside of his diaper (a few tiny spots of blood on his diapers for a few days, however, is perfectly normal). Ordinarily, you'll need to keep the penis dry, and the tip lubricated with petroleum jelly or antibiotic ointment and wrapped in gauze to protect it from urine, which is very irritating. The person who performed the circumcision or the hospital nursing staff will be able to tell you how long to keep the penis covered and how often to change the bandages.

THE UNCIRCUMCISED PENIS

Even if you elect not to circumcise your son, you'll still have to spend some time taking care of his penis. The standard way to clean an uncircumcised penis is to retract the foreskin and gently wash the head of the penis with mild soap and water. However, 85 percent of boys under six months have foreskins that don't retract, according to the American Academy of Pediatrics. If this is the case with your son, do not force it. Check with your pediatrician immediately and follow his or her hygiene instructions carefully. Fortunately, as boys get older, their foreskins retract on their own; by age one, 50 percent retract, and by age three, 80 to 90 percent.

Notes:

MONTH

Getting to Know You

What's Going On with the Baby

Physically

- ◆ Most of your baby's physical movements are still reflexive. But sometime this month, while flailing his arms around he'll accidentally stick his hand into his mouth. After getting over the initial shock, your baby will realize that sucking—even when there's no milk involved—is downright fun. By the end of the month, he'll probably be able to get his hand in his mouth— on purpose—fairly regularly.
- ◆ Lying on his tummy, he's now able to lift his head just enough to turn it so his nose won't be smashed into the mattress.
- ◆ If you put him in a sitting position, he'll try to keep his head in line with his back, but he won't be able to hold it steady for more than a second or two without support.
- ◆ Waste production is way down: 2 to 3 bowel movements and 5 to 6 wet diapers per day.

Intellectually

- ◆ Your baby is already beginning to express an interest in finding out what's new in the world—he'll stare at a new object for much longer than a familiar one.
- ◆ According to psychiatrist Peter Wolff, an object exists for a baby only as "something to suck, or something to see, or something to grasp, but not as something to grasp *and* to see at the same time."

Verbally

♦ As his vocal chords mature, your baby will be able to expand his collection of animal sounds to include some small, throaty, and incredibly cute noises.

♦ He is already beginning to differentiate between language and the other kinds of noise he hears all day.

♦ Still, his main form of using his vocal chords will be to cry—something he'll do for a total of about three hours a day.

Emotionally/Socially

♦ Don't expect many hints from your baby about what he's thinking—most of the time his expression is pretty blank.

♦ Not quite ready for the cocktail circuit, your baby is probably sleeping 16 to 20 hours a day. In fact, he may use sleep as a kind of self-defense mechanism, shutting down his systems when he gets overstimulated.

What You're Going Through

Bonding with the Baby

In one of the earliest studies of father-infant interaction, researcher Ross Parke made a discovery that shocked a lot of traditionalists: fathers were just as caring, interested, and involved with their infants as mothers were, and they held, touched, kissed, rocked, and cooed at their new babies with at least the same frequency as mothers did. Several years later, Dr. Martin Greenberg coined a term, *engrossment,* to describe "a father's sense of absorption, pre-occupation, and interest in his baby."

Over the years a number of other researchers have confirmed these findings about father-infant interaction and have concluded that what triggers engrossment in men is the same thing that prompts similar nurturing feelings in women: early infant contact. "In sum," writes Dr. Parke, "the amount of stimulatory and affectional behavior depends on the opportunity to hold the infant."

Not surprisingly, Parke and others have found that men who attended their babies' birth bonded slightly faster than those who didn't. But if you weren't able to be there for the birth, don't worry. "Early contact at birth is not a magic pill," writes Ellen Galinsky. "It does not guarantee attachment. Neither does lack of contact prevent bonding."

But What If I Don't Bond Right Away?

If you haven't established an instant bond with your baby, there's absolutely nothing wrong with you. In fact, in a study by psychiatrists Kay Robson and

Remesh Kumar, 25 to 40 percent of new parents—mothers *and* fathers—admitted that their first response to the baby was "indifference." Putting it in slightly stronger terms, researcher Katherine May says, "This bonding business is nonsense. We've sold parents a bill of goods. They believe that if they don't have skin-to-skin contact within the first fifteen minutes, they won't bond. Science just doesn't show that."

This really makes more sense than the love-at-first-sight kind of bonding you hear so much about. And anyway, there's no evidence whatsoever that your relationship with or feelings for your child will be any less loving than if you'd fallen head over heels in love in the first second. So, just take your time. Don't pressure yourself, and don't think for a second that you've failed as a father.

In addition, there's a lot of evidence that parent-child bonding comes as a result of physical closeness. So if you'd like to speed up the process, try carrying the baby every chance you get, taking him with you whenever you can, and taking care of as many of his basic needs as possible.

My Baby Doesn't Love Me

For about the first six to eight weeks of life, your baby probably won't give you much feedback about how you're doing as a father: he won't smile, laugh, or react to you in any noticeable way. In fact, just about all he will do is cry. This can result in your feeling unloved and, surprisingly often, feeling a need to "get even" with the baby by deliberately withholding your own love.

As the grown-up, it's your job to nip this destructive cycle in the bud. "The relationship between parent and child is interactive," writes Ellen Galinsky. "What the child does affects what the parent does, which in turn affects what the child does." So if you find yourself feeling unloved or unappreciated by your newborn, here are a few things to keep in mind:

- Although your baby can express preferences for sounds, tastes, or patterns (see pages 13–14, 19), he is not yet capable of expressing love.
- Your baby's needs and wants are fairly limited at this stage—feed me, change me, hold me, put me in bed—and he has a different way of letting you know which one he wants. If you pay close attention, you'll soon be able to figure out what he's "telling" you. Getting to know your baby in this way will make you feel less anxious and more confident as a parent, which will make the baby more comfortable with you, which in turn will make your mutual attachment more secure.
- Another important way to get to know your baby is by carefully reading the "What's Going On with the Baby" sections of this book. Knowing what your baby is capable of—and what he isn't—at various stages can go a long way

Attachment and Bonding Are *Not* the Same Thing

While there's no question that bonding with your baby is an important goal, it is essentially a one-way street: you establish a relationship with the infant and don't get much back. But attachment is more of a two-way street: you and the baby establish relationships with each other.

In our attachment relationships with adults (including our partners), both players have "relatively equal positions in providing an emotionally satisfying relationship with each other," write Barbara and Philip Newman of Ohio State University. But the attachment you have with your baby is not—by any stretch of the imagination—equal. It is, however, balanced in very interesting and delicate ways.

Basically, it works like this: as you learn to read your baby's signals and satisfy his needs in an appropriate way, he learns to view you as a reliable and responsive person—someone he can count on in times of trouble. And he'll find some way (babies always do) to get you the message that you're needed and wanted.

This exchange of information is what psychologist Bertrand Cramer and pediatrician T. Berry Brazelton call "synchronous communication." And according to them, parents who have synchronous communication with their babies "experience their own competence. . . . When they achieve it for themselves, the most insecure parents can feel a sense of control, over their baby's vulnerabilities and over their own."

Meanwhile, babies who have synchronous "chats" with their parents come to prefer them over any of the other adults around who might be able to satisfy a need or two. Over time, this kind of preference (based on feelings of security and the parents' reliability) develops into self-confidence and becomes the foundation for all of the growing baby's future relationships.

toward helping you understand your baby's behavior and establish reasonable expectations.

♦ Change your perspective a little. The fact that your baby often stops crying when you pick him up and that he loves to fall asleep on your chest are signs that he feels close to you and trusts you—critical steps on the way to the love you want him to feel. Allow yourself the pleasure of stroking his incredibly soft skin, of admiring his tiny fingers, and of filling your lungs with his clean, new baby smell. If that doesn't hook you, nothing will.

Bonding, Attachment, and Adoptive Parents

It's extremely common for adoptive couples—particularly those who adopted because of infertility—to feel insecure or inadequate as parents. They often believe that the process of bonding and forming an attachment with a baby comes "naturally" to birth parents, and that since they weren't with the baby from the beginning, they'll never be as close to their child as a biological parent would.

The good news is that this isn't true. "Most infants, if adopted before the age of nine months," write adoption psychotherapists Judith Schaffer and Christina Lindstrom, "will take to their new parents as if they were born to them, developing an attachment to them as they would have done to their birth parents."

There are things, of course, that can interfere with adoptive parent-child attachment. Among the most common are the feelings of inadequacy discussed above, and the age and physical health of the child at adoption. But remember: as we've discussed earlier in this chapter, the processes of bonding and attachment don't happen automatically. They take time—and often a lot of work—to develop. In all but the rarest cases, the desire for attachment to a child can overcome even the most formidable obstacles.

So if you're worried for any reason about your abilities as a parent or about anything else that might get in the way of your relationship with your adopted child, call the National Adoption Information Clearinghouse, at (301) 231-6512, or The National Adoption Center, at (800) TO-ADOPT. Either of these organizations can refer you to resources—including support groups and counseling services—in your area. A few other adoption-related resources are listed in the Resources appendix of this book.

The Incredible Shrinking Baby

In their first week or so of life, most babies lose some weight—often as much as 25 percent of their birth weight. This can be pretty scary, especially since babies are generally supposed to get bigger over time, not smaller. This shrinking baby thing is perfectly normal (in the first few days the baby isn't eating much), and your baby will probably regain his birth weight by the time he's two weeks old. After that, the rate of growth—for the next few months, at least—is phenomenal: about an ounce a day and an inch per month. Doesn't sound like much, but if he continued growing at this rate, by his eighteenth birthday your baby would be nearly twenty feet tall and weigh in at about 420 pounds.

During every visit to the pediatrician your baby will be weighed, his overall length and head circumference will be measured, and the results will be given not only in inches (or centimeters) but in *percentile.* (If your baby is in the 75th percentile for weight, that means that he's heavier than 75 percent of babies the same age.) Try not to get too caught up with these numbers. As with most things, bigger isn't necessarily better; more important, it's normal for different parts of a baby's body to grow at different rates. Both my daughters, for example, were built like nails—90th percentile for both height and head size, but 40th percentile for weight.

Keep in mind also that the numbers on these charts generally apply to formula-fed babies, who tend to bulk up a little more quickly than their breastfed agemates.

You and Your Baby

The most important thing you can do for your baby is to make him feel loved and cared for. And the best way to do this is to continue to do the activities listed on pages 19–20, only more so.

Reading

At this age, you can read just about anything to your baby—even *War and Peace* or those *New Yorker* profiles you're so behind on. "What is important . . . is that the child becomes accustomed to the rhythmic sounds of your reading voice and associates it with a peaceful, secure time of day," writes Jim Trelease, author of *The New Read Aloud Handbook.* So set up a regular reading time and place. And as with most baby-related things, your baby will let you know whether she's interested or not, so don't force her to sit through the end of a chapter.

Toys and Games

Giving your baby a rattle, stuffed animal, or anything else that needs to be grasped is a total waste of time. She simply isn't interested in toys right now. That doesn't mean, however, that she doesn't want to play. If you pay close attention, you'll soon figure out when she's telling you she wants to play. "She'll look you straight in the eye and 'talk' to you," write Drs. Art Ulene and Steven Shelov. "The talk may be only a syllable or two, or it may be a

"You have the right to remain silent . . ."

prolonged cooing, but you'll know from the tone and intensity whether she's in a good mood or a bad."

It's even more important that you learn to recognize the clues your baby gives you when she wants to quit. "At first she'll look away," say Ulene and Shelov. "Then she may become glassy-eyed or look right through you. She may move her body to physically turn away or simply go limp. Finally, if all else fails, she may wail for escape. By getting to know and respect your baby's early warning signals, you can spare both of you a lot of needless discomfort."

Visual Stimulation

Since your baby still isn't capable of grabbing hold of much of anything, she's doing most of her learning with her eyes. Here are a few ways to stimulate your baby visually:

♦ Fasten an unbreakable mirror securely to the inside of the baby's crib.

♦ Make sure the baby has a lot of different things to look at. For the first few months, infants are particularly responsive to high contrast, so black-and-white toys and patterns are often a big hit.

♦ Have your baby show you what she prefers. Hold up different patterns

12 to 18 inches from the baby's face for a few seconds. Which ones does she stare at intently? Which ones does she turn away from?
♦ Play some visual tracking games. With the baby on his back, hold a small object 12 to 18 inches from his nose. Move the object slowly to one side. Does the baby follow the object with his eyes? Does he move his head? Do the same thing for the other side.

Whatever games you're playing with the baby, keep in mind that your baby is not a trained seal and that these activities are games, not college entrance exams.

Mobiles

Mobiles are among the most popular furnishings in almost any baby's room. And this is the perfect time to put some up: one over the bed and perhaps another, smaller one over the changing table. When considering mobiles, keep these ideas in mind:
♦ Get mobiles that allow you to change the figures. As your baby gets older his taste will become more sophisticated and you'll need to keep up. My wife and I found that mobile characters were quite expensive; we could have bought a year's worth of clothes for the baby with what it would have cost us to buy five or six sets of mobile characters. The solution? Make your own.
♦ When buying or making mobile characters, keep in mind that the baby will be looking at them from underneath. Quite a number of manufacturers produce mobiles that are gorgeous when viewed from the parents' perspective, but from the baby's perspective they're essentially blank.
♦ At this point, your baby is still interested in simple lines: stripes, large squares, and the outlines of things. Intricate patterns or complicated designs are not appropriate now.
♦ Keep the mobile 6 to 18 inches above the baby's face and put it slightly to the side; babies don't like to look straight up for long.

Fun with Reflexes

"The newborn is faced with two fundamental and simultaneous challenges during the first weeks of life," writes child psychiatrist Stanley I. Greenspan. "The first is self-regulation—the ability to feel calm and relaxed, not overwhelmed by his new environment. The second is to become interested in the world about him."

Unfortunately, babies can't do much to accomplish either of these goals on their own. That's your job. And you'll do it by caring for and responding to your baby, and by providing him with a stimulating environment. But because your baby can't be expected to sit around waiting for you, he came fully equipped with a wide range of reflexes to get him started.

Yes, all that wild, seemingly random arm and leg flailing really has a purpose: "Many reflexes are designed to help infants to survive and lead them on to more complicated sequences of voluntary behavior," write the Newmans. "The sucking reflex is a good example. At birth, inserting something in an infant's mouth produces the sucking reflex. This reflex helps infants gain nourishment relatively easily before sucking behavior is under voluntary control."

Understanding these reflexes can give you greater insight into your baby's behavior. And by keeping track of when they disappear, you'll be able to monitor his development. Best of all, they're a lot of fun—for you as well as the baby.

In addition to these reflexes, there are a few more that the experts haven't yet figured out what to do with. For example, babies seem able to determine the path of an oncoming object; they will take defensive action (leaning back hard, turning away, closing eyes, bringing arms up in front of the face) if the object is going to hit them. But if the object isn't on a path that will hit the baby, he'll ignore it. If you want to try this, strap your baby into his car seat and, from a few feet away, move a ball or other fairly large object straight at his head and again past him.

If you want to experiment with any of these reflexes, the best time is during your baby's active alert stage (see page 18). Remember to be extra careful of the baby's head and to respect his desire to quit.

Family Matters

Crying

Since the moment your baby was born she's been trying to communicate with you. That's the good news. The bad news is that she settled on crying as the way to do it. It will take you a while to teach her that there are more effective, and less annoying, ways of getting your attention. In the meantime, though, if she's like most babies, she's a real chatterbox: 80 to 90 percent of all babies have crying spells that last from twenty minutes to an hour every day.

Of course, not all of your baby's tears mean that she is sad, uncomfortable, or dissatisfied with something you've done. Nevertheless, holding an inconsolably crying baby can bring out a range of emotions, even in the most seasoned parent, running from pity and frustration to fury and inadequacy.

Exploring Your Baby's Reflexes

IF YOU	THE BABY WILL
◆ Tap the bridge of your baby's nose (gently, please), turn on a bright light, or clap your hands close to his head	◆ Close his eyes tightly
◆ Make a sudden, loud noise or give the baby the sensation of falling	◆ Fling legs and arms out and back, throw head back, open eyes wide, and cry
◆ Straighten the baby's arms and legs	◆ Flex arms and legs
◆ Pull baby up to a sitting position (be sure to support baby's head while doing this)	◆ Snap eyes open, tense shoulders, try (usually unsuccessfully) to right head
◆ Stand baby up (while holding under the arms) on a solid surface; works just as well holding baby against a wall (but be sure to support her head)	◆ Lift one leg, then the other, as if marching
◆ Put baby on tummy on flat surface or support baby's chest on a water surface (if trying in water, *do not let go*—baby can't really swim); *never do this on a beanbag or other soft surface—baby can suffocate*	◆ Turn head to side and lift it slightly; wiggle arms around as if swimming
◆ Stroke back of hand or top of foot; gently poke sole	◆ Withdraw hand or foot and arch it
◆ Stroke leg or upper body	◆ Cross opposite leg or hand to push hand away
◆ Stroke palm or sole of foot	◆ Grasp with hand or foot; hand grasp may be strong enough to allow you to pull baby to sitting position (be sure to support head)

WHAT IT MEANS	HOW LONG UNTIL IT'S GONE
◆ Protects baby's eyes from being injured by an object or a harsh light	◆ 1–2 months
◆ A fairly primitive way for the newborn to call for help	◆ Called the Moro or startle reflex, disappears within 3 or 4 months
◆ Probably the body's attempt to resist being held down	◆ 3 months
◆ Attempts to get self upright	◆ Called the China Doll reflex, disappears within 1–2 months
◆ Baby can protect herself by kicking away potentially dangerous things; has absolutely nothing to do with real walking	◆ About 2 months
◆ A way for the baby to protect self against smothering	◆ 2–4 months
◆ Protection against pain	◆ 2–4 months
◆ Protection against pain	◆ 3–4 months
◆ Encourages baby to start understanding the shape, texture, and weight of whatever she's grasping	◆ 2–4 months

(continued on next page)

Exploring Your Baby's Reflexes *(continued from pages 40–41)*

IF YOU	THE BABY WILL
◆ Stroke cheek or mouth	◆ Turn head toward side being stroked, open mouth and start sucking
◆ Place an object over baby's face (be *very careful* while doing this)	◆ Open and close mouth vigorously, twist head, flail arms
◆ Place baby on his back and turn his head to one side (don't force anything)	◆ Straighten arm on the side he is looking, bend arm and leg on other side

Fathers are likely to experience these feelings—especially inadequacy—more acutely than mothers. As with so many mother/father differences, the culprit is socialization: most men come into fatherhood feeling less than completely confident in their own parenting abilities, and a baby's cries are too easily seen as confirmation that daddy is doing a less-than-adequate job.

As difficult as crying can be to deal with, you obviously don't want your baby to be completely silent (in fact, if your baby doesn't cry at least several times a day, have a talk with your pediatrician). Fortunately, there are a few things you can do to make your baby's crying a less unpleasant experience for both of you:

◆ **When (not if) your child starts to cry, resist the urge to hand him or her to your partner.** She knows nothing more about crying babies than you do (or will soon enough). Since each of you instinctively has a different way of interacting with the baby, your hanging in there through a crying spell will double the chances you'll find new ways to soothe the baby.

◆ **Learn to speak your baby's language.** By now, you can almost always tell your baby's cry from any other baby's, and you can probably recognize her "I'm tired," "Feed me now," and "Change my diaper" cries. And while the language she speaks isn't as sexy or as vocabulary-rich as French, your baby has added a few more "phrases" to her vocabulary, including "I'm as uncomfortable as hell," "I'm bored out of my mind," and "I'm crying because I'm mad and I'm not going to stop no matter what you do." Responding promptly when your baby cries will help you learn to recognize which cry is which. You'll then be able to tailor your response and keep your baby happy.

◆ **Carry your baby more.** The more you hold them (even when they're not

WHAT IT MEANS	HOW LONG UNTIL IT'S GONE
♦ Called rooting reflex, helps baby get ready to eat	♦ 3–4 months
♦ Attempt to keep from suffocating	♦ 5–7 months
♦ Called the tonic neck reflex or fencer's pose, encourages baby to use each side of body and to notice own hands	♦ 1–3 months

crying), the less likely they are to cry. In one study, researchers found that a two-hour increase in carrying time per day resulted in a 42 percent decrease in crying time.

♦ **Get to know your baby's routine.** Keeping a diary of when your baby cries, how long the crying spells last, and what (if anything) works to slow them down can really help. Some babies like to thrash around and cry a little (or a lot) before going to sleep; others don't.

♦ **If your partner is breastfeeding, watch what she eats.** This is especially important if the baby suddenly and inexplicably deviates from her normal crying routine. Broccoli, cauliflower, brussels sprouts, and milk, when consumed by nursing mothers, often result in gastrically distressed (and weepy) babies.

After you've tried soothing, feeding, changing the diaper, checking for uncomfortable clothing, and rocking, the baby may still continue to howl. Sometimes there's really nothing you can do about it (see the section "Coping with Crying," pages 44–45), but sometimes all it takes is a new approach. Here are a few alternatives you might want to try:

♦ **Hold the baby differently.** Not all babies like to be held facing you; some want to face out so they can see the world. One of the most successful ways I've learned to soothe a crying baby—and I've tried this on many kids besides my own—is to use Dave's Magic Baby Hold. (Dave, the father of a close friend, supposedly used the Hold to calm his own three children.) Quite simply, have the baby "sit" in the palm of your hand—thumb in front, the other fingers on the baby's bottom. Then have the baby lie face down on the inside of your forearm, with his or her head resting on the inside of your elbow. Use your other hand to stroke or pat the baby's back.

♦ **Distraction.** Offer a toy, a story, a song. If the baby is diverted by a story or song, you'd better be prepared to repeat it over and over and over. . . .

♦ **Give the baby something to suck on.** Just take a guess why they call them "pacifiers." If you don't approve of pacifiers, you can either help the baby suck on his or her own fingers, or loan out one of yours (for more on pacifiers, see page 137).

♦ **Give the baby a bath.** Some babies find warm water soothing. Others freak out when they get wet. If you do decide to try bathing a crying infant, don't do it alone. Holding onto a calm soapy baby is no easy chore. Keeping a grip on a squirming, screaming, soapy baby takes a team of highly trained specialists.

♦ **Invest in a frontpack.** No matter how strong you think you are, carrying a baby around—even a newborn—is rough on the arms and back.

♦ **Take the baby for a walk or a drive.** A word of caution: this doesn't work for all babies. When she was an infant, my elder daughter would fall asleep in the stroller or the car in a heartbeat. But my younger daughter hates riding in the car, especially when she's tired, and cries even more when she's put in her car seat. If you don't feel like going out, try putting the baby on top of a running washing machine or dryer. There's also a special device called SleepTight that, when attached to the baby's crib, simulates the feel (and sounds) of a car going fifty-five miles an hour. Call 1-800-NO-COLIC for more information.

Coping with Crying

If you've tried everything you can think of to stop the baby from crying but to no avail, here are some things that may help you cope:

♦ **Tag-team crying duty.** There's no reason why both you and your partner have to suffer together through what Martin Greenberg calls "the tyranny of crying." Spelling each other in twenty-minute or half-hour shifts will do you both a world of good. Getting a little exercise during your "time off" will also calm your nerves before your next shift starts.

♦ **Let the baby "cry it out."** If the crying has gone on for more than twenty minutes, you might put the baby in his crib and give yourself a break. If the baby doesn't stop screaming in ten minutes, pick him up and try to soothe him some other way for fifteen more minutes. Repeat as necessary. Note: The "crying it out" approach should be used only after you've tried everything else. Generally speaking, you should respond promptly and

"See what Daddy has for you, if you stop crying?"

lovingly to your baby's cries. Several studies show that babies who are
responded to in this way develop into more confident youngsters.

♦ **Get some help.** Dealing with a crying child for even a few minutes can
provoke incredible rage and frustration. And if the screams go on for hours,
it can become truly difficult to maintain your sanity, let alone control your
temper. If you find yourself concerned that you might lash out (other than
verbally) at your child, call someone: your partner, pediatrician, parents,
baby-sitter, friends, neighbors, clergy person, or even a parental-stress
hotline. If your baby is a real crier, keep these numbers handy.

♦ **Don't take it personally.** Your baby isn't deliberately trying to antagonize
you. It's all too easy to let your frustration at this temporary situation permanently interfere with the way you treat your child. "Even if your powerful
feelings don't lead to child abuse," write the authors of *What to Expect the
First Year,* "they can start eroding your relationship with your baby and your
confidence in yourself as a parent unless you get counseling quickly."

Dealing with Postpartum Blues and Depression

About 70 percent of new mothers experience periods of mild sadness, weepi-
ness, moodiness, sleep deprivation, loss of appetite, inability to make decisions,
anger, or anxiety after the baby is born. These postpartum blues, which many

Colic

Starting at about two weeks of age, some 10–20 percent of babies develop colic—crying spells that, unlike "ordinary" crying, can last for hours at a time. Although many colicky babies limit their crying to certain times of the day, many others cry all day or all night. The duration and intensity of crying spells peaks at about six weeks, and usually disappears entirely within three months.

Since there's no real agreement on what causes colic or on what to do about it, your pediatrician probably won't be able to offer a quick cure. Some parents, however, have been able to relieve (partially or completely) their colicky infants with an over-the-counter gas remedy for adults. Talk to your doctor about whether he or she thinks taking this medication would benefit your child. Here are a few other approaches to dealing with colic (or crying babies in general).

♦ Use the methods described in the "Crying" and "Coping with Crying" sections.

♦ If you're bottle-feeding the baby, try taking her off cow's milk. Some pediatricians feel that colic may be linked to a milk intolerance and suggest switching to a non–cow's milk formula.

♦ Hold the baby facing you, with his head over your shoulder and your shoulder pressing on his stomach.

♦ Hold the baby a little *less*. One school of thought maintains that some babies cry because their nervous systems aren't mature enough to handle the stimulation that comes with being held and stroked and talked to. But don't do this unless your physician advises you to.

♦ Put a hot water bottle on your knees, place the baby face down across it to warm his tummy, and stroke his back.

♦ Baby massage (see pages 59–60).

♦ Try swaddling. Being enveloped in a blanket may make the baby feel more comfortable.

♦ See the section on anger (pages 199–202).

believe are caused by hormonal shifts in a new mother's body, can last for hours or days, but in most cases they disappear within a few weeks. If you notice that your partner is experiencing any of these symptoms, there's not much you can do except be supportive. Encourage her to get out of the house for a while and see to it that she's eating healthily.

In a small number of cases, postpartum blues can develop into postpartum depression. According to the American College of Obstetricians and Gynecologists, postpartum depression, if not recognized and treated, may become worse or last longer than it needs to. Here are some symptoms to watch out for:

♦ Postpartum blues that don't go away after two weeks, or feelings of depression or anger that surface a month or two after the birth.

♦ Feelings of sadness, doubt, guilt, helplessness, or hopelessness that begin to disrupt your partner's normal functioning.

♦ Inability to sleep when tired, or sleeping most of the time, even when the baby is awake.

♦ Marked changes in appetite.

♦ Extreme concern and worry about the baby—or lack of interest in the baby and/or other members of the family.

♦ Fear of harming the baby or thoughts of self-harm.

Again, most of what your partner will go through after the birth is completely normal and nothing to worry about. If you're really concerned, however, encourage your partner to talk with you about what she's feeling and to see her doctor or a therapist.

Even Guys Get the Blues

Although postpartum blues or depression are almost always associated with women, the fact is that many men also get the blues after their babies are born. Men's blues, however, are not hormonally based like their partner's. The feelings of sadness, the mood swings, and the anxiety you may be experiencing are more likely the result of coming face to face with the reality of your changing life.

"The hearty congratulations at work last a few days," writes S. Adams Sullivan, author of *The Father's Almanac*, "but then your status as a celebrity wears off and you begin to notice that you're coming home every night to a demanding baby and a distraught wife, and the bills are piling up. . . . You look at your wife and . . . the healthy, radiant glow that made her beautiful while she was pregnant has disappeared, and you're tempted to agree with her when she gripes about her looks . . . you're getting maybe four and a half hours of sleep, total, and that's broken up into hour-and-a-half naps, so that you're nodding off every day at work and falling behind."

Fortunately, most men (and women, for that matter) don't suffer from any kind of postpartum depression. But if you do, you can take some comfort in knowing that it will eventually pass: you'll get caught up at work, the baby will settle into a routine, you'll get more sleep, and your wife's body will somehow get back to looking pretty much the way it did before she got pregnant.

Safety First

It may seem strange to talk about safety at a time when the baby is practically immobile and probably can't get into any serious trouble. But even at this age babies can do the most surprising things. Here are a few precautions you should take now to start making your home a little safer:

♦ Avoid beanbags. Most beanbag chairs and baby rests have been taken off the market, but there are still plenty of them in garages all over the country. There is more than a coincidental link between beanbags and suffocation deaths.

♦ Never leave the baby's car seat—with the baby in it, of course—balanced on anything. A flailing arm or leg, even a sneeze, might move the car seat enough for it to tip over.

♦ Put together a good first aid kit. You can find a list of items on page 140.

♦ Take an infant CPR class. Instruction is usually available at your local Red Cross or YMCA.

♦ Take a quick look at the safety measures described in later chapters (pages 138–41, for example). Start putting together the materials you'll need and get into the habit of doing such things as pointing pot handles toward the rear of the stove.

Notes:

First Smiles

What's Going On with the Baby

Physically

♦ By the end of this month, most of your baby's innate reflexes will have disappeared. Sad but true. Nevertheless, she still holds her arms and legs away from her body, and there's plenty of twitching to go around.

♦ Lying on her tummy, she can now hold her head at a 45-degree angle for a few minutes. And when she's sitting (a position she probably prefers by now), she's getting a lot better at keeping her head straight.

♦ Your baby is now beginning to reach for objects. Grasping, which was once purely a reflex action, is now becoming voluntary. She even may be able to hold small objects for a few minutes at a time.

♦ Although her vision is still limited to what's directly in front of her face, just about everything is now in focus. And because you're such an interesting sight, she'll follow you with her eyes everywhere you go.

Intellectually

♦ As her brain develops, your baby will prefer more complex patterns. Instead of the simple, relatively motionless outline of your face, she now prefers your eyes and mouth, which are constantly changing shape.

♦ If you touch her cheek now, she probably won't start sucking—an indication that she can now tell the difference between your finger and a milk-bearing nipple.

♦ She is also now able to accommodate herself to various situations. If you're holding her upright against your shoulder, she'll hold herself differently than if you're resting her on your knees.

♦ She gets excited when she sees familiar objects, but she has no sense of "object permanence" (which means that as far as the baby is concerned, anything she can't see simply doesn't exist).

Verbally

♦ Leaving behind the grunting and squeaking, your baby is adding to her repertoire some delightful cooing (a combination of a squeal and a gurgle), as well as some impressive oohs, ohhs, and ahhs.

♦ Crying, however, is still one of her favorite ways of communicating.

Emotionally/Socially

♦ And now, the moment you've been waiting for: your baby is finally able to smile at you (sorry, but until now those things you thought were smiles were probably just gas).

♦ As she becomes more and more interested in learning about her world (a process that hopefully won't stop for the rest of her life), your baby will really enjoy regular changes of scenery; she's also very capable of expressing excitement—and distress.

♦ She's awake about 10 hours a day; although she's stimulated more by touch than by social interaction, she'll stay awake longer if there are people around to amuse her.

What You're Going Through

Thinking about Sex

Most OB/GYNs advise their patients to refrain from intercourse for at least six weeks after giving birth. But before you mark that date on your calendar, remember that the six-week rule is only a guideline. Resuming intercourse ultimately depends on the condition of your partner's cervix and vagina, and, more important, on how you're both feeling. Many couples begin having sex again in as little as three or four weeks, but it's not at all uncommon for couples to take as long as six months to fully reestablish their prepregnancy sex life.

Many factors—both physical and psychological—influence when and how a couple decides to resume their sex life. Here are a few:

♦ When you had sex with your partner before, she was the woman you loved. Now she's also a mother—a thought that may remind you of your own

> ## Nonsexual and Almost Nonsexual Affection
>
> Professors Phil and Carolyn Cowan have found that many couples need practice finding sensual ways to please each other short of intercourse. Hand-holding, back rubs, hair stroking while watching TV, or even gentle, nonsexual kissing are good for those times one of you isn't in the mood. If you're not in the mood but want to give—or receive—some nonsexual affection, tell your partner up front that there are no strings attached. Researchers have found that men and women who don't want sex are frequently afraid that the kiss or hug they need from, or want to give to, their partners will be misinterpreted as a sexual overture.

mother and can be a big turn-off. At the same time, in your new capacity as parent, you may remind your partner a little too much of her own father. She may also find it tough to reconcile her roles as lover and mother, and may see herself as unsexual.

♦ Your partner may not have fully recovered from her episiotomy or C-section.

♦ Your partner may be embarrassed if milk flows from her breasts when she's aroused.

♦ A lot of men find leaking breasts erotic. But if you don't—and she senses your feelings—she may worry that you don't find her desirable anymore.

♦ Some men have "emotional difficulty being sexual with the part of their wives that produced their children," says psychologist Jerrold Shapiro. And a lot of women find it difficult to think of their vaginas as sexual organs after seeing babies come out of them.

♦ You may resent your baby's unlimited access to your partner's breasts and feel that your partner is focusing more on the baby than on you.

♦ Your (or your partner's) motivation to have sex may have changed since your baby was born. If, for example, you or she were motivated to have sex because you really wanted to be a parent, sex after having a baby may feel a little anticlimactic, so to speak.

♦ Now that you have concrete proof (the baby) of your virility, you may feel more intimate with your partner than ever before.

When You and Your Partner are Out of Sync

Just as you and your partner can't always agree on what movie you want to see or what you want to have for dinner, you can't expect that you'll both feel sexually aroused at the same time. She might want to make love at a time when

The First Time . . . Again

When you do finally get around to making love, you should expect the first few times to be a period of tentative rediscovery for both of you. Her body has changed, and she may respond differently than she used to. Some studies have shown that after giving birth women experience a slightly decreased interest in vaginal stimulation and an increased interest in clitoral and breast stimulation. Also, women who experienced multiple orgasms before giving birth are less likely to do so, or will do so less frequently, now.

She may also be worried that having sex will hurt, and you may be afraid of the same thing or that those extra pounds she hasn't lost yet will interfere with her pleasure. Go slowly, take your cues from her, and give yourselves plenty of time to get used to each other again.

Sex researchers William Fisher and Janice Gray found that nursing mothers generally resume their sexual lives sooner than women who don't breastfeed. This is a little odd, considering that nursing mothers produce lower levels of ovarian hormones, which are responsible for producing vaginal lubrication. As a result, if your partner is nursing, her vagina may be much drier than before, making intercourse painful. Obviously, this doesn't mean she isn't aroused by you; it's simply a common postbirth condition. In situations like these, a little K-Y Jelly, Astroglide, or other over-the-counter lubricant will go a long way.

you're simply too tired to move. Or you might want to have sex when she's feeling "touched out," having spent an entire day with a baby crawling all over her, sucking her breasts.

The months right after the birth of a baby are a particularly vulnerable time for your sex life. "If you had a good sex life before and during the pregnancy, it is important to be intentional about keeping a positive sex life after the birth of your child," says Dr. William Stayton, a professor of human sexuality at the University of Pennsylvania. "If you did not have a good sex life before the pregnancy, then it is very likely that it will not get better after the birth of your child unless you intentionally give time and energy to your sexual relationship." Here are a few suggestions that might help smooth over some of the rough spots you'll invariably encounter:

♦ Figure out what, exactly, is motivating you to want to have sex. "Sex can be an expression of monogamy, intimacy, love, or even an affirmation of one's sexual identity ('I'm a man and this is what men do')," says Linda Perlin

Alperstein, an associate professor at the University of California, San Francisco. "It can also be the only way some of us ever get held and touched lovingly in our culture." And for some people (this is pretty rare, though) sex is thought of exclusively as a way to reproduce.

♦ Talk. "Unless the couple can talk about their sex life, their entire relationship may suffer, and that in turn will compound their sexual problems," write psychologists Libby and Arthur Colman.

♦ Negotiate. If you really want to have sex and she doesn't, ask her—without putting a lot of pressure on her—what, if anything, she'd be willing to do. Would she, for example, be willing to masturbate you? Would she hold you in her arms or let you touch her breasts while you stimulate yourself? It goes without saying (or at least it should) that you should be prepared to reciprocate. The object here is not to convince her to have sex with you; the two of you should be working toward creating an environment in which you both feel safe expressing your desires and in which each of you can turn the other down without fear of causing offense or hurting feelings.

♦ Be completely honest. If you and your partner agree that you'll hold each other like spoons and kiss, but that you won't touch each other's genitals, don't go over the line. Doing so will only make her tense and not trust you.

♦ Change your attitude. A lot of men have the idea that every erection has to be paired up with an ejaculation. "But the truth is that just being aroused can be nice—and quite enjoyable," says Linda Alperstein. "So rather than have no sexual life if you can't have the one you fantasize about, enjoy what you can have; just enjoy the fact that you can get aroused again. You don't have to actually reach an orgasm to experience pleasure."

♦ Take it easy. "While a positive sexual relationship is a very nice and important component of an enduring and happy marriage," writes psychologist Brad Sachs, "it will not, by itself, ensure one."

♦ Ask for—and give your partner—some nonsexual affection (see page 51).

Not Ready to Be a Father

One of the most consistent findings by researchers is that new fathers almost always feel unprepared for their new role. Personally, I would have been surprised if it were otherwise. As writer David L. Giveans says, "It is both unfair and unrealistic to expect a man . . . to automatically 'father' when his life experiences have skillfully isolated him from learning how."

When most of our fathers were raising us, a "good father" was synonymous with "good provider." He supported his family financially, mowed the lawn, washed the car, and maintained discipline in the home. No one seemed to care

"You're not real experienced at this father business, are you?"

whether he ever spent much time with his children; in fact, he was *discouraged* from doing so, and told to leave the kids to his wife, the "good mother."

Yesterday's "good father" has now retroactively become an emotionally distant, uncaring villain. And today's "good father," besides still being a breadwinner, is expected to be a real presence—physically and emotionally—in his kids' lives. This, in a nutshell, is exactly what most new fathers want. Most of us have no intention of being wait-till-your-father-comes-home dads and want to be more involved with our children than our own fathers were. The problem is that we just haven't had the training.

The solution? Quit complaining and jump right in. The "maternal instinct" that women are supposedly born with is actually acquired on the job. And that's exactly where you're going to develop your "paternal instinct."

Confusion

If there's one thing that set my first few months of fatherhood apart from the next few years, it was the confusing and often conflicting emotions I felt:

- ♦ On the one hand, I had a sense of incredible virility, power, and pride at having created a new life. On the other, I often felt helpless when I couldn't understand—let alone satisfy—the baby's needs.

♦ Most of the time I felt the most powerful kind of love for my tiny child. But sometimes I also felt ambivalent. And once in a while I felt a powerful anger—one that seemed to come out of nowhere—at the very same baby.

♦ Most of the time I felt particularly close to my wife—especially when we would admire our children together. But every so often I'd get suspicious that she loved them more than she did me.

Apparently I wasn't the only confused new dad around. "Almost all new fathers express some level of confusion," says psychologist Bruce Linton, who runs workshops for expectant and new fathers. But as if feeling confused isn't bad enough, Linton has found that new fathers "consistently express anxiety and concern that there's something wrong with them or that they're abnormal because they're confused."

Before you go off and check yourself into a mental hospital, there are a few things you should know. First, being confused isn't abnormal at all. After spending the day in Linton's workshop discussing their concerns with other men, new fathers are greatly relieved to find out that their feelings aren't all that different from those of any other new father. (And anyway, doesn't it seem logical that if almost everyone thinks he's abnormal, then being abnormal must really be the norm?) Second, this state of confusion—and the accompanying suspicions about your sanity—usually disappear by the end of the third month.

Fears—Lots of Them

The combination of feeling unprepared and confused at the same time can be rather frightening, and the first few months of fatherhood are riddled with fears. Here are some of the most common:

♦ Fear of not being able to live up to your own expectations.

♦ Fear of not being able to protect your children from physical harm as they grow and develop.

♦ Fear of not being able to deal with the most basic parenting responsibilities: feeding, clothing, earning enough money, dealing with the baby's illnesses.

♦ Fear of not being able to shield your child from some of the more abstract horrors of modern life: poverty, war, disease, the destruction of the environment . . .

♦ Fear of simply not being "ready" to assume the role of father.

♦ Fear of picking up the baby because you think you might hurt him.

♦ Fear of your anger at the baby.

Don't Panic

Taken together, the feelings of unpreparedness, the fears, and the confusion so many new fathers experience can be overwhelming. Unfortunately, some men respond to this turmoil by running away—emotionally, physically, or both—from their kids and their partners. If you're feeling unable to deal with your anxieties and your feelings, do *not* run. Find yourself a more experienced father about your age and ask him to help you sort things out (see pages 133–35 for information on fathers' groups). If you can't find another father, talk to your partner. And if none of those alternatives work, find a good therapist, preferably one with experience dealing with men's concerns. There *is* help out there; you just have to find it.

♦ Fear of not being able—or willing—to love the baby enough.

♦ Fear of not being in control (see pages 73–74).

♦ Fear of repeating the mistakes made by your own father (see pages 71–72).

♦ Fear that if you discuss your fears with your partner, she'll misinterpret them and think you don't love her or the baby.

Some fears—such as fear of poverty and war, or of not being ready—you just can't do anything about. But others you can. For example, fear of not being able to handle the little things can be overcome by practice; fear of hurting the baby can also be overcome by spending more time carrying, stroking, picking up, and holding him—babies are not nearly as fragile as they look; and the fear of discussing things with your partner can be cured (to a certain extent) by taking a deep breath and telling her what you feel. She's going through many of the same things you are and will be relieved to find that she's not alone. Guaranteed.

Whatever your fears, you need to start by admitting to yourself that they exist and remembering that all new fathers are afraid sometimes. In his book *Fatherjournal*, David Steinberg eloquently describes coming to terms with himself and his fears. "I was going to be the perfect father: loving, caring, nurturing, soft. . . . I was going to do it right. . . . Tonight I see how scared I am. There is so much to do for this little creature who screams and wriggles and needs and doesn't know what he needs and relies on me to figure it out. . . . I need to accept my fear, my reluctance, my instinct to flee. I have to start from where I am instead of where the model new-age father would be."

Rethinking What It Means to Be a Man

There are two major reasons why so many of us would prefer to drive ten miles down the wrong road rather than stop and ask for directions. First, from the time we were little boys, we've been socialized to associate knowledge with masculinity—in other words, real men know everything, so admitting to being lost is a sign of weakness (and, of course, a lack of masculinity). Second, and even worse, we've also been socialized to be strong, independent, and goal-oriented, so asking for help is a sign of weakness (and, again, a lack of masculinity).

Nothing in the world can bring these two factors into play faster than the birth of a baby. Because of the near-total absence of active, involved, nurturing male role models, most new fathers can't seriously claim that they know what to do with a new baby (although never having cooked before didn't prevent my father from insisting he could make the best blueberry pancakes we'd ever taste; boy, was he wrong).

Getting help seems like the obvious solution to the ignorance problem, but most men don't want to seem helpless or expose their lack of knowledge by asking anyone. Now toss in a few more ingredients:

♦ The confusion and fears we've been feeling lately.

♦ The prevailing attitude that a man who is actively involved with his children—especially if he's the primary caretaker—is not as masculine as his less-involved brothers.

♦ Psychologist Henry Biller's observation that "too many men get caught up in the idea that to be an effective parent they must adopt a more maternal or mothering role."

It's easy to see how the whole experience of becoming a father can lead so many new fathers to wonder secretly (no one would ever *openly* admit to having these thoughts) whether or not they've retained their masculinity. All too often the result of this kind of thinking is that fathers leave all the child-rearing to their partners and thereby leave their kids essentially without a father. As Biller writes, "Children are at a particular disadvantage when they are deprived of constructive experiences with their fathers. Infants and young children are unlikely to be provided with other opportunities to form a relationship with a caring and readily available adult male if their father is not emotionally committed to them."

So you have a choice. Either accept the hardest yet most rewarding challenge you'll probably ever face by becoming an actively involved father and taking on a significant share of the responsibility for raising your children, or take the easy way out and leave it all to someone else. What would a "real" man do?

You and Your Baby

Awakening the Senses

Your baby was born equipped with the same five basic senses you were. And although his senses would probably develop pretty well without any additional help, there's a lot you can do (while having fun at the same time) to encourage development by exposing him to a broad range of sensory stimulation.

TASTE

By putting drops of various foods (in liquid) on babies' tongues, researchers have proven that babies have definite likes and dislikes. You're not going to try this, of course. At this age, your baby has no business eating anything but breast milk or formula. Save the experiments with real taste sensations for when you wean your baby (see pages 205–7). In the meantime, give the baby lots of different objects to put in his mouth. But be extremely careful that none of them is small enough to be a choking hazard or has removable pieces or sharp edges.

SMELL

Offer the baby a wide variety of things to smell:
+ If you're cooking, let her smell the spices and other ingredients.
+ If you're out for a walk, let her smell the flowers.
+ Try some experiments to see whether she prefers sweet smells to sour ones.
+ Be careful, though. Make sure she doesn't get any of these things in her mouth, and don't experiment with extremely strong smells. Also, stay away from ammonia, bleach, gasoline, paint thinner, pool or garden chemicals, and any other toxic materials you may have around the house.

SIGHT

+ Experiment with the baby's sight. Regularly change the patterns and keep track of which ones he prefers. Over the course of the next few months he'll advance from simple shapes and patterns to more complex ones.
+ Show him mirrors, pictures, and photographs.
+ Take the baby out for a walk and let him see what's going on in the world.

TOUCH

Expose the baby to as many textures as possible: the satin edges of his blanket; the plastic (or cloth) on his diaper; the family dog; a window; your computer keyboard. Let the baby feel each object for as long as he's interested. And don't

> ## No Baby Talk, Please
> Whenever you talk to your baby, pay close attention to your voice. Your natural, conversational voice is best because it exposes the baby to English as it is actually spoken. For some reason I've never been able to understand, many people can't bring themselves to speak naturally to a baby. Instead, they smile the biggest fake smile they can and say things like "Cootchie-cootchie widduw baby-poo, can I pinchy-winchy your cheeky-weeky?" Is that really the way you want your baby to learn how to speak? Need I say more?

limit yourself to the baby's hands; you can gently rub objects on the baby's cheeks, arms, or legs. (From a very young age, both my daughters loved me to rub the bottoms of their feet on my two-day beard growth.) Again, use common sense here. Be gentle and don't leave any objects with the baby.

HEARING
+ Expose the baby to as wide a variety of sounds as possible: the radio; any musical instruments you have around the house; construction sites (if they're not too loud). Does your baby seem to prefer one kind of noise—or music—over another?
+ For fun, take a small bell, hold it behind the baby, and ring it gently. Does he try to turn around? Now move the bell to one side. Did the baby notice the change?
+ Don't forget about your own voice. Make sounds, changing the pitch of your voice; sing; and even have leisurely chats (okay, monologues) with the baby.
+ Play imitation games. Make a noise (a Bronx cheer is always a good place to start) and see whether the baby responds. It may take a few minutes or even a few days to get a reply. Once you do, try the same noise a few more times and then switch roles, having the baby initiate the "conversation" so you can imitate her.

Baby Massage
Many parents in Africa, Asia, and India massage their babies every day. But in the United States this idea is just catching on. And in the eyes of some, it's about time. According to researcher Tiffany Field, massage:
+ Facilitates the parent-infant bonding process and the development of warm, positive relationships.

> ## Massage for Preemies
>
> Over a dozen researchers have seriously explored the question of whether baby massage could help preterm infants. One study found that preemies who had daily ten-minute sessions of neck, shoulder, back, and leg massage, and five minutes a day of gentle limb flexing gained 47 percent more weight than preterm babies who got no massage, even though the two groups did not differ in calorie intake. In addition, massaged infants were awake and active a greater percentage of the time, developed more quickly, and required six fewer days of hospitalization.

♦ Reduces stressful responses to painful procedures like vaccines (at least for the baby).

♦ Reduces pain associated with teething and constipation.

♦ Reduces colic.

♦ Helps induce sleep.

♦ Makes parents feel good while they're massaging their infants.

Sounds like it's at least worth a try, doesn't it? Here's how to do it:

1. With your fingertips, gently massage the baby's forehead, nose, and mouth.
2. Starting in the middle of your baby's chest, use a flat hand to stroke outward.
3. Do the same thing on his back—start from the middle and stroke outward.
4. Take one of the baby's feet with one hand. With the other, hold the baby's ankle like a baseball bat and slide your hand toward the thigh. Repeat with the other foot.
5. Do the same thing for the arms: start at the wrist and move toward the shoulder.

The best time to massage is when the baby is calm. You might want to rub a little baby oil or lotion on your hands before you start, and be sure to use a combination of straight and circular strokes.

It's especially important to keep the pressure gentle yet firm. Babies respond negatively to a very light touch, which they perceive as tickling. If at all possible, try to do some massage every day (or split the duties with your partner). If you're interested in learning more about baby massage, several books on the subject are probably available at your local library. One of the best is Vimala McClure's *Infant Massage: A Handbook for Loving Parents.*

The Importance of Squirming Around

Most two-month-old babies are not really mobile. They can raise their heads about 45 degrees, but rolling over is still a ways away. Nevertheless, it's a good idea to let your baby exercise her muscles. Here are a few ways to do this:

♦ Stop swaddling (if you haven't already). Your baby needs to practice using her arms and hands, something she won't be able to do if she's all bundled up in a blanket.

♦ When putting the baby down, alternate among front, back, left side, and right side. This encourages the baby to use as many different muscles as possible. Babies who spend all day on one side (including front or back) generally don't learn to lift their heads as quickly as those who are shifted from side to side.

Introducing the Doctor

If you went to all your partner's prenatal doctor visits, the schedule of visits to your baby's pediatrician will seem quite leisurely—only eight (usually called well-baby checkups) the entire first year. Whether or not you got into

Vaccinations

There has been a lot of controversy lately about vaccinations (Are the vaccines themselves dangerous? Are the risks worth the rewards?), and a small but growing number of people are electing not to have their children inoculated. On pages 62–65 you'll find a chart listing the vaccines, the possible side effects, and what might happen to someone who's not inoculated. If you're thinking of skipping the vaccinations, keep these points in mind:

♦ Almost all public schools, and many private ones, require proof of vaccination before admitting a child.

♦ Not vaccinating your kids can be a viable option only if everyone else's kids *are* vaccinated, thus reducing the chance that your child will be exposed to health risks. This is known as "herd immunity": if enough people are immune, they'll protect the rest of the "herd." Imagine what would happen if everyone decided not to vaccinate.

VACCINE	RISKS (👎) / REWARDS (👍)
Diphtheria, Pertussis, Tetanus (DPT) or Diphtheria, Tetanus (DT) or DTaP: same as above, minus pertussis part for babies who have: ♦ history of seizures ♦ suspected or known neuro-logical disease ♦ reactions to previous shot	👍 almost all protected after 3 doses plus booster 👎 you'll need to observe baby carefully for 72 hours after shot 👎 some fussiness, drowsiness, soreness, or a lump at injection site 👎 fever for 24 hours after the shot is common 👎 irritation of the brain occurs in 1 in 100,000 kids, and rarely (1 in 310,000), permanent brain damage results. *Note:* Most of the risks are associated with the pertussis component. The only risk associated with the diphtheria and tetanus parts is local (injection site swelling)
Hepatitis B: a noninfectious vaccine produced from cultures	👍 almost all children protected after 3 doses 👎 no adverse reactions, but occasional fussiness 👎 possible soreness at injection site, low-grade fever, or headache
Haemophilus (HiB)	👍 90–100 percent protection rate after the full series of shots 👎 soreness and/or lump at the injection site 👎 fever (rarely above 101 degrees) for 12–24 hours after shot
Measles	👍 over 95 percent protected after one dose 👎 10–20 percent have mild fever or rash 10 days after shot 👎 1 in 1,000,000 may develop a brain disorder

WHAT IT PREVENTS	RISKS IF YOU GET THE DISEASE
Diphtheria	• extremely contagious • attacks the throat and nose, interferes with breathing, and causes paralysis • damages heart, kidneys, nerves • 10–35 percent death rate
Pertussis (whooping cough): prior to the invention of this vaccine, pertussis caused as many deaths as all other contagious diseases combined	• can cause brain damage, pneumonia, and seizures • can cause death (1–2 percent) • most severe in young babies
Tetanus (lockjaw), caused by dirt getting in cuts	• causes painful muscle contractions • 20–60 percent of kids die
Hepatitis B	• important cause of viral hepatitis • complications include cirrhosis, chronic active hepatitis, and liver cancer
Haemophilus Influenza type B, bacterial infection of children under 5	• causes 12,000 cases of meningitis and 8,000 cases of deep-seated infections (bones, joint, heart, lungs, throat) each year • 5 percent mortality rate
Measles	• a most serious, common childhood disease • high fever (103–105 degrees) and rash for up to 10 days • may cause pneumonia or ear infection • 1 in 100 kids becomes deaf or develops brain disorders

(continued on next page)

(continued from pages 62–63)

VACCINE	RISKS (👎) / REWARDS (👍)
Mumps	👍 99 percent protected after one dose
	👎 rare fever, rashes, and swelling of glands after vaccination
Rubella	👍 over 95 percent protected after one dose
	👍 getting it now protects future fetuses of girl babies
	👍 children of pregnant women can be vaccinated without risk to mother
	👎 1 percent of young children will have temporary leg, arm, joint pain
MMR measles, mumps, rubella vaccines	👍 protection is as good as when vaccines are given separately
	👍 side effects are same as when given separately
Oral Polio (OPV): three kinds of polio virus—your child needs all 3 vaccines to be protected	👍 drops, not shots
	👍 95 percent receiving all 3 doses are protected
	👍 no common reactions
	👎 1 in 4 million chance of paralysis
	👎 1 in 12 million chance of actually getting polio

the doctor-visit habit before the baby was born, make every effort to go to as many well-baby visits (and not-so-well-baby visits) as you can. Your doing so is good for everyone, says James Levine, head of the Fatherhood Project at the Families and Work Institute.

♦ Your baby will know that he can turn to you for help and that you'll be there to comfort him when he needs it.

♦ Your doctor will be able to get some of *your* family history to apply to the

WHAT IT PREVENTS	RISKS IF YOU GET THE DISEASE
Mumps	♦ causes fever and swelling of salivary glands ♦ may cause irritation of heart, pancreas, or thyroid ♦ can cause permanent deafness and temporary brain disorder
Rubella (German measles)	♦ can cause birth defects in fetus of pregnant women ♦ symptoms are mild, often missed
Mumps, Measles, Rubella	
Polio	♦ causes paralysis of arms and legs ♦ interferes with breathing ♦ 1 in 10 kids with polio dies

baby. And since most of what pediatricians know about their young patients comes from what the parents tell them, your input doubles the amount of information the doctor can use to make a diagnosis.

♦ You'll be more in touch with your child and more involved in his life.

Most doctor visits will be pretty much the same: the nurse will try to convince the baby to lie flat enough to be measured, and to sit still on a scale long enough to get weighed. Then the doctor will poke the baby's stomach, measure his head, and ask you a series of questions about the baby's health. The big events at most doctor visits for the first several years are the vaccinations.

We'll discuss some specific medical questions in later chapters. But for now, here's a fairly typical schedule of well-baby checkups and the vaccinations your baby will receive at each visit:

AGE AT TIME OF VISIT	VACCINATION(S) GIVEN
birth–2 weeks	Hepatitis B
2 months	DPT and Hepatitis B
3 months	OPV and Haemophilus Influenza B
4 months	DPT and Hepatitis B
5 months	OPV and Haemophilus Influenza B
6 months	DPT and Hepatitis B
8 months	OPV and Haemophilus Influenza B
12 months	MMR and TB test

Notes:

Let the Games Begin

What's Going On with the Baby

Physically

♦ As more and more of his reflexes disappear, your baby's body is changing. He can now keep his hands open (instead of balled up in tiny fists), and when you put him down on his tummy, he extends his legs instead of automatically rolling up into a little ball like a pill bug.

♦ But he can't yet tell one side of his body from the other, and he moves both legs or both arms together.

♦ When you pull him from a reclining position, he'll try to stand up, pressing his feet against whatever he was lying on.

♦ His head is bobbing around a lot less, and if you can get him into a sitting position, he can probably sit fairly well for a few seconds (he'll still need plenty of support). He may also be able to clap his hands.

♦ Your baby is getting much better at grasping things—a development some experts feel is a new reflex, designed to develop your baby's hand-eye coordination. "Everything that the child grasps is brought to the eyes and everything he sees evokes an effort to grasp," says Dr. Wolff.

Intellectually

♦ Moving objects are a source of nearly endless fascination. Your baby will follow with his eyes and head an object moving from one side of his head to the other.

♦ One day your baby will catch sight of his own hand on its way into his mouth. Until this very moment, he had no idea that the thing he's been sucking on for the past few months actually belongs to him. Best of all, he now realizes that objects (or at least his hand) can exist for at least two reasons at the same time: to look at *and* to suck on.

♦ As a result of this startling, and incredibly important, revelation, your baby will spend as much as 15 minutes at a stretch intently staring at his squiggling fingers and then shoving them into his mouth. He'll repeat the process over and over and over.

♦ The baby is now able to tell the difference between various objects; he prefers circular shapes to stripes.

♦ He is also able to make associations between certain objects and qualities linked to them. For example, he may associate your partner with food and you with play, and will react differently to each of you.

Verbally

♦ Although most of your baby's vocalizing is crying, he's making some delightful, soothing, single-syllable sounds.

♦ He's now beginning to use his vocalizing for a purpose—if you listen carefully, you should be able to tell the difference between his "I'm hungry," "I'm tired," and "Change my diaper" cries.

♦ He's now also attentively listening to all the sounds around him and distinguishes speech from any other sound.

Emotionally/Socially

♦ At this point your baby's schedule of eating, sleeping, diaper filling, and being alert is fairly regular.

♦ When it comes to people, he has strong likes and dislikes, crying or calming down depending on who holds him. He'll also smile at familiar people, stare at strangers.

♦ He'll stare, absorbed with his surroundings, for up to 30 minutes at a time.

What You're Going Through

Worried about SIDS

Every year seven thousand children die of SIDS (Sudden Infant Death Syndrome). Striking one out of every thousand babies, it is the most common cause of death of children between one week and one year old.

Although government and private agencies spend millions of dollars each year in the fight against SIDS, scientists have been unable to figure out what, exactly, causes the disease. And there's no medical test to determine which babies are at the greatest risk. Here is what scientists *do* know:

♦ SIDS is most likely to strike infants two to four months old.
♦ Ninety percent of deaths happen by six months, but SIDS still strikes children up to one year old.
♦ It is more likely to occur to boys than girls, to preterm babies, to multiple-birth babies, and to babies from families in which a parent or caretaker smokes or bottle-feeds.
♦ The disease is more common in cold weather, when respiratory infections and overheating are more common. Both have been linked to SIDS.

Although two-thirds of all SIDS babies have no risk factors, there are a few things you can do to minimize the risk:

♦ Make sure your baby sleeps on his back. When my older daughter was born in 1990, the then-current wisdom was that babies should not sleep on their backs because of the risk of choking if the baby spit up. But by the time my second was born in 1993, the spit-up theory had been debunked. If your baby has been sleeping on his stomach, it's not too late to change (sure, he's been doing it all his life, but still, it's been only three months). After four months, making the stomach-to-back shift is far less critical.
♦ Don't smoke and don't let anyone else smoke near the baby.
♦ Don't overdress the baby (see the section on dressing, pages 79–80).
♦ Have your baby sleep on a firm mattress: no pillows, fluffy blankets, cushiony sofas, waterbeds, thick rugs, or beanbags. Make sure the mattress fits snugly into the crib so that the baby can't slip between the mattress and the crib frame. And take out of the crib all the plush animals, extra blankets, and other things that might accidentally cover the baby.
♦ Breastfeed.
♦ Don't panic. Although SIDS is a horrible, devastating experience for any parent, remember that 999 out of 1,000 babies *don't* die of it.

What to Do If You Lose Your Baby to SIDS

The loss of a child is a terrible thing, something that will affect you and your partner for the rest of your lives. Too often SIDS affects couples who haven't been together very long, and the strain can be especially taxing to their new relationship. But no matter how long a couple has been together, the loss of a child will have a devastating effect on their relationship.

"Surviving grief does not mean escaping from it," says Amy Hillyard

Grief: Not for Women Only

For better or worse, men and women are socially and culturally conditioned to behave in certain ways in certain situations. We could spend a lot of time arguing about the advantages and disadvantages of our socialization, but one thing we can all agree on is that men, generally, aren't allowed to experience or express grief in a way that is healthy to themselves or to those who love them.

Women are more likely to talk about their grief—they have more intimate friends and are more willing to ask for help. They're also more likely to get offered help. Men, however, are less likely to talk about their grief, preferring to internalize it and remain silent. They have fewer intimate friends and avoid asking for help. They also get offered a lot less help.

Men have some very specific needs when it comes to grieving. Here are some wonderful suggestions from the SIDS Alliance in Baltimore:

♦ Talk to your family—especially your wife. "Grief is the stone that bears one down, but two bear it lightly," said William Hauff in the nineteenth century. Let people know you're doing as much as you can and let them know how they can help you.

♦ Have quality "alone" time. You need time to sort through all

Jensen, author of *Healing Grief.* "Grief itself is the healing process and you must go through it. Grief will change you, but you have some control over whether the changes are for better or for worse."

Marion McNurlen of the Minnesota SIDS Alliance suggests that grieving couples do as many of the following as possible:

♦ Don't assume the other doesn't know what you're feeling or what you're going through.

♦ Schedule some time to talk to each other. You and your partner have experienced the same physical loss, but you won't grieve at the same pace, or at the same time. You need to check in with each other often.

♦ Have other people to talk to. Your partner can't be there for you (nor you for her) all the time. Call your friends, clergy person, or therapist.

♦ Touch each other. Often, the completely normal feelings of blame (either of yourself or of your partner) lead to not wanting to touch or be touched. At the same time, though, you and your partner may be nearly screaming inwardly for the other's touch, but you're afraid to ask, afraid of burdening the questions running through your brain. Think about keeping a journal.

♦ Decrease your social activities. Many men seek out new hobbies or other activities, but these only detract from the grieving you really need to do.

♦ Cry. It's just about the hardest thing to do for most of us, but don't try to keep down that lump in your throat or swallow your tears. Crying releases some tension and can actually make you feel better.

♦ Get angry. Anger is a natural part of the grieving process and holding it back or ignoring it won't make it disappear. There's nothing wrong with being angry; it's what you do with the feeling that counts, so find a way to express your anger that won't hurt others. Exercise is perhaps the best outlet for it.

♦ Find a support system. For many men, asking for help is even tougher than crying. But research has shown that what men find most helpful is a caring listener, someone patient, someone, perhaps, who is going through (or has recently gone through) the same experience. Local hospitals are an excellent source of referrals to support groups. So is the SIDS Alliance, which has counselors available twenty-four hours a day. You can reach them at (800) 221-SIDS (7437).

the other with your own needs. Physical closeness may be more important now than at any other time in your relationship.

♦ Try to have some fun. "It is common for grieving parents to have a strong sense that it is disrespectful of their child for them to laugh," says McNurlen. "But laughter is very healing, you can deeply miss your child and have fun once in a while."

Examining Your Relationship with Your Father

As you continue to grow and develop as a father, you may find yourself spending a lot of time thinking about your own father. Was he the kind of father you'd like to use as a role model, or was he exactly the kind of father you don't want to be? Was he supportive and nurturing, or was he absent or abusive? Like it or not, it is the relationship you had with your father when you were young that sets the tone for your relationship with your own children.

Depending on your perspective, this is either good news or bad news. If you are satisfied with your relationship with your dad and you'd like to be the kind

Well, Dad, I'll tell you: Every time I face a dilemma about parenting, I ask myself, "What would Dad do?"... And then I do the opposite.

SIPRESS

of father he was, you don't have much to worry about. "A cohesive boyhood home atmosphere in which the father and mother worked together," writes researcher John Snarey, "predicts that the boy who grew up in it will provide more care for his own children's social-emotional development in adolescence."

But if your relationship with your father was not everything it should have been, you may be afraid that you are somehow destined to repeat your father's mistakes. And you may have started to act accordingly. Psychologist Bruce Linton has observed that if a man's father was abusive, he may begin to withdraw or disengage from parenting his own infant out of "an unconscious or conscious desire to protect his child from his own fear of being abusive." And when the son of an absent father becomes a father himself, says Linton, "He often carries a deep grief or longing for the father he never had, and this feeling is activated as he experiences his own infant."

If you're finding yourself doing—or not doing—things with your baby out of fear, you can relax. At least a little. Dr. Snarey found that new fathers seem to take the good from their fathers and throw away the bad. In fact, many new fathers are able to turn to their advantage the example of a less-than-perfect relationship with their fathers. Here are some common scenarios:

♦ Men whose fathers were distant or non-nurturant often provide high levels of care for their children's social-emotional and intellectual-academic development in adolescence.

♦ Men whose fathers provided inconsistent or inadequate supervision tend to provide high levels of care for their children's physical-athletic development in childhood.

♦ Men whose fathers used or threatened to use physical punishment that instilled fear in them as boys generally provide high levels of care for their own children's physical-athletic development in childhood.

Taking On More Responsibility

Nearly two-thirds of the men in Dr. Bruce Drobeck's research studies stated that the biggest change in their lives since they became fathers was that they had taken on more responsibility. Drobeck doesn't say where "taking on more responsibility" ranked for the remaining third, but I can't imagine any new father not experiencing at least *some* increase. Then again, it depends on how one defines the term.

If you think, for example, that "taking on more responsibility" means only that you are spending the same amount of time on child care as your partner, you may not view those two extra dinners you plan and prepare or the three extra loads of laundry you now do each week as an increase. But I do. One new father, a man who had been out of work for four years, became more responsible when he started looking more realistically at his employment situation. "I just have to lower my sights," he said. "I can't hold out for the exact position I want." Sounds quite responsible to me.

Whatever definition of responsibility you settle on, you'll undoubtedly find that you're focusing much more on your family now, and you're spending more time thinking about the consequences of your actions. "A D.W.I. would put a hardship on the family," said one new father who quit having a few drinks before driving home from the golf course.

For me, being more responsible meant obeying the speed limits (or trying to) and not accelerating at yellow traffic lights. For you, however, it might mean anything from giving up bungee jumping or alligator wrestling to reducing the aggressiveness of your investments.

So whether you call it "taking on more responsibility," "changing your priorities," or "putting your family first," these completely normal behavioral changes all have at least one thing in common. Each, in Bruce Drobeck's words, gives the new father "a positive motivation for personal improvement and growth."

Losing Your Grip

"The baby cries, the parent answers," writes Ellen Galinsky. "The baby is hungry, the parent provides food. The baby is awake most of the night, so is the parent. Parents feel as if their old life, their ability to plan, to have a reliable pattern to their days, is slipping away. . . . They don't know how to gauge themselves. The chores, the repetitive cycles of feeding, changing, putting the baby to sleep, seem endless. Night blurs into day. Time and their ability to control it, even count on it, seem far beyond their grasp, perhaps forever." Sounds like a horror story, doesn't it?

Of course, no one wants to lose control. But the feeling of losing one's grip on one's own life is particularly hard for men. Although there aren't any guaranteed cures for feeling out of control, there are two deceptively simple things you can do to at least take the edge off the feeling:

♦ Sit down with your partner and schedule some regular breaks for each of you: from the baby, from each other, from the house. You'll be amazed at how rejuvenated you'll feel after even just a couple of hours alone, doing something non-baby-related. This isn't a one-shot deal—try to schedule breaks once a week or more often, if you need to.

♦ Learn to accept that some things are within your control and that some things aren't. Babies—at least at this age—aren't.

You and Your Baby

Let the Games Begin

Playing with your baby is one of the most important things you can do for him. Researchers have found that early parent-child play can speed up the attachment process. In addition, kids who are played with a lot as babies are more attentive and interactive as they grow up, and end up with higher self-esteem than kids who weren't played with as much.

But before you mount that basketball hoop, remember that at this stage of life babies have literally just discovered themselves, and watching and experimenting with their own little bodies are quite enough to keep them occupied for a big chunk of their waking time.

At this age, the first "game" you play with your baby starts off with nothing more than his giving you a smile. If you respond nicely, he'll smile at you again. After repeating this a few times (it may even take a few days), your baby will learn that what *he* does can lead to a response from *you*. That seemingly simple realization is the basis for any kind of meaningful interaction your baby will have with other people.

Nuts and Bolts

For now, most babies have no idea what to do with rattles, keys, or anything else that needs to be grabbed. This doesn't mean, however, that you shouldn't make regular attempts to introduce some objects into the baby's life. Just don't take it personally if your gesture is completely ignored.

You don't really need any more equipment or supplies than last month. However, you might want to hang a few more pictures of faces where the baby can see them easily. Also, be sure to review the "Awakening the Senses" section, pages 58–59.

A fun experiment: tie one end of a ribbon loosely to the baby's ankle and the other to a mobile. Make the ribbon taut enough so that if the baby moves his leg, he'll also move the mobile. After a few minutes, most (but definitely not all) babies at this age will begin to see a cause and effect relationship developing and will begin to move the tied leg more than the other. Move the ribbon to the other leg, then to the arms, and see how well the baby adapts. A note of caution: never leave the room—even for a minute—with the baby tied to the mobile.

Music

While it's way too early to introduce your baby to music in any serious way, it's not too early to acclimate him. And if you pay attention, you'll notice that he already has a rudimentary sense of rhythm. Lay him on the floor and turn on the stereo (not too loud, please). Notice how he moves his arms and legs rhythmically—not in *time* to the music, but definitely in *response* to it. Try different types of music. Do his movements change as you change the style?

Here are a few things to keep in mind as you're thinking about introducing your baby to music:

- Kids are surrounded by language from their first days (in fact, there's plenty of research showing that kids respond to linguistic rhythms and patterns they heard even before they were born).
- Kids learn music in much the same way as they do language: they start off by listening and absorbing. And remember: "It is not possible to harm a child by allowing her to listen to too much music," says music education researcher Edwin Gordon.
- Play a wide variety of music. Major or minor keys, fast or slow tempos, simple or complex rhythms, and the types of instruments are not important at this stage.
- Select music you like too (after all, you'll be listening as well).

♦ Some babies this age may try to imitate tones they hear. This is, however, extremely rare.

Reading: From Birth through Eight Months

Feeling a little silly about the prospect of sitting down and reading to your baby? Consider this: "When children have been read to, they enter school with larger vocabularies, longer attention spans, greater understanding of books and print, and consequently have the fewest difficulties in learning to read," writes Jim Trelease, author of *The New Read Aloud Handbook*. And in 1985, a U.S. Department of Education report stated, "The single most important activity for building the knowledge required for eventual success in reading is reading aloud to children."

Still not convinced? How about this: 60 percent of prison inmates are illiterate, 85 percent of juvenile offenders have reading problems, and 44 percent of adult Americans do not read a *single* book in the course of a year. Clearly, reading is an important habit to develop, and it's never too early to start.

What to Read When

For the first few months of your baby's life, your reading probably won't seem to be having much effect on him. Sometimes he'll stare at the book, sometimes not. Once in a while a flailing arm might hit the book, but it's completely accidental. It doesn't really matter what you read at this stage, just as long as you do it. It's a great opportunity for you and the baby to snuggle together and for him to get to know the rhythm and feel of our language.

At about three months, your baby may start holding your finger while you read to him. While it doesn't seem like much, this tiny gesture is a clear indication that he's starting to become aware of the book as a separate object and that he likes what you're doing. Look for books with simple, uncluttered drawings as well as poetry and nursery rhymes.

At four months, your baby will sit still and listen attentively while you're reading. He may even reach out to scratch the pages of the book. Don't get too excited, though, he's a while away from being able to identify anything on the page. Nursery rhymes, finger plays (this little piggy went to market and so on), and books with pictures of other babies are big hits at this stage.

At about five months most babies are just starting to respond to your pointing. There are two ways to take advantage of this new development: first, watch your baby's eyes, then point to and talk about what he is already focusing on. Second, point to something and encourage the infant to look where you're pointing.

At six months babies will respond to what you're reading by bouncing up and down or chuckling before you get to a familiar part of the story. If you've been reading regularly to your baby for a few months, you may notice that he has developed clear preferences for books and will let you know which one he wants you to read. A word of warning: at this age babies have an irresistible need to put everything into their mouths, and books are no exception. But first they'll want to scratch, tear, pat, rub, hit, and get into a serious tug-of-war with you over the book. To avoid these problems before they start, give your baby something else to put in his mouth while you're reading to him, and try to distract him with noise books (the cow says "moo," the airplane goes "whooosh").

At about seven months your baby's grabbing and tearing are now slightly more purposeful, and you may notice an occasional attempt to turn pages. It will be another month or two, though, until he's actually able to do so. Plot is pretty well wasted on babies this age. But he'll like books with brightly colored pictures of familiar objects, as well as those that encourage you to make different sounds.

READY, SET . . .

Here are a few things to keep in mind when you're getting ready to read:
- Select a regular place for reading.
- Set aside a regular time, when you will be able to devote your full attention to the baby and the book. Just before or just after a nap is usually good.
- Try to read for at least fifteen minutes each day. Be prepared: you may have to do this in several installments. Kids' attention spans average only about three minutes at this age, but vary widely (my older daughter would sit in my lap for an hour at a time, whereas my younger couldn't sit still for more than three seconds).
- Reading to your child is for *her*, not for you. So if she arches her back, squirms, lurches forward, or does anything to let you know she's not happy, stop immediately—you're wasting your time. If you don't, the baby will begin to associate reading with discomfort.
- Don't read things that are developmentally inappropriate. "The difference between whether kids enjoyed it or not," say researchers Linda Lamme and Athol Packer, "was whether or not the parents adjusted their bookreading behavior to the developmental levels of their infants."

A list of appropriate titles follows. This is by no means a definitive list. With about five thousand new children's titles published each year, the pool of good books never stops growing. I strongly urge you to get to know your local librarians, who are always up to date, or to subscribe to *Children's Literature*, a wonderful newsletter that reviews current children's books (the address is in the resource guide at the end of the book).

. . . GO!

GENERAL INTEREST FOR THE FIRST SIX TO EIGHT MONTHS

Baby Animal Friends, Phoebe Dunn (board book)
The Baby (and others), John Burningham
Baby Farm Animals, Garth Williams
Baby's Book of Babies, Kathy Henderson
Baby's First Words, Lars Wik
Baby's First Year, Phyllis Hoffman
Baby's Home, Tana Hoban
First Things First, Charlotte Voake
Hand Rhymes, Marc Brown
Happy Baby, Angie and Sage
I See (and others), Rachel Isadora
Pat the Bunny, Dorothy Kunhardt
Pat the Cat, Edith Kunhardt
Peek-a-Boo!, Janet and Allan Ahlberg
Spot's Toys, Eric Hill
This Is Me, Lenore Blegvad (board book)
Ten Little Babies, Debbie MacKinnon (board book)
Trot Trot to Boston: Play Rhymes for Baby
Welcome, Little Baby (and others), Aliki
What Do Babies Do? Debby Slier (board book)
What Is It? Tana Hoban (board book)

MOTHER GOOSE, LULLABIES, POETRY AND SONGS, FINGERPLAYS

These are great for kids of all ages. Start now and return to them as often as you like.

The Baby's Bedtime Book, Kay Chorao
A First Caldecott Collection: The House That Jack Built and *A Frog He Would A-Wooing Go*
A Second Caldecott Collection: Sing a Song of Sixpence and *Three Jovial Huntsmen*
A Third Caldecott Collection: Queen of Hearts and *The Farmer's Boy*
The House that Jack Built, Janet Stevens

The Mother Goose Treasury, Raymond Briggs
Old Mother Hubbard, Alice and Martin Provensen
The Random House Book of Mother Goose, Arnold Lobel
Read-Aloud Rhymes for the Very Young, selected by Jack Prelutsky
Ring a Ring O-Roses, Flint Public Library
Sing a Song of Popcorn: Every Child's Book Of Poems, selected by
    Beatrice S. De Regniers et al.
The Complete Story of the Three Blind Mice, John Ivimey
Three Little Kittens, Lorinda Cauley
Singing Bee! A Collection of Favorite Children's Songs
Tail Feathers from Mother Goose: The Opie Rhyme Book, Iona and Peter Opie
Tomie De Paola's Mother Goose, Tomie De Paola
A Week of Lullabies, Helen Plotz
Wendy Watson's Mother Goose, Wendy Watson

Hittin' the Road

Despite what your mother or mother-in-law might tell you, you can take your
baby out at any age. The trick is in knowing how to dress him.

One of the great myths about babies is that you have to bundle them up
like Nanook of the North every time you take them out of the house. Here's the
truth: overdressed babies are at risk of getting heat stroke, which can result in
abnormally high fevers and even convulsions. This risk is especially high if
you're taking the baby out in a sling, backpack, or frontpack, where he'll be
even hotter.

Of course, underdressing can be a problem, too. The answer is to dress your
baby just as you would dress yourself (except that you're probably not going
to wear any of those cute little booties). When the weather's cold, it helps to
dress the baby in various layers rather than one or two very heavy items. That
way you can remove a layer or two if the baby gets overheated.

Most important, because you're the grown-up, you're going to have to pay
close attention. If you underdress your baby, he'll probably let you know about
it; babies usually complain loudly when they're too cold. Babies who are too
hot, though, tend *not* to complain, preferring, instead, to lie there listlessly.

SUMMER

For the first six months, your baby should be kept far away from direct sun-
light. Because babies' skin is at its thinnest and lightest during this period,
even a little sun can do a lot of damage. This applies to babies of all races
and skin tones.

When you go out, dress your baby in lightweight and light-colored long-sleeved shirts and long pants. From the time they were a few months old, neither of my kids would let me put any kind of hat anywhere near them. But if you can get your baby to wear a cute hat with a wide brim, so much the better. And if you're brave enough to try putting sunglasses on her, get the kind that shield her eyes from UVA and UVB rays. For extra protection, consider getting a parasol or sunshade for your stroller and try to stay indoors during the hottest parts of the day (about 11 A.M. to 3 P.M.).

When you're putting together your supplies for an outdoor summertime excursion, throw in a sweater and some warm pants for the baby. Sounds a little strange, but if you step into any kind of air-conditioned building (such as a supermarket or your office building) after having been outside for a while, you're going to feel awfully cold—and so will the baby.

Oh, and by the way, if you were thinking that your baby can't get a sunburn on a cloudy or overcast day, think again. Studies have shown that 60 percent of the sun's UV rays make their way down here, regardless of clouds, fog, or anything else.

Skin Problems

SUN

Despite all your precautions and good intentions, your baby may still end up with a minor sun-related condition:

- **Sunburn.** If it's minor, cover the affected area with a cool compress. If there are blisters, if the baby is running a fever, or if he's listless or nonresponsive, call your doctor immediately.
- **Prickly heat (heat rash).** A direct result of overdressing, prickly heat looks like tiny red blisters on a flushed area. It occurs anywhere sweat can build up: where the neck meets the shoulders, under the arms, inside elbows and knees, inside diapers. If your baby has heat rash, try to keep him as cool as possible. Lotions and creams probably won't help much, but putting a cool, damp washcloth or some cornstarch on the affected area may make your baby more comfortable.

INSECTS

The sun isn't the only potentially dangerous element that comes out in the summer. Here are some tips for preventing your baby from being consumed by insects:

- Don't use any kind of scented powders, lotions, or even diaper wipes. Bugs love them.

Sunscreen

Until she's six months old, don't use any sunscreen on your baby at all (that's why it's so important to keep infants out of the sun). Because they are usually so filled with chemicals, sunscreens frequently cause allergic reactions.

After six months, the risk of an allergic reaction from sunscreen is much lower, but stick with one that's unscented, alcohol- and PABA-free, and hypoallergenic, or made specially for infants. Hawaiian Tropic, Johnson & Johnson, and Water Babies all make acceptable formulas.

Lube your baby up with sunscreen about half an hour before going outside, and add some more every three hours or so. Pay special attention to feet, hands, legs, and arms—even if they're completely covered. Socks can roll down, and sleeves and pant legs can hike up all by themselves, exposing baby's skin to the elements.

♦ Avoid insect repellent if at all possible. A long-sleeved shirt and long pants can provide just about the same level of protection and are a lot easier on infant skin.

♦ Stay away from clothes with floral patterns: most bugs aren't smart enough to tell the difference between a real flower and your equally delicious flower-covered child. Light colors are far less attractive to bugs than dark colors.

DIAPER RASH

In the pre-disposable-diaper era, when a baby urinated the moisture stayed right there against her skin. Partly because of the acid in urine and partly because it's uncomfortable to sit in something wet, the baby would soon start complaining. And if she made what my older daughter used to call "a big dirty" (a bowel movement), her discomfort was greater, and her complaints voiced sooner. This raised the chances that she'd get changed fairly quickly.

But with disposables, a lot of the moisture is whisked away from the baby (just like in the commercials) and converted into some kind of nonliquid gel. Still, the digestive acids in the baby's waste, especially in her stool, continue to irritate her skin until—voilà!—diaper rash. But because the baby isn't uncomfortable enough to complain, her diapers somehow don't manage to get changed quite as often.

Unlike sunburn or insect bites, no matter what you do or how hard you try, one of these days your baby is going to get diaper rash. Just about the only thing you can do to keep it to a minimum is to check your baby's diapers every few hours and change them even if they're only slightly wet. Also:

- ♦ If you're using cloth diapers, don't use rubber or plastic pants. Your baby's bottom needs good air circulation.
- ♦ When diaper rash develops, let your baby frolic for a few minutes sans diaper (on a towel, perhaps, just in case . . .). The extra air circulation will help.
- ♦ Apply some diaper cream with each change, but be especially gentle: irritated skin doesn't like to be rubbed. A piece of advice: after you've applied diaper rash cream to the baby's bottom, wipe any residual cream on your fingers onto the inside of the diaper. If any of the cream gets onto the plastic fasteners of a disposable diaper, they won't stick to the diaper.

Notes:

 **MONTHS**

Born to Be...

What's Going On with the Baby

Physically

- ♦ Lying on her back, she can now track moving objects, coordinating the activities of her eyes and head as well as an adult can.
- ♦ She's making better use of her hands, using them to finger each other, and to grasp small objects (most of which immediately end up in her mouth). But she hasn't yet figured out what to do with her opposable thumb. So, for the next few months at least, she won't be using it much, making her grasping a little clumsy.
- ♦ By the end of this month, though, she will have figured out that the two sides of her body are separate—a discovery she's glad to demonstrate by passing things back and forth between her hands.
- ♦ While on her tummy, she can lift her head 90 degrees and prop herself up on her forearms.
- ♦ She may be able to roll from her tummy to her side, and may occasionally make it onto her back.
- ♦ She still tries to stand when you pull her up, and when she's sitting, her back is straight and her head hardly wobbles.

Intellectually

- ♦ Your baby is developing a physical sense of her body, recognizing that her hands and feet are extensions of herself. And she'll spend a great deal of time every day using her hands to explore her face, her mouth, and whatever other parts of her body she can reach.

♦ She can retain objects in her hands voluntarily.

♦ She's beginning the long process of understanding cause and effect relationships. If she accidentally kicks a toy and it squeaks, she may try to kick it again, hoping to get the same reaction.

♦ She's begun to draw small distinctions between similar objects. She can clearly tell the difference between a real face and a picture of one, and she can distinguish nearby objects from distant ones.

♦ She is also starting to differentiate herself from some other objects in her world. She may, for example, find a special toy particularly soothing.

Verbally

♦ The amount of time your baby spends crying has decreased dramatically and she's just about ready to hold up her end of a conversation.

♦ When she hears a sound—especially a voice—she actively searches for it with her eyes.

♦ And if you wait a few seconds after saying something to her, she may "answer" you, making ample use of her expanding vocabulary of squeals, chuckles, chortles, giggles, and clicks.

♦ She's trying as hard as she can to imitate one or two sounds and, if she's got something on her mind, may take the initiative and start a "conversation" with you.

Emotionally/Socially

♦ Overall, your baby is a pretty happy kid, smiling regularly and spontaneously and anticipating pleasurable encounters by vigorously kicking her arms and legs.

♦ She's also so anxious to socialize that she can actually suppress other interests in order to play. If you talk to her while she's eating, for example, she'll gladly stop for half an hour or so to chat.

♦ She now tries to extend her playtime by laughing or holding her gaze on a desired object, and she may protest loudly if you stop doing what she wants you to.

♦ Despite this hedonistic streak, she's still got clear preferences among playmates. Some will be able to soothe her, others won't.

♦ This is an extremely busy developmental time for your baby, and you may notice some interruption in her sleep patterns as she wakes up in the middle of the night to practice her new tricks.

What You're Going Through

Reevaluating Your Relationship with Your Job

Remember the shift in focus and priorities we talked about last month—from self to family? Well, once that shift has begun, the very next thing most new fathers do is take a long, hard look at their jobs.

In a small number of cases, fathers make a renewed commitment to their jobs—longer hours, increased productivity, more responsibility—motivated by a need to provide for their growing families. A far more common scenario, however, is the one Bruce Drobeck found in his research. Most new fathers, he says, "were looking for ways to reduce or restructure their work hours in order to achieve a balance between work and family."

This, of course, flies in the face of a lot of the stereotypes we often hear about fathers. But if you don't believe me, consider the results of a few national polls:

♦ 65 percent of fathers in one national poll said they believe they are being asked to sacrifice too much family time for the workplace.

♦ 57 percent of the men surveyed at one major corporation (up from 37 percent five years earlier) wanted work-schedule flexibility that would allow them to spend more time with their families.

♦ A recent survey by *Forbes* magazine found that 30 percent of fathers with kids under twelve had personally turned down a job promotion or transfer because it would have reduced the time they spend with their families.

Based on these statistics, it shouldn't come as much of a surprise that, as researcher John Snarey found, "a majority of husbands now experience fathering as more psychologically rewarding . . . than their occupations."

However, lest you think that all this is just a bunch of optimistic rhetoric, here's an example of the lengths to which some new fathers will go in order to spend more time with their families. A recent study by the Families and Work Institute stated that "some men had told friends at work they were going to a bar when in fact they were going home to care for their children."

Coming to Terms with Breastfeeding

Before their babies are born, nearly all expectant fathers feel that breastfeeding is the best way to feed a baby and that their partners should do so as long as possible. After the baby comes, new fathers still feel that breast is best, but many are also feeling a little ambivalent.

Most new fathers feel that breastfeeding "perpetuates the exclusive relationship the mother and infant experienced during pregnancy," writes Dr. Pamela Jordan, one of the few researchers ever to explore the effects of breastfeeding on men.

Given all this, says Dr. Jordan, a new father is likely to experience:

♦ A diminished opportunity to develop a relationship with his child.

♦ A sense of inadequacy.

♦ A feeling that the baby has come between him and his partner.

♦ A feeling that nothing he does to satisfy his child can ever compete with his partner's breasts.

♦ A sense of relief when his partner weans the baby, giving him the opportunity to "catch up."

♦ A belief in what Jordan calls the "hormonal advantage theory"—the idea that women are born with certain knowledge and skills that give them an advantage in parenting, including guaranteed success with breastfeeding.

SIPRESS

Whether or not you're experiencing these or any other less-than-completely-positive feelings, there's a good chance that your partner is having a few ambivalent feelings of her own about breastfeeding. Here are some of the things she may be feeling:

♦ Exhaustion. It may look easy and relaxing to you, but nursing a baby is tough work.

♦ Despite the images of smiling, happy nursing mothers, your partner simply may not be enjoying the experience. And if she isn't, she may be feeling guilty or inadequate. (Just goes to show you that fathers aren't the only ones boxed in by socialization.)

♦ She may resent the way nursing interferes with some of the other things she'd like to do.

♦ She may want to run as far away from the baby as possible. If so, she's also likely to feel guilty or selfish (socialization again . . . mothers are always supposed to be happy to be with their children).

♦ She may not be interested in answering your questions about the process. (I had a million for my wife: How does it feel? How much comes out in each feeding? Does the milk come out from one hole or more than one?)

"Preparing a meal and feeding someone is a powerful symbolic act," writes

Dr. Jordan. "Feeding the infant is often perceived by parents as the most important aspect of infant care, the most meaningful interaction." If your partner is breastfeeding, there's no question that you're at a bit of a disadvantage when it comes to feeding the baby. There are, however, a few ways you can help your partner and yourself make breastfeeding as pleasant an experience as possible for everyone:

♦ You can bottle-feed your baby with breast milk if your partner is willing to express some. But don't insist on this. Many women find expressing milk— manually or with a pump—uncomfortable or even painful.

♦ Don't take it personally if your baby doesn't seem interested in taking a bottle from you. Some babies need a few days to get used to the idea of sucking on a plastic nipple instead of a real one. Other babies, like my younger daughter, simply refuse to take a bottle at all. But don't give up without a fight. Plastic nipples—like real ones—come in all sorts of shapes and sizes. So you may have to do a little experimenting before you and your baby discover the kind she likes best (which may or may not have anything in common with the kind you like best).

♦ Make sure you get some private time with your baby for activities that provide regular skin-to-skin contact, such as bathing, cuddling, playing, putting to bed, and even changing diapers. According to Dr. Jordan, establishing rituals like these with your baby may help you feel that "the mother does not have exclusive rights to a special relationship." It can also help your partner by giving her some needed time off.

♦ Compare notes with other men whose partners breastfed their babies.

For Women Only (you can read this, but only if you promise to show it to your partner when you're done)
"The breastfeeding mother has the control of parenting and must realize that she has the power to invite the father in or exclude him," writes Dr. Pamela Jordan. "She can play a vital role in establishing exclusive father-infant time, often while simultaneously meeting her own needs for time away and alone. Just as the father is viewed as the primary support of the mother-infant relationship, the mother is the primary support of the father-infant relationship . . . supporting the father during breastfeeding may help improve his, and consequently, the mother's, satisfaction with breastfeeding, the duration of breastfeeding, and the adaptation of both parents to parenthood."

Worried That Your Life Will Never Be the Same Again (It Won't)

Before my kids were born, just about everybody my wife and I knew with kids pulled us aside and tried to warn us that our lives would change forever once we became parents. They told us about how hard it is to shift from worrying about only ourselves to being responsible for the safety and well-being of a completely helpless little person. They told us that we'd lose a lot of sleep and even more privacy. And they told us that we'd better go to a lot of movies and read a stack of books because we might not have another chance for a while. Everything everyone said was absolutely correct, but none of it really prepared us for our transition to parenthood.

What I often find most interesting about the changes I underwent when I became a father is the way my memories of my prefatherhood past have been subtly altered. It's not that I can't or don't remember life before children, it's just that that life, in retrospect, seems somehow incomplete.

I have clear, fond memories of taking long walks on the beach by myself, sleeping in all day, and going out at midnight for a beer with friends—things I haven't done much since becoming a father. It's as though those things happened to someone else, however. I don't really miss my other life, but in a way I wish I could have shared it with my children (not the beers, perhaps, but the walks on the beach and the sleeping in).

You and Your Baby

Your Baby's Temperament

About forty years ago a husband-and-wife team of psychiatrists, Stella Chess and Alexander Thomas, theorized that children are born with a set of nine fundamental behavioral and emotional traits they called "temperamental qualities." These qualities, which experts now believe remain fairly consistent throughout life, combine differently for each child and determine, to a great extent, a child's personality and whether he will be "easy" or "challenging." In addition, Chess and Thomas found that a child's temperament has a major influence on his parents' behavior and attitudes.

Over the past few decades, Chess and Thomas's original research in temperament has been expanded, refined, and improved upon. Here, then, are the nine temperament traits, adapted from Chess and Thomas, the Temperament Program at the Center for Parenting Excellence, and the work of Jim Cameron, head of The Preventive Ounce, a nonprofit mental health organization for children.

The Nine Temperament Traits of Babies

APPROACHING
♦ separate easily from parents
♦ are excited to meet and interact with new people
♦ greet new foods eagerly
♦ seem perfectly "at home" in new situations

WITHDRAWING
♦ are usually shy, cling to their parents in new situations or around strangers
♦ have difficulty separating from parents
♦ need time to warm up to new experiences
♦ may be extremely picky eaters and spit out food with new taste sensations

FAST ADAPTING
♦ fall asleep easily and without fussing, no matter where they are
♦ don't mind changes in routines
♦ can be fed easily by different people
♦ don't mind being handled by different people or passed around
♦ smile back quickly when talked to

SLOW ADAPTING
♦ may refuse to fall asleep in a strange place (or even a moderately familiar one like grandma and grandpa's)
♦ are slow to get back to sleep after being awakened
♦ don't like being picked up and held by strangers
♦ take a long time to warm up to new situations, and once upset, may take a long time to calm down

LOW INTENSITY
♦ display their emotions, but are often hard to read
♦ have subdued moods
♦ seem fairly nonchalant

HIGH INTENSITY
♦ react strongly (positively or negatively) to strangers, loud noises, bright lights
♦ do everything—shrieking with delight or crying—so loudly it hurts your ears

POSITIVE MOOD
♦ laugh and smile at just about everything
♦ are happy even when having their diapers changed
♦ seem genuinely happy to see you

NEGATIVE MOOD
♦ cry when being changed
♦ are fussy or cranky most of the time
♦ whimper or cry a lot, sometimes seemingly for no reason
♦ complain during hair brushing

LOW ACTIVITY
♦ seem content to lie still while nursing or getting changed
♦ will sit calmly in the car seat
♦ prefer less physical play (swings instead of wrestling)

HIGH ACTIVITY
♦ move around a lot while sleeping, frequently kicking their blankets off
♦ move around a lot while awake, and are hard to dress, change, bathe, or feed
♦ often reach physical developmental milestones earlier than lower-activity kids

PREDICTABLE

* get hungry, tired, and move their bowels at about the same times every day
* love regular eating and bedtime schedules
* struggle with changes in eating and sleep routines

UNPREDICTABLE

* may or may not take naps
* have frequent sleep problems and get up several times during the night
* may not be hungry at mealtimes and may want to eat at different times every day
* have irregular bowel movements

HIGH SENSORY THRESHOLD (OBLIVIOUS)

* love loud events (basketball games, circuses, bands . . .)
* aren't bothered by wet or dirty diapers
* are emotionally stable
* don't seem to be able to differentiate between two voices
* aren't bothered by clothing labels or scratchy fabrics
* don't seem bothered by pain

LOW SENSORY THRESHOLD (VERY AWARE)

* are easily overstimulated
* are awakened easily by gentle touch or by turning on lights
* may get extremely upset at loud noises
* notice tiny variations in the taste of food
* are extremely uncomfortable in wet or dirty diapers
* are very sensitive to fabrics, labels, and the fit of their clothes

LOW DISTRACTIBILITY

* are quite hard to soothe
* seem completely oblivious to interruptions (noise, familiar voices) when involved in something important (like nursing)

HIGH DISTRACTIBILITY

* have short attention spans
* are easily distracted while nursing
* are easily soothed when upset

HIGH PERSISTENCE

* are able to amuse themselves for a few minutes at a time
* like to practice new motor skills (like rolling from back to front) for a minute or more
* pay close attention (for more than a minute) to rattles and mobiles
* pay close attention to other children when playing
* cry when you stop playing with them

LOW PERSISTENCE

* can't amuse themselves for very long in crib or playpen
* have short attention spans and are frustrated easily, even by simple tasks
* quickly lose interest in playing, even with favorite toys
* won't spend much time working on new skills (rolling over, sitting up)

1. Approach/Withdrawal: Your child's usual *initial* reaction to a new experience, such as meeting a new person, tasting a new food, or being in a new situation.
2. Adaptability: Similar to Approach/Withdrawal, but deals with your child's longer-term reactions to changes in routines or expectations, new places, and new ideas.
3. Intensity: The amount of energy a child commonly uses to express emotions—both positive and negative.
4. Mood: Your child's general mood—happy or fussy—over the course of a typical day.
5. Activity level: The amount of energy your child puts into everything he does.
6. Regularity: The day-to-day predictability of your baby's hunger, sleeping, and filling diapers.
7. Sensitivity: Your baby's sensitivity to pain, noise, temperature change, lights, odors, flavors, textures, and emotions. Note: it's quite possible for your baby to be highly sensitive to one sensation (bright lights, for example) but not at all sensitive to others (noise).
8. Distractibility: How easy is it to change the focus of your baby's attention.
9. Persistence: Similar to Distractibility, but goes beyond the initial reaction and concerns the length of time your baby will spend trying to overcome obstacles or distractions.

Now that you know what to look for, spend a few minutes rating your baby on the following scale. And have your partner do it, too.

TRAIT	RATING						
Approach/Withdrawal	Approaching	1	2	3	4	5	Withdrawing
Adaptability	Fast	1	2	3	4	5	Slow
Intensity	Low	1	2	3	4	5	High
Mood	Positive	1	2	3	4	5	Negative
Activity Level	Low	1	2	3	4	5	High
Regularity	Predictable	1	2	3	4	5	Unpredictable
Sensitivity	Oblivious	1	2	3	4	5	Very Aware
Distractibility	Low	1	2	3	4	5	High
Persistence	High	1	2	3	4	5	Low

ENFANT TERRIBLE.

MUELLER

If you have a lot of 1s and 2s, you're one lucky guy. You've got an "easy" child (about 40 percent of parents do), and having an easy child is, well, easy. The baby's always smiling and happy, sleeps through the night, eats at the same time every day, and loves playing and meeting new people. When he does get upset or fussy, you can usually calm him down almost immediately. You're madly in love with your baby and you're feeling confident about your parenting skills.

But if you ended up with a lot of 4s and 5s, you most likely have a "challenging" child (only about 10 percent of parents do), and things are not nearly as rosy. She doesn't sleep through the night, has trouble eating, freaks out at the slightest noise or change in her surroundings, cries for hours at a time (and nothing you try seems to make it any better), and is generally fussy. Meanwhile, you're exhausted and depressed, angry at the baby for her "malicious" behavior, embarrassed at the way people stare at your unhappy child, guilty about your unparental feelings, and jealous of your friends and their easy babies. In short, you're not finding your parenting experience very satisfying, you're discouraged and frustrated, and you think you must be a complete failure as a father. You may even feel trapped and fantasize about running away.

As bad as it sounds, there are some things you can do to help you overcome a lot of your frustration and negative feelings:

♦ Recognize that challenging children are challenging because of their innate makeup. Their temperament exists at birth. It's not their fault, it's not your fault, and it's not your partner's fault. It's just the way things are.

♦ Stop blaming yourself, your partner, or your baby. There's probably nothing wrong with any of you. The problem is that the way you're interacting with your child simply isn't working.

♦ Get to know your child's—and your own—temperament and look for similarities and differences. If you're both Highly Distractible, you may never get through that book you're reading—and neither of you will care. But if you're Highly Approaching and the baby is Highly Withdrawing, you may have some real problems taking her to meet your boss for the first time.

At the very least, these steps will enable you to modify your approaches to your child's behavior and to anticipate and avoid conflicts before they occur. The result will be a far happier, more loving, and more satisfying relationship with your child. Guaranteed.

Putting Your Knowledge of Temperament to Good Use

Following are some of the most common, difficult-to-handle traits you're likely to encounter during your baby's first year, along with some suggestions for how to handle them, loosely based on the work of researchers Stanley Turecki and Leslie Tonner.

INITIAL WITHDRAWAL/SLOW ADAPTABILITY

Just because your baby initially spits out new foods and refuses to play with new toys doesn't mean he'll never change. Before you give up, try gently introducing new foods a few times at different meals, and give the baby a chance to "meet" a new toy from a distance before letting him touch it. (This process will help you figure out whether your child is Withdrawing and Slow-Adapting or has a Low Sensory Threshold.)

Your Withdrawing/Slow-Adapting baby will probably begin experiencing *stranger anxiety* (see pages 149–50) earlier—and it will last longer—than more Approaching and Fast-Adapting babies. Tell new visitors, and even those the baby knows a little bit, not to approach too quickly, not to try to pick him up right away, and not to take it personally if the baby reacts negatively.

One warning: Think about your baby's temperament before making any major changes in your appearance. Shaving your beard, getting a haircut, or even replacing your glasses with contact lenses can trigger a strong, negative reaction. When my older daughter was six months old, her baby-sitter—whom she absolutely adored—got a haircut, and it took her more than a week to recover.

HIGH INTENSITY

Short of leaving the room or getting ear plugs (both of which are perfectly reasonable approaches), there's not much you can do about your High-Intensity baby.

NEGATIVE MOOD

Not much can make you happier than going out with a smiling, happy baby. But a baby who isn't a smiler, and who whimpers and cries all the time, can be a real challenge to your self-confidence. It's hard to take pleasure in a baby with a Negative Mood, or even to feel proud of her. And it's certainly tempting to think that if the baby doesn't smile at you all the time, she doesn't love you.

If you're feeling this way, resist the urge to get angry with your baby for her whining, or to "get even" with her by withholding your love. (I know it sounds silly, but it happens.) The truth is that the lack of a smile doesn't necessarily mean there's a lack of love. And the whining *will* subside as your baby's verbal skills improve, enabling her to get your attention in more productive ways.

HIGH ACTIVITY

Because your High-Activity baby will spend his sleeping moments doing laps in his crib, it's important to install some big, soft bumpers (pads designed to protect babies' heads from banging into the bars). You'll also need to make sure there's nothing in the crib (or nearby) that could fall on top of the baby's head. And, if your house tends to be a little cold at night, dress the baby in something thick so he'll be warm when he kicks the covers off.

Never, never leave your baby unattended—even for a second—on a changing table or bed; she could very well roll off. Once, when my older daughter was seven months old, I was tickling her in her bassinet when the phone (located about three feet away) rang. I stepped over, said "Hello," and heard a loud thump behind me: my daughter, who had never given any indication that she could pull herself up, had done exactly that, and toppled over the side of the bassinet. No harm was done, but we never used that bassinet again.

UNPREDICTABILITY

Since your Unpredictable baby seems to be eating, sleeping, and filling his diaper at random, it's up to you to try to establish a regular schedule. Although he may not want to eat, try to feed him something at times that are more convenient for you. If you schedule meals at the same times every day, you may be able to help him create a modified routine.

When it comes to getting your baby to sleep, establishing a routine is also important. When you go into his room at night, don't turn on the lights, don't pick him up, don't play, and get out as soon as you can. Once you stumble on a getting-back-to-sleep routine, stick with it. If your baby's sleep irregularities are truly serious, you and your partner should divide up the night, each taking a shift while the other sleeps. If that doesn't help, talk with your pediatrician about a mild sedative. For the baby, not you.

LOW SENSORY THRESHOLD

For the first few months of a Low-Sensory-Threshold baby's life, you'll never know what's going to set her off. Sounds, smells, and sensations you might hardly notice can cause her to explode into tears: turning on the car radio, the crowd applauding at a basketball game (yes, you can take babies to basketball games), even too many toys in her crib.

One way to make your baby's life a little less jarring is to modify the amount and type of stimulation in her environment. Avoid neon colors when decorating her room, get opaque drapes to keep daytime light out during nap time, and don't play actively with her right before bedtime. When dressing your baby, stay away from tight clothes, brand-new clothes (they're often too stiff), wool, synthetic fabrics, or anything with a rough texture. Cotton blends usually offer the best combination of washability and softness. And be sure to clip off scratchy labels and tags.

HIGH DISTRACTIBILITY AND LOW PERSISTENCE

These traits are usually not much of a problem for you or your baby at this stage.

For most readers, this discussion of temperament should be sufficient to identify and begin to deal with their child's behavior patterns. But if you're seriously concerned about your child's temperament, or would be interested in exploring the subject in greater detail, I suggest you contact Temperament Talk, in Portland, Oregon, or Jim Cameron at The Preventive Ounce.

Family Matters

Sleeping Tight

We all love our children, but let's face it, sometimes we want them to go to sleep—and stay that way for a while. There are all sorts of factors (many of which are beyond your control) that influence whether your child will be a "good" sleeper or a "bad" one. Fortunately, though, there are a few rules of thumb that can help tilt the odds in your favor:

*"And so the big bad wolf ate Little Red Riding Hood, Hansel and Gretel,
Cinderella, and the three little pigs, and that was the end of
fairy tales forever. Now good night!"*

♦ Don't become the baby's sleep transition object. Baby's last waking memory should be of her crib or something familiar in it (blankie, toy, a picture on the wall). That way, if she wakes up in the middle of the night, she'll see the familiar object and be able to associate it with sleep. If you were the last thing she saw before dropping off, she'll want you again, even if you happen to be sleeping.

♦ It's perfectly natural for babies to fuss or be restless for fifteen or twenty minutes after being put down. (Please remember that fussing is one thing, screaming is another. If the baby begins to really wail, pick her up and soothe her, but try to get her back in her crib while she's still awake. It's absolutely impossible to spoil a baby by picking her up or soothing her in the first three or four months of life.)

♦ Keep nighttime activity to a minimum. Whether your baby is sleeping with you or not, she needs to learn that nighttime is for sleeping, not for playing.

♦ Don't turn on the lights. If the baby wakes up for a middle-of-the-night breast or bottle, do it in the dark.

♦ Don't change diapers unless you absolutely have to (such as when you're trying to treat a particularly nasty case of diaper rash). In most cases, your baby will be perfectly fine until the morning.

♦ Establish a routine. You'll need to make up your own, depending on what works best for you. Here's a fairly simple routine that is good for babies this age as well as for toddlers: change diapers, get sleepsuit on, read a story or two, go around the room and say "goodnight" to all the toys and animals, give a kiss goodnight, and into bed.

♦ When your baby is about six months old, start leaving the door to her room open. Kids this age get scared if they feel they're trapped in a small space, especially if they aren't sure you're just outside the door.

♦ In case of nightmares or other middle-of-the-night scares, respond promptly and be as reassuring as possible. Unless your child is hysterical with fear, try to keep things brief and resist the urge to take the baby out of the crib. You can do a lot of soothing by rubbing the baby's back or head—all from your side of the bars.

♦ During the day, gently wake up—and entertain—your baby if she tries to nap more than two or three hours at a stretch. The idea is to make her longest sleep of the day occur at night.

But What about Those Middle-of-the-Night Wake-Ups?

The most common reason babies wake up in the middle of the night is that they want to eat. If your partner is breastfeeding, do everything you can to stay in bed and let her handle things. I realize that this sounds positively insensitive, but the truth is that there's really nothing you can do to help out. If your partner wants some adult company (and who wouldn't?), try not to give in. Instead, offer to give her a few extra hours of sleep while you handle the early-morning child-care shift (which usually lasts a lot longer than a 2 A.M. feeding).

Of course, if you're bottle-feeding your baby (either with formula or expressed breast milk), you should do your fair share of the feedings. And since there's no sense in both you and your partner getting up at the same time, you

---

Naps and Sleep Schedules

At four months your baby has probably only recently settled into a regular sleep routine. Every baby has her own sleeping schedule, but a typical one for a baby this age might include a ten-hour stretch at night plus, if you're lucky, two two-hour naps—one midmorning, the other midafternoon.

Keep an eye on these naps, however; if they get too late, they may start upsetting the night-sleeping routine. You can't expect a baby to take a nap from 4 to 6 P.M. and then go to bed for the night at 7.

should be able to negotiate breakfast in bed (or at least a couple of hours of sleep) on those days when you do the 2 A.M. feeding.

Sometimes, no matter what you do, your baby is going to wake up at two or three in the morning for no other reason than to stay awake for a few hours and check things out. As with the feeding situations, try to split the entertainment duty as much as you can (unless one of you really needs to catch up on TV reruns or order a slicing, dicing, memory-improving, income-boosting workout machine).

No matter what it is that gets your baby (and you) up at three thirty in the morning, be sure to keep your middle-of-the-night encounters as boring as possible. Until they're old enough to have sex, kids need to know that nighttime is for sleeping.

Sleeping Arrangements

As hard as it may be to imagine, there exists a rather basic parenting issue that regularly generates even more controversy than the disposable versus cloth diapers debate: whether or not to have your child sleep in the same bed as you and your partner.

The argument goes something like this: Proponents of the "family bed" say that kids are being forced to be independent too early, that human evolution simply can't keep pace with the new demands our culture is placing on its children. "Proximity to parental sounds, smells, heat, and movement during the night is precisely what the human infant's immature system expects and needs," says James McKenna, an anthropologist and sleep researcher. They also add that in most countries (comprising about 80 percent of the world's population), parents and children sleep in the same bed.

Opponents of the family bed, however, say that what works in other countries doesn't always work here. In America early independence is critical, and babies should therefore quickly learn to be away from their parents, especially if both work and the children have to be in day care.

Fortunately (or unfortunately, depending on where you stand on the issue), there's absolutely no consensus on which of these two opposing views is the "right" one. And just to make sure that there's no real way to decide this issue once and for all, there's no serious scientific data supporting either position.

Our older daughter slept in a bassinet in our room for a month or so until we moved her into her own room. Our younger daughter, however, slept in bed with us for six months before being asked to leave. Personally, I kind of liked being able to snuggle up with a warm, smooth baby, but after being kicked in the head, stomach, back, face, and chest every night for six months I was glad to go back to an adults-only sleeping arrangement.

Here are some of the most common issues that come up in discussions of the family bed:

♦ **Independence.** Critics of family sleeping claim that parents who let their kids sleep with them are spoiling their children, who will grow up clingy and dependent. "Sleeping alone is an important part of a child's learning to be able to separate from his parents without anxiety and to see himself as an independent individual," writes Dr. Richard Ferber, one of the most well-respected anti-family-bed people around. Proponents of family sleeping, however, make nearly the opposite claim, maintaining that before a child can become independent she must feel that the world is a safe place and that her needs will be met. Kids who sleep in a family bed, proponents argue, turn out to be more independent, more confident, and more self-assured than those who don't.

♦ **Sleep: the baby's.** Despite what you might think, co-sleeping children tend to sleep more lightly than children who sleep alone (blankets rustling and parents turning over in bed wake them up). But light sleeping isn't necessarily a bad thing. In fact, there seems to be a correlation between lighter sleep and a lower incidence of SIDS.

♦ **Sleep: yours.** It's perfectly normal for even the soundest-sleeping kids to wake up every three or four hours for a quick look around the room. The vast majority (about 70 percent) soothe themselves back to sleep after a minute or two. But about 30 percent will spot something they just have to play with (you or your partner, for example), and they're up for hours.

♦ **Safety.** Many parents are afraid that they'll accidentally roll over their sleeping child if the whole family is sharing the same bed. While this is a perfectly legitimate concern, most adults—even while asleep—have a highly developed sense of where they are. It's probably been quite a while since you fell out of bed in the middle of the night. However, a recent study published in the *New England Journal of Medicine* found that adult overlying (non-alcohol and non-drug-related) was the probable cause of death in almost 20 percent of infants whose death had initially been attributed to SIDS.

♦ **Sexual spontaneity.** No kidding. But there are plenty of other places to make love besides your bed.

♦ **Breastfeeding.** There's no question that it's a lot easier for a nursing mother to reach across her bed for the baby than to get up and stagger down the hall. Problems arise, however, when fathers feel (and they often do) displaced by the nursing baby and decide that the only place to get a good night's sleep is on the couch.

♦ **Think before you start.** Once your baby has been sleeping in your bed for six to eight months, it's going to be awfully hard to get her out if you change your mind.

A Few Things to Consider If You're Thinking about Sharing Your Bed with Your Child

♦ Keep politics out of your decision-making. Sleep with your child because you and your partner want to, not because you feel you have to.

♦ Don't be embarrassed. You're not being soft, negligent, or overindulgent— it's a choice made by millions of fine parents.

♦ Make sure your bed is large enough to accommodate everyone. (But no waterbeds—baby could roll between you and the mattress.) Put the bed against the wall and have the baby sleep on the wall side, or get a guard rail if she's going to sleep on the outside edge. And remember, overly soft mattresses and pillows may pose a risk of suffocation.

♦ Make sure everyone's toenails are trimmed.

♦ Rethink your decision right now if you're obese, you drink or take any medication that might make you hard to wake up, or if you're generally such a sound sleeper that you're worried you might roll on top of your baby without noticing.

A Few Things to Consider If You're Thinking about Not Sharing Your Bed with Your Child

♦ Don't feel guilty. You're not a bad or selfish parent for not doing it.

♦ There is absolutely no evidence that sleeping with your child will speed up the bonding/attachment process.

♦ It's okay to make an occasional exception, such as when a child is ill or has had a frightening experience.

♦ If you're making your decision because of safety issues, you may be able to compromise by setting up the baby's crib in your bedroom.

 **MONTHS**

Work and Family

What's Going On with the Baby

Physically

♦ This month's big discovery is, yes, toes. And just as your baby spent hours fondling and sucking his own fingers, he'll repeat the process with his lower extremities.

♦ He's getting a lot stronger and is now able to roll from his stomach to his back at will. He can also get himself from his tummy to his hands and knees. Once there, he may rock back and forth as if anxious for some kind of race to begin.

♦ When you pull him to a standing position, he'll try to help you out by leaning his head forward and bending at the waist. Once standing, he may stamp his feet up and down.

♦ He's almost able to sit without support and can now pick up objects while sitting.

♦ His hands continue to get more coordinated. He now plays with a toy in either hand and can turn his wrist (it's harder than it sounds), thus enabling him to get a better look at what he's picked up.

♦ There are now longer and more regular intervals between feedings and bowel movements.

Intellectually

♦ For the past four months, your baby's world has been "a series of things that mysteriously disappear and reappear," writes child development expert Frank Caplan. But now he's no longer content to sit back and stare at objects, nor is he satisfied when you put something in his hand. In an attempt to actively engage in his world, he's starting to reach for things. Watch carefully as he looks back and forth between an object and his hand—inching the hand slowly toward the object. As mundane as it sounds, reaching is a critical intellectual stage, introducing the baby to the idea that, says Caplan, "things are beyond and apart and, therefore, separate" from him.

♦ Handling and turning an object teaches the baby that even though something looks different from different angles, its shape remains the same.

♦ With these newfound skills, the baby will now anticipate (and get excited by) seeing only a small part of a familiar object and will try to move small obstacles out of his way. He's also learning that objects can move, and he may lean over to find a toy he's dropped instead of staring at his hand. But if the object is out of his sight for more than just a few seconds, it ceases to exist and he forgets about it.

Verbally

♦ It's finally happened: your baby is babbling. Besides the vowel sounds *(eee, aaa, ayy)* he's been making, he's added a few consonants *(bbb, ddd, mmm)* to the mix.

♦ He's found his voice's volume switch and will practice modulating his voice.

♦ Although he's still trying to imitate more of the voice sounds you make to him, the noises he produces sound nothing like actual language.

♦ He's so delighted with his newfound language skills that he'll babble for 20 to 30 minutes at a stretch. Don't worry if you're not there to enjoy it— he's perfectly content to talk to his toys or, in a pinch, to himself.

♦ He may understand, and respond to, his name.

Emotionally/Socially

♦ He's capable of expressing a growing number of emotions: fear, anger, disgust, and satisfaction. He'll cry if you put him down and calm down if you pick him up.

♦ He also has—and readily expresses—strong preferences for toys and people. And he deliberately imitates faces and gestures.

♦ If he feels you're not paying enough attention to him, he'll try to interrupt whatever you're doing with a yelp or a cry. If he does start crying, you can usually stop his tears just by talking to him.

♦ He knows the difference between familiar people and strangers, and associates friends with his pleasure.

♦ Unfortunately, he doesn't remember that his friends started off (to him, at least) as strangers. Consequently, he's a little slow to warm to new people.

♦ He may spend some time trying to soothe himself—either by talking to himself or by clutching a favorite toy.

What You're Going Through

Worried about Doing Things Wrong

Just a few months ago your baby didn't make very many demands, so satisfying them wasn't all that tough. But now his needs are far more complex, and at times you may feel that it's nearly impossible to react promptly and appropriately.

With so much to respond to, it's perfectly normal to worry that you're not reading your baby's signals correctly and that you're doing everything wrong. These feelings, of course, are made worse by a baby who won't stop crying (a reflection of inadequate fathering skills?) or by a dissatisfied or seemingly hostile look on the baby's face (possibly a reproach that you've made some terrible mistake).

Perhaps the best way to overcome your worries is to spend more time with the baby. The more practice you get, the better you'll be at understanding the baby's "language" and the more confident you'll be in responding.

Also, learn to go with your gut feelings. There's almost always more than one solution to a given problem, and you'll undoubtedly settle on a good one. Even if you make a few mistakes, they aren't likely to have any long-term effects. After all, just because your partner burps the baby over her shoulder doesn't mean you can't do it with the baby sitting on your knees.

Of course, if you're really sure you're making *serious* mistakes, ask for some help. But spending too much time analyzing things and worrying that you've done something wrong can get you into trouble. According to psychiatrist Stanley Greenspan, excessive worrying can destroy your self-confidence and lead to doing nothing at all or to adopting a hands-off attitude toward the baby. (That way, the twisted logic goes, at least you won't make any *more* mistakes.) This, of course, can have a decidedly negative effect on your baby's development—and on your development as a father.

Finally, before you toss in the towel, consider this: If you think you're having trouble reading your baby's signals, how can you be so sure that his crying and odd looks mean all the horrible, negative things you think they do?

Striking a Balance Between Work and Family

Most new fathers, writes author David Giveans, are "torn between the need to provide economically for the family and the desire to be a nurturing father." And finding the right balance between these two seemingly mutually exclusive options is something you'll be working on for the rest of your life.

As mentioned in the previous chapter (pages 85–86), most men place a high value on their family life and claim that they're willing to make sacrifices to spend more time with their children. But by six months after their children's birth, about 95 percent of new fathers are back working full-time. (Phil and Carolyn Cowan found that at the same point in time only 19 percent of women are employed full-time, and another 36 percent are working part-time.)

At first glance it seems that there's a major contradiction between what men say and what they do. But researcher Glen Palm found that the work/ family trade-off isn't nearly so cut-and-dried. Many new fathers, Palm says, are "taking time off from friendships, recreation, and sleep to devote to their children, while they continue the time commitment to a full-time job."

Clearly there's something keeping fathers from spending less time at the office. One explanation, of course, is financial. Since the average working woman makes less than the average working man, if one parent is going to take time off from work, many families conclude that they can better survive the loss of the woman's salary.

Another important explanation is that in our society men and women have very different choices about the relative value of career in their lives. According to Dr. Warren Farrell, author of *Why Men Are the Way They Are,* women can choose between having a full-time career, being a full-time mother and homemaker, or some combination of the two. Men's choices, says Farrell, are a bit more limited: career, career, or career.

While this may be a bit of an exaggeration, the truth is that we simply expect men to show their love for their families by providing for them financially. "To many people, 'working mother' means conflict," says the Fatherhood Project's Jim Levine. "But 'working father' is a redundancy."

Perhaps the most interesting explanation (and my favorite) for why we keep fathers tied to their jobs and away from their families is offered by anthropologist Margaret Mead: "No developing society that needs men to leave home and do their thing for society ever allows young men in to handle or touch their newborns . . . for they know somewhere that if they did the new fathers would become so 'hooked' they would never go out and do their thing properly." Hmmmm.

Just because most fathers are trapped at the office doesn't mean that they aren't affected by what's going on at home. Radcliffe professor Rosalind Barnette found that men are just as likely as women to worry about family problems at the office. And according to researcher Joseph Pleck, 36 percent of fathers (and 37 percent of mothers) say work/family conflicts have caused them "a lot of stress." Pleck also says that "when stress occurs it has more negative consequences for men than for women."

Making Some Changes

Although you may never be able to resolve your work/family conflicts completely, there are a few ways you can maximize your time with your family, minimize your stress, and avoid trashing your career.

SCHEDULE CHANGES

"One of the conditions for men to become and stay highly involved in childrearing is for their work hours to be and continue to be flexible," writes John Snarey. Here are a few rather painless flexible scheduling options to run by your employer:

- ◆ Work four ten-hour days instead of five eight-hour days.
- ◆ Work from 5:00 A.M. to 1:00 P.M. (or some other schedule) instead of the usual 9:00–5:00.
- ◆ Consider a split shift, for example, work from 8:00 A.M. to noon and from 5:00 P.M. to 9:00 P.M.

"It's your husband. The baby won't burp for him.'

WORKING LESS THAN FULL-TIME

If you can afford to, you might want to consider one of the following options:

♦ Job sharing. You and another person divide up the responsibilities of the job. You would probably use the same office and desk. A typical job-share schedule might have you working two days one week and three days the next, while your workplace partner does the opposite. One warning: be very careful to negotiate a continuation of your health benefits. Many employers drop them for less-than-full-time employees.

♦ Switch to part-time, which is more or less the same as job sharing, except you probably won't have to share a desk with someone else.

♦ Become a consultant to your current employer. This can be a great way for you to get a lot of flexibility over your workday. There are also lots of tax advantages, particularly if you set up a home office (see more on this in the next section). At the very least, you'll be able to deduct auto mileage and a percentage of your phone and utility bills. But be sure to check with an accountant first; the IRS uses certain "tests" to determine whether someone is an employee or a consultant. If, for example, you go into the office every day, have a secretary, and get company benefits, you are an employee. Also, remember that if you become a consultant, you'll lose your benefit package. So be sure to build the cost of that package (or the amount you'll have to pay to replace it) into the daily or hourly rate you negotiate with your soon-to-be-former employer.

WORKING AT HOME (TELECOMMUTING)

Far too many managers believe in the importance of daily "face time" (actually being seen at the office). The truth is that face time is highly overrated and often unnecessary. In all the years I've been writing, I've worked for dozens of magazines and newspapers, most of which are several thousand miles from my home. And in most cases I've never even met my bosses.

I'm certainly the first to admit that being a writer isn't a typical job. But millions of Americans do work that doesn't require their physical presence in any particular place at any particular time (engineers, computer programmers, and just about anybody else who sits at a desk). If you're not a construction worker or a retail salesman, you might be a prime candidate for telecommuting.

If You're an Employer (or a Supervisor)

"Companies compete to woo skilled women," says *Wall Street Journal* columnist Sue Shellenbarger. "But many still assume that men will continue to work regardless of how they are treated as fathers." The ultimate responsibility for changing this Neanderthal attitude and helping men get more involved with their families rests at the top—with you.

♦ Change your own schedule. Many of your male employees will be reluctant to approach you with proposed schedule changes. So if you know someone has just become a father, raise the issue with him first. Chances are he'll be grateful.

♦ Make some changes. If you have enough employees, organize classes and support groups for new parents. Even if you don't have many employees, you can still offer free (or subsidized) on-site or near-site child care. You can also encourage your employees to take advantage of part-time, job-sharing, or flexible scheduling options. Overall, your company's policies should recognize that *all* parents (as opposed to just mothers) are responsible for their children's care and development.

♦ Don't worry about the cost. Companies with family-friendly policies find that the costs of implementing such programs are more than compensated for by increased morale and productivity, reduced absenteeism, and lower turnover. They're also a great recruiting tool.

Now don't get too excited: it's not as if you and your boss will never see each other again. Most telecommuters are out of the office only a day or two a week. And if it's going to be a workable option at all, telecommuting is something you'll have to ease yourself (and your employer) into. Like the other flexible work options discussed in this chapter, telecommuting is designed to give you more time with your family. But if you think you'll be able to save money on child care or have your baby sit on your lap while you crunch numbers, you're sorely mistaken.

If you want to give it a try, here's what you'll probably need:

♦ A computer (compatible with your employer's system)
♦ An additional phone line or two
♦ A modem
♦ A fax machine (or a send/receive fax/modem)
♦ A quiet place to set things up

Besides the convenience aspect, one of the major advantages of telecommuting is that you don't have to shave and you can work in your underwear. There are, however, a few disadvantages. Primary among them is lack of human contact: you may hate that train ride into the city or the annoying guy in your carpool, but after a few months alone in your house, you might actually miss them. You might also miss going out to lunch with your co-workers or even just bumping into them in the halls. And if you have a tendency to be obsessive about your work (as I do), you'll have to train yourself to take frequent breaks. I can't tell you how many times I've realized—at ten o'clock at night—that I haven't eaten all day and that the only time I went outside was to take the newspaper in from the porch.

Putting It All Together

No matter how you try to keep your work life separate from your family life, there's going to be plenty of spillover between the two. This isn't necessarily a bad thing. In his four-decade-long study of fathers, John Snarey found that, "contrary to the stereotype of rigid work-family trade-off, a positive, reciprocal interaction may exist between childrearing and bread-winning."

Other researchers have come to similar conclusions. "Before they became fathers, men did not appear to be conscious that home and work life often require different personal qualities," writes Phil Cowan. After becoming fathers, however, many men "described new abilities to juggle conflicting demands, make decisions, and communicate quickly and clearly both at home and at work. . . . Some described themselves as more aware of their personal relationships on the job, and more able to use some of their managerial skills in the solution of family problems."

You and Your Baby

Time for Solids

When I was a baby, the current wisdom about introducing solid foods was to do it as early as possible, often as soon as five or six weeks. One of the explanations was that babies who ate solid foods supposedly slept longer than those on bottles (almost no one was being breastfed then). Today, people are more interested in the baby's health than in whether he sleeps through the night (which eating solid food doesn't affect anyway), and most pediatricians now recommend that you delay introducing solids until your baby is anywhere from four to six months old. The recommended delay may be even longer if you or your partner has a history of food allergies (for more on food allergies, see page 112).

Even if you're tempted to start solids earlier than four to six months, resist. "Introducing solids to the younger baby can interfere with his desire to suck," says Frances Wells Burck, author of *Babysense.* "Solids may also crowd out room for milk without making up for its nutritional loss." According to Burck, there are a few other reasons to keep your baby off solids until he's truly ready:

♦ Because younger babies' digestive systems are immature, solid food—along with their nutrients—passes undigested through their systems.

♦ Babies' young kidneys have to work harder to process solid foods than they do for milk or formula.

♦ Delaying especially allergenic foods (see page 113) can reduce the likelihood of developing allergies later on.

♦ Breast- and bottle-feeding is a great opportunity for parents to cuddle with their babies, although it's nearly impossible for *you* to cuddle the baby while your partner is breastfeeding.

♦ With breasts, there's nothing to clean up; with bottles, only the bottle. But with solids, you have to wash spoons, dishes, high-chair trays, bibs, and perhaps even the floor and nearby walls.

Here's how you can tell if your baby is really ready for solids:

♦ Her weight has doubled since birth (indicating that she's getting plenty of nutrition).

♦ She's very underweight for her age (indicating that she's not getting enough nutrition).

♦ She's drinking more than a quart (32 ounces) of formula or breast milk per day.
♦ She chews on nipples (either your partner's or the bottle's) while sucking.
♦ She pays close attention when you're eating.

Remember, introducing solids does not mean that breast- or bottle-feeding will end (see pages 205–8 for information on weaning). In fact, most of your baby's nutrients will still come from milk or formula for a few more months.

Getting Started

Getting your baby to eat solid foods isn't going to happen overnight. For starters, he'll probably take a few days to get used to the strange new taste and texture. Then he's got to figure out how to move it from the front of his mouth to his throat (liquids kind of know where to go by themselves), where he can swallow it. Here's the way to do it:

♦ Your baby's first food should be a single-grain cereal (no, not Cheerios)— oatmeal, barley, or rice. For the first few days, add breast milk or formula— but *not* cow's milk—to make the cereal especially liquidy. If you're buying packaged baby cereal, get the kind that's iron fortified.
♦ Offer new foods at the beginning of the meal, when the baby is likely to be at his hungriest.
♦ Three days after you actually manage to get some cereal down the baby's throat, start adding vegetables—one at a time, three to five days apart. Make sure the baby gets a good mix of yellow (carrots, squash) and green (peas, spinach, zucchini) veggies. Many people prefer to make bananas baby's first noncereal food. The problem with bananas is that they are fairly sweet, and babies may become so fond of them that they won't be interested in any other foods you may introduce thereafter.
♦ After a week or so on vegetables, introduce the bananas and some other noncitrus fruits (again, one at a time, three to five days apart). Until he's a year old, your baby can't digest raw apples, but applesauce is okay. Hold off on the oranges for a few more months.
♦ If you absolutely must give your baby juice (see page 28 for a few reasons not to), be sure to dilute it fifty-fifty with water.
♦ When your baby is about seven months old, introduce yogurt. It's an important source of protein and can easily be mixed with other foods. Although most babies like yogurt, mine didn't, and we had to trick them into eating it by putting a blueberry (always a favorite food) at the back of the spoon.
♦ Breads and cereals (yes, Cheerios are okay now) are next.

Allergies and Intolerances:
What They Are and How to Prevent Them

Despite the claims of about 25 percent of American parents, fewer than 5 percent of children under three are truly allergic to any foods. True allergies are abnormal responses by the immune system to ingested proteins. The most common symptoms are nasal congestion, asthma, skin rashes (eczema and hives), chronic runny nose or cough, vomiting, and severe mood swings. In contrast, symptoms such as headaches, excess gas, diarrhea, or constipation are generally caused by intolerances, which are usually the result of an enzyme deficiency.

While you may be tempted to say, "What's the difference? A reaction is a reaction," the distinction between an allergy and an intolerance is critical and subtle. Allergies often begin in infancy and get progressively worse with each encounter with the offending food. Intolerances don't. Fortunately, most kids—except those allergic to peanuts and fish—usually outgrow their allergies altogether by age five. (Only about 2 percent of children over five have true food allergies.)

The consensus among pediatricians is that the way to deal with allergies and intolerances is to prevent them before they happen. Complete prevention, of course, is impossible. But here are a few things you can do to better the odds:

- Breastfeed your baby and withhold solid foods for at least four to six months.
- If your partner has a history of true allergies, she should reduce or completely eliminate high-risk foods (see page 113) while breastfeeding.
- Introduce only one new food at a time. That way, if your baby has a reaction, you'll know right away what caused it.
- After introducing a new food, wait three to five days before introducing another.
- If your baby has any of the negative reactions mentioned above, eliminate the food right away and call your pediatrician. He or she will probably tell you to take the baby off the food and reintroduce it in six months. By then, your baby may have built up the necessary defenses.

MOST ALLERGENIC FOODS	LEAST ALLERGENIC FOODS
♦ Egg whites	♦ Rice
♦ Wheat and yeast	♦ Oats
♦ Milk and other dairy products	♦ Barley
♦ Citrus fruits	♦ Carrots
♦ Berries	♦ Squash
♦ Tomatoes	♦ Apricots
♦ Chocolate	♦ Peaches
♦ Nuts	♦ Apples
♦ Shellfish	♦ Lamb

♦ At about one year, your baby can eat almost any kind of food, but in small pieces. Some foods, such as grapes, raw carrots, nuts, and hot dogs, can still present choking hazards.

♦ One big warning: Do not give your baby honey or corn sweeteners for at least the first year. They often contain tiny parasites that an adult's digestive system exterminates with no problem. But the baby's still-immature system won't be able to handle the chore.

I Wanna Do It Myself

When your baby is ready to feed himself, he'll let you know, usually by grabbing the spoon from your hand (babies are quicker than you'd think) or mushing around anything that's dropped on to the high-chair tray. When this happens, prepare yourself; in the course of the next few weeks, your baby will discover the joys of sticking various kinds of food in his nose and eyes, under his chin, behind his ears, and in his hair. And it won't be much longer until he learns to throw.

One way to minimize the mess is to put a large piece of plastic under the high chair; a large trash bag cut open along the side is good. But don't relax yet; your baby will soon learn to use his spoon as a catapult to launch food beyond this protective boundary. There's really nothing you can do about this, so avoid wearing your best clothes while the baby is eating.

Making Your Own

You can, of course, buy pre-prepared baby food in those tiny jars. But they're expensive and often filled with preservatives, chemicals, and other nasty stuff. Some companies, such as Earth's Best, offer organic, pesticide- and preservative-free foods. They're even more expensive.

Two Small Warnings

First, when you begin giving your baby solids, she's going to make an incredible array of faces: horror, disgust, fear, betrayal. Try not to take them personally. Your baby is probably reacting to the new and unknown and not criticizing your cooking.

Second, don't make a ton of food the first few times. You'll probably end up feeding the baby the same spoonful over and over again (you put some in her mouth, she spits it out; you scrape it off her cheek and put it in her mouth again . . .). This can be frustrating, but try to remember what comedian Dave Barry says: "Babies do not take solid food through their mouths. . . . Babies absorb solid food through their chins. You can save yourself a lot of frustrating effort if you smear the food directly on your baby's chin, rather than putting it in the baby's mouth and forcing the baby to expel it on to its chin, as so many uninformed parents do."

The solution: be patient and keep your video camera ready at all times.

By far the cheapest alternative is to make your own. After all, the major ingredient of most baby food is cooked vegetables. You can even do it in bulk. All you have to do is boil some vegetables, mash them up, and put the mash into an ice-cube tray. Whenever you need to, just pop out a cube, thaw, and serve.

A word of caution: Microwaves heat food unevenly, leaving hot spots right next to cold ones. So if you're using a microwave, make sure you stir well and test anything you're planning to give the baby.

Notes:

 **MONTHS**

Gaining Confidence

What's Going On with the Baby

Physically

- By the end of this month she'll probably be able to sit by herself in "tripod position" (feet splayed, hands on the floor in between for balance). She may even be able to right herself if she tips over.
- She can turn herself from back to front or front to back at will, and may even be able to propel herself short distances (usually backward at first) by creeping or wiggling. Be prepared, though: she'll be demonstrating a lot of these new moves when you're trying to change or dress her.
- She can probably get herself to her hands and knees and will spend hours rocking back and forth, picking up an arm here, a leg there—all in preparation for crawling.
- She can clap her hands and bang two objects together. And whatever isn't being banged is sure to be in her mouth.

Intellectually

- With so many new things to do and learn, your baby is now awake about 12 hours a day and spends most of that time finding out about her environment by touching, holding, tasting, and shaking things. According to Frank Caplan, this is proof that "the need to learn is at least as important as pleasure-seeking in determining behavior."
- The idea that she is separate from other people and other objects is slowly sinking in. But she still thinks she has absolute control over all she sees or

ouches. As if to rub it in, she'll endlessly drop toys, dishes, and food from her high chair and revel in the way she can make you pick them up.

♦ Another way your baby demonstrates her complete power over the world and everything in it (especially you) is to cry for attention whether she needs any or not.

♦ Both these activities show that your baby is able to formulate plans and can anticipate the consequences of her actions.

Verbally

♦ She's now more regularly adding consonants to vowels and creating single-syllable "words" such as *ba, ma, la, ka, pa.*

♦ She's getting pretty good at imitating sounds and also tries—with some success—to imitate your inflections.

♦ She's getting so familiar with language that she can easily tell the difference between conversational speech and any of the other noises you make. She might, for example, laugh when you start making animal noises.

♦ She's also learning to like other sounds; music in particular will cause her to stop what she's doing and listen.

Emotionally/Socially

♦ Until this month, your baby really didn't care who fed her, changed her, played with her, or hugged her, just as long as it got done. But now, for about 50–80 percent of babies, *who* satisfies their needs is almost as important. You, your partner, and perhaps a few other very familiar people may now be the only ones your baby will allow near her without crying. This is the beginning of *stranger anxiety.*

♦ She'll wave her arms to let you know to pick her up, cling to you when you do, and cry if you take away a toy or stop playing with her.

♦ Despite all this, she's still incredibly curious in new situations, and will spend as much as ninety minutes taking in her surroundings.

♦ Her desire to imitate what you do has led to an interest in eating solid food.

What You're Going Through

Growing Up

There's nothing quite like having a kid to make you realize that you're a grown-up. It also makes you realize that besides being a son, you're also a father. That may sound like a painfully obvious thing to say, but you'd be

SIPRESS

surprised at how many men have a hard time with the concept. After all, we've spent our whole lives looking at our fathers as fathers and at ourselves as sons.

Here's how a friend of mine describes becoming aware that he had made the transition: "One day I slipped my arm into the sleeve of my jacket and my father's hand came out the other side."

Feeling Like a Father

According to Bruce Drobeck, a large percentage of men see the fatherhood role as that of a teacher of values and skills. Until they can actually communicate with their children, these men don't quite feel that they've become fathers. And since it's hard to communicate with a helpless and essentially nonresponsive baby, caring for one doesn't seem very fatherly.

But by the time your baby is six months old, she's no longer unable to communicate. She turns her head when you call her, she gets excited when you walk into the room. And when you wrestle with her, build a tower together, or tickle her, she'll give you a smile that could melt steel—a smile that's only for you. You're starting to feel confident that your baby needs you and that you're playing an important and influential role in her young life. You're finally starting to feel like a father; and the more you and your baby interact, the more you'll feel that way.

Jealousy

"The single emotion that can be the most destructive and disruptive to your experience of fatherhood is jealousy," writes Dr. Martin Greenberg in *The Birth of a Father.*

There's certainly plenty to be jealous about, but the real question is: Whom (or what) are you jealous of? Your partner for her close relationship with the baby and the extra time she gets to spend with her? The baby for taking up more than her "fair share" of your partner's attention and for having full access to her breasts while they may be "too tender" for you to touch? The baby-sitter for being the recipient of the baby's daytime smiles and love—tokens of affection you'd rather were directed at you? Or maybe it's the baby's carefree life. The answer, of course, is: All of the above.

Like most emotions, a little jealousy goes a long way. Too much can make you feel competitive toward or resentful of your partner, the baby-sitter, even the baby. Do you feel you need more attention or emotional support from your partner? Do you need more private time with the baby? Whatever or whomever you're jealous of, it's critical to express your feelings clearly and honestly and to encourage your partner to do the same. If for some reason you feel you can't discuss your feelings on this issue with your partner, take them up with a male friend or relative. You'll be surprised at how common jealousy is. Jealousy's "potential for destruction," writes Greenberg, "lies not in having the feelings but in burying them."

Gaining Confidence

I don't remember every day of my children's childhoods, but there's one day in particular—when my older daughter was about six months old—that I recall quite clearly.

It really wasn't all that different from any other day. I gave her a bottle and dressed her. When she threw up all over her clothes, I dressed her again. Five minutes later she had an explosive bowel movement that oozed all the way up to her neck, so I cleaned her up and dressed her for the third time. Over the course of the day I probably changed five more diapers and two more outfits, gave her three bottles, calmed her from crying four times, took her in and out of the car eight times as I drove all over town doing errands, put her down for two successful naps during which I managed to do a few loads of laundry and wash the dishes. I even managed to get some writing done.

All in all, it wouldn't have been a very memorable day if it weren't for what happened at the end of it. As I sat in bed reading, I remember thinking to myself, "Damn, I'm really getting a pretty good handle on this dad stuff." The truth is that I was. And by now, you probably are too.

Things that would have had you panicking a few months ago now seem completely ordinary. You've learned to understand your baby's cues, you can predict the unpredictable, and those feelings of not being able to do things right are nearly gone. You probably feel more connected and attached to your baby than ever before. The feeling is one of confidence and stability, and

signals that you've entered what some sociologists and psychologists re
as the "honeymoon period" with your baby.

For many men, feelings of confidence as fathers lead them to feel more confident in their relationships with their partners as well. A majority of men in
fatherhood researcher Bruce Linton's studies felt that their relationships with
their partners had gotten "easier" and described a sensation of connection and
attachment to both baby and partner—kind of "bonding as a family."

You and Your Baby

Playing Around

As your baby develops her reaching, grabbing, and shoving-things-into-her-
mouth skills, she'll gradually lose interest in face-to-face play and become
more focused on the objects around her (or at least the ones she can reach)
and on exploring her environment.

The first, and perhaps most important, lesson your baby will learn about
objects is that she can, to a certain extent, control them. Of course, this
startling epiphany comes about as a complete accident: you put a rattle in her
hand and after swinging her arms around for a while, she'll notice that the
rattle makes some noise. But over the course of several months, your baby will
learn that when she stops flailing, the rattle stops rattling and that she can—
just because she wants to—get it to rattle again, and again, and again.

Your baby will learn quite a bit about objects all by herself. But if you're
interested, there are a number of games you can play with your baby that,
besides being fun, will encourage object awareness and perception.

REACHING GAMES

To encourage your baby to reach and to expand her horizons, try holding attractive toys just out of her reach: above her head, in front of her, to the sides. See
how close you have to get the toy before she makes her move. Remember, the
object here is not to tease or torture the baby, it's to have fun.

TOUCHING GAMES

Try this: Let your baby play with a small toy without letting her see it (you
might want to do this in the dark or with her hands in a paper bag). Then put
that toy together with several other toys she's never played with. Many babies
this age will pick up the familiar toy. Although this may sound fairly easy, it
isn't. You're asking your baby to use two senses—touch and vision—at the

same time. If your baby isn't ready for this one, don't worry. Just try it again in a few weeks.

IF . . . THEN . . . GAMES

There are thousands of things you can do to reinforce cause-and-effect thinking. Rattles, banging games, rolling a ball back and forth, and splashing in the pool are excellent. So is blowing up your cheeks and having the baby "pop" them. Baby gyms—especially the kind that make a lot of noise when smacked—are also good, but be sure to pack them up the moment your baby starts trying to use the gym to pull herself up; they just aren't sturdy enough.

Give the Kid a Break

Don't feel that you have to entertain your baby all the time. Sure it's fun, but letting her have some time to play by herself is almost as important to her development as playing with her yourself. And don't worry; letting her play alone—as long as you're close enough to hear what she's doing and to respond quickly if she needs you—doesn't mean you're being neglectful. Quite the opposite, in fact. By giving her the opportunity to make up her own games or to practice on her own the things she does with you, you're helping her learn that she's capable of satisfying at least some of her needs by herself. You'll also be helping her build her sense of self-confidence by allowing her to decide for herself what she'll be playing with and for how long.

GOOD TOYS	BAD TOYS
♦ Blocks	♦ Anything made of foam—it's too
♦ Dolls with easy-to-grasp limbs	easy to chew off pieces
♦ Real things: phones, computer	♦ Anything small enough to swal-
keyboards, shoes, etc.	low or that has detachable parts
♦ Toys that make different sounds	♦ Anything that could possibly
and have different textures	pinch the baby
♦ Musical toys	♦ Anything that runs on electricity
♦ Balls	♦ Stuffed animals and other furry
♦ Sturdy books	things that might shed (stuffed
	animals that *don't* shed are fine)
	♦ Toys with strings, ribbons,
	elastic—all potential choking
	hazards

OBJECT PERMANENCE

When your baby is about six or seven months old, the all-important idea that objects can exist even when they're out of sight slowly starts sinking in.

♦ Peek-a-boo and other games that involve hiding and finding things are great for developing object permanence. Peek-a-boo in particular teaches your baby an excellent lesson: when you go away, you always come back. This doesn't sound like much, but making this connection now lets her know she can count on you to be there when she needs you and will help her cope with *separation anxiety* (see pages 154–55).

♦ Object permanence develops in stages. If you're interested in seeing how, try this: Show your baby a toy. Then, while she's watching, "hide" it under a pillow. If you ask her where the toy is, she'll probably push the pillow out of the way and "find" it. But if you quickly move the toy to another hiding place when she's not looking, the baby will continue to look for it in the first hiding place.

TRACKING GAMES

Hold an object in front of the baby. When you're sure she's seen it, let it drop out of your hand. At five or six months, most babies won't follow the object down. But starting at about seven months, they'll begin to anticipate where things are going to land. When your baby has more or less mastered this skill, add an additional complication: drop a few objects and let her track them down. Then hold a helium balloon in front of her and let it go. She'll look down and be rather stunned that the balloon never lands. Let her hold the string of the balloon and experiment.

Again, if your baby doesn't respond to some, or any, of the activities suggested here, don't worry. Babies develop at very different rates, and what's "normal" for your baby may be advanced—or delayed—for your neighbor's.

Family Matters

Finding Quality Child Care

Most parents instinctively feel (and there's plenty of research to back them up) that to have one or both of them care for their baby in their own home would, in a perfect world, probably be the best child-care option. But most couples can't afford the traditional dad-goes-to-work-while-mom-stays-at-home option or the less-traditional mom-goes-to-work-while-dad-stays-at-home scenario. So chances are that, sooner or later, you'll need to consider some form of day care for your child. Here are some of the options, along with their advantages and disadvantages.

IN-HOME CARE

Unless you work at home, in-home care is probably the most convenient option for parents. You don't have to worry about day-care schedules, and your baby can stay in the environment to which he or she has become accustomed. In addition, your baby will receive plenty of one-on-one attention, and, if you stay on top of the situation, the caregiver will keep you up to date on your child's development. Finally, by remaining at home, your child will be less exposed to germs and illness.

Leaving your child alone with a stranger can be daunting and traumatic, especially the first time. On the one hand, you might be worried about whether you really know (and can trust) the caregiver. You might also be worried—as I was—that no one will be able to love or care for your child as well as you and your partner. On the other hand, you might experience what psychologist and parenting guru Dr. Lawrence Kutner calls the "natural rivalry" between parents and caregivers. "As parents, we want our children to feel close (but not too close) to the other adults in their lives. We worry that, if those attachments are too strong, they will replace us in our child's eyes."

Fortunately, no one will ever be able to replace you—or your love. But

Au Pairs

Au pairs are usually young women who come to the States on yearlong cultural exchange programs administered by the United States Information Agency (USIA). Legally, au pairs are nonresident aliens and are exempt from social security, Medicare, and unemployment taxes (see below for more on taxes and payroll).

What an au pair provides is up to forty-five hours per week of live-in child care. In exchange, you pay a weekly stipend (currently about $155) as well as airfare, insurance, an educational stipend, program support, and full room and board. On average, having an au pair will set you back about $12,000 for the full year.

You can hire an au pair through one of only eight USIA-approved placement agencies. You could hire one through a non-USIA agency, but the au pair would be subject to immediate deportation and you to a $10,000 fine.

Having an au pair can be a wonderful opportunity for you and your baby to learn about another culture. One drawback, however, is that they can stay only a year; then it's *au revoir* to one, *bonjour* to another. In addition, it's important to remember that from the young woman's perspective, being an au pair is a cultural thing. In theory she's supposed to do a lot of child care and other work, but in reality she may be far more interested in going to the mall with her new American friends or hanging out with your neighbor's teen-age son.

there are many wonderful caregivers out there who can give your baby the next best thing. You just need to know how to find them.

HOW TO FIND IN-HOME CAREGIVERS

The best ways to find in-home caregivers are:

♦ Agencies
♦ Word of mouth
♦ Bulletin boards (either caregivers respond to your ad, or you respond to theirs)

The first thing to do is to conduct thorough interviews over the phone— this will enable you to screen out the obviously unacceptable candidates (for example, the ones who are only looking for a month-long job, or those who don't drive if you need a driver). Then invite the "finalists" over to meet with you, your partner, and the baby in person. Make sure the baby and the prospective caregiver spend a few minutes together, and pay close attention to how they interact. Someone who approaches your baby cautiously and speaks to her reassuringly before picking her up is someone who understands, and cares about, your baby's feelings. And someone who strokes your baby's hair and strikes up a "conversation" is a far better choice than a person who sits rigidly with your baby on her knee.

Another good "test" for potential caregivers is to have them change your baby's diapers. Does the applicant smile or sing or try some other way to make getting changed interesting and fun for the baby, or does she seem disgusted by the whole thing? And be sure that she washes her hands when she's done.

When you've finally put together your list of finalists, get references—and check at least two (it's awkward, but absolutely essential). Ask each of the references why the baby-sitter left his or her previous jobs, and what the best and worst things about him or her were. Also, make sure to ask the prospective caregiver the questions listed below.

When you make your final choice, have the person start a few days before you return to work so you can all get to know each other, and, of course, so you can spy.

WHAT TO ASK THEM

Here are a few good questions to ask prospective in-home caregivers. You may want to add a few more from the sections on other child-care options.

♦ What previous child-care experience have you had (including caring for younger relatives)?
♦ What age children have you cared for?
♦ Tell us a little about your own childhood.
♦ What would you do if . . . ? (Give several examples of things a child might do that would require different degrees of discipline.)
♦ When would you hit or spank a child? (If the answer is anything other than "Never," find yourself another candidate.)
♦ How would you handle . . . ? (Name a couple of emergency situations, such as a gushing head wound or a broken arm.)
♦ Do you know baby CPR? (If not, you might want to consider paying for the caregiver to take a class.)
♦ What are your favorite things to do with kids?
♦ Do you have a driver's license?

♦ What days/hours are you available/not available? How flexible can you be if an emergency arises while we're at work?

♦ Are you a native speaker of any foreign language?

OTHER IMPORTANT ISSUES TO DISCUSS

♦ Compensation (find out the going rate by checking with other people who have caregivers) and vacation.

♦ Telephone privileges.

♦ Complete responsibilities of the job: feeding, bathing, diapering, changing clothes, reading to the baby, and so on, as well as what light housekeeping chores, if any, will be expected while the baby is sleeping.

♦ English-language skills—particularly important in case of emergency (you want someone who can accurately describe to a doctor or 911 operator what's going on).

♦ Immigration/green card status (more on this and other legal complications below).

You might want to draw up an informal contract listing all of the caregiver's responsibilities—just so there won't be any misunderstandings.

LIVE-IN HELP

Hiring a live-in caregiver is like adding a new member to the family. The process for selecting one is similar to that for finding a non-live-in caregiver, so you can use most of the questions listed above for conducting interviews. After you've made your choice, try out your new relationship on a non-live-in basis for a few weeks, just to make sure everything's going to work out to everyone's satisfaction.

To Grandmother's (or Grandfather's) House We Go

If your parents, in-laws, or other relatives live in the neighborhood, they may provide you with a convenient, loving, and low-cost child-care alternative. According to a recent survey by the U.S. Census Bureau, about 16 percent of children under five years old are being cared for by their grandparents while their parents are working—half of them in their grandparents' homes. Other relatives account for an additional 8 percent of all child-care arrangements for preschoolers.

FAMILY DAY CARE

If you can't (or don't want to, or can't afford to) have someone care for your child in your home, the next best alternative is to have your child cared for in someone else's home. Since the caregiver is usually looking after only two or three children (including yours), your baby will get the individual attention he needs as well as the opportunity to socialize with other children. And since the caregiver lives in his or her own house, personnel changes are unlikely; this gives your baby a greater sense of stability.

Be sure to ask potential family-day-care providers what kind of backup system they have to deal with vacations and illness (the provider's). Will you suddenly find yourself without child care or will your baby be cared for by another adult whom both you and your baby know?

GROUP DAY CARE

Many people—even those who can afford in-home child care—would rather use an out-of-home center. For one, a good day-care center is, as a rule, much better equipped than your home, or anyone else's for that matter, and will undoubtedly offer your child a wider range of stimulating activities. But remember, "There is absolutely no relationship between the amount of money a child-care center charges and the quality of care your baby will receive," writes Lawrence Kutner. "The best child-care centers invest in hiring and retaining the best people, not buying the most toys."

Many parents also prefer group day care because it usually offers kids more opportunities to play with one another. In the long run, most parenting experts agree that being able to play with a variety of other kids helps children become better socialized and more independent. The downside, of course, is that your child won't get as much individual attention from the adult caregivers; and since your six-month-old won't really be playing with other kids for a while longer, adult-baby contact is more important. In addition, interacting with other kids usually means interacting with their germs: children in group day care tend to get sick a lot more often than those cared for at home (whether yours or someone else's).

Where to Find Out-of-Home Caregivers

You're most likely to find out-of-home child-care facilities through word of mouth or by seeing an ad in a local parenting newspaper. Perhaps the easiest (and safest) alternative is through Child Care Aware, a nationwide campaign created to help parents identify quality child care in their communities. Contact them at 1-800-424-2246.

However you find out about a potential child-care facility, there's no substitute for checking it out for yourself in person. Here are some of the things Child Care Aware suggests you keep in mind when comparing child-care facilities:

ABOUT THE CAREGIVERS
♦ Do they seem to really like children? And do the kids seem to like them?
♦ Do they get down on each child's level to speak to the child?
♦ Are the children greeted when they arrive?
♦ Are the children's needs quickly met even when things get busy?
♦ Are the caregivers trained in CPR, first aid, and early childhood development?
♦ Are they involved in continuing education programs?
♦ Does the program keep up with children's changing interests?
♦ Will the caregivers always be ready to answer your questions?
♦ Will they tell you what your child is doing every day?
♦ Are parents' ideas welcomed? Are there ways for you to get involved if you want to?
♦ Are there enough caregivers for the number of kids? (One adult for four kids is the absolute maximum ratio you should accept; if there are two or more infants the ratio should be less.)

ABOUT THE FACILITY
♦ Is the atmosphere bright and pleasant?
♦ Is there a fenced-in outdoor play area with a variety of safe equipment?
♦ Can the caregivers see the entire playground at all times?
♦ Are there different areas for resting, quiet play, and active play?
♦ What precautions are taken to ensure that kids can be picked up only by the person you select? Do strangers have access to the center?
♦ Are there adequate safety measures to keep children away from windows, fences, and kitchen appliances and utensils (knives, ovens, stoves, household chemicals, and so forth)?

ABOUT THE PROGRAM
♦ Is there a daily balance of play time, story time, and nap time?
♦ Are the activities right for each age group?
♦ Are there enough toys and learning materials for the number of children?
♦ Are the toys clean, safe, and within reach of the children?

ABOUT OTHER THINGS
♦ Do you agree with the discipline practices?

Taxes and Government Regulations

If you hire an in-home caregiver or family day-care provider, here are some of the steps you have to take to meet IRS, INS, and Department of Labor requirements:

+ Get a federal ID number (you may be able to use your social security number)
+ Register with your state tax department
+ Register with the Department of Labor
+ Calculate payroll deductions (and, of course, deduct them)
+ File quarterly reports to your state tax board
+ Calculate unemployment tax
+ Get a worker's compensation policy and compute the premium (usually a percentage of payroll rather than a flat fee for the year)
+ Prepare W-2 and W-4 forms
+ Demonstrate compliance with Immigration and Naturalization Service guidelines

If the prospect of doing all this doesn't make you want to quit your job to stay home with the baby, nothing will. There is, however, an alternative: get in touch with Alan L. Goldberg, president of NannyTax, Inc. (phone: 212-867-1776; fax: 212-867-2045). His organization takes care of all these matters and any other pesky details that may arise.

+ Do you hear the sounds of happy children?
+ Is the program licensed or regulated? By whom?
+ Are surprise visits by parents encouraged?
+ Will your child be happy there?

Try to visit each facility more than once, and after you've made your final decision, make a few unannounced visits—just to see what goes on when there aren't any parents around.

A FEW THINGS TO GET SUSPICIOUS ABOUT

+ Parents are not allowed to drop in unannounced. You need to call before visiting or coming to pick up your child.
+ Parents dropping off kids are not allowed into the care-giving areas.
+ Your child is unhappy after several months.

♦ There seem to be new and unfamiliar caregivers almost every day.
♦ You don't get any serious response when you voice your concerns.

Finding a good child-care provider is a lengthy, agonizing process, and it's important not to give up until you're satisfied. "Half to three-quarters of parents who use daycare feel they have no choices and must settle for what they can find," writes Sue Shellenbarger, author of the Work & Family column for the *Wall Street Journal.* The result? Most infants get mediocre care. A recent study by the Work and Families Institute (WFI) found that only 8 percent of child-care facilities were considered "good quality," and 40 percent were rated "less than minimal." According to WFI's president, Ellen Galinsky, 10 to 20 percent of children "get care so poor that it risks damaging their development." So be careful.

Notes:

A Whole New Kind of Love

What's Going On with the Baby

Physically

- He's getting so good at sitting that he doesn't need his hands for balancing anymore. Instead, he can—and will—use them to reach for things.
- He can get himself to a sitting position from his stomach.
- He's starting to crawl, but don't be surprised if he goes backward at least some of the time, or, instead of crawling, scoots around on his bottom, using one arm to pull, the other to push.
- If you hold him upright, supported under the arms, he can bear some weight on his feet and will stamp and bounce up and down.
- He now uses his opposable thumb almost like you do, and is able to pick up what he wants confidently and quickly. He still prefers objects he can bang together and, of course, put into his mouth.

Intellectually

- As his brain develops, so does his ability to make associations. He recognizes the sound of your approaching footsteps and starts getting excited even before you come into his room.
- If confronted with blocks of different sizes, he will pick each one up, manipulate them a bit, then line them up to compare them to one another.
- He's so thrilled with his newfound ability to pick up and hold objects, he just can't get enough. He spends a lot of time examining objects upside

down and from other angles. And if he's holding a block in one hand, he'll reach for a second one and eye a third—all at the same time.

♦ The idea that objects may exist even when he can't see them is just beginning to take shape. If he drops something, he no longer thinks it's gone forever. Instead, he'll grope around for it or stare intently at the place it disappeared from, hoping to bring it back. But if it doesn't show up within 5 to 10 seconds, he'll forget about it.

Verbally

♦ A few months ago, your baby was capable (with practice) of producing any sound that a human can produce. But since he spends all his time trying to make the sounds *you* make, he's forgetting how to make the ones you don't (like rolled Rs or the clicks of the African bush people).

♦ In English, though, your baby's babbling is shifting from single-syllable to multisyllable (*babababa, mamamama, dadadada* . . .). He's able to modulate the tone, volume, and speed of his sounds and actively tries to converse with you, vocalizing after you stop speaking and waiting for you to respond to him.

♦ Your baby's passive language skills are also improving. He now turns when he hears his own name and understands several other words.

Emotionally/Socially

♦ Although he's fascinated with objects, your baby really prefers social interactions and one-on-one activities, such as chasing and fetching.

♦ He can now tell the difference between adults and children, and may be interested in playing with (actually, alongside) kids his own age.

♦ He recognizes, and reacts differently to, positive and negative tones of voice and happy or sad facial expressions.

♦ Shyness or anxiety around strangers continues.

♦ Continuing on his mission to imitate everything you do, your baby now wants to finger-feed himself or hold his own bottle or cup.

What You're Going Through

A New and Different Kind of Love

Sooner or later, almost every writer takes a crack at trying to describe love. And for the most part, they fall short. The problem is that there are so many different kinds. The love I feel for my wife, for example, is completely different from the love I feel for my sisters, which is different from the love I feel for my parents. And none of those seems even remotely similar to the love I have for my children.

I usually describe my love for my children in fairly happy terms, but periodically I experience it in a completely different way—one that sometimes frightens me.

Here's how it happens: I'm watching one of my daughters (either one will do) play in the park, her beautiful, innocent face filled with joy. All of a sudden, out of nowhere, I begin to imagine how I would feel if something terrible were to happen to her. What if she fell and broke her neck? What if she got hit by a truck? What if she got horribly sick and died? The loss is almost palpable, and just thinking about these things is enough to depress me for the rest of the day.

And there's more. Sometimes my imagination goes a step further and I wonder what I would do if someone, anyone, tried to hurt or kidnap or kill one of my children. At the very instant that that thought pops into my head, my heart suddenly begins beating faster and so loudly I can almost hear it, my breathing quickens, and my teeth and fists clench. I haven't hit another person outside a Karate studio for more than twenty-five years. But during those brief moments when my imagination runs loose I realize that I would be perfectly capable of killing another human being with my bare hands and without a moment's hesitation.

Feeling Isolated

When my older daughter was still quite young, she and her baby-sitter spent several mornings a week at Totland, a nearby park that had become something of a Mecca for caretakers and children. Most afternoons I'd come to pick up my daughter at the park, and I'd stay for an hour or so watching her play with the other kids.

The other caregivers—almost all of whom were women—would be gathered in groups of four or five, chatting, sharing information, and learning from each other. And newcomers—as long as they were female—were quickly welcomed into these groups. But despite the nodding relationships I had developed with a few of the women, I was never made completely welcome. "It's strange being a man in this woman's place," writes David Steinberg, describing a trip to the park with his baby. "There is an easy-going exchange among the women here, yet I am outside of it. . . . Maybe it's all in my head, just me being uncomfortable about integrating this lunch counter. Whatever it is, it leaves me feeling strange and alone."

Once in a while another father would come to the park with his child, and we'd nod, smile, or raise our eyebrows at each other. We probably had much in common as fathers, shared many of the same concerns, and could have learned a lot from each other. But we didn't. Instead, we sat ten yards apart; if we ever spoke, it was about football or something equally superficial. Each of us was afraid to approach the other for fear of seeming too needy, too ignorant, or not masculine enough. What a couple of idiots.

Unfortunately, the majority of new fathers in the same situation would do exactly the same thing. "Most men," says Bruce Linton, "turn to their wives, not to other men, to help them understand their feelings about fatherhood." That approach, however, is often less than completely satisfying. Even if their wives are supportive, most men report that "there's something they are not 'getting,'" says Linton. The result is that many new fathers feel isolated; they have all sorts of concerns, worries, and feelings they don't completely understand, and they think there's no one else they can share their experience with. Fatherhood, it seems, can be a lonely business at times.

Getting Together with Other Men

One of the best ways to overcome your feelings of isolation or loneliness as a father is to join or start a fathers' group. Even in California, where there are so many support groups that there are support groups for people who belong to too many support groups, the idea of being involved in a fathers' group still sounds a little risky. But according to Doug Spangler, author of *Fatherhood: An Owner's Manual*, there are many important reasons to do it:

- ◆ Education. Women get a ton of parenting (and other) advice from other women: where to buy the best used children's clothes, places to take the kids on rainy days, surefire cures for illnesses, ways to soothe crying babies, finding and hiring baby-sitters. You'd be surprised how much you already know, and how much you'll be able to help other men.
- ◆ Perspective. It won't take long for you to learn that you're not the only father who is having the feelings or thoughts you are. Yet because each of us has a different way of looking at or doing things, you'll have plenty of unique insights to contribute to the other guys in the group.
- ◆ Opportunities for sharing. Like most men, you probably have a few things you just can't talk about with your wife. When those issues arise, you need a couple of guys who are—or have been—experiencing some of the same things you have.
- ◆ Encouragement. If you're having a tough time with something, or you need help making a decision, you'll be able to tap into the collective wisdom of other men who have made fatherhood a priority in their lives.

*"Gotta go, guys. I've had about all the male bonding
I can take for today."*

♦ Accountability. The other fathers in your group will support you, but because they're guys, they'll also let you know if you're screwing up.

Finding other fathers to join a group probably won't be easy. But if you put the word out you're sure to get some responses. Here are some likely sources of new (or existing) fathers:
♦ Your church or synagogue
♦ The hospital where your baby was born
♦ Your partner's OB/GYN
♦ Your pediatrician
♦ Leaders of mothers' groups

If you aren't comfortable joining a group (and there are plenty of us who aren't), it's still important to make regular contact with other fathers. You can do this one-on-one with another father, or, if you've got a computer, by logging on to the Internet. There are discussion groups, lists, and Web pages dealing with just about every aspect of parenting: some for both mothers and fathers, some just for fathers. Almost all of these services are available for free. There's a listing of good Internet addresses in the Resources appendix at the end of this book.

According to Bruce Linton, "A father's need for friendships with other fathers is critical to his continued development." In addition, there's plenty of research indicating that fathers who join support groups are generally happier. So don't think you can handle by yourself every fatherhood-related matter that comes up. You can't. And trying to do so will only hurt your kids and yourself.

You and Your Baby

A (Very) Brief Introduction to Discipline

"Discipline is the second most important thing you do for a child," says pediatrician T. Berry Brazelton. "Love comes first." There's no question in my mind that Brazelton is absolutely right. But before we go any further, let's clarify one thing: Discipline does *not* mean "punishment"; it means "teaching" and "setting limits."

According to pediatrician Burton White, there is absolutely no need to discipline kids under seven months. There are two main reasons for this. First, your child simply isn't capable of understanding that she's doing

"Your father and I have come to believe that incarceration is sometimes the only appropriate punishment."

something wrong. She has no idea at this point what "right" and "wrong" mean. Second, babies under about seven months have very short memories. So by the time you've disciplined the baby, she's already forgotten what she did to get you so upset.

Starting at about seven months, though, White suggests slowly beginning

---

Your Baby's Teeth

Although your baby's little chompers started forming when your partner was four months pregnant, they probably won't make their first appearance ("eruption" in dental lingo) until about six or seven months. And it's not at all uncommon for a child to be toothless until his first birthday. One thing you can count on, though: whenever your baby's teeth show up, they'll be followed immediately by plaque. Yes, the same stuff that your dentist has to chip off your teeth with a chisel.

It's way too early to start taking your child to a dentist, but you should use a small piece of gauze to clean each of his teeth once a day. When he's a year old, use a toothbrush with a very soft bristle. Flossing won't be necessary for a while.

TEETHING

There are two important things to know about teething. First, your baby's teeth start showing up in a fairly predictable order: first the two lower central incisors, then the two top central incisors, and then the ones on either side. Most kids will have all eight incisors by the end of their first year.

Second, teething isn't usually much fun for your baby or for anyone else nearby. Most kids experience at least some discomfort around the tooth for a few days before it breaks through the gum. For many, those pre-eruption days are marked by runny noses, loose stools, a low-grade fever, and some general crankiness.

Fortunately, teething discomfort doesn't last long and is relatively easily dealt with. Most babies respond quite well to acetaminophen (ask your pediatrician how many drops to give and don't waste your time rubbing it on the baby's gums—it doesn't work). Teething rings are also helpful, especially the kind that are water filled and can be frozen, and so, for that matter are frozen bagels (although if you go the bagel route, you'll be finding crumbs all over your house for a month).

Pacifier Safety

Generally speaking, there's nothing wrong with giving your baby a pacifier. A lot of babies have a need to suck that can't be satisfied by breastfeeding or shoving their own (or even your) fingers into their mouths.
And don't worry about damaging your baby's soon-to-be-dazzling smile;
most dentists agree that sucking on a pacifier isn't a problem until
about age four.

Thumbs, on the other hand, are a bit more problematic. First of all,
because thumbs don't conform to the shape of your baby's mouth as well
as pacifiers do, there's a greater chance that thumbsucking will damage
your baby's teeth (although not until he's five or so). And if your baby is
a constant thumbsucker, there's a chance it will have an impact on the
way he speaks. Finally, most illness-causing germs get into our bodies
from our hands. Need I say more?

There are, however, some potential dangers involved in using pacifiers. Here's what to do to avoid them:
- Nipples should be made of a single piece of nontoxic material.
- The shield (the part that stays on the outside of the baby's mouth)
  should be nondetachable and have several holes for saliva.
- Check the nipple for holes, tears, or other signs of wear. If you find
  any, replace the pacifier immediately—you don't want baby to chew
  off pieces and swallow them.
- Never, never, never tie the pacifier around your baby's neck or use
  string to attach the pacifier to your baby—it can pose a serious
  strangulation risk. But if you're tired of picking the pacifier up off
  the floor thirty-eight times a day, buy yourself a clip-on holder, one
  that detaches easily.

to set limits. Nothing rigid—just some basic guidelines to get your baby
used to the idea.

The best way (in fact, it's really the only serious option at this age) to
discipline and set limits for your baby is to distract him; take advantage of
his short memory while you still can. So if he's gotten hold of that priceless
Van Gogh you accidentally left on the floor, give him a teddy bear; and if he's
making a break for the nearest busy street, pick him up and turn him around
the other way. Chances are, he won't even notice. And even if he does, he'll
be disappointed for only a few seconds.

Walkers

I had a walker when I was a baby and both my kids did too. But there's a lot of controversy about whether walkers are safe or not. Supposedly, 15,000 emergency room visits per year are attributed to them. This has less to do with the actual walker and more to do with falling down the stairs. So if you keep your stairs securely gated, walkers shouldn't be a problem.

Another common complaint about walkers is that babies can build up some real speed and fly around the house smacking into everything in sight—fun for them, not so fun for you. In addition, they can be a source of great frustration for the baby: he may have a hard time going over thresholds or making the transition from smooth floor to carpet; and because walkers are usually fairly wide, babies always seem to be getting stuck behind the furniture.

If you're worried, most of the potential problems can be resolved by buying a "jumper"—essentially a walker with a bouncy seat and no wheels.

Childproofing Your House

Once your baby realizes that he's able to move around by himself, his mission in life will be to locate—and make you race to—the most dangerous, life-threatening things in your home. So if you haven't already begun the never-ending process of childproofing your house, you'd better start now.

The first thing to do is get down on your hands and knees and check things out from your baby's perspective. Don't those lamp cords and speaker wires look like they'd be fun to yank on? And don't those outlets seem to be waiting for you to stick something in them?

Taking care of those enticing wires and covering up your outlets is only the beginning, so let's start with the basics.

ANYWHERE AND EVERYWHERE

♦ Move all your valuable items out of the baby's reach. It's not too early to try to teach him not to touch, but don't expect much compliance at so young an age.

♦ Bolt to the wall bookshelves and other freestanding cabinets (this is especially important if you live in earthquake country); pulling things down on top of themselves is a favorite baby suicide attempt.

- Don't hang heavy things on the stroller—it can tip over.
- Get special guards for your radiators and raise any space heaters and e. tric fans off the floor.
- Install a safety gate at the bottom and top of every flight of stairs. After a few months, you can move the bottom gate up a few steps to give the baby a low-risk way to practice climbing.
- Adjust your water heater temperature to 120 degrees. This will reduce the likelihood that your baby will scald himself.
- Get a fire extinguisher and put smoke alarms in every bedroom. If you want to be extra cautious, consider a carbon monoxide detector.
- If you have a two-story house (or higher), consider getting a rope escape ladder.
- Take first aid and CPR classes; they're usually offered by the local Red Cross, YMCA, or hospital.
- Put together a first aid kit (see page 140 for the ingredients).

ESPECIALLY IN THE KITCHEN

- Install safety locks on all but one of your low cabinets and drawers. Most of these locks allow the door to be opened slightly—just enough to accommodate a baby's fingers—so make sure the kind you get also keeps the door from *closing* completely as well.
- Stock the one unlocked cabinet with unbreakable pots and pans and encourage your baby to jump right in.
- Keep baby's high chair away from the walls. His strong little legs can push off the wall and knock the chair over.
- Watch out for irons and ironing boards. The cords are a hazard and the boards themselves are very easy to knock over.
- Get an oven lock and covers for your oven and stove knobs.
- Use the back burners on the stove whenever possible and keep pot handles turned toward the back of the stove.
- Try to keep the baby out of the kitchen when anyone is cooking. It's too easy to trip over him, drop or spill something on him, or accidentally smack him with something.
- Never hold your baby while you're cooking. Teaching him what steam is or how water boils may seem like a good idea, but bubbling spaghetti sauce or hot oil hurts when it splashes.
- Put mouse and insect traps in places where your baby can't get to them. Better yet, set them after he's asleep and take your kill to the taxidermist before he gets up.

What Every Good First Aid Kit Needs

- ace bandages
- acetaminophen (Tylenol) drops and tablets
- adhesive strips
- adhesive tape
- antibiotic ointment
- antiseptic ointment
- antibiotic wash
- butterfly bandages
- clean popsicle sticks (for splints)
- cleansing agent to clean wounds
- cotton balls (sterile if possible)
- cotton cloth for slings
- disposable instant ice packs
- disposable hand wipes (individual packets)
- emergency telephone numbers
- gauze rolls or pads (sterile if possible)
- mild soap
- syrup of ipecac (to induce vomiting, if necessary)
- tweezers (for splinters and the like)
- pair of clean (surgical) gloves
- scissors with rounded tip
- sterile 4 × 4-inch bandages

It's also a good idea to have an emergency treatment manual around the house. Here are a few good ones:

- *Emergency Treatment: Infants* (for kids birth–12 months), $7.95.
- *Emergency Treatment: Children* (for kids 1–9 years), $7.95.
- *Emergency Treatment: Infants, Children, and Adults* (for the whole family), $12.95. Available in English and Spanish from Mosby/EMT, 200 North La Salle Street, Chicago, IL 60601. (800) 767-5215.
- *The American Medical Association Handbook: First Aid/Emergency,* $10.00 plus $4.00 shipping and handling. Available from Random House Ordering Department, 400 Hahn Road, Westminster, MD 21157. (800) 733-3000.

- Use plastic dishes and serving bowls whenever you can—glass breaks, and, at least in my house, the shards seem to show up for weeks, no matter how well I sweep.
- Post the phone numbers of the nearest poison control agency and your pediatrician near your phone.

ESPECIALLY IN THE LIVING ROOM

- Put decals at baby height on all sliding glass doors.
- Get your plants off the floor: more than seven hundred species can cause

illness or death if eaten, including such common ones as lily of the valley, iris, and poinsettia.

◆ Pad the corners of low tables, chairs, and fireplace hearths.

◆ Make sure your fireplace screen and tools can't be pulled down or knocked over.

◆ Keep furniture away from windows. Babies will climb up whatever they can and may fall through the glass.

ESPECIALLY IN THE BEDROOM/NURSERY

◆ No homemade or antique cribs. They almost never conform to today's safety standards. Cribs with protruding corner posts are especially dangerous.

◆ Remove from the crib all mobiles and hanging toys. By five months, most kids can push themselves up on their hands and knees and can get tangled up in (and even choke on) strings.

◆ Keep the crib at least two feet away from blinds, drapes, hanging cords, or wall decorations with ribbons.

◆ Check toys for missing parts.

◆ Toy chest lids should stay up when opened (so they don't slam on tiny fingers).

◆ Don't leave dresser drawers open. From the baby's perspective, they look a lot like stairs.

◆ Keep crib items to a minimum: a sheet, a blanket, bumpers, and a few *soft* toys. Babies don't need pillows at this age and large toys or stuffed animals can be climbed on and used to escape from the crib.

◆ Don't leave your baby alone on the changing table even for a second.

ESPECIALLY IN THE BATHROOM

◆ If possible, use a gate to keep access restricted to the adults in the house.

◆ Install a toilet guard.

◆ Keep bath and shower doors closed.

◆ Never leave water standing in the bath, the sink, or even a bucket. Drowning is the third most common cause of accidental deaths among young children, and babies can drown in practically no water at all—even an inch or two.

◆ Keep medication and cosmetics high up.

◆ Make sure there's nothing your baby can climb up on to gain access to the medicine cabinet.

◆ Keep razors and hair dryers unplugged and out of reach.

◆ Never keep electrical appliances near the bathtub.

◆ Use a bath mat or stick-on safety strips to reduce the risk of slipping in the bathtub.

Perpetual Motion

What's Going On with the Baby

Physically

♦ At this stage, your baby is in motion just about every waking minute. She's an excellent crawler and will follow you around for hours.

♦ Having mastered crawling, she's now working on getting herself upright.

♦ She'll start by pulling herself up to a half-standing crouch and letting herself drop back down. Sometime in the next few weeks, though, she'll pull herself up to a complete standing position.

♦ If she's really adventurous, she'll let go with one hand or even lean against something and release both hands. Either way, she'll be shocked to discover that she can't get down.

♦ She now uses a "pincer grip" to pick things up and, because of her increased dexterity, becomes fascinated by tiny things.

♦ If she's holding a toy and sees something new, she'll drop what she's got and pick up the second. She may even retain the first toy and pick up the second with her other hand.

♦ Her finger-feeding and bottle- or cup-handling skills are improving fast.

Intellectually

♦ Your baby's increased mobility has opened a new range of possibilities for exploration and discovery. She now gets into drawers and cabinets and can empty them amazingly quickly.

♦ Her mobility also lets her get better acquainted with some of the objects she's heretofore seen only from afar. Crawling around on the floor, for example, a baby will stop underneath a chair and examine it from every possible angle. Then, writes child psychologist Selma Fraiberg, "Upon leaving the underside of the chair, he pauses to wrestle with one of the legs, gets the feel of its roundness and its slipperiness and sinks his two front teeth into it in order to sample flavor and texture. In a number of circle tours around the chair at various times in the days and weeks to come, he discovers that the various profiles he has been meeting are the several faces of one object, the object we call a chair."

♦ Now able to pick up a different object in each hand, your baby will spend a lot of time comparing the capabilities of each side of her body.

Verbally

♦ She now babbles almost constantly, using your intonation as much as she can.

♦ She can also use sounds to express different emotions.

♦ She continues to concentrate on two-syllable "words"; *b*, *p*, and *m* are her favorite consonants.

♦ Her name is not the only sound she knows. She'll also turn her head in response to other familiar sounds, such as a car approaching, the phone ringing, the television "speaking," and the refrigerator opening.

Emotionally/Socially

♦ With so much to keep her busy during the day, your baby may feel she doesn't have time for naps anymore. The lack of sleep, together with the frustration at not being able to do everything she wants with her body, may make her cranky.

♦ When she's in a good mood, she really wants to be included in socializing; she may crawl into the middle of a conversation, sit up, and start chattering.

♦ She can anticipate events and will, for example, wriggle her entire body when she thinks you're getting ready to play with her.

♦ She may actually be frightened by the developing idea that she and you are separate, and may cling to you even more than before. At the same time, her fear of strangers is peaking.

What You're Going Through

Learning Flexibility and Patience

Before my older daughter was born, I was incredibly anal about time; I always

*"Hey, would you kids mind holding down
the quality-time racket?"*

showed up wherever I was supposed to be exactly when I was supposed to, and I demanded the same from others. But as you now know, going on a simple trip to the store with baby in tow takes as much planning as an expedition to Mt. Everest. And getting anywhere on time is just about impossible.

It took a while, but eventually I learned that trying to be a father and Mr. Prompt at the same time just wasn't going to work. And somehow, simply accepting that fact made me a lot more forgiving of other people's lateness as well.

Interestingly, this new flexible attitude about time began to rub off on other areas of my life. Overall, since becoming a father I think I'm far more tolerant of individual differences and can more easily accept other people's limitations, as well as my own.

Whatever you're most rigid and impatient about, you can bet that your baby will figure it out and push all your buttons. That leisurely walk in the park you planned might have to be cut short when the baby panics and won't stop crying after a friendly dog licks her face. Or you might end up having to stay a few extra hours at a friend's house so as not to wake the baby if she's sleeping or, if she's awake, not to upset her nap schedule by having her fall asleep in the car on the way home.

"As soon as I get oriented to one of Dylan's patterns, he changes and a whole new pattern begins to evolve," writes David Steinberg about his son. "It's like standing up in a roller coaster. I'm finding that the more I accept this constant change, the more I can enjoy the dynamics of it, the constant growing. Dylan is deepening my sense of change as a way of life."

Not everyone, however, finds change as pleasant or as easy to accept as David Steinberg. For some, any sort of deviation from an orderly schedule, or any lack of continuity, can be very discombobulating. If you're in this category, you've got a rather Zen-like choice to make: you can bend or you can break. Babies are, almost by definition, irrational and not at all interested in your timetables. "I can't impose my rules on Dylan," writes Steinberg. "All the persuasive skills I use to get other people to do things my way are totally irrelevant to him. I am forced to accept the validity of his rules, and then to learn to integrate that with my real needs. The trick is to become less of a control freak without entirely sacrificing myself." True, true, true.

Thinking about How Involved You Are

Before I became a father, I don't think I had ever held an infant. I babysat two or three times when I was a teenager, but only when my young charges were fast asleep. And I certainly had never changed a diaper, filled a bottle, or pushed a stroller.

Whenever I imagined myself with a child of my own, she was always two or three years old and we were walking on the beach holding hands, wrestling, playing catch, telling stories. The thought that babies start off as tiny, helpless infants never really crossed my mind, and I wouldn't have been able to describe what I—or anyone else, for that matter—would do with a baby.

Most fathers-to-be know just about as much about babies as I did. But despite our ignorance, we spend a lot of time thinking about how we want to be involved with our kids. In his research, Bruce Drobeck found that although "being involved" means different things to different people, most men agreed that they:

♦ Don't want their partner to raise the kids alone.
♦ Don't want to be stuck in the role of the "wait-till-your-dad-comes-home" disciplinarian they may have grown up with.
♦ Want to be more open and communicative than their fathers were with them.
♦ Want to be involved with their children in a meaningful manner, from the earliest stages of development.

So how are you doing? Are you as involved with your baby as you want to be? As you planned to be? As we discussed earlier, new fathers generally do less child care than either they or their partners had predicted during pregnancy (to review the reasons why, see pages 105–6). Jay Belsky describes one study in which 74 percent of new fathers said that child care should be shared equally. But when asked whether or not they actually shared child care with their partners, only 13 percent said yes.

If you're in that 13 percent, you're probably feeling pretty proud of yourself, and you have every right to. But many new fathers—especially those who have to return to work sooner than they'd like, or have to work longer hours to bring in extra money—experience a profound sadness and longing for their families.

It's Hard to Make Up for Lost Time

There's nothing like a long day at the office to make you realize just how much you miss your baby. And when you get home, you might be tempted to try to make up for lost time by cramming as much active, physical father/baby contact as you can into the few hours before bedtime (yours or the baby's). That's a pretty tall order, and just about the only way you'll be able to fill it is to be "overly controlling, intrusive, and hyper-stimulating," writes psychiatrist Stanley Greenspan. So before you start tickling and wrestling and playing with the baby, spend a few minutes reading or cuddling with her, quietly getting to know each other again—even at eight months, a day away from you is a looooong time for your baby. You'll both feel a lot better if you do.

Besides making you miss your baby, a long day at the office can also make you feel guilty about the amount of time you're away from her. Now a little guilt is probably a good thing, but far too many parents let their guilt get out of hand. And the results are not good at all. "In order to make the emotional burden easier," writes Greenspan, "they distance themselves from their children."

Although there's no practical way for you to make up for lost time, it's important that you find some middle ground between being overly controlling and distancing yourself from your baby. The best way to do that is to make sure that whenever you're with your child, you're there 100 percent. Forget the phone, forget the newspapers or the TV, forget washing the dishes, and forget eating if you can. You can do all those things after the baby goes to sleep.

He Says, She Says

Remember the story about the five blind men and the elephant? Each of them approaches an elephant and bumps into a different part—the leg, the tail, the ear, the trunk, the side—and then authoritatively describes to the others what he thinks an elephant *really* looks like. The moral of the story, of course, is that two (or more) people looking at exactly the same object or situation may see very different things.

The same moral applies when couples are asked to rate the husband's level of involvement in the home: men are more likely to be satisfied with their contribution and women are more likely to be disappointed. The problem here is not one of blindness, however. Instead, it's that men and women, according to Jay Belsky, are using different yardsticks to measure.

"A wife measures what a husband does against what she does. And because what a man does looks small . . . the woman often ends up . . . unhappy and disgruntled," writes Belsky. "The man, on the other hand, usually measures his contribution to chores against what his father did." And because he's sure to be doing more, he ends up feeling "good about himself and his contribution."

Another factor that Belsky feels contributes to a new father's tendency to overrate his participation is that ever since the baby was born, he has probably been the main, even the sole, breadwinner. And since he's been socialized to equate breadwinning with parenting, going to work "makes the 20 percent he does at home seem like 200 percent," says Belsky.

Circumstances may make it impossible for you to make any changes in the time you can spend with your family. But if you have any flexibility at all, take another look at the work/family options on pages 106–9. On his deathbed, no father ever wishes he'd spent more time at the office.

You and Your Baby

Reading

At eight to nine months of age, children who have been read to regularly can predict and anticipate actions in a familiar book and will mimic gestures and noises. So at this age it's a good idea to involve your baby more actively in the

"The weasel represents the forces of evil and the duck the forces of good,
a surrogate for American air and naval superiority."

reading process. Talk about the things on the page that aren't described in the text and ask your baby a lot of identification questions. If you can, show your baby real-life examples of the objects pictured in her books.

At around ten months, your baby may be perfectly content to sit with a book and turn pages—probably two or three at a time. Don't worry if she seems not to be paying any attention to what she's "reading"; she's learning a lot about books' structure and feel. If you put a book upside down in front of your baby she'll turn it the right way. Singing, finger plays, and rhythmic bouncing while reciting nursery rhymes are still big hits.

At eleven months, your baby may be able to follow a character from page to page. This is also the age at which she may start demanding that you read specific stories or that you reread the one you just finished. Board books and sturdy flap books are great for this age.

By the time she's a year old, your baby may be able to turn the pages of her books one at a time. She will point to specific pictures you ask her to identify and may even make the correct animal sounds when you ask her, "What does a . . . say?" Be sure to respond positively every time your baby makes any attempt to speak—animal noises included.

As you've probably noticed already, reading provides you and your baby with a wonderful opportunity for close physical contact. The best position I've found (it's the one with maximum snuggle potential) is to put the baby on your lap and, with your arms around her, hold the book in front while you read over her shoulder.

When considering the next few months' reading, look for books with bright, big, well-defined illustrations, simple stories, and not too much text. Besides your baby's current favorites (which you should keep reading for as long as she's interested), you might want to check out a few of these books:

Baby Animals (and many others), Gyo Fujikawa

The Baby's Catalog, Janet Ahlberg, Allan Ahlberg

Baby's Bedtime Book, Kay Chorado

The Ball Bounced (and many others), Nancy Tafuri

Daddy, Play with Me (and many others), Shigeo Watanabe

Dressing (and many, many others), Helen Oxenbury

Goodnight Moon, Margaret Wise Brown

"More, More, More," Said the Baby: 3 Love Stories, Vera B. Williams

"Paddle," Said the Swan, Gloria Kamen

Sam's Bath (and other books in the Sam series), Barbro Lindgren

Sleepy Book, Charlotte Zolotow

Step by Step, Bruce McMillan

Spot Goes Splash (and many other Spot books), Eric Hill

Tickle; All Fall Down; Say Goodnight; Dad's Back (and many others), Jan Ormerod

What Sadie Sang; Sam Who Never Forgets (and others), Eve Rice

Wheels on the Bus, adapted by Paul O. Zelinsky

Who Said Meow? Maria Polushkin

CONCEPTS

The ABC Bunny, Wanda Gag

Clap Hands (and many others), Helen Oxenbury

First Words for Babies and Toddlers, Jane Salt

Ten, Nine, Eight, Molly Bang

Dealing with Stranger Anxiety

At about seven or eight months, you'll probably notice a marked change in your baby's behavior around strangers. Only a few weeks ago, you could have handed him to just about anyone and he would have greeted the new person with a huge smile. But now, if a stranger—or even someone the baby has seen before—comes anywhere near him, he'll cling tightly to you and cry. Welcome to *stranger anxiety,* your baby's first fear.

What's happening is that your baby is just beginning to figure out that he and you (and his other primary caretakers) are separate human beings. It's a scary idea, and he's simply afraid that some person he doesn't like very much might take you—and all the services you provide—away.

Stranger anxiety affects 50–80 percent of babies. It usually kicks in at around seven or eight months, but sometimes not until a year. It can last anywhere from a few weeks to six months.

Your baby is more likely to experience stranger anxiety if he's withdrawing, slow-adapting, or has low sensory threshold (see the "Temperament" section on pages 89–96). He'll be less likely to be affected if he's approaching or fast-adapting or if he's been exposed to a steady flow of new people since early infancy.

Here are a few things you can do to help your baby (and yourself) cope with stranger anxiety:

♦ If you're getting together with friends, try to do it at your own house instead of someplace else. The baby's reaction will be less dramatic in a familiar place.

♦ Hold your baby closely whenever you enter a new environment or anyplace where there are likely to be other people.

♦ When you enter a new place, don't just hand the baby off to someone he doesn't know. Let him cling to you for a while and use you as a safe haven.

♦ Warn friends, relatives, and strangers not to be offended by the baby's shyness, crying, screaming, or overall reluctance to have anything to do with them. Tell them to approach the baby as they might any other wild animal: slowly, cautiously, with a big smile, talking quietly, and perhaps even offering a toy.

♦ Be patient with your baby. Don't pressure him to go to strangers or even to be nice to them. And don't criticize him if he cries or clings to you.

♦ If you're leaving the baby with a new sitter, have her or him get to your house at least twenty minutes before you have to leave. This will (hopefully) give baby and sitter a few minutes—with you nearby—to get to know each other.

♦ If your partner stays at home with the baby while you're at work, you need to understand that your baby might lump you in with the people she considers strangers. Don't take it personally. Just follow the steps above on how strangers should approach the baby, and be patient.

Family Matters

Money

Without a doubt, money is the number one issue couples fight about. And financial squabbles are especially common during the early parenthood years, while both parents are getting settled.

Many factors contribute to quarrels over money. Here are some of the most common:

♦ **Frustration.** Women who have put their careers on hold to take a more active role at home may resent having their income (and the associated power) reduced. This goes double for men because of the still-lingering "good provider" pressures.

♦ **Your childhood.** The way you were raised can have a big impact—positive or negative—on the way you raise your own kids. If you grew up in a poor family, you may feel weird spending money on anything more than the bare necessities. Or you may feel obligated to give your child all the things you never got—at least the ones that money can buy. And if your parents were big spenders, you may be inclined to bury your baby in gifts, or you may be afraid of spoiling your child and cut way back. Whatever your overall attitude toward money, if your partner's differs considerably from yours, look out.

♦ **Differences in spending habits.** You like Cheerios and eating lunch out; your partner wants you to buy the generic brand and bring lunch from home. She makes long-distance calls in the middle of the day; you want her to wait until the rates go down.

♦ **Differences in definitions.** My wife loves to get things "half off"; the way I figure it, half off of something that costs three times more than it should is still no deal.

♦ **Gender differences.** Generally speaking, fathers and mothers have different ideas about money and what should be done with it. Fathers tend to worry about enhancing the family's long-range financial outlook and to be more concerned than mothers about savings. "Often for women new baby clothes represent a sensible economic choice because they advance another of the new mother's priorities: social presentation," says Jay Belsky. "This is the name given to her desire to present her baby—her creation—to the larger world of family and friends for admiration and praise." The big problem here is that your partner may interpret your not wanting to spend money on clothes as a sign that you don't love your baby (and, by extension, that you don't love her either).

Avoiding Money Problems, or at Least
Learning to Live with Them

♦ Be realistic. Having a baby can have a major impact on your financial life. Food, clothing, medical expenses, and day-care or preschool tuition all add up pretty quickly.

♦ Make a budget (there are plenty of good budgeting software packages, Quicken being among the best). Keep track of everything coming in and going out—even your cash expenditures.

♦ Hold regular monthly meetings to discuss your financial situation. Listen to each other's concerns and remember that whatever your differences, you both have the best interests of your family at heart. No blaming or yelling, and stay away from discussion-killing phrases like "You always" and "You never."

♦ Rearrange your priorities. Take care of the absolute necessities—food, clothing, shelter—first. If there's anything left over, start saving it for ice cream cones, vacations, private school education.

♦ Negotiate and compromise. You give up Cheerios and take a brown bag to lunch; she makes her long-distance calls after 11 P.M. or before 8 A.M. And remember, there are plenty of ways to cut back without having to skimp. Why pay full price for a pair of pants your child is going to outgrow in a few months when you can get a perfectly good used pair for less than three bucks?

♦ Make a plan. Set realistic and achievable savings goals, and make sure you're adequately insured.

Notes:

The Building Blocks of Development

What's Going On with the Baby

Physically

♦ As if recovering from the frantic developmental pace of the past two months, your baby will probably not add many new skills this month. Instead, he'll spend his time perfecting the old ones.

♦ By the end of this month he'll be such a confident crawler that he'll be able to buzz around the house grasping a block or other toy in one hand. He'll be able to crawl backward and may even make it up a flight of stairs.

♦ He easily pulls himself to an upright position and can stand (briefly) while holding your hand. He can cruise (sidestep) along furniture and walls, and when he's done, he no longer has any trouble unlocking his knees and sitting down.

♦ Now able to move his fingers separately, he has discovered that the house is filled with holes and cracks that are just big enough to accommodate his index finger.

♦ The biggest development this month (and this is pretty important) is that your baby is now coordinated enough to build a "tower" of two or three blocks (which he'll knock down immediately).

Intellectually

♦ In previous months your baby would learn a new skill and then repeat it endlessly. At this point, though, he'll begin to experiment with new ways of doing things. For example, instead of repeatedly dropping his spoon off his high-chair tray, he may start with the spoon, then drop his bowl off the other side, and finish up by tossing his cup over his shoulder.

♦ He's just beginning to come to terms with the idea that he is not the power behind everything that happens. He may, for example, bring you a wind-up toy to wind up.

♦ He's also beginning to shake his if-I-can't-see-it-it-doesn't-exist attitude, but just barely. Now if he watches you hide a toy, he will look for it. But if you hide the same toy in a second hiding place, he will continue looking in the first hiding place. In his mind, something out of his sight can exist, but only in one specific place.

♦ He's also learning about actions and their consequences. If he sees you putting on a coat, he'll know you're going outside and he may cry.

♦ As his memory gets better, you'll be able to interrupt him in the middle of an activity and he'll go back to it a few minutes later.

Verbally

♦ He's developing a distinctive "voice" in his babbling and may identify certain objects by the sound they make (*choo-choo* for train, *moo* for cow).

♦ Besides recognizing his name, your baby now understands and responds to other words and phrases, such as "No" and "Where's the baby?" He also understands and might even obey simple commands such as "Bring me my pipe."

♦ Although he's several months away from saying anything truly understandable, your baby already has a good grasp of the rhythm and sound of his native language. German researcher Angela Friederici found that even at this young age, babies are sensitive to the structure of words in their own language and can listen to a string of speech and break it down into wordlike units.

Emotionally/Socially

♦ This baby loves to play. He'll shout if he thinks you should be paying more attention to him and imitates such acts as blowing out candles, coughing, and sneezing.

♦ He may be able to get you to understand—by pointing, grunting, squealing, or bouncing up and down—that he needs something specific.

♦ Preferences are becoming more distinct, and he'll push away things (and people) he doesn't want.

♦ Perhaps a little scared of the new world he's discovering, he clings to you more than ever and cries if you leave him alone; it's the beginning of *separation anxiety* (different from the stranger anxiety of the past few months).

What You're Going Through

Feeling More Attached to Your Baby

As your baby gets older and becomes more and more responsive and inter-active, your attachment to her will deepen. As we discussed earlier, however, parent-child attachments are a little bit lopsided: "It is fairly obvious," write psychologists Barbara and Philip Newman, "that soon after a child's birth the parent's attachment to the child becomes quite specific, that is, the parent would not be willing to replace his or her child with any other child of similar age."

But what the Newmans and I—and you, too—really want to know is, "At what point does the child make this kind of commitment to the *parent?*" The answer is somewhere between six and nine months. By that time, the baby has developed the mental capacity to associate you with having his needs and wants satisfied and can summon up a mental image of you to keep him company when you're not there.

But don't think that this means you needn't bother trying to establish an attachment to your baby right away. On the contrary. Attachment doesn't just happen overnight; it's a gradual process that takes months to develop, and the sooner you get started, the better. "A healthy attachment in infancy is likely to turn out a healthier adult," write the husband-wife/pediatrician-nurse team of William and Martha Sears. And the way you react and respond to your baby will have a great influence on the kind of attachment you and she eventually establish.

As you might imagine, the single most successful strategy for forming last-ing, secure attachments with your children is to spend time with them one-on-one, doing everything you possibly can together, from the mundane to the exciting. "The earlier the father can feel involved with the infant," says Henry Biller, "the more likely will a strong father-child attachment develop."

Attachment theories were first developed in the 1950s by researchers John Bowlby and Mary Ainsworth, who conducted detailed studies of the interactions between several hundred parents and their children. Bowlby and Ainsworth concluded that there are two basic types of attachment: *secure,* meaning that

Attachment Basics

ATTACHMENT	TWELVE-MONTH-OLDS
Secure (about ⅔ are securely attached, but that doesn't mean they won't have any problems when they grow up)	◆ Are confident that their parents will be there when needed. ◆ Know they can depend on their parents to respond to their pain, hunger, and attempts at interaction. ◆ Readily explore their environment using parents as bases. ◆ Don't cry much and are easy to put down after being held.
Avoidant (⅙)	◆ May avoid physical contact with parents. ◆ Don't depend on parents to be secure base. ◆ Don't expect to be responded to caringly. ◆ Learn not to act needy no matter how much they may want to be held or loved.
Ambivalent (⅙)	◆ Cry a lot but don't know whether their cries will get a response. ◆ Are afraid of being abandoned physically or emotionally. ◆ Are worried and anxious, easily upset. ◆ Cling to parents, teachers, other adults. ◆ Tend to be immature and mentally scattered.

the child feels confident that the parent will respond appropriately to her needs; and *insecure*, meaning that the child is constantly afraid her needs *won't* be met by the parent. They further divided the insecure category into two subcategories: *avoidant* and *ambivalent*. (See the chart above for a more detailed explanation.)

TODDLERS	PARENTS
◆ Are independent and trusting. ◆ Learn early how people treat other people. ◆ Are open to having their behavior redirected. ◆ Mix well with all age groups. ◆ Become social leaders. ◆ Are curious and eager to learn.	◆ Respond to children sensitively and consistently. ◆ Pick up the baby when he cries, feed him when he's hungry, hold him when he wants to be held.
◆ Are less curious. ◆ Are frequently distrusting. ◆ Can be selfish, aggressive, manipulative. ◆ May have few friends.	◆ Deny their (and others') feelings and needs. ◆ Believe children should be independent early. ◆ Don't like to cuddle with the baby or pick him up when he cries. ◆ Can be emotionally cold.
◆ Lack self-confidence. ◆ May experience uncontrolled anger. ◆ May either overreact emotionally or repress feelings. ◆ Are frequently less adaptable.	◆ Are wildly inconsistent and unpredictable in their parenting. ◆ Are frequently self-involved. ◆ Hope to get from the baby the love that they never had from their own parents and that they may not be able to get from each other.

Based on the information they gathered by observing babies in their first months of life, Bowlby and Ainsworth were able to predict accurately the specific behavior patterns those same babies would exhibit as they grew. Bowlby's and Aisworth's theories are just as applicable today as they were when articulated nearly fifty years ago.

In Case You Thought You Were Alone . . .

There isn't a single animal species in which the female doesn't produce the eggs. But eggs aren't worth much without the male's sperm to fertilize them. In most cases, once the eggs are laid, neither parent sticks around to watch it hatch or to meet their babies. Sometimes, though, eggs need more specialized care or they'll all perish. In these cases, one or both parents are required to pitch in. Here are just a few examples of some of the dozens of species of animals in which the father plays an important role in carrying, raising, protecting, and educating his young.

Long before the male three-spined stickleback has even met his mate, he sets to work building an attractive little house out of algae. When he's finished, he hangs out in front and makes a pass at the first female who happens by. If she's interested, the male invites her in, but, not being much of a romantic, he asks her to leave after she's laid her eggs, which he quickly fertilizes as soon as she's gone. For the next few weeks, the father guards his nest, keeping it well ventilated and repairing any damage. Until his babies hatch, the father never leaves the nest, even to eat.

Like the stickleback, the male giant water bug does everything he possibly can to attract females. If one shows any interest, he fertilizes her eggs. The female then climbs onto her lover's back and lays nearly a hundred eggs, securing each to his back with a special glue. For the next two weeks the father is completely responsible for the eggs' safety and well-being. When they finally hatch, the babies stick close to dad until they feel confident enough to swim away.

Unlike the stickleback, a cichlid (pronounced SIK-lid) doesn't need a nest. As soon as the female lays the eggs, the male scoops them up into his mouth. Because his mouth is so full, the father can't eat until the babies hatch—sometimes up to two weeks. And after they're born and can swim by themselves, dad still protects his children by carrying them in his mouth. He spits them out when it's time to eat, get some air, or just have a little fun. And when play time is over (or if danger is lurking), he sucks them back in again.

Frogs are famous for having involved fathers. After the eggs of the two-toned poison-arrow frog hatch, the tadpoles crawl onto their father's back, where they hang on with their suckerlike mouths as dad carries them through the jungle. Darwin's frogs take things one step further. Just as his tiny, jelly-covered eggs are about to hatch, the future father snaps them up with his tongue and slides them into a special pouch inside his body. The eggs hatch and the tiny tadpoles stay inside the pouch until they lose their tails and jump out of their father's mouth.

Among birds and mammals, there is a high rate of co-parenting. For example, male and female geese, gulls, pigeons, woodpeckers, and many other birds work as a team to build their homes, brood (sit on the eggs to keep them warm), and feed and protect the young after they're born. In a similar fashion, the male California mouse is responsible for bringing food into the nest and for huddling with the young to keep them warm (the babies aren't born with the ability to regulate their own body temperatures). These mice have at least two things in common with human parents. First, they are both generally monogamous. Second, the presence of an involved father has a major impact on the babies: pups weigh more, their ears and eyes open earlier, and they have a greater survival rate than pups who are separated from their fathers.

"They're hatching! Quick, Albert, get the camcorder!"

The Generational View

Like it or not, the type of attachment you establish with your baby will be influenced (not set in stone, just *influenced*) by your own attachment experience with your parents. So as you read this section, spend some time thinking about *your* childhood. Doing so may help you understand a few things about yourself and your parents. More important, it may help you avoid making some of the same mistakes with your own children that your parents made with you.

Your attachment with your child may also be influenced by your relationship with your partner. Dozens of studies confirm that the better the couple relationship, the more secure the parent-child relationship (see pages 210–12 for more on couple relationships).

The Father-Child Connection

Although the vast majority of research on attachment has focused on mothers and children, some researchers are now beginning to study father-child attachment. Their findings confirm what active, involved fathers have known in their hearts for years—that the father-child bond is no less important than the mother-child bond. Here's what the experts have to say:

- Researcher Frank Pedersen and his colleagues found that th involved a six-month-old baby has been with his father, the h baby's scores on mental and motor development tests.
- Fatherhood pioneer Ross Parke found that "the more fathers v in the everyday repetitive aspects of caring for infants (bathin dressing, and diapering), the more socially responsible the babies were and the better able they were in handling stressful situations."
- Researcher Norma Radin found that greater father involvement leads to increased performance in math. She also found that active fathering contributed to better social adjustment and competence, to children's perception that they were masters of their own fates, and to a higher mental age on verbal intelligence tests.

There are also factors that may interfere with father-child attachments, and researcher Glen Palm has identified several of them:

- Many fathers experience some tension in their relationships with their children because they feel excluded by the mother-infant bond, or because they feel that they have to compete with their partners to form a relationship with the child. Others say it's hard to form a close relationship because they feel they are unable to comfort their children adequately.

"Really, Howard! You're just like your father."

A lot of these fathers were able to form close attachments only after their children were weaned.

♦ Fathers who have to be away from home a lot during the week find that "re-attaching" with the kids on the weekends takes a lot of time and energy.

♦ Temperament. No matter how much you love your child, you'll find it easier to attach to an "easy" child than to a "difficult" one. (See pages 89–96 for more on temperament.)

♦ A small but significant percentage of fathers feel that their in-laws are overprotective of their adult daughters and get in the way too much.

♦ There is a glaring lack of information and support for new fathers.

You and Your Baby

Playing Around . . . Again

For the first seven or eight months of your baby's life, he had to be content with staring at things from across the room and waiting for you to bring them to him. But now that he's mobile, he's going to try to make up for lost time. He's incredibly curious about his world, and no obstacle can stand between him and something to touch, squeeze, gum, or grab. (If your baby *isn't* very curious, however, let your pediatrician know. But don't be alarmed if you catch the baby staring off into space once in a while. According to Burton White, babies this age spend about 20 percent of their waking time soaking up information visually.)

Although our society doesn't value play nearly as highly as some other parent-child pastimes such as feeding and diaper changing, it is, neverthe-less, critical to your baby's development. "Many children who do not have much chance to play and who are only infrequently played with suffer severe intellectual arrest or setbacks," writes developmental psychologist Bruno Bettelheim.

One of your major goals should be to expose your baby to the most varied, enriching play environment possible. But perhaps even more important is your basic philosophy about play. "Parents' inner attitudes always have a strong impact on their children," says Bettelheim. "So the way parents feel about play, the importance they give it or their lack of interest in it, is never lost on their child. Only when parents give play not just respect and tolerance but also their personal interest, will the child's play experience provide a solid basis upon which he can develop his relation to them and further to the world."

Brain Builders

These games and exercises can stimulate your baby's capacity to
ent skills at the same time (seeing, hearing, thinking, and remem
for example):

♦ Get two toys that are nearly identical except that they react in different ways
(one might need to be squeezed to make noise, the other shaken). Let the baby
play with one of them for a few minutes, then switch. Did he get confused?

♦ Ring a bell, squeeze a toy, or shake a rattle. When the baby looks to see
what made the sound, put the toy into a group of things he's familiar with.
Will he go for the one that made the noise or will he get sidetracked by
the other toys?

♦ More hiding games. A few months ago you discovered that if you hid a toy
under a pillow or towel, your baby would push the obstacle out of the way

Vive la Différence!

As we've discussed earlier, fathers and mothers generally have distinctive but complementary styles of playing with their children: fathers
tend to be more physical; mothers, less. But besides the physical nature
of play, there are some other male-female differences you should be
able to see now.

Fathers tend to encourage their children to do things for themselves,
take more risks, and experience the consequences of their actions.
Mothers, in contrast, tend to want to spare their children disappointment, be more protective of them, and steer clear of encouraging
risk-taking.

To see how these differences might play out, imagine that your baby
is building a tower that is just about to collapse. You'll probably let the
tower fall, hoping your baby will learn from his mistakes. Your partner,
though, will probably steady the tower as it teeters.

Many researchers have found that the differences in father-child
and mother-child play styles can have a significant impact on the child.
"There were indications that children's intellectual functioning was
stimulated more in families with high father involvement," writes researcher Norma Radin. "We attribute this effect to the fact that fathers
appear to have a different way of interacting with children; they tend to
be more physical, more provocative, and less stereotyped in their play
behavior than mothers."

to "find" the toy (see page 121). Now that he's a little older and more sophisticated, you can up the ante a little by hiding an interesting toy under three or four towels. The look on his face when he pulls the first towel off and doesn't see what he was expecting will be priceless. Until he's about a year old, he'll probably get confused by the extra obstacles and forget what he was looking for in the first place.

♦ Imitating and pretend games. According to Bettelheim, engaging in this type of activity is an important developmental milestone. When our children imitate us, they're trying to figure out who we are and what we're doing. "When they imitate an older sibling or friend, they're not only trying to understand them, but they're figuring out what it's like to be older," he writes. When playing with blocks, for example, be sure to include some nonblock things such as people, cars, trucks, animals.

♦ Show him that objects can have more than one function. Envelopes, for example, can be shredded or used to contain other things.

♦ Encourage him to use tools. For example, tie a string around a toy that is well out of reach. Will he crawl to get the toy or will he pull the string to bring it closer? What happens if you demonstrate what to do? A word of caution: once your baby has mastered the idea that there are new and exciting ways to get hold of things, watch out for low-hanging tablecloths and other dangling stuff.

Exercises for the Major Muscle Groups

It's taken a while, but your baby is finally getting around to discovering that he has control over his feet. And over the next few months, he'll be making more and more use of his feet by learning to walk. He'll do this all by himself, of course, but helping him build up his muscles and coordination can be great fun for both of you:

♦ Put some toys near his feet and see if he'll kick them.

♦ Roll a ball far enough out of your baby's reach so he has to crawl to get it.

♦ Supervised stair climbing is great. But stay nearby and be extremely careful. This is a good time to start teaching your baby to come down stairs backward. But be prepared to demonstrate yourself and to physically turn your baby around a few dozen times a day.

♦ Play alternating chasing games: you chase him; he chases you. At the end, "reward" him with a big hug and—if he doesn't protest—a little wrestling. Besides being fun, these kinds of games teach your baby a valuable lesson: when you go away, you always come back. The more that idea is reinforced, the less he'll be impacted by separation anxiety (see pages 154–55).

> ### Crawling
> Although you may be in a hurry to see your baby walk, be patient. Crawling (which includes just about any type of forward movement, such as slithering, "hopping" along on the butt, or "rowing" forward with one leg) is a major developmental stage, and you should encourage your baby to do it as much as possible. There's also some evidence that makes a connection between crawling and later proficiency in math and sciences. Kids who don't crawl apparently don't do as well in those fields.

Getting Those Little Hands and Eyes to Work Together

There are plenty of activities you and your baby can do that stimulate hand-eye coordination:

- Puzzles. The best ones for this age are made of wood, have a separate hole for each piece, and a peg for easy lifting.
- Nesting and stacking toys. These help improve gentle placement skills.
- Things to crush, tear, or crinkle—the noisier the better.
- Weave some string between baby's fingers or tape two of his fingers together. Can he "free" himself?
- Stock your bathtub with toys that squirt or spin.
- Get toys that can be used in the bathtub or a sandbox to pour stuff back and forth. Measuring cups and spoons are also good.
- When you're shopping, have the baby help you put things in the grocery cart.
- If you're brave, let the baby change channels on your stereo or TV (supervised, of course).
- Play hand-clapping games.

More Experiments from the Land of Consequences

The idea that different actions produce different effects is one that can't be reinforced often enough. Here are a few ways that are especially appropriate for your nine-to-twelve-month-old.

- Jack-in-the-boxes—especially the kind with four or five doors, each opened by a push, twist, poke, or some other action. These are also good for hand-eye coordination. Be cautious the first few times, though; some babies may be frightened.
- Balls are a big hit. They roll, they bounce off things, they can knock over other things. For your baby's protection (and to reduce the chance of breaking your good dishes) make sure the balls you use are soft.

The Building Blocks of Development

There are literally dozens of cutting-edge, high-tech (and expensive) toys and games that claim to be essential to your baby's physical and mental development. Some are worthwhile, others aren't. But there's one toy—just about the least cutting-edge, lowest-tech, cheapest thing going—that truly is an essential part of every nursery: blocks. Here's why:

- They help your baby develop hand-eye coordination as well as grasping and releasing skills.
- They teach your baby all about patterns, sizes, categories (big ones with the big ones, little ones with the little ones); gravity, balance, and structure. These brief lessons in math and physics lay the foundation for your baby's later understanding of how the world works.
- They teach good thinking skills. "Taken from a psychological viewpoint," wrote Albert Einstein, "this combinatory play [erector sets, blocks, puzzles] seems to be the essential feature in productive thought—before there is any connection with logical construction in words or other kinds of signs which can be communicated to others."
- They can help babies grasp the difference between things they have control over and things they don't. "In building a tower, a child has had to deal with the laws of gravity, size, balance, etc.—laws he cannot control," says Bruno Bettelheim. "And when he knocks the tower down, he is trying to regain control over the situation."
- They teach perseverance. Building a tower—or anything else—out of blocks can be an excruciatingly frustrating experience for a baby. But along the way, he'll learn that if he keeps working on something long enough, he'll eventually succeed.

- Pots, pans, xylophones, or anything else the baby can bang on. He'll learn that different things make different noises when smacked and that hitting something hard sounds different from hitting something soft.
- Doors (and anything else with a hinge)—provided you're there to make sure no one gets pinched. Books operate on the same basic principle. (If you've been reading to your baby lately, you've probably noticed that he's more interested in turning the pages than in looking at what's on them.)

The bigger your baby's world gets, the more interested he'll become in objects and the less interested in you. And why not? After all, you always

> ### Success and Failure
> Whatever your baby is doing, be sure to praise his *efforts* as well as his *accomplishment*. Kids need to learn that trying to do something can often be just as important as actually doing it. Confining your praise and happiness only to successful completion of a project can make your baby less likely to take risks or try new things for fear of failing.

seem to be around, but one of those exciting new toys might disappear before he gets a chance to grab it.

Giving up the number one position in your baby's heart and mind can be tough on the ego, especially if you're being replaced by a stuffed animal or a toy car. But instead of pouting, take a more aggressive, if-you-can't-beat-'em-join-'em attitude: if you're having trouble keeping your baby interested in playing with you, use a toy to get his attention. But don't be in a hurry; wait until the baby has begun to lose interest in whatever (or whomever) he's playing with before replacing it with something new.

Family Matters

The Division of Labor
About 90 percent of new parents experience an increase in stress after their babies are born. And the number one stressor—by a huge margin—is the division of labor in the home.

Oh, How Much Work Could a Baby Really Be?
Before your baby was born, you and your partner probably anticipated that having a baby would increase the amount of household work you'd both have to do. But I'll bet you were *way* off on your estimates.

Psychologist Jay Belsky found that for most new parents, dishwashing increased from once or twice a day to four times, laundry from one load a week to four or five, shopping from one trip per week to three, meal preparation from two times a day to four, and household cleaning from once a week to once a day.

And that's just the nonbaby areas of your life. When you factor in all the baby-related stuff, things really start to get out of control. "On average, a baby needs to be diapered six or seven times and bathed two or three times per day, soothed two or three times per night and often as many as five times per day,"

writes Belsky. In addition, the baby's helplessness makes just about every task, from going to the bank to getting dressed in the morning, take five times longer than it used to.

One woman in Belsky's studies summed up the discrepancy between her prebirth workload estimate and the postbirth reality as essentially the difference between "watching a tornado on TV and having one actually blow the roof off your house."

And Who's Going to Do It?

Another thing you and your partner may have agreed upon before your baby was born was that you'd both be sharing responsibility for all the extra work the baby would require. That was a good thing: the more equitably domestic tasks are divided up, the happier couples are with their marriages. Unfortunately, though, you were most likely wrong about this one too.

"Women ended up doing more of the housework than before they were mothers," write Phil and Carolyn Cowan. "And men did less of the baby care than they or their wives predicted." Researcher Ross Parke confirmed these findings: "The birth of a baby seems to bring even egalitarian parents back to traditional roles," he writes. "There was a marked return to the customary division of labor for a variety of functions."

Everyone Knows that Women Do More Around the House, Right?

It seems that every few months or so there's a new study telling us that although women have dramatically increased the hours they work outside the home, men have barely changed the number of hours they spend working *inside*. The most widely quoted figure for men's contribution to child care, for example, is twelve minutes a day.

Pretty incriminating, eh? Well, it's not nearly as bad as it sounds. The twelve-minutes-a-day figure comes from data analyzed by Arlie Hochschild in her book *The Second Shift: Working Parents and the Revolution at Home.* And to call Hochschild's conclusions "flawed" would be charitable. Here's why:

♦ Hochschild based her findings on data gathered in 1965, although there was much more recent, and accurate, data available.

♦ When tallying *men's* hours, Hochschild "neglected" to include weekends, times when men are more likely to be actively involved with their kids.

♦ She also didn't include the hours men spend playing with their kids as child care. So if your partner is cooking dinner and you're playing with the baby, her hours are counted as household work, yours aren't. Doesn't seem very fair, does it?

♦ Even if she had counted weekends and playtime, Hochschild failed to make a distinction between *accessibility* (being on duty and available) and *engagement* (active involvement with a child). Most kids don't need or want to be entertained every second of the day, but an adult still needs to be around.

Here's what happens to Hochschild's twelve minutes a day when her errors of omission are corrected:

♦ Researchers McBride and Mills found that fathers were *accessible* an average of 4.9 hours per day on weekdays and 9.8 hours per day on Saturday and Sunday.

♦ McBride and Mills found that fathers were *engaged* with their children an average of 1.9 hours on weekdays and 6.5 hours per day on Saturday and Sunday.

♦ In the 1960s and 1970s fathers spent one-third as much time engaged with and half as much time accessible to their children as their partners. These numbers went way up in the 1980s and 1990s, to 40 percent as much time engaged and two-thirds as much time accessible. One study found that fathers were engaged 83 percent as much as mothers and accessible 82 percent as much as mothers.

That's a very different story. Of course, researchers can come up with statistics to back up just about any claim. Still, no matter how you crunch the division-of-labor numbers, the bottom line is that women do a greater share of the household and child-related work.

What's important to remember, though, is that in most cases this inequity is *not* a function of men's lack of interest in their families. Phil and Carolyn Cowan have identified five significant barriers that prevent men from taking on a completely equal role in the home:

♦ Both men and women can't seem to shake the age-old idea that child-rearing is women's work and that breadwinning is men's work. Many men, therefore, are afraid of committing career suicide by openly expressing a desire to spend more time with the family and less at work.

♦ Mothers step in quickly to take over when either the father or the baby looks a little uneasy. At the same time, men—who hate feeling incompetent and who expect their wives to be competent with babies right from the start—are all too glad to hand over the baby to the "expert." Jay Belsky adds that "a woman's significant biological investment in the child can make her so critical of her husband's parenting that, without intending to, she drives him away." As a result, says Belsky, "men who find themselves continually criticized for their inadequate diapering, bathing, and dressing skills . . . feel humiliated and often conclude that the best (and safest) policy to adopt vis-à-vis child-care chores is a hands-off policy."

♦ The roles available to men are considered second-rate and discourage male involvement. As discussed on pages 86–88, feeding the baby—something women generally have a lock on—is considered the most important task, whereas soothing the baby and changing her diapers—tasks available to men—don't seem nearly as important.

♦ The more men attempt to take an active role in the care of their children, the more mixed or negative feedback they receive from their own parents. During my first few years as a father, my own parents, for example, would wonder—just loud enough for me to hear—when I'd be going back to work, or whether taking so much time off would have a negative effect on my career.

♦ The economics of the workplace and the lack of quality child care encourage fathers to work and mothers to stay home while the children are young.

The Cowans recognize that some men are willing to buck the traditional roles and do whatever it takes to get more involved. "Unfortunately, they are swimming upstream," write the Cowans, "fighting off a formidable array of forces as they try to make their way forward."

As a result, far too often *both* parents give up and adopt a more traditional division of labor. That, in turn, can lead to a decline in marital satisfaction.

Notes:

Forming an Identity

What's Going On with the Baby

Physically

♦ Unless you have a very active baby, the slowdown in motor learning that began last month will continue this month, says Frank Caplan. But don't be deceived: she's "really gathering strength to carry herself through that big step of walking."

♦ She may be able to get herself to a standing position from a crawl and, once upright, can stand with little support.

♦ She can "cruise" (sidestep while holding on to something) just about everywhere, and if you hold both her hands, she'll walk and walk and walk.

♦ She's getting to be a fairly confident climber as well, getting up and down from couches and chairs almost without fear.

♦ She's also getting much better at manipulating her hands now, and can grasp two objects in one hand.

♦ She is beginning to discover that each side of her body can be used differently. And she may even be exhibiting an early "handedness" preference. She can, for example, use one hand for picking up and manipulating toys, the other for holding.

♦ If both hands are full, she may put down one object in order to pick up a third.

♦ Although she's quite graceful in her grasping, her releasing is still fairly clumsy.

Intellectually

♦ Although she still isn't completely convinced that things she can't see do exist, she's starting to suspect as much. This month, she'll look for a toy she sees you hide. If she's seen you move the toy to a second hiding place, she'll look for it there as well.

♦ She now understands that objects of different sizes need to be treated differently. She'll approach small objects with her fingers, but large ones with both hands.

♦ She's also intrigued by the idea that objects can exist for several reasons at the same time (they have properties as well as functions). Paper, for example, can be chewed, crumpled, and torn. And crayons can be held, eaten, and, best of all, used to scribble on things. This ability enables the baby to organize things into two categories ("things I can chew on" and "things that are too big to get into my mouth")—a realization that gives her a bit of control and predictability in her life.

♦ As her memory improves, she's getting more persistent. It's harder to distract her from whatever she's doing, and, if you manage to turn her attention to something else, she'll go right back to her original activity as soon as you quit bugging her.

♦ She's now capable of *symbolic thinking* (associating something you can see with something you can't). For example, a few months ago, your baby would probably cry when seeing the nurses at her pediatrician's office. She associated nurses with shots. But now she may recognize the doctor's office from the street and will start crying as soon as you pull into the parking lot.

Verbally

♦ Although she's been saying "dada" and "mama" for a while, she really didn't know what those words meant. But now "dada," "mama," "bye-bye," "no," and possibly a few others have a definite meaning that she uses deliberately.

♦ She now understands what she hears and may actually cooperate (but probably not in front of friends you're trying to impress) in a game of Identify the Baby's Body Part ("Where's your belly button?").

♦ She's also able to combine words and gestures: a head shake with "no," a hand wave with "bye-bye."

♦ She listens actively to adult conversation and will frequently butt in with a few "words" of her own.

Emotionally/Socially

♦ With physical development on hold for this month, says Frank Caplan, your baby is spending most of her energy on social and personal growth.

♦ Her mimicking skills are growing by leaps and bounds, and she'll now try to imitate just about everything you do: rubbing her hands together under running water, saying "brr" and shivering after getting out of the bath, and talking on the phone.

♦ When she cries (which she does much less frequently than a few months ago), it's less to get you to come running and more out of fear—of unfamiliar places or things, or of separation from you.

♦ She's becoming more sensitive to your emotions and is better able to express her own. If you're happy, she will be too. But if you scold her, she'll pout; if you do something she doesn't like, she's capable of genuine anger; and if you leave her alone for too long (only she knows how long that is), she may "punish" you by clinging and crying at the same time.

What You're Going Through

Feeling Irreplaceable

You've been a father for most of a year now, and, as we briefly discussed a few months ago (pages 118–19), you should be feeling pretty good about your fathering skills. If you're lucky, your partner, your friends, and your relatives have been telling you what a great father you are. But there's one person whose opinion of your abilities probably means more to you than anyone else's: the baby.

As a grown man, you'd think you wouldn't need to have your ego stroked by a baby. But the fact is that there is absolutely nothing in the world that will ever make you feel better, more powerful, or more loved than the feeling of being needed by your own child. "In the family, children send a message that you are really irreplaceable—no one has the meaning and value to your child that you do," write Barbara and Philip Newman. "The feeling that your life has meaning because of your role as a parent makes an important contribution to your sense of psychological well-being."

A Sense of Fulfillment

If feeling needed and appreciated by your boss and co-workers can give you a sense of self-worth and security at the office, feeling needed and appreciated as a father has the same result at home. In fact, nearly half the men in Bruce

*"I've never once demanded respect from you simply because
I'm your father. You should respect me for that."*

Drobeck's studies described fatherhood "as giving them more of a sense of
fulfillment and/or purpose in their lives."

For some, becoming a father was the achievement of their fondest dreams
and long-term goals. One man said, "I finally feel like I'm where I want to be
and doing what I want to be doing." Another added that having a baby "kind
of puts a reason to everything."

A New Kind of Feeling Left Out, or Mr. Baby's Father

It's hard for any father to discuss his children objectively, but you're just
going to have to take me at my word when I tell you that my older daughter
has always been exceptionally well behaved, good-tempered, and social
(my younger is pretty much the same, but this story's not about her). From
the time she was just a few months old, people would stop me on the street to
tell me how gorgeous and engaging she was. Even in France, the Parisians,
who I'm convinced share W. C. Fields's legendary love for children (he preferred them fried), were enraptured by her easy smile and made special
trips across the Champs Elysées to tickle her under the chin.

Having a baby who attracts this kind of attention (and we all do, of course) has some interesting side effects. The most common is the feeling of being completely ignored by the people who come over to gawk at your baby. This can be especially disconcerting if you actually want to meet the people who don't seem to have noticed that you're alive.

A few years ago I had a rather intense exposure to these feelings while visiting the set of *The Linguini Incident,* a movie written by one of my sisters and starring David Bowie and Roseanna Arquette. My sister had written a small scene for my wife, my daughter, and me, and the three of us had flown to L.A. for our fifteen minutes of celluloid fame.

Over the course of our twelve hours on the set, Roseanna Arquette must have taken my daughter away from me ten times, each time muttering under her breath, "Oh, my womb, my aching womb." We hardly saw our daughter all day.

At nearly midnight, we finally finished shooting, and Roseanna began saying her good-byes. She hugged the director and then came over to the table my wife, baby, and I were sitting at. Again, she took my daughter out of my arms, told her that she'd miss her, that she'd been a great little baby, that she was the best, the cutest . . . all the time kissing and kissing her. After about two minutes, Roseanna handed my baby back, said a flat "Goodnight" to me and left.

There is a strange, if false, sense of closeness that one establishes with someone who has held one's child. Roseanna had held my baby for hours, she'd told me about her womb, and I felt that we'd shared something that day— forged a kind of bond. So when I didn't get a goodnight kiss, I felt slighted.

A few months later, at the preview screening of the movie, I approached Roseanna to say hi. She gave me an icy stare and walked away. But a few minutes later she was back, smiling almost apologetically, "Oh, you're that incredibly gorgeous baby's father, aren't you?" she said. "How is she?"

You and Your Baby

Exposing Your Child to Music

By the time your baby started babbling verbally, she had already been babbling *musically* for several months—cooing happily, adjusting her pitch up or down to match yours. You'd sing or coo back and the two of you would have a little "duet."

For your baby, there is little if any difference between musical and verbal babbling. But for most parents, the difference is enormous. And the minute parents get even the slightest hint that their babies are beginning to understand language, the cooing and singing stops and they focus their attention on developing the baby's verbal skills. "Consequently," says Ken Guilmartin, president of Center for Music and Young Children, "the singing form is not reinforced and becomes developmentally delayed, or even atrophies completely."

Even if you and your partner don't have any particular musical talent, there's no reason why you can't stimulate your baby's musical potential. Now before you protest that you can't carry a tune to save your life, keep in mind that "potential" and "achievement" are *not* the same thing. Unfortunately, this is a distinction that far too many parents fail to make. And the result, says music education researcher Edwin Gordon, "can be fatal to a child's music development."

According to Gordon, every child is born with at least some musical apti-tude: 68 percent have perfectly average aptitude; 16 percent well above; and 16 percent well below. "Just as there are no children without intelligence," he says, "there are no children without musical aptitude."

Good, bad, or indifferent, your baby's musical aptitude is greatly affected by the environment you provide. Even if you're so tone deaf that you're embarrassed to sing in the shower, you can easily provide your baby with a rich musical atmosphere—and you'll probably enjoy yourself in the process. Here's how:

♦ As you started when your baby was three months old (see pages 75–76), continue exposing her to a wide variety of musical styles. But now try to choose recordings that have frequent changes in rhythm, tempo, and dynamics (loudness/softness). At ten months your baby's attention span is still quite short and these contrasts will hold her interest longer and more easily, says Guilmartin.

♦ Never force your baby to listen to music. Your goal here is not to teach her (just like you won't be teaching her how to speak, crawl, or walk); rather, it is to guide and encourage her and let her develop at a natural pace.

♦ Don't turn off the music if the baby doesn't seem to be paying any atten-tion. "There is little doubt that young children derive as much from listening to music when they appear not to be paying attention as when they appear to be paying attention," says Dr. Gordon.

♦ Try to avoid songs with words. Because your baby is rapidly developing her language skills, she may pay more attention to the words than to the music.

♦ Sing. Whenever and wherever you can. And don't worry about being in tune—your baby doesn't care. As above, use nonsense syllables—dum-dee-dum kinds of things—instead of real words.

♦ Listen to music *you* like. Your baby will be paying close attention to the way you react to the music and will know if you've selected some "good-for-you" piece that you hate.

♦ Watch your baby's reaction to the music. She's moving much more actively than a few months ago. Her arm and leg movements may seem (to adults, anyway) to have no connection to the music, but they are actually internally rhythmic.

♦ Be patient. "The process of learning music is much the same as the process of learning language," write Gordon and his associates Richard Grunow and Christopher Azzara. Here are the steps they've identified:

◊ Listening. From birth (and before), you absorbed the rhythm and inflections of your language—without any expectation of response.

◊ Imitating. You weren't too successful at first, but you were encouraged to babble even though no one understood a single "word" you said.

◊ Thinking (understanding). As you got more proficient with language, you were able to decipher the muddle of sounds coming out of people's mouths into meaningful words and phrases.

◊ Improvising. You made up your own words and phrases and sometimes other people actually understood them.

◊ Reading and writing. But not until you'd been listening, imitating, improvising, and thinking for more than five years.

Don't try to mess with the order—it's set in stone. If your parents had insisted on trying to teach you to read before you could speak, you might never have learned to do either.

Your Role in Molding Your Kids' Sexual Identity

Everyone knows that little girls are sugar and spice and all that's nice, while little boys are frogs and snails and puppy-dogs' tails, right? Well, as with most stereotypes, there is, at the core, a kernel of truth there: girls and boys *are* different and they *do* seem to behave differently, even in early infancy. Girls tend to respond to sights and sounds earlier and more intensively than boys, and they also learn to talk earlier. Boys tend to cry more and are somewhat more physical and aggressive. But what accounts for these differences—biology (nature) or the way boys and girls are treated by their parents (nurture)?

Without going into all the gory details of the debate, suffice it to say that the generally accepted view is that "sex differences in infant behavior are more a function of differential treatment than of innate biological predispositions," writes psychologist Henry Biller. "Parents may exaggerate relatively minor sex differences by talking to their girls more and handling their boys more vigorously."

Well, that was easy. But here's a much more provocative question: are the differences we see in boys' and girls' behavior—however they got there— real, or are we just imagining them?

Researchers John and Sandra Condry showed a group of more than two hundred adults a videotape of a nine-month-old baby playing. Half were told that they were watching a boy, half that they were watching a girl. Although everyone was viewing the exact same tape, the descriptions the two groups gave of the baby's behavior were startlingly different. The group that was watching a "boy" saw more pleasure and less fear in the baby's behavior than the group that was watching a "girl." And when the baby displayed negative emotions, the boy group saw anger; the girl group saw fear.

So do these imagined differences affect the way adults interact with children? The Condrys think so. "It seems reasonable to assume," they write, "that a child who is thought to be afraid is held and cuddled more than a child who is thought to be angry."

Other researchers have confirmed that adults do indeed behave differently with (perceived) boys than with (perceived) girls. Hannah Frisch conducted essentially the same experiment as the Condrys, except that in hers the adults actually played one-on-one with two different children. One time the adults were told they were playing with a boy, one time with a girl. "The general picture which emerges," writes Frisch, "is one in which adults are playing in masculine ways with children whom they think are boys and in feminine ways with children whom they think are girls."

In another study, Beverly Fagot found that by treating boys and girls differently adults may inadvertently reinforce sex stereotypes. For example, parents tend to react more positively to their daughters' attempts to communicate and more negatively to similar attempts by their sons, thus "confirming" that girls are more verbal than boys. Parents also react more positively when their sons engage in physical play and more negatively when their daughters do, thus "confirming" that boys are more physical than girls. So do boys play with trucks and girls with dolls because *they* want to or because that's what their parents want them to? Think about that the next time you're looking for a gift for your baby.

Although mothers and fathers generally treat their sons and daughters in

*"I gotta go play with my doll now, so that I'll be a
really great Dad someday."*

the same sex-stereotyped ways—pushing girls to be more "feminine" and boys
to be more "masculine"—fathers have a greater tendency to do it. "Fathers
are likely to cuddle infant daughters gently but to engage in rough-and-tumble
activities with sons," writes Biller. In addition, Biller has found that "fathers
are more apt to accept a temperamentally difficult male infant but to withdraw
from a female infant who presents similar problems (see pages 89–96 for
more on temperament).

Biller warns, however, that fathers are not always discriminating when treating boys and girls differently. "The child's reaction can be a major factor; in
general, infant sons may actually display more positive emotional reactions
than daughters do when fathers engage them in physically stimulating play."

The whole point of this section is to get you to see how easy it is to fall into
sex-stereotype traps. Sure, you'll still probably treat girls a little differently
from boys; that's normal. But hopefully, now that you're a bit more aware of the
dynamics, you'll be able to avoid the larger problems and give your kids a
richer childhood experience.

If you have a boy, encourage him to communicate as much as he can. Don't
discourage him from crying or from playing with dolls, and teach him that
asking for help isn't a bad (unmanly) thing. If you have a daughter, encourage

"We're calling her Fred, after her father."

her to play physically and teach her that assertiveness and independence aren't unfeminine.

But whether you have a boy or a girl, make sure you aren't forcing your child into a type of behavior that doesn't fit his or her character or temperament. "Trying to force a boy or a girl into a straightjacket conception of appropriate sex-role behavior is certainly not in the child's best interests," writes Biller. "But neither is trying to pressure a child into behaving in a so-called nonsexist manner when he or she naturally appears comfortable with more traditional expectations." The bottom line is that some boys, if you give them a Barbie to play with, will tear her head off and use her legs as a double-barreled shotgun; and some girls are going to want to wear lace everywhere they go.

Planes, Trains, and Automobiles

What's Going On with the Baby

Physically

- Your baby is still conserving a lot of his physical energy in preparation for taking his first steps.
- He can nevertheless get himself to a standing position by straightening his legs and pushing off from his hands, and may even be able to stand up from a squatting position.
- He may be able to stand without any support and will try to do two activities at the same time, such as standing and waving. He may even try to squat down to pick up a toy.
- He can climb up stairs holding on to a railing and can walk holding on to only one of your hands.
- He adores rough play—wrestling, rolling around on the floor, being held upside down, and bouncing on your knees.
- He can turn the pages of a book, but not as accurately as he'd probably like to.
- He still can't release grasped objects exactly when and how he wants to.

Intellectually

- One day this month, your newly upright baby will be leaning against a chair and he'll accidentally make it move a little. He'll immediately understand that *he's* the one responsible and will do it again. And again. He may, in fact, spend the rest of the day (and the month, for that matter) pushing the chair around the house.

♦ Imitation reaches new heights this month. But rather than mimicking specific actions, he's now able to imitate *concepts,* or even a series of actions. He'll now hide things and get you to look for them, feed you, and try to brush his own teeth and get himself dressed.

♦ He'll spend a lot of time this month dropping small objects into larger containers, learning the difference between big and small, container and contained, "in" and "out."

♦ He's also expanding his knowledge about symbols. He's fascinated by books but doesn't really know what to make of them. He'll poke at the pictures in a book, intrigued by the idea that he can *see* an object but can't pick it up.

♦ Although still convinced that he's running the world, he's discovering that his body has certain limitations. If some precious object is out of reach, he'll push you toward it, trying to get you to reach it for him, thus using you as a tool.

Verbally

♦ Although his vocabulary is growing, he's nowhere near being able to put together sentences. But he'll babble in long "paragraphs" and toss in an occasional recognizable word.

♦ Interestingly, the sounds he uses in his babbling are specific to his native language, and he can no longer produce some of the ones he could even a few months ago.

♦ Whenever he learns a new word, he'll repeat it to himself dozens of times.

♦ He recognizes the symbolic use of words: he'll say "yum" if you're talking about ice cream, "meow" if you point out a cat.

♦ He's developed an incredible ability to hear what he wants to: he'll completely ignore a shouted "get away from that stove," but will stop whatever he's doing and rush to your side if you whisper "ice cream" from another zip code.

Emotionally/Socially

♦ Besides happy and sad, your baby is now capable of other, more sophisticated emotions. If you play with another baby, for example, he'll become jealous and protest loudly. He's also getting much more demonstrative, and will show genuine tenderness and affection to you as well as to his stuffed animals.

♦ He also understands approval and disapproval. When he cleans his plate, he'll joyously shout for you to come look, and he'll beam with pride at having done something good. If he's done something he shouldn't have, though, he knows it and will bow his head sheepishly in anticipation of a few sharp words. Generally, he wants to please you, but he also needs to displease you to learn how you'll react.

♦ He may also be afraid of growing up and may regress emotionally as well as physically to a time when he was a baby and you took care of him.

♦ Strange as it sounds, your baby is already beginning to establish his or her own sexual identity. Girls begin to identify with their mother and other females and do what they do, while boys will identify with you and other men and want to do what you do.

What You're Going Through

Fear of Sexual Feelings

This may very well be the most controversial section in this book. So before you continue, you've got to promise that you'll keep an open mind and read all the way to the end.

Imagine this: you're rolling around on the floor with your baby, having the time of your life, or you're standing by your sleeping child's bed, stroking his beautiful, perfect cheek. Then, without warning, you get, well, aroused.

Now before you throw this book down and report me to the police, keep in mind that the overwhelming majority of mental health professionals say that it is *perfectly normal* for a parent to experience brief sexual feelings toward his or her child. "Most parents feel physical pleasure toward their babies," writes psychiatrist Stanley Greenspan. "For some, these pleasures are translated into fleeting sexual feelings."

Normal or not, feeling sexual desire—even briefly—for a child can be especially terrifying for men. You might be afraid that someone will accuse you of being a child molester, or that you actually are one and won't be able to control your unnatural "urges." Or that you might have to be locked up to protect your children. Or that you're completely insane.

Despite everything we hear about the "epidemic of sexual abuse," the truth is that well over 99 percent of parents never abuse anybody. So the odds are pretty slim that you'll do anything even remotely improper. Nevertheless, many men (and women as well) are so afraid and feel so guilty about their feelings that they withdraw from their children and stop playing with them, picking them up, or cuddling with them.

If you find yourself reacting in this way, stop it right now. "If you withdraw

"I did ask her and she said to ask you where I came from."

your physical displays of affection," says clinical psychologist Aaron Hass, "your child may believe there is something wrong with being affectionate in that manner. And if you stop hugging your child, you will miss the opportunity to enhance, in a very primal way, the bond between the two of you."

By reading this section you have, without even being aware of it, taken a very important step toward understanding and dealing with your momentary sexual feelings. Simply being aware of how normal these feelings are, says Dr. Greenspan, can "inhibit you from acting inappropriately" and "keep your special relationship with your baby from being dominated by fear."

Of course, if you're seriously worried that your feelings toward your child are inappropriate, and/or if you're having trouble managing them, get some professional help quickly. And don't worry, telling your therapist about your feelings will not get you arrested.

More Worries about the Baby's Health

For the first few months of your baby's life, you depended on your doctor to keep you informed as to how the baby was doing. And had there been any major problem (neurological defects, Down syndrome, and so on), or anything amiss with your baby's growth or development, you would have heard about it by now.

But most problems that affect children aren't easy to spot. And now that your baby is older and his well-baby checkups are farther apart, your pediatrician will rely more on you and your daily observations about your baby's behavior to make any diagnoses. Here are the kinds of things you should be looking out for:

♦ Is the baby having trouble manipulating objects or moving around? Delays in developing sensory/motor skills can cause delays in language development as well.

♦ Is the baby using her body fairly symmetrically? Does she use one hand (or foot, or eye) more than the other?

♦ Is the baby having trouble eating or swallowing food? Besides resulting in nutritional deficiencies and general health problems, these problems may interfere with your baby's using his jaw, lips, and tongue. Once again, language and cognitive skills can be seriously (negatively) affected.

♦ Has your baby lost previously attained skills? Did he used to babble and coo but suddenly stop? Does she no longer react when people come and go? This could be an indication of a hearing problem, which, again, can affect language development.

♦ Is the baby not achieving, within a month or two, the milestones described in the "What's Going On with the Baby" sections in this book?

♦ Does the baby seem uninterested in exploring his surroundings?

♦ Has your baby undergone a major change in temperament? (See pages 89–96.) But remember: difficult temperament by itself is *not* an indication of any kind of disability.

In most cases, the "problem" behaviors you identify will turn out to be perfectly normal. But that doesn't mean you should stop paying attention. Here are some things you can do to reassure yourself:

♦ Spend some time studying the "What's Going On with the Baby" sections of this book. The more you know about what your baby is and isn't capable of, the less you'll worry.

♦ Don't worry that your doctor—or your partner—will think you're asking too many questions or becoming overly concerned. You (or your insurance company) are paying your doctor more than enough for him or her to listen respectfully to any questions you might have.

♦ If, after talking to your doctor, you're still not satisfied (or you think you're being ignored), get another opinion.

♦ Keep a detailed log of things your child does (or doesn't do) that concern you, when they happen, and under what circumstances.

♦ Men have a tendency to ignore their own health concerns either because they hope whatever's worrying them will go away or because they're afraid the doctor will confirm their worst suspicions. If you want to ignore something that's been bothering you, that's your own prerogative. But don't apply the same standard to your baby. You may not be the most experienced parent in the world, but your gut reactions about what ails your children are usually pretty good and should be acted on. Of course, this doesn't mean bringing the baby into the emergency room every day, but an occasional call to your doctor's advice nurse is fine. If there is something to worry about, you're better off knowing sooner than later, when the problem will be much harder to deal with.

You and Your Baby

Planes, Trains, and Automobiles

When my older daughter was only six months old, my wife and I decided it was about time to take that honeymoon trip we'd been putting off since we'd gotten married. So we traded in a few years' worth of frequent-flier miles, and the three of us took off on a month-long trip to New York, France, Israel, and Phoenix. All in all, it was a great trip.

While your first trip with your baby is not likely to be as big an expedition as ours, sooner or later you're going to want to pack up the family and go somewhere.

What to Do Before You Go

♦ Spend some time planning your itinerary. You can take babies under about seven months just about anywhere anytime. After your baby has learned to walk, however, it's best to limit your destinations. Seven cities in four days is hard for even the most seasoned adult traveler.

♦ If possible, pick destinations that won't be terribly crowded; large groups of unfamiliar people may spook babies and toddlers alike.

♦ Get your tickets in advance. There's no sense standing in lines if you don't have to.

♦ Travel during off-peak times. Christmas Day, New Year's Day, and Thanksgiving Day (as opposed to the days before or after), for example, are good. If you're driving, there'll be less traffic on the road; if you're traveling some other way, you'll find a lot more empty seats, meaning more room to stretch out or run around.

♦ Red-eye flights may increase the chances your baby will sleep on the plane, and can also help get the jet-lag acclimation process under way.

♦ Prepare for jet-lag/time differences before you leave. You can keep the kid up late, put him to bed early, and so forth. Also adjust meal times.

♦ Prepare your child for the upcoming trip by talking about it regularly. Make it sound like it's going to be the most fun anyone has ever had.

♦ Schedule a doctor's appointment (for your child) for a few weeks before you leave. Tell your pediatrician where you're going and ask for the names of a few good local doctors. Also ask him or her to suggest any medical supplies you should bring along. If your child is taking any medication and will come anywhere near running out while you're on the road, get an extra prescription.

What to Bring

No matter where you go, the trick to making things run smoothly on a trip away from home is to surround your baby with as many familiar things as possible. This will help minimize the shock of the new routine and scenery. Whatever your destination, then, you'll probably need most of the following:

♦ Eating utensils and bibs.

♦ If you're traveling overseas and will be using powdered formula, plan on bringing some bottled water.

♦ Car seat. Doubles nicely as a high chair if you really need to restrain your baby while she's eating.

♦ A good backpack. It'll free up both your arms so you can schlep the six tons of other baby-related stuff you'll be needing.

♦ A portable crib. Or, if you'll be staying in a hotel, call ahead to reserve one.

♦ A first aid kit (see page 140 for the ingredients).

♦ A stroller that collapses compactly enough so you can take it on the plane.

♦ Lots of familiar toys, stuffed animals, favorite foods.

♦ Bring only what you're absolutely sure you'll need. If you aren't going trekking in the Himalayas, for example, there's really no sense taking along a large number of disposable diapers—they're available just about anywhere. The first thing my wife and I did when we arrived in New York was get a huge cardboard crate and ship home about half of the stuff we'd brought.

Once You Get There

♦ Keep up the routines you've established at home. Read, sing, play at the same times if you can. This is especially important for predictable babies (see page 91).

♦ Don't overbook activities. One or two excursions a day is plenty.

♦ Pick up local parenting publications (they're usually free) in whatever city or cities you're going to. You can order copies of these publications before you go by contacting Parenting Publications of America, 12715 Path Finder Lane, San Antonio, TX 78230-1532, (210) 492-3886, 492-3887 (fax); parpubs@aol.com.

♦ Keep a sharp eye on baby/relative contact. If friends and relatives haven't seen the baby for a while or are meeting him for the first time, they'll all want to hold, squeeze, cuddle, and entertain. This can freak out even the calmest of babies. Be especially sensitive if your baby is going through a period of stranger or separation anxiety.

♦ If you're planning to leave the baby with a sitter or a relative, have her or him come early so the two of them can get to know each other for a few minutes.

♦ Stay away from meats, fish, eggs, and dairy products. If you're going to get food poisoning on the road, it'll probably come from one of those food groups. And if you're traveling overseas, stay away from water, milk, juice, raw foods, and anything served by street vendors.

Traveling by Car

♦ For short trips, try to leave an hour or so before your baby's usual nap time and, once he falls asleep, drive as far as you can while his nap lasts.

♦ For longer trips, consider doing your driving from 4 P.M. to midnight. That way, you'll only have a few hours of entertainment and stops for feedings before baby goes to sleep for the night.

♦ If you need to drive during the day, you or your partner should ride in the back seat with the baby in hour or two-hour shifts to keep him amused and awake. Car travel tends to knock babies out and can really screw up their sleep schedules.

♦ Take lots of breaks and make sure everyone has plenty of opportunity to stretch, unwind, and relax. Stop at interesting places, pet the cows, watch the road-repair crews, point out new sights (forests, cloud shapes, and so forth), sing songs, read stories. Going through an automatic car wash can be a thrill for some kids, but for others it can be terrifying. Whatever you do, have fun.

♦ Put the car seat in the middle of the back seat; it's safest there.

♦ Lock car doors from the inside.

♦ Never, never leave your child alone in a car. Babies can suffocate a lot faster than you might think.

GOOD THINGS TO BRING IN THE CAR

♦ Lots of food and drink.

♦ Lots and lots of books.

♦ Stickers, markers, crayons, paper, and other art supplies.

♦ Magnetic puzzles.

♦ A battery-operated tape recorder (if you don't have one in the car) and a good selection of music. Make sure to bring some you like as well.

One warning: if you have to slam on your brakes at sixty miles an hour, every object you have in your car is a potential projectile. So before you bring anything into the car, think about whether you'd like to be hit in the head by it.

Traveling by Plane

♦ Get to the airport early. Let the baby run around and tire himself out. This may make the flight a little easier on everyone.

♦ Try to get bulkhead seats (usually the first row)—they generally offer a little more room, and you won't have to worry that your child will kick the seat of the people in front of you. Also, ask to be seated next to an empty seat if possible. Be sure to hold your absolutely adorable baby in your arms while you're asking—this can improve your chances of getting what you want.

♦ *Don't* board early. Instead, send your partner on with the carry-on stuff while you stay out in the lounge, letting the kids run themselves ragged until the last minute. Why spend any more time cooped up in the airplane than you absolutely have to?

The All-Purpose Travel Bag

If there's ever any danger of getting separated from your luggage (even if most of it is just in the trunk of your car), you should have a well-stocked bag with the necessary "emergency" supplies:

♦ Diapers and wipers.

♦ Toys (one for each hour of travel time); mirrors and suction-cup rattles are big hits with babies.

♦ Food.

♦ Something to suck on (pacifiers, teething rings, and so forth).

♦ A few books.

♦ Some favorite comfort items (blankets, teddy bears, and so on).

♦ If you're going on a long trip and your child is particularly restless or active, schedule a stopover or two to give you all a chance to get off the plane, stretch, and run around.

♦ Every child under two years old should suck on something—breast, bottle, or pacifier—on the way up and the way down. This will counteract the pressurization and reduce the chances of painful earaches.

♦ Make sure your child drinks a lot on board. Airplane travel can dry out your baby's (and your) mucous membranes, making her more susceptible to colds or sinus infections.

♦ Check as many bags as you can, but carry on the all-purpose travel bag (see page 190).

WHAT TO BRING

♦ Same as for cars (see page 190).

♦ Some extra food. The meals you ordered might not show up, or, if you're taking a short flight, there might not be any food at all.

DEALING WITH JET LAG

♦ If you're traveling for only a few days, keep baby doing things at the time he would be doing them at home. This will make it easier to return to your regular schedule when you get back home.

♦ Spend time outside. Natural light helps acclimate people to new time zones more quickly.

Family Matters

Life Insurance

Becoming a parent does some interesting things to your mind and to your outlook on life. On the one hand, having a child makes you want to live forever and not miss a single second with your child. On the other hand, watching your child grow older is like a hard slap in the face; it makes you realize that no matter how much you want to, you're not going to live forever.

Simply put, the purpose of life insurance is to make sure that after your death at least some of your survivors' financial needs are taken care of. But according to the National Insurance Consumer Organization, more than 90 percent of Americans have the wrong kind of insurance coverage and in the wrong amounts.

Unfortunately, there really aren't any hard-and-fast rules or secret formulas

"Greetings, stockholders."

to help you determine how much insurance you need. But spending some time thinking about the following questions will put you in the top 10 percent (it's really not that hard) of insurance consumers:

- Do you need or want to pay off your mortgage? Could your partner make the full payment on what she makes?
- Do you have a lot of debts you want to pay off?
- Do you need or want to leave an estate large enough to pay fully for your kids' college education?
- How many years of your income do you want your insurance to replace?
- What do you expect your tax situation to be? If you have a huge estate, your heirs will have to come up with a tidy sum to cover inheritance taxes.

There are two basic ways to make sure your insurance needs are properly taken care of:

- Read a few good personal finance guides (or at least sections of them). Despite what you might think, it's not all that complicated. Eric Tyson's *Personal Finance for Dummies* (IDG Books) is one of the best.
- Get yourself a financial planner (see pages 194–95 for some helpful tips).

Either way, you should at least be aware of your insurance options. Basically, there are two types of life insurance on the market: term and cash value; each is further divided into several subcategories. Here's a brief overview:

TERM

There are three types of term insurance, and they all share these features:
- Fairly low cost, especially in the early years.
- Premiums increase over time as your odds of dying go up.
- Policies are in effect only for a specified period of time.
- No cash value accumulation.

Here are your basic term insurance choices:
- Renewable term. You can renew the policy annually. Death benefit generally remains level, while premiums increase over time.
- Level premium. The death benefit and the premium remain the same for a specified period of time, usually five, ten, or twenty years.
- Decreasing premium. The death benefit decreases each year, while premiums remain the same.

CASH VALUE

There are an increasing number of cash value insurance products available. Despite their differences, they all share the following features:
- These policies are essentially a combination of term insurance and a savings plan. A portion of your premium pays for pure term insurance. The balance is deposited into some kind of side fund on which you can earn interest or dividends.
- These policies tend to offer—initially—very competitive interest rates. The rate is usually guaranteed for a year, but then drops to whatever the market is paying.
- You can pay pretty much whatever you want to. But if your payment isn't enough to cover the insurance cost, the balance is taken out of your side fund, reducing your cash value.
- The cash benefit accumulates tax-free, and you can borrow against it or withdraw from it during your lifetime.
- If properly placed in trust, the entire cash and accumulated savings can go to your heirs free of income tax.

Here are your cash value choices:
- Whole life. Locks in a death benefit, cash values, and premium. The side fund is invested by the insurance company.

Picking a Financial Planner

Since most states don't have laws regulating or accrediting financial planners (who may also call themselves "advisors," "consultants," or "managers"), just about anyone can set up shop to dole out financial advice and sell products.

Most financial planners are paid on a commission basis, meaning that there's always at least the possibility of a conflict of interest. (In other words, whether or not your investments do well, the financial planner is assured his commission.) Commissions typically range from as low as 4 percent on some mutual funds to the entire first year's premium on a cash value life insurance policy. Others are paid on a fee basis and typically charge from $50 to $250 per hour.

This doesn't mean, of course, that fee-based planners are inherently better than their commission-based colleagues (although many experts believe that you'll be happier, and possibly richer, with someone who charges a fee). Your goal is to find someone you like and who you believe will have your best interests at heart. Here are a few things you can do to help you weed out the losers:

♦ Get references from friends, business associates, and so forth. Alternatively, the Institute of Certified Financial Planners (800) 282-7526 will give you some local references, and the National Association of Personal Financial Advisors (800) 366-2732 makes referrals only of fee-based (as opposed to commission-based) planners.

♦ Select at least three potential candidates and set up initial consultations (which shouldn't cost you anything). Then conduct tough interviews. Here's what you want to know:

♦ Universal life. Similar to Whole life, except that you can change the premium payment and death benefits anytime. And since the side fund is invested in fixed-income home securities (bonds and so forth), your cash values can fluctuate.

♦ Variable life. Similar to Universal, except that you have a bit more input into how your side fund is invested. Your choices usually include money markets, government securities, corporate bonds, growth, fixed-income, or total-return portfolios.

So how can you possibly make a choice between term and cash value?

◊ Educational background. Not to be snobby here, but the more formal the education—especially in financial management—the better. Watch out for fancy initials: many planners prominently display the letters CFP (for Certified Financial Planner) after their names. Forbes magazine recently called the CFP credential "meaningless."

◊ Level of experience. Unless you've got money to burn, let your niece break in her MBA on someone else. Stick to experienced professionals with at least three years in the business.

◊ Profile of the typical client. What you're looking for is a planner who has experience working with people whose income level and family situation are similar to yours.

◊ Compensation. If fee-based, how is the fee calculated? If commission, what are the percentages on each product offered? Any hesitation to show you a commission schedule is a red flag.

◊ Get a sample financial plan. You want to see what you're going to be getting for your money. Be careful, though: fancy graphics, incomprehensible boilerplate language, and expensive leather binders are often used to distract you from the report's lack of substance.

◊ References. How long have customers been with the planner? Are they happy? Better off? Any complaints or weaknesses?

♦ Check your prospective planner's record with state and federal regulators. You can call the federal Securities and Exchange Commission (202) 272-7450 or your state's equivalent to check on disciplinary action and to see whether your candidates have ever been sued.

Financial author and counselor Eric Tyson has some fairly strong views on the subject: "Cash value insurance is the most oversold insurance and financial product in the history of the industry," he writes. His solution?

Unless you have a high net worth, get yourself a term insurance policy with the following features:

♦ Guaranteed renewable (you don't want to be canceled if you get sick).

♦ Level premiums for five to ten years (that way you won't need to get a physical exam every year).

♦ A price you can live with. Costs for the very same policy can vary by as much as 200–300 percent, so shop around. (Since a rather big chunk of your premium is going to some agent in the form of commission, you can cut your costs way down by buying a "no load" or "low load" policy.)

WHEN YOU SHOULD BUY CASH VALUE INSURANCE

♦ Currently, an individual can leave up to $600,000, and a couple can leave up to $1,200,000 to beneficiaries *without* having to pay federal estate taxes. If you aren't worth this much, or don't expect to be when you die, stick with term.

♦ If you own a small business that's worth more than $1 million, cash value insurance makes sense, unless you have enough in liquid assets to pay off the estate taxes your heirs will owe.

Notes:

12 MONTHS

There Now, That Wasn't So Bad, Was It?

What's Going On with the Baby

Physically

♦ Still building toward walking, your baby can now get to a standing position from a squat and can lower herself gracefully from standing to sitting.

♦ She's also getting more confident about combining standing and walking. She can turn 90 degrees, stoop to pick things up, and walk holding on to you with one hand while clutching a favorite toy (or two or three) in the other. She might even experiment with taking a few backward steps.

♦ If your baby does take a few steps this month, she'll still use crawling as her main means of transportation.

♦ She can take simple covers off containers (but probably not screw-tops), and she'll help you dress and undress her (well, at least she *thinks* she's helping . . .).

♦ She's finally mastered her opposable thumb and can now pick up tiny objects between her thumb and pointing finger.

♦ She's also expressing a strong preference for "handedness," using one hand for grasping, the other for manipulating. If you put an object in her "passive" hand, she'll transfer it to the "active" one.

♦ She's now learned to store objects. If she's holding one thing in each hand and you offer her a third, she now wants to get control of all three; she'll transfer the contents of one hand to her mouth or armpit and *then* pick up the third object with the free hand.

Intellectually

♦ One of the most important intellectual accomplishments of your baby's first year is her ability to retain a visual image of an object she has seen before but that is currently out of sight.

♦ By the end of this month, your baby will be able to demonstrate this ability by searching—in more than one place—for objects she has seen but that she didn't see you hide.

♦ In another major intellectual leap this month, your baby will begin using trial and error to solve her problems and overcome obstacles.

♦ As annoying as it may get, it's important to recognize that your baby's constant banging, building and knocking over, and putting things in and dumping them out are important learning activities that are teaching her more about the multiple properties of the objects in her world. Adding water to sand changes the way the sand feels (and tastes); dropping marbles into a metal can produces a much different sound than dropping them into a plastic box; and dumping them onto the living room rug isn't nearly as much fun as watching them bounce and roll around after dumping them on the vinyl kitchen floor.

Verbally

♦ She probably has a vocabulary of six to eight real words, as well as five or six more sound words, such as *moo, woof,* or *boom.*

♦ Her passive vocabulary is significantly larger, and she'll gleefully identify quite a few of her body parts, as well as such familiar objects as you and your partner, her bottle, and her crib.

♦ She still doesn't know much about the symbolic use of words. If you point to a book at a friend's house and say, "Look at the book," your baby may be confused. In her world, the word *book* applies only to the ones at home.

Emotionally/Socially

♦ She actively tries to avoid doing things she knows you don't like, and loves your applause and approval.

♦ She's not always cooperative and will regularly test your limits (and your patience). She also is developing a basic sense of right and wrong and shows guilt when she does something wrong.

♦ She's developing a sense of humor and finds incongruities most entertaining. If you tell her a dog says "moo," or if you crawl or pretend to cry, she'll laugh hysterically.

♦ In her home, where she feels most secure, your baby will play with other kids and may share some of her toys with them. In less secure environments, however, she's not nearly as sociable and will not stray far from you.

♦ She's got some pretty firm ideas of what she wants and will do what she can (cry, have a tantrum, smile sweetly) to influence your decisions.

What You're Going Through

Anger

While my wife was pregnant with our first child, I spent a lot of time thinking about the things I would never do once I became a father. First on my list was No Hitting the Kids. Then I thought about all those parents (including my own) I'd seen over the years scream at their children in the grocery store or

"If you ask me, this kid isn't lost. His parents just made a run for it."

the post office. "How weak," I remember thinking to myself. "If people can't control themselves any better than that, they really shouldn't be parents." I quickly and rather smugly added No Yelling at the Kids to my list.

One afternoon my daughter woke up from her nap crying like she never had before. I knew she wasn't tired, so I checked to see if her diaper was full (it wasn't), whether her clothes were binding her (they weren't), and even took her temperature (normal). She didn't respond to my comforting words or my requests to stop crying and tell me what was wrong (at six months, why should she?), and she continued howling. I was alone in the house, and after half an hour I'd had enough. I was frustrated and angry. So angry, in fact, that I felt like throwing my baby out the window and driving away.

Almost immediately, though, I was nearly overcome with feelings of embarrassment and disappointment for having let my emotions get away from me. I also felt like a complete failure as a father for having had such horrible thoughts about my own baby. It's no wonder that, in the words of psychologist Lawrence Kutner, "Anger—no, fury—is among the 'dirty little secrets' of parenthood."

"While parents talk about and glorify their feelings of love and protectiveness, their normal and often predictable moments of rage toward their children are seldom brought into the open," writes Kutner. "It is as if acknowledging the intensity of their anger is an admission of inadequacy or failure. If we deny it, perhaps it will go away, or we can convince ourselves that it never happened at all."

COPING WITH ANGER

"The conflicts that trigger the most intense responses often tell us more about ourselves than about our children," says Kutner. "Our most dramatic reactions to our children's behavior often come when we're feeling hurt. The child most likely to set off that strong, emotional response is the one who is most like us—especially when that child reminds us of things we don't particularly like about ourselves."

In addition, of course, things like job pressures, financial difficulties, health problems, or even car trouble can be redirected toward our kids and make us lash out at them. Whatever the reason for your anger, remember that there's nothing wrong with *feeling* it—even when it's directed at your kids. It's what you *do* with your anger, however, that can be a problem. Here are some suggestions that will help you understand, and better deal with, your anger.

♦ **Change your perspective.** Although your child may periodically do something deliberately to annoy you, many of his actions are really beyond his control. "A child's ability to bring out anger in his parents is usually

If You Lose Control . . .

Even parents with the best intentions accidentally lose control. If you do:

♦ Apologize. Explain to your child that you lost your temper. Make sure she knows that it was her *behavior* you didn't like, not her as a person, that you love her, and that you'll never hit her again.

♦ Don't go overboard, though. Resist the urge to punish yourself for your mistakes by being extra lenient with your child. You're only human, so lighten up.

Remember, anger can be just the first step in a vicious circle: something angers you enough that you lose control; feeling out of control makes you angrier; and feeling angry makes you feel even more out of control.

Unchecked, this process can escalate into physical and emotional abuse (which, besides screaming, can include insulting, humiliating, or withholding love). If you're worried that you might lose control again, get some help immediately: call a friend, a therapist, your child's pediatrician, or even a local parental-stress hotline (see also some of the suggestions for dealing with crying on pages 44–45). And if you're worried that your partner might prove to be violent, suggest she do the same.

a sign of normal development," says Kutner. "A toddler who is testing the limits of her independence will reject her parents occasionally, ignoring their pleas."

♦ **"Keep your sense of humor,"** says Ellen Galinsky. It may be a pain to clean up, but drawing on the walls with lipstick can be funny—if you let it.

♦ **Take regular breaks.** This can help keep minor annoyances from accumulating and boiling over. Make sure your partner gets plenty of time off too.

♦ **Give yourself a time-out.** Remove yourself from the situation and your child *before* you do something you'll regret for a long, long time.

♦ **Watch what you say.** Don't insult or humiliate your child. If you must criticize her, do it in private. Contrary to the old adage "Sticks and stones may break my bones, but names will never hurt me," calling your baby names can, in fact, have greater long-term negative impact than hitting.

◊ Use "I" messages: "*I* don't like it when you scratch me—it hurts," is a much more effective message than "*You're* a bad girl because you scratched me."

◊ Saying things like "You always . . ." or "You never . . ." can fill a child with a sense of futility, a conviction that she'll fail no matter what she does or how hard she tries.

◊ Avoid mixed messages. Yelling at your child to stop yelling will probably not do you a lot of good.

♦ **Watch what you do.** "Children learn as much or more about the expression of anger from watching their parents when they are angry as they do from verbal explanations or punishment," say Barbara and Philip Newman. So don't let your toddler see you vent steam in a physical way; he won't be able to understand your anger and might even be afraid that you'll turn on him. He could also try to imitate you, and might hurt himself, someone else, or someone's property.

♦ **Get physical.** Taking a long jog, punching a pillow, and taking a boxing class are good ways to let off some steam. If there are any batting cages nearby, try them out—if you squint, slow-moving softballs can look an awful lot like a human head . . .

You and Your Baby

Discipline Update

When I was a kid, one of my father's favorite sayings was, "You're free to swing your arms around any way you want. But that freedom ends right where someone else's nose begins." In a nutshell, teaching your child this lesson—to be respectful of other people's noses—is the primary goal of discipline.

A few months ago this was a concept your baby couldn't possibly have grasped. And the only way for you to control his evil impulses was to distract him with a toy and hope he'd forget about whatever it was he shouldn't have been doing. But your baby's memory has been improving every day, and by the time he's a year old one toy just won't do the trick anymore; now you'll need two or three. And pretty soon, toys won't work at all.

When this happens, you'll face two major challenges, say the Newmans: making a smooth transition from "nurturing protector to the force for law and order," and combining "empathic caring" with "firm protectiveness."

The first step toward accomplishing these goals is to set reasonable, consistent limits. Here are a few things that will make this a lot easier:

♦ Limit potential risks. Basically, this means childproofing the hell out of your house and keeping anything you really want to stay in one piece as far away from the baby as possible. (To minimize problems elsewhere, ask your parents and in-laws to take similar preventive measures.)

- Give the baby a safe place to explore.
- Have plenty of substitutes available: old phones and remote controls, spare computer keyboards, and so on. But be prepared: some kids can tell instinctively that what you're giving them isn't the real thing, and they won't be amused.
- Stop dangerous behavior immediately, but *subtly.* If your baby is pounding on a plate-glass window with his toy hammer and you scream, drop your coffee, and leap across the room to wrestle him to the ground, he'll find your reaction so much fun that he'll be sure to repeat exactly the behavior that provoked it the first time.
- Be tolerant of your baby's "negativity." Your baby's "no's" are an important part of his developing identity. Giving your baby some decision-making control will help him accept the limits you set.
- Spend some serious time trying to figure out what the baby needs. Researcher Donelda Stayton and her associates found that early obedience (in nine-to-

twelve-month-olds) was related to the sensitivity of responsiveness to infant signals, *not* to the frequency of commands or forcible interventions.

While setting limits is important, it's really only half the battle. "If children are to correct their own behavior," write the Newmans, "they must know what acts are considered appropriate as well as how to inhibit their inappropriate acts." And the way your child will learn these lessons is by watching you. "Parental modeling and reinforcement of acceptable behavior are significant in the development of internal control," write the Newmans.

Biting and Hitting

For some strange reason, right around their first birthdays, almost all babies go through a phase when they bite and/or hit people—strangers and loved ones alike. If (when) your baby starts, the first thing you need to do is find out why. Your baby may be biting or hitting because she's:

+ Trying to express affection (you probably nibble gently on her and she may simply be trying to imitate you).
+ Frustrated that she can't express herself verbally.
+ Teething and trying to relieve her discomfort.
+ Simply conducting an experiment to see how others will react.
+ Tired, overstimulated, or frustrated.
+ Trying to defend herself or her property.
+ Imitating an older friend or sibling.

Fortunately, the hitting-and-biting phase usually lasts no longer than a few months (although, when you're getting bitten a few times a day, that can seem like a very long time). Here, however, are a few dos and don'ts that may make this painful period a little shorter:

+ Don't get angry; it will only make her defensive.
+ Don't slap or spank.
+ Don't bite back or have the baby bite herself "to show her what it feels like"; this sets a rotten example and will only reinforce the behavior by implying that it's really okay.
+ Do remove the baby promptly. If she's sitting on your lap and bites you, put her down for a minute (no longer); if she's hit or bitten someone else, take her away from that person for a minute.
+ Don't say, "You're bad" or any variation on that theme. Instead say, "*Biting* is bad."
+ Don't insist on an apology. There's almost no chance that your baby has

Keep Your Mouth Running

There's plenty of evidence that talking to your baby can have some very positive long-term effects. So as you go through the day, identify everything you can, tell the baby what you're doing, where you're going, what's going on outside, what the weather's like, who won last night's baseball games, and so on.

According to pediatrician Burton White, parents who raised babies who turned out to be gifted or at least bright did the following things to build their children's language skills from infancy:

♦ They identified the things their children were interested in and talked about them a lot.

♦ They engaged in fifteen to twenty verbal interchanges each hour, most lasting between twenty and thirty seconds.

♦ They rarely "taught" or lectured children. Instead, they spoke casually and conversationally.

♦ They spoke in full sentences, using words slightly above the child's apparent level of comprehension.

♦ They read picture books and stories from infancy, even though most of the kids didn't seem to be paying much attention until they were two.

any idea what regret is or that biting really hurts (babies this age are completely incapable of imagining anything from any other perspective than their own).

♦ Don't overreact. The baby might find your reaction so amusing that she'll bite or hit again just to get your attention.

♦ Do spend some time trying to figure out why your baby is biting or hitting. Is it happening at certain times of the day (right before nap time, for example)? Does she do it only to certain people?

♦ Do rethink your discipline policies. You may be setting so many limits that your baby may be trying to bite her way to freedom.

Weaning Your Baby from Breast or Bottle

Most pediatricians today agree that new mothers should breastfeed their babies for as long as possible—generally between six months and a year. What to do after that, however, is the source of far less agreement.

So should you stop breastfeeding completely now or gradually phase it out? Should you transition your baby from breast to bottle, or skip the bottle and go directly to cups? And if you've been bottle-feeding from the start, when should you stop? The answers, of course, are up to you, your partner, and your baby.

We're assuming here that your baby is eating at least *some* solid foods in addition to her breast- or bottle-feeding. Eventually, she'll get all her food via cup and utensils, but the process of weaning her completely can take months or even years. (My wife nursed our older daughter for nine months and our younger for two years.)

Why to Wean the Baby from the Breast (or at Least Cut Back Some)

♦ By one year, the baby's gotten most of the long-term health benefits from breastfeeding. At this point, breastmilk alone can't satisfy all the baby's needs and may, in fact, suppress her appetite for solids.

♦ Babies who fall asleep with a breast in their mouth (and many do), often leave their teeth soaking in a pool of milk—this can lead to tooth decay.

♦ Most babies nurse in some kind of reclining position. This allows fluid from the mouth back up into the Eustachian tubes and can cause ear infections.

♦ The baby may start (or may already be) using the breast as a comfort or sleep aid, thus delaying development of the ability to comfort herself or fall asleep by herself.

♦ You may be feeling that enough is enough: your partner's breasts have been at least partially off-limits for a year, and it's time to unlatch that baby. You may see your wife's refusal to do so as a kind of slap in your face.

Why to Wean the Baby from the Bottle (or Start Cutting Back)

♦ Babies tend to let formula or juice slosh around in their mouths for a while. Little teeth that soak up too much can rot.

♦ Your baby may fill herself up on liquids so much that she will lose interest in all those solid foods she needs for a well-balanced diet.

♦ By about fifteen months your baby may begin forming an emotional attachment to her bottle (just as she might to a blanket, thumb, or favorite stuffed animal). Emotional attachments are nice, but breaking an attachment to a bottle will be a lot easier now than in a few months, when the baby starts getting stubborn and contrary.

♦ Some experts believe that overdependence on the bottle can interfere with physical and mental developmental milestones and advise giving it up entirely by eighteen months.

Introduction to Potty Training

Have you heard the one about the kid who was toilet-trained at eight months? If you haven't, you soon will. But prepare yourself: it isn't a joke—or, at least, it isn't *supposed* to be one. People will tell you all sorts of things about the babies they knew who were out of diapers before they could walk. But no matter what anyone says, or how much you might want to believe the stories, they just aren't true.

First of all, there's no such thing as potty training; your child will learn to use the toilet on her own only when she's ready. And at eight months or even a year, she's simply incapable of controlling her bowels or bladder. Sure, she may grunt and groan while producing a bowel movement, and everyone in the house (except her, of course) will be able to smell it, but she has no idea there's any connection between the feeling she gets when she's filling a diaper and the actual contents. If anybody's being "trained" at this age it's the parents, who may have learned to recognize their baby's signals and rush her to the toilet. But rest assured, the baby can't do it on her own.

At about fifteen months your baby will begin associating what's in her diaper with herself and may announce from time to time that she's produced something. But only after the fact. At eighteen months she may occasionally announce that she is *about* to do something, but she still hasn't learned how to hold it in long enough to get to a toilet. For the best results, unless your child is extremely interested, wait until she's at least two before seriously starting to toilet "train" her.

In the meantime, however, you can help increase your child's awareness of what's going on in her diapers by talking about the process as it's happening. As you're changing her, show the baby what she's done, but don't emphasize the yuckiness of it. Instead, say something admiring, like "Hey, that's a pretty impressive load—someday you'll do this in the toilet like me and mommy."

♦ A hint for easing the process of giving up the bottle: If the baby protests her missing bottle, offer her some solid food first. The theory here is that if she's full before starting the bottle, she won't be as interested in it and will miss it less when it's gone.

Perfectly Good Reasons to Continue Limited Breastfeeding

- The baby likes it.
- Your partner likes it, likes the contact and connection with the baby, and doesn't want to give it up.
- It's more natural, cheaper, and more convenient than prepared food.

Making the Switch

On one occasion while my wife was still nursing, she got held up in meetings and couldn't get home to feed the baby. If our daughter had been used to taking a bottle, this wouldn't have been a problem. But I'd only tried once or twice to get her to take a bottle and hadn't put up much of a fight when she'd spit it out. My punishment for having been so lax was that I had to drive

---

Temperament Tidbits

How well your baby makes the transition from breastfeeding to bottle-feeding or cups may depend more on his temperament than on any other factor. According to temperament researcher Jim Cameron:

- Extremely active toddlers with high-frustration tolerance (they aren't easily frustrated) usually wean themselves. They prefer bottles to breast because of the convenience.
- Highly active, slow-to-adapt kids also like the independence and convenience of a bottle or cup during the day. But they'll still want to nurse in the morning and at night.
- Active kids who don't tolerate frustration as well, however, know that parents are quite helpful in overcoming frustration. To them, giving up nursing means giving up support and help from parents and they won't be in any hurry to do it.
- Slow-adapting kids see the breast as security and won't want to give it up without a fight, especially at night. A gradual phase-out is particularly important for these kids.
- Moderately high-energy, high-adjustability kids wean themselves naturally.
- Kids who are moderately high in activity level and moderately low in frustration tolerance are fairly ambivalent about weaning. They'll generally take their direction from you and your partner.

twenty miles to my wife's office—with the baby screaming at the top of her lungs—so she could nurse. The moral of the story is: start getting the baby used to taking a bottle as early as possible (but not before she's completely comfortable with the breast). Here are some things you can do to get even the most committed breastfeeder to give the bottle a try:

- Use smaller bottles and nipples. Keep experimenting until you find a size and style the baby likes. If she's got a pacifier, try a bottle nipple that is shaped like the one on her pacifier.
- When introducing the bottle, hold the baby in the position she's in for breastfeeding.
- Ease the transition by filling bottles or cups with expressed breast milk. Some women find pumping very painful, so leave this one up to your partner.
- Go slow. Introduce the bottle for a few minutes at first, then add a minute or two every day.
- Phase out gradually. Kids tend to be more attached to the morning and evening feedings, so start by eliminating your baby's midday feeding(s) first. If that goes well for a few days, drop the morning feeding next. Of course, exceptions can be made: we dropped the evening feeding first because our daughters were getting up at five in the morning to eat anyway. So why not nurse (and hope the baby goes back to sleep again), rather than get out of a warm bed.
- A tip: Make sure your partner is out of the house (or at least out of sight in another room) when you're trying to give the baby a bottle. If your partner (actually, her breasts) are within smelling distance, your baby may refuse the bottle.
- A warning: The American Academy of Pediatrics suggests not starting your baby on cow's milk until after the baby's first birthday.

When *Not* to Wean Your Baby

No matter how old your baby is or how long he's been breast- or bottle-feeding, there are a few really rotten times to try to wean him:

- Any impending or recent major transition that might make the baby feel vulnerable, out of control, and in need of extra parental support. Moving to a new home, the birth of a younger sibling or the announcement of pregnancy, a new baby-sitter, and starting day care are good examples.
- If the baby has been sick.
- If you or your partner are under some kind of extreme pressure.
- If the baby is teething.

Family Matters

Ch-Ch-Ch-Changing Relationships

Considering how small and helpless babies are, it's sometimes surprising just how much of an impact they can have on the lives of the adults around them. Just think, for example, about how different things are for you now compared to your prefatherhood life.

Babies create new relationships in people's lives simply by being born: you and your partner have gone from being children to being parents, your parents are now grandparents, your brothers and sisters are uncles and aunts, and so on. And naturally, those relationships (as well as the rights and responsibilities that go with them) will take some getting used to.

But perhaps babies' greatest power is their ability to change profoundly the relationships that had existed long before they were born.

Your Changing Relationship with Your Partner

"Most couples approach parenthood imagining the new baby will bring them closer together, giving them a new and deeper sense of 'us,'" writes researcher Jay Belsky. For most families, things ultimately work out this way. But Belsky found that in the early stages of parenthood a new baby "tends to push his mother and father apart by revealing the hidden and half-hidden differences in their relationship."

Not surprisingly, says Phil Cowan, "differences between partners lead to feeling distant, that feeling distant tends to stimulate conflict, and that increased conflict, in turn, affects both partners' feelings about the marriage."

Some of the differences are aggravated because, although their feelings about their relationship with each other are very similar, men and women rarely feel the same thing at the same time. Many women, for example, tend to experience a major drop in their level of satisfaction with the marriage within six months of the baby's birth. Among the common reasons for this are a woman's feelings about her postbirth body, her perception that her partner is less interested in her, and her dissatisfaction with the workload around the house.

Many men, too, go through a decline in satisfaction with their marriages, but usually not until twelve to eighteen months after the baby's birth. This is when financial issues, fears about not being loved by the baby, and feelings of being left out by their partners are uppermost in their minds.

Although declining satisfaction with a marriage sounds bad, Phil Cowan believes it doesn't necessarily have to be so. "Given that men's and women's

Baby's First Birthday Party

Let's get one thing straight: your baby's first birthday party is really more for you than for her. She won't help you put together the guest list, is too little to play Pin the Tail on the Donkey or to bob for apples, and will probably be more interested in the wrapping paper than in what's inside it.

Here are a couple of first birthday dos and don'ts:

♦ Don't knock yourself out planning special activities. At this age your baby will prefer the familiar to the new almost every time.

♦ Don't invite too many kids—two or three is plenty. And limit the adults to six or seven. Any more and you run the risk of overwhelming the baby.

♦ Don't make a huge cake (unless the adults plan to eat it). And remember: no nuts, honey, or cow's milk.

♦ Save the clowns and masks for next year or the year after. Kids under two or three are more often scared by masks than entertained.

♦ Keep the party short (no more than an hour) and try not to have it conflict with nap or sleep times or any other time when your baby tends to be cranky.

♦ Don't go overboard on gifts. And don't demand or even expect wild declarations of thanks or any other great performances for the cameras. It's just not going to happen.

♦ Give identical party favors to any other child guests. Make sure your baby gets one as well.

♦ Get presents (smaller ones) for any older or younger siblings.

♦ Keep a list (or have someone else do it) of who gave what so you can send thank-yous later.

energies are not infinitely expandable," he writes, "it may be adaptive for some energy to be diverted from the couple relationship in the service of attending to the needs of the infant or young child. . . . Those who can adopt the perspective that placing the marriage on the back burner is a regrettable but temporary state of affairs may be able to return to enhanced relationship satisfaction and quality in the future."

Here are a few of the very positive ways the baby can affect your life and your relationship with your partner.

♦ You may feel a sense of gratefulness to the baby for enabling you to feel what it's like to be loved and to love more deeply than you ever have before.

♦ For some men having a baby is like having a great new toy and may give you a chance to relive certain parts of your childhood.

♦ The baby may bring you and your partner closer together and may make the two of you feel more deeply committed to the marriage and to making it work. You now also have someone to pass along new and old family traditions to.

♦ The baby may give you and your partner a sense of tremendous pride at having jointly created something absolutely amazing.

Parent/Grandparent Relationships

THE GOOD . . .

♦ After becoming parents, most men feel closer to their parents, especially their fathers. Even those who don't feel closer are usually at least willing to end, or put behind them, long-running family disputes.

♦ Seeing your parents in action with your child may bring back happy memories of your own childhood. You may also be pleasantly surprised at how

"Do you remember any of those things people said we'd tell our grandkids someday?"

your parents have changed since you were young. The father who may not have had much time for you, for example, may now spend hours with his grandchild. And the mother who limited your junk food intake to half a stick of sugarless gum a week may be a little more relaxed now.

♦ Now that you know exactly how much work it is to be a parent, you may be feeling a bit more appreciative of what your own parents did—and sacrificed—for you.

♦ After all these years of being a child, you're in charge now; if they want to be with the baby, they'll have to do things *your* way.

♦ You'll develop a closer relationship with your in-laws.

THE BAD . . .

♦ Seeing your parents in action with your child may bring back unhappy memories of your own childhood. And if your parents are treating the baby differently than they treated you, you may be jealous, feeling that the love your baby is getting should really be yours.

♦ Your parents may not be supportive or accepting of your increased role in your child's life.

♦ They may want to assume a role in your child's life—either too involved or not involved enough—that you aren't happy with. Grandparents are free to love their grandchildren without any of the restrictions of parenthood, says psychologist Brad Sachs.

♦ There may be some friction between your parenting style and that of your parents, between the way you react to the baby's needs and the way they do. It's not uncommon to hear from one's parents statements such as: "I did a pretty good job of raising my own kids, so don't tell me how to . . ." or "Don't you think it's time she [your partner] stopped nursing that child?"

♦ If you think they did a lousy job as parents, you may be afraid of repeating their mistakes.

♦ If your parents live nearby, they may always be "in the neighborhood," and you might be seeing them more than you really care to.

♦ There may be disputes and power struggles between your parents and your partner's about their grandparental roles.

However your relationship with your parents and/or in-laws changes, remember this: "A loving and vigorous bond between the grandparent and grandchild," writes Sachs, "is not just related to, but *essential* to, the emotional health and stability of *all three generations.*"

Other Relationships

Without really thinking about it, you and your partner will find that your relationships with friends and other nonimmediate family members have changed.

+ You may be interested (or at least more interested than you were before becoming a parent) in getting together with relatives your own age, especially those with kids, so that the next generation can get to know their cousins.

+ Your circle of closer friends will gradually change to include more couples, especially couples with kids.

+ While your child is young, she'll be happy to play with whomever you introduce her to, and her first friends are most likely going to be *your* friends' kids. But as she gets older and starts meeting other kids on her own in parks and preschools, your child will take on a more active role in the family social committee, and all of a sudden you'll find yourself socializing with *her* friends' parents.

+ Relationships between you and other adults may continue longer than they otherwise might because the kids like getting together.

+ Relationships can be affected by competition: whose kid walks, talks, reads, or even sings first. As minor as it sounds, this can have a dramatic effect on your friendships. My wife and I used to get together fairly regularly with a couple whose two kids were just a few months older than ours. We all had a lot in common and got along fine, but the woman couldn't stop comparing her kids to ours—usually right in front of them—and hers, surprisingly, always came up on the short end. It was all very nice to hear how great our kids were, but after a while my wife and I couldn't stand it any more and the friendship eventually fizzled out.

Going Public with Fatherhood

In the concluding chapter of *The Expectant Father* I painted a rather gloomy portrait of the ways men and women—both individually and collectively as a society—actively discourage men from getting involved with their children. Sadly, in the several years since the publication of that book, little has changed. Men still don't get the support and encouragement they so sorely need to assume a greater nurturing role.

Fortunately, though, more and more men are expressing their dissatisfaction with this Neanderthal status quo. And we're just now starting to see the results of a modest revolution that's been going on quietly for more than twenty years.

Today, some 90 percent of fathers (even those who don't or won't live with

their kids) are present at their children's births—more than triple the percentage in 1974. Seventy-five percent of men say their jobs conflict with their
family responsibilities—up from only 12 percent in 1977; 74 percent say
they'd give up their fast-track job for a "daddy-track" job that would allow
them to spend more time with their families; and 30 percent reported actually
having turned down a job promotion or transfer for the same reason.

Of course, some of these dramatic changes may have been born out of
economic necessity: more and more mothers are entering the workplace and
someone else has to step in to share the child-care burden. But in my view,
the more significant reason for the nurturing-father revolution has to do with
men themselves.

Most men, especially those whose fathers were physically or emotionally
absent, instinctively know what they missed when they were young. And just
as they know they were deprived of a relationship with their fathers, they
know that their fathers were deprived of relationships with them.

More than turning down a job promotion or transfer, the real measure of a
man's commitment to a new kind of relationship with his kids is how he feels
about being a father and about the impact fatherhood is having on his life.

In one major study, researchers found that fathers generally see fathering as
an important and satisfying experience. They disagree that only mothers should
be responsible for discipline or for caring for a sick child; rather, they consider
parenting a partnership experience to be shared equally with their wives.

Clearly, things are changing for fathers—perhaps not as quickly as we
would like, but they are changing. "Discussion is growing on on-line computer
networks. Men's centers and private-practice therapists are beginning to offer
fathers' groups," writes Steven Harris, editor of *Full-Time Dad* magazine.
"Fathers are tentatively pushing their way into play-groups and other informal
gatherings, once the domain of mothers exclusively. The life of the father is
expanding, slowly but surely."

Still, far too many men continue to devalue the importance of the role they
play in their children's lives. Too many children have missed having a relationship with their fathers, and too many fathers have missed having relationships
with their children.

As a new father, you are in a unique position to break this cycle and to
make the word *fatherhood* as synonymous with childrearing and nurturing as
motherhood. And there's no better time to start than right now.

For most new fathers, the last few months of their first year as parents are
a time of relative calm. They've dealt with the big emotional, professional,
and personal hurdles of fatherhood and are now comfortably juggling their

*"My father wakes up the sun every morning.
What does your father do?"*

roles as husband, father, provider, and son. In short, they're finally feeling "like a family," and are entering what Bruce Linton calls the "community phase" of fatherhood.

As a result, says Linton, at this stage many new fathers feel ready to socialize—along with their partners and children—with other families, and use their fatherhood as a way to participate more actively in the public domain. They typically take on a more active role in their churches or synagogues, and they experience a heightened sense of *public* responsibility. Issues such as the quality of schools, city planning and zoning, the environment, and public safety become much more pressing than before.

Other researchers have confirmed Linton's theory. "Parenting brings new levels of insight and social commitment," write Barbara and Philip Newman, "that contribute in positive ways to the overall evolution of the culture."

In the introduction to this book, I quoted author Michael Levine, who said that "having children makes you no more a parent than having a piano makes you a pianist." Well, at this point you may not be any closer to being a pianist than you were a year ago. But there's no doubt that you're a parent. And a pretty good one at that.

Selected Bibliography

Books

Ames, Louise Bates, and Carol Chase Haber. *Your One Year Old: The Fun-Loving, Fussy 12- to 24-Month-Old.* New York: Delta, 1982.

Barry, Dave. *Bad Habits.* New York: Henry Holt, 1985.

Belsky, Jay, and John Kelly. *The Transition to Parenthood: How a First Child Changes a Marriage: Why Some Couples Grow Closer and Others Apart.* New York: Delacorte, 1994.

Berman, Phyllis W., and Frank A. Pedersen. *Men's Transitions to Parenthood: Longitudinal Studies of Early Family Experience.* Hillsdale, N.J.: Erlbaum, 1987.

Bettelheim, Bruno. *A Good Enough Parent: A Book on Child-Rearing.* New York: Vintage, 1987.

Biller, Henry B. *Fathers and Families: Paternal Factors in Child Development.* Westport, Conn.: Auburn House, 1993.

Biller, Henry B., and Robert J. Trotter. *The Father Factor: What You Need to Know to Make a Difference.* New York: Pocket Books, 1994.

Bluestine, Eric. *The Ways Children Learn Music: An Introduction and Practical Guide to Music Learning Theory.* Chicago: GIA Publications, 1995.

Bornstein, M. H., ed. *Handbook of Parenting.* Hillsdale, N.J.: Erlbaum, 1995.

Brazelton, T. Berry, and Bertrand Cramer. *The Earliest Relationship: Parents, Infants, and the Drama of Early Attachment.* Reading, Mass.: Addison-Wesley, 1990.

Bronstein, Phyllis, and Carolyn Pape Cowan, eds. *Fatherhood Today: Men's Changing Role in the Family.* New York: John Wiley & Sons, 1988.

Britton, James. *Language and Learning: The Importance of Speech in Children's Development.* New York: Penguin, 1970.

Brott, Armin, and Jennifer Ash. *The Expectant Father: Facts, Tips, and Advice for Dads-to-Be.* New York: Abbeville Press, 1995.

Butler, Dorothy. *Babies Need Books.* New York: Atheneum, 1980.

Canfield, Ken. *The Heart of a Father.* Chicago: Northfield, 1996.

Caplan, Frank, ed. *The First Twelve Months of Life.* New York: Grosset & Dunlap, 1973.

Cath, Stanley H., et al., eds. *Fathers and Their Families.* Hillsdale, N.J.: Analytic Press, 1989.

———. *Father and Child: Developmental and Clinical Perspectives.* Hillsdale, N.J.: Analytic Press, 1994.

Cowan, Carolyn Pape, and Philip A. Cowan. *When Partners Become Parents: The Big Life Change for Couples.* New York: HarperCollins, 1992.

Cullinan, Bernice E., and Lee Galda. *Literature and the Child,* 3d ed. Orlando, Fla.: Harcourt Brace, 1994.

Cutchins, Judy, and Ginny Johnston. *Parenting Papas: Unusual Animal Fathers.* New York: Morrow Junior Books, 1994.

Drobeck, Bruce. "The Impact on Men of the Transition to Fatherhood: A Phenomenological Investigation." Dissertation, 1990.

Eisenberg, Arlene, et al. *What to Expect the First Year.* New York: Workman, 1989.

Flint Public Library. *Ring a Ring O'Roses: Finger Plays for Pre-School Children.* Flint, Mich.: Flint Public Library, n.d.

Fraiberg, Selma H. *The Magic Years: Understanding and Handling the Problems of Early Childhood.* New York: Scribner's, 1959.

Galinsky, Ellen. *Between Generations: The Six Stages of Parenthood.* New York: Times Books, 1981.

Gordon, Edwin E. *A Music Learning Theory for Newborn and Young Children.* Chicago: GIA Publications, 1990.

Greene, Ellin. *Books, Babies, and Libraries: Serving Infants, Toddlers, Their Parents, and Caregivers.* Chicago: ALA Books, 1991.

Greenspan, Stanley, and Nancy Thorndike Greenspan. *First Feelings: Milestones in the Emotional Development of Your Baby and Child.* New York: Penguin, 1985.

Hanson, Shirley M. H., and Frederick W. Bozett. *Dimensions of Fatherhood.* Beverly Hills, Calif.: Sage, 1985.

Hass, Aaron. *The Gift of Fatherhood: How Men's Lives Are Transformed by Their Children.* New York: Fireside, 1994.

Hochschild, Arlie. *The Second Shift: Working Parents and the Revolution at Home.* New York: Viking, 1989.

Jacob, S. H. *Your Baby's Mind.* Holbrook, Mass.: Bob Adams, 1991.

Jordan, Pamela L. "The Mother's Role in Promoting Fathering Behavior." In *Becoming a Father: Contemporary Social, Developmental, and Clinical Perspectives,* J. L. Shapiro, et al., eds. New York: Springer Publications, 1995, pp. 61–71.

Karen, Robert. *Becoming Attached: Unfolding the Mystery of the Infant-Mother Bond and Impact on Later Life.* New York: Warner Books, 1994.

Kitzinger, S. *The Experience of Breastfeeding.* Middlesex, England: Penguin, 1987.

Kropp, Paul. *Raising a Reader: Make Your Child a Reader for Life.* New York: Doubleday, 1996.

Kutner, Lawrence. *Your School-Age Child.* New York: William Morrow, 1996.

Lamb, Michael E., ed. *The Role of the Father in Child Development.* New York: John Wiley, 1981.

Leach, Penelope. *Babyhood.* New York: Knopf, 1974 (1983).

Lehane, Stephen. *Help Your Baby Learn: 100 Piaget-Based Activities for the First Two Years of Life.* New York: Prentice Hall, 1976.

Linton, Bruce. "The Phases of Paternal Development: Pregnancy Through Twelve Months Post-Partum." Dissertation, 1991.

Marino, Jane, and Dorothy F. Houlihan. *Mother Goose Time: Library Programs for Babies and Their Caregivers.* New York: H. W. Wilson, 1992.

Marzollo, Jean. *Fathers and Babies.* New York: HarperPerennial, 1993.

Minnesota Fathering Alliance. *Working with Fathers: Methods and Perspectives.* Stillwater, Minn.: nu ink unlimited, 1992.

Newman, Barbara M., and Philip R. Newman. *Development Through Life: A Psychosocial Approach,* 6th ed. Pacific Grove, Calif.: Brooks/Cole Publishing, 1994.

Pagnoni, Mario. *Computers and Small Fries: A Computer-Readiness Guide for Parents of Tots, Toddlers and Other Minors.* Wayne, N.J.: Avery Publishing, 1987.

Parke, Ross D. *Fathers,* rev. ed. Cambridge, Mass.: Harvard University Press, 1996.

———. "Fathers and Families." In *Handbook of Parenting,* M. H. Bornstein, ed. Hillsdale, N.J.: Erlbaum, 1995.

Parke, Ross D., and Barbara R. Tinsley. "The Father's Role in Infancy: Determinants of Involvement in Caregiving and Play." In *The Role of the Father in Child Development,* Michael Lamb, ed. New York: Wiley, 1981.

Platt, Harvey J. *Your Living Trust and Estate Plan: How to Maximize Your Family's Assets and Protect Your Loved Ones.* New York: Allworth Press, 1995.

Pleck, Joseph H. "Are 'Family Supportive' Employer Policies Relevant to Men?" In *Men, Work, and Family*, Jane C. Hood, ed. Newbury Park, Calif.: Sage, 1993.

Pruett, Kyle D. "The Nurturing Male: A Longitudinal Study of Primary Nurturing Fathers." In *Fathers and Their Families*, Stanley Cath et al., eds. Hillsdale, N.J.: Analytic Press, 1989.

Sachs, Brad E. *Things Just Haven't Been the Same: Making the Transition from Marriage to Parenthood*. New York: William Morrow, 1992.

Schaffer, Judith, and Christina Lindstrom. *How to Raise an Adopted Child*. New York: Crown, 1989.

Sears, William, and Martha Sears. *The Baby Book: Everything You Need to Know about Your Baby—From Birth to Age Two*. New York: Little Brown, 1993.

Snarey, John. *How Fathers Care for the Next Generation: A Four-Decade Study*. Cambridge, Mass.: Harvard University Press, 1993.

Spangler, Doug. *Fatherhood: An Owner's Manual*. Richmond, Calif.: Fabus, 1994.

Spock, Benjamin, and Michael B. Rothenberg. *Dr. Spock's Baby and Child Care*. New York: Pocket Books, 1992.

Steinberg, David. *Fatherjournal*. Albion, Calif.: Times Change Press, 1977.

Sullivan, S. Adams. *The Father's Almanac*, rev. ed. New York: Doubleday, 1992.

Trelease, Jim. *The New Read-Aloud Handbook*. New York: Penguin, 1989.

Tyson, Eric. *Personal Finance for Dummies*. Foster City, Calif.: IDG Books, 1995.

Ulene, Art, and Steven Shelov. *Discovery Play: Loving and Learning with Your Baby*. Berkeley, Calif.: Ulysses Press, 1994.

White, Burton L. *The First Three Years of Life: The Revised Edition*. New York: Prentice Hall, 1985.

Journal Articles

Bailey, William T. "Fathers' Involvement and Responding to Infants: 'More' May Not be 'Better.'" *Psychological Reports* 74 (1994): 92–94.

———. "Psychological Development in Men: Generativity and Involvement with Young Children." *Psychological Reports* 71 (1992): 929–30.

Barrett-Goldfarb, Minna, and Grover J. Whitehurst. "Infant Vocalizations as a Function of Parental Voice Selection." *Developmental Psychology* 8, no. 2 (1973): 273–76.

Baumrind, Diana. "Current Patterns of Parental Authority." *Developmental Psychology Monograph* 4, no. 1, part 1 (1971): 1–101.

Cohn, Deborah A., et al. "Working Models of Childhood Attachment and Couple Relationships." *Journal of Family Issues* 13, no. 4 (1992): 432–49.

Condry, John, and Sandra Condry. "Sex Differences: A Study of the Eye of the Beholder." *Child Development* 47 (1976): 812–19.

Condry, John, and David F. Ross. "Sex and Aggression: The Influence of Gender Label on the Perception of Aggression in Children." *Child Development* 56 (1985): 225–33.

DeLuccie, Mary F. "Mothers as Gatekeepers: A Model of Maternal Mediators of Father Involvement." *Journal of Genetic Psychology* 156, no. 1 (1994): 115–31.

Deutsch, Francine M., et al. "Taking Credit: Couples' Reports of Contributions to Child Care." *Journal of Family Issues* 14, no. 3 (1993): 421–37.

Dickstein, Susan, and Ross D. Parke. "Social Referencing in Infancy: A Glance at Fathers and Marriage." *Child Development* 59 (1988): 506–11.

Fagot, Beverly I. "The Influence of Sex of Child on Parental Reactions to Toddler Children." *Child Development* 49 (1978): 459–65.

———. "Sex Differences in Toddlers' Behavior and Parental Reaction." *Developmental Psychology* 10, no. 4 (1974): 554–58.

Fagot, Beverly, and Richard Hagan. "Aggression in Toddlers: Responses to the Assertive Acts of Boys and Girls." *Sex Roles* 12, nos. 3–4 (1985): 341–51.

———. "Observations of Parent Reactions to Sex-Stereotyped Behaviors: Age and Sex Effects." *Child Development* 62 (1991): 617–28.

Field, T., S. Schanberg, et al. "Tactile/Kinesthetic Stimulation Effects on Preterm Neonates." *Pediatrics* 77, no. 5 (1986): 654–58.

Frisch, Hannah L. "Sex Stereotypes in Adult-Infant Play." *Child Development* 48 (1977): 1671–75.

Gambill, Lionel. "Can More Touching Lead to Less Violence in Our Society?" *Human Touch* 1, no. 3 (1985): 1–3.

Goldbloom, Richard B. "Behavior and Allergy: Myth or Reality?" *Pediatrics in Review* 13, no. 8 (1992): 312–13.

Gordon, Betty Nye. "Maternal Perception of Child Temperament and Observed Mother-Child Interaction." *Child Psychiatry and Human Development* 13, no. 3 (1983): 153–65.

Hall, Wendy A. "New Fatherhood: Myths and Realities." *Public Health Nursing* 11, no. 4 (1994): 219–28.

Haugland, Susan W. "The Effect of Computer Software on Preschool Children's

Developmental Gains." *Journal of Computing in Childhood Education* 3, no. 1 (1992): 15–20.

Jewett, Don L., et al. "A Double-Blind Study of Symptom Provocation to Determine Food Sensitivity." *New England Journal of Medicine* 323, no. 7 (1990): 429–33.

Jordan, Pamela L. "Laboring for Relevance: Expectant and New Fatherhood." *Nursing Research* 39, no. 1 (1990): 11–16.

Jordan, Pamela L., et al. "Breastfeeding and Fathers: Illuminating the Darker Side." *Birth* 19, no. 4 (1990): 210–13.

———. "Supporting the Father When an Infant is Breastfed." *Journal of Human Lactation* 9, no. 1 (1993): 31–34.

Krupper, Jan C., and Ina C. Uzgiris. "Fathers' and Mothers' Speech to Young Infants." *Journal of Psycholinguistic Research* 16, no. 6 (1987): 597–614.

Lamme, Linda, and Athol B. Packer. "Bookreading Behaviors of Infants." *Reading Teacher* 39, no. 6 (1986): 504–9.

Lovestone, S., and R. Kumar. "Postnatal Psychiatric Illness: The Impact of Partners." *British Journal of Psychiatry* 163 (1993): 210–16.

McBride, B. A., and G. Mills. "A Comparison of Mother and Father Involvement with Their Preschool Age Children. *Early Childhood Research Quarterly* 8 (1993): 457–77.

MacDonald, Kevin, and Ross D. Parke. "Parent-Child Physical Play: The Effects of Sex and Age of Children and Parents." *Sex Roles* 15, nos. 7–8 (1986): 367–78.

McKenna, James J., and Sara Mosko. "Evolution and Infant Sleep: An Experimental Study of Infant-Parent Co-Sleeping and Its Implications for SIDS." *ACTA Paediatrica: An International Journal of Paediatrics* 82, supplement 389 (June 1993): 31–35.

Medoff, David, and Charles E. Schaefer. "Children Sharing the Parental Bed: A Review of the Advantages and Disadvantages of Cosleeping." *Psychology: A Journal of Human Behavior* 30, no. 1 (1993): 1–9.

Newman, Philip R., and Barbara Newman. "Parenthood and Adult Development." *Marriage and Family Review* 12, nos. 3–4 (1988): 313–37.

Nicolson, P. "A Brief Report of Women's Expectations of Men's Behaviour in the Transition to Parenthood: Contradictions and Conflicts for Counselling Psychology Practice." *Counselling Psychology Quarterly* 3, no. 4 (1990): 353–61.

Palm, G. "Involved Fatherhood: A Second Chance." *Journal of Men's Studies* 2 (1993): 139–54.

Palm G., and Bill Joyce. "Attachment from a Father's Perspective." *Typescript,* 1994.

Papousek, Mechthild, et al. "Didactic Adjustments in Fathers' and Mothers' Speech to Their 3-Month-Old Infants." *Journal of Psycholinguistic Research* 16, no. 5 (1987): 491–516.

Power, Thomas G., et al. "Compliance and Self-Assertion: Young Children's Responses to Mothers Versus Fathers." *Developmental Psychology* 30, no. 6 (1994): 980–89.

Power, Thomas G., and Ross D. Parke. "Patterns of Early Socialization: Mother- and Father-Infant Interactions in the Home." *International Journal of Behavioral Development* 9 (1986): 331–41.

———. "The Paternal Presence." *Families in Society* 74, no. 1 (1993): 46–50.

Reis, Myrna, and Dolores Gold. "Relationship of Paternal Availability to Problem Solving and Sex-Role Orientation in Young Boys." *Psychological Reports* 40 (1977): 823–29.

Sampson, Hugh A., et al. "Fatal and Near-Fatal Anaphalyctic Reactions to Food in Children and Adolescents." *New England Journal of Medicine* 327, no. 6 (1992): 380–84.

Sorce, James F., et al. "Maternal Emotional Signaling: Its Effect on the Visual Cliff Behavior of 1-Year-Olds." *Developmental Psychology* 21, no. 1 (1985): 195–200.

Stayton, Donelda, et al. "Infant Obedience and Maternal Behavior: The Origins of Socialization Reconsidered." *Child Development* 42 (1971): 1057–69.

Whaley, Kimberlee K. "The Emergence of Social Play in Infancy: A Proposed Developmental Sequence of Infant-Adult Social Play." *Early Childhood Research Quarterly* 5, no. 3 (1990): 347–58.

Whitehurst, G. J., et al. "Accelerating Language Development Through Picture Book Reading." *Developmental Psychology* 24, no. 4 (1988): 552–59.

Resources

Adoption

NATIONAL ADOPTION CENTER offers a great list of questions to ask adoption agencies; addresses tax issues, single-parent issues, and legal issues; provides photos of kids waiting to be adopted, book reviews, lists of state and local contacts, and links to other adoption-related organizations.

1500 Walnut Street, Suite 701
Philadelphia, PA 19102
Tel.: (215) 735-9988
e-mail: nac@adopt.org
http://www.inetcom.net/adopt/nac/nac.html

Advice

FAMILY PLANET has a stable of columnists who dispense advice on just about every topic you can imagine.

http://family.starwave.com/experts/index.html

PARENTSPLACE.COM has one of the largest clearinghouses of parenting advice on the Net.

http://parentsplace.com/

At-Home Dads

"AT-HOME DAD" NEWSLETTER has just about everything a stay-at-home dad could want to know.

Peter Baylies, Publisher
61 Brightwood Ave.
North Andover, MA 01845
Tel.: (508) 685-7931
e-mail: athomedad@aol.com

NATIONAL AT-HOME DADS ASSOCIATION. A resource for all at-home dads who are the primary care providers to their children, this association is designed to help at-home dads connect with one another. NAHDA sponsors a national network for at-home dads and offers an extensive and growing resource list. Contact them for details at:

P.O. Box 1876
Coppell, TX 75019-1876
e-mail: fulltdad@aol.com

or write to Curtis Cooper, founder of the NAHDA, at:
120 Ashbrook Lane
Roswell, GA 30075
Tel.: (770) 643-6964

Babies
FAMILY INTERNET'S BABYCARE CORNER
http://www.familyinternet.com/babycare/babycare.htm

PARENTS' PAGE
http://members.aol.com/AllianceMD/parents.html

Two fact-filled resources written by pediatricians for parents of infants who need basic information fast (treating diaper rash, growth patterns, immunizations, introducing solid foods).

Computers
COMPUTERTOTS
Tel.: (800) 531-5053

Death and Grief
AMERICAN SUDDEN INFANT DEATH SYNDROME (SIDS) INSTITUTE
6065 Roswell Road, Suite 876
Atlanta, GA 30328
Tel.: (800) 232-7437
Fax: (404) 843-0577
e-mail: prevent@sids.org
http://www.sids.org/#Bereavement

SIDS NETWORK
  9 Gonch Farm Road
  Ledyard, CT 06339
  http://sids-network.org/net.htm

Both organizations offer great resources, information, references, and support to help parents and other surviving family members deal with the tragedy of the death of a child.

Divorce

CHILDREN'S RIGHTS COUNCIL has a well-stocked catalog of resources, including a listing of great books on the subject for kids and their parents.
  http://www.vix.com/crc/catalog.htm

SINGLE FATHERS HOMEPAGE
  http://www.pitt.edu/~jsims/singlefa.html

Fun Stuff

BRITE has quite a comprehensive line of parenting aids, child development tools, phonics programs, and teaching ideas.
  http://users.aol.com/clintg777/private/brite.html

CREATIVE CREATIONS has a constantly changing list of twenty fun things to do with kids of all ages.
  http://www.waidsoft.com/funkids.html

ELLEN DAVIS also offers a bunch of fun activities.
  http://ucunix.san.uc.edu/~edavis/kids-list/crafts/easy-and-fun.html

KIDS CRAFTBASE has great suggestions, advice, and products for doing art with kids of all ages.
  http://www.vistek.com/kidcraft.htm

PARENTSPLACE.COM is the parents' resource center on the World Wide Web. It offers a constantly growing collection of articles, advice, and links to other great sites, as well as a newsletter.
  http://www.parentsplace.com

General Fatherhood

FATHER TO FATHER is a wonderful source of information, referrals, and support.

12 McNeal Hall
1985 Buford Avenue
St. Paul, MN 55108
Tel.: (612) 626-1212
http://www.cyfc.umn.edu/FatherNet.htp

FATHERS HOTLINE can refer you to father-friendly organizations in your state or community.

Tel.: (512) 472-DADS (3237)
e-mail: dads@fathers.org

FATHER'S RESOURCE CENTER offers parenting classes, support groups, workshops, legal clinics, and reading lists, and publishes the quarterly newsletter "FatherTimes."

430 Oak Grove Street, Suite 105
Minneapolis, MN 55403
Tel.: (612) 874-1509
e-mail: frc@freenet.msp.mn.us
http://freenet.msp.mn.us/org/frc/index.html

FATHERWORK is a new home page designed to encourage good fathering. The folks at FatherWork view fathering not so much as a social role men play, but as the work they do each day to care for the next generation.

http://fatherwork.byu.edu

NATIONAL CENTER FOR FATHERING has resources designed to help men become more aware of their own fathering style and then work toward improving their skills. Call for a free issue of NCF's quarterly magazine, "Today's Father."

10200 West 75th Street, #267
Shawnee Mission, KS 66204-2223
Tel.: (913) 384-4661
Fax: (913) 384-4665
e-mail: ncf@aol.com
http://www.fathers.com

NATIONAL CENTER ON FATHERS & FAMILIES is a great source of research
and data on fathers, father involvement, and so forth.

    c/o University of Pennsylvania
    3700 Walnut Street, Box 58
    Philadelphia, PA 19104-6216
    Tel.: (215) 898-5000

NATIONAL FATHERHOOD INITIATIVE offers membership that includes the
quarterly newsletter "Fatherhood Today"; updates on family issues and
political/legislative developments; the Fatherhood Resource Catalog of books,
videos, and audio tapes, offering a discount on all items; and updates on
activities and events.

    600 Eden Road, Building E
    Lancaster, PA 17601
    Tel.: (800) 790-DADS or (717) 581-8860
    Fax: (717) 581-8862

General Parenting

ERIC CLEARINGHOUSE. More information on parenting than you could ever
possibly go through.

    Tel.: (800) 583-4135 or (217) 333-1386
    e-mail: ericeece@ux1.cso.uiuc.edu
    http://ericps.ed.uiuc.edu/ericeece.html

FAMILY PLANET offers links, articles, and resources on just about everything
from stranger anxiety to child safety.

    http://family.starwave.com/resource/pra/Table_of_Contents.htm

NATIONAL COUNCIL ON FAMILY RELATIONS
    Minneapolis, MN
    Tel.: (612) 781-9331

"SMART FAMILIES" is a great newsletter published by Family University.
    P.O. Box 500050
    San Diego, CA 92150-0050
    Tel.: (619) 487-7099
    Fax: (619) 487-7356
    e-mail: FamilyU@aol.com

Health Concerns

NATIONAL ORGANIZATION FOR RARE DISORDERS
P.O. Box 8923
New Fairfield, CT 06812-1783
Tel.: (800) 999-6673

NORTHWEST COALITION FOR ALTERNATIVES TO PESTICIDES (NCAP)
publishes the *Journal of Pesticide Reform* as well as the information packets
"Children and Pesticides" and "Planning for Non-chemical School Ground
Maintenance."
P.O. Box 1393
Eugene, OR 97440
Tel.: (503) 344-5044
Fax: (503) 344-6923
e-mail: ncap@igc.apc.org

WEB DOCTOR will answer your specific questions on line.
http://www.parentsplace.com/readroom/health.html

Music

ADVENTURE KIDS MUSIC AND STORIES
http://www.rmii.com/dreamweaver/colors.gif

CENTER FOR MUSIC AND YOUNG CHILDREN
217 Nassau Street
Princeton, NJ 08542
Tel.: (609) 924-7801

MUSIC FOR PEOPLE
David Darling
Tel.: (203) 672-0275

On-line Conferences, Mailing Lists, and Newsletters

FATHER-L is an e-mail conference dedicated to discussing the importance of
fathers in kids' lives. Send e-mail to listserv@vm1.spcs.umn.edu and write
"subscribe father-l" in the body of the message. If you need more info, send a
message to father-l@tc.umn.edu

PARENTING-L is a great way to get fifty quick, informative answers to just
about any nonemergency question you might have. To subscribe, send e-mail
to listserv@postoffice.cso.usuc.edu with "subscribe parenting-l" in the
subject line.

THE PARENTS' LETTER is published by a pediatrician and filled with good, basic information on such topics as health maintenance, immunizations, illness, behavior, and parenting skills. To subscribe, send e-mail to majordomo@pobox.com with a blank subject line and "subscribe letter" in the body of the message.

OTHER PARENTING LISTS:
    kids-newborn (0–2/3 months)
    kids-infant (3 months–1 year)

To subscribe to one or more of the above, send e-mail to
    listserv@vm.ege.edu.tr using the following format (substituting your own
        name for mine, of course):
    sub kids-newborn Armin Brott
    sub kids-infant Armin Brott

Reading and Other Media

CHILDREN'S LITERATURE provides reviews of the latest kids' books, videos, and computer games.
    7513 Shadywood Road
    Bethesda, MD 20817-9823
    Tel.: (800) 469-2070 or (301) 469-2070 (yes, it's the same number)
    Fax: (301) 469-2071

Temperament

TEMPERAMENT TALK
    1100 K Avenue
    La Grande, OR 97850
    Tel.: (541) 962-8836
    Fax: (541) 963-3572

Toys

VTECH has a wonderful array of high-tech toys for kids six months and older. For a catalog, write or call:
    101 E. Palatine Road
    Wheeling, IL 60090
    Tel.: (800) 521-2010

Travel

FAMILY WORLD HOMEPAGE offers calendars (broken down into four regions) that include information on all sorts of fun places for families to visit in different parts of the country.

http://family.com

Twins

TWINLINE parenting consultation.

http://www.parentsplace.com/readroom/twins/twinline.html

For many more interesting web sites, check out Jean Armour Polly's *Internet Kids Yellow Pages* (Osborne McGraw-Hill, 1996). Despite the title, it's a wonderful source of resources for parents too.

If you have any comments or suggestions about the topics discussed in this book, you can send them to

Armin Brott
P.O. Box 2458
Berkeley, CA 94702
e-mail: armin@pacbell.net

Index

A

abuse, 72, 184, 201
acne, 29
active alert state, 18, 22
active sleep, 19
activity level, 90, 92, 95, 208
adaptability level, 90, 92, 94, 150, 208
adoption, 35
aggression, 11
Ainsworth, Mary, 155–57
allergies: food, 27, 110, 112–13; to sunscreen, 81
Alperstein, Linda Perlin, 52–53
ambivalent attachment, 155–56
anger: at baby, 55, 199–202; after death of baby, 71
animals: co-parenting by, 158–59; pets, 24
apologies, 204–5
apples, 111
approach/withdraw level, 90, 92, 94, 150
Arquette, Roseanna, 176
attachment, parent-child, 34, 74, 101, 155–62; adoption and, 35; factors interfering with father's development of, 161–62;

forming of, 155; importance of, 160–61; influenced by other relationships, 160; types of, 155–57
au pairs, 123
avoidant attachment, 155–56
Azzara, Christopher, 178

B

babies: at 1 week, 13–30; at 1 month, 31–48; at 2 months, 49–66; at 3 months, 67–82; at 4 months, 83–101; at 5 months, 102–14; at 6 months, 115–29; at 7 months, 130–41; at 8 months, 142–52; at 9 months, 153–71; at 10 months, 172–81; at 11 months, 182–96; at 12 months, 197–216; anger at, 55, 199–202; attachment between parents and, 34, 35, 74, 101, 155–62; bathing, 29, 44, 167; biting and hitting by, 204–5; bonding with, 28, 32–35, 59, 101; child care for, 108, 122–29; crying of (see crying); dental care for, 136,

206; development of, 10. *See also* emotional/social development; intellectual development; physical development; verbal development); diapering (*see* diaper changing; diapers); discipline for, 135–37, 202–4, 205, 215; dressing, 69, 79, 80, 81, 96; exposing to music, 75–76, 176–78; feeding (*see* bottle-feeding; breast-feeding; feeding); first birthday party of, 211; growth rate of, 35–36; impact of father's involvement on, 10–11; jealousy of, 118; love for, 131–32, 135; massage of, 59–61; pacifiers for, 44, 137; pediatrician visits of, 61–66; playing with (*see* games; playing; toys); potty training and, 21, 207; reading to, 36, 76–79, 147–49, 205; reflexes of, 38–39, 40–42, 49, 67; relationships changed by, 210–14; senses of, 13–14, 58–59; sexual feelings toward, 184–85; sexual identity of,

178–81, 184; sleeping of (*see* sleeping); strangers feared by, 94, 116, 131, 143, 149–50, 189; talking to, 19–20, 59, 205; teething of, 60, 136, 204, 209; temperament of, 89–96, 150, 162, 180, 186, 208; traveling with, 187–91; vaccinations for, 60, 61–65; walkers for, 138; workload increased by, 167; worries about health of, 185–87. *See also* newborns
baby food: making your own, 113–14
baby gyms, 120
baby talk, 59
backpacks, 79
balls, 165
bananas, 111
Barnette, Rosalind, 106
Barry, Dave, 17, 114
bathing baby, 29, 44, 167
bathrooms: childproofing of, 141
beanbags, 48
bedrooms: childproofing of, 141
Belsky, Jay, 146, 147, 151, 167–68, 170, 210
Bettelheim, Bruno, 162, 164, 166
Biller, Henry, 57, 155, 179, 180, 181
birthmarks, 29
biting, 204–5
blisters, 29
blocks, 130, 131, 153, 166
blotches, 29
bonding: as family, 119
bonding with baby, 32–35, 101; adoption and, 35; attachment vs., 34; attendance at childbirth and, 32; breastfeeding and, 28; delay in, 32–33; massage and, 59; physical contact and, 32, 33
books: playing with, 22, 166, 183. *See also* reading to baby
bottle-feeding: breastfeeding vs., 25–28; with breast milk, 88, 209; introducing solids and, 110, 111; middle-of-the-night wake-ups and, 98–99; transition from breastfeeding to, 205–6, 208–9; weaning from, 206–7, 208
Bowlby, John, 155–57
boys: caring for penis of, 30; sexual identity and, 178–81
brain builders, 163–64
Brazelton, T. Berry, 11, 34, 135
breads, 111
breastfeeding, 22, 23, 24, 69, 86–88, 137; benefits of, 25–28; crying and, 43; family bed and, 100–101; father's ambivalence about, 86; father's support in, 26, 27; food intolerances and, 112; getting hang of, 27; growth rate and, 36; introducing solids and, 110, 111; making into more pleasant experience, 88; middle-of-the-night wake-ups and, 98; mother's ambivalence about, 87; resumption of sexual life and, 52; weaning from, 205–6, 208–9
breast milk: bottle-feeding with, 88, 209
budgeting, 152
Burck, Frances Wells, 110

C
Cameron, Jim, 89, 208
Canfield, Ken, 16–17
Caplan, Frank, 103, 115, 172, 174
car rides, 289–90: crying and, 44
car seats, 48, 189
cash value insurance, 193–95, 196
cause-and-effect games, 75, 84, 120, 165–66
cereals, 111
Cesarean sections, 23, 51
challenging children, 93–94, 180
change: acceptance of, 145
chasing games, 164
Chess, Stella, 89
childbirth, 16; blaming baby for problems in, 14–15; father's presence at, 32, 215; recovery from, 23–25
child care, 108, 122–29; au pairs and, 123; family day care, 126; finding out-of-home caregivers for, 127–29; group day care, 126; in-home, 122–25; taxes and, 128
childproofing home, 138–41, 202
choking hazards, 113
circumcision, 30
climbing, 164, 172, 182
colic, 46, 60
Colman, Libby and Arthur, 53
colostrum, 27
Condry, John and Sandra, 179
confidence: father's feelings of, 118–19
confusion: father's feelings of, 54–55
constipation, 60

consulting: as work option, 107–8

control: new parents' loss of, 73–74

Cowan, Phil, 51, 105, 109, 169, 170–71, 210–11

Cowan, Carolyn, 51, 105, 169, 170–71

cow's milk, 46, 209

CPR: for infants, 48

cradle cap, 29

Cramer, Bertrand, 34

crawling, 115, 142, 143, 153, 165, 197

cribs, 95, 101, 141

cruising, 153, 172

crying, 17, 18, 32, 33, 34, 39–45, 50, 84, 103, 174; colic and, 46, 60; coping with, 44–45; holding baby and, 42–44, 46; keeping diary of, 43; as means of communication, 39, 42; parents' emotional response to, 39–42, 45, 104, 105; soothing tactics for, 43–44

D

day care. *See* child care

death of child: grieving after, 69–71; SIDS and, 68–71, 100

delivery. *See* childbirth

dental care, 136, 206

depression: postpartum, 23, 47

development: differences in rate of, 10. *See also* emotional/social development; intellectual development; physical development; verbal development

diaper changing, 20, 29, 81, 82, 97, 167, 170; potty training and, 207;

as test for potential caregivers, 124

diaper rash, 81–82, 97

diapers: of breastfed babies, 28; disposable vs. cloth, 20–21

diarrhea, 28

diphtheria, pertussis, tetanus (DPT) vaccines, 62–63, 66

discipline, 135–37, 202–4, 205, 215

distractibility level, 91, 92, 96

division of labor, 167, 168–71

doors: playing with, 166

dressing baby, 69, 79; insect protection and, 81; sensory threshold and, 96; sun protection and, 80

Drobeck, Bruce, 73, 85, 117, 145, 174–75

drowsiness state, 18

E

Einstein, Albert, 166

emergency treatment manuals, 140

emotional/social development: at 1 week, 14; at 1 month, 32; at 2 months, 50; at 3 months, 68; at 4 months, 84; at 5 months, 103–4; at 6 months, 116; at 7 months, 131; at 8 months, 143; at 9 months, 154–55; at 10 months, 174; at 11 months, 183–84; at 12 months, 198–99

engrossment, 32

exercises: for major muscle groups, 164

F

Fagot, Beverly, 179

family: bonding as, 119; increase in household workload and, 167–68; money matters and, 151–52, 191–96; *See also* partner, relationship with

family bed, 99–101

family day care, 216

Farrell, Warren, 106

fatherhood: dealing with reality of, 16–17, 47; new father's feelings about, 133

fathers: ambivalent about breastfeeding, 86; anger felt by, 199–202; attachment between baby and, 34, 74, 101, 155–62; attention paid to baby vs., 175–76; changes in societal role of, 214–16; at childbirth, 32, 215; confidence gained by, 118–19; confusing and conflicting emotions of, 54–55; control lost by, 73–74; division of labor between mother and, 167, 168–71; examining your relationship with your own father, 71–73; fears felt by, 55–56; feeling like a father, 117; flexibility and patience needed by, 143–45; fulfillment felt by, 174–75; grandparents' relationship with, 212–13; growing up by, 116–17; guilt felt by, 146; impact of parenting by, 10–11; involvement level of, 145–47; irreplaceable feeling of, 174; isolation felt by, 132–33; jealousy felt by, 117–18; love felt by, 131–32; manhood's meaning for, 57; parenting by mothers vs., 9; partner's relationship with (*see* partner, relationship with); play style of mothers vs., 163; postpartum blues in, 47–48; public responsibility of, 216; resources for, 56; responsibility taken on by, 73; sexual feelings of, toward baby, 184–85; support groups for, 133–35; unpreparedness felt by, 53–54; in various animal species, 158–59; work issues and, 85–86, 105–10, 146–47, 170–71, 215; worried about doing things wrong, 104–5; worried that life will never be same again, 89

feeding baby, 110–14, 131, 142, 170; establishing regular schedule for, 95; juice and, 28, 111; in middle of night, 98–99; new foods and, 94; playing with food during, 113; solid foods and, 110–13, 116, 206, 207. *See also* bottle-feeding; breastfeeding

Ferber, Richard, 100
Field, Tiffany, 59
financial planners, 192, 194–95
first aid kits, 48, 140
first birthday party, 211
Fisher, William, 52
flexibility: parents' need for, 143–45
flexible schedule options, 106, 108
food allergies, 27, 110, 112–13
food intolerances, 112
formula, 28, 36, 46, 188. *See also* bottle-feeding

Fraiberg, Selma, 143
Friederici, Angela, 154
friendships: of parents, 214
Frisch, Hannah, 179
frontpacks, 44, 79
fruit juice, 28, 111
fruits, 111
fussing: at bedtime, 97

G

Galinsky, Ellen, 16, 32, 33, 73, 129, 201
games, 36; brain builders, 163–64; chasing, 164; hiding, 121, 154, 163–64, 173, 198; if . . . then . . . , 75, 120, 165–66; imitation, 17, 19, 59, 164; pretend, 164; reaching, 119; touching, 119–20; tracking, 38, 121–22
gender differences, 178–81; interacting with baby and, 22, 163, 179–81; money and, 151; real vs. imagined, 179; stereotypes and, 178
girls: sexual identity and, 178–81
Giveans, David L., 53, 105
Gordon, Edwin, 75, 177, 178
grandparents: accepting help from, 25; as caregivers, 125; negative feedback from, 170–71; parents' relationship with, 71–73, 212–13
grasping, 31, 49, 67, 83, 142, 172, 197
Gray, Janice, 52
Greenberg, Martin, 32, 44, 117, 118
Greenspan, Stanley I., 38, 105, 146, 184, 185
grieving: after death of baby, 69–71

group day care, 126
growing up: by new father, 116–17
Grunow, Richard, 178
Guilmartin, Ken, 177
guilt, 146, 198
gut feelings: going with, 105

H

haemophilus influenza B (HiB) vaccines, 62–63, 66
"handedness" preference, 172, 197
hand-eye coordination, 165
Harris, Steven, 215
Hass, Aaron, 185
hats, 80
Hauff, William, 70
head: lifting, 31, 49, 61, 83; of newborns, 22
health matters: traveling and, 188; vaccinations and, 60, 61–65; well-baby checkups and, 61–66; worries about, 185–87
hearing, 13, 17, 59
heat rash, 80
hepatitis B vaccines, 62–63, 66
hiding games, 121, 154, 163–64, 173, 198
hitting, 204–5
Hochschild, Arlie, 169
holding baby, 19, 32, 56; bonding and, 32; crying and, 42–44, 46
home: childproofing of, 138–41, 202; working in, 107, 108–9
honeymoon period, 119
hormonal advantage theory, 86
household chores, 24; accepting outside help with, 25; division of labor and, 167, 168–71; increased by baby, 167–68
humor, 11, 198, 201

I

if . . . then games, 75, 120, 165–66
imitation games, 17, 19, 59, 164
independence: family bed and, 99, 100
in-home care, 122–25; au pairs and, 123; finding caregiver for, 123–25; live-in help for, 125
in-laws, 162, 213; accepting help from, 25; as caregivers, 125. *See also* grandparents
insect repellent, 81
insects, 80–81
insecure attachment, 155–56
intellectual development: at 1 week, 13–14; at 1 month, 31; at 2 months, 49–50; at 3 months, 67–68; at 4 months, 83–84; at 5 months, 102–3; at 6 months, 115–16; at 7 months, 130–31; at 8 months, 142–43; at 9 months, 153–54; at 10 months, 173; at 11 months, 182–83; at 12 months, 198
intensity, 90, 92, 95
Internet, 134
IQ, 10–11
isolation: father's feelings of, 132–33
"Is This Really My Baby?" phase, 15–16

J

jack-in-the-boxes, 165
jaundice, 29
jealousy, 117–18
Jensen, Amy Hillyard, 69–70
jet lag, 188, 191

job. *See* work
job sharing, 107, 108
Jordan, Pamela, 16, 86, 87
juice, 28, 111
jumpers, 138

K

kitchen: childproofing of, 139–40
Kitzinger, Sheila, 26
Klaus, Marshall, 17, 19
Klaus, Phyllis, 17
Kumar, Remesh, 33
Kutner, Lawrence, 126, 200–201

L

Lamme, Linda, 77
language development. *See* verbal development
Levine, James, 64, 106
Levine, Michael, 9, 216
life insurance, 191–96; cash value, 193–95, 196; term, 193, 194–96
Lindstrom, Christina, 35
Linton, Bruce, 55, 72, 119, 133, 134–35, 216
live-in help, 125
living room: childproofing of, 140–41
lotions, 21
love, 131–32, 135

M

McClure, Vimala, 61
McKenna, James, 99
McNurlen, Marion, 70–71
manhood: rethinking meaning of, 57
massage, 59–61
mattresses, 69
May, Katherine, 33
Mead, Margaret, 106
measles vaccines, 62–63, 64–65, 66
memory, 19, 154, 173, 202
microwaves, 114

middle-of-the-night wake-ups, 84, 98–99
milk intolerance, 46
MMR (measles, mumps, rubella) vaccines, 64–65, 66
mobiles, 38, 75, 141
money matters, 151–52; financial planners and, 192, 194–95; life insurance and, 191–96; quarrels over, 151
mood, 17, 90, 92, 95
mothers: breastfeeding by (*see* breastfeeding); division of labor between father and, 167, 168–71; handling of baby by fathers vs., 22; parenting by fathers vs., 9; partner's jealousy of, 117–18; partner's relationship with (*see* partner, relationship with); physical recovery of, 23–25; play style of fathers vs., 163; postpartum blues and depression in, 23, 45–47; working, 105, 215
motor development. *See* physical development
multiple-birth babies, 69
mumps vaccines, 64–65, 66
music, 116: exposing baby to, 75–76, 176–78

N

naps, 98, 143
newborns, 13–48; at 1 week, 13–30; at 1 month, 31–48; bonding with, 28, 32–35; capabilities of, 13–14; childbirth problems and, 14–15; cleaning, 29; crying by, 17, 18, 32, 33, 34, 39–45, 46; diapering,

20–21, 29; disappointment with sex of, 16; head of, 22; interacting with, 19–20, 21–22; male, caring for penis of, 30; parent feeling unloved by, 33–34; physical appearance of, 15–16, 28–29; physical contact with, 19, 32; playing with, 19, 21–22, 36–38; reading to, 36; reflexes of, 38–39, 40–42, 49; six behavioral states of, 17–19; skin problems of, 28–29; talking to, 19–20; visual stimulation and, 37–38; weight loss in, 35

Newman, Barbara and Philip, 34, 39, 155, 174, 202, 204, 216

nightmares, 98

noise books, 77

nonsexual affection, 51

nursery: childproofing of, 141

O

obesity, 27

object permanence, 50, 121

oranges, 111

P

pacifiers, 44, 137

Packer, Athol, 77

Palm, Glen, 105, 161–62

Parke, Ross, 11, 32, 161, 169

partner, relationship with, 11; changed by baby, 210–12; division of labor and, 167, 168–71; nonsexual affection and, 51; sexual intercourse and, 23, 50–53, 100

part-time work, 107

patience: parents' need for, 143–45

Pedersen, Frank, 161

pediatricians, 186, 188; visits to, 61–66

peek-a-boo, 121

penis: caring for, 30; circumcision and, 30

persistence level, 91, 92, 96

pets, 24

physical development, 161; at 1 week, 13; at 1 month, 31–48; at 2 months, 49; at 3 months, 67; at 4 months, 83; at 5 months, 102; at 6 months, 115; at 7 months, 130; at 8 months, 142; at 9 months, 153; at 10 months, 172; at 11 months, 182; at 12 months, 197; exercises for major muscle groups and, 164

plane travel, 190–91

playing, 74–75, 84, 119–22, 154, 162–67; alone, 120; baby's interest in objects vs. you during, 166–67; with blocks, 130, 131, 153, 166; brain building games and exercises, 163–64; cause-and-effect in, 75, 120, 165–66; exercising major muscle groups in, 164; in first few weeks, 19, 21–22, 36–38; gender differences and, 163, 179–81; hand-eye coordination and, 165; importance of, 162; with other babies, 126, 131, 198–99; parents' inner attitudes about, 162. *See also* games; toys

Pleck, Joseph, 106

polio vaccines: oral (OPV), 64–65, 66

Popenoe, David, 9

postpartum blues and depression: in new fathers, 47–48; in new mothers, 23, 45–47

potty training, 21, 207

powders, 21

praise, 167

preterm babies, 29, 60, 69

pretend games, 164

prickly heat, 80

punishment, 135. *See also* discipline

puzzles, 165

Q

quiet alert state, 17–18, 22

quiet sleep, 18–19

R

Radin, Norma, 161, 163

rashes: diaper, 81–82, 97; heat, 80

rattles, 119, 120

reaching games, 119

reading to baby, 36, 76–79, 147–49, 205; physical contact during, 149; suggested books for, 77–79, 149; tips for, 77

recovery: from childbirth, 23–25

reflexes, 38–39, 49, 67; exploring, 40–42

regularity level, 91, 92, 95–96

relationships: baby's impact on, 210–14. *See also* partner, relationship with

relatives: accepting help from, 25; baby's contact with, 189; as caregivers, 125. *See also* grandparents; in-laws

responsibility: of new fathers, 73

Robson, Kay, 32–33

rolling over, 61, 83, 102
routines: establishing of, 95–96, 97–98
rubella vaccines, 64–65, 66

S

Sachs, Brad, 53, 213
safety: childproofing home and, 138–41, 202; family bed and, 100, 101; in first month, 48; pacifiers and, 137; solid foods and, 113; walkers and, 138
Schaffer, Judith, 35
Sears, William and Martha, 155
seborrheic dermatitis, 29
secure attachment, 155–57
senses, 13–14, 58–59
sensory threshold, 91, 92, 96, 150
separation anxiety, 121, 154–55, 189
sex of baby: disappointment with, 16
sexual feelings: toward baby, 184–85
sexual identity, 178–81, 184. *See also* gender differences
sexual intercourse, 51–53; family bed and, 100; painful, 23, 52; resumption of, 50–51, 52
Shapiro, Jerrold, 51
Shellenbarger, Sue, 108, 129
Shelov, Steven, 36–37
SIDS (Sudden Infant Death Syndrome), 68–71, 100
sight, 14, 17, 31, 49, 58, 67–68, 83; visual stimulation and, 37–38
Silverstein, Louise B., 11
singing, 177–78
sitters, 150, 189
sitting, 49, 67, 83, 102, 115

skin: protecting from sun, 79–80
skin problems, 80–82; diaper rash, 81–82, 97; insect-related, 80–81; in newborns, 28–29; sun-related, 80
sleep, 13, 32, 60, 95–101; active, 19; on back vs. stomach, 69; establishing regular schedule for, 95–96, 97–98; family bed and, 99–101; middle-of-the-night wake-ups and, 84, 98–99; quiet, 18–19; rules of thumb for, 96–98
SleepTight, 44
slings, 79
smell, 14, 58
smiles, 50, 74, 95
smoking near baby, 69
Snarey, John, 72, 86, 106, 109
social development. *See* emotional/social development
solid foods, 110–13, 116, 206, 207; determining readiness for, 110–11; making your own, 113–14; reasons for delaying introduction of, 110; tips for, 111–13
soothing, 97, 104, 170
Spangler, Doug, 133
splotches, 29
spoiling, 100
squirming around, 61
stair climbing, 164, 182
standing, 67, 83, 102, 142, 153, 172, 182, 197
Stayton, Donelda, 203–4
Stayton, William, 52
Steinberg, David, 56, 132, 145
stranger anxiety, 94, 116, 131, 143, 149–50, 189

sucking, 31, 49, 68; on pacifiers, 44, 137; as reflex, 39; on thumbs, 137
Sullivan, S. Adams, 47
sun: protecting baby from, 79–80
sunburn, 80
sunglasses, 80
sunscreen, 81
support groups, 133–35
swaddling, 46, 61
symbolic thinking, 173
synchronous communication, 34

T

talking to baby: avoiding baby talk in, 59; in first week, 19–20; positive long-term effects of, 205
taste, 13, 58
taxes: child care and, 128
TB tests, 66
teething, 60, 136, 204, 209
telecommuting, 107, 108–9
temperament of baby, 89–96, 180; attachment and, 162; major change in, 186; nine traits of, 90–92; overcoming your negative feelings about, 93–94; stranger anxiety and, 150; temperament of parents vs., 94; using your knowledge about, 94–96; weaning and, 208
term insurance, 193, 194–96
Thomas, Alexander, 89
thumbsucking, 137
touch, 58–59
touching games, 119–20
toys, 22, 36, 75, 119–20; good vs. bad, 121; new, refusing to play with, 94; safety concerns and, 141. *See also* games; playing

tracking games, 38, 121–22
Trelease, Jim, 36, 76
trips, 187–91; activities at destination in, 188–89; all-purpose travelbag for, 190; car travel and, 189–90; plane travel and, 190–91; planning for, 187–88; what to bring on, 188
Tyson, Eric, 195

U
Ulene, Art, 36–37
umbilical cord stump, 29
universal life insurance, 194
unpredictability level, 91, 92, 95–96

V
vaccinations, 60, 61–65; electing not to have, 61; list of (chart), 62–65; typical schedule for, 66
variable life insurance, 194

vegetables, 111
verbal development: at 1 week, 14; at 1 month, 32; at 2 months, 50; at 3 months, 68; at 4 months, 84; at 5 months, 103; at 6 months, 116; at 7 months, 131; at 8 months, 143; at 9 months, 154; at 10 months, 173; at 11 months, 183; at 12 months, 198
vision. *See* sight
visitors, 25
visual stimulation, 37–38

W
walkers, 138
walking, 197
walks: crying and, 44
waterbeds, 101
weaning, 205–9; bad times for, 209; from bottle, 206–7, 208; from breast, 205–6, 208–9; reasons for, 206

weight: growth rate and, 35–36; lost by newborns, 35
well-baby checkups, 61–66
White, Burton, 135–37, 162, 205
whole life insurance, 193
wipers, 21
withdraw/approach level, 90, 92, 94, 150
Wolff, Peter, 31, 67
work: arriving home from, 146; balancing family and, 105–10, 146–47, 170–71, 215; in home office, 107, 108–9; less-than-full-time options for, 107–8; reevaluating relationship with, 85–86; schedule changes and, 106, 108; spillover between family life and, 109–10

Y
yogurt, 111

CARTOON CREDITS

© 1997 George Abbot from The Cartoon Bank,™ Inc.: pp. 15, 199; © 1997 Donna Barstow from The Cartoon Bank,™ Inc.: p. 159; © 1997 Frank Cotham from The Cartoon Bank,™ Inc.: pp. 24, 37; © 1997 Joseph Farris from The Cartoon Bank,™ Inc.: p. 107; © 1997 Ed Frascino from The Cartoon Bank,™ Inc.: pp. 175, 180, 185, 192, 212, 216; © 1997 Anne Gibbons from The Cartoon Bank,™ Inc.: p. 168; © 1997 William Haefeli from The Cartoon Bank,™ Inc.: pp. 26, 54; © 1997 John Jonik from The Cartoon Bank,™ Inc.: p. 120; © 1997 Arnie Levin from The Cartoon Bank,™ Inc.: p. 161; Robert Mankoff © 1986 from The New Yorker Magazine, Inc.: p. 134; © 1997 Peter Mueller from The Cartoon Bank,™ Inc.: pp. 93, 203; © 1997 J. P. Rini from The Cartoon Bank,™ Inc.: p. 85; © 1997 David Sipress from The Cartoon Bank,™ Inc.: pp. 2, 8, 72, 87, 104, 117, 160; © 1997 Peter Steiner from The Cartoon Bank,™ Inc.: p. 135; © 1997 Mick Stevens from The Cartoon Bank,™ Inc.: p. 181; © 1997 Jack Ziegler from The Cartoon Bank,™ Inc.: pp. 45, 97, 144, 148.

About the Author

Armin Brott, author of *The Expectant Father: Facts, Tips, and Advice for Dads-to Be* and a contributing writer to *BabyTalk* magazine, has written on fatherhood for the *New York Times Magazine, Newsweek,* the *Washington Post, American Baby* magazine, *Parenting* magazine, and many other periodicals. His weekly radio show on parenting is carried by one of the largest radio stations in the San Francisco Bay area. He and his family live in Berkeley, California.

The Complete

Retirement
Survival
Guide

Second Edition

Everything You Need to Know to
Safeguard Your Money, Your Health,
and Your Independence

PETER J. STRAUSS

AND

NANCY M. LEDERMAN

Checkmark Books®

An imprint of Facts On File, Inc.

The Complete Retirement Survival Guide, Second Edition

Checkmark Books
An imprint of Facts On File, Inc.
132 West 31st Street
New York NY 10001

Library of Congress Cataloging-in-Publication Data
Strauss, Peter J.
    The complete retirement survival guide : everything you need to know to safeguard your money, your health, and your independence / Peter J. Strauss & Nancy M. Lederman.—2nd ed.
        p. cm.
Rev. ed. of : The elder law handbook. c1996.
Includes index.
        ISBN 0-8160-4803-7 (hc)—ISBN 0-8160-4804-5 (pbk.)
1. Aged—Legal status, laws, etc.—United States—Popular works. I. Lederman, Nancy M. II. Strauss, Peter J. Elder law handbook. III. Title.
KF390.A4.S755 2003
346.7301′3—dc21   2002033929

Checkmark Books are available at special discounts when purchased in bulk quantities for businesses, associations, institutions, or sales promotions. Please call our Special Sales Department in New York at (212) 967-8800 or (800) 322-8755.

You can find Facts On File on the World Wide Web at
http://www.factsonfile.com

Text design by Erika K. Arroyo
Cover design by Cathy Rincon

Printed in the United States of America

MP Hermitage 10 9 8 7 6 5 4 3 2 1

This book is printed on acid-free paper.

Contents

Dedication and acknowledgments   xv

Preface   xvii

Introduction: Planning for your future   xxi

The demographic imperative   xxi
Future shock, future anxieties   xxi
Planning lessons from elder law   xxii
Multiple strategies for survival   xxiv
How to use this book   xxvii

PART 1: PLANNING FOR YOUR HEALTH
CARE NEEDS   1

Chapter 1. Doctors and hospitals   2

Choosing a doctor   2
Checking on your doctor   5
Getting the medical information you need   6
Your medical records   8
Privacy   8
How your doctor charges   9
Choosing a hospital   10
In an emergency   11
How hospitals are organized   12
Patient's Bill of Rights   13
Patient advocates   16
Regulating doctors and hospitals   16

Chapter 2. Making health care decisions   18

The emergence of patient rights   19
Consenting to treatment   20
Experimental procedures   23

Refusing treatment   24
The Patient Self-Determination Act   24
The "right to die"   26
Enforcing your rights   27

Chapter 3. Home and community care   29

Identifying your need   30
Activities of daily living (ADLs)   30
Types of programs   31
Senior centers   32
Adult day care   32
Hospice services   33
Respite services   34
Family caregiving   34
Community-based services and care   35
How to find home care   36
How to evaluate a home care agency   37
Private care managers   38
Paying for home care   39
Where to complain   40

Chapter 4. Nursing homes   41

Identifying your need   42
Finding a nursing home   42
How to evaluate a nursing home   43
Nursing home reforms   45
The nursing home contract   46
Admissions and discrimination   46
Waiting lists   47
Deposits and payments   47
Quality of care   48
Chemical and physical restraints   50
Bed-hold and bed reservations   51
Transfers and discharge   52
Resident's Bill of Rights   53
Sex in nursing homes   55
Nursing home abuse   56
Regulating nursing homes   56
Enforcing your rights   57

PART 2: MANAGING AND PAYING FOR HEALTH CARE
61

Chapter 5. Medicare
62

Eligibility for Medicare	63
Enrollment (Part A hospital coverage)	64
Enrollment (Part B medical insurance)	65
Medicare Buy-in Program	66
Coverage and exclusions	67
Medicare and Alzheimer's disease	69
Prescription drugs	70
Deductibles and copayment	71
Outpatient (ambulatory) care	72
Physician fees	73
Hospital costs and treatment	75
Discharge	76
Expedited review before discharge	77
Appealing a Medicare decision	79

Chapter 6. Health insurance
85

Types of health insurance	86
Policy terms and conditions	87
Preexisting conditions and waiting periods	89
Renewability	91
Checking the insurance company	92
Filing an insurance claim	93
Insurance regulation	95
Continuing coverage when you stop working	96
Medical savings accounts	98
Medigap supplemental insurance	99
Medicare coverage when you're working	103

Chapter 7. Managed care, HMOs, and Medicare + Choice
104

What is an HMO?	104
HMO coverage	105
Utilization review	106
Medicare + Choice	106
Enrolling in Medicare + Choice	106
Medicare + Choice coverage	107
Your Medicare + Choice rights	107

Switching Medicare + Choice coverage 108
Appealing an HMO decision—external review 109
Appealing a Medicare + Choice plan decision 110
Accreditation 111
Assessing the Medicare + Choice program 111

PART 3: FINANCING LONG-TERM CARE 113

Chapter 8. Medicare and long-term care 114
Post-hospital care under Medicare 114
Home health care under Medicare 116
Medicare and hospice services 119

Chapter 9. Medicaid and long-term care 120
Medicaid coverage 121
"Spending down" for Medicaid 122
Applying for Medicaid 122
Qualifying for Medicaid 123
Your home and other exempt assets 124
Protecting spousal resources 125
Protecting spousal income 128
Transferring assets 129
Trusts and Medicaid planning 131
Claims for recovery 134
Appealing a Medicaid decision 135
Medicaid's future 136

Chapter 10. Long-term care insurance 138
Evaluating the long-term care policy 139
Public-private partnership policies 142

Chapter 11. Reverse mortgages, annuities, and life insurance 145
Reverse mortgages 145
Qualifying for a reverse mortgage 147
Loan amount and payment options 147
Truth in Lending requirements 149
Reverse mortgages and government benefits 150
Finding a reverse mortgage 150
Annuities 151
Using life insurance 152

PART 4: LIFE PLANNING FOR YOU AND YOUR FAMILY   155

Chapter 12. Advance directives for health care   156

The three basic directives   157
Living wills   157
Specific treatment instructions   160
Instructions on nutrition and hydration   162
"Do not resuscitate" orders   162
Physician responsibility and liability   164
Living will statutes and legal formalities   165
5 Wishes   170
Health care proxies   171
Appointing a health care agent   172
Proxy formalities   175
Surrogate and family consent   176
Organ and tissue donation   178
Assisted suicide   180
Oregon Death with Dignity Act   181
Supreme Court rulings on physician-assisted suicide   183
Pain management statutes   186
End-of-life care   187
Enforcing your rights   188

Chapter 13. Property management systems   190

Power of attorney   190
Durable power of attorney   191
Springing power of attorney   192
Appointing an agent   193
Legal capacity and formalities   198
Dealing with banks   199
Revoking a power of attorney   200
Trusts   200
The role of trusts   202
Joint accounts   202
Designating a representative payee   204

Chapter 14. Planning for the disabled child   205

Services and entitlements   205
Supplemental needs trust   206
Appointing trustees   208

How a trust works   208
Education and housing   210
Legal protections   211
Finding help   212

Chapter 15. Guardians and protective services   213

The law of guardianship   214
The nature of incapacity   215
Determining incapacity   216
The role of the guardian   216
Choosing the guardian   218
The hearing process   219
Monitoring guardianship   221
Alternatives to guardianship   222
Elder abuse and the law   223
Identifying elder abuse   224
Reporting elder abuse   226
Investigation and services   226
Abuse in nursing homes   227

Chapter 16. Wills and estate planning   228

Understanding the basics   228
Your will and estate taxes   231
Bequests to spouses, children, and other family members   232
Disposing of your personal effects   235
Burial instructions   236
Disinheriting your heirs   236
Bequests to charities   237
Jointly owned property   237
Community property states   238
Witnesses and other formalities   238
Dying without a will   241
Renouncing an inheritance   242
The use of trusts   244

PART 5: YOU AND YOUR TAXES   247

Chapter 17. Planning and tax implications   248

Gift and estate taxes   249
Using the lifetime exclusion and marital deduction   252
Selected trust strategies   253

Income taxes   255
State taxes   259

PART 6: WORKING AND RETIREMENT   **261**

Chapter 18. Protections in the workplace   262

Age Discrimination in Employment Act   263
Your rights under the ADEA   263
Americans with Disabilities Act   267
Your ADA rights   268
Enforcing your rights   272
Back pay and other relief   275
Mediating employment disputes   276
State discrimination laws   278
Family and Medical Leave Act   279
State family leave laws   282

Chapter 19. Pensions, benefits, and IRAs   283

ERISA—the law of pension plans   284
Your right to participate   285
Vesting rules   287
Receiving pension benefits   288
Survivor pensions   289
Making a claim   290
Getting information on your pension   290
Appealing a claim decision   291
Pension plan terminations   292
Benefits and welfare plans   294
Changing employee benefits   295
Retiree benefits   296
IRA and retirement plan distributions   297

Chapter 20. Social Security and disability   303

Social Security eligibility and benefits   304
Retirement and early retirement   306
Applying for Social Security benefits   307
Working past retirement age   308
Taxing Social Security   309
Spousal benefits   309
Survivor benefits   310

Social Security overpayments   311
Social Security disability insurance   312
Disability eligibility and benefits   312
Determining disability   313
Continuing disability review   316
Supplemental Security Income   316
SSI eligibility   317
New transfer rules for SSI   318
Applying for SSI   320
SSI benefits   320
SSI disability rules   321
Ticket to Work program   321
Appealing a Social Security decision   322
Creditor protection for your benefits   324
Your Social Security number   324

PART 7: MEETING YOUR HOUSING NEEDS   **327**

Chapter 21. Tenants and homeowners   **328**
Tenants' rights   328
Housing regulation   329
Rental assistance   329
Shared housing   332
Help for homeowners   333
Sale leaseback   334
Selling your home   335
Moving to another state   336
Zoning and age discrimination   337
Fair housing laws   337
Some help from the ADA   340

Chapter 22. Adult living communities   **343**
Types of communities   345
Contractual agreements   346
Financial soundness   347
Entrance fees and payments   348
Housing and related services   349
Social and support services   350
Assisted living and nursing services   351
Government benefits   352
Residents' rights   352

Changes in your family   353
Regulating adult living communities   353

PART 8: GETTING HELP   355

Chapter 23. Protecting your rights   356

Asserting your position   356
"In-house" assistance   357
Appealing decisions   357
Federal and state help   358
The Older Americans Act   358
Legal problems of the elderly   358
Hiring a lawyer   359
Aging organizations and agencies   361

Appendix I. Where to get information or help   363

Appendix II. State agencies   374

Index   396

Dedication and Acknowledgments

To my family, young and not so young, who created the framework for my values and ideas

—P.J.S.

To my grandmother Freda Weinstein (1902–1992)

—N.M.L.

A lawyer's career is influenced by many persons, beginning with family, friends, and teachers in school, college, and law school, and later with mentors at the bar. This is certainly true for me, and I acknowledge my debt to all those who in their own way helped shape my life as a lawyer. But in particular, I wish to acknowledge the small group of lawyers who were the pioneers in elder law in the late 1970s when only a handful of us were working to develop this new area of expertise. Alan Bogutz of Tucson, Arizona; Steven Feldman of Philadelphia; Michael Gilfix of Palo Alto, California; Charles Robert of New York; and my former partner Robert Wolf of New York were just a few of those early practitioners who I worked with then to shape the development of elder law. To them and all the others who were part of the 1988 group of 26 founders of the National Academy of Elder Law Attorneys, I owe a great deal.

Before lawyers discovered the elderly, social workers and other gerontologists had served them for many years as counselors, advocates, and experts on the issues of aging. I was fortunate to have met these social worker–gerontologists early on and was deeply affected by their knowledge, expertise, and values. In the early 1980s I worked with the group that had formed the New York Network on Aging that later broadened its scope to build the National Association of Professional Geriatric Care Managers, an organization with which I have been proud to be affiliated for many years. Those first "care managers"—Lenise

Dolen, Adele Elkind, Jerie Charnow, Sarah N. Cohen, Leonie Nowitz, Ellen Lurie Polivy, and Bernice Sheppard—have left an indelible mark on our senior citizen population as well as on me.

Lastly, I must recognize the physicians, nurses, and psychologists who have led the medical profession in creating the specialty of geriatric medicine. By acknowledging that the medical needs of the elderly are different from others', and developing approaches and treatment strategies that recognize their different needs while respecting their rights and values, they have contributed greatly to the quality of life of our aging population.

—Peter J. Strauss

I join with Peter in saluting the lawyers, social workers, and medical professionals who pioneered services for the elderly. Their work laid a foundation that changed the way this country views its older citizens and those with disabilities.

In addition, I would like to acknowledge my personal debt to the many friends and colleagues who influenced my own career in education and elder law, and helped me shape my legal work to the needs of clients rather than neat little pigeonholes of law. Among them are Anthony Alvarado, Selma Belenky, Doreen DeMartini, Ellen Estrin, Shelley Greif, Charles Schonhaut, Peter Strauss, Jane Stern, Robin Willner, and Carol Ziegler. An added note of thanks goes to Jeanne Frankl for her role at the inception of this project. I also pay tribute to Jack Lipson, who was my best friend and teacher.

My family deserves special mention, particularly my parents, Marilyn and Paul Lederman; my sisters, Sherri Mandell and Loren Fogelson; and my brother, Elliot Weinstein. A unique debt of gratitude is reserved for my grandmother Freda Weinstein, who taught me what it is like to be an older person negotiating the world. As her caretaker in her final years, I drew much from her counsel and worldview as she benefited from my more "practical" help. This book is dedicated to her.

Sincere thanks go to our editors, Caroline Sutton, Bob Shuman, Drew Silver, and James Chambers, for their help in shepherding this book to publication.

Lastly, I must thank those older friends, relatives, and clients who have generously helped me to see the world through their eyes.

—Nancy M. Lederman

Preface

"I've got enough money for the rest of my life,
unless I want to buy something."

When Milton Berle says it, it's funny. For the rest of us, the financial and legal dilemmas of our later years are no laughing matter. That's why we've written *The Complete Retirement Survival Guide*—to give you something more than a punchline with which to face your future. This book provides what you and your family need, access to the vast array of legal rights, tools, and strategies available to face those dilemmas.

For both of us, writing this book represents a commitment spanning our professional lives and our personal beliefs. For Peter, it's the natural culmination of years spent on the front lines treating the problems of older people. When Peter first hung out his shingle as a specialist in legal problems of the aging, no one had ever heard of "elder law." It simply didn't exist.

There was only the growing subterranean culture of older Americans, neither rich nor poor, with multiple legal needs relating to aging. Peter's first elder law case, in 1980, gave him a memorable introduction to this world. Sally and David Franklin[1] were a retired couple faced with a common tragedy when David had a stroke. His condition left him needing help with simple tasks such as eating, toileting, and bathing.

The problem was money. The Franklins lived on a fixed income, nowhere near the price of the continued institutional care that David needed. They couldn't pay. Medicare wouldn't pay—not for the so-called unskilled care that David required. Medicaid would pay, but it was a welfare program. In order to qualify, David would have had to relinquish his income, leaving Sally with barely $300 a month on which to live. It was only a matter of time before she would be out on the street.

---

[1] Not their real names.

As a lawyer, Peter was able to devise a legal solution for the Franklins. Sally sued David for support, which rendered her court-ordered support immune from Medicaid. For the Franklins, it was a lifesaver. For Peter, it was an eye-opener. Here were people who had believed in the American dream, worked and struggled their whole lives trying to earn some needed security in their later years. Yet the system designed for their care, Medicare, excluded the very coverage they actually needed.

It was the unfairness that troubled him. Who decided that acute care patients would be favored over those with long-term needs? Wasn't that the very heart of discrimination against the elderly, punishing them for the very conditions to which they were most vulnerable? What kind of system, he asked himself, encouraged divorce, impoverishment, dependency?

Peter's questions led him away from courthouses and legal chambers to hospitals and nursing homes, to retirement communities and senior centers. He met couples trying to find help for their disabled children, older people trying to manage chronic illnesses on their own, patients fighting "the system" to get the care they wanted—and to end the care they didn't—and social workers trying to find patchwork solutions to insoluble problems. Again and again he heard how little was being done to meet the simplest needs of the elderly (and disabled people of all ages, often caught in the same trap). Over the next decade, elder law evolved as the Franklins' story was repeated again and again in law offices and hospital wards and the homes and communities of older people across the country.

For Nancy, a slip on the ice provided her entry to the world of elder law. Her 85-year-old grandmother Freda Weinstein was hospitalized for a month, then discharged to her home with no help. Nancy's years as an attorney didn't prepare her for the toll of caretaking. From finding home care to paying her grandmother's bills, making plans for future needs, dealing with doctors over medical treatment, and exercising her grandmother's health care proxy, Nancy was on the front lines as a consumer and as her grandmother's advocate.

Although by this time Peter had been joined by other practitioners working on the legal problems of the aging, for consumers there was little help or information available. What was available was generally useless, or worse, misinformation. Nancy was able to get the guidance she needed because of her legal experience in the field of public education, working on behalf of children and the disabled. As an attorney, she knew where to go. The contrast was stark: on the one hand, lack of information—and a ton of misinformation; on the other, information and help for those who knew how to get it.

So we teamed up to write *The Complete Retirement Survival Guide,* to get that information to the people who need it. It could not have been written 20 years before. It had to wait for elder law to develop as a separate area. But it could not have waited another minute. We could not have been more gratified by the response to the first edition. People literally came up to us on the street to thank us for the advice they found in the book. It was as if a door had been opened and they had been allowed to enter. For both of us, elder law is about more than enforcing the laws written in books; it's about helping people shape their lives and their destinies. Whether dealing with a crisis or planning for the future, we believe in forcing changes through traditional and not-so-traditional solutions and educating the community about the need for change.

Education is key. Americans' rising awareness of the problems facing the elderly has forced the passage of dozens of laws on nursing home practices, patients' rights, age discrimination, and insurance reform. Since this book was first published, there have been sweeping changes in Medicare, long-term care insurance, assisted living, retirement plans, and health care laws. Educating the public about these subjects is as important now as ever before.

Today, David Franklin's bills would be paid, and Sally Franklin would have a "community spouse resource allowance," which in New York would allow her to keep up to $90,660 of marital assets, a monthly income of at least $2,266.50, and her home. These rights came into being *because of* Sally and David and all the others like them who fought back.

As we go to press on this second edition, some politicians are now advocating rolling back these reforms. Yet who could sensibly argue for return to a system that would allow David Franklin to be cared for in an unsafe or unsanitary nursing home? What moral argument could justify forcing Sally Franklin to the poorhouse?

Injustice invariably creates legends out of ordinary people caught in extraordinary circumstances. The aging community has just such a pantheon of heroes and martyrs:

- *Estelle Browning, the Florida widow whose living will was ignored by the hospital, which insisted on administering artificial hydration and nutrition against her expressed wishes.*
- *Jean Elbaum, the comatose patient who was continued on a feeding tube against her wish not to be kept alive by tubes and medication.*

- *Murray Elbaum, who was forced to court to enforce his wife Jean's rights and then given a bill by the nursing home for $120,000 for her medical care, care that had been administered over his objections and in contradiction to his wife's wishes.*
- *Edward Winter, who after watching his wife's death in horror, had executed a do-not-resuscitate order on his own behalf. Hospital workers ignored his written orders, causing him to live on in pain for two years after an unwanted resuscitation.*
- *John Kingery, the 82-year-old man suffering from Alzheimer's disease who was abandoned at a racetrack by a daughter unable to care for him.*
- *Maggie Kuhn, forced to retire from a church job at age 65, who went on to found the Gray Panthers.*
- *Karen Ann Quinlan, age 21, kept alive in a persistent vegetative coma by artificial feeding, whose parents' fight to disconnect their daughter's respirator led to the first judicial decision on the right to die.*
- *Nancy Cruzan, age 25, kept alive in a persistent vegetative coma by artificial feeding, whose parents fought to the United States Supreme Court for the right of their daughter's wishes to determine her fate.*
- *Timothy Quill, the Rochester, New York, physician who went public at great personal risk to himself to tell the story of how he helped Diane, his terminally ill patient suffering with painful cancer, to die.*

The list goes on and on. Add to it Sally and David Franklin and Freda Weinstein and the thousands of anonymous older Americans relying on Medicare for their health care and unprotected when illness struck, or being tube-fed in nursing homes against their will, or left in the care of abusive caretakers, or left without any help at all for the simple tasks involved in managing their lives.

For both of us, elder law is about educating people about their rights—and giving them the tools to advocate on their own behalf. We dedicate this book to all of them and the rights they've helped win for all of us.

—Peter J. Strauss
—Nancy M. Lederman

Introduction:
Planning
for Your Future

Planning for the future, once just a matter of a steady job and a savings passbook, today requires a cadre of experts to steer you through the unknown. The prospects are hardly glowing. As you grow older, you and your family face the possibility of reduced spending power, rising health care and insurance costs, loss of health benefits both on the job and in retirement, pensions in jeopardy, and changing housing needs. If you're feeling the pinch, you're not alone. According to a recent *New York Times* poll, three out of four workers expect they or their colleagues will face a financial crisis when they retire.

THE DEMOGRAPHIC IMPERATIVE

To some extent, this is the result of phenomenal demographic changes in the United States. During the last two decades the older population has grown more than twice as fast as the rest of the population. The median age in the country, 35.3 years in 2000, is expected to top 40 by 2030. Life expectancy, less than 50 years in 1900, reached an all-time high of 76.9 years in 2000.

In sheer numbers, the increase is staggering. At the beginning of the 20th century, only one out of 25 Americans was over 65. By the year 2000, one out of every seven—a whopping 35 million—was 65 or older. In 2020, 70 million Americans will be over 65. The fastest-growing part of the population, those over 85, at 4.5 million now, will reach 8.5 million in the next 25 years.

FUTURE SHOCK, FUTURE ANXIETIES

These changes have been accompanied by a host of new problems that cut across all lines in American society. One of the greatest of these is health care. One-third of the nation's annual health care expenditures—now reaching upward of $1.3 trillion in 2002—goes to those over 65. Yet despite these enormous outlays, the health care system fails the elderly and people of all ages with disabilities because funding is not available for their long-term and custodial care—forcing them into poverty to obtain needed assistance from Medicaid.

The cost of this system has sent Congress scrambling for changes to limit Medicaid spending and force reforms in Medicare. Yet Medicare, the Great Society program designed for the elderly, does not provide enough. Worse, it discriminates against the elderly. Medicare funding is provided solely for acute illness and is not available for the long-term and custodial care that characterizes the needs of so many elderly people. It does not cover what they actually need—help with managing their lives. Nearly 70 percent seek or receive help with day-to-day tasks such as preparing meals or dressing or managing money.

One out of five Americans over 65 have disabilities; an estimated 43 percent of this sector will need long-term care during their lifetimes. Only 1.5 million currently reside in nursing homes, representing 4–5 percent of the nation's elderly population. In the next five years, the number will reach 2 million; by the year 2025, 3 million beds will be needed to deal with a population of nearly 70 million older Americans.

In the absence of home care and community assistance, caretaking falls disproportionately on wives and daughters—today's working women. Of 25 million caregivers in the United States, an estimated two-thirds are juggling careers or taking early retirement in order to provide care for an elderly relative. Nearly 40 percent of women workers over 55 are working part time. Elder abuse, largely unreported, is on the increase both at home and in institutions; an estimated 1.5 million older Americans are victims of financial or personal abuse.

At the same time, medical technology has posed new dilemmas in medical ethics, raising issues about treatment at the end of life and pushing courts and legislatures to address a whole new batch of ethical questions about personal autonomy—your right to make decisions to control your life. And the questions become even more difficult for the increasing number of family and friends who are called upon to make decisions for others.

PLANNING LESSONS FROM ELDER LAW

If you're like most people, you've planned for good times and ignored the possibility of bad, hoping they wouldn't catch up with you. The irony is that the longer you live the longer the odds are against you, especially if you aren't prepared.

Consider these questions:

- Can I get decent care for my parents, in or out of a nursing home? Where will the financing come from?
- Is my money protected in the event of a health crisis in my family?
- Will my wishes about my health care treatment be respected if I'm incapacitated?
- How secure is the future of my disabled child?
- Will I be able to find appropriate housing or living arrangements as my needs change?

Elder law was founded on these dilemmas, to help find solutions for these problems and to find a way to safeguard your own future and the future of your parents and your children. This rapidly evolving area of law deals with legal and management problems that may result from aging, illness, or incapacity, reflecting the pace of change affecting older Americans.

The problems of older people tend to fall into more than one category, creating multiple dilemmas that demand creative and unconventional strategies. Elder law offers solutions for many of these problems—on a short- and long-term basis—that cut across traditional legal categories:

- Living wills and health care proxies to ensure you have a say in your medical treatment
- Powers of attorney and trusts to help manage your property and secure your assets
- Enforcing rights to Medicare and other government benefits
- Medicaid planning to qualify for government benefits
- Long-term care insurance and other financing tools
- Home care and support programs for staying in the community
- Nursing home reforms
- Reverse mortgages to obtain financing on your home

Since Medicare and Medicaid were signed into law in 1965 and the Older Americans Act in 1966, laws passed on behalf of the elderly have included reforms in supplemental Medicare ("Medigap") insurance, long-term care insurance, nursing home reforms, guardianship protections, prohibitions on age discrimination and discrimination on account of disability (on the job and in housing), family leave laws, employee retirement laws, pension guarantees, fair housing laws, and living will statutes.

MULTIPLE STRATEGIES FOR SURVIVAL

Older people face daily decisions ranging from health care issues to financial planning to basic living arrangements. Unfortunately, too little information about how to deal with these questions—or too much misinformation—has found its way to the general public. People facing retirement need hard facts to protect their independence and their resources. So do people already retired, people over age 55 or with a parent over age 55, anyone who is disabled, or anyone with a disabled family member. That's what the following pages are about. An understanding of the universe of life planning can help you identify your goals and formulate strategies to achieve them. Specific planning and action steps will help you to focus on your concerns and explain how financial strategies and legal protections work for your benefit—so you can understand what your options are and how you can proceed.

Part 1: Planning for Your Health Care Needs

For older Americans and their families, health is their most precious asset—and the one most vulnerable. This part is devoted to a discussion of your health care needs—from identifying your needs and getting appropriate care to financing the health care you receive.

We begin in Chapter 1 with a brief tour of the health care system, including the doctors and hospitals who provide your first line of defense. In Chapter 2, we discuss your rights in making medical decisions about your care. Chapter 3 tells you about options for care in your home and the community, and Chapter 4 describes nursing homes and your rights and options under federal and state law.

Part 2: Managing and Paying for Health Care

For most people, the most important questions are how to find quality care and how to pay for it. These questions assume even greater urgency in a crisis. In Part 2, we show you how to make sure you can pay for the health care you need. In Chapter 5, we discuss your rights under Medicare and the insurance coverage provided by the United States government for those over 65 and younger persons with disabilities, and note recent changes and trends. In Chapter 6, we discuss private insurance and supplemental coverage and explain the protections designed to help you hold onto that coverage. In Chapter 7, we extend our analysis to managed care programs, HMOs, and Medicare + Choice.

Part 3: Financing Long-Term Care

In this section, we introduce you to a number of tools that may be useful for long-term care financing. In Chapter 8, we take a look at the options that may be available to you through Medicare, and in Chapter 9, we explain the ins and outs of Medicaid planning, to ensure you and your family won't have to be impoverished to receive the health care services you may need. In Chapter 10, we discuss the benefits of long-term care insurance, and in Chapter 11, we take a look at a few other financing ideas that may be of help—reverse mortgages, annuities, and life insurance.

Part 4: Life Planning for You and Your Family

Many people believe, mistakenly, that life planning is for the wealthy. But most people, rich or not, have the same goals—health, enough assets and income to ensure support for themselves and their spouses, and a cushion for a possible crisis or chronic long-term care needs.

Life planning is about tools that can help you achieve your goals. We start with health: In Chapter 12, we tell you about health care decision making, how you can protect yourself with advance directives, and how these same documents can help you make decisions on behalf of others.

Then we turn to other planning tools. Chapter 13 tells you about financial planning—and the use of the power of attorney, perhaps the most important legal tool you'll ever need. We explain what a trust is, what it can and cannot do for you, how to avoid common pitfalls, and whether "avoiding probate" is really the best course for you.

Chapter 14 gives you a short tour of planning instruments for a disabled child. In Chapter 15, we talk about options available for those no longer able to make their own decisions, from guardianships to other protective services. We also discuss the increasing problem of personal and financial elder abuse, among families and in institutions, and describe options available for its many victims.

For many, making a will is the primary vehicle for financial planning for a spouse or children. This becomes even more difficult when you consider the possibility of your spouse's need for greater health care in the future—and how provisions you make may affect his or her eligibility for needed government benefits. We discuss wills and estate planning, and the implications for taxes and Medicaid, in Chapter 16.

Part 5: You and Your Taxes

One element of planning for the future is a consideration of potential tax obligations. Shifting funds for Medicaid planning, creating trusts, using financial strategies such as reverse mortgages or accelerated death benefits to reap cash flow—all of these may have significant implications for your tax situation. Chapter 17 discusses taxes for older citizens—including gift and estate taxes, income taxation of Social Security benefits, and the effect of tax laws on Medicaid planning.

Part 6: Working and Retirement

Recent years have seen a small revolution in work in the United States. The linear path from trainee to retiree has been replaced with a new and often bewildering maze of options. Already one in three workers is over 55—more than 21 million people currently in the workforce—and the number will increase by 50 percent over the next two decades. Another 4 million unemployed Americans over the age of 55 are ready and able to work.

This section offers a short course on issues that you may face while you're working and after you retire. Chapter 18 tells you how to identify and deal with age discrimination practices at work and the ins and outs of family leave. Chapter 19 discusses pension and retirement plans and benefit protections. In Chapter 20, we give you the grand tour of Social Security retirement and disability benefits.

Part 7: Meeting Your Housing Needs

Surveys indicate that more than 90 percent of people over 55 want to remain in their own homes, and most do. For older people, housing expenses represent a major budget item. Those who do stay in their own homes often feel a financial pinch. For others, frailty and insecurity make other housing alternatives a necessity.

In Chapter 21, we discuss your status if you rent or if you own your home, explaining both the rights you have and the opportunities available to help you maintain control over your living arrangements. In Chapter 22, we discuss alternative housing arrangements for older Americans, ranging from continuing care facilities to assisted living communities. As these have gained in popularity, they have become a $15 billion industry.

Part 8: Getting Help

In order for your rights to be respected, you have to know how to enforce them. In Chapter 23, we explain the process of filing claims and making appeals, how to go about finding a lawyer when you need one, and what agencies you may contact for help.

Resources: Appendixes I and II

At the end of this book, you will find a comprehensive list of government agencies, not-for-profit organizations, legal advocacy groups, aging societies, and other sources offering information and support. In the past few years, the Internet has developed as a major resource for older people seeking help. In this revised edition, we have included website addresses that should prove an invaluable resource for any problems you may encounter.

HOW TO USE THIS BOOK

One of the keys to planning your future is identifying the problems and knowing the options available to you. We help you sort through laws and regulations pouring forth from government to find the strategy fitted to your problem. Where state requirements vary, we point you to the law in your state. Where federal mandates rule, we tell you. We explain your rights at various levels of government so you can deal with complicated requirements as well as understand the amendments and reforms being discussed. Where your future is concerned, you need information about your rights today—and the consequences of government action on your rights tomorrow.

Your rights depend on the actions you take to enforce them. Throughout this book, we explain how to enforce your rights, from keeping accurate records and making your grievances known to filing claims with the right agencies.

This book was not written to replace a lawyer or to provide legal advice for any particular case. Interpretation of laws often turns on the facts of a particular case. And, as we've pointed out, laws change. With 51 legislatures at the federal and state level, it would be hard to imagine otherwise. Although we note some likely areas for change, we can't predict all possible changes nor what they may look like. But we do promise that if you follow the advice we've laid out for you, you'll be better prepared for any changes that may come.

In many cases, we recommend getting the advice of a professional—whether a lawyer, accountant, financial planner, or private care manager. But regardless of who you call, the responsibility for your life and your future is yours. Don't leave it to chance or depend on others to make the best decisions for you. Start planning now, before a crisis. And keep planning and revising your plans. Control of your future depends on your taking action in the present.

Part 1

Planning for Your Health Care Needs

For older Americans and their families, health is their most precious asset—and their most vulnerable one. We begin this part with a blueprint for ensuring good health care, from identifying your needs to getting appropriate care to exercising your right to determine what treatment you will and will not receive. (Later on, in Part 2, we'll show you how to make sure you can pay.)

We start with a brief tour of the health care system. Chapter 1 describes the system you must deal with, healthy or ill, when you go to the doctor and when you enter a hospital. Chapter 2 discusses your right to determine your own treatment—and your right to refuse treatment. (We'll show you even more ways to protect your rights to make decisions about your health care in Chapter 12.)

In health crisis, the most important question is how to find quality care. Chapters 3 and 4 tell you about available home and community care programs and nursing homes, and describe your rights and options under federal and state law.

1

Doctors and Hospitals

For most of us, the health care system is represented by doctors. They are the front-line troops who administer the prescriptions, the check-ups, the sage advice that keeps us well when we're healthy and gets us better when we're not.

Doctors, specialists, and hospitals, along with nurses and lab technicians—that's the health care system. Other major players in the system are the insurance industry and the government. In today's medical marketplace, whether you can get access to the doctor you want or an experimental treatment or a specific facility often depends on your insurance. The government provides medical benefits for millions of Americans through the Medicare and Medicaid programs.

Don't forget the most important participant in the health care community—the patient. With all our technological advances, we're still likely to treat the patient as the problem to be solved rather than as a participant in finding a solution.

Seeking and getting health care today is not so much knowing the system as understanding the pieces of a puzzle. In order to take care of your health and your family's health, you need to know how the puzzle fits together—so that you can understand your options and exercise your rights and responsibilities as a consumer as well as a patient.

CHOOSING A DOCTOR

Your choice of doctor may be the most important health care decision you will make. Everything else flows from that one decision. Your primary physician is the one who in all likelihood will give you routine medical care, treat you in illness and emergencies, perform laboratory tests and make diagnoses, refer you to specialists, and find you other services and facilities as needed. In everyday matters and crisis situations, this is the doctor who will be monitoring your care and explaining your options to you.

People are often forced to search for a doctor when they are least capable of doing it. Either they are sick or they are in an emergency situation, forced to rely solely on a blind recommendation or the luck of the draw at the local emergency room. Part of good health care planning is choosing ahead of time.

It's important to have a doctor you know and trust, and one you can talk to. In searching for and choosing a suitable doctor, the recommendations of family and friends can be very useful. So can referrals from your county medical association or local hospital.

Even if you are joining a health maintenance organization (HMO) or are covered by an insurance plan that restricts your choice of doctors, you generally can choose a primary care physician from among a roster of participating doctors. Remember, before choosing a doctor or allowing one to treat you, there are certain things you are entitled to know.

Education and experience. A doctor has completed four years of medical school following college, most likely followed by two years or more of postgraduate practice in residency. Upon passing a qualifying examination, he or she is licensed to practice medicine by the state.

Theoretically that's all a doctor needs to perform even the most difficult procedures, like open-heart surgery. However, that shouldn't be enough to satisfy you (nor would it be allowed by most hospitals).

Board certification. A doctor with expertise in a particular area of medicine may have certification of the specialized knowledge and qualifications to practice in that particular area. Board certification provides an extra measure of assurance that a doctor is trained and proficient in an area of practice. In order to become a board-certified specialist, a doctor must complete a prescribed course of training as a resident in that specialty, pass an examination, and satisfy other requirements established by the board in question.

Primary-care specialties include internal medicine, pediatrics, and obstetrics/gynecology, as well as family practice for those who specialize in care of the individual or family. You can get referrals to local members from the American Board of Internal Medicine (telephone 800/441-ABIM [2246]) and the American Academy of Family Practice (telephone 888/995-5700), or you can contact the American Geriatrics Society's Physician Referral Service online at http://www. healthinaging.org.

Certification in subspecialties is available from a number of boards. For example, the American Board of Internal Medicine certifies subspecialties in gastroenterology and medical oncology. The American Board of Internal Medicine and the American Board of Family Practice also certify competence in geriatric medicine. In order to have subspecialty certification, a doctor must first have certification in the umbrella specialty.

Certification is not available in some areas of practice and is relatively new in others. All together, approximately 124 specialty boards provide certification, although with significant variations in their requirements. The American Board of Medical Specialties is an umbrella organization of 24 specialty boards, such as the American Board of Internal Medicine, which are generally accepted as setting industry standards. In addition to specialty certification, member boards offer 50 subspecialty certifications.

How can I find out if my doctor is certified?

The American Board of Medical Specialties runs a special certification hot line at 866/ASK-ABMS (275-2267) or online at http://www.abms.org to check whether your doctor is certified with one of their boards.

If my doctor is board-certified, does that guarantee knowledge of all the latest technology and advances in the field?

Not necessarily. Your doctor's certification may be old, and once certified, not all doctors need to be recertified.

A number of specialty boards do require periodic recertification. For instance, in internal medicine, physicians must be certified every 10 years. Many doctors who are currently board-certified were "grandfathered" in under old rules, meaning they do not need to be recertified to keep their standing. Good doctors do keep up with changes in their field, regardless of their recertification requirements.

Don't the states have some sort of recertification procedure?

No. A number of states do impose continuing education requirements that compel doctors to complete a minimum number of continuing medical education course credits in order to keep their licenses. (State regulation is discussed later in this chapter.)

Is membership in a medical society or academy the same thing as certification?

Not all societies or academies are certifying boards, and it's difficult to distinguish among them. In general, membership in a medical society helps a doctor keep up with advances in the profession. There are some with rigorous requirements amounting to board equivalence.

Hospital affiliation. Affiliation ("privileges") with a particular hospital allows your doctor to admit you to that hospital and to treat you there as your attending physician (sometimes called *voluntary physician*). An internist or other primary care physician who is affiliated with a medical center is more likely to offer you greater access to a broad range of specialists. It's generally your primary care physician who makes these recommendations when you need them—and who will troubleshoot any medical problems you have.

A hospital can be held legally responsible for the actions of a doctor affiliated with it, especially where the hospital knew or should have known about any deficiencies in the doctor's performance. A hospital has an obligation to review the credentials of its attending physicians, including education credentials, any disciplinary actions and malpractice suits, and references. The hospital may limit an attending physician to those procedures the physician is qualified to perform, although there is no obligation that a hospital restrict a doctor's privileges for any given reason. Usually a hospital bases its decision on the type of practice the doctor has and whether the hospital will be able to handle admissions from that particular doctor.

Traditionally, attending physicians have been doctors in private practice. Recent changes in hospital organization have dramatically altered the relationship between hospitals and doctors, with more and more hospitals affiliated in networks with doctors. Thus far, networks have been shielded from legal accountability, but a 2002 Supreme Court ruling allowing state review may cause greater scrutiny and responsibility of both networks and member hospitals for doctors with whom they are more closely affiliated.

CHECKING ON YOUR DOCTOR

The general unavailability of public information concerning doctors is one of the disgraces of the medical profession. Oversight of doctors varies from state to state, and reporting requirements are generally minimal. Some states, such as New York and Pennsylvania, publish limited information on heart surgeons' mortality rates. Reports concerning doctors with outstanding malpractice claims against them are generally not made available to the public, although California, Florida, Idaho, Massachusetts, and Tennessee have begun providing data on malpractice suits.

Disciplinary information is one of the emerging consumer success stories of the technological age. All state medical boards now have websites, either their own sites or through the state department of health, and all but two have doctor-specific information on disciplinary charges. (The exceptions are South Dakota and Michigan.) Thirty-nine states have 10 years of information posted.

It's still hard to track those doctors who have been found guilty of professional misconduct in one state and moved to another. Hospitals have access to information on disciplinary actions against doctors through the National Practitioners Data Bank. Under law, the public is not entitled to this information. Only a handful of states—California, Florida, Idaho, and Massachusetts—report actions taken by hospitals against doctors.

You should check with your state department of health or licensing agency to determine whether your doctor has been charged with or found guilty of any disciplinary charges. Public Citizen's Health Research Group has developed a databank called *Questionable Doctors,* which offers summary information on doctors who have been disciplined. The online edition currently includes information on doctors from 12 states: California, Connecticut, Hawaii, Illinois, Indiana, Maine, Massachusetts, Michigan, New Hampshire, Ohio, Rhode Island, and Vermont. (See Appendix 1.)

GETTING THE MEDICAL INFORMATION YOU NEED

If you think your doctor is not paying enough attention to you, don't dismiss the thought as only in your imagination. Studies show that many doctors just don't listen to their patients. This is not just bad manners. It's bad medicine. It restricts the ability of the doctor to glean necessary information from the patient interview. This is especially important for older patients, who often have multiple complaints. A doctor who hears only the main symptom may be missing the big picture. Doctors who treat the elderly must be alert to underlying and additional symptoms.

Today's doctors have less time for patients in both managed care plans and traditional fee-for-service practices. Find one who will give you enough time. Don't let your doctor monopolize the conversation. You should do your part, too. Be prepared with a list of your complaints and symptoms, and have your questions written down in advance. Write down the doctor's answers, too, and any instructions you may be given.

Speaking up can be especially important for women. According to one study published in the *New England Journal of Medicine,* women have a 50 percent higher risk than men of getting inadequate levels of relief for pain.

Drug prescriptions. The *Journal of the American Medical Association* reports that almost one-quarter of patients 65 older are given inappropriate prescriptions. Older patients are also more susceptible to undesirable interactions from multiple drug prescriptions. Don't assume a reaction is the result of your old age. Make sure your doctor takes a complete drug history and discusses all your medication and possible side effects with you.

Diet and nutrition. Nutritional assessment and training have been shown to be useful in illness prevention and treatment for older patients. Yet doctors are for the most part uninformed about nutrition and fail to inquire about the nutritional habits of their patients. Insist that diet and nutrition be included in your discussions with your doctor.

Treatment in catastrophic illness. A recent study found that many doctors routinely prescribed aggressive treatment in end-of-life cases, regardless of patient wishes. Only a small percentage of physicians even knew when their seriously ill patients wanted to avoid cardiopulmonary resuscitation. Make sure your wishes are discussed with your doctor. (Your doctor should also be given a copy of your living will. Living wills are discussed in Chapter 12.)

Is a second opinion always necessary before surgery?

Yes. It may also be the last bargain in medicine. You should seek another opinion before surgery and whenever you diagnosis is serious or uncertain, your treatment is undesirable or simply not working, or you have any questions about your doctor's competence. Insurers support second opinions, which often save unnecessary surgery and other costly and unwanted procedures. If you can't find a doctor, the Medicare hot line at 800/MEDICARE (633-4227) will supply you with local referrals.

How can I find out more about my condition?

The information explosion has had one enormous benefit. Medical information once inaccessible to the layperson is no longer unavailable. Not only are research journals easy to locate, but there are any number of agencies to give you information on specific diseases, conditions, and symptoms.

If you have access to a computer and modem, health-related information databases will let you research specific diseases and print out articles from medical journals. A number of private companies also have emerged that offer to conduct research for you, for a fee. These can be very expensive, however, and are not covered by insurance. Medical journals and public access databases may also be available at your public library. (See appendixes at the end of this book.)

YOUR MEDICAL RECORDS

Reviewing your records increases your participation in and control of your health care. It also allows you to question or correct inaccurate information, a not uncommon occurrence. The use and dissemination of patients' medical records are regulated by the states. Many state and federal laws prescribe strict confidentiality concerning information and limiting release of your medical records.

- More than half the states have laws granting you direct access to your medical records, including Alaska, California, Colorado, Florida, Michigan, Minnesota, New Jersey, New York, South Carolina, and Wisconsin.
- In others, you may be restricted to a summary prepared by your doctor or the hospital, or you may have to obtain release through a physician or a lawyer.
- Federal law grants nursing home residents in Medicare and Medicaid facilities access to their medical records.
- Patients are also granted access to medical records held in federal facilities such as Veterans' Administration hospitals.

Ask! Many doctors and medical facilities will give you copies of your records if you just ask for them.

PRIVACY

With the rise of technology, the privacy of medical records has raised concerns. Medical records contain personal information about you—including any disabilities or disease, alcohol or drug abuse—information that can be used by current or prospective employers, insurers, creditors, and others to make decisions that might affect your life. For some, that may include abuse. Despite laws governing confidentiality, the risk of disclosure with advanced medical information systems and electronic claims processing is much higher.

To address some of these concerns, the federal government issued a so-called Privacy Rule as part of implementing the Health Insurance Portability and Accountability Act (HIPAA). As of April 2003, the rule guarantees patients access to their medical records and restricts the use of personal information. Health care providers must give patients a written privacy notice, explaining their right to protect their personal health information from unauthorized use or disclosure. Incidental use will still be allowed, and researchers will be allowed access to medical records with all personally identifiable information redacted, under certain circumstances. (A controversial provision requiring doctors to get written consent from patients before using their health information for treatment, payment, and health care operations was dropped from the final version.)

Some additional protection can be found in the rule. Information from your medical records cannot be disclosed to your employer without consent. Drugstores are forbidden from selling your personal information to pharmaceutical companies or other commercial ventures.

Don't rely on others to protect your privacy! Always read medical forms and insurance claims before you sign them. You have always had the right to limit disclosure of information for treatment or reimbursement purposes.

And be careful when you're answering marketing calls or surfing the Internet. Several types of databases already have confidential information about you. Don't answer intimate questions on the phone or give out personal information. Be especially wary online. Make sure you know a site's privacy policies before you provide any confidential data.

HOW YOUR DOCTOR CHARGES

Because of upheavals in the health care industry, many doctors are joining with other doctors in managed-care organizations and networks, changing their fee structures and the nature of their medical practice. In addition, government regulations are setting more requirements on doctors, while insurers are second-guessing once-sacrosanct medical decisions.

For consumers, it's a very confusing time. Some of the changes you may find at your doctor's office may affect the quality or cost of the care you receive, and should be considered when choosing your doctor.

Traditionally, doctors have charged patients on a per-service basis with few controls. This led to a spiral of rising charges for overtesting, overtreating, and overprescribing. There was little incentive for doctors to practice preventive care to keep healthy patients well.

HMOs and managed care. Many doctors have joined managed-care organizations such as health maintenance organizations (HMOs) or more loosely configured networks of health care providers. In many of the groups, doctors or hospitals receive per-person payment instead of per-service payment. This is called *capitation.*

By joining, the doctor has agreed to accept certain lower fees. The patient may be liable for a small share of the cost, known as *copayment.* Under capitation, there is a shared financial risk and greater incentives for physicians to practice preventive medicine. The downside of this system is that it may result in less incentive to provide quality care on an individual basis.

Doctors' fees. A large portion of health care reforms has focused on lowering health care costs in general, and doctors' fees in particular. Insurance companies apply fee limits through their reimbursement rates, paying a percentage of what they deem to be "standard and customary." We explain how to deal with your insurance company in Chapter 6, but remember that you can also negotiate with your doctor for lower rates so you won't be unreasonably out-of-pocket.

As a result of federal reforms, there are fee limits for the amounts *all doctors* can charge Medicare patients. A number of states also restrict fees. (For an explanation of fee limits for Medicare patients, see Chapter 5, Physician Fees.)

CHOOSING A HOSPITAL

In choosing a hospital in nonemergency situations, you have two options. One is to have a doctor affiliated with a good hospital located near your home. Remember that when you pick your primary care doctor, you're picking a hospital, too. The hospital your doctor is affiliated with is not only where you may likely wind up if you need hospitalization, but where your doctor may send you for laboratory tests, CT scans, and other outpatient procedures.

The other choice (when you have time to plan for hospital services) is to go where the type of surgery or procedure you need is performed most often. The more complex the procedure, the smarter it is to go where the specialty is. Hospitals have specialties in which their work and reputations are excellent. Studies have shown that the more often a doctor or hospital does a procedure, the more likely the results will be better for the patient.

Another consideration for older patients is *discharge planning.* This is especially important for those going to rehabilitation services. Many hospitals offer special programs for senior citizens.

What information is available? Hospitals are evaluated and accredited by the Joint Commission on Accreditation of Healthcare Organizations, which accredits four out of every five of the nation's hospitals. Accreditation is dependent on inspection every three years, based on a variety of measures. The Centers for Medicare and Medicaid Services (CMS), which certifies facilities for federal reimbursement purposes, publishes quality-of-care data for Medicare patients. States publish some information on hospital patients. New York has consumer information guides to its hospitals, which show the most common procedures and their cost.

IN AN EMERGENCY

Emergency rooms are busy places. In 2000, 95 million people went to an emergency room. For many, the emergency room (ER) *is* their health care system. Unfortunately, for them and for you, this drives up the cost of ER care—and makes getting in harder and more time-consuming.

Under federal law any institution with emergency facilities must treat you if you have an urgent medical problem. This is commonly referred to as the "antidumping" law, although its formal title is the Emergency Treatment and Active Labor Act (EMTALA). It prohibits private hospitals from turning away uninsured patients needing emergency care.

No matter what the particular intake procedures of the hospital you go to, you will begin with *triage,* where someone—most likely a nurse or a physician's assistant—will make a preliminary evaluation of your medical condition. This evaluation determines how long you will wait. ER workers can be wrong. If you're in pain or think you need to see someone sooner, speak up! It's easy to be forgotten in an ER. Insist on having a doctor examine you to assess the urgency of your condition.

Do all hospitals have emergency rooms?

No. One response of strapped hospitals to antidumping laws has been to eliminate their emergency care service altogether. However, some states require all hospitals to have an emergency room.

In an emergency, am I entitled to be admitted for treatment?

You're entitled to medical screening and treatment for an emergency medical condition. If you have an urgent medical problem and present yourself at a hospital with an ER, you may have the legal right to be treated. And you can't be transferred to a different facility, unless you're in stable condition (or a doctor certifies that the benefit of transfer outweighs the risk and the receiving hospital has agreed to accept you). But beware—proposed changes to federal regulations threaten to limit the services available to you, and at least one federal court has ruled that your right to "stabilization" treatment only applies if you are transferred.

Make sure a doctor examines you to determine appropriate treatment! If you aren't treated and suffer damage, you may still have grounds for a malpractice suit against the hospital. Some jurisdictions also provide penalties for hospitals that deny you emergency care.

Once the emergency is dealt with, you may need continued care. This no longer qualifies as an emergency, and whether you must be admitted to the hospital at that point varies from state to state.

Can I be refused emergency care if I can't pay?

No. You have a right to emergency treatment for an emergency condition regardless of your ability to pay. One little-known fact is that many hospitals receive construction funding under the federal Hill-Burton Act, passed in 1946, which requires them to accept a number of indigent patients free of charge. You can inquire at the hospital about eligibility and how to apply for these services. (If you can't pay, you may also be able to qualify for Medicaid. For more, see Chapter 9.)

HOW HOSPITALS ARE ORGANIZED

Hospitals are going through dramatic changes, as is the rest of the nation's health care system. In many parts of the country, hospitals have cut costs, merged with other institutions, and redefined the services they offer. In some communities, they are going under. Across the board, traditional notions of hospital structure—like the delivery of all health care services—are being questioned. These changes have both direct and indirect implications for consumers.

Traditionally, hospitals have been classified by both ownership (whether they are public or private) and specialties. In regard to ownership, don't be confused by misleading nomenclature. *Voluntary* or *charitable* hospitals are generally private, nonprofit organizations. Private hospitals are called *proprietary.* Not all hospitals provide all services. Specialty institutions may treat a particular disease or condition, such as heart disease. Some *teaching hospitals* maintain close affiliations with medical schools.

Who's in charge of my care?

Although a hospital as a corporation is run by its board and management, your health care is in the hands of the medical staff. This may be either your private physician or resident doctors, or a combination of both. Your attending physician, if you have one, is in charge of your care. If you don't have an attending physician and you've been admitted to the hospital, there will be a doctor, generally a resident on staff, assigned that responsibility. You have the right to know who that person is.

Do I have to be examined by residents, interns, and medical students?

You can refuse to be examined by medical students or hospital staff such as interns and residents (also known as PGY-1, PGY-2, and so on, for their "postgraduate year"). The person with the responsibility to make decisions about your care is the attending physician. But remember, hospitals are caught between the dual missions of training doctors and providing patient care. Your care may be improved by the attention that comes with additional help.

PATIENT'S BILL OF RIGHTS

One of the first initiatives in the patient rights movement was the development of a bill of rights. This was developed over the years and has been adopted by the American Hospital Association as the Patient's Bill of Rights.

Most hospitals have adopted some version of it, and many states have adopted statutes enumerating patients' rights, including the right to know who's treating them, to reject care by students, to be informed about doctors' financial interests in hospitals if it would affect health care, to consent to or refuse treatment ("informed consent"), to be told about the alternatives for treatment and surgery, and to receive a copy of hospital medical records.

Federal law has also adopted some portions. Hospitals are required by federal law to notify patients of their right under state law to refuse medical treatment.

Legislative note: *As of 2003, passage of a federal Patients' Bill of Rights has become a political football, and both houses of Congress have passed competing versions. The key difference between the two bills are that the Senate bill gives patients more rights for holding HMOs accountable. We predict more action in this area, following the judicial determination by the U.S. Supreme Court that states can regulate HMOs. At least one federal appeals court has already ruled that HMOs can be sued for medical malpractice when they made treatment decisions.*

PATIENT'S BILL OF RIGHTS*

1. The patient has the right to considerate and respectful care.

2. The patient has the right to and is encouraged to obtain from physicians and other direct caregivers relevant, current, and understandable information concerning diagnosis, treatment, and prognosis.

   Except in emergencies when the patient lacks decision-making capacity and the need for treatment is urgent, the patient is entitled to the opportunity to discuss and request information related to the specific procedures and/or treatments, the risks involved, the possible length of recuperation, and the medically reasonable alternatives and their accompanying risks and benefits.

   Patients have the right to know the identity of physicians, nurses, and others involved in their care, as well as when those involved are students, residents, or other trainees. The patient also has the right to know the immediate and long-term financial implications of treatment choices, insofar as they are known.

3. The patient has the right to make decisions about the plan of care prior to and during the course of treatment and to refuse a recommended treatment or plan of care to the extent permitted by law and hospital policy and to be informed of the medical consequences of this action. In case of such refusal, the patient is entitled to other appropriate care and services that the hospital provides or transfer to another hospital. The hospital should notify patients of any policy that might affect patient choice within the institution.

4. The patient has the right to have an advance directive (such as a living will, health care proxy, or durable power of attorney for health care) concerning treatment or designating a surrogate decision maker with the expectation that the hospital will honor the intent of that directive to the extent permitted by law and hospital policy.

   Health care institutions must advise patients of their rights under state law and hospital policy to make informed medical choices, ask if the patient has an advance directive, and include that information in patient records. The patient has the right to timely information about hospital policy that may limit its ability to implement fully a legally valid advance directive.

5. The patient has the right to every consideration of privacy. Case discussion, consultation, examination, and treatment should be conducted so as to protect each patient's privacy.

6. The patient has the right to expect that all communications and records pertaining to his/her care will be treated as confidential by the hospital,

---

*These rights can be exercised on the patient's behalf by a designated surrogate or proxy decision maker if the patient lacks decision-making capacity, is legally incompetent, or is a minor.

except in cases such as suspected abuse and public health hazards when reporting is permitted or required by law. The patient has the right to expect that the hospital will emphasize the confidentiality of this information when it releases it to any other parties entitled to review information in these records.

7. The patient has the right to review the records pertaining to his/her medical care and to have the information explained or interpreted as necessary, except when restricted by law.

8. The patient has the right to expect that, within its capacity and policies, a hospital will make reasonable response to the request of a patient for appropriate and medically indicated care and services. The hospital must provide evaluation, service, and/or referral as indicated by the urgency of the case. When medically appropriate and legally permissible, or when a patient has so requested, a patient may be transferred to another facility. The institution to which the patient is to be transferred must first have accepted the patient for transfer. The patient must also have the benefit of complete information and explanation concerning the need for, risks, benefits, and alternatives to such a transfer.

9. The patient has the right to ask and be informed of the existence of business relationships among the hospitals, educational institutions, other health care providers, or payers that may influence the patient's treatment and care.

10. The patient has the right to consent to or decline to participate in proposed research studies or human experimentation affecting care and treatment or requiring direct patient involvement, and to have those studies fully explained prior to consent. A patient who declines to participate in research or experimentation is entitled to the most effective care that the hospital can otherwise provide.

11. The patient has the right to expect reasonable continuity of care when appropriate and to be informed by physicians and other caregivers of available and realistic patient care options when hospital care is no longer appropriate.

12. The patient has the right to be informed of hospital policies and practices that relate to patient care, treatment, and responsibilities. The patient has the right to be informed of available resources for resolving disputes, grievances, and conflicts, such as ethics committees, patient representatives, or other mechanisms available in the institution. The patient has the right to be informed of the hospital's charges for services and available payment methods.

How do I enforce my rights?

Even where a written bill of rights is routinely distributed, patient rights may not always be respected. Too often, health care providers do not receive adequate training. One of the advances that has most helped in this area is the "patient advocate," described in the next section.

PATIENT ADVOCATES

Most hospitals have a *patient advocate* (also called a *patient representative* or *patient ombudsman*), who can provide the communications link between the patient and the hospital. Often this is just of a matter of taking the time to explain to you and your family what is going on. If you have a complaint, the patient advocate will discuss it with you and take it to hospital administrators or doctors.

Patient advocates are knowledgeable about the options available to you and can explain your rights in exercising those options, help you obtain a second opinion, or assist you in challenging a hospital decision to discharge you. They can be of particular help in situations in which you are refusing treatment or making decisions on behalf of someone else. (See Chapter 12 on health care directives.)

One caveat: Patient advocates, social workers, and others you encounter in a hospital may offer you helpful advice on qualifying for Medicaid. Before you follow *anyone's* advice on transferring or spending funds to make yourself Medicaid-eligible, make sure you consult a lawyer knowledgeable in the field. (Medicaid planning is discussed in Chapter 9.)

How do I find the patient advocate?

Information on how to find the patient advocate will be included in your hospital admission papers and posted or placed in your hospital room.

REGULATING DOCTORS AND HOSPITALS

State regulation comes in a variety of forms. In the first instance, states license doctors and hospitals, usually under the authority of the state department of health. If standards or conditions of licensure are not maintained, licenses can be suspended or revoked. While action against a hospital is rare, an increasing number of doctors have been disciplined for professional misconduct by state regulatory agencies. In 2001, more than 2,700 American doctors received reprimands or had their licenses suspended or revoked.

A 1996 report by Public Citizen's Health Research Group, however, charges that only one-third of those doctors found to have given substandard or negligent care were required to stop practicing temporarily or permanently; most retain their licenses and continue to treat patients. There is great variation in penalties from state to state.

Health care reforms and related economies are forcing states to look harder at their regulations. Hospitals, for example, are finding it harder to justify new or expanded services. Doctors who make referrals of patients for medical services in which they have a financial interest, a practice called *self-referral*, are finding themselves under criticism for conflict of interest. One survey showed that nine out of 10 doctors who write treatment guidelines have financial ties to the pharmaceutical industry, a relationship that is not usually disclosed.

Under federal law, doctors are prohibited from referring Medicare patients for clinical laboratory and radiological services in which they have a financial interest, and current proposals would broaden categories of prohibited services. Some states prohibit self-referrals or fee-splitting, while others have laws mandating disclosure.

If you have a problem with medical treatment or any other action by a doctor or hospital, you can make a complaint to the state department of health or your local medical society. Remember, complaints you make to the proper authorities may help protect the next unwary patient. (Check the appendixes at the end of this book.) If your complaint is of possible malpractice, you should also consult an attorney to determine if you have a valid claim or grounds for a lawsuit. (We discuss how to find an attorney in Chapter 23.)

2

Making Health Care Decisions

Decision making about one's life and medical care is a basic right of an autonomous human being. In health care as in many areas involving experts and professionals, individuals are only recently learning to make their own decisions and, perhaps more important, questioning the decisions of others in areas that have a direct bearing on their lives.

Each day medical science offers new technologies, new technologies offer new options, and new options create new dilemmas. With advanced technologies capable of keeping more and more people alive longer and longer, life-and-death issues have become both more complex and more common.

At the same time, patients have fought for and won the right to make decisions about their own health care, decisions that were formerly the exclusive province of medical practitioners. Compounding the difficulty for patients, they have to make these decisions at times of crisis, often under extreme stress.

Under optimal circumstances it would be hard to absorb all the information thrown at you—options, therapeutic benefits and risk factors, possible side effects—and all in scientific terms guaranteed to alarm even the most stout-hearted. Medical crises are rarely optimal circumstances. The more life-threatening the situation, the more difficult the decision; the more difficult the decision, the more stressful the situation. It's a vicious cycle.

While you're trying to determine what's best to do, others may be undermining your efforts, trying to take the choice away from you. When it comes to confronting life-and-death issues, there are no easy answers. But there are legal techniques that will empower you to assert your rights.

18

THE EMERGENCE OF PATIENT RIGHTS

The history of patient rights is surprisingly brief. Not so long ago patients could be subject to experimentation by doctors, without their knowledge or consent. Although the role of the patient has changed, the concept of patient rights is not new. As far back as 1914, in a landmark decision, New York's highest court ruled:

> Every human being of adult years and sound mind has a right to determine what shall be done with his own body; and a surgeon who performs an operation without his patient's consent commits an assault for which he is liable in damages.

The author of those words was Judge Benjamin Cardozo, renowned jurist of the New York State Court of Appeals who later served on the United States Supreme Court. In that one opinion, Judge Cardozo established your absolute right as a patient to determine your own treatment and the liability of those who fail to respect that right.

Patient rights and patient autonomy. Nancy Cruzan at the age of 25 had a tragic automobile accident in Missouri. She fell into what doctors call a "persistent vegetative state" and was kept alive only by artificial feeding. When her parents sought to disconnect the feeding tube, citing their daughter's wishes in the matter, the hospital refused. The Cruzans went to court.

Cruzan provided the ultimate test between medical authority and patient rights. Eventually the Missouri case went to the United States Supreme Court, which in 1990 ruled that there was a constitutional right to refuse artificial life support. The liberty interests of the individual under the 14th Amendment were held to be paramount. Nancy Cruzan had the constitutional right to determine her own care (in this case through her parents as her surrogate).

Not everyone is comfortable with patients' and their families' exercising their rights to make these "medical" decisions. Changes to the traditional patient-doctor relationship are resisted both within and outside the medical community. As the decision-making role of the doctor has diminished, patients have been transformed from unquestioning supplicants to wary consumers in dealing with doctors, hospitals, and insurance companies. There continues to be a large "care gap" between what patients want and what they get. That's why it's so important for patients to learn how best to exercise their rights—and the responsibilities that come with them.

CONSENTING TO TREATMENT

When you go to a doctor, there are certain assumptions that are understood by both parties. You have entered a relationship with expectations of each other.

- The doctor will examine you, either as part of a routine checkup or in response to specific complaints, or a combination of both.
- The doctor will evaluate your medical condition and, if appropriate, attempt to offer a diagnosis and possible treatment, or further tests to aid in diagnosis or treatment.
- The doctor will offer you treatment recommendations and options, fully explaining advantages and disadvantages, benefits and risks.
- You will decide whether to accept or reject the doctor's advice.
- You (or your insurance company, or Medicare) will pay for the service.

That's the extent of the relationship. If you don't want to have your blood drawn or X ray taken, you can refuse. No one may force you. In a nutshell, that's *informed consent:*

- *Informed:* Doctors provide information to patients to help them understand their condition and proposed treatments
- *Consent:* Patients agree to a course of treatment before it starts, to protect doctors from liability for things that go wrong

Before you undergo *any* medical treatment or procedure, you need to know what is planned for you and you need to agree to it. Informed consent requires full disclosure to you, the patient, of the risks and benefits of the proposed treatment, as well as any possible alternative treatments. Without this information, your assent is worthless, because you haven't been given the information that would make your consent "informed."

The average encounter soliciting your approval for a procedure will have more emphasis on the *consent* side of the equation than on the *informed.* This is due to the inherently unequal nature of the doctor-patient relationship.

Don't put your faith blindly in experts and professionals. Hospitals have systems to prevent errors, but systems break down. *Things go wrong.* Doctors prescribe medicines and forget to ask about allergies or other medications. Medicine gets delivered to the wrong patient, or the wrong patient gets delivered to the operating room. From *St. Elsewhere* to *E.R.,* comedies and dramas depict incompetence, larceny, and medical malpractice on a regular basis. Unfortunately, such horror stories are not confined to television.

A report published in the *New England Journal of Medicine* found that thousands of hospital patients have suffered similar negligence. Several well-known institutions have received national publicity for performing the wrong surgery on patients—wrong limb, wrong brain hemisphere, wrong patient—with tragic results. Medical errors are responsible for 44,000 to 98,000 deaths a year, according to a study by the Institute of Medicine. Often a big error is the result of a series of small mistakes, system flaws like inadequate recordkeeping, or mislabeled medications.

Don't assume that a procedure that you haven't approved is intended for you at all! Make sure anything that your primary doctor has not discussed with you beforehand is in fact intended for you.

And always get a second opinion before you agree to any high-risk treatment. Most insurance policies now require this, because it cuts down on unnecessary surgery.

Is informed consent required by law?

Yes. Treating you without your consent may constitute assault or battery. It may be grounds for a malpractice lawsuit. The right to informed consent is included in the American Hospital Association's Patient's Bill of Rights (see page 14). Written consent is merely documentation of your agreement. In most cases other than experimental treatments, writing itself is not required by any statute or regulation.

Nevertheless, you can wind up signing as many as three or more consent forms when you're in the hospital. Whether any of these is legally valid depends on the circumstances. Although a signed form can be used as "evidence" of informed consent, it does not necessarily preclude you from bringing a suit after treatment.

How specific does informed consent have to be?

You need to be informed of the risks and potential benefits of planned treatments, and of alternative treatments or procedures. These include the option and probable outcome of receiving no treatment. Serious side effects, however unlikely, should always be disclosed.

Consent is not simply a blanket agreement to treatment. If you're undergoing surgery, you have the right to authorize what will be done to you—and the right to say what will *not* be done to you. The law grants some leeway to surgeons confronting unexpected problems. If there is any question, discuss these matters with your surgeon beforehand.

For the most part, general consent forms prepared by hospitals have limited legal validity. The more specific your consent, the more likely it will be upheld as valid in any subsequent court proceeding. From a legal point of view, what counts is whether you were given the information you needed to make your consent meaningful.

Are there exceptions to the requirement that a patient give informed consent?

In an emergency situation, where there is no one available to authorize treatment, doctors may proceed without consent. This emergency authority is sometimes abused in institutional settings to give unwanted medication. Problems also arise in emergency situations when elderly people are given treatment by doctors and other personnel without knowledge of or in disregard of contrary prior instructions.

In cases where the patient is unable to give consent due to incapacity, doctors may sometimes proceed with consent from a designated health care agent or family members (*substituted consent*). Many adults with mental illness receive drug treatments with the consent of relatives or friends. (See Chapter 12.)

Doctors sometimes cite "therapeutic privilege" to withhold information. This may be done in limited circumstances when the doctor believes that disclosing it would have an adverse effect on the patient's condition, for example, on a depressed or critically ill patient.

My doctor is pressuring me to sign a consent form. What are my options?

If no medical emergency exists, get a second opinion. This is always your right. Your consent must be voluntary, without any coercion. Most insurance companies will back you up on this. Ask to talk with the hospital's patient advocate, who will explain your rights to you. Ask for time to think about it. And remember you can always alter the form, deleting or editing the words that make you feel uncomfortable.

The most important step to take with a consent form, as with any other paper you may be asked to sign, is: *Read it before you sign.* Your signature signifies both your understanding and your agreement.

- Don't sign what you don't understand.
- Don't sign what you don't agree with.
- Always get a copy of what you sign.

You are as important as the physician standing before you, and your wishes and requests for information must be respected and honored. That's only fair—and it's the law!

Remember, signing does not keep you from changing your mind during your treatment or bringing a lawsuit afterward if you were not properly advised or if you received negligent treatment.

EXPERIMENTAL PROCEDURES

Codes of behavior against human experimentation date back to two philosopher-physicians practicing in the 11th and 12th centuries, when Avicenna, who was Islamic, and Maimonides, who was Jewish, warned against using patients for medical discoveries and not treating them for their own good. Unhappily, this advice has not always been taken. In the United States, notorious examples of such experiments include syphilis treatment withheld from black sharecroppers at Tuskegee in the 1930s, penicillin withheld from servicemen in the 1950s, and cancer cells injected into elderly patients as recently at the 1960s, all in the name of research.

The doctrine of informed consent was developed in part to remedy this sorry history of human exploitation. In cases where experimentation is involved, more detailed and complete information is required. The patient must fully understand the experimental nature of the proposed treatment, the existence of other approved treatments in the protocol of the trial, the potential for known and unknown risks, and the probability of success.

In the institutional setting, federal regulations mandate review by an institutional review board (IRB) established to approve and monitor research projects. There are between 3,000 and 5,000 IRBs in this country, each composed of at least five members (one not affiliated with the organization). Most IRBs are associated with a hospital, university, or research institution, although they can also be found in managed-care organizations and government agencies. Specific review criteria must address the rights and welfare of the individual research subjects, the methods used to obtain informed consent, and the risks and potential benefits of the investigation. Approval by the institutional review board only signifies approval of the research being conducted; it does *not* mean that you have to consent to being a part of it. (In some cases, you may have no choice. There are some research projects for which IRBs waive the informed consent requirement, such as where only review of medical records is involved and there is no risk to patients.)

REFUSING TREATMENT

The corollary to informed consent is the right to refuse treatment. *If you have the right to consent to treatment, it necessarily follows that you have the right to refuse it.*

Traditionally, the right to refuse treatment has been based on your common-law right to bodily integrity, your constitutional right to privacy, and, under certain circumstances, your constitutional right to the free exercise of your religion. Theoretically at least, treatment performed against your will could be a form of negligence or assault.

According to the law—upheld in the Supreme Court's 1990 *Cruzan* decision—the decision to reject lifesaving treatment is protected by the guarantee of the right to liberty embodied in the 14th Amendment to the Constitution. The right to refuse treatment is included in the American Hospital Association's Patient's Bill of Rights (see page 14), and included in most individual hospitals' patient bill of rights. Hospitals are required by federal law to notify patients of their right under state law to refuse medical treatment.

What kinds of treatments can I refuse?

Any kind. Whether it's good or bad for you, you can refuse it. You are free to refuse treatment even if it puts your life in jeopardy.

Is there any exception?

Only a very limited one, to protect public health, as in vaccinations required by the board of health. Even this kind of requirement may be overridden in some cases by objections based on religious belief.

Is the right to refuse treatment lost when a person becomes incompetent?

No. If a person's wishes were expressed when he or she was competent, either through a document such as a living will or orally to another person, those wishes must be respected. Decisions for incapacitated adults or children who have not expressed their wishes are usually made by relatives pursuant to *family consent laws* or the doctrine of *substituted judgment*. You can preserve your rights though a health care proxy, in which you can designate an agent in advance to make decisions on your behalf if you later become incapacitated. We discuss these issues in Chapter 12, Advance Directives for Health Care.

THE PATIENT SELF-DETERMINATION ACT

The Patient Self-Determination Act (PSDA) was enacted by Congress on the heels of the Supreme Court's *Cruzan* decision, in an effort to avoid repeats of Nancy Cruzan's situation by spelling out those rights to refuse medical treatment and encouraging patients to exercise those rights through advance directives. Under the law, all hospitals, nursing homes, home health agencies, hospices, and prepaid health care organizations receiving federal aid must notify patients of their right to receive or refuse medical treatment. The Patient Self-Determination Act mandates that health care facilities that participate in Medicare and Medicaid must

- Provide *written information* to all adult patients as to their rights under state law to make decisions about their medical care, including the right to accept or refuse care and their right to sign advance directives—living wills and health care proxies—for health care decisions
- Provide a *written description* of state law and their own internal policies governing patients' rights
- Inquire whether any advance directives have been signed, document the existence of any directives, and avoid discriminating in the kind of care provided based on whether the patient has executed advance directives
- Ensure compliance with state law on advance directives

The PSDA applies only when a patient is admitted to the hospital. Outpatient services are not covered. Under federal law, health care facilities that do not comply risk loss of funding. Hospitals and nursing homes are not required to provide forms for patient use, although materials for the public are prepared by the Department of Health and Human Services.

In many respects, the law has been a disappointment. Studies show little if any improvement in public understanding of advance directives or doctor-patient communication about these important end-of-life medical decisions. Legislation to strengthen the law has been stalled in Congress for several years.

Under what circumstances can I leave a hospital?
If you want to leave the hospital, the hospital can't stop you. Some people prefer not to stay in the hospital, risking unwanted infections; others want to be far away from possible extraordinary lifesaving measures. Provided you're of sound mind, you can leave anytime. You can sign yourself out of hospital "AMA" (against medical advice).

Most hospitals will ask you to sign a form saying "discharge against medical advice." You don't have to sign this or any other form to leave the hospital, even if you haven't paid the bill. Keeping you against your will would be false imprisonment.

Can the hospital kick me out for not following its advice?

No. The hospital cannot discharge you for other than medical reasons. Antidumping laws guarantee that the hospital will continue to provide medical care if you need it. You can be transferred to another hospital only if you're in stable condition.

THE "RIGHT TO DIE"

The phrase "right to die" means different things to different people. It is used and misused by advocates and opponents alike, as the Cheshire Cat explained to Alice, to mean what they want it to mean. What it means to patients who assert their rights when they are critically ill— and to the lawyers who help them—is this: *it is your right to determine what treatment you will get and what treatment you may refuse.*

In simple terms, this is just an extension of the "informed consent" rights you've had all along to situations in which refusing treatment could result in your death. Consider this common scenario. People with chronic diseases live longer, sicker lives. The terminally ill, once left at home to die among their loved ones, are now ensconced in hospitals and nursing homes, at the mercy of technology available to save them and strangers ready to administer it.

For many, the end is preceded by prolonged discussions and negotiations among patients, their families, and their doctors about how much treatment to pursue and when to call a halt. An estimated 70 percent of deaths today are "negotiated" in this manner.

Does determining my own treatment mean that I must cease treatment?

No. While that may be the most common outcome, your right to determine the medical interventions you will and will not allow may include determining that you want to continue treatment, even though doctors may not want to continue. What's called the right to die can also be called the right to treatment as you choose. (Partnership for Caring can provide you information about life-sustaining technology and how to enforce your wishes. For information, telephone 800/989-9455 or go online at http://www.partnershipforcaring.org)

Do I have the right to treatment?

There is a point at which further treatment may be so medically futile that it should be ended, although where society will draw the line between appropriate and futile treatment is thus far unresolved. In a recent Virginia case, a federal appeals court ruled that doctors are *required* to treat and stabilize all emergency conditions, regardless of their medical belief that no treatment is warranted, under the federal antidumping law. Other courts have held that patients do not have a right to demand treatment that the physician deems medically inappropriate. We expect to see much litigation about this issue.

What's the difference between the right to die and suicide?

Refusing treatment is not suicide. The right to die does not mean the right to kill yourself, or to be assisted in your own hastened death. It is *not* the right to suicide, or to assisted suicide. *It is the right to determine what treatment you will get, and what treatment you may refuse,* in accordance with your personal values and wishes. (Assisted suicide and recent rulings on the rights of terminally ill patients are discussed in Chapter 12.)

Do I have to have a living will to enforce the right to die?

No. You enforce your right to die, or your right to determine what treatment you'll accept or refuse, by telling the doctor your decision and discussing it with him or her. (Advance directives—living wills and health care proxies—are your protection when and if you become incapable of making or communicating decisions about your health care. We discuss these in Chapter 12.)

ENFORCING YOUR RIGHTS

Laws and policies protecting patients, however well motivated, are not generally what lawyers call "self-executing." Nor are they types of laws for which you can scream "Call a cop!" and expect enforcement.

Rather, these are laws that require the participation of the people they're designed to protect in order to ensure that they are followed. They are civil laws with remedies available through bureaucratic processes, agency hearings, and administrative law.

This applies generally to all topics we discuss in this book, but especially so in health care decision making, when your health is at stake—raising the ante at a time when you're least likely to be in a position to fight recalcitrant agencies.

What can you do? Well for starters, there are some basic principles to apply. These may sound simple, but you'd be surprised how often people neglect to do just these things that would in fact directly deal with the problem.

- **Assert your rights.** You have them. Shyness is not appropriate here. We're talking about your health and your life. Talk to your doctor and nurses and the hospital administrators. Tell them your wishes. Ask questions, even if you think they are dumb. And if you don't understand the answer, get a clearer one. Make sure to ask this question: "Do you agree to respect and honor my wishes?"
- **Make yourself heard.** Studies show that doctors often ignore patient wishes, often administering unwanted aggressive treatment to terminally ill patients. Insist on the care you want and the care you don't want for you or your spouse or parent—and keep insisting on it. Repeat yourself until you are sure the message is getting through.
- **Write it down.** Make a record of both the treatment or care you're objecting to and the conversations you have about it—including *who* you're dealing with, *when* the conversation or action takes place, *what* people say to you, and *what* you say to them. And be prepared to put it in writing—to the doctor or the hospital. One of the things we do as lawyers is to write letters for people. You'd be surprised how often that makes a difference.
- **Get a lawyer.** You may want to consult a lawyer to be sure of your grounds and to help you assert your rights against a recalcitrant bureaucracy. The mere presence of a lawyer may get you action. (For more on seeking legal help, see Chapter 23.)
- **Plan ahead.** We can't say this often enough. Waiting to deal with these matters until you are hospitalized, especially for critical care, is a mistake. There are a number of techniques, such as living wills and health care proxies, that will help you avoid some of the problems discussed here. (See Chapter 12 for a discussion of these advance directives.)

Don't wait to get outside help. Start with the patient advocate in the hospital, who can help you cut through any number of problems. If he or she is unable to help you, see if there is a hospital ethicist or ethics committee, and contact them. You may try to be transferred to another doctor or facility. This is generally your right, if a doctor or hospital will not comply with your legal wishes. Although it may feel you are fighting the entire medical establishment in trying to assert your legal rights, remember that the law is a powerful ally.

3

Home and Community Care

Many people need care for a chronic condition or recovery from an illness but dread the prospect of a nursing home. Although in some cases nursing home care may be necessary, it is by no means the only option for all cases. The care you (or your spouse or your parent) need may be available at home or in community settings other than an institution.

With an estimated 2.5 million people receiving care at home each year, home health care has mushroomed into a $30 billion a year industry with more than 17,000 home care agencies. Hundreds of communities across the country have developed programs that provide specific services to elderly residents in their homes. An estimated 2 million home care aides are currently working in the United States.

Home care that is not provided directly through government programs is often financed by government benefits, making recipients vulnerable to budget and service cuts. Many of those who need home care services don't receive them. Home health care is allotted only a small portion of the billions spent for long-term care under Medicare and Medicaid, most of which goes to more costly nursing home services. Massive cuts in public home health spending in the late 1990s caused a 24 percent decline in home care recipients and left some 800,000 people to fend for themselves, potentially forced into nursing homes. Many home care agencies were forced to close. The National Institute of Medicine estimated that if all those entering nursing homes waited an extra month, the United States would reap $3 billion in savings. (For more on financing home care, see Chapters 8 and 9.)

More recent attention has been given to community programs as a way to provide support for the rapidly increasing population of aging individuals for whom neither homebound services nor institutional care provides the solution and who cannot be served in regular senior centers programs.

IDENTIFYING YOUR NEED

The warehouse model is of little appeal to most people with any choice in the matter. One reason the nursing home population has more than doubled in the past quarter of a century is that the Medicare and Medicaid laws are structured to encourage institutionalized rather than community-based care. The result is less money to help you stay at home.

Most older people—even most of those over 85—live at home and get some kind of help for both their medical and functional problems. One-third of them live alone. More than three-quarters of older people report changing their behavior and using other strategies to adapt to their changing needs as they age. Some try to cope on their own or limit their activities. Although only 23 percent have problems with basic activities of daily living, nearly 70 percent seek or receive help with day-to-day tasks such as preparing meals or dressing or managing money.

You may be one of them. Or you may need greater monitoring of your health situation. Depending on your circumstances, alternatives may be available to meet your specific needs, and at lesser cost than institutionalized care.

What many of the home care options discussed in this chapter have in common is that they are modeled on individual needs, not the needs of an institution into which you must fit yourself. And by providing services at home and in the community, they operate to maximize independence and autonomy.

ACTIVITIES OF DAILY LIVING (ADLs)

Home care is often prescribed for people recuperating after illnesses or hospital stays and requiring some medical services and the assistance of trained medical personnel. But home assistance is needed just as urgently by many who don't need these skilled interventions but who do need help with *activities of daily living*. These ADLs, as they are known, are the many functional tasks of everyday life, the performance of which may diminish with age.

ADLs include activities as basic as walking, dressing, bathing, eating, breathing, transferring (moving from bed to chair), cooking, shopping, and daily money management. Cooking, shopping, and money management are sometimes called *instrumental activities of daily living*, or IADLs. You'll note that a number of ADLs refer to activities requiring mobility. In fact, more than a quarter of older people report that their biggest problem as they age is walking.

ADLs are used often to determine eligibility for home care services under insurance, Medicare, Medicaid, or other programs. Assessment of a person's ADLs provides a *functional* measurement. The reliance on ADLs came about largely because of the efforts of advocates to replace unhelpful labels with professional assessment techniques to identify people's specific needs. With proper assistance, many people with functional disabilities (whether physical or cognitive) can continue in their homes and their lives with help tailored to their needs. Often all they need is task-specific help—and recognition of that fact.

ADLs are an important concept for you to understand, for they are used to measure a person's level of functioning in a number of situations and determine the appropriate level of assistance, such as

- Determining the need for a guardian
- Providing long-term care insurance benefits
- Making nursing home assessments
- Making accommodations at work
- Finding appropriate housing in a retirement community

TYPES OF PROGRAMS

Some programs provide traditional care delivered in the home, and others provide services in community settings convenient to the home. A third category offers help for family members—spouses, adult children, and others—who care for their relatives at home.

From home care to a variety of forms of assisted living, a number of options may be available through public and private agencies in your area:

- At-home services, including meal programs, home repair services, transportation
- Personal care and homemaker services, including shopping, bathing, cleaning, cooking
- Home health care, either live-in 24-hour care or part-time care
- Adult day care
- Daily money management services
- Hospice services

- Foster homes
- Respite services for caretakers

Home health care can include both health-related nursing services as well as help with ADLs by home health aides, on a full- or part-time basis. If it is not covered by insurance or government benefits, it can be very expensive. (But you may be able to qualify for financial help. See Chapters 8 and 9.)

Not all the services listed above are offered in the home. Senior centers in your community may have a host of services to offer, including a social worker and other therapists. Other community-based care may include adult day care.

SENIOR CENTERS

Senior centers play an important role in community-based care. First set up under the Older Americans Act (OAA), senior centers are connected to community centers, hospitals, churches, synagogues, city and county councils on aging, housing agencies, and recreation organizations. There are more than 15,000 senior centers across the country, largely funded by OAA federal dollars, as well as state and local monies, and often supported in part by sponsoring organizations.

Don't overlook the senior center as an invaluable resource, for everything from general information to specific service provider. Centers are often the first line of service for the elderly in the community, offering information and referral, social and recreation programs, mental health counseling, case management and advocacy, as well as daily dining and transportation. Many operate intergenerational programs or wellness centers; several sponsor lecture series, which include professionals such as lawyers, accountants, and nutritionists who specialize in the elderly. A senior center can give you a meal, if that's what you need, but it can also give you companionship or counseling, as needed.

ADULT DAY CARE

Adult day service (ADS) programs offer significant health and social benefits, providing much needed care and activity for patients and relief for caretakers. These are community-based programs offering supervision, socialization, assistance with daily living activities, and related support and intensive services enabling individuals to continue to live at home rather than in an institution despite reduced functioning.

These programs fill an important gap in the care available for physically frail or cognitively impaired elderly people in the community. ADS programs potentially improve or maintain an individual's highest level of functioning and independence, preventing or delaying costly long-term care alternatives, while providing respite help for overburdened caregivers and working caregivers and substantial savings to employers of working caregivers.

The majority of programs operate part time, often as half-day or once-weekly programs. Scheduling and transportation are especially difficult for the population most in need of these services. Programs are about equally divided between those serving the physically frail and those serving the cognitively impaired, with staff supported by volunteer help. National ADS models have been developed by the Robert Wood Johnson Foundation and the Brookdale Foundation.

There are approximately 2,200 adult day care programs in the country. Most programs are located in senior centers, naturally occurring retirement communities (NORCs), settlement houses, churches, and other nonprofit agency sites.

HOSPICE SERVICES

Hospice services can be given at a hospice facility or in the home. Some hospitals have hospices. A hospice provides palliative care and pain management, treating symptoms and giving support to the terminally ill. Terminally ill patients may elect to receive hospice care. The premise underlying hospice care is broader than just dealing with pain. Hospice care is designed to help those patients continue as normal a life as possible and remain at home for as long as possible.

Hospice services include physical, occupational, and speech therapy, physician services, skilled nursing services, counseling (dietary, spiritual, bereavement, and other services), medical social services, drugs and biologicals for pain control and symptom management, home health aide and homemaker services, and inpatient respite care.

The word *hospice* derives from *hospitium,* Latin for "guest house." Hospice care is a specialized type of home health care. There are more than 2,500 certified hospice programs, serving nearly a half-million people in 2001. About one-half of the hospices are associated with home health agencies or hospitals; 90 percent of hospice care is provided in the patient's home. Hospice services are generally covered by Medicare. (For more on hospice services, see Chapter 8.)

RESPITE SERVICES

Of increasing importance are *respite services* for the caretaker. Respite programs provide a home care professional or aide to substitute for a caretaker, who gets a much-needed break. Some plans offer a three- or four-hour break once or twice a week, or a month. These are especially welcome for caretakers of people with chronic conditions such as Alzheimer's disease. (For more options for family caretakers, see the next section.)

FAMILY CAREGIVING

The first line of help for many older people is their families. Yet caretaking for older people puts enormous burdens on a family's resources, emotional as well as financial. Caretaking is a stressful responsibility, often falling on the family member least able to handle the frustrations and difficulties.

- **The young old.** Many caretakers are themselves older, the so-called young old, who at 65 find themselves taking care of their 85- and 90-year-old parents.
- **The sandwich generation.** Many women performing caretaking chores are working as well, often part of the "sandwich generation" tending both children and elderly parents.

  These women perform superhuman feats. There are 25 million caregivers, providing 80 percent of the care for elderly in this country. According to a study by the United Hospital Fund, they provide services that would be worth $200 billion. A MetLife study estimated the productivity losses for American companies at $29 billion.

Public policies pay lip service to caretakers but do not support family members in this important role. Caretakers are unprepared and unaware of supports that may be available to help them, such as training, counseling, peer support, or even practical help with transportation and respite services.

For many caretakers, respite care is the only break they get, while the patient is in attendance at an adult day care program. A number of corporations have begun to offer respite care and other services for their employees that may be available for you. Some programs have been developed to give payment or financial assistance to family and informal caretakers in North Dakota, Washington, and Pennsylvania. The

National Family Caregiver Support Program supports some services, such as respite care and day care. (See Appendix I.)

For those acting as or relying on working caretakers, the Family and Medical Leave Act also gives employees up to 12 weeks of unpaid leave to tend to a parent or other immediate family member with a serious health condition. This time need not be taken consecutively but can generally be used in smaller time periods to tend to the needs of a chronically ill parent. (For more on this law, see Chapter 18.)

If you are taking care of an older relative or you are being taken care of, you should consider helpful life planning tools such as a power of attorney. (For more, see Part 4, "Life Planning for You and your Family.")

Caretaking often falls to family members poorly prepared for or inadequate to the task; 30 percent of domestic abuse occurs within the family. One recurring problem in such families is personal and financial elder abuse. There are a number of programs and services available to provide information and needed intervention. (See Chapter 15.)

COMMUNITY-BASED SERVICES AND CARE

In a recent case, *L.M. v. Olmstead,* the U.S. Supreme Court held that states must provide community-based treatment for persons with mental disabilities, under the Americans with Disabilities Act (ADA). The Court decision in *Olmstead* was a wake-up call for the need for community alternatives for all people with a disability or long-term illness. An executive order was issued promoting community-based alternatives other than institutions for individuals with disabilities. It directed the states to develop comprehensive plans so that residents are assessed for, informed of, and given the choice to receive long-term care services in the community.

These reform efforts are designed to enable persons of any age who have a disability or long-term illness to:

- Live in the most integrated community setting appropriate to their individual support requirements and preferences
- Exercise meaningful choices about their living environment, their service providers, the types of supports they receive, and the manner in which supportive services are provided and
- Obtain quality services in a manner consistent with their living preferences and priorities

Unfortunately, lofty goals do not translate immediately into programs. State and local models of long-term support are being showcased on the Centers for Medicare and Medicaid Services (CMS) website; a repository of promising practices can be seen at www.cms.hhs.gov. The site includes system reform efforts as well as programs targeted to individuals. Programs include cash allowances and support services for people with disabilities in Arkansas, Florida, and New Jersey, and "one-stop shopping" programs in Illinois, New Jersey, and Wisconsin. Unfortunately, neither the court ruling nor the executive order required the states to come up with the money to meet the demand for services.

HOW TO FIND HOME CARE

Many home care and community programs are available through the Older Americans Act, which provides grants to State and Area Agencies on Aging and to more than 10,000 senior centers. These programs include meal and transportation services, respite care, housekeeping and personal care services, shopping, money management, and related caregiving services, all of which help maintain people in the community. Services in these centers are usually free, although limited by funding and staff.

A number of states have developed home care options for elderly with disabilities. Oregon has pioneered home care as part of its assisted living program, which provides daily help for Medicaid patients formerly in nursing homes. Wisconsin provides an ambitious array of services, on a sliding scale, to keep people in their homes. New York State's model home care program cares for more than 200,000 elderly.

Nearly 700 Area Agencies on Aging nationwide have been set up under the Older Americans Act to administer nonmedical services. Many offer case management services and may be able to coordinate services for you. Your Area Agency on Aging can refer you to available services in your community. Another possibility is a private care manager, discussed below. (See Appendix II for a list of State Agencies on Aging.)

A number of home care and community services are also available through other program and funding sources in your state and locality. One possible source of information is your employer. A number of corporations have set up programs to counsel employees caring for elderly parents and to make referrals. You can also try the Administration on Aging's National Eldercare Locator at 800/677-1116, which makes referrals for adult day care.

HOW TO EVALUATE A HOME CARE AGENCY

Approximately 45 percent of home care is funded or paid for by public programs, and 55 percent is paid for privately. All together, there are an estimated 17,000 home health agencies across the nation. In evaluating an agency to meet your needs, there are a number of things to keep in mind.

Certification. Approximately half of the home care agencies in the United States are Medicare- or Medicaid-certified home care agencies. This certification means that Medicare or Medicaid will pay for home care provided by them. Although certification is not conclusive, it means the agency has met certain minimum requirements imposed by the federal government in patient care and finances.

Certified agencies can provide specified home health services for both Medicare and Medicaid recipients. You can inspect a copy of an agency's Medicare Survey Report by contacting your state health department.

Licensure. Home health care agencies are licensed in many states. Licensure means it is subject to state standards and regulation, although as a general rule, oversight of even licensed facilities is generally poor and not a good indicator of quality.

Accreditation. There are a number of accrediting agencies for home care, depending on the services provided. Check to see whether an agency is accredited by the Community Health Accreditation Program, the Joint Commission on Accreditation of Healthcare Organizations, the National HomeCaring Council, or the Accreditation Commission for Health Care. If so, it has voluntarily submitted to compliance with standards promulgated by the accrediting organization.

Some of these home care accreditation programs have begun to develop hospice accreditation as well. The National Association of Adult Day Services has entered into an agreement with the Rehabilitation Accreditation Commission to offer accreditation for ADS programs. In addition, local authorities may issue standards for their own adult day programs. (See Appendix I for accreditation agency contact information.)

Staff qualifications, selection, and training. As a general rule, certified agencies are more selective and demanding in their hiring, in part due to government-imposed requirements on who may work as home health aides under their programs. Federal law requires aides to pass competency tests in patient care and to have at least 75 hours of classroom and practical training. Training and testing requirements vary by state and may be stricter in your locality. For example, New York's model home care program has rigorous requirements in training, certification, and benefits for home care workers.

Training is important to ensure that all workers can perform the tasks necessary for your needs. Non-certified agencies may charge lower fees, but without certification requirements, they often provide less training and less trained staff. The National HomeCaring Council has developed standards for home care services, which require adequate training. It also offers a national certification program for home care aides.

Note that terminology for home care workers is often a function of funding source and not function. For example, "home health aides" are generally employed in certified agencies to perform health-related services, while "home attendants" perform so-called personal care. As a practical matter, both may perform the same services.

Plan of care. An important service is a written plan of care, detailing the services that will be provided and the specific tasks performed. A copy of this plan should be available for you and your family.

Availability of staff in emergency. This is very important. Check what the agency's plans are to deal with emergency care, if needed, and whether 24-hour backup help will be available.

Information. Check to see if family members are informed about care, any other services are provided, or if you are given any written information, including a bill of rights for patients and information about fees and charges.

Ask for and consult references. Inquire in the community and at local senior centers. If you are seeking help following a hospital stay, remember to consult with professional staff at the hospital such as discharge planners or social workers.

PRIVATE CARE MANAGERS

One profession that has emerged along with the aging population is *geriatric care management.* A care manager is a professional with training in gerontology, usually as a social worker, nurse, or psychologist, who specializes in assisting older people and their families with long-term care arrangements. You can hire a private care manager to help you with managing your care needs.

A care manager can evaluate your needs, formulate a care plan, locate appropriate services, and arrange care for you—even fill out the applications for you. The care manager can help you evaluate the options available to you and can also monitor care after it's been arranged. These services are particularly useful for people caretaking their parents in faraway cities.

The case management approach is beneficial for elderly patients. With community and medical services coordinated, care is assured and problems that arise may be identified promptly. Professional care managers are skilled in finding and coordinating needed care, and despite the emphasis on geriatric care, may also be useful for people trying to find services for persons of any age with disabilities.

Private care managers have raised some ire in the traditionally non-profit social work community, but they perform a useful and valuable function. In recent years, their value has been recognized by the corporate world, which has begun to employ geriatric care managers or offer their employees access to care managers (usually for assessment of employees' parents) as part of a benefits package. Professional standards for practice have been developed by the National Association of Professional Geriatric Care Managers. You can find a private care manager from social service agency referrals, or you can contact the association (telephone 520/881-8008 or online at http://www.caremanager.org).

PAYING FOR HOME CARE

You can always pay for home care yourself, which may be an option if your needs are limited and you're not strapped for cash. But costs mount up swiftly, year in and year out, and you should be aware of other options open to you.

Some home care is available through the community or the government, either free or for a limited charge. Many of the programs available through the Older Americans Act are not means-tested, which means you don't have to plead poverty to qualify. Some require fees, payable on a sliding scale according to need.

Home care is also available under Medicare and Medicaid, subject to stated conditions. Medicare especially tries to limit home nursing care. Community-based programs are generally not coordinated within the larger continuum of care for the elderly community. So-called waiver programs have covered home and community long-term care services provided by health providers, but payment for community-based services is usually limited to low-income recipients. Adult day care may also charge you fees, often on a sliding scale, to offset their costs. We discuss your coverage under Medicare and Medicaid, and how much the government is paying for care, in Chapters 8 and 9. Broader coverage for home care services is also included in more recent long-term care insurance policies. (See Chapter 10.)

WHERE TO COMPLAIN

If you have a complaint about home health care services, you should always start at the source, with the agency itself. If the agency does business in your community, it will be in its best interests to respond promptly and fully to your complaint.

If the agency is Medicare-certified, you can complain to Medicare. If your agency is licensed by the state, you can also notify the appropriate state agency, usually the state department of health. Certified and licensed agencies are required to comply with federal and state standards for operations.

4

Nursing Homes

The longer you live, the more likely it is you will spend some time in a nursing home. If you're a woman, your chances are even greater. Women not only live longer than men, they care for men outside of institutions in far greater numbers than they are cared for. Not surprisingly, women account for nearly two-thirds of the nursing home population.

According to studies, nearly half of those turning 65—43 percent in one survey—will use a nursing home in the future. One out of four will spend one year in a nursing home, and one out of 11 will spend as long as five years in a nursing home. An estimated 1.6 million people live in 17,000 nursing homes, a one-third increase in the span of a decade. And that's *before* the onslaught to come as the past century's baby boomers turn into the 21st century's senior citizens.

The good news is that the nursing homes of the past—badly managed, frightening places for warehousing souls—are no longer the rule. Today, with federal and state reforms spurred by heightened consumer awareness and greater treatment options for older patients, many nursing homes are well-run places. Nevertheless, problems persist. A significant number still offer a poor or questionable level of care. According to a 2002 report by the Department of Health and Human Services, more than 90 percent of nursing homes have inadequate staffing; there are simply too few workers to care for residents. Estimates put the shortfall at upward of a half-million nurses or nursing aides. And some legislators want to turn back reforms, eliminating federal protections along with Medicaid benefit cutbacks.

The search for a nursing home therefore poses these questions: (1) how to find a good nursing home, (2) when you do, what your rights are to quality care and services, and (3) how to enforce those rights. (The all-important question of cost and your options for financing long-term care are discussed in Part 3 of this book.)

IDENTIFYING YOUR NEED

A nursing home provides nursing, rehabilitative, and other health-related services, along with room and board. Depending on your circumstances, other alternatives may be available to meet your specific needs and at lesser cost.

We've seen that health care is available in settings other than a nursing home. In today's competitive marketplace, some nursing homes are beginning to offer specialized services in addition to custodial and skilled nursing care (e.g., assisted living services, adult day care). If a facility doesn't offer health services, however, it's *not* a nursing home. (Chapter 3 describes the number of options available in home and community-based care. For more on adult living communities, see Chapter 22.)

If institutionalized nursing care is needed, then by all means follow our recommendations in this chapter. But make sure you explore whether the alternatives may be the answer for you—or your spouse or parent. For most people seeking to maintain their independence and autonomy in later years, a nursing home is the least desirable option.

FINDING A NURSING HOME

Your first source for facilities in your area may be the social worker at the hospital, senior center, or other agency with which you have contact. If you're in a hospital, your discharge plan will seek to locate and identify an appropriate facility. In addition, your State or Area Agency on Aging or local or state aging department should be able to provide you with a list of nursing homes in your area. You can also try the Administration on Aging's Eldercare Locator, at 800/677-1116, which will provide referrals in your area.

One helpful resource may be your state's long-term care ombudsman. Under the Older Americans Act, the long-term care ombudsman serves as an advocate for those in nursing homes and will know of those facilities which have been subject to repeated complaints or found to provide substandard care. *Consumer Reports* also provides ratings for national chains and not-for-profit groups operating 4,000 nursing homes. The federal government has a website that offers information on a facility's status, residents, inspection results, and staff. (See the appendixes for contact information.)

No matter what the source, you must visit and inspect the facility in person. If you cannot go, send someone in your place. An on-site visit is critical to an informed decision about whether to enter a particular facility—and offers the added benefit of a display of concern.

HOW TO EVALUATE A NURSING HOME

Some people need nursing home care during short-term rehabilitation following illness or injury. Others need day care while family members work. Others need round-the-clock medical care or custodial care or both. Few nursing homes offer a complete range of services, although services may be coordinated with outside agencies. Other specific services include rehabilitation programs specifically for older people, assessment services, and social work programs.

Credentials. Facilities are both licensed by the state and certified by Medicare and Medicaid. More than 10,000 nursing homes are certified by Medicare. A nursing home that is not certified may not meet minimum standards of care required for federal reimbursement.

Quality of care, services, and activities. Quality is critical to your health. In a nursing home, you need good nursing and medical services, as well as adequate food and shelter.

As important as the physical structure of the facility and the extent of its services is the staff providing them. It's important to know whether medical staff and supervisors are on premises or "on call." Are rehabilitative services furnished by nursing home staff or outside providers? Is there an activities program to meet your interests as well as your physical, mental, and psychosocial well-being? Is there a qualified therapeutic recreation specialist or activities professional on staff? Remember, you should be receiving social services designed to meet your needs.

Staffing rates are published, but you should verify those reports for yourself. Find out about staff levels and schedules of nurses, assistants, social workers, and other full- and part-time staff. In a worst-case scenario, low staff ratios can result in bedsores, malnutrition, dehydration, and pneumonia. Many nursing home residents need help to move, eat, or bathe; without enough staff, they can be left in their beds, food uneaten, without having showered.

Physical environment. The ideal nursing home will provide a safe, clean, and homelike environment, allowing you to keep and use your personal belongings to the greatest extent possible. Federal regulations require housekeeping and maintenance services to keep rooms not just sanitary but comfortable, with clean bed and bath linens in good condition, adequate and comfortable lighting levels in all areas, and comfortable sound and temperature levels (generally between 71° and 81°F). You are entitled to private closet space in your room.

Be sure to check the physical conditions of the nursing home, inspecting for sanitation and comfort. Rooms, furnishings, common areas, and toilet and bathing facilities should all be on your checklist.

Rules and restraints. Another area of concern is rules. A nursing home has policy and rules that govern such aspects of resident life as eating, sleeping, participation in activities, use of telephone and mail. You want to examine these rules to gauge whether they are flexible enough to meet your needs or unduly restrictive.

Of special note is a nursing home's policy on restraining devices—both the physical and chemical variety—for patients. It should be unacceptable at the start of the 21st century that we continue to allow our elder citizens to be routinely subjected to this horrible indignity. Yet restraints are commonplace in nursing homes, where they are almost always used, improperly, for the convenience of staff rather than the welfare of patients. Despite reforms, a substantial proportion of facilities continue to use restraints on their patients inappropriately and illegally. Make sure you ask about the home's policy—and observe whether patients are indeed free of restraints. (We discuss the law on using restraints later in this chapter.)

Another area of concern is an institution's policy on sexual activity of residents. Don't assume the subject is irrelevant or inappropriate. Although few homes have written guidelines, questions about sex and how a home handles sensitive situations deserve your attention. For more on this subject, see page 55.

Shopping for a nursing home, whether for yourself or a relative, is a very traumatizing experience for most people. If possible, go with a friend or family member when you make your inspection—and take notes. Ask questions and write down the answers. If you proceed in a deliberate way, you maximize your chances of making an informed and wise decision.

Subjective attributes. A nursing home may be a home, but it is not your home. Even with recent improvements, nursing homes by nature are impersonal places, designed to offer production-line, albeit humane, services marketed to the least common denominator.

We say this not by way of criticism, but to remind you that personal contact, caring, and interest are qualities that are hard to measure but very important for you to consider. A facility that has compassionate staff, that manages to engage its residents in activities of interest to them, that establishes some sense of warmth in individual quarters and common rooms—these are things that cannot be quantified but will be invaluable, literally lifesaving, to residents.

- Visit as many nursing homes as you can. Be sure to schedule a weekend or evening visit, as well. Observe the staff and the residents, and ask them about staffing, activities, and scheduling. Their comments should prove extremely useful to you.
- Ask administrators and staff their attitudes about personal rights of residents in the home and make your own observations about rights being exercised by residents. For most people, their most important human right is freedom. Loss of autonomy is the greatest indignity imposed by a stay in a nursing home. A few years back, the National Citizens Coalition for Nursing Home Reform surveyed residents for qualities they thought important in a good nursing home. The responses included food, activities, staff—and choice and autonomy.
- Do your homework. Get copies of annual state reviews and quality care surveys of individual facilities. These reviews should provide valuable information on quality of life and quality of care issues. Ask to see copies of the facility's most recent survey, available at the nursing home and from the state. The federal government has a "Nursing Home Compare" website (http://www.medicare.gov/nhcompare/home.asp), which includes substantial information on nursing homes. Don't let an inspection report substitute for a personal visit.

NURSING HOME REFORMS

The Nursing Home Reform Act of 1987 enacted a comprehensive series of standards for nursing homes. The law was designed to address the most prevalent abuses occurring in the nursing home industry as well as to establish a basic standard of care and rights due to all nursing home residents.

The rights established by this law include the basic human rights to dignity, choice, privacy, and autonomy, as well as to quality services. Just as important, the act outlaws discrimination against residents who are or may become Medicaid recipients.

The reforms cover a number of areas:

- Increased staff qualifications
- Quality of care
- Residents' rights

- Use of restraints
- Information and access

The Nursing Home Reform Act is sometimes referred to as OBRA '87, because it was passed as part of the Omnibus Budget Reconciliation Act of that year. The law applies to all nursing facilities and their owners and operators who receive Medicare or Medicaid funds.

THE NURSING HOME CONTRACT

When you enter a nursing home, a contract (the "admissions agreement") is signed. There are a number of considerations in signing this contract, which we describe below. Remember that entering or admitting someone to a nursing home is an act done in a time of stress. In the urgency of the moment, you may not be exercising your best critical abilities. A number of nursing home contracts routinely include illegal clauses, such as those concerning advance payments or requiring guarantees.

Often, such clauses are unenforceable. But not always. Be aware that nursing home admission agreements are contracts, and should be read and considered in detail before signing.

Don't confuse a nursing home with a *continuing care facility* (sometimes called a *lifecare community*). These generally provide housing and some medical care—less than a nursing home—for an unspecified, lifetime term. Some of these facilities do have nursing homes as well. Many states provide some regulation of continuing care facilities, governing items such as entrance fees, probationary periods, and refunds. (Some of the protections in these statutes may apply to nursing home contracts as well.) If you are applying for entry to a nursing home, you should not be asked to sign a lifecare contract. (For more on continuing care facilities, see Chapter 22.)

ADMISSIONS AND DISCRIMINATION

Discrimination against Medicaid recipients is prohibited by federal regulations banning discrimination on the basis of source of payment. This discrimination is sometimes referred to as *Medicaid discrimination*. The prohibition applies to admissions, services, transfer, and discharge.

Despite these prohibitions, residents applying under private pay rates, which are not regulated, will find it easier to obtain nursing home care. Although in theory all applicants have equal access to quality care, courts have been generally unwilling to hold nursing homes to identical standards for Medicaid and non-Medicaid applicants due to lower reimbursement rates provided by Medicaid.

Some safeguards against discrimination based on source of payment are described below. Prohibitions against discrimination that are mandated by other federal, state, and local laws continue to apply in nursing homes.

WAITING LISTS

Many nursing homes have waiting lists. Whether a bed is available is a function of where you live and the quality of the facility. It may also be a function of payment—if you are a private payer, you will find it easier than if you (or your parent or spouse) are already on Medicaid. The pressures on hospitals to discharge Medicare patients had led to increased referrals to nursing homes.

In some cases (and depending on where you live), it may also be a function of the extent of services needed or anticipated, and government reimbursement structures. For example, the less care you need, the more likely you are to find a bed. However, some states encourage facilities to take residents needing greater care by providing higher reimbursement rates for them.

Many states require a minimum percentage of Medicaid patients. For example, New York requires that the percentage of Medicaid patients in a nursing home be at least 75 percent of the percentage of Medicaid patients in nursing homes in the county as a whole. A nursing home's admissions policy should be available upon request, including an explanation of its waiting list, where one is used.

DEPOSITS AND PAYMENTS

Under the reform law, if you enter a nursing home covered by either Medicare or Medicaid, you cannot be asked for a "security deposit," "contribution," or any other form of advance payment.

This is what the law says. It is not what happens. Typically nursing homes do ask for upfront payments and other forms of "guarantees" from applicants or their relatives. These may run in the thousands of dollars, in some areas reaching $10,000 or $20,000. Some homes try to charge you for a minimum number of days or months. These deposits and charges are against the law.

The law also says that you cannot be asked to sign anything giving up any of your rights to Medicaid. For example, some homes ask that you agree not to transfer your personal funds or to apply for Medicaid for a given period of time. This is illegal. (Keep in mind, however, that giving away your funds could make you ineligible for Medicaid. We discuss this in Chapter 9.)

If you are a friend or relative helping a nursing home applicant in the admissions process, make sure you don't sign anything making you personally responsible for payment. These third-party guarantees are also illegal.

Residents who are covered by Medicaid may nevertheless be asked to pay for "extra" services, such as laundry or hair care, which in fact are covered by government benefits. These supplementary fees are also illegal. (Note that some added fees may not be illegal, such as for a TV in your room. But they cannot be required for your admission, either.)

Many states also have laws restricting or banning nursing home deposits. Check with your long-term care ombudsman for the requirements in your state. (See Appendix II at the end of this book.)

My stay is not covered by Medicare and I'm not eligible for Medicaid. The nursing home wants a deposit. Is this permitted?

In most states, yes. Under these circumstances, your ability to pay is a legitimate concern for a nursing home. However, many states limit the size of the deposit that can legally be requested. For example, Florida provides for a $1,500 maximum security deposit. Some (Connecticut and California) establish an outright ban on security deposits. Under New York law, any deposit remains your property and must be treated as such.

Make sure that you really are not covered by Medicare. You have the right to ask that a "demand bill" be submitted to Medicare for a determination concerning your coverage.

QUALITY OF CARE

The difference between quality services and inadequate services can be as critical as getting adequate medical treatment or being afforded the dignity of your own personal space. Reforms have attempted to codify both a process and plan for providing quality services for nursing home residents. Your involvement, as a resident or a family member, ensures that nursing home staff get the information they need to provide quality services.

Preadmission screening and annual resident review (PASARR). Screening and review are mandated to ensure that individuals with mental illness or retardation are not inappropriately placed in nursing homes.

Assessments. Individual patient assessment is critical for the delivery of quality patient care. Assessment measures a patient's ability to function and perform activities of daily living (ADLs), including abilities as basic as walking, dressing, bathing, eating, and breathing.

Each resident must be assessed by the nursing home staff at the following times:

- Within 14 days of admission and
- At least once a year thereafter and
- Upon any significant change in mental or physical condition. In such cases subsequent three-month reviews are required

The assessment must be administered or coordinated by a registered nurse (RN). In addition, each person performing a portion of the assessment must certify its accuracy. The form and content of the assessment is specified by state requirements, in compliance with federal regulations.

Plan of care. A plan of care spells out strategies, tasks, and responsibilities as part of an overall design to allow each resident to maintain the highest practicable physical, mental, and emotional well-being. The plan of care should address both medical and nonmedical issues, including daily schedules, staff, personal care, medications, and activities. A program of activities must be provided to meet the interests and physical, mental, and psychosocial well-being of each resident.

The law requires that a written comprehensive plan of care be prepared by the attending doctor, an RN with responsibility for the resident, and any other facility staff who may be involved in a resident's care, as well as the resident and a family member or lawyer as his or her representative.

A plan of care (also called a "care plan") must be done within seven days of an assessment. Care plan conferences must occur every three months and whenever there is a significant change in a resident's mental or physical condition.

Physician choice. You are entitled to free choice of an attending physician. The nursing home can't prevent you from exercising this right by imposing unreasonable practice rules before allowing your doctor to see you on the premises.

Staff requirements. Federal law requires minimum nursing staff 24 hours a day, including an RN as director of nursing, an RN on duty at least one shift a day, and a licensed nurse on duty at all times. Homes with more than 120 beds must also employ full-time social workers. In many cases, however, these requirements have been circumvented by waivers.

Nursing home administrators must be licensed by the state. The law specifies training and competency requirements for both full- and part-time workers in nursing homes. States are made responsible for training and evaluating nursing home nurses' aides. Training is required for all nurses' aides employed more than four months. Retraining and reevaluation is required after more than two years' absence.

States must also establish and maintain registries of nurses' aides who have completed training and evaluation. Registries must also include individuals who have neglected or abused residents, or misappropriated resident funds. Nursing homes must check state and other available registries for employee history of patient neglect or abuse.

Rehabilitation, dental, and pharmacy services. You must get any physical therapy or other rehabilitative services specified in your care plan. This may include speech language pathology, occupational therapy, and mental health rehabilitative services. The nursing home can either provide the service by staff or arrange to have it furnished by qualified outside personnel. You must get necessary routine and 24-hour emergency dental care (for which Medicare patients may be charged). This includes a prompt referral for residents with lost or damaged dentures. If necessary, you are entitled to assistance in making appointments and arranging transportation to and from the dentist's office. You must also be provided with medication, as needed.

Other services. Dietary services are prescribed as to the number and time of meals. The physical environment is also regulated. A room can have no more than four beds, and a minimum amount of space must be allotted for each resident. Rooms must be adequately furnished, with toilet and bathing facilities nearby and accessible. There must also be a system in place for residents to summon help.

CHEMICAL AND PHYSICAL RESTRAINTS

In an industry long noted for abuses, the biggest abuse is one that continues to this day. That is the practice of keeping nursing home residents "under control," a euphemism for the physical and chemical restraints that keep thousands of institutionalized persons "roped up and doped up" for the convenience of those who tend them.

Federal law prescribes the use of both *physical restraints* and *chemical restraints*. Physical restraints are ropes, jackets, and mittens that tie a patient to a chair or bed. Chemical restraints are psychotropic drugs. They are both used for the same purpose, keeping the patient subdued and passive.

Hospital and nursing home operators who routinely order restraints justify them as needed to prevent patients, especially elderly patients, from falling or injuring themselves or pulling out tubes. But restraints are mostly used as a convenience for staff rather than to safeguard the health of patients. In egregious cases, they have been used as discipline for "misbehaving" residents. In nursing homes, especially, antihistamines have been misused to keep patients drowsy and tractable.

In some cases, restraints can keep patients from harming themselves. But there are alternatives. Reducing the use of restraints may require training staff to meet individual needs through innovations such as environmental alterations, positioning devices, or redeploying nursing assistants. As simple an idea as a regular walking program can benefit many residents. The Jewish Home and Hospital for the Aged (JHHA) in New York City has proved that a restraint-free environment can lead to more independence and autonomy, without increasing and in fact lessening injuries and accidents. (JHHA has developed programs seeking to minimize the use of restraints. You can also get information on reducing restraint use from the National Citizens' Coalition for Nursing Home Reform in Washington, D.C. See Appendix I for contact information.)

Under federal law, blanket orders for restraints "as needed" may no longer be issued. Before restraints may be used on a patient, there must be an individual order *for that patient* that explains the need for restraints and when their use will be discontinued. Orders for drug restraints are good for no longer than 12 hours.

Except in an emergency situation to protect patient life or safety, restraints must be ordered by a doctor, in writing, specifying the need and the duration. Under no circumstances should restraints ever be used as "discipline." Nursing homes are required to report on alternatives and plans for ending restraints.

BED-HOLD AND BED RESERVATIONS

An important factor for residents in a nursing home, and one with potentially serious consequences, is the facility's *bed-hold and bed reservation* policy. If a nursing home resident has to be hospitalized, what are the resident's rights to have his or her bed held open until he or she returns from the hospital? What are his or her rights to the next available bed?

The answer is tied to money. Homes will generally hold beds for as long as they are paid for. If you are paying privately, this is covered by your pocketbook or by your insurance. Note that charging you for holding a bed is *not* a violation of law. As a general rule, Medicaid will cover a minimum number of days. For example, in New Jersey it will cover 10 days. A resident who remains in the hospital longer becomes entitled to the next available bed in the same nursing home. Generally, the hospital will keep him or her until the next bed is available.

Residents have a right to know the nursing home's policy. They have a right to readmission to the next available bed.

Many state laws also govern bed reservation and bed-hold policies. Some require that beds be held for a minimum number of days (seven days in California for Medicaid patients; 15 days in Florida, 30 days for private pay).

If I am waiting in the hospital for a space in a specific nursing home, can I decline one that another nursing home offered me?

If you decline an appropriate placement without a good reason, you will be obligated to pay for your hospital stay. An "appropriate" placement is one within a 50-mile radius of your home.

TRANSFERS AND DISCHARGE

Under the law, there may be no arbitrary transfer or discharge from a nursing home. Transfers and discharges against your will (known as "involuntary transfers") are only allowed under certain conditions:

- If you present a risk to the safety or health of yourself or others
- If you regain your health, making a nursing home stay inappropriate
- If you fail to pay (for Medicare and Medicaid residents, this applies only to allowable charges)
- If the nursing home closes

If you are to be transferred or discharged, you must be given 30 days' advance notice. You have the right to appeal a transfer or discharge through an appeal process established by the state and to be granted a hearing. (This right does not apply to transfers to other floors or rooms within the same facility.) Procedures for a hearing apply to all nursing home residents, regardless of the source of payment.

My elderly uncle is being discharged from his nursing home for being disruptive. Is this legal?

Not if he doesn't present a risk to his own or others' safety or health. At least one court has ruled that merely being disruptive is not cause to discharge a resident from a nursing home.

RESIDENT'S BILL OF RIGHTS

By its nature, a nursing home robs people of their independence and their autonomy. Once in a nursing home, a resident's whole life is subject to regulations and schedules imposed by others. The new resident loses control of such simple things as choosing meals, taking medication, and keeping personal possessions.

This situation has been partly addressed by provisions in federal law that seek to establish a minimum standard of personal rights—a "bill of rights" for nursing home residents. Among the most important rights are

A statement of your rights. You are entitled to a copy of your legal rights when you enter a nursing home, and any revisions thereafter. This includes a statement of your right to make a complaint to the state about abuse or neglect. You have the right to a description of how your personal funds will be protected.

A written statement of fees, charges, and services. You are entitled to this before entering. If you are on Medicaid or Medicaid eligible, you must be informed of available coverage as well as all other fees and services.

Quality of life, dignity, and self-determination. You are entitled to receive care in a manner and an environment that promotes maintenance or enhancement of your quality of life, dignity, and respect in full recognition of your individuality.

Self-determination means that you have the right to choose activities, schedules, and health care consistent with your interests, assessment, and plan of care. You are entitled to interact with members of the community both inside and outside the facility, and make choices about aspects of life in the facility of significance to you.

Right to privacy. Privacy is the most sought-after and elusive goal in a communal setting like a nursing home. You have the right to privacy in your room (although not to a private room), as well as in telephone calls, mail, and visitors. You also have rights to confidentiality concerning your medical records.

Financial control. You have the right to manage your own finances to the extent that you can. As protection of resident funds, the law provides that you must be given information about your personal funds.

Visits. You have the right to visitors at any reasonable hour. You also have the concomitant right *not* to have visitors—to refuse to see family or friends if you don't want to.

Access and visitation. Reasonable access must be granted to anyone providing you service, such as legal services. Your personal physician and a long-term care ombudsman or other state representative must be given immediate access to you. The patient's attorney or state officer can examine the resident's records, with the resident's permission.

Meetings and participation in resident and family groups. You and your family have the right to meet to discuss problems or any matters that concern you. You and your family also have the right to form councils to discuss your problems and to bring them to the attention of administrators, as necessary. The nursing home is required to make space available and to designate a staff person responsible for providing assistance and responding to written requests that may result from group meetings.

I am considering nursing home services, which I may need for an undetermined period of time. If I enter a nursing home, do I have the right to come and go as I please?

Yes. You are a resident, not an inmate. Except where your health renders you incapable to leaving the facility, you have an absolute right to leave whenever you want. This includes shopping excursions or visits to friends.

The nursing home can be held liable for your supervision, however, and some nursing homes will limit your right to remain in the home if you stay away for an extended period of time. You should make sure you know the nursing home policy in regard to leaving the premises.

If I am in a nursing home, what rights do I have concerning my medical treatment? Do I have to go along with whatever "the doctor orders"?

No. You have the right to participate in making your plan of care. You also have the right to give or refuse consent to any treatment or procedure, as you would outside the nursing home. Make sure that you, your representative, and your health care proxy, if you have appointed one, are aware of your rights in this regard. (See Chapter 12 on health care directives.)

If I enter a nursing home, will I lose the right to manage my finances?

Not because you enter a home. You still have the right to manage your finances, although your cash allowance within the home may be limited. However, this does not restrict your right to manage, direct, and otherwise administer your business affairs and your assets and income.

SEX IN NURSING HOMES

One issue not commonly addressed in nursing homes is sexual behavior of residents. Despite studies revealing that nearly half of Americans over 60 are sexually active, stereotypes and taboos persist that older people don't have sex or shouldn't have sex. As a result, the issue is ignored except when a situation arises, to be "dealt with" by unprepared staff members, who may be uncomfortable or disapproving. Adult children may disapprove, also compounding the problem for unprepared staff.

In 1995, the Hebrew Home for the Aged at Riverdale in New York City produced the country's first written policy and guidelines on resident sexuality. Under the policy, residents have the right to "seek out and engage in sexual expression, including words, gestures, movements or activities that appear motivated by the desire for sexual gratification." The home has also produced a training video narrated by actress Anne Meara, which has been distributed to nursing homes throughout New York.

In any group setting, the need for intimacy must be balanced against the rights of others, and questions of privacy, consent, and the potential for abuse must be addressed. The Hebrew Home's policy bans relationships with minors or people with seriously declining mental faculties, as well as public displays and nonconsensual acts.

Make sure you understand what the policy is in the nursing home, whether you or your parent are already a resident or shopping for an appropriate facility. Don't be too shy about asking if you are visiting a home on your own behalf—these are your needs that must be met and your privacy that must be respected. If you are a child of a potential resident, don't assume the subject has no importance to your parent. Few homes have adopted guidelines or offered training to staff, but there is an increasing recognition of the importance of sex to physical and mental health and more willingness to discuss questions of sexuality and how to handle sensitive situations. These discussions should take place in every nursing home.

NURSING HOME ABUSE

An alarming problem that persists is the possibility of physical and sexual abuse of nursing home residents. According to a 2002 report by the General Accounting Office, nursing home residents have suffered serious injuries or, in some cases, have died as a result of abuse. One out of three of the nation's nursing homes has been cited by state inspectors for violations serious enough to harm residents or place them in immediate jeopardy, although reports indicate that less than 2 percent of cases resulted in any harm.

Nursing home abuse is a particularly vicious exploitation of vulnerable individuals. The report says that many incidents are not reported, at least not until a sharp-eyed relative or employee complains, and fewer are prosecuted. Residents may be abused by staff or other residents. Residents fear retribution, while managers fear publicity and lawsuits. The system offers few penalties, and employees fired from one job find it easy to gain employment in another area or state. Nursing homes are supposed to post the telephone number for reporting abuse, but few do.

What can you do? Vigilance should begin on your first visit to the facility, whether you are a relative, a friend, or a prospective resident. Ask about verification of staff credentials and references. Check to see if the number to call to report abuse is posted. Ask whether the nursing home has a policy on resident abuse, whether any incidents have occurred, and if so, how they were handled. And if anything happens, don't hesitate to report it. Report your observations to the nursing home director, and if you believe a crime has been committed, make sure the police are called in to investigate. You can also call the Medicare hotline at 800/MEDICARE and the long-term care ombudsman in your state.

REGULATING NURSING HOMES

Nursing homes are licensed by the state and must be inspected yearly. States are now required to conduct annual reviews and perform quality care surveys of nursing homes under federal guidelines.

All states have a long-term care ombudsman, whose powers and duties are set forth by statute. States must investigate complaints of violation and allegations of neglect and abuse and monitor deficient nursing homes. Where facilities have been found to provide substandard care, notice is required to the long-term care ombudsman, administrative licensing board, and the attending physicians of residents.

Under federal law, each state must maintain a registry of nursing aides who have been found abusive. Other health care professionals, including nurses, doctors, and administrators, who have been found guilty of abuse, neglect, or misappropriation of funds must be reported to the appropriate state agency.

States have their own nursing home statutes, many with nursing home bills of rights (either parallel to the federal law or adding specific rights). These generally include a requirement that the law be posted in the nursing home, a process for making complaints, and sanctions for noncompliance with standards, including Medicaid sanctions, other fines and penalties, and licensure suspension or revocation for violations. Many also specify a prohibition on discrimination in nursing home admissions and services based on age, race, national origin, handicap, or sex. In several states, separate funds have been created to protect nursing home residents, financed by fees and penalties.

ENFORCING YOUR RIGHTS

Implementation of the federal law has not been easy and is still ongoing. Reforms cost time and money, education and training are needed, and politicians and industry lobbyists debate the law's effectiveness.

How does this affect you? It makes your active participation all the more important. Oversight is as much a responsibility of the individual as of the government. It's crucial that individuals know their rights, and their closest friends and relatives know what those rights are so that objections can be voiced strongly when standards of care, basic quality services, and legally mandated rights are not met.

You should be aware that there are specific sanctions in place for violation of the law. States may order a plan of correction and take steps to ensure compliance (under threat of loss of federal Medicaid funds).

One of the problems with sanctions for nursing homes is that the cure may be worse than the disease. Even with substandard facilities, it is often not in the best interest of residents for a facility to be closed or residents moved. Other possible sanctions include fines, denial of payment, and temporary takeover of management.

Complaints and grievances within the nursing home or institution. A statement of rights is good only if you have a mechanism that backs it up. A nursing home must have a formal complaint and griev-ance procedure in place for dealing with complaints from residents. This means that you should be able to identify the place and the person to whom you should make your complaint, and what the home's responsibility is to investigate and respond. Nursing homes are required to provide immediate efforts to resolve resident grievances.

Don't think that because someone has a title, that individual knows what he or she is talking about. Remember, many of these reforms are very new, and implementation has been sporadic. Often, what seems to be a violation of your rights and flagrant disregard of law is merely ignorance. Your job at the outset is to make your complaint. If the offi-cials with whom you speak profess lack of interest or ignorance, your job is to educate them. Both the residents and the facility staff should know the requirements of the law. Residents have the right to voice grievances without reprisal.

State investigation. Each state must institute a process for inves-tigating complaints of violation and allegations of neglect and abuse. The state regulatory system must provide for corrective plans where needed and appropriate sanctions. State action can originate from inspections and surveys, or upon a complaint by an individual. State action can lead to improvements—or to closings.

Long-term care ombudsman. Every state must have a long-term care ombudsman, who serves as an advocate for those in nursing homes and other long-term care facilities. This is required under the Older Americans Act. (See Chapter 15 on the long-term care ombudsman's role in elder abuse and protective proceedings.)

Other state agencies. Your state department of health regulates and licenses nursing homes, and may be some help. The state also licenses nursing home administrators, nurses, nurses' aides, and other health care professionals. State human rights agencies are given respon-sibilities for enforcing discrimination laws.

Criminal action. Medicaid fraud and other financial irregularities have long been the object of criminal investigations and prosecutions in the nursing home industry. Although not as common, an increasing number of prosecutions have been initiated against nursing home administrators and staff charging neglect or abuse of residents so fla-grant as to constitute criminal misconduct.

Private action. If neglect or abuse or serious injury has occurred, you may have a private right of action. Depending on the circum-stances, you may bring a lawsuit based on negligence, breach of con-tract, or violation of the statutory requirements (or a combination of those). There have been several successful suits where aggrieved parties have won significant awards against nursing homes.

A number of states provide an additional private right of action for violation of their nursing home residents' rights statutes. In states such as Florida or Missouri, for example, an aggrieved resident can sue for violation of statutory protection, although damages may be limited. If you believe you have a case warranting a private lawsuit, you should consult an attorney for advice.

Part 2

Managing and Paying for Health Care

In our free enterprise system, medical care is a commodity, bought and sold like any other. Yet it is a commodity whose economic fortunes have the power to affect every part of your life. Health care costs can influence your choice of doctors, the frequency of your medical checkups, and the kind of care you and your family will receive during an illness. If you need to protect health care insurance coverage you receive through employment, the impact of medical costs may dictate where you live and work.

Health care costs have accelerated at an unprecedented pace over the last decade. For crisis situations requiring high-tech interventions and chronic conditions demanding long-term care, costs have risen exponentially. In New York State, the average daily cost of a nursing home is $200; that translates into $73,000 yearly. Across the country, as many as 2.8 million people can be expected to use a nursing home during the course of a single year—fewer than half covered by Medicare and insurance.

This section shows you how to make sure you can pay for the health care you need. Chapter 5 discusses Medicare, the insurance coverage provided by the United States government for people over 65. Chapter 6 describes supplemental coverage and other private health insurance, and details current law designed to help you hold onto that coverage. In Chapter 7, we review HMOs and managed-care plans and the rules governing them.

5

Medicare

Medicare has been an accepted part of later life for nearly 40 years, so much a feature of the health care landscape that legislators are wary of the political fallout of program changes. When it was signed into law in 1965 it was historic legislation. President Lyndon Johnson took the occasion to predict:

> Every citizen will be able, in his productive years when he is earning, to insure himself against the ravages of illness in his old age. No longer will illness crush and destroy the savings they have so carefully put away over a lifetime so that they might enjoy dignity in their later years.

If you're over 65 and retired, Medicare is your primary health insurance. Under Part A (hospital coverage) and Part B (medical insurance), nearly 40 million disabled and elderly have Medicare coverage, providing payment to doctors and hospitals, either directly or via reimbursement to patients. (A third program, Medicare + Choice, is discussed in Chapter 7.)

At its creation, Medicare was a revolutionary scheme by the government to insure older people, with contributions provided by citizens when they are working and after their retirement. The financing of Medicare reflects the shared responsibility of employer and employee, citizen and insured. Medicare's hospital coverage (Part A) is financed by payroll taxes of 2.9 percent per worker, split between the employer and the worker. The medical insurance program, which covers doctor fees (Part B), is paid for in part from general tax revenues and from monthly premiums paid by enrollees.

Health care costs attributed to Medicare have been staggering, and tax revenues are hard-pressed to keep pace with growing costs. The program faces an uncertain financial future. The hospital insurance trust fund is in jeopardy, and current predictions are that its funds will be depleted by 2030.

Yet for all the expense, Medicare has failed to fulfill the promise articulated by President Johnson. Medicare pays only for "skilled" care for "acute" illness, contributing to only 44 percent of personal health care expenses. With no coverage for "unskilled" care, such as help with personal hygiene or household chores, and insurance picking up only some of the gap, the burden of health care costs on American families today looms greater than ever.

ELIGIBILITY FOR MEDICARE

Medicare consists of two programs: Part A, hospital insurance, and Part B, medical insurance. Each program involves different kinds of treatment for which enrollees are partially or fully covered.

You're eligible for Medicare if you're

- Over 65 and entitled to retirement benefits under the Social Security Act (even if you don't actually receive benefits because you've earned too much income)
- Under 65 but permanently and totally disabled for 24 months

Can I get Medicare if I'm not a citizen?

Medicare is available only to United States citizens or permanent aliens who have resided here more than five years.

My spouse has enrolled in Medicare. Am I eligible for Medicare as a spouse?

Medicare benefits are available only to the individual applying for them. If one marital partner is 65 and the other is not, the younger spouse is not eligible to purchase Medicare insurance. Don't give up private insurance for yourself or your spouse until you know you are both covered by Medicare.

My son was injured in an accident more than two years ago. Is he eligible for Medicare?

It depends on the severity of the injury. Your son qualifies if he has been permanently and totally disabled for 24 months. Although our emphasis throughout this book is on the elderly, what we say about government entitlements is generally applicable to the disabled as well.

ENROLLMENT
(PART A HOSPITAL COVERAGE)

For most people, enrollment in Medicare is a fairly straightforward process that accompanies enrollment in the Social Security system. The Social Security Administration handles applications to both Social Security and Medicare. Once you've established your entitlement to Social Security, you should be enrolled in Medicare without having to file a separate application. Social Security disability recipients who receive benefits for 24 months are also enrolled automatically. You'll automatically receive Part A hospital coverage. Part A covers all in-hospital services, discussed later in this chapter. (Social Security is discussed in Chapter 20.)

If you're not enrolled in Social Security, you must file an application for Medicare with the Social Security Administration. Apply during your *initial enrollment period,* which begins three months before the month of your 65th birthday and runs for seven months (through the three months following your birthday month).

Applying is as simple as making a phone call to your local Social Security office. All you have to supply is proof of eligibility, including your age and some record of your earnings. The Social Security office does the rest—it even fills out the forms for you.

It pays to enroll before the month of your birthday. If you do, coverage will begin on the first day of the month of your 65th birthday. If you wait until your birthday month, coverage won't begin until the next month; if you enroll in the following months, coverage will begin in the second month following your enrollment; and if you wait until the last two months, coverage will begin in the third month following your enrollment.

After you've enrolled, your contact with Medicare will be primarily through claims filed with your *intermediary* or *carrier.* These are private insurance companies under contract with Medicare to process claims and handle information requests. Whether you will be dealing with an intermediary or a carrier depends on the type of claim you're filing: intermediaries handle Part A claims, and carriers are responsible for Part B claims. (It's a distinction without a difference; a company can be both an intermediary and a carrier.) Intermediaries and carriers report to the Centers for Medicare and Medicaid Services (CMS), formerly the Health Care Financing Administration, the federal agency that administers Medicare.

I'm not eligible for Social Security benefits. Can I purchase Medicare privately?

Yes. You can buy Medicare insurance if you're 65 or older. The premiums are expensive, but may well be worth it when you factor in the rising cost of health insurance and the scarcity of other forms of insurance available to the elderly. In 2003, Part A coverage comes to $316 a month. For those with 30 quarters towards Social Security, there is a reduced $174 monthly premium. The premium cost for Part B is the same as for Medicare-eligible enrollees.

Medicare can't refuse to accept you because of your previous health history. Don't underestimate the importance of this guarantee. If you live in a state that allows medical underwriting, this may be the only insurance you can get.

Will I be notified by the government when it's time for me to apply?

Don't count on the government to tell you you're eligible or remind you to enroll. One way the government saves money is by neglecting to do just that. If you're not automatically enrolled as a Social Security recipient, you'll have to make that call to Social Security.

Can I get retroactive benefits?

Yes, for Part A hospital coverage. If you apply within six months, benefits will be retroactive to the first month of eligibility. If you apply later, they'll be retroactive to the sixth month of potential eligibility. In order to receive retroactive benefits, you must apply for them. (Only living individuals can apply; estates are not eligible for retroactive benefits.)

ENROLLMENT
(PART B MEDICAL INSURANCE)

Part B medical insurance covers physician and surgeon services and other specified services (discussed later in this chapter). Enrollment in Part B is automatic with your Medicare enrollment. No separate application is necessary.

Part B charges premiums like those you would pay for traditional medical insurance. The rates, which are established by statute, are increased each year to reach 25 percent of Part B costs. In 2003, the monthly premium is $58.70. The premium is expected to more than double in the next 10 years.

Premiums are deducted from your monthly Social Security check. If you're not receiving Social Security, premiums will be billed directly to you on a quarterly basis.

Part B coverage is optional. If you don't want Part B coverage, you can opt out. The Social Security Administration will send you a letter granting you a specific time, at least two months, for you to decline.

If you don't enroll in Part B during your initial enrollment period when you reach age 65, you can enroll thereafter only during a *general enrollment period* from January 1 to March 31 of each year, with coverage to start July 1. There is a *premium penalty* of 10 percent for each year in which you're eligible but fail to enroll. (There is no penalty for those covered by a company plan after reaching age 65.)

Medicare Part B is administered nationwide by 32 carriers, including Blue Shield plans and private insurers such as CIGNA, Aetna, and Transamerica. Carriers are responsible for paying your claims and providing information on your coverage.

Can I get retroactive benefits for Part B?

No. Retroactive benefits are available for Part A hospital coverage only. There are no retroactive benefits available for Part B.

If I'm working, do I have to pay for Medicare Part B?

No. Part B is optional, whether you are working or not. And there's no premium penalty for older workers who delay enrollment because they're covered under group health plans through their (or their spouses') current employment. If you are covered by a company plan, you needn't enroll in Medicare Part B. When you stop working, you can apply through a *special enrollment period.*

Are Part B costs tax deductible?

Yes, Part B premiums are tax deductible to the same extent that medical insurance premiums are.

MEDICARE BUY-IN PROGRAM

If you can't afford Medicare premiums, you may be able to have the government pick up the check. Under the Medicare Buy-in Program (also called the *Qualified Medicare Beneficiary Program,* or *QMB*), states cover specified Medicare charges for qualified individuals. In order to qualify, you must be Medicare eligible with an income no more than 120 percent of the poverty level.

The potential for savings is great. The Medicare Buy-in Program pays for premium costs, as well as deductibles and copayments. This can run into the thousands. (Deductibles and copayments are discussed later in this chapter.)

An estimated 4 million elderly poor are believed to be eligible. If you think you or a member of your family may be eligible for the Medicare Buy-in, contact your local Medicaid office and ask for an application. Or call Medicare's toll-free hot line at 800/MEDICARE. The Buy-in Program is separately administered from Medicare, through your state's Medicaid program.

I'm 65 years old. I'm not on Medicaid and I can't afford Medicare. Can I get help?

The Medicare Buy-in Program may pay for your Medicare premiums—and also cover your deductible and copayment. This is like getting Medicare *and* supplemental insurance. Call now to see if you're qualified. You don't have to be on Medicaid to qualify for the program.

COVERAGE AND EXCLUSIONS

What does Medicare insurance provide? Coverage under both Part A and Part B entitles participants to a number of services. One caveat: in order to qualify for coverage, all services must be provided in an appropriate facility and by personnel with Medicare certification and licensed by the state.

Part A hospital insurance covers inpatient hospital care, including:

- Semiprivate room and meals
- Special care units
- Diagnostic procedures, X rays, laboratory services
- Anesthesia
- Operating and recovery rooms
- Rehabilitation services
- Post-hospital skilled nursing facility care (under specific conditions only)
- Home health care (under specific conditions only)
- Hospice care
- Blood

Part B medical insurance covers

- Physician and surgeon services
- Clinical laboratory services
- Ambulatory (outpatient) services

- Physicians' assistants and nurse anesthetists
- Psychiatric social services
- Physical and speech therapists
- Chiropractic care
- Ambulance services
- Screening mammograms, Pap smears
- Specific preventive services, including diabetes, colorectal, and prostate cancer screening
- Injectable drugs to treat osteoporosis
- Durable medical equipment, medical supplies, and prosthetic devices
- Blood
- Home health care (under specific conditions only)

Medicare has announced coverage for some additional services:

- Eye treatments for age-related macular degeneration
- Foot care for some diabetics
- Ambulatory blood pressure monitoring
- Home testing of blood thinness for mechanical heart valves
- Sleep disorder devices

For an up-to-date listing of available services and devices, you can check Medicare's website at www.list.nih.gov.

It's also vital to know what's not covered by Medicare. Medicare does *not* cover

- Long-term nursing home care
- Full-time home nursing care or personal care
- Homemaker services (except hospice patients)
- Home-delivered meals
- Most checkups and preventive care
- Routine eye exams, eyeglasses, and contact lenses (except for some cataract surgery patients)
- Hearing exams, hearing aids and fittings
- Routine foot care and orthopedic shoes
- Dental care and dentures
- Over-the-counter drugs
- Prescription drugs used at home (except hospice patients)
- Self-administered injections such as insulin
- Most immunizations

- Experimental procedures
- Chiropractic services
- Acupuncture
- Private hospital rooms
- Private duty nursing

These exclusions can be fairly daunting to those in need of the care they represent—and in some circumstances even the care included on the list of covered services may be denied. Medicare coverage for home health care and post-hospital care in particular is limited in most cases due to extensive restrictions. Be prepared to fight for benefits you're entitled to. You may need to appeal an adverse decision or seek professional legal assistance. Appeals are discussed later in this chapter. (See Chapter 8 for information on obtaining Medicare for home health and post-hospital care.)

MEDICARE AND ALZHEIMER'S DISEASE

Alzheimer's disease, a brain disorder that destroys memory, impairs cognitive ability, and alters personality, afflicts nearly 4 million Americans. The Alzheimer's Association estimates that as many 10 percent of people over 65—and nearly half of those over 85—have Alzheimer's or some form of behavior and cognitive decline. Yet until very recently, people with Alzheimer's disease have been without help from Medicare. In 2002, the CMS announced a policy change, authorizing Medicare coverage for the treatment of Alzheimer's disease.

Under the new policy, costs of medical services will not be denied on the basis of the Alzheimer's diagnosis. Medicare will pay for medically necessary services, such as physical, occupational, and speech therapy; mental health services; and hospice care.

The rationale? In the past, claims were automatically denied on the assumption that treatment was futile and that individuals with Alzheimer's disease could not benefit from interventions. But studies show that Alzheimer's patients can benefit from psychotherapy; physical, speech, and occupational therapy; and other services. For example, physical therapy can help some patients who have "forgotten" how to walk to walk again.

People claiming benefits will still have to show medical need for treatment. And with cutbacks in home health care, expectations of major services are illusory. Nevertheless, with patients able to receive benefits that were once denied, the hope is that new services will enable many to live longer on their own, with greater ability to function. Possible services include evaluation, management visits, physical, occupational, and speech therapy, psychotherapy, and behavior management therapy.

Will the new policy cover prescription drugs?

As a general rule, Medicare will not cover prescription drugs for any illness, including Alzheimer's disease.

Will it pay for day care or nursing home care specially designed for Alzheimer's patients?

Medicare will not pay for adult day care. Medicare will not pay for room and board in an assisted living facility, custodial care in a nursing home, or 24-hour personal care in the home. But it may cover some limited home health care, if the individual is homebound and requires a skilled service, such as nursing services, or physical, occupational, or speech therapy, even if the beneficiary attends adult day care.

PRESCRIPTION DRUGS

Prescription drugs are the fastest-growing area of health care spending. National spending has tripled in the last decade and doubled in the last five years. The medicine cabinets of the elderly, some 13 percent of the population, hold more than one-third of the prescriptions.

For most, out-of-pocket costs have skyrocketed. The average per-person cost topped $1,000 in 2002. Although many have some sort of insurance to help defray the cost of drugs, an estimated 38 percent of Medicare beneficiaries have no coverage. Nearly one out of four report skipping doses or not filling prescriptions because of costs. (Prescription drug benefits available through Medigap supplemental insurance are described in Chapter 6.)

Medicare does pay for some drugs. Under Part B, it assumes payment for some 450 drugs, most of which are chemotherapy agents or immune-suppressor drugs that patients cannot administer themselves. It also pays for drugs for hospice patients.

Many states already have a drug subsidy program for low-income seniors, mostly financed by state money, including New York's EPIC, New Jersey's PAAD, and Connecticut's Conspace programs. Illinois and Washington are among states participating in a federal matching program, which grants money to states for drug coverage for people who are not eligible for Medicaid. A number of states have applied to join the program, which will operate like a Medicaid waiver program, allowing drug benefits to seniors not eligible for Medicaid (and siphoning off benefits to Medicaid).

Check also with your local hospital and drug manufacturers. Major drug companies in particular often have savings programs that offer deep discounts for seniors, although the programs are not well publicized. The National Council on the Aging (NCOA) has a website to connect older adults with prescription savings programs at http://www. BenefitsCheckUp.org.

Legislative note: *Prescription drugs are the forerunner of Medicare's future. Prescription drugs have been a hot-button issue in the last nationwide election campaigns. Democrats have pushed for increased drug benefits, while Republicans have wanted to include prescription benefits within a larger reform package. What happens within this political fight may forecast the future of Medicare.*

The myriad bills addressing prescription drugs are as similar and varied as the ills they purport to tame. One proposal would add a prescription drug benefit to Medicare, carrying a $40 monthly premium charge and a $250 deductible (eliminated or reduced for those at or near the poverty level). The benefit would cover 70 percent, then 50 percent of costs, up to a maximum of $5,000 for those at or near the poverty level. An alternative proposal would limit the premium to $25 a month, with no deductible, beginning with a 50 percent copayment and with a stop loss limit of $4,000.

Details go to the heart of Medicare. One proposal has "pharmacy benefits managers" allocated among the Medicare regions, another would administer the program through competing private health plans. One would give CMS the authority to negotiate drug prices, like the Veterans Administration (VA) does, while still another would fold the drug benefit into a new agency, along with Medicare + Choice plans (see next chapter). Still another version would limit benefits to Medicare recipients who agree to enter HMOs or other private plans.

A few reform bills are aimed at the drug companies themselves, trying to encourage research or permit pharmacies to purchase drugs from Canada.

In general, the argument is between increased government benefits, which would guarantee the services but with a costly high price tag, versus free market insurance, spreading the risk and the cost but less likely to provide the services needed. The upshot for Medicare recipients is bound to be a disappointment, because no matter what the eventual structure, it will cover only part of each person's bill.

DEDUCTIBLES AND COPAYMENT

Medicare is a cost-sharing program, its expenses borne by the government and contributed to by Medicare participants. These contributions are in the form of premiums (discussed above) and deductibles and copayments for which participants are liable.

Deductibles. A deductible is the amount you must pay before Medicare assumes responsibility for payment. For medical services under Part B, you have to pay the first $100 in charges each year. For hospital care under Part A, you have to pay a deductible ($840 in 2003) for *each* benefit period. Part B deductibles are waived for some services, such as mammograms, home health care, and vaccines.

A *benefit period* is a measure of your use of hospital services. A benefit period starts when you're admitted to the hospital and ends after you've been out of the hospital (or the skilled facility you went to after leaving the hospital) for 60 days.

If you're readmitted to the hospital within the 60 days following your discharge, that counts as part of the same benefit period. If you're readmitted more than 60 days after your discharge, you've entered a new benefit period—and you'll have to pay a new $840 deductible. After the new deductible is met, you once again have a full 60 days at full reimbursement before copayment is required.

Copayment. Copayment requires you to pay a share of the costs. Under Part B, you generally have to pay 20 percent of the approved amount of doctors' costs. Some services have no coinsurance requirements, including home health care and diagnostic laboratory tests.

For Part A hospitalization, you have to pay a set amount ($210 a day in 2003) after 60 days. If you need more than 90 days, you will have to use a one-time bank of 60 "lifetime reserve" days, for which you have to pay $420 per day (in 2003). You are responsible for total costs over 150 days. (We'll explain how Medicare supplemental insurance can pay these amounts in Chapter 6.)

For skilled nursing facility expenses under your Part A coverage, you have to pay a set amount after 20 days ($105 a day in 2003). Beyond 100 days, you're liable for total costs.

OUTPATIENT (AMBULATORY) CARE

Watch out for outpatient costs! If you go for ambulatory, outpatient treatment, you will pay higher copayments than for other treatment.

As of August 1, 2000, the new hospital Outpatient Prospective Payment System (OPPS) was put into place. The system is designed to balance services with access to new drug and device technologies, increasing payments to hospitals while reducing beneficiary copayments. Generally, coinsurance amounts are based on 20 percent of the national median charge billed by hospitals for the service. In 25 years, coinsurance will be 20 percent of the prospective payment amount, but that's of little help today. Your copay may be 50 percent, or as high as 90 percent for services such as radiology and chemotherapy. The only limitation is that your copay for an individual service may not exceed the amount of the deductible for inpatient hospital services.

The OPPS also covers some services provided by home health agencies and hospices, such as antigens, vaccines, casts, and splints. It does not cover ambulance services, for which a new fee schedule is being developed.

PHYSICIAN FEES

Under Medicare Part B, the patient is responsible for paying an initial $100 deductible and 20 percent of the approved amount of the doctor's fee. As a Medicare patient, your costs will be dependent on

- The approved rate set by Medicare
- Whether your doctor participates in Medicare
- Fee limits imposed by federal and state law

Medicare-approved rate. This is the rate set by Medicare for the particular medical service performed by the doctor, whether it is an office visit or outpatient or in-hospital surgery. The Medicare-approved rate governs how much the doctor may bill Medicare and how much the patient will be charged. Depending on the state you live in and your choice of doctor, patient charges may range from 20 to 35 percent of the Medicare-approved rate (not including liability for the yearly $100 deductible).

Participating doctors. A participating doctor is one who accepts assignment for all patients, who will then be charged at the Medicare-approved rate. By accepting assignment, the doctor agrees to accept the Medicare-approved rate in full payment for services rendered. The doctor submits all Medicare claim forms to CMS for direct payment, and the patient is billed for any deductible and copayment unpaid by Medicare.

With a participating doctor, there is no cost to you above the $100 Part B deductible and 20 percent copayment. Participating doctors must take assignment on all the services they render.

A doctor who doesn't accept assignment or who accepts it in select cases only is a *nonparticipating* doctor. If your doctor refuses assignment, you may have to pay the whole amount of your doctor's charge (subject to fee caps, discussed below) and wait for Medicare to reimburse you. You'll be responsible for the annual deductible and 20 percent copayment amount, plus the cost over what Medicare approves for the service. This is called *balance billing.*

If your doctor is nonparticipating but accepts assignment on your case, for all practical purposes it works the same as with a participating doctor. The doctor must submit the bill to Medicare, and you will be charged only the applicable deductible and copayment of 20 percent of the Medicare-approved rate.

Fee limits. Whether or not a doctor accepts assignment, the federal government and a number of states have imposed additional fee limits (also called *fee caps*) on the amount doctors may charge Medicare patients.

Federally imposed fee limits apply to all doctors treating Medicare patients, even if they don't accept assignment:

- A doctor who accepts assignment is limited to the Medicare-approved fee. Medicare will pay 80 percent, which leaves you liable for 20 percent.
- A doctor who doesn't accept assignment can charge you more than the Medicare rate, but *no more than 115 percent* of the Medicare-approved rate. Medicare will still pay 80 percent, which leaves you liable for no more than 35 percent.

A number of states specify more restricted fees than the federal law or eliminate additional fees ("balance billing") totally:

- **Fee restrictions.** Massachusetts requires doctors to accept assignment for all Medicare patients. Pennsylvania prohibits any billing above the Medicare-approved rate. New York imposes fee limits of 105 percent of the Medicare-approved rate (limits are not applicable to home and office visits).
- **Means-tested restrictions.** Rhode Island requires assignment for all those below a certain income. Connecticut and Vermont also have eligibility requirements by income. (Vermont does not apply limits to home and office visits.)

Florida, Minnesota, and Ohio laws also limit balance billing.

How can I find a participating doctor?

A directory of participating physicians is made available to all Medicare recipients. Between one-quarter and one-third of physicians are participating doctors. Even if your doctor is not a participating doctor, you can always try to negotiate with your doctor to accept assignment on your case.

My doctor does not participate in Medicare and insists on my paying upfront. Are there any limits on the fees I can be charged?

Yes. Fee limits set by federal law apply to *all* Medicare patients, regardless of whether your doctor is a participating doctor or accepts assignment in your case. Your state may impose additional restrictions on the amount you are charged.

What do I do with these Medicare forms?

Under recent law, all doctors must fill out and submit Part B Medicare forms for their Medicare patients, whether they've accepted assignment or not. The law allows doctors one year to file a claim.

I have an insurance policy that will pay the balance above the rate allowed by Medicare. What should I tell my doctor?

If you are covered by insurance, your doctor can bill your insurance company for the extra amount, despite the fee limits. But with statutory limits on the fees you can be charged anyway, why pay extra for that kind of coverage?

The doctor I used to go to refuses to accept Medicare patients. Is this legal?

Yes. Doctors are not obligated to treat Medicare patients.

My doctor has joined an HMO. Can he still treat me? What options do I have?

You have the right to join an HMO in lieu of Medicare services. More than 5 million Medicare recipients nationwide have joined HMOs. (For more on managed care and Medicare, see the next chapter.)

HOSPITAL COSTS AND TREATMENT

Once you're in the hospital, you have the right to the treatment and services you need. Medicare Part A covers these inpatient hospital services, subject to your deductible and copayments not covered by insurance. This is what you will pay.

Don't confuse your charges with the amount Medicare pays the hospital. In order to control hospital costs, Congress has established a payment system based on patient diagnosis. When you enter the hospital, a flat fee is determined in advance by whether you're being admitted for a hernia or heart surgery or any one of more than 500 different groups (called *Diagnosis Related Groups,* or *DRGs*). Under this "prospective payment" or "DRG system," the hospital gets the same flat rate from Medicare no matter how long you stay in the hospital or how many or how few services you receive.

How does the DRG system affect your treatment? Theoretically, it shouldn't. If you need treatment, you are legally entitled to it even if your "DRG days" are used up. When the DRG system was first introduced, critics charged that hospitals were discharging patients "quicker and sicker." Although the prevalence of these abuses has since lessened in response to intense consumer outcry and government monitoring, the economic incentive for hospitals is still there—and so is the opportunity for abuse. Remember, your discharge date must be determined by your medical needs, not by your DRG category or Medicare coverage.

You will have to pay, however, for any service or treatment you receive that isn't approved by Medicare. Medicare pays only for hospitalization that is medically necessary. If the hospital believes the particular treatment or service you're being prescribed is not covered by Medicare, it must inform you in writing.

- If you haven't already been treated, you'll have to forgo the service or pay privately. The catch-22 of this alternative is that if you can't afford and don't pay for the service, you have nothing to appeal later.
- If the decision on your treatment amounts to a denial of your right to remain in the hospital, you can appeal your discharge as premature to the hospital's Quality Improvement Organization (QIO) through an *immediate review* process designed to help you remain in the hospital if discharge is inappropriate. You can make this appeal whether you're being discharged to a skilled nursing facility, to home health care, or to your home.

DISCHARGE

You have the absolute right to *discharge planning* before you're discharged from the hospital. What services will or won't be covered should be discussed at your consultation. The plan must be discussed with you and placed in your record. Under law, it must be finished in time for arrangements to be made for your transfer to a nursing home or skilled nursing facility or to your home with home care services before discharge. (See Chapter 8 for information on your rights in this regard.)

The hospital wants to discharge me, but I'm still sick. Can they do this?

It depends on your medical condition. In more egregious cases, patients have been transferred from the hospital before their conditions were stable. This kind of "dumping" is strictly against the law.

Am I limited to the number of days in the DRG for my illness?

No. You're not limited to the number of days in your DRG and you cannot be charged extra if your stay exceeds them. So long as your medical condition requires hospital care, the hospital cannot discharge you.

The hospital wants to discharge me, but I don't have a bed to go to. Can they charge me?

If you're awaiting placement in a skilled nursing facility, you're entitled to stay in the hospital without charge until a skilled nursing bed is available. It's the responsibility of your doctor and the hospital to find an appropriate placement for you. That doesn't necessarily mean the facility of your choice. You will not be allowed to remain in the hospital once an appropriate nursing home bed is found, even if it's not where you'd prefer to go.

EXPEDITED REVIEW BEFORE DISCHARGE

Once you've received a decision turning down a claim submitted to Medicare, you can challenge that decision through an appeals process set forth in the Medicare law (and described in the following section). However, if you are in the hospital and the decision amounts to denial of your right to remain in the hospital, you may also be entitled to an *expedited review.*

If you receive a "Notice of Noncoverage" while you're in the hospital, one option is to stay on and pay privately, appealing later if you wish. Another option, for those unable to foot the bill even temporarily, is to ask for an immediate, or *expedited,* review.

How to proceed with your expedited review depends on whether your doctor agrees or disagrees with the hospital's determination to discharge you.

- **If the hospital and your doctor agree** that you should be discharged, you must request a review by noon of the first workday after you receive the written Notice of Noncoverage. You can make your request by phone or in writing, but the deadline is very important. If you meet the deadline, you can't be made to pay hospital charges until a committee called the Quality Improvement Organization (QIO, formerly the Peer Review Organization, or PRO) reviews your case.

  The QIO is a group of doctors who review treatment decisions on behalf of Medicare. Although these are usually statewide groups, some QIO decisions are made by hospital utilization review committees that have been delegated that task.

The QIO will ask your views before making its decision, which it will communicate to you by phone or in writing. If it agrees with you, you'll be allowed to remain in the hospital without paying. If not, you're not billed until noon of the day after you receive their decision.

You can gain at least one day more of coverage if you do not appeal on the day you receive your notice but wait until the morning of the following day. If your appeal is denied on the same day, you are liable as of noon of the next day. You must file before noon.

- **If the hospital and your doctor disagree** about your discharge, your case has probably already been reviewed by the QIO. With your doctor opposed to discharge, the QIO had to agree with the hospital for a Notice of Noncoverage to have been issued. Because of this, the hospital is allowed to bill you as of the third day after you receive your notice, even if you've requested another review.

To limit your potential liability to one day, you should request reconsideration immediately, by phone or in writing. The QIO has three working days to complete its review.

If you receive a Notice of Noncoverage while you're in the hospital, contact the hospital's patient representative immediately. The patient representative (also called *patient advocate* or *ombudsman*) will help you understand the notice and explain the options available to you if you want to stay longer.

I've received a Notice of Noncoverage from the hospital. What happens now? What are my legal obligations?

If you don't request a review, the hospital may bill you for all the costs of your stay beginning the third day after you receive the written notice.

The hospital says I'm not covered by Medicare for any more time, but I haven't received anything in writing. Am I legally obligated to pay?

If you don't receive a written Notice of Noncoverage, you don't have to pay.

I want to request my review right away. Why can't I just go ahead and do that?

You can. But there are financial reasons to delay. If you do request an expedited review and it's decided against you right away, you may lose those extra days that delay might gain you.

What happens if I don't ask for an immediate review and stay in the hospital and pay for the noncovered days?

You can still appeal Medicare's decision to end payment later on, through the regular appeals process described in the following section.

APPEALING A MEDICARE DECISION

As noted above, Medicare contracts out its claims administration to private insurance companies, called *intermediaries* and *carriers*. (Intermediaries process Part A claims; carriers process Part B claims.)

Once you've submitted a claim and received an initial determination from the Medicare carrier or intermediary, you can challenge that decision through an appeals process set forth in the Medicare law. If you go to a participating doctor or if your doctor has accepted assignment for your treatment, the doctor handles appeals; you only have to appeal on unassigned claims.

You can appeal decisions about

- Doctor bills under Medicare Part B
- In-hospital admission or continued hospital stay
- Decisions about hospital payment
- Admission to skilled nursing facility and continued stay
- Home health agency coverage and payment

The Medicare appeal process is multilevel. The rules differ slightly depending on whether you're appealing a Part B claim decision, a Part A claim decision for in-hospital services, or any other part A claim decision. Each step has different rules, including minimum amounts that must be "in controversy" and deadlines which must be observed. The time runs from the receipt of the prior decision.

New appeals procedure were enacted in 2000 as part of the Beneficiaries Improvement and Protection Act (BIPA). The law's reforms include:

- A uniform process for claims under Medicare Parts A and B
- New time frames for filing appeals
- New time frames for decisions
- A uniform amount in controversy for administrative law judge (ALJ) hearings
- A new review level by qualified independent contractors (QICs)

Concerns about current backlogs and scarce resources have caused CMS to delay implementation of many of these changes, causing considerable confusion. Specific provisions that have been postponed include the new QIC level of review, as well as the time frames for filing appeals and rendering decisions (decisions and notices by intermediaries and carriers 45 days after receipt of the claim, redeter-

MEDICARE APPEALS

Part B Claims

Steps	Deadline to file (from receipt of prior decision)	Minimum amount in controversy
Initial denial		
Review	120 days	None
Fair hearing	6 months	$100
Administrative hearing	60 days	$500
Appeals Council	60 days	$500
Federal Court	60 days	$1000

Part A Claims (In-Hospital)

Steps	Deadline to file (from receipt of prior decision)	Minimum amount in controversy
Initial denial		
Reconsideration	120 days	None
Administrative hearing	60 days	$100
Appeals Council	60 days	$200
Federal Court	60 days	$2000

Part A Claims (All Others)

Steps	Deadline to file (from receipt of prior decision)	Minimum amount in controversy
Initial denial		
Reconsideration	120 days	None
Administrative hearing	60 days	$100
Appeals Council	60 days	$100
Federal Court	60 days	$1000

minations by contractors of initial determinations within 30 days, 90-day deadline for ALJ and Appeals Council decisions, and expedited determinations of provider decisions to terminate care). Existing appeals processes, as specified below, include new rules that went into effect October 1, 2002.

Although the appeal process uses different nomenclature for different steps (e.g., "review" of Part B claims, "reconsideration" of Part A claims), there is no legal significance to the names used. They are primarily used to distinguish one appeal step from another. Medicare provides forms to request review, reconsideration, or appeal. These forms are not required; you can use any other forms or letters that state your case. However, you may wish to use them for your convenience or as a guide to help prepare your appeal.

1. Review and Reconsideration

Review of Part B claims. You should request a review if Medicare denies your coverage of a Part B claim, or if it pays you less than 80 percent of your doctor's (or other health provider's) charges. This happens when Medicare says the "reasonable charge" is less than what your doctor billed.

You can get a review simply by requesting it within 120 days after the date of the initial denial. Simply write to your Medicare carrier. The carrier can extend the deadline 60 days if you request additional time to gather necessary medical records. The carrier will have your claim reviewed by a different employee than the one who made the initial determination. You'll get a written response within six to eight weeks.

Always request a review if your claim is denied. There is no minimum amount that need be in dispute. More than 63 percent of Part B reviews are successful at this first review level, winning money for the claimants.

Reconsideration of Part A claims for inpatient hospital care. For determinations concerning the necessity of inpatient hospital care, you may request reconsideration by the QIO.

You can get a reconsideration of your claim upon request within 120 days. Expedited review of admission or continued-stay denials is also available upon request by the patient. The QIO will issue its written reconsideration determination within 30 days, within 10 days for skilled nursing facility patients, and within three days for admissions candidates and hospital patients. There is no minimum dispute amount for reconsideration.

Reconsideration of Part A claims for other than inpatient hospital care. You may request reconsideration by the intermediary. Again, there is a 120-day period in which you must make your request for reconsideration; there is no minimum dispute amount. These will be decided "on paper," which means you don't have to appear anywhere. The decision will be made by an intermediary employee, *not* the one who made the initial determination. The reversal rate for these appeals is only 15–20 percent.

2. Fair Hearing (Part B claims only)

If the review of your Part B claim has not been successful and your claim is at least $100, you're entitled to a fair hearing from the carrier. You must request a hearing within six months of the review determination.

For this kind of hearing, courtroom rules of evidence do not apply. The hearing officer is appointed by the carrier, usually a paid employee. The hearing officer has no subpoena power. In making a decision, the hearing officer applies Medicare policies and guidelines. The hearing is recorded and transcribed.

The hearing is usually held at the carrier's office or a Social Security office, although it can be held elsewhere on request. The hearing may be in person or "on the record," which means the appeal is decided solely on documents submitted to the hearing officer.

Your odds on success at a fair hearing are good. The reversal rate for claimants at a Part B hearing is 60 percent.

3. Administrative Hearing

If you're still not satisfied after your review and/or hearing, you're entitled to an administrative hearing before an administrative law judge (ALJ) employed by the Social Security Administration. You may bring a lawyer.

You must request an administrative hearing within 60 days of the prior determination made concerning your claim. The minimum amount that must be in dispute depends on the type of claim: $500 for a Part B claim, $200 for a Part A inpatient claim, and $100 for all other Part A claims.

An administrative hearing is similar to a regular civil suit, including sworn testimony by the parties. You have the right to submit testimony, the opportunity for cross-examination, and the right to object to admission of evidence. An ALJ can issue subpoenas on the written request of counsel, made at least five days before the scheduled hearing date. Your doctor may be required to testify.

The hearing is usually held near your home, although you may be required to travel up to 75 miles. You or your lawyer will get 10 days notice of the time and the place of the hearing from the ALJ.

The hearing may be in person or "on the record." There is a 40 percent success rate for those who request in-person hearings.

4. Appeals Council Review

Within 60 days of the ALJ's decision, you may appeal the ALJ's decision to the Medicare Appeals Council of the Departmental Appeals Board. There is no additional dollar minimum. Review by the Appeals Council of a decision by an ALJ is usually based on errors of law, abuse of discretion, and policy issues. For the most part, it's an on-the-record hearing. More than 10,000 cases are heard annually by the Appeals Council. The Appeals Council is the last step required before you go to federal court.

5. Federal Court

If the Appeals Council rules against you or if it refuses a hearing, you may appeal to the federal courts. If you meet the minimum amount requirements ($2,000 for in-hospital Part A claim, $1,000 for all others), you or your lawyer can request a federal court hearing. If the district court finds in your favor, it can reverse Medicare's decision or order a new hearing.

Medicare denied my claim. How do I decide whether to appeal?

In most appeals, the question being reviewed is the medical necessity of your care. In order to show that your treatment or care meets that standard, you will have to produce letters from your doctor attesting to your condition as well as any other medical documentation. In later stages of an appeal, your doctor may be called to testify.

Other possible issues include whether Medicare covers the particular treatment or service, whether you're entitled to it under the rules, and what amount you're entitled to. You might be arguing about deductibles, copayments, days used in a benefit period, or duration of a benefit period. Whatever the issue, it's important that you focus on that question and not get sidetracked by extraneous matters.

How can I appeal when I don't know why they denied my claim?

You have a right to the information on which Medicare based its decision. You should ask for a copy of your file when you request a review or recommendation.

I missed the deadline for review. What do I do?

Requests for review or reconsideration, or other appeal, must be filed within certain time limits set forth in the law. The time limits are important, although a late filing may be allowed for "good cause." What constitutes good cause may be death or serious illness in the family or misunderstanding, but there is no requirement that you be allowed a late filing. The safest bet is to meet the deadline in the first place.

My claim is for $2,000. Can I go directly to federal court?

No. You have to start with the first step of the appeals process (review or reconsideration) and proceeding to each subsequent step in order. Before going to court, you must first complete the administrative process. This is called *exhausting your remedies.*

Of course if you prevail at any step, you stop at that stage. If Medicare doesn't appeal, then you win. If Medicare appeals, you have to continue on to the next step.

Should I get legal help?

You may represent yourself throughout the entire process or use a lawyer for each step. As a general rule, the initial stages of appeal don't require sophisticated legal help. In admission and continued-stay determinations, where the consequences are more immediate and the stakes are higher, you may welcome professional assistance at early stages.

A number of Medicare advocacy programs provide free legal services. American Association of Retired Persons (AARP) has a Medicare assistance program, which helps with Medicare problems, processing payments and paperwork. Assistance is also available with Medicare appeals. (See the appendixes at the end of this book for a listing of agencies that may be of help.)

6

Health Insurance

For most older retired Americans, primary health insurance is provided by Medicare. For charges that Medicare does not cover and charges that it covers only in part, they rely on other insurance supplemental to that primary coverage.

Insurance made available through employment provides the primary coverage and protection for many older workers, retirees, and their spouses. For those age 65 to 69, that insurance is their primary coverage and protection. For those with other insurance coverage, Medicare provides secondary coverage, covering services and charges not paid for by their private carrier. At age 70, no matter what your employment status, Medicare becomes your primary insurance coverage.

No matter which category you fall into, an understanding of the protection afforded by hospitalization, major medical policies, Medigap supplemental policies, and long-term care policies (discussed in Chapter 10) is crucial to your health care planning.

This is especially true now, when corporations and insurers are experimenting with new arrangements to keep costs down, including self-insurance, health maintenance organizations and managed care, direct administration of company plans, and utilization review and monitoring. You need to be able to assess what type of insurance will meet your needs and to know how to evaluate policies, what your rights are, and how to assert them. There's no excuse for ignorance—and less for not asserting rights you've paid for.

Your benefits depend on these factors:

- The type of coverage you have
- The terms and conditions of your individual policy
- The fiscal integrity of your insurance company
- Laws affording you protection as a consumer

A number of laws govern the benefits you receive and rights you are afforded under health policies, including HIPAA (Health Insurance Portability and Accountability Act), which affords you certain rights in policy terms; COBRA, which affords you rights when you stop working; and Medicare law, which governs Medicare supplemental insurance (Medigap).

TYPES OF HEALTH INSURANCE

Traditional fee-for-service coverage is structured so that the health care provider—doctor, hospital, therapist—is paid for services on a per-service basis. The fee is generally determined by the doctor, and if you are not self-insured, how much you will have to pay depends upon your insurance.

Your insurance will cover some or all of the fees, subject to the policy definition of eligible expenses, the doctor's fee, and your copayment and deductible. The benefit to you is that you choose the health care provider and the hospital. (Managed care, the opposite of fee-for-service, is discussed in Chapter 7.)

Under the new HIPAA, passed in 1997, certain provisions of your contract are spelled out by federal law. HIPAA limits exclusions for pre-existing conditions and guarantees renewability and access to insurance for certain employees and individuals.

Hospital-surgical insurance covers inpatient hospital services and surgical procedures. Charges for room and board, surgeons' fees, nursing services, X rays, and lab and diagnostic tests should also be included. Almost always excluded are services provided outside the hospital, even follow-up visits.

Your coverage under a hospital-surgical policy may be limited to a fixed number of days in the hospital. Double-check reimbursement rates. This type of policy often pays at the low end of the scale, leaving you with a hefty balance due.

Comprehensive/major medical insurance provides coverage for basic hospital services and for doctor services in and out of the hospital. Coverage generally includes room and board, operating and recovery, doctor visits, nursing care, lab tests, X rays, anesthesia, and other costs commonly associated with hospital services.

Policies vary widely. Some offer supplemental items such as prescription drugs or post-hospital coverage. If you're over 65 and receiving Medicare benefits, comprehensive policies may be needed for your under-65 spouse's coverage.

Medigap insurance is designed to supplement Medicare coverage for older people and may provide some additional benefits as well.

These are the most common forms of insurance. Stick with a basic hospitalization plan, or a comprehensive major-medical if you can get one. Others include the following:

- *Hospital indemnity policies* pay a fixed dollar amount for each day you're in the hospital. Some are designed to pay a fixed amount per service. Coverage is often linked to a waiting period for which you cannot collect benefits, and the amounts are often too small to cover hospital costs.
- *Dread disease insurance* is linked to the possibility that you might catch a specific disease. You can buy cancer insurance, or insurance against other specific diseases. Not only are the odds against your contracting the particular disease for which you're covered, the benefits are usually pitifully small, the premiums comparatively high, and there's usually a qualification period of six months or more before you would be eligible to collect benefits. These are banned in New York and a number of other states.

POLICY TERMS AND CONDITIONS

An insurance policy is a contract. It binds both you and your insurer to certain obligations enforceable under the law. The terms of your policy determine whether you'll collect on any claims and how much you'll collect.

Your policy may have exclusions for eligible expenses, deductibles and copayment amounts, and newly instituted review boards. There are any number of possible variations, and it's important for you to know what coverage you have and what coverage you're buying.

Eligible expenses. Health coverage is typically linked to a determination by the insurance company of eligible expenses. An eligible expense is one for which the treatment or service is covered by your policy. It's generally subject to the condition that the treatment must be *medically necessary,* often limited to treatment of an illness or injury, as defined by the insurer.

Even if the procedure is determined to be medically necessary, you have another hurdle to cross. Your expenses are limited to *reasonable and customary charges.* What constitutes a reasonable and customary charge differs among insurers and among policies. The amount is theoretically set on doctors' fees in your area. You're liable for what the doctor charges above the insurance company–determined eligible expense.

Make sure you know how much your insurance will pay before you commit to any high-ticket procedures. If the amount is appreciably out of sync with your doctor's fee, you should ask why. Either your doctor is overcharging or your insurance company is not paying enough. You can negotiate with your doctor or your insurance company, and ask them to reconsider their decision.

Deductibles and copayment. You will be reimbursed subject to your deductible and copayment share. The deductible is the amount you pay before the insurance company reimbursement begins. The higher the deductible, the lower the premium.

The copayment is the portion or amount of medical charges you are required to pay once the deductible is met. Many policies pay 80 percent of eligible expenses, leaving your copay share at 20 percent. Other policies provide 70–30 or 50–50. More recent policies, including many managed-care policies, require a higher percentage if you don't use panel-approved doctors or hospitals.

An upper cap on the copayment amount you're liable for per year is called a *stop loss*. Above a given amount, for example, $5,000 or $10,000, 100 percent of eligible expenses will be paid. With stop loss protection, your maximum outlay is limited to the total of your premiums, deductible, and copayments within a given range. Some policies exclude certain expenses, such as for mental health, from stop loss protection. (One proposal before Congress would require coverage for mental illness to be equivalent to that provided for other conditions, eliminating it as a category for separate treatment.)

Case management/utilization review. More and more insurance companies are issuing policies requiring review for your health care to be covered. A case management or utilization review program incorporated into your health insurance policy is intended to ensure that proposed medical services are necessary, reasonable, and cost-efficient: the most "appropriate" level and amount of care at the least cost. This kind of review is similar to the controls established by HMOs and other managed-care organizations.

Often the case management requirement is limited to inpatient hospital treatment. Preadmission review or admission review following emergency admission commonly includes second opinions (covered by insurers), precertification, and testing. There may be a penalty when the insurance company is not notified of an inpatient stay.

Many policies, which include an appeals process for claim conflicts, set up an additional, special appeals process to handle denials of this kind. Check your policy: *it may require a special appeal to be made within as short a time as 24 hours.* If you miss this deadline and go ahead with your treatment without utilizing the special appeals process, you can avail yourself of the regular appeals machinery later on. (See "Filing an insurance claim," later in this chapter.)

PREEXISTING CONDITIONS AND WAITING PERIODS

Preexisting conditions are health problems for which you were diagnosed or received advice or treatment prior to the effective date of your insurance. Insurance companies often will issue a policy that (1) defines a preexisting condition as one diagnosed or treated within a specified period of time before the effective date of coverage and (2) requires a waiting period before allowing coverage for preexisting conditions. The length of time for defining a preexisting condition generally varies from six months to two years before coverage begins. Waiting periods may vary from 90 days to as much as two years.

A number of states limit both the length of time prior to coverage for a preexisting condition and the waiting period after coverage begins to a specified duration. About half the states limit the length of time for preexisting conditions to the six-month period before coverage, and another 11 states limit it to 12 months in laws governing small employer health insurance. Waiting periods after the effective date of coverage are restricted to a maximum of 12 months in half the states, and to six months in six states.

Under HIPAA, the only preexisting conditions that may be excluded from your coverage are those for which medical advice, diagnosis, care, or treatment was recommended or received within the six months before your enrollment date. Your enrollment date is your first date of coverage. If your plan has a waiting period, then your enrollment date is the first date of your waiting period (usually your date of hire).

If you have an exclusion period for a preexisting condition, HIPAA sets a maximum time limit of 12 months during which the exclusion may apply (18 months for "late enrollees" who miss the first opportunity to enroll in the plan).

The period of any exclusion would be eliminated or reduced under various laws. HIPAA reduces the duration of any exclusion by the amount of "creditable coverage" received under another health policy.

You receive credit for coverage—group health plan, HMO, Medicare, Medicaid, COBRA continuation coverage—that occurred without a break of 63 days or more.

Your former health plan or insurance company is required to give you a certificate of creditable coverage to document your coverage. Usually, the information will just be transferred by telephone, between the two insurance plans.

A number of states also have additional "portability" provisions, in which waiting periods and limitation or exclusion of coverage for preexisting conditions are waived for individuals who have had continuous health insurance coverage for up to 30 or 60 days (in some states, 90 days) prior to the date of new coverage. Some states prohibit waiting periods and limitations in coverage for preexisting conditions altogether.

It's very important to disclose any preexisting conditions on your insurance application. In some states, insurance companies are permitted to delay checking on an applicant's medical history until a claim is filed. This is called *medical underwriting*. If you have a preexisting condition that is later uncovered, the company could rescind your policy.

I have a long-term condition, for which I've received treatment in the past, but none in the past six months. Is this a preexisting condition?

Under HIPAA, no. No exclusion can be applied against you.

Am I covered for preventive care such as checkups and routine examinations?

Probably not. Most traditional forms of insurance cover only medically necessary care, defined as treatment for illness or injury. Alternative forms of coverage such as managed care are beginning to include coverage for preventive care. Some state laws require coverage for specific items such as Pap smears, mammograms, and other screening services. If so, your policy will state this.

I told my insurance agent about my condition and was told to leave it off the application, that it would be all right. Should I follow my agent's advice?

No. Lying on an application is fraud. Remember, your prior treatment is a matter of record. It doesn't do you any good to get a policy that won't pay later.

The Medical Information Bureau maintains a database on more than 15 million insurance applicants. The information is disseminated to nearly 700 insurance companies, which may in turn base coverage decisions and premium charges on it.

These files often contain errors. It's a good idea to obtain a record of your application and policy claims information to make sure the contents are accurate. You can obtain a copy of the record of your insurance coverage by contacting the Medical Insurance Bureau at 617/426-3660 or online at http://www.mib.com.

I'm changing jobs. Do I have to worry about changing insurance?

It depends. A new job may give you benefits even if you have a medical problem, but there might be a waiting period for a preexisting condition. And you may not be covered for some period of time, often six to 12 months. You may need to get COBRA "continuation" coverage or "conversion" coverage from your former employer to cover you in the interim. COBRA coverage may also help you avoid a 63-day break in coverage to reduce your waiting period. (We discuss COBRA later in this chapter.)

RENEWABILITY

An insurance policy is a contract, in force for a period of time specified in the contract. Traditionally, some *optionally renewable* policies could be canceled by the insurer at the end of the policy year or premium period, for no reason at all. In a *conditionally renewable* policy, the contract could be canceled only if all other similar policies in your group, category, or state are canceled. A policy that's *guaranteed renewable* could not be canceled, but this kind of policy was harder to find. No more. Under HIPAA, individual health coverage must be renewed or continued in force. A number of states also have extended "guaranteed renewal" protections to insurance obtained through small employers.

I have a health insurance policy that is guaranteed renewable. I missed a few payments and the insurance company canceled it for lack of payment. Can they do that?

Yes. Even if your policy is guaranteed renewable, it can be canceled if you fail to pay your premium or commit fraud. Also, if you move out of the service area or terminate membership in a bona fide association (as defined by your state rules), your coverage can be terminated. (One exception: some long-term care policies provide for a waiver of premiums if you're collecting benefits. See Chapter 10.)

Am I protected once my rate is set?

Insurers set premiums for the contract period, generally one year. There's little protection against premium raises, which can force strapped policyholders to cancel. However, the law allows insurance companies to raise rates only by class of policyholders; your company cannot raise your rates just because you've made numerous claims.

There's limited protection for older workers in federal law, which grants to those who work for employers of 20 or more the right to the same coverage offered to those under 65 and under the same conditions, whether or not they're covered by Medicare.

CHECKING THE INSURANCE COMPANY

When you buy an insurance policy, you're buying an insurance company. Unfortunately, failures of health insurers have become more common. You don't want to be left in the position of paying the bill for that failure. While all the states have established guarantee associations to fund benefits and limited coverage for those whose insurance companies have failed, there are significant gaps in the protections afforded you by those funds. Policyholders have been held responsible for unpaid claims.

How can I tell if an insurance company is fiscally sound?

First, check with the insurance company. Ask for copies of financial statements filed with your state's insurance department. Check with your state insurance department to find out if the health insurance company is licensed in your state. The insurance department can also provide you with information on pricing and service. Insurance departments also conduct financial reviews of insurers within the state. Ask about any problems or complaints. (See Appendix II for a list of state insurance departments.)

Make sure you check with a rating service. Although not perfect, they're an indispensable source of information if you're researching a company. Among the companies that furnish reports on insurance companies' solvency are A.M. Best, Standard & Poor's, Moody's Investors Service, Fitch Ratings (formerly Duff & Phelps), and Weiss Ratings.

Highest ratings for each company are

- Standard & Poor's   AAA
- Moody's   Aaa
- A.M. Best   A++
- Fitch Ratings   AAA

Rating reports are available online and in public libraries. (See the resources section for rating service contact information.)

Am I protected if the company is backed by a larger insurance company?

Not necessarily. Check with the larger company about its relationship with the smaller one. Don't take it for granted that because it's written in a brochure it must be so. In some cases, companies have claimed to be guaranteed by a respectable-sounding insurance company, or to have links with one, which on closer examination turned out to be tenuous.

Are there any protections from government?

Some state insurance departments are vigorous monitors on behalf of consumers. Others don't see their function the same way. Still others are underfunded and can't perform adequate oversight. State "guarantee associations" are supposed to absorb the liability of bankrupt companies and provide some benefits and coverage for stranded policyholders. Check with your state insurance department to see if your insurance company has contributed to your state's fund.

I work for a firm that is "self-insured," but the plan is administered by Blue Cross. Does this make Blue Cross my insurer?

No. Don't confuse your insurer with your insurance plan administrator. Many health plans are administered by third-party administrators, which may be local insurers or Blue Cross. If so, it doesn't mean your plan is underwritten by the insurance company or subject to state regulation; self-insured plans are exempt from state standards. More than half of all employees in the United States work for companies that are fully or partially self-insured. Businesses like self-insurance because it saves money in premiums and assets can be used to pay claims.

FILING AN INSURANCE CLAIM

When a claim is filed with an insurance company, it's generally reviewed based on (1) whether the service is covered under your policy and (2) whether the service was "medically necessary."

Services must be included in your contract coverage for you to receive payment for them. States often have express requirements for health insurance policies that insurers must write into their policies. For example, on the theory that preventive care saves money in the long run, some states require that mammograms or other preventive tests be covered by all insurance policies. If the terms of your policy conflict with state law, the law overrides the provisions of the policy.

Once a claim is made and meets the test of medical necessity, the actual charges are reviewed based on a standard of "customary and reasonable." The company will provide reimbursement at the contract rate (for example, 80 percent) against that standard. Unlike Medicare, there are no restrictions on fees charged in relation to the insurance reimbursement or approved rate.

Check in advance. With an eye on the corporate bottom line, more and more insurance companies are rejecting claims, in whole or in part. If at all possible, check in advance about your basic coverage and the amount you will be covered for.

Research costs. If a portion of your doctor's charges is disallowed as unreasonable and you believe your doctor's fees are similar to those of other doctors in the same geographic area, write a letter to your insurance company asking it to review the reasonable and customary allowance. Get letters from your doctor and survey costs in your area. (If it turns out your doctor's fees exceed charges in your area, you can ask your doctor to lower the charges.)

Keep a record. Remember to put everything in writing. If you make a telephone call, keep a record of it. Maintain a log of your medical treatment, payments made and received, and copies of claims submitted to your insurance company. These will be essential for any appeal.

Appeal. You have the right to appeal any decision by your insurance company. It never hurts to appeal an adverse decision. An estimated 30 percent of insurance company rejections are the result of error. Insurance companies will often back down if they get reasonable, written objections.

The process you will have to follow will be in the policy, and it may also be explained in the company's letter to you. You will also be given instructions on when and where to appeal. Check out your appeal rights before you sign up. Remember to file by the deadline!

Pursue your claim. If you can't get any action from the insurance company or feel you're not being treated fairly, try contacting the president of the insurance company, your state insurance department, or your congressional representative. Your employer or plan administrator may also be of help. Remember, most people are too busy or too intimidated to pursue their complaints—and companies rely on that.

My insurance company has given me less than half of my doctor's charges, based on their estimation of "reasonable and customary charges," less my 20 percent copayment. Is this legal? Is there anything I can do about it?

It's legal, but that doesn't mean there's nothing you can do about it. Ask the insurance company to provide you with the supporting data it used to arrive at its determination. Compare the data and your own survey results of doctor's charges. If the company doesn't reconsider, file a formal appeal.

INSURANCE REGULATION

Insurance regulation is a primary responsibility of the states, which oversee the activities of insurance companies operating in their jurisdictions through their state insurance departments.

States license insurance companies, setting standards for financial operations and approving rates and policies issued by insurers. Policies are also subject to review to make sure they comply with state minimum requirements for benefits and other safeguards. Insurance agents are also licensed by the state.

More than 30 states have passed limits on rate increases for people with costly illnesses, while a smaller number have passed laws mandating uniform rates. New York, for example, requires insurance companies to accept all applicants—individuals and small companies—at the same "community rate," regardless of age, gender, or health history. Other states with similar laws include Hawaii, Vermont, Maine, and Oregon.

Some states are more active than others on behalf of consumers, providing closer oversight and monitoring of insurance companies. All state insurance departments have review procedures to assist consumers and investigate their complaints.

The National Association of Insurance Commissioners (NAIC) has adopted accreditation standards that have accredited some two-thirds of the states but have stirred opponents in state legislatures that have refused to adopt NAIC's model laws. The General Accounting Office has found NAIC's accreditation standards inconsistent. New York, New Jersey, and Connecticut are among the states not accredited.

If you have a complaint against an insurance company, make sure you notify your state insurance department by phone and in writing. And make sure the company knows it, by forwarding it a copy of the letter. Your letter may provide just the leverage you need to get the response you want from the insurance company.

We mentioned the guarantee associations that states have set up to provide help for ex-policyholders. Some states also have programs to provide subsidies toward insurance or managed care for uninsured residents who don't qualify for other insurance or Medicaid benefits.

CONTINUING COVERAGE
WHEN YOU STOP WORKING

The loss of a job no longer has to mean the loss of health insurance. If your job is in jeopardy, you may be eligible to continue in your group plan or convert to an individual policy.

Contract. You may be able to continue your policy under the terms of the policy itself. Some insurance contracts have special provisions allowing retirees or others to continue or convert their coverage after they leave their employment.

Whether you or the company will pay the premiums depends on the language of the contract. Make sure you consult your policy before you agree to any other arrangements. Don't sign away health insurance benefits that are rightfully yours.

Federal law. Under the "Comprehensive Omnibus Budget Reconciliation Act" (COBRA), if your past employer has more than 20 employees, you can remain in the same group plan for 18 months or longer. You'll pay a monthly premium, which is figured at 102 percent of your current premium cost and subject to the same deductible.

You must apply for continuation coverage during an election period that begins before your initial coverage ends and extends at least 60 days after it would end or when you've been given notice, whichever is later. Continuation coverage begins the date your prior coverage ends.

The chart below highlights eligibility for COBRA benefits and the duration of benefits for employees and dependent family members under different circumstances. Some of the provisions reflect changes made by HIPAA.

Continuation coverage is commonly purchased for those who lose their jobs, or whose spouses are not yet eligible for Medicare. It may also be useful for those who are changing jobs but have a preexisting condition not covered for a period of time under their new employer's policy. However, limits on plan exclusions for preexisting conditions mandated by the 1997 Health Insurance Portability and Accountability Act (HIPAA) have cut into COBRA's effectiveness in this regard. If a group health plan limits or excludes benefits for preexisting conditions but because of the new HIPAA rules those limits or exclusions would not apply to (or would be satisfied by) an individual receiving COBRA continuation coverage, then the plan providing the COBRA continuation coverage can stop making the COBRA continuation coverage available.

State law. Even if COBRA doesn't apply, a number of states mandate that you be given continuation benefits—at your employer's expense or your own—for a limited period of time ranging from three

COBRA ELIGIBILITY

Qualified beneficiary	Circumstances	Duration of coverage
Employee*	Your employment is terminated (except for gross misconduct)	18 months
	Your hours are reduced so that you no longer qualify for coverage	18 months
	You're disabled and eligible for Social Security benefits when your Employment ends or at any time during the first 60 days of COBRA continuation coverage**	29 months
	Your former employer commences bankruptcy	36 months
Spouse of an employee***	Your spouse dies or becomes entitled to Medicare	36 months
	You divorce or become legally separated	36 months
Dependent child of an employee	You lose "dependent child" status and exceed the age for coverage under the employee's plan	36 months

* These rules and time periods apply to employees and to their spouses and dependent children, including children born to or adopted by covered employees during COBRA continuation coverage.
** Nondisabled family members entitled to COBRA coverage are also entitled to the 29-month disability extension. You may have to pay as much as 150 percent for the additional months of coverage.
*** These rules and time periods also apply to dependent children.

to as many as 26 months (Connecticut). Your state department of insurance will be able to tell you what your state requires and what your rights are.

Conversion insurance. Once your continuation coverage ends, you may be able to convert to an individual policy from the same insurance company under state law. A conversion policy allows the purchase of a health policy without waiting periods, medical underwriting, or preexisting condition requirements. A majority of states require that you be offered a conversion option allowing you to convert to an individual policy. To find out about your rights to a conversion policy, check with your state insurance department or go to the National Association of Insurance Commissioners (NAIC) website at http://www.naic. org/regulator/usamap.htm. (See appendixes.) Remember that this right may be included in your insurance contract.

Employers who offer leaving employees conversion policies must also make them available to former employees when their continuation coverage under COBRA ends. You'll usually be given a time limit of 30 days for enrollment in a conversion policy. But you may be better off with a new policy. Keep in mind that the benefits offered under conversion policies may not be as good as your employer's group policy.

I thought that when I got Medicare my company had to cover me the same as before. But I'm told by my former employer that my coverage is going to end. Is this legal?

Under the law, your right to continuation coverage ends when you become entitled to Medicare or obtain coverage under a new policy. If your COBRA coverage is better than Medicare will be, you might try arguing with your employer that "entitled to Medicare" requires you actually to enroll—and that until you do, you're still entitled to your continuation coverage. Your benefits are also not protected when your former employer goes out of business and discontinues health insurance for other workers.

My former employer has fewer than 20 employees. Do I have any right to continuation coverage?

Although you're not covered by federal law, which is limited to businesses with 20 or more employees, some states require continuation benefits for three to as many as 26 months. If not, you may have to buy a new policy. Check with your state insurance department.

My former employer is self-insured. Does he have to provide continuation coverage?

Yes. Although employers who serve as their own health insurers are generally exempt for insurance regulation, they are still required to cover you for these purposes.

MEDICAL SAVINGS ACCOUNTS

One recent innovation is the *medical savings account,* in which money is earmarked for an individual's medical expenses by an employer, who funds all or part of the account. Medical savings accounts were originally authorized by Congress as part of a demonstration project, available to individuals and those in firms with fewer than 50 employees.

The medical savings account is not insurance. When combined with health care coverage (usually a high deductible plan with a lower premium), the medical savings account provides a savings for employers while giving "account holders" an incentive to "save" rather than spend the amounts in their accounts. At the end of the year, the unused balance in the account can be retained by the employee.

For people with few health care needs, it may save money, but it is potentially more expensive for those with greater needs. And if the use of medical savings accounts becomes widespread, there is also a potential indirect cost as greater numbers of healthy people in cheap account plans would leave older people and others in need of services paying higher costs. Even more troublesome, medical savings accounts may operate to discourage the preventive care that might keep you healthy now and avoid the need for costlier treatment down the road.

The political interest elicited by medical savings accounts was ultimately not matched by market interest. Although the law authorized 750,000 plans, fewer than 60,000 were sold. Nevertheless, the demonstration project has been renewed. At least one-quarter of the states have passed bills authorizing the use of medical savings accounts.

My employer has a flexible plan that establishes a tax-free medical benefits account for me. Is this the same as a medical savings account? Is it a good deal?

Many employers already offer "flexible plans" that allow employees to put some part of their pay into a tax-exempt account for medical benefits; however, in those plans, money not spent generally goes back to the employer. If you are right on target in estimating your costs, you can save on your tax bill, but if you're not, you can lose money you've earned. It's a good deal only if you keep your deposits into the account on the low end. If you're betting your salary against your health, it's not a fair deal.

MEDIGAP SUPPLEMENTAL INSURANCE

Medicare supplemental insurance, often called "Medigap," supplements your Medicare coverage by picking up the tab for a large portion of your health care and treatment that Medicare doesn't cover. Depending on your policy, it pays for coinsurance and deductibles; additional benefits not covered by Medicare, such as prescription drugs; and charges exceeding Medicare-approved rates.

Medigap coverage is only supplemental to what Medicare covers. If you have expenses not covered in the first place by Medicare (such as nonessential cosmetic surgery), your Medigap policy generally won't pay for the coinsurance or deductible. As a general rule, Medigap policies don't cover custodial care or long-term nursing home or home care.

The law guarantees the availability of Medigap policies to all new Medicare enrollees without any medical examination if you enroll within six months of your 65th birthday. You can't be denied a policy or charged more because of your health. In those states that have eliminated medical underwriting entirely, you don't have to worry about the six-month limitation.

There's a six-month limitation on the time you can be excluded from collecting benefits or otherwise limited for a "preexisting condition." If you switch your policy, any preexisting condition you have will be credited with the time elapsed under your original policy.

You have the right to return a Medigap insurance policy within 30 days of its delivery. You're also entitled to a full refund of any premiums you've paid. Your Medigap policy is renewable yearly as long as you pay the premiums.

As a result of abuses in sales of Medigap policies, federal law allows the sale of only 10 basic Medigap model policies (called A through J), as shown on the chart on page 102.

Each policy must offer you these basic benefits, provided in Plan A:

- Part A hospitalization coinsurance for 60–90 days and one-time "lifetime reserve" for days 91–150
- 365 lifetime hospital days (100 percent reimbursable) after Medicare benefits ends
- Part B doctor bill coinsurance
- Three pints of blood yearly

The menu of benefits available in Plans B through J is as follows:

- *Plans C–J.* Skilled nursing care coinsurance (in 2003, $105 a day for days 21–100)
- *Plans B–J.* Part A deductible
- *Plans C, F, J.* Part B deductible
- *Plans F, G, I, J.* Excess of Part B doctor bills beyond Medicare limits. (All are 100 percent reimbursable except G, which is reimbursable at 80 percent.) These are of limited value, given the limits on doctor fees to Medicare patients. The law makes it illegal for doctors to charge Medigap insurers more that 115 percent of Medicare's approved rate.
- *Plans C–J.* Foreign travel emergency (80 percent of costs after a $250 deductible, up to a lifetime benefit of $50,000)

- *Plans D, G, I, J.* At home recovery. This is somewhat limited, offering up to eight weeks beyond Medicare coverage, limited to 28 hours a week, at $40 an hour, up to $1,600 a year. You can receive these benefits only if you receive Medicare home care benefits.
- *Plans H, I, J.* Prescription drugs. This is expensive, offering only a 50 percent copayment and subject to a $250 deductible. Plans H and I have a $1,250 annual limit; Plan J goes up to $3,000
- *Plans E, J.* Preventive care such as flu shots and tests for cancer, diabetes, and hearing disorders, up to $120 a year

In addition, Plans F and J have a high deductible option ($1,620 in 2002) under which beneficiaries also pay deductibles for prescriptions ($250 per year for Plan J) and foreign travel emergency ($250 per year for Plans F and J).

These are now the only Medigap policies that may be sold. Not all insurers supply all policies, although each must give you the basic plan.

Which of the 10 models is best?

Every additional benefit increases the premium. You should buy a policy based on your individual medical history and expenses. Why spend extra dollars for foreign travel benefit if you never go anywhere? Prescription drug expenses may be of greater importance to you. If you want to ensure benefits for the future, you may want to purchase comprehensive policies now.

If the policies are uniform, does that mean I don't have to shop around for rates?

No. Coverage is uniform, but premiums may vary considerably among different insurers. We've seen variations in premium costs as high as $60 monthly—a whopping $720 a year—for the same policy. Over the past few years, the price of Medigap policies has risen at an alarming rate. You should investigate thoroughly before you buy a Medigap policy. The law makes comparison shopping relatively easy, with a ready basis for comparison provided by the 10 models.

You can get a list of carriers offering Medigap insurance from your state insurance department or office of aging. Use the chart to compare what you're being offered by different insurers, and make sure you try at least three or more companies before purchasing a policy. Some policies purchased through organizations such as AARP may be less expensive because there are no sales commissions built into the premium.

I'm disabled and getting Medicare. Should I buy Medigap coverage?

Medigap coverage has generally been available only to Medicare-eligible people over 65. Some states do allow Medigap insurance to be

MEDICARE SUPPLEMENTAL INSURANCE MEDIGAP POLICIES AND BENEFITS*

Plan	A	B	C	D	E	F	G	H	I	J
Coverage										
Core policy										
Part A coinsurance (for days 61–90 and "lifetime reserve" days 91–150)										
365 lifetime hospital days										
Part B coinsurance 3 pints of blood yearly (Parts A & B)	•	•	•	•	•	•	•	•	•	•
Skilled nursing care coinsurance (for days 21–100)			•	•	•	•	•	•	•	•
Part A deductible		•	•	•	•	•	•	•	•	•
Part B deductible			•			•				•
Excess Part B bills						•	•		•	•
Foreign travel emergency			•	•	•	•	•	•	•	•
Home health care			•			•			•	•
Outpatient prescription drugs								•	•	•
Preventive medical care					•					•

Source: GAO

* This chart does not apply in Massachusetts, Minnesota, and Wisconsin, where alternate standards for supplemental health policies exist.

bought through their pool (a big help to the disabled who are otherwise ineligible), and a few companies do offer it.

I have a health plan from my former employer. Do I need a Medigap policy?

Check your coverage. Health care plans available through your employer may supply more supplemental coverage than you can get through a Medigap policy.

Can my Medigap policy be canceled?

By law, Medigap insurance policies must be guaranteed renewable.

I'm moving to Florida next year. Can I buy new Medigap insurance?

You can, but it's not necessary. You have the right to keep the same Medigap policy you have for the rest of your life, regardless of where you move.

I'm canceling my Medigap insurance to join an HMO under the Medicare + Choice program. If I leave the HMO, can I return to my old Medigap policy?

If you terminate your Medigap policy to join an M+C plan, you may return to your original policy. But if it's not available, you're only guaranteed access to A, B, C, and F plans (all without prescription drugs).

How do I know what I'm getting?

Under the law, you can get help in deciding about Medigap policies through counseling programs set up through your local Social Security office. These should provide an objective source of information on Medigap policies. You can also call the Medigap Hotline at 800/MEDICARE.

MEDICARE COVERAGE WHEN YOU'RE WORKING

For employees aged 65 to 69 and covered by insurance, and for their spouses covered by the employer's health plan, Medicare is the secondary payer. The employer's plan must be the primary payer. Medicare will pay the difference between what the primary payer approves and pays and the doctor's charges, up to the Medicare-approved amount. At age 70, Medicare becomes the primary payer.

Medicare is also secondary to any automobile, liability, or no-fault insurance you may have, as well as to workers' compensation. If you are trying to collect through the courts, your medical expenses will be advanced by Medicare, which you must reimburse from the eventual settlement or judgment.

7

Managed Care, HMOs, and Medicare + Choice

More and more employees are leaving traditional insurance plans and enrolling in managed-care programs, from health maintenance organizations (HMOs) to wider networks of doctors and hospitals offering discounted fees. HMOs and other managed-care organizations now enroll as many as 50 million Americans, an increase of nearly 40 percent in five years. According to one survey, nearly two out of three employees and their families are now enrolled in managed-care plans.

So prevalent have they become that many doctors who first resisted participating are now trying to get in. The resistance of many groups to including all comers has resulted in a legislative push for statutes requiring managed-care organizations to admit any and all doctors who want to participate.

Managed care, originally touted as a cost containment strategy, quickly became the object of much criticism, ranging from quality of care to over-bureaucratization. Financial incentives and utilization review compromised patient care, while organizations were shielded from accountability by laws.

WHAT IS AN HMO?

A *health maintenance organization (HMO)* is not insurance in the traditional sense, but an alternative to insurance. It's an organization of health care providers—doctors, surgeons, hospitals, and other providers and facilities—that provide you with comprehensive services for a fixed, prepaid fee. It functions both as insurance and as the health care delivery system for its members.

In today's market-driven era, a number of other types of organizations have been created. *Preferred provider organizations (PPOs)* are groups of doctors and other health care providers who continue in their private practice but have contracts with employers, insurers, or other third-party payers to deliver services, usually to employee groups, at reduced rates. With a PPO you can choose a doctor from a wider range of participating doctors than available through HMOs. If you use a designated doctor, you get a discount and may not have a copayment; if you choose from off the list, you'll have to pay more in coinsurance. A PPO is not prepaid but reimbursed, as with traditional insurance.

There are also hybrid systems, sometimes called *managed medical systems* or *competitive medical plans.* These combine elements of managed care with provisions allowing you to choose nonparticipating providers for a greater fee. Each has its own set of rules and regulations, with which you should be fully familiar before enrolling.

The rationale underlying HMOs is that they are dedicated to maintaining your health rather than paying for your illness. The emphasis on prevention and early diagnosis is both a cost and health measure. However, perceptions of reduced time, services, and quality of care persist.

In fact, reports suggest that elderly members of Medicare HMOs are spending even more money for medical care. Out-of-pocket costs have risen steeply, as HMOs have cut drug plans or limited coverage. For those in poor health, the effects on their pocketbooks have been disastrous.

HMO COVERAGE

An HMO provides nearly all of a person's medical needs through designated doctors and hospitals. All costs are covered by a preset monthly premium, which is the same no matter how much or little medical care you receive. The only requirement is that members must use only HMO doctors and facilities to be covered (except for emergency care or urgently needed care outside the HMO's geographic service area). A primary care provider selected by the patient is responsible for coordinating all medical care, services, and referrals for specialists and tests. Some HMOs charge a nominal fee per visit (such as $2 or $5); other than that there are no deductibles or copayment requirements.

Most states have laws requiring that basic information be provided to consumers. HMOs are also required to have enough providers in their networks to ensure enrollees enough access to the services, and to offer "point of service" (POS) options (allowing out-of-network services).

UTILIZATION REVIEW

Utilization review is used to determine if proposed treatment is both medically necessary and delivered in the most effective manner. Common examples include hospital admission precertification, specialist referrals, and second opinions.

Theoretically, there's no limit based on duration or intensity of care, even if you have to go to a hospital. However, utilization review may be tougher than with regular insurance, limiting your stay and care. Problems arise when review of prospective treatment delays treatment, too often at cost to the health of patients.

MEDICARE + CHOICE

Since 1997, there has been a new letter in the Medicare alphabet, Medicare + Choice (M+C), providing a range of managed-care alternatives to Medicare recipients.

The M+C program is designed to offer Medicare beneficiaries access to a wide range of health plan services in addition to traditional fee-for-service. Beneficiaries select a private health plan to provide services that would be available under Medicare Part A and B. Medicare pays the plan a per-beneficiary rate, regardless of the costs incurred by the beneficiary.

The services provided under M+C must include all Medicare-covered services. Plans may provide additional benefits such as prescription drugs or preventive care.

- HMOs and coordinated care plans, including PPOs and POS plans.
- Private fee for service. Private plans, although eligible plans will allow the selection of any willing provider.
- Medical savings accounts. A demonstration project for medical savings account (just renewed as Archer MSAs) to be combined with a high-deductible plan.

ENROLLING IN MEDICARE + CHOICE

If you're eligible for Medicare, you have the right to enroll in an HMO in lieu of Medicare services. About 12.5 percent of the 40 million Medicare recipients are currently enrolled in and receiving their health care benefits through HMO plans nationwide.

As a Medicare recipient, you can only join an HMO or other plan that has a contract with Medicare. The premium for the HMO is paid by Medicare. You have to be enrolled in Part B as well as Part A—that's where payment is coming from. The government pays the HMO to provide you with coverage, the HMO pays the doctors and hospitals and does the paperwork. You continue to pay your Medicare Part B premium, but you don't have to pay any deductibles or copayments. You can't be denied enrollment in an HMO because of your health.

MEDICARE + CHOICE COVERAGE

All Medicare + Choice organizations must provide you with a "low-option plan" at least equal to Medicare benefits (without deductibles and copayments). If you want any services that Medicare doesn't cover, you may have to pay an extra premium for them.

Basic benefits provided under federal law include

- Physician services, including "consultant and referral services by a physician"
- Hospital services, both inpatient and outpatient
- Diagnostic laboratory and therapeutic radiology services
- Home health services
- Preventive health services, including periodic health exams
- Medically necessary emergency health services
- Short-term outpatient mental health services
- Alcohol and drug abuse treatment and referral
- Supplemental services provided by that M+C organization's individual plans, such as prescription drugs or dental services

YOUR MEDICARE + CHOICE RIGHTS

As a Medicare recipient, you have these rights:

- You can't be denied enrollment in a plan because of your health (although you can be limited to a low-option plan).
- Your coverage cannot be terminated because of health or treatment.
- Emergency services must be available 24 hours a day.
- You're entitled to the plan's written procedures for resolving complaints, which you may utilize in addition to the appeal rights you have under Medicare.

Does my employer have to give me an HMO option?

Federal law requires that all employers with at least 25 employees (living in the service area, full or part time) and having some health benefit plan provide the option of enrolling in an HMO. Your employer must contribute an amount equal to the contribution that would have been made to your health insurance, as well as supplemental continued benefits for any services you can't get through the HMO. A number of HMOs and other managed care plans are also available to individuals during a prescribed open enrollment period.

I'm on Medicare and have supplemental Medigap insurance. I plan to switch over to a Medicare + Choice HMO. How does this affect my Medigap insurance?

For Medicare recipients, it eliminates the need for supplemental insurance. (See Chapter 6 on Medigap insurance.)

Will the services be the same?

You have to check with your specific plan. Not all have 24-hour medical care available. Check the hours and whether the plan offers access to 24-hour medical attention, with doctors on call.

Also, you should note that Medicare + Choice is not for frequent travelers. As a general rule, you're not covered for services outside the plan's service area except for severe emergency. Even then, you'll have to get approval by phone. If you're a frequent traveler, you may also want to get Medigap insurance with the foreign travel emergency benefit.

SWITCHING MEDICARE + CHOICE COVERAGE

If you're not happy with the HMO or other Medicare + Choice plan, you can always drop out and return to Medicare. If you choose to disenroll or move out of the service area, your standard Medicare coverage automatically resumes on the date of the termination of your plan, which can be as early as the calendar month following your request. If you enroll in M+C and leave within one year, you are guaranteed access to any Medigap policy without medical underwriting.

Retroactive disenrollment is also possible under certain circumstances. If you go to a hospital outside of the network and your plan refuses to cover you, you can get Medicare to pay if you can prove you didn't know the rules.

I don't like my plan and a friend said I could change at the end of the month, but the plan said only once a year.

Changes to and from M+C plans were allowed on a monthly basis through 2001. As of 2002, you're limited to change during the annual election period (once in the first three months of 2003).

APPEALING AN HMO DECISION—EXTERNAL REVIEW

Under law, HMOs were required to adopt procedures to ensure hearing of patient grievances. However, these were often inadequate, failing to provide fair process to ensure real investigation and opportunity for the patient to be heard.

One of the stumbling blocks to consumer acceptance of HMOs is that organizations that are in effect making medical decisions about your care have nevertheless been exempt from accountability for those decisions. This is because the federal ERISA law which governs employee benefits has long acted as a shield against state law.

Several states have stepped in where Congress has failed to act and passed various Patient Bills of Rights to mandate independent review of HMO decisions, forcing second opinions and in some cases payment for needed care. Florida, New Jersey, and New York are among the 42 states that have external appeal procedures.

In New York, the law has established an independent process for such appeals.

- All adverse decisions by an insurer must contain instructions for filing an external appeal.
- An application fee is allowed, up to $50, returnable if the appeal is won and waivable if the claimant can't afford it.
- There is a 45-day limit to initiate the review process.
- A decision must be made within 30 days (three days if delay would provide an imminent and serious threat to the health of the patient).
- Special teams will allow peer review for "experimental procedures."

One study found that independent reviews overturn insurers' decisions about half the time (ranging as high as two decisions overturned out of every three in Maryland), but their existence is not well publicized. In June 2002, the Supreme Court upheld the validity of state laws providing external review of coverage decisions, rejecting the argument that reviews are preempted by federal ERISA law governing pension benefits. In February 2003 the Second Circuit Court of Appeals in New York ruled that HMOs that make mixed eligibility and treatment decisions can be held liable under state standards of medical malpractice. The decision comes as a welcome step on the road to a nationwide Patient's Bill of Rights, which would make it easier for patients to bring action against health plans for the decisions they make affecting patient health.

APPEALING A MEDICARE + CHOICE PLAN DECISION

Appealing a Medicare + Choice plan decision is similar to the appeals of other Medicare decisions described in Chapter 5. After an initial determination by a plan, you have the right to a reconsideration review by an external entity.

HMOs sometimes process Medicare appeals incorrectly as grievances, subject only to their internal review processes. Make sure your plan gives you a written notice of your appeal rights for Medicare-covered services.

Reconsideration. You have 60 calendar days from a determination to request a reconsideration (more if you can show "good cause"). You are entitled to a decision as expeditiously as your health requires, and no later than 14 calendar days after a request for service has been made. Requests for payments must be decided within 60 days from receipt of the request. If a reconsideration is in your favor, the service must be provided within 30 days (a 14-day extension will be allowed at your request or if the plan requires additional information for your benefit).

Appeal. An unfavorable decision will be sent to the Center for Health Dispute Resolution (CHDR), a private contractor, which will make its determination within 30 calendar days. If it is in your favor, the service must be authorized within 72 hours and provided within 14 days of receipt of the decision.

If CHDR's decision is not favorable, you may appeal through the regular Medicare appeal process to an administrative law hearing, appeals council, and court review. Deadlines, procedure, and minimum claims are detailed in Chapter 5.

Expedited appeal. You may also be entitled to an expedited review for a refusal to provide or pay for services or discontinuance of a service. For cases in which the standard time frame would seriously jeopardize the patient's life or health, or his or her ability to regain maximum functioning, a decision must be made within 72 hours of receipt of the request. You are not entitled to an expedited review as a matter of right, but a physician's request must be honored. Agreement to grant or deny an expedited review must be made within 72 hours, and you have the right to resubmit with physician support. A request for an expedited review can be made orally or in writing.

ACCREDITATION

CMS has approved standards for Medicare managed-care organizations promulgated by the National Committee on Quality Assurance (NCQA), a private, national accreditation organization. The NCQA will provide assurance that a Medicare + Choice organization meets or exceeds requirements established by the Medicare program.

Can I check on an HMO like an insurance company?

Yes. A.M. Best Company and Weiss Ratings provide ratings of HMOs. These ratings reflect the financial soundness of organization as well as its ability to deliver services; ratings do not measure the quality of services provided.

The Joint Commission on the Accreditation of Healthcare Organizations provides accreditation services for HMOs. The NCQA, which sets accreditation standards for HMOs, also provides "quality of care and service" report cards for HMOs. (See appendixes for contact information.)

ASSESSING THE
MEDICARE + CHOICE PROGRAM

The range of options for seniors and the disabled never materialized in the way it was expected. Nearly all plans currently in effect are HMOs (other than the pilot effort described below). Rates and benefits vary across the country and across states, and health plans complain of inadequate federal payments. In large areas—in populous states such as New York, Florida, California—recipients still have a choice of plans. But in other locations, even in those states, many plans have pulled out or reduced benefits, throwing customers into confusion and disarray. Some areas have no plan at all. In 2002, 40 percent of Medicare beneficiaries lived in counties with no Medicare + Choice plans. Estimates are that one out of three have no access to an M+C plan. Barely 12.5 percent of the 40 million Medicare recipients are enrolled in M+C; a total of 2.4 million have been dropped by HMOs.

For many, the promise was a lie. Studies show that Medicare out-of-pocket costs increased 50 percent in three years, to $1,438 in 2001, and to $3,578 for those in poor health. Medicare contracts have declined from 346 in the year after the program was enacted to 148 contracts in 2002, and enrollment from an estimated 6 million to 5 million.

Thus far the government has been unable to stanch the withdrawal of private plans from the M+C program. In January 2003, a three-year pilot program was begun in 241 counties in 23 states, offering Medicare recipients new PPO plans, which allow them to go outside of network for an extra charge. CMS hopes to attract enrollees who seek greater flexibility and choice from among 11 million Medicare recipients who are eligible for the new plans.

Part 3

Financing Long-Term Care

Long-term care comes in many forms, with interventions available along a continuum of services that range from home care services to services in a skilled nursing facility. Whether the care takes place at home or in a nursing facility, it will be expensive.

Although most nursing home stays average less than a year, with costs for long-term care averaging $50,000 a year and approaching as much as $120,000 annually in some areas, financing home care or even a short stay in a nursing home can mean a quick trip to the poorhouse. Studies show the average family spends its resources in a health care crisis *in 13 weeks.*

What many do not realize, often to their detriment, is that Medicare and health insurance do not cover long-term care. Medicare, even supplemented by Medigap insurance, covers skilled care only and that only for a limited time. We discuss Medicare's role in long-term care in Chapter 8.

With spiraling health care costs, planning for long-term care is critical. In Chapter 9, we explain the ins and outs of Medicaid planning, to ensure that you and your family won't have to be impoverished to receive needed care. In Chapter 10, we describe long-term care insurance, and in Chapter 11, we introduce to you other financing options, including annuities, life insurance, and reverse mortgages.

8

Medicare and Long-Term Care

As we described in Chapter 5, Medicare provides you with basic hospital care, home health care benefits to a maximum of 35 hours a week, and post-hospital skilled nursing facility benefits up to 100 days. Days 21 through 100 in a facility require some payment from you, but with Medigap insurance you receive 100 percent coverage.

You should apply for these benefits if you are eligible or think you may be. The potential savings can be significant. In 1995, an estimated 3.5 million people received health care under Medicare, more than double the number from a decade before.

However, Medicare's role in long-term care planning is a limited one. For purely custodial cases, coverage may be wholly unavailable. Restrictions on coverage and benefits (for both home health care and care in a skilled nursing facility) limit Medicare's value as a planning tool.

POST-HOSPITAL CARE UNDER MEDICARE

If you need further care after being in the hospital, Medicare Part A also covers post-hospital care in a skilled nursing facility, including:

- Bed and board
- Nursing care by registered nurses
- Medical care by interns and residents
- Physical, occupational, or speech therapy

Up to 100 days in a skilled nursing facility may be covered per benefit period. Days 1–20 are fully paid by Medicare; days 21–100, you pay

114

$101.50 a day in copay. (Medigap insurance may be available to pay this amount, which increases each year; see Chapter 6 for more information.) After day 100, you must pay all costs.

There are several restrictions on receiving this benefit:

- Your post-hospital care must be for skilled nursing care or rehabilitative services.
- Your care must be received daily in a skilled nursing facility.
- You must enter within 30 days after having had a hospital stay of three days or longer (not counting the day of discharge).

Prior hospitalization/spell of illness. In order to qualify for Medicare coverage the same condition ("spell of illness") must necessitate your stay in the hospital and your admission for post-hospital care. A spell of illness must be continuous, without a break in services of more than 60 days. If there is a break of 60 days, you'll need another hospital stay prior to entering a skilled nursing facility or you will not be covered under Medicare.

Skilled nursing care. The difference between skilled and custodial care is crucial. Basically, your care will be deemed "custodial" if it is the kind of care that a layperson can perform without special professional training or experience. For example, helping you to dress is custodial care.

Because Medicare doesn't cover custodial care, you must be receiving daily skilled care or rehabilitative services that can be provided only on an inpatient basis. It is not required that a patient be capable of recovery or even improvement for services to be covered. Physical therapy to prevent deterioration is enough to justify the provision of skilled care.

Skilled nursing facility. A critical requirement for Medicare coverage is that you must need and receive care in a skilled nursing facility (SNF). An SNF is engaged primarily in providing skilled nursing care or rehabilitative services such as physical or occupational therapy to help restore a person's health. It provides RNs, LPNs, and nurses' aides on a 24-hour basis. Medicare covers care at the skilled level only, in a Medicare-certified program. It does not cover care in a custodial or residential care facility. Assisted living facilities do not qualify.

Changes in your status. If the SNF believes a service is not covered by Medicare, it must inform you in writing. You have the right to demand that the SNF bill Medicare regardless, and you don't have to pay for the service until Medicare denies payment. If the SNF fails to give you the required "notice of noncoverage," you cannot be charged.

When a level-of-care determination "demotes" you from skilled to nonskilled, ending your Medicare coverage, you have the right to an immediate review. An appeal from an SNF must be decided within 10 days.

Can I enter a nursing facility directly from home and receive coverage from Medicare?

No. Your admission must follow a hospital stay.

Do I have to be admitted to the hospital again for the same thing?

Only one hospital visit is necessary. Should you leave the skilled nursing facility and have to return for continued services for the same condition within 60 days, you don't need to satisfy the three-day hospital requirement again.

Should I appeal?

If you have the resources to stay in a nursing home and pay for services after Medicare cuts you off, you can still appeal the payment decision. The skilled versus custodial care battle is one Medicare loves to fight. Only 3 percent of all nursing home stays are Medicare-covered. But appeals are a good bet. A large number are successful.

HOME HEALTH CARE
UNDER MEDICARE

Medicare's home health care benefit provides some coverage for care in your home. Although it often follows a hospital stay, prior hospitalization is not required for home health care benefits.

Home health care benefits include

- Part-time or intermittent skilled nursing care
- Physical therapy, speech therapy, and occupational therapy
- Home health aides, part-time or intermittent
- Medical social services
- Medical supplies and equipment

Home health benefits are provided under both Part A and Part B. Assuming you're covered, Medicare pays the full amount of these services, subject only to the $100 deductible for Part B services. There is a 20 percent copayment you have to make on medical equipment only.

The purpose of home health care is to supply you with some of the medical services that will allow you to remain at home. To qualify under Medicare's rules, there are a number of conditions that must be met.

- You (or the patient) must be homebound, confined to home except for going for medical treatment with some kind of assistance. You do not have to be bedridden, but you do have to be confined to home.
- You must need and receive either skilled nursing care, physical therapy, or speech therapy. This means that you may get the services of a home health aide (for your custodial care needs) only if you need one or more of these skilled services.
- Your condition does not need to be "curable" or even capable of improvement; what is required is that you need care or therapy to maintain your condition without deterioration.
- Your care must be provided by a home health agency certified by Medicare.

Medicare will cover up to 35 hours per week of part-time or intermittent care. Medicare will cover up to 35 hours per week of *combined* home health aide and skilled services if you're required to have at least intermittent skilled services pursuant to a home health plan set up by your doctor. Intermittent skilled care must be for fewer than five days a week and may be as infrequent as once in 60 days. If services are needed for a finite and predictable period up to 21 days, then up to seven days a week are allowed, and as many as 56 hours in the week may be covered.

That's what the law says, but the coverage you can expect to get is a lot more limited. Medicare guidelines try to limit number of visits and hours per visit, now more than ever. This is the result of dramatic changes in the home health care arena over the past several years. Following a surge in home health care in the 1990s, a newly instituted prospective payment structure coupled with massive budget cuts and tightened eligibility rules helped shut down 30 percent of the certified home care agencies and left the remaining ones with a 24 percent smaller client base and reduced services to offer those who were left.

Before the plan is established, the agency makes an evaluation visit, which operates to limit the prospective services to what the agency anticipates will be covered by Medicare. As a result, visits are generally limited to a few hours weekly, not really sufficient to maintain a patient at home. Be prepared to fight for what the law allows.

Check with your local aging agency to see if your state or locality has any programs that provide similar assistance that may be of help to those needing home health care services, such as Meals on Wheels or transportation to get medical services. (See Chapter 3 for more on home care programs.)

If the agency says Medicare won't cover your care and payment is demanded in advance for services that you believe should be covered, you must decide whether to accept or decline those services. The catch-22 is that appeal is only allowed for services actually received, and agencies commonly refuse to provide services. They're actually penalized for submitting claims that are denied.

- You are entitled to demand that the home health agency bill Medicare so you can appeal any adverse decision.
- The reversal rate for home health care decisions on appeal is quite good, as high as 70 percent.
- If you don't get the service, there's nothing to contest—and no appeal process.

If the outlook doesn't sound optimistic, that's because outlays for home health care are now at one-half what they were five years ago. Nearly 30 percent of Medicare-certified home care agencies throughout the country have closed as a direct result of the 1997 Balanced Budget Act requirements.

Government reports indicating stable market conditions and a lack of problems accessing care do not reflect the experiences of any of the older clients we know, nor do they track what happened to the 800,000 people no longer eligible for home care.

What if I need another type of service?

You must need and receive one or more of the three specified services (skilled nursing care, physical therapy, or speech therapy). Coverage is also available for occupational therapy, but it must be linked to a need for skilled nursing care, physical therapy, or speech therapy. Once established, occupational therapy may continue after these other services have lapsed.

May I receive personal or custodial care from a Medicaid health aide?

Incidental household chores performed by a covered home health aide are permissible.

My doctor is part owner of a home health agency. Can he refer me there?

Under federal law, your doctor cannot certify the need for treatment in any home health agency in which he or she may have a share (unless it is the only one in the community).

MEDICARE AND HOSPICE SERVICES

Hospice services are covered by Medicare Part A. These include

- Physical, occupational, and speech therapy
- Physician services
- Skilled nursing services
- Counseling (dietary, spiritual, bereavement, and other counseling services)
- Medical social services
- Drugs and biologicals for pain control and symptom management
- Home health aide and homemaker services
- Inpatient respite care

Eligibility. Beneficiaries must be certified to have a life expectancy of no more than six months. To be eligible for hospice, beneficiaries must give up other services related to treatment designed to cure their condition. Medicare will still pay for other unrelated care.

Generally, certification will be for a 90-day period, followed by another 90-day period, followed by 60-day periods. There is no limit on the total time so long as the patient's prognosis meets the six-month test.

The benefit may be extended beyond the six-month term, so long as certification of terminal illness can be made by the physician or medical director based on clinical judgment concerning the normal course of the individual's illness.

My mother is scheduled to enter hospice, which will be provided at home. Am I liable for copay?

There are no coinsurance or deductibles for hospice care, whether you receive services in the hospital or in your home. Exceptions are drugs and biologicals, which are subject to copay, with a $5 per prescription limit.

9

Medicaid and Long-Term Care

Medicaid is a public assistance grant program, the twin Great Society benefit signed into law along with Medicare by President Lyndon B. Johnson in 1965. Financed jointly by federal and state moneys, it provides health benefits to 40 million low-income people who are aged, blind, or disabled, as well as those who are poor.

Although designed to serve low-income people of all ages, Medicaid has become a lifeline for the elderly, providing essential services that Medicare doesn't—home health care and long-term nursing home care.

Don't make the mistake of thinking that Medicaid benefits are limited to the very poor. Medicaid is a complex, confusing, but important government program that has become essential for many middle-income families who need help paying for long-term care in order to avoid impoverishment.

Medicaid is the major payer of long-term care for those who can't afford the average yearly cost of $50,000 or more (more than double that amount in some areas). Medicaid covers the "nonskilled" but unbelievably expensive custodial care services that Medicare doesn't. Thousands of middle-income Americans have found themselves divesting themselves of their assets or "spending down" to eligibility levels in order to qualify for benefits under Medicaid. Medicaid pays for 46 percent of all nursing home costs nationwide. It covers more than 70 percent of all nursing home patients.

Administered by the states, Medicaid represents the fastest-growing component of state budgets, reaching 20 percent in 2002. States pay approximately 45 percent and the federal government 55 percent of Medicaid costs. About 20 states pass part of this cost on to counties. Nearly one-third of Medicaid spending goes to home health services and long-term nursing home care. Total costs for Medicaid topped $200 billion in 2000.

Medicaid rules must be understood in context. One target for budget cuts has been the benefits furnished to middle-income people who have made themselves eligible for Medicaid to avoid the astronomical costs of long-term care. Stricter eligibility rules have made qualifying for benefits harder than ever before, and service and program cuts have affected both home care and nursing home care as well as programs such as adult day care. Additional changes and restrictions are being contemplated by Congress and several states. These events make it more important than ever that you understand the rules and how Medicaid works.

There may be any number of reasons not to apply for Medicaid, including personal, family, and psychological reasons, quality-of-care issues, and tax consequences. Nevertheless, it is an option that deserves serious consideration. While access to Medicaid is complicated and may not be available to or right for everyone, it is a possible source of financing for long-term care—even for those who may not now imagine they can take advantage of it.

MEDICAID COVERAGE

Before learning how to qualify for Medicaid, you should understand what the benefits are you're trying to obtain. In general, Medicaid pays for doctors and hospital stays, like Medicare. It also provides coverage for long-term nursing home care not covered by Medicare. Nursing homes operate according to a Medicaid plan that requires doctor certification of the need to enter the facility and periodic review of the need for continued care.

Medicaid also covers home health care services, medical supplies, and equipment. It commonly pays for at-home services supplied under state plans for people who would otherwise be institutionalized, covering part-time skilled nursing, home health, and homemaker services provided by certified home health agencies.

A number of limitations are imposed by states to restrain costs and eliminate unnecessary and inappropriate treatment. Depending upon where you live, this may include copayments for mandatory as well as optional benefits, restrictions on physician visits, and limits on other services such as lab tests, prescriptions, or transportation costs. A number of states have enrolled Medicaid recipients in HMO and managed-care plans and instituted other program restrictions.

What else does Medicaid cover?

Each state has its own program, providing a different menu of services, subject to minimum federal standards. Your state's program may cover dental care, medical equipment, prescription drugs, foot care, optometry services, eyeglasses, clinic services, and various diagnostic, screening, and rehabilitative services, as well as transportation to obtain medical care.

Emergency services are also covered. Federal law prohibits states from limiting the number of emergency room visits for Medicaid recipients, but watch for periodic efforts to lift the ban.

Who needs Medicaid?

The poor and the not-so-poor. This includes people who do not have Medicare, who cannot get or cannot afford health insurance, and who need Medicaid for all of their health care needs. Those who do have Medicare (and Medicare supplemental insurance) but have long-term care needs not met by Medicare are also turning in increasing numbers to Medicaid as the payer of last resort.

"SPENDING DOWN" FOR MEDICAID

For millions of older Americans, Medicaid is the only means by which long-term custodial care can be supported. Each year half a million people "spend down" their assets in order to qualify for long-term care assistance available under Medicaid. Some actually pay for their care until their assets are used up. Others purchase "exempt" items or transfer their assets, all legitimate Medicaid-planning strategies to allow them to keep their independence and autonomy without sacrificing their life savings.

These strategies all follow from one basic rule. *All* your income and assets above specified levels must be spent to pay for care before you will qualify for Medicaid. Various planning strategies using statutory exemptions, spousal protections, and asset transfers are described below.

Plan ahead! This is one area in which advance planning is critical. Depending on your circumstances, it may take time to spend down or otherwise divest yourself of your assets in order to meet eligibility levels—and the law imposes penalty periods after transfers before you can qualify for benefits. Last-minute action may not work.

Although financing long-term care in this manner is entirely legal, Medicaid planning has become a major political issue. So many people have been forced to try to qualify for Medicaid benefits that the various methods for achieving that goal are under continuous attack.

APPLYING FOR MEDICAID

Medicaid is administered by state or local Medicaid offices. States have their own application processes to ensure eligibility, including applications that are often lengthy and complex. (Only those who qualify for Medicaid based on their Supplemental Security Income status, as described in the next section, don't have to make a separate application.)

Applying for Medicaid entails verification of your financial resources as well as citizenship and residency requirements. You must be a United States citizen, lawfully admitted permanent resident, or residing permanently in the United States under color of law.

Financial requirements are strict. You will be asked for your bank statements, tax returns, and other financial records reflecting your income, assets, and expenses. Often this will be required in a short time period, although extensions can be granted. Make sure you have the documentation you need—and make sure you go to any scheduled interviews. Eligibility determinations can go against you solely on your failure to provide required documentation or to appear at interviews.

More and more older people seeking Medicaid for nursing home and home care services are enlisting professional help in obtaining Medicaid, using lawyers or social workers familiar with the process and its requirements. We recommend this approach highly. Regardless of whether you need to avail yourself of other Medicaid planning strategies to protect assets, you want to ensure that you get the health care coverage you need.

QUALIFYING FOR MEDICAID

As we've described, Medicaid is a *means-tested* program. In order to qualify, you must establish financial eligibility by meeting income and assets tests set by the states. Depending on where you live, you can qualify for Medicaid under one or more of these programs:

Categorical needy program. All states provide health care coverage for those who meet the financial eligibility tests and are either aged, blind, or disabled. In 37 states and the District of Columbia, income and asset standards match guidelines for the Supplemental Security Income (SSI) program, which is welfare provided by the federal government for the aged, blind, or disabled. In these states, if you qualify for SSI, you automatically qualify for Medicaid. (See Chapter 20 for more on SSI.)

In the remaining 13 states, guidelines differ from those for SSI; most are more restrictive, although some are less so. (The 13 states are Connecticut, Hawaii, Illinois, Indiana, Minnesota, Missouri, Nebraska, New Hampshire, North Carolina, North Dakota, Ohio, Oklahoma, and Virginia.)

Medically needy program. In 37 states, people whose incomes are too high to qualify for "categorically needy" Medicaid coverage but whose medical bills are so great that in effect they've reduced their incomes to that level, may qualify for Medicaid under this standard. These states have "medically needy" programs with spend-down or "share of cost" provisions that generally operate in the applicant's favor. (This category includes California, Massachusetts, and New York.)

Income caps. Some states do not have a "medically needy" program at all. According to the Medicaid laws in these states, if your income is one cent above the state's "income cap," you cannot get Medicaid at all. (In most cases, the cap is set at three times the federal SSI benefit, a limit of $1,656 a month in 2003.) Income cap states include Arizona, Colorado, Florida, Kansas, Nevada, Oregon, and Texas.

Eligibility rules in the states are confusing even for experts. Many states distinguish between nursing home and other home- and community-based care in determining Medicaid eligibility for those services. In some states there is a "medically needy" option for nursing home care only but not for general services. Eight states have a partial "medically needy" program for services other than nursing homes. These are Arizona, Arkansas, Florida, Iowa, Kansas, Louisiana, Oklahoma, and Oregon.

The income cap has caused much hardship and generated even more controversy, although the harshness of these rules has been universally acknowledged. In 1993, Congress provided a way for people living in income cap states to set up certain kinds of trusts (called Miller trusts) to allow them to qualify for Medicaid despite the harsh income cap rules. We discuss trusts and Medicaid planning later in this chapter.

My mother is a legal immigrant but not a citizen. Is she eligible for Medicaid benefits?

It depends on where you live. The 1996 law that denied Medicaid coverage for most legal aliens was struck down by New York's Court of Appeals. Many states had already passed laws to give them equivalent benefits, among them Pennsylvania, California, and Massachusetts.

YOUR HOME AND OTHER EXEMPT ASSETS

Medicaid allows you to hold on to certain resources. Under the rules, these assets are *exempt,* which means that you can keep them and still qualify for Medicaid. An individual may retain

- $2,000 in assets (higher in a dozen states)
- A burial fund of $1,500 or prepaid burial trusts

- Certain assets, including a car, jewelry, and clothing
- A home

A couple applying for Medicaid can retain

- $3,000 in assets (higher in a dozen states)
- Two $1,500 burial allowances or prepaid burial trusts
- Certain assets, including a car, jewelry, and clothing
- A home

If my home is exempt, can I transfer it to my adult child and still qualify for Medicaid?

No. Owning exempt assets doesn't mean that you can transfer these assets without penalty. Your home is yours and is not counted so long as you, your spouse, or your minor, blind, or disabled child resides there. If an individual is on or applying for Medicaid, it cannot be transferred without losing Medicaid eligibility or incurring a penalty period unless it is transferred to

- A spouse
- A child under 21 or who is blind or disabled
- A child living there for two years prior to institutionalization who cared for the parent, enabling the parent to remain at home
- A sibling with an equity interest who has resided there for one year prior to institutionalization

Transfers of assets are discussed later in this chapter.

PROTECTING SPOUSAL RESOURCES

At one time, a married couple faced impoverishment when one partner went into a nursing home. In 1988, Congress acted to protect assets and income of people whose spouses are institutionalized.

When one member of a married couple moves to a nursing home and applies for Medicaid, the couple's total resources are reviewed for Medicaid purposes. A "snapshot" of the total assets of the couple is taken (leaving out exempt assets). The rules state that the *total nonexempt assets* of both the spouse who enters a nursing home (the *institutionalized spouse*) and the spouse who remains at home (the *at-home* or *community spouse*) are considered available for the institutionalized spouse's care, except for the *community spouse resource allowance (CSRA)*.

The CSRA is deducted from the couple's total assets. Assets above the allowance are deemed excess resources. The CSRA is determined by a set of complicated regulations and varies from state to state. The community spouse may retain

- A CSRA of up to $90,660 in assets (maximum amount is less in some states)
- The home and other exempt assets

The institutionalized spouse may keep

- The exemption amount ($2,000 in most states)
- A burial account of $1,500

Allowances are indexed for inflation; they are increased each year by the same percentage as Social Security benefits. These figures are from 2003.

Community spouse resource allowances vary considerably from state to state, from as low as $18,132 to as high as $90,660. (The income allowance is discussed in the next section.)

Determining the exact amount of your assets is critical. States also vary in how they treat different assets for purposes of Medicaid. For example, an individual applicant's retirement funds are generally treated as assets, if they can be withdrawn. The possibility of a withdrawal penalty is irrelevant, except to the total worth of funds. If the funds are in payout status, however, they will be treated as income. (See the next section for treatment of income.) In some states, the retirement accounts of a community spouse will be treated as assets countable as part of the couple's total assets; in others, they will be exempt and not included in the calculation of the CSRA. In New York, retirement funds of a community spouse are counted toward the CSRA but are not counted as excess resources.

My husband requires long-term nursing home care. Must all our assets except for the CSRA be spent on his nursing home care before Medicaid takes over?

No. There are a number of steps you can take to protect yourself and your assets. The CSRA can be increased via a court order or an order obtained through a Medicaid "fair hearing," in cases of hardship or special need or to permit you to have enough assets to earn the spouse's allowable monthly income allowance.

Depending on where you live, other techniques may be used. For example, in some states you can invest the excess assets (the assets over the CSRA) in an annuity payable to you for your lifetime which would not need to be spent down on your husband's care.

In some states, you are allowed to "refuse" to use the excess assets for your spouse's care. This is called a *right of refusal.* New York was a pioneering state in spousal refusal. Medicaid still gets all the information about your assets and income, and asks the institutionalized spouse to assign to the state rights of support. State laws differ considerably on the scope and nature of an individual's obligation to support his or her spouse. Under the law, Medicaid must pay for your institutionalized spouse's care but has a right to take you (the at-home spouse) to court and seek a support order.

If I do refuse support, is Medicaid likely to seek a support order?

Yes. In recent years, Medicaid has tightened up on the states to pursue recovery from spouses who have refused to pay for their institutionalized spouses. For the most part, states have complied, seeking assets from refusing spouses for their share. When West Virginia resisted, Medicaid threatened to withhold funding if the state did not implement estate recovery provisions.

Although using this option will no longer allow you to escape liability totally, there are still reasons to go this route. The first is that you can negotiate your payback. This is very important, especially for spouses with large bills and uncertain incomes. Medicaid will only seek the amount paid out by Medicaid, not the amount of your assets, and it will only seek payment from your assets in excess of the CSRA.

Also, you're being asked to pay back at the Medicaid rate, which is significantly lower than the rate you would be charged as a private payer. Often settlement may be possible, at a rate of 25 percent of your income above the monthly income you are allowed to keep. Make sure you consult with an attorney.

If your spouse is being institutionalized now, you don't know what the ultimate bill will be. Action is never brought right away, because there is no bill due right away. Medicaid may wait six months or longer, or even until after the death of the institutionalized spouse, to pursue repayment.

If I transfer resources, doesn't that amount to fraud?

You have the right to transfer assets belonging to you for any reason. But several states have taken the position that if you know your spouse has benefits, any transfer by you elsewhere is subject to recovery proceedings.

What about transfers made after my spouse is declared eligible for Medicaid?

Any transfer after your spouse's institutionalization ("post-eligibility transfers") will no longer affect the eligibility of your institutionalized spouse. But don't forget, any transfers that you make may affect your own eligibility for Medicaid. In these cases, however, the courts tend to be fairly protective, requiring proof that you as the at-home spouse can truly afford to pay for the care.

PROTECTING SPOUSAL INCOME

Income is treated differently than assets, although Medicaid rules also apply to income. Medicaid applies a "name on the check" rule, counting only the income that is paid directly to the ill spouse as his or hers for eligibility and spending-down purposes. If income is received in both names, each is considered to own one-half of the total amount. The community spouse may retain his or her income in most cases.

Under the law, each state must establish a *monthly income allowance* for the community spouse (technically called the "minimum monthly maintenance needs allowance"). In calculating the amount, the states are given an option, under which the income allowance must be at least

- *A basic allowance* of 150 percent of the nonfarm poverty level for a family of two, amounting to $1,492.50 a month (as of July 2000), plus an *excess shelter allowance* of $447.75 for housing costs for the spouse's primary residence (equal to the amount by which combined rent, taxes, utilities, and related expenses exceeds 30 percent of the basic allowance), or
- A flat $2,266.50 monthly (in 2003).

There is also a family income allowance for minor children. Amounts are indexed to inflation and increase each year.

If the community spouse's separate income is below the monthly income allowance, enough of the institutionalized spouse's income will be automatically assigned to the community spouse to raise his or her income to that state's income allowance. The community spouse's monthly income allowance can also be raised above the state allowance in cases of hardship or special need, through a court proceeding or Medicaid fair hearing. (For this to occur, the institutionalized spouse must have more income that can be assigned to the at-home spouse.)

Determining whether income or assets are counted first can be critical. In the *Blumer* case, Wisconsin's "income first" rule was upheld by the U.S. Supreme Court. The rule requires that the institutionalized spouse's income had to be used to raise the community spouse's income to minimum levels before resources to the community spouse could be increased.

In many cases, this rule constitutes a real hardship for community spouses. The income of an institutionalized spouse, such as pension, could cease upon the individual's death. By requiring the community spouse to rely on this income first, the assets that would otherwise have provided equivalent income indefinitely are no longer available. As a lower court noted, the purpose of spousal impoverishment rules would be lost if after an institutionalized death, income is gone and so are the resources.

TRANSFERRING ASSETS

One of the ways in which an applicant with assets above the specified amount can qualify for Medicaid is to transfer them to another person. Medicaid has rules about these kinds of transfers. Making a transfer triggers a period of ineligibility, called a *penalty period*, before Medicaid will pay for care. Any transfer, *other than to your spouse or blind or disabled child*, creates a penalty period.

The penalty period is triggered only if you make a transfer within 36 months of making an application for Medicaid benefits (60 months for transfers to trusts). This 36-month period is called the *look-back period*. When you apply, you will be asked for your financial records dating back 36 months. A transfer within that 36 months will trigger the penalty period. A transfer before that time will not. (These rules apply to transfers made after August 1993; transfers before that date were subject to a 30-month look-back period.)

Transfer Penalties

If you apply for Medicaid within 36 months following the date of transfer, you will be ineligible for Medicaid for a period of time determined by dividing the value of the property transferred by the monthly cost of nursing home care in your area. (This cost is determined by the state Medicaid agency.)

For example, if you transfer $60,000, and the average cost of nursing homes in your area is $3,000 a month, you would divide $60,000 by $3,000. The resulting number, 20, is the number of months you are ineligible for Medicaid.

The penalty period begins on the first day of the month following the month in which the transfer takes place (or, in some states, the first day of the month of the transfer). Thus, if the $60,000 transfer described above was made in the first month of the 36-month look-back period and it is now 21 months later, the penalty period will have passed and the person who made the transfer would be eligible. In other words, you don't have to wait 36 months in all cases, just until the month after the number of penalty period months has passed.

If you apply for Medicaid within the look-back period, there is *no limit* on the duration of the penalty period. Although there once was a 30-month limit on ineligibility, the law has changed and there is no maximum period. For example, in a state with a monthly cost factor set at $3000, if you transfer $200,000 and file your application before 36 months have gone by, you would be ineligible for 66 months.

If you apply for Medicaid after 36 months following the date of transfer, there is no penalty period. You need not disclose the transfer, and it will not be considered in your application.

It is critical never to apply within the look-back period if the amount of the transfer is more than 36 times the state's average cost factor.

Transfer rules for spouses and disabled children. Exceptions to the above rules are made for transfers to spouses and blind or disabled children. An institutionalized spouse can transfer resources at any time to his or her spouse or to a child who is blind or totally and permanently disabled without limit or penalty.

It's important to distinguish between transfers *to* a spouse and *by* a spouse. Transfers by the spouse of a person who receives or applies for Medicaid within 36 months can also disqualify the applicant.

Transfers of jointly held assets are also treated as transfers by the applicant. The full value of the assets will be treated as a transfer unless the co-owner can show contribution.

Home care and community services. Individuals who transfer assets and seek non–nursing home Medicaid benefits (such as home care or hospital benefits) are not subject to any federally imposed period of ineligibility. Your state may choose to apply transfer prohibitions in determining eligibility for these "community" Medicaid benefits. Certain community programs (known as "waiver programs") are covered by the transfer rules just as nursing home situations.

If a person remaining in the community receives Medicaid and subsequently enters a nursing home, Medicaid may be cut off if transfers have been made within the 36-month look-back period and he or she is admitted within a penalty period.

Do the same rules apply to transfers to trusts?

Different rules apply to transfers to certain types of irrevocable trusts, making them subject to a look-back period of 60 months. (See Trusts and Medicaid Planning in the next section.)

How does the look-back period relate to transfers?

A penalty period is calculated for nonexempt transfers made within the look-back period. Ineligibility is measured from the date the penalty period begins. Once the penalty period passes, you may apply for Medicaid.

A transfer made before the look-back period is not used to figure eligibility. For sufficiently large amounts, you may just wait the 36 months before making an application, at which time you need not disclose the transfer.

Do all transfers result in a penalty?

No. Remember, there is an exception for transfers to spouses and blind or disabled children. Your home can also be transferred to certain other individuals without penalty. In addition, only transfers for which there was no legal consideration (such as gifts) will be penalized. For example, selling something is not a Medicaid transfer. Giving something to a child who gives you something in return is not a Medicaid transfer to the extent of the value of what you get back. If you give your daughter $50,000 but she promises to allow you to live with her for your lifetime, you will not have a penalty period so long as the "value" of your right to live with her approximates $50,000.

If you make a transfer for reasons having nothing to do with Medicaid (for example, giving a $25,000 wedding gift to your grandchild when you are perfectly healthy), it will not result in a penalty period should you subsequently need to apply for Medicaid. Only transfers that were intended to make you eligible for Medicaid result in a penalty. But you must be able to show that your gift was not intended to qualify you for Medicaid.

TRUSTS AND MEDICAID PLANNING

One of the earliest and still common forms of Medicaid planning is to establish a trust. A trust works by establishing a fund to be administered under the direction of a trustee or trustees. In broad outline, a trust makes provision for distribution of the income, usually on a regular basis to the named beneficiary, and eventual disposition of the principal.

By this means, ownership of assets can be transferred away from the Medicaid applicant—and away from Medicaid—and yet remain within reach. For these purposes, trusts are used in two basic types of situations:

- *Third-party trusts.* These are trusts set up by one party to benefit another. For example, a parent may set up a trust to benefit a disabled adult child, or an adult child may establish a trust for an aging parent or a sibling. Since the person setting up the trust has no obligation to support the beneficiary, the trust can specify that it be used to supplement, not replace, Medicaid benefits for the adult child, parent, or sibling who is the beneficiary. (These "supplemental needs trusts," discussed later in this chapter, may be established during your lifetime or by your will.)
- *Self-settled trusts.* These are trusts by which a person in need of Medicaid seeks to protect his or her own assets. The rules governing these trusts are much more restrictive. In general, you cannot set up a trust with funds that belong to you or funds to which you're entitled, have them remain "available" to you, and gain protection.

Depending on the purpose of the trust, the degree of discretion granted to the trustees, and restrictions on that discretion or use of the funds, trust principal can be sheltered and will not disqualify the trust donor once the statutory period of ineligibility following transfer of assets into the trust has expired.

Discretionary trusts were always subject to challenge by the government, which argued that any possible exercise of discretion by the trustees would make trust assets available and therefore countable as assets of the potential beneficiary when he or she applied for Medicaid. For Medicaid purposes, the resources in a *revocable trust* are considered available to the creator of the trust, who can revoke or undo the trust, and therefore count as his or her assets in determining eligibility. Income paid from the trust to any person is considered income of that person. Payments to others are treated as transfers subject to the transfer rules. It doesn't matter whether the trustee has actually exercised discretion or not. The mere possibility operates to disqualify the applicant from eligibility for benefits. These so-called *Medicaid qualifying trusts* are really *Medicaid disqualifying trusts.*

Theoretically an *irrevocable trust,* which by definition cannot be revoked, removes all control from the trust's creator. Subject to the trust provisions, the property is out of his or her hands. Therefore, only the income and principal that can be paid to the creator from the trust would be counted as available to the Medicaid applicant for eligibility determining purposes.

Because of the proliferation of so-called Medicaid qualifying trusts, Congress acted to tighten the rules of eligibility for transfers involving trusts. Tougher new Medicaid rules for trusts create a 60-month look-back period (and possible longer penalty periods) for transfers and other restrictions on their use. The new rules apply to trusts created with assets of the individual regardless of whether the trust is established by

- The individual
- The individual's spouse
- A person with legal authority to act in place of the individual or individual's spouse, such as a guardian or attorney in fact
- A person acting at the direction or request of an individual or individual's spouse, such as a guardian or attorney in fact

Despite restrictions, trusts may work in limited situations. A properly drafted "income only" trust, in which the trustee has no power to use any of the principal for the income beneficiary, will protect the trust funds after a penalty period (figured on the value of the assets placed in the trust).

How does the look-back period relate to transfers to trusts?

Remember, it's not just the look-back period that's critical but the penalty period. Thus, if you transfer $150,000 to a trust where you will get the income on the trust for your life but cannot access the principal, and the "average cost factor" for your state is $3,000 a month, the look-back period will be 60 months—but the penalty period will be no longer than 50 months.

In fact, the value of the "Medicaid transfer" to the trust will be less than $150,000 because it is reduced by the value of your lifetime right to the trust income. This reduction will be based on your age and life expectancy as set forth in tables used by Medicaid. If you are age 70 when you set up this "income-only" trust the value of the transfer to the trust for penalty period calculation purposes would be only $59,250, resulting in a penalty period of only 19 months. (Not all states permit this reduction in value.)

Do penalty rules apply to all trusts?

Medicaid rules apply to living trusts only. Trusts created by wills, called *testamentary trusts,* are not subject to these restrictive Medicaid rules. (Testamentary trusts are described in Chapter 16.)

Supplemental needs trusts. These trusts are traditionally set up for the use of disabled persons, often from the assets received from judgments or settlements arising out of accident or medical malpractice suits, or from assets accumulated by the disabled person before becoming ill. In the past, people would often be rendered ineligible for Medicaid by virtue of their ownership of these assets or settlements, which would dissipate quickly and not last the course of their lifetime.

The law protects assets of a Medicaid applicant placed in these trusts so long as the state's Medicaid outlay will be repaid out of the total amount of money left in the trust upon the individual's death. Two types of such trusts are authorized under law:

- A trust set up for a disabled person under age 65 by a parent, grandparent, legal guardian, or court
- A trust established and managed by a not-for-profit association for the benefit of a person of any age (a "pooled trust")

Assets placed in either type of trust are not treated as "available" for Medicaid eligibility purposes and can be used to pay for the "supplemental" needs of the disabled person (see Chapter 14). Transferring assets to such trusts is not subject to the transfer penalty rules *if* the trust beneficiary who is applying for Medicaid is under age 65 at the time that person's assets are placed in the trust. A transfer by a person more than 65 years old to such a trust could result in a penalty period, but the look-back period will be only 36 months.

Trusts are legal instruments governed by complicated rules. A person cannot and should not draw up a trust without the advice of an attorney expert in estate and trust planning and Medicaid law. For a full discussion of trusts, see Chapter 13; Chapter 14 describes setting up a trust for a disabled child.

CLAIMS FOR RECOVERY

Medicaid will pursue recovery from estate claims, personal injury liens, and real property, as well as any mistaken overpayments. One exception: the assets of the owner of a long-term care policy issued under a public-private partnership are protected from recovery (see Chapter 10).

Under Medicaid law, states are now required to have estate recovery programs, whereby assets from an individual's estate may be sought for Medicaid outlays made on his or her behalf. How can a Medicaid recipient have an estate if he or she is not allowed more than nominal assets to be eligible in the first place? In most cases there will be no "estate," but in some, there may be. For example, the home is exempt and may be owned by the Medicaid recipient at the time of death. Medicaid law also instructs the states to seek recovery from those assets in which the recipient had any interest at the time of death, raising complicated legal issues. No lien is allowed until after the death of the surviving spouse (except in spousal refusal cases).

I have a life estate in my former house, now owned by my child. Is the house vulnerable to state action?

This part of the Medicaid law is poorly written and very confusing, even to Medicaid experts. State interpretations vary. One interpretation is that the state can seek recovery from "nonprobate" assets such as trusts and annuities from which you received some benefits during your lifetime even if those benefits pass to someone else later on. Another is that the state has the right to go after jointly owned property or real estate in which the recipient has a life estate. If you have exempt assets or a partial interest in any assets, you need to get competent legal advice.

APPEALING A MEDICAID DECISION

Under Medicaid, you have the right to a fair hearing, with due process guarantees, for a denial of application for benefits or for termination, suspension, or reduction of eligibility or covered services. Basically, almost any denial, downgrade, or cessation of benefits can be appealed. (One exception: The state can always terminate optional benefits for lack of funding without giving you a hearing.)

The process for appeal under Medicaid is different than that of Medicare, which relies on its intermediaries and carriers to make determinations and hear appeals. In Medicaid, an appeal is made directly to the government.

Notice. Under federal regulations, you're entitled to receive 10 days notice before cessation or reduction of your benefits takes place. The notice must specify the action to be taken, the reasons for it, the legal grounds supporting the action, and your rights to a hearing and to continuation of benefits pending a hearing. You should also be informed of any legal assistance available to you.

The notice will also inform you of the date by which you must request a hearing. Your request should be in writing. Upon request, you should also be allowed access to your file at a reasonable time in advance of the hearing, and to any other relevant documents to be used at the hearing.

Fair hearing. A fair hearing is an informal process, conducted by an impartial hearing officer. The burden of proof is on the government to show that its action was supported by applicable law and regulations. You have the right to appear in person, to be represented by counsel, and to call and cross-examine witnesses. Formal rules of evidence don't necessarily apply.

The law states that the hearing must be held and a written decision issued by the hearing officer within 90 days of your initial request for a hearing, although these rules are not always followed. If the decision goes against you, you may file for a rehearing or administrative appeal. Any further appeal is made to the courts for judicial review.

Don't be misled into thinking you don't need a lawyer. Despite the informal nature of administrative review, Medicaid eligibility rules are extraordinarily complex and state regulations sometimes more so. If at all possible, you need the assistance of a lawyer familiar with Medicaid cases. This is an adversarial proceeding, and depending on the circumstances, the consequences may be severe.

What happens to my benefits during the hearing?

You usually have the right to continuation of your benefits pending the hearing, but *you must ask for it.* You must claim your right by asking for continuing aid when you request a fair hearing appeal. If your request for continuing aid is received within 10 days, your benefits must be continued.

MEDICAID'S FUTURE

Originally intended for the poor, Medicaid has become the payer of last resort for persons of modest means. Spousal protections for resources and income clearly indicate congressional intent that Medicaid continue as a program for middle-income Americans. Yet the use of Medicaid to finance long-term care, particularly nursing home costs, has had a profound impact on state budgets and resulted in attempts to restrict access to the program and limit benefits.

Despite intended overhaul, with the federal government unlikely to increase Medicare benefits in the foreseeable future, Medicaid is likely to continue as the only government-funded program that deals with long-term care.

A number of states already impose restrictions on benefits and services to restrain costs and treatment. Even if the Medicaid structure remains intact and federal guarantees stay in place, the poor can expect to feel the pinch in access to health care.

The real change for older Americans of modest means may be expected in eligibility for and access to long-term care under Medicaid. However, we can predict that access will be more limited and many transfer rules will be tightened. In 2003, for example, Connecticut is expected to win approval of a demonstration project that would increase restrictions on Medicaid transfers, change the start date of penalties, and extend the look-back period for transfers of real estate to 60 months.

That makes it imperative for you to start planning now—and consult with an experienced attorney about your plans.

Don't let yourself feel embarrassed about all this Medicaid planning. Consider this quote from New York's highest court, a decision (*Matter of Shah*) that allowed a wife, as guardian of her institutionalized husband, to transfer assets to herself.

> The complexities [of the law] . . . should never be allowed to blind us to the essential proposition that a man or a woman should normally have the absolute right to do anything that he or she wants to do with his or her assets, a right which includes the right to give those assets away to someone else for any reason or for no reason. . . . no agency of the government has any right to complain about the fact that middle class people confronted with desperate circumstances choose voluntarily to inflict poverty upon themselves when it is the government itself which has established the rule that poverty is a prerequisite to the receipt of government assistance in the defraying of the costs of ruinously expensive, but absolutely essential, medical treatment.

10

Long-Term Care Insurance

Long-term care insurance can provide a shield for the high costs of health care. This is a brand of insurance that's intended to fill in the gaps left by general insurance coverage and government benefits, paying for your care in a nursing home or at home. Depending on the policy, long-term care insurance can be extremely valuable, offering coverage not just for nursing home care but for home care, adult day care, and care in assisted living facilities.

Long-term care insurance differs from Medicare and general health insurance in several ways. First, it's intended to cover you for custodial, nonskilled care. It also is designed to provide benefits for a longer period of time. Benefit periods in long-term care policies generally provide three years of coverage for nursing home care and six years for home health care. Longer benefit periods and lifetime benefits are available.

The virtue of a longer benefit period is twofold. In the first place, it pays for your nursing home care during a crucial period—and the typical three-year coverage is more than the average person will need. The other real advantage to long-term care insurance is that *it buys you time.* If Medicaid will ultimately have to finance your long-term care needs but you don't wish to transfer funds to make yourself eligible at the present time, purchasing long-term care insurance now will allow Medicaid transfers to be postponed until a later date. (Under present Medicaid rules, you generally need to wait as long as three years between transferring money and applying for Medicaid benefits. We explain transfers and qualifying for Medicaid in Chapter 9.)

If you then need care, the three years of insurance coverage gives you a financial cushion to pay for it while transfers can be made and Medicaid eligibility kicks in. With long-term care insurance, planning must be done now, but transfers can be made later.

One question is cost. Long-term care policies are expensive and considered most suitable for middle-income buyers. Wealthier individuals have resources to cover their expenses and will probably not need Medicaid in the future, while annual premiums of $1,500—and approaching $6,000 for an initial purchase at age 75—may be too costly for those with less in assets and less income. Long-term care insurance is generally recommended for those with incomes of more than $20,000 yearly and assets of more than $100,000.

Long-term care insurance is still a relatively new product. But with budget cuts on the horizon, long-term care insurance offers more appeal to consumers worried about future home care and nursing home care needs. Cutbacks and changes in Medicaid laws may spur innovations and increased interest. One such innovation, pioneered in Connecticut and available in some other states, is the "public-private partnership" (see page 142).

EVALUATING THE LONG-TERM CARE POLICY

The business of long-term care insurance has grown from the 100,000 policies sold in 1986. Today some 6 million are in force from more than 130 insurance companies. Major sellers include John Hancock, Unum, CNA, Amex Life Assurance, and GE Capital.

Nearly all the states have passed laws and regulations governing long-term care insurance. While many of these laws are similar, modeled on recommendations of the National Association of Insurance Commissioners, specifics vary from state to state. Policies offer various options in coverage, benefits, deductibles, and protection, leaving you with a number of factors to consider when shopping for a long-term care policy.

The insurance company. The most important consideration is the fiscal soundness of your insurer. You do not want to be in a position in which your insurer fails and you are left holding a stack of unpaid claims. Check with your state insurance department, which is responsible for monitoring the solvency of insurers operating within the state. Make sure you check with one or more of the insurer rating services as well: A.M. Best, Standard & Poor's, Moody's, Fitch Ratings, or Weiss Ratings. And make sure you know how each rating service ranks companies—rating systems differ. (For more on insurer solvency and rating services, see Chapter 6.)

Level of care. You want to make sure the policy covers both nursing home and home health care. Some policies now cover adult day care and assisted living as well. Check what benefits are paid for each level of care.

The home care benefits under the policy should be of particular concern to you. Policies differ significantly in the "triggering event," which determines your coverage and how quickly they will pay on it (see below). Some companies may utilize a "care manager," who may or may not be an employee of the insurer, to review your claim and determine the care you will get.

Conditions covered. Early policies covered only certain medical conditions and excluded others, such as Alzheimer's disease. Make sure the policy includes language providing coverage for cognitive impairment and functional impairment as measured by activities of daily living (ADLs).

Restrictions on coverage. Some policies restrict benefits by mandating preconditions, for example, requiring prior hospitalization or skilled services before coverage will be provided. This is unacceptable—and now illegal in many states. Another restriction which is not acceptable is that you receive nursing home or home care from Medicare or otherwise "certified" facilities.

When benefits begin. In all policies, there is the *triggering event.* The triggering event is the injury, illness, or condition that must occur before coverage is provided and a claim is payable. It may be based upon establishment of either cognitive impairment or functional disability (for ADLs such as dressing, eating, and transferring). Medical necessity as a triggering event is no longer permitted.

Post-claims underwriting. This is a practice under which a company insures you but requests more detailed information about your application upon your filing a subsequent claim. At that time, it can then try to rescind the policy. This is illegal in some states. Avoid these policies.

Preexisting conditions. Policies may restrict benefits for conditions for which medical advice was or should have been sought within a given period of time preceding the effective coverage date. For older people, many with multiple ailments, this may exclude the very condition or conditions for which they seek coverage. Make sure that any restriction on preexisting conditions is itself subject to a fixed period with a so-called sunset clause, after which coverage will be granted.

Benefit payouts and deductible period. Payouts should be daily, starting at $100 a day. The *elimination* or *deductible period,* measuring the number of days before you can begin receiving benefits, is generally anywhere from 0 to 100 days. Make sure the benefit is realistic. A nursing home benefit of $75 a day will do little good if the daily cost in your community is $150 a day, unless you can afford to pick up the difference.

Since the cost of care will certainly increase over the years, you need *inflation protection* in the form of an inflation rider so that the benefit will increase each year. The most common form of this benefit is a 5 percent annual increase in the daily benefit, at either simple or compounded interest, although a compounding increase rider is preferable. Some policies also offer the right to purchase additional coverage later on with no medical examination necessary (although premiums for the additional coverage will be higher based on your age).

Duration of benefits. This refers to the maximum benefit period allowed under your policy. Although three years of nursing home care or six years of home care (with various combinations) is the most common, some policies offer variations ranging from two years to lifetime benefits. Your age, resources, and projected costs should be factors in your consideration. Remember that if you are using long-term care insurance as a delaying strategy to allow you time to transfer funds for Medicaid eligibility, you must have a minimum benefit period of three years to cover the usual Medicaid look-back period.

Premium costs. The older you are, the more your insurance will cost you at the time of purchase. Under the law, long-term care policies are *guaranteed renewable.* This means that the policy can't be canceled, as long as you pay the premium. The law does allow an insurance company to increase the premium for the class of *all* policyholders with the same policy.

The only time you don't have to pay the premium is if the policy has a waiver of premium feature, which allows you to stop paying when you are receiving benefits under the policy.

Inflation. The older you are, the more your insurance will cost. With rising costs, you need to know about future increases. Two provisions are of importance: *inflation protection* and *waiver of premium* for collection of benefits. Inflation protection ensures that rising costs will not outstrip future payments. A waiver of premium allows you not to have to pay the premiums while you are collecting benefits.

Group policies. An estimated 2,100 employers offer *group* long-term care policies for employees. There are a number of considerations that may make this a better deal for you. The premium cost may be substantially lower under a group than for an individual policy, even if you are asked to contribute in whole or in part to the premium cost. And the benefits may be better, regardless of premium costs.

Some group policies are offered *guaranteed issue*—meaning you can purchase the insurance even if you are not healthy (although you will probably have a preexisting condition waiting period). One disadvantage, however, is that if your company drops the plan and you have no conversion privilege, you may not be able then to buy an individual policy.

If you are considering a group policy, be sure to check the terms to see if it can be canceled, and if so, what your rights are to convert to an individual policy. State law may also provide additional protections for you.

PUBLIC-PRIVATE PARTNERSHIP POLICIES

An innovative project pioneered in Connecticut and also available in California, Indiana, and New York is the "public-private partnership" for long-term care financing.

If you live in one of these four states, the partnership offers you the opportunity to

- Buy long-term care insurance and
- Get Medicaid after your insurance benefits are used up—without having to "spend down" or give away your assets

If you have and use this long-term care insurance and its benefits, you may be able subsequently to qualify for Medicaid *automatically,* without having to spend down. Three states—California, Indiana, and Connecticut—match your protection dollar for dollar. In the fourth state, New York, your asset protection through this program is unlimited.

Under the partnership, public agencies join with private insurers to market long-term care policies that guarantee certain minimum benefits. An "approved" partnership insurance policy must meet certain standards, including at a minimum these basic components:

- Coverage for at least three years' nursing home benefits or six years' home care benefits (two days of home care equal one day of nursing home coverage)
- A minimum daily benefit of $110 for nursing home care and $60 for home care, with a 5 percent compounded inflation rider (these are 1995 minimums)

Medicaid benefits and asset protection. Once you use up the policy benefits, your assets will be protected as follows:

- **Dollar-matching.** In California, Connecticut, and Indiana, your assets will be protected up to the amount that your insurance pays for your medical expenses. Thus, if your insurance pays for $150,000 of nursing home costs, you can keep $150,000 of your assets (in addition to your home) and still be eligible for Medicaid.
- **Total asset protection.** In New York, all your assets will be exempt and fully protected. New York's program gives you unlimited asset protection.
- **Hybrid program.** Indiana offers either dollar-for-dollar or, for those who purchase a given amount, total asset protection. Indiana's total asset protection is afforded for policies bought in 1998 or before for $140,000, and goes up each year:

2002	$170,171
2003	$178,679
2004	$187,613
2005	$196,994
2006	$206,644
2007	$217,186
2008	$228,045
2009	$239,447
2010	$251,419

Can I buy a partnership policy in New York and use its benefits if I move to Florida and become ill there?

Yes and no. If you purchase a partnership policy, the home health and nursing home care insurance benefits can be used anywhere, subject to your qualifying for them. However, if you subsequently apply for Medicaid and wish to protect your assets under the plan, you must apply for benefits from the state that approved and sponsored the partnership policy.

Income restrictions. Although you receive assets protection, your income is not protected under the partnership programs. In fact, you may have to spend down your income. This may not be critical if you are single and living in a nursing home, but it will be a problem if you are married and your spouse will need your income to continue to live in the community.

Future partnerships. The public-private partnership is designed to encourage people to buy long-term care insurance. Because the average nursing home stay is two and a half years, the states expect to achieve savings through reduced Medicaid costs covered by the policies purchased under the program. Depending on your circumstances, it may also be of great value to you as a private individual, saving you a considerable amount of your resources.

Unfortunately, the federal government has seen fit to bar additional states from adopting new partnership programs. In 1993, it acted to restrict the program to the four states in which it now exists.

11

Reverse Mortgages, Annuities, and Life Insurance

Long-term care may be in your home, in another's home, or in another home that you purchase expressly to obtain services. But wherever it is provided, financing is needed.

One option for financing long-term care is the reverse mortgage. For older homeowners who are house rich but cash poor, home equity conversion mortgages, or *reverse mortgages*, permit them to tap the equity in their homes without having to sell them. With a reverse mortgage, you *receive* payments—either in a lump sum or at monthly intervals over the course of a fixed term or your lifetime. The total amount generally becomes due when you sell or leave your home.

Reverse mortgages may be a source of funds for financing long-term care. It may provide the additional cash you need to pay for help in your home, to cover premiums on long-term care insurance, or to place your spouse or parent in a nursing home or other living facility. On the minus side, once your home equity is spent, it is no longer available to you. And your home is protected only as long as you live in it.

This chapter discusses reverse mortgages and some other financing options, including the use of annuities and life insurance.

REVERSE MORTGAGES

Many older homeowners find themselves in the dubious position of being house rich and cash poor. With their houses paid off and no money owed to a bank, they are suddenly faced with unanticipated housing costs ranging from increased tax payments to roof repairs for which they simply don't have the money. At the same time, they may incur significant expenses for other unexpected needs, such as home care.

One solution designed to supplement other income is the reverse mortgage. Reverse mortgage programs permit elderly homeowners to convert the equity in their homes into cash, without having to sell their homes. A reverse mortgage is a type of home equity loan designed expressly for older homeowners. Using their homes as collateral, homeowners can borrow money and postpone repayment until a future time.

Technically, this is a *home equity conversion mortgage.* The reason it's called a *reverse mortgage* is that it reverses the way a regular mortgage works. Instead of your making a payment to your lender each month, the lender pays you.

The benefit is that, unlike other home equity loans, you're not required to pay back the loan for as long as you live in the house. And reverse mortgages can be used for any purpose. If you qualify, you can continue to own and live in your home while receiving either a lump sum or periodic payments. Under most plans, repayment is not due until the home is sold or the owner dies.

Reverse mortgages have been on the market for more than a quarter of a century. The most recent figures indicate that 10,000 reverse mortgages were issued in 2001.

There are three basic types of reverse mortgages offered by banks and savings and loan associations. These are

- *FHA-insured reverse mortgages.* Reverse mortgages insured by the Federal Housing Administration (FHA) provide funds in a lump-sum payment, monthly, or whenever you choose. The FHA puts limits on the amount of cash you may get, as a condition of its insuring such loans. This insurance is an important guarantee: if the lender defaults, you will continue to be paid. Home equity conversion mortgages sponsored through the Department of Housing and Urban Development (HUD), of which the FHA is a part, are available through FHA-approved lenders nationwide. Under FHA rules, independent counseling is also provided.
- *Private insurance.* Reverse mortgages backed by private insurance may offer greater cash advances than FHA-insured reverse mortgages. The biggest disadvantage of such insurance is the risk connected to the financial stability of the lender. As with any insurance, you should check the financial soundness of the company.

- *Uninsured.* Uninsured reverse mortgages are for fixed terms. Monthly payments are available for terms varying from three to 10 years, and the loans must be repaid in full when the term ends. Unlike standard reverse mortgages, these do not allow you to continue to live in your home for as long as you want—in most cases, a major drawback. Uninsured reverse mortgages may be found in Arizona, California, Massachusetts, and Minnesota.

QUALIFYING FOR A REVERSE MORTGAGE

Different programs apply different qualifying restrictions. Basic eligibility requirements are

- Borrowers must be at least 62 years old.
- Borrowers should owe little or no money on their homes. (As you're not expected to make regular payments, income is not a factor in your eligibility for a reverse mortgage.)
- Homes must be single-family, one-unit, owner-occupied dwellings or two- to four-unit owner-occupied dwellings.
- Condominiums, planned unit developments, and manufactured homes must be FHA-approved to be eligible.

I live in a cooperative apartment. Am I eligible for a reverse mortgage?

Under the American Homeownership and Economic Opportunity Act, signed into law in 2000, cooperative units are now eligible for FHA-insured reverse mortgages. But don't be surprised if you can't find a reverse mortgage on your co-op. Regulations to implement the law have not yet been issued.

LOAN AMOUNT AND PAYMENT OPTIONS

Total loan amount. Loans made as reverse mortgages are calculated on an amount fixed at the maximum the FHA will insure. The total amount you may receive depends on

- The value of your home
- Your age
- The area in which you reside

The maximum amount varies per locality, from $78,660 in low-cost rural areas to $155,250 in costlier housing markets. This cap determines the total amount from which your cash payments will be made. If your home value is less, the cap will be less.

The amount will also vary depending on your age. Payments are based on actuarial tables. The percentage you receive will vary from 37 percent of the limit for a 62-year-old to 83 percent for a 95-year-old.

Payment options (what you get). Once approved, the homeowner has various options for receiving payment. The type of payment chosen also alters the amount.

- Lifetime monthly payments (*tenure plans*). These will vary depending on your age. The older you are, the higher the monthly amount will be. (For couples, the younger person's age will determine the payout, as his or her life expectancy is how long the house is likely to be kept.) In some plans, monthly payments may be increased in later years
- Monthly payments for a fixed term
- A one-time lump-sum payment
- A line of credit, from which withdrawals may be made

These same options are available through FHA-backed and private lender reverse mortgages. A combination is also possible, such as monthly payments and a line of credit. Under FHA rules, options can be changed, at an administrative fee of no more than $20. As a general rule, the federally insured Home Equity Conversion Mortgage offers the largest payouts, state and local government programs the smallest. Private-sector mortgages vary considerably. All come with a wide variety of costs (application fee, closing, appraisal), although these can be charged to the loan amount.

Amount due (what you owe). In addition to the full loan amount, you are liable for fees, as with any mortgage, including application fees, points, closing costs, insurance premiums, plus all interest. Interest and closing rates are generally higher than those in conventional mortgages.

Your potential liability is limited to the value of your home. You can't be made to pay from other assets you may have. No costs, including insurance premiums, are collected until the loan is due.

Counseling. You must get counseling from a mortgage counselor from an HUD-approved agency. This protects both you and the bank. Call 888/466-3487 for the name and location of a HUD-approved housing counseling agency near you.

Warning. A reverse mortgage is a loan. It becomes due when you move, sell your home, or die, or in some cases, at the end of a determinate loan period. You could lose your home if the reverse mortgage is not repaid, or use up your equity and have to move. Remember, once your home equity is spent, it is no longer available to you or your heirs. Make sure you consult with your lawyer or accountant before agreeing to a reverse mortgage.

Who pays property taxes?

As the owner, you are still responsible for property taxes, insurance, and repairs. If you fail to pay your property taxes or keep your house insured and maintained in good repair, your loan could become due and payable in full. Lenders may reduce your loan advances to pay for these expenses.

What happens when my spouse dies?

In most reverse mortgages, no repayment is due until the last surviving borrower dies or sells or moves from the home.

Is my home safe? What if I have to go to a nursing home or a facility? Should I sell my home?

Most reverse mortgage plans address the issue of what will happen when your home is unoccupied for a long period of time. Depending on the provisions in your plan, you might be required to repay the loan amount. A forced sale under equity conversion may force spend-down of proceeds. And any equity you use up will not be available to your spouse or heirs.

TRUTH IN LENDING REQUIREMENTS

The federal Truth in Lending Act requires lenders to inform you about the terms, conditions, and costs of your reverse mortgage plan. This includes an explanation of payment terms, annual percentage and variable rates, credit charges, and other fees. There is a Truth in Lending form that tells you what the loan actually costs.

The law also requires mortgage counseling from a third party who is not the lender. The information you are given must include

- Other options available to you, including home equity conversion
- Financial implications of the plan
- Tax and estate consequences of the plan
- The consequences of the plan for your eligibility for government benefits

Your right to *rescission* is also spelled out in the notice from your lender. You have three business days after signing and receiving your Truth in Lending disclosures to reconsider your decision to take out the loan.

Reverse mortgages are complicated legal transactions, combining elements of home equity loans, life insurance, and annuities. You should not proceed without a professional adviser to counsel you concerning the terms and their implications for you.

REVERSE MORTGAGES AND GOVERNMENT BENEFITS

Reverse mortgage payments are not taxable. Nor are they counted as income for purposes of determining eligibility for Social Security, SSI, Medicare, or Medicaid benefits. However, reverse mortgage payments may nevertheless affect your eligibility in the following way. Although the monthly payments you receive from a reverse mortgage are not "income" for Medicaid or SSI purposes, if the funds are not spent, you may accumulate assets in excess of the allowable amounts (see Chapter 9). By the same principle, annuity payments or a lump-sum payment to you may jeopardize your eligibility. This is an important issue, so make sure you consult a lawyer familiar with federal SSI requirements and your state's Medicaid regulations before getting a reverse mortgage.

FINDING A REVERSE MORTGAGE

At the present time, FHA-insured reverse mortgages are offered through lenders in 47 states and the District of Columbia. Privately insured and uninsured reverse mortgages are also available in several states.

A list of programs offering reverse mortgages is available from the National Center for Home Equity Conversion (telephone 612/953-4474). The names of FHA-insured lenders are available from the Federal National Mortgage Association, or Fannie Mae (telephone 800/7-FANNIE). The American Association of Retired Persons (AARP) also supplies information on private and public reverse mortgage lenders (telephone 202/434-6030). (See the appendixes of this book for complete listings.)

A listing of reverse mortgage counseling agencies, approved by HUD, can be obtained from lenders in your area. Nonprofit agencies that provide information and initial contacts for reverse mortgages are also available in your area. Complaints or questions should be directed to the Federal Trade Commission.

ANNUITIES

An annuity is simply an agreement to pay given sums at stated intervals for a period of time, in return for valuable consideration. Annuities are sold for a variety of reasons, primarily for tax deferral. An annuity can be fixed or variable (that is, paying a set or variable amount), and it can be immediate or deferred (payments starting now or later). Although most annuities are sold commercially by insurance companies, in fact private annuities are also valid.

One benefit of an annuity is that, if properly constructed, it does not count as an asset for Medicaid purposes. That means that if you purchase an annuity, you can convert vulnerable assets into an income stream, which is more protected.

Federal law expressly authorizes the purchase of an annuity for this purpose. Under federal rules, the test of whether an annuity will receive protection is whether it is "actuarially sound," meaning the amount being received is a fair market value of what could be expected over the expected term of life of the beneficiary.

- It must be an immediate annuity, payable immediately.
- It must be irrevocable and nonassignable.
- It must be for a term certain not to exceed the life expectancy (as determined by Social Security Administration tables or, in some states, state tables).

If the annuity fails to meet this test, the purchase cost will be considered a transfer subject to Medicaid penalties.

State law may add a few wrinkles. Some states, such as Maine and Connecticut, consider the purchase of any annuity a transfer. Some such as Indiana, prohibit private annuities. Make sure you know what your state law provides before you purchase an annuity for Medical planning purposes.

What are the disadvantages of an annuity?

The biggest one is loss of control of the assets. Once an irrevocable annuity is purchased, you have no access to those funds, for any purpose. You are limited to the income stream. Changing interest rates may also pose a disadvantage.

How does an annuity for a community spouse work with the community spouse resource allowance (CSRA)?

The annuity should be used with the CSRA. Make sure that you calculate the exact figures. An annuity purchased before a Medicaid application, effective before that date, will ensure that those assets are not included in the snapshot that determines the ceiling amount of the allowance. Purchasing the annuity before the application could lower the CSRA amount if you live in a state where the rate is fixed as "one-half the total assets" up to a given amount and your combined assets fall below that given amount. Retain assets that can be transferred after determination of the allowance amount (for example, for a funeral or burial plot).

Timing is important. If a community spouse gets an annuity too far in advance of application, the first payments may be made in time to count toward the assets and income again. Payments will be income, reducing the minimum income to which the spouse would be otherwise entitled.

USING LIFE INSURANCE

One idea that has gained popularity in recent years is the receipt of death benefits under a life insurance policy *before death*. This is also known as *living benefits* or *accelerated death benefits*.

Holders of existing life insurance policies and purchasers of new policies are being offered living benefits riders. More than 200 companies now offer them.

Triggering event. As with long-term care and health insurance, policies pay living benefits upon the occurrence of a triggering event. Some policies, especially earlier ones, required proof of terminal illness before benefits could be paid out. Over the years, these requirements have altered, and payouts are allowed for chronic care needs.

Determination of benefit. The amount of benefits you can receive, usually a percentage of the face value of the policy, depends on the controlling language of the policy. It may vary from 25 to 100 percent of the full benefit under the life insurance policy.

Accelerated death benefits are regulated by the states. To some extent, payouts are limited. With a living benefits rider, you can get either a lump sum benefit or payment through installments. Installments are preferable for those entering long-term care.

I have a standard life insurance policy, without riders. Can I get an accelerated benefit payout?

Check with your insurance company. It may be willing to issue a rider. Or you may be able to "sell" your policy to a company that will give you a *viatical settlement*. Viatical settlements are based on the same concept as accelerated benefits riders, allowing you to collect on your policy in advance of death. The policy is *viaticated,* that is, sold by the owner to the company, at a discounted rate. As a general rule, payout under a viatical settlement is conditioned on terminal illness (or permanent transfer to a long-term care facility). Often, a life expectancy of no more than two years is required. The percentage the owner gets depends on his or her life expectancy: the shorter, the greater in cash terms. Payouts are generally from 60 to 80 percent of the policy death benefit.

Viatical settlements are regulated in California and New York, as well as Kansas and New Mexico, where they were originally pioneered. Viatical settlements are prohibited in Utah.

Part 4

Life Planning for You and Your Family

Many people believe, mistakenly, that life planning is for the wealthy. But most people, rich or not, have the same goals—good health, income and assets to ensure security for themselves and their spouses, and a cushion for a possible crisis or chronic long-term care needs. Planning can help identify those goals and formulate strategies to achieve them.

In Chapter 12, we'll tell you about tools for health care decision making, how you can protect yourself with advance directives, and how these same documents can help you make decisions on behalf of others. Chapter 13 tells you about financial planning—and the use of the power of attorney and trusts, among other property management systems. In recent years, living trusts and other trust instruments have become increasingly popular among financial planners and advisers to the elderly. We explain what a trust is, what it can and cannot do for you, and how to avoid common pitfalls. Chapter 14 gives you an introduction to planning strategies for a disabled child. In Chapter 15, we talk about options available for those no longer able to make their own decisions, from guardianships to other protective services.

For many, making a will is the primary vehicle for financial planning. This becomes even more difficult when you consider the possibility of your spouse's needing increased health care in the future—and the Medicaid implications. We discuss the implications of wills and estate planning in Chapter 16.

12

Advance Directives for Health Care

In Chapter 2, we described your rights to determine what medical treatment you will get and what treatment you will refuse. The decision by the United States Supreme Court in the *Cruzan* case upheld your constitutional right to determine your own care, including the right to refuse life support.

If you're able to communicate with your doctors, you can tell them your views on the treatment they offer. In the best of all possible worlds, they'll make a diagnosis, discuss treatment options and their advantages and disadvantages with you, and give you ample time to come to a decision after obtaining a second and even a third opinion and discussing the options with your family and loved ones.

Unfortunately, medical decisions are not usually made at leisure. Nor are they always made when the patient is in a position to understand, make, and communicate decisions about his or her health.

Your right to have your wishes respected continues even if you are incapacitated. If you are no longer in a position to state them, others may assert them on your behalf as your *surrogate*. In the *Cruzan* case, Nancy Cruzan's parents spoke on behalf of their daughter, who was in a persistent vegetative coma and incapable of articulating her wishes. The decision made it clear that she had that right—that her own prior statements were in fact the best evidence of her present wishes, were she able to communicate them.

If a person's wishes are expressed when he or she is competent, either through a document such as a *living will* or orally to another person, those wishes must be respected. In this chapter, we discuss the use of living wills and *health care proxies,* and what happens when decisions

156

must be made on behalf of incapacitated adults or children who have not expressed their wishes through such *advance directives.*

The rules may vary, depending on the state you live in. We've tried to note some of the differences here, but be aware that state legislatures make frequent changes in this area. If you find yourself in a situation where you're making decisions for someone else or having decisions made for you by someone else, doctors, hospital administrators, and other health care professionals may be overzealous in resisting your legal rights. That's when you'll need help in enforcing your rights. Patients have learned to use legal documents such as living wills and health care proxies to assert their rights to receive or refuse medical treatment according to their values and wishes.

THE THREE BASIC DIRECTIVES

To deal with possible future incapacity, lawyers have come up with documents called *advance directives* that allow people to make their wishes known when they are no longer in a position to express them themselves. Advance directives commonly used include

- **Living will.** The living will states your desires concerning future medical care, specifying what procedures you want or don't want. These are sometimes called *health care directives, medical directives,* or *instructional directives.* We use the expression *living will* because that's what most people call them.
- **Health care proxy.** Also called a *durable power of attorney for health care,* the health care proxy allows you to designate an agent in advance to make decisions on your behalf if you later become incapacitated. The proxy designates someone else to *ensure that the wishes you have expressed—in your living will or otherwise—are carried out,* and to *make health care determinations on your behalf, if you're not capable or don't have a living will, or for things not anticipated in your living will.* The power of attorney for health care is sometimes combined with a living will.
- **Power of attorney.** This is an advance directive primarily for use in financial planning. (This type of power of attorney is discussed in Chapter 13.)

LIVING WILLS

Living wills have become common since Nancy Cruzan's death provided the legal authority to recognize patients' wishes expressed through living wills. Both Jacqueline Onassis and Richard Nixon had living wills, which illustrates how accepted living wills have become.

How does it work? If you're well enough and competent, you tell your doctors what you want and don't want. If you're not able, your living will does it for you.

A living will speaks for you when you can't. It ensures that your family and your doctor—and any other doctor or medical facility treating you—knows your wishes in the event you aren't able to make your own medical decisions. It protects you if you are in a coma or incompetent.

What do you need to know about a living will?

- *When* and under what conditions it becomes effective
- *What* medical care is authorized and what medical care is not authorized
- *How* the living will itself is sanctioned, by what form and with what necessary signatures

Living wills are governed by state law. Forty-seven states and the District of Columbia have specific laws authorizing and regulating their use. The other states recognize them and rely on interpretation of court decisions. Whether you live in a state with or without a living will statute, it's important to understand that *all states recognize living wills.*

Remember, you should talk with those closest to you about your wishes ahead of time—that's why your written expression of your wishes is called an "advance directive." Take the time now to talk to family, physicians, and clergy. A living will is your protection when and if you become incapable of making or communicating decisions about your health care.

When does a living will become effective?

When you're incapable of making or communicating the necessary health care decision. In other words, when you have lost the capacity to give informed consent. If you could speak for yourself, you wouldn't need that piece of paper.

What is the definition of capacity? For health care purposes, a person with capacity is able to understand the illness, the nature and effect of the proposed treatment, and the risk in accepting or refusing it.

Several states impose restrictions on the use of living wills. In most states, the statutes say a living will may be used only if the patient is terminal; in some states, death must be imminent. The intent of these statutes is to preclude using the living will to refuse treatment for a patient who is seriously ill and with no hope of recovery, but not on the brink of death. Thus, a person in an irreversible coma or with advanced Alzheimer's might be given artificial hydration and nutrition even against his or her wishes.

Language such as this is clearly not binding. Under the *Cruzan* decision, you have the right to refuse treatment, through stating your wishes or through your living will, whether you are in a terminal condition or not. You do not have to agree to "heroic measures" that you do not want. (The model living will in this chapter covers a broad set of circumstances.)

Many states impose very specific requirements concerning use of a living will. Colorado's statute, for example, requires the person be terminal for seven days, and then imposes a 48-hour waiting period on removal of life-sustaining treatment. Alaska, Arizona, and California also have requirements concerning the duration of the patient's condition and additional procedures for certifying it. Other states are becoming more and more flexible, broadening the circumstances under which a living will may be invoked in the wake of the *Cruzan* decision.

Once I've signed a living will, can my doctor "pull the plug" at any time?

No. A living will (and any other medical directive you may sign) becomes effective only when and if you are incapable of making or communicating decisions about your health care. If you are so incapable *and* you are terminally ill, in a persistent vegetative state, or suffering persistent mental incapacity, *then* it can be used as an indicator of your wishes.

Can the state prevent my wishes from being honored? What do I do then?

You (or your family acting as your surrogate) may need a lawyer to enforce your rights. In Florida, Estelle Browning left specific written instructions not to give her tube feeding. Because she was in a vegetative condition but death was not imminent, as she specified in her living will, her instructions were ignored and she was kept alive against her wishes. Subsequent legal action, unfortunately too late for Mrs. Browning, upheld her right to refuse all life-sustaining treatment.

One important lesson of the *Browning* case is that the language of your living will should not be limited to preconceived ideas about your state law but should express your views so that they may stand as the true expression of your intentions.

SPECIFIC TREATMENT INSTRUCTIONS

People do not generally think about the specifics of illness and dying. They generally phrase their thoughts in vague expressions like "I don't want to be kept alive like that," which may refer to anything from being mentally incapacitated to receiving artificial respiration. Drafting and executing a living will forces you to confront these issues.

In cases of serious or terminal illness, doctors may prescribe diagnostic tests ranging from relatively straightforward procedures such as blood tests, X rays, MRI, and CT scans to biopsies and exploratory surgery. Other possible treatment choices may include radiation, chemotherapy, or hormone therapy, all of which have potentially undesirable side effects. Or comfort care may be ordered to deal exclusively with alleviating pain.

A living will usually discusses these kinds of treatment and life-support options—procedures, medicines, technologies, foods, or any combination of those—and whether or not the individual wants them, and under what conditions. Treatments and other options often discussed in a living will can include respirators or ventilators, nutrition and hydration, cardiopulmonary resuscitation (CPR), and so forth.

Treatments don't have to be painful or unpleasant to be specified in a living will. For example, antibiotics have relatively harmless side effects but are commonly refused because of their very effectiveness in prolonging lives.

Your living will applies also to treatments that you would want to help you. At least one hospital has gone to court for permission to take someone off life-sustaining treatment because the hospital thought that continued treatment was futile. The court refused the hospital's request, specifically citing the patient's expressed desire for continued treatment.

In drafting your living will and discussing its provisions with your lawyer or your family, don't gloss over the specifics. Remember, details count. They count when you're deciding to accept or refuse treatment. They count even more when you're in no position to make the decision and someone else has to make it for you.

Do I have a right to demand treatment through my living will?

Yes, at least to the extent you have the right to demand it at all. As we discussed in Chapter 2, the limits to "treatment on demand" are still uncertain. Courts have refused to take a patient off life-sustaining treatment, despite medical evidence of its futility. Treatment has also been ordered by courts for patients in a persistent vegetative state. New Jersey laws sanction continued treatment for those of Orthodox Jewish faith who believe that the cessation of heart and lung function, rather than of brain activity, determines legal death.

Forcing doctors to treat patients in medically unacceptable ways creates numerous ethical dilemmas as yet unresolved. At least one lawsuit has been instituted charging a failure to provide requested care, and more may be predicted. A disturbing survey reported in the *New York Times* found that 80 percent of doctors had withdrawn care over the objections of family members, and 14 percent had withheld or withdrawn care they considered "futile" without discussion.

Are there any special rules for pregnant women?

Many states exclude pregnant women from their living will statutes and do not allow them to refuse life-sustaining treatment during pregnancy. Some expressly make viability of the fetus or viability with life support the point at which treatment cannot be refused. Arizona, Maryland, and New Jersey allow pregnant women to refuse life support.

How do religions feel about living wills?

Organized religion for the most part respects the right to die in dignity, without prolonging suffering by artificial means. Yet some Catholic, Orthodox Jewish, and fundamentalist Protestant groups remain opposed. One organization has drafted a living will form for use by Orthodox Jews, which includes a hierarchy of rabbinical boards to determine issues of Jewish law for end-of-life decisions. The validity of this document in court is open to question.

Statutes deal with religion in two ways.

- First, they exempt physicians and hospitals from having to comply with directives that go against their personal religious beliefs. Patients under the care of doctors and institutions who are unsympathetic to their views can either seek another doctor or transfer to another institution. The Patient Self-Determination Act addresses this problem by requiring health care facilities to take certain steps to ensure that advance directives are respected.
- Second, some statutes modify the definition of death (usually "brain death") for those whose belief system would insist the person is still alive. In New Jersey, for example, an otherwise dead person whose heart and lungs are still functioning may be considered alive. This has obvious implications for when to end life support.

INSTRUCTIONS ON NUTRITION AND HYDRATION

People have special feelings about eating and drinking. Although many people have no qualms about refusing medication or ending aggressive measures for very ill patients, they balk at ending basic support of nutrition and hydration.

The *Cruzan* court made clear that there was no legal distinction between nutrition and hydration and other forms of life-sustaining treatment (such as respiration). Recent studies indicate that competent hospital patients eat and drink little at the end of their lives and do not experience additional discomfort by avoiding artificial nutrition and hydration. According to some medical experts, there is no evidence that individuals dependent on artificial nutrition and hydration would experience any discomfort if these treatments were foregone; in fact, the imposition of artificial nutrition and hydration may actually contribute to an uncomfortable death.

Nevertheless, problems arise with artificial or tube feeding. In some states, you must expressly indicate in your living will that that you don't want nutrition and hydration. This is the requirement in Alaska, Florida, Maine, Minnesota, Ohio, Oregon, South Dakota, and Tennessee.

Most state statutes are silent on the subject. In those states where withdrawal of nutrition and hydration is not authorized, courts have split on recognizing the patient's wishes. A generic living will may also be prepared, which may help as an added precaution. (See our model living will in this chapter.)

What is the difference between withdrawing and withholding life-sustaining treatment?

From a legal or moral point of view, there is no difference. The Supreme Court made clear that there is no valid legal distinction between withholding a treatment (refusing to start it) and withdrawing it once it has begun. Yet withdrawing treatment is often resisted by health care workers who feel more deeply implicated morally by actually turning off a machine than by just not turning it on in the first place. Drafting your living will to address both possibilities can help alleviate this problem.

"DO NOT RESUSCITATE" ORDERS

"DNR" stands for *do not resuscitate,* a code for an order commonly used in a hospital or nursing home. DNR indicates that if the patient's heart or breathing stops, he or she is not to be revived. These orders are known as *DNR codes, No codes,* or *Hollywood codes.* Hospitals used to routinely enter DNR on the charts of severely ill elderly patients, without asking.

Living wills can authorize DNR orders, naming resuscitation as one of the life-sustaining procedures refused. Many states have laws requiring hospitals and nursing homes to withhold emergency cardiopulmonary resuscitation from patients who note their refusal in advance.

Interestingly, New York, which has no living will statute, has a DNR law covering hospitals and nursing homes as well as nonhospital DNR situations. Extending DNR regulation to homes as well as hospitals was intended to benefit many people with advanced medical conditions who die at home or in hospices. Emergency medical service workers are no longer required to resuscitate them.

A number of other states have passed laws prescribing guidelines for DNR orders outside health care facilities. These include Arizona, Colorado, Florida, Illinois, Maryland, Ohio, Pennsylvania, and Virginia.

A DNR order outside the hospital or institutional setting is hard to enforce. Emergency workers generally have no knowledge of a patient's wishes unless the patient is in a position to tell them, and often this is not possible. Some patient wear bracelets with the order on it or carry a card in their wallet so that emergency service workers will be sure to see it. Laws generally grant immunity to health professionals who carry out a DNR order in good faith, as well as to those who attempt resuscitation unaware of the order. Nevada law provides misdemeanor penalties for emergency medical service personnel who willfully fail to comply or who conceal or withhold knowledge of a DNR order.

How can I make sure a DNR order is respected?

The unhappy fact is that when it comes to DNR orders, patient preferences are routinely ignored.

Make sure your doctor understands your wishes, and, if you are in a hospital, make sure the order is entered in your medical chart. In a study reported in the *New York Times,* although three out of 10 patients said they didn't want cardiopulmonary resuscitation, 80 percent of their doctors either ignored or misunderstood their instructions. Only 48 percent of the physicians could accurately identify their patients' preferences for CPR. Nearly *half* the patients requesting it did not get DNR orders entered on their charts.

Speak up! Giving physicians more information failed to significantly affect their knowledge of patients' wishes or treatment decisions.

Does "do not resuscitate" mean "do not treat"?

DNR should not be confused with DNT ("do not treat"). In practice, some hospitals or health care providers may be casual about the difference, assuming that if you sign a DNR, meaning you don't want resuscitation, you don't want treatment. But this is not necessarily so. You may very well want continued treatment, for infections or for life-threatening situations other than cardiac arrest, particularly if there is a chance of recovery. Not all ways to go are equally bad. Make sure the people who are treating you know the difference.

What if I am resuscitated against my will? Do I have any recourse against the hospital?

Not under current law. Edward Winter saw his wife die after painful resuscitation years before and determined to avoid that fate himself. The Cincinnati man left clear instructions that no such effort was to be made on his behalf, and when he was hospitalized they were entered on his chart and posted behind the monitor. Nursing personnel were not informed and acted against his instructions, resuscitating him and saving his life for two more years. He brought a personal injury suit against the hospital, charging "wrongful living." The suit was dismissed by the court.

However, several newer cases have challenged the right to give aggressive treatment such as CPR in the face of express refusals, citing theories of negligence, intentional infliction of emotional distress, and battery.

PHYSICIAN RESPONSIBILITY AND LIABILITY

As a general rule, state laws relieve doctors and families of responsibility in the patient's decision, specifically providing that withholding or withdrawing life-sustaining treatment in compliance with a living will does not constitute assisted suicide or homicide. Often the statute provides immunity from liability for health care providers.

A bigger problem for patients is the number of doctors who ignore the instructions in the advance directives of their patients. A number of states impose penalties upon doctors for failure either to comply with medical directives in a living will or to transfer a patient to a facility that will comply. Some states sanction health providers for failure to record the terminal condition with criminal misdemeanors and penalties.

An interesting question of liability arose in the unfortunate case of Jean Elbaum, who was given medical services over her express objections. The nursing home said her wishes were not expressed in a way that met New York's "clear and convincing" standard of proof and kept her alive through a series of legal battles until the courts ruled that the treatment was unwanted and should be discontinued. The nursing home then presented her husband with a bill for more than $120,000. Astonishingly, the obligation of Mr. Elbaum to pay the bill—*even for treatment that was found to be unwanted*—was upheld by New York's highest court.

More recently, several lawsuits have sought to challenge doctors, hospitals, and health care providers who have ignored living wills and other advance directives, and hold them liable for damages. In one case, a Michigan woman was awarded a verdict of $16.5 million for unauthorized treatment by a hospital against the patient's wishes.

LIVING WILL STATUTES AND LEGAL FORMALITIES

Let's clear up one common misunderstanding right now. There are states with so-called living will statutes and states without such statutes. But all states *recognize* living wills. All states are subject to the *Cruzan* decision of the United States Supreme Court allowing self-determination in refusing life-sustaining treatment.

Those states with statutes authorizing living wills look to their statutes to determine issues that arise. The fact that the state you live in has no law concerning living wills does not mean that you shouldn't have one. Those states without living will statutes look to prior court decisions. A living will can be just as important, if not more so, in a nonstatute jurisdiction, where it will count as evidence to the court of the patient's intentions.

The states without statutes authorizing living wills are New York, Massachusetts, and Missouri (Nancy Cruzan's home state). New York, for example, has no living will statute, but in fact the New York Court of Appeals, the state's highest court, declared in a landmark decision that the ideal situation to establish a patient's intentions to decline medical assistance would be one in which the person's wishes were expressed in some form of writing such as a living will when he or she was still competent. (Without a writing, "mere statements" about not being maintained on artificial life support were not sufficient to constitute the "clear and convincing" level of proof needed to assure the court that the patient had indeed made this determination.)

LIVING WILL AND HEALTH CARE DECLARATION

Know all people by these presents that I, _____, residing at _____, hereby declare my will with respect to my medical care and treatment in the event I am unable for any reason to make known my will at the time medical decisions must be made.

1. *Directive to forgo or discontinue life-prolonging medical treatment when recovery is unlikely.*

In the event I suffer from an injury, disease, or illness, including intractable pain, which renders me unable to make health care decisions on my own behalf, which leaves me unable to communicate with others meaningfully, and from which there is no reasonable prospect of recovery to a cognitive and sentient life (even if my condition or illness is not deemed to be "terminal" and even if my death is not imminent), I direct that no medical treatments or procedures (except as provided in paragraph 3 below) be utilized in my care or, if begun, that they be discontinued.

2. *Definition of medical treatment.*

By "medical treatments or procedures," I mean interventions by medical doctors, nurses, paramedics, hospitals, residential health care facilities, or any other health care provider, in the care of my body and mind, including all medical and surgical procedures, mechanical or otherwise, treatments, therapies, including drugs and hormones, which may substitute for, replace, supplant, enhance, or assist any bodily function. This specifically includes maintenance of respiration, nutrition, and hydration by artificial means. With respect to all medical treatments or procedures, I include both existing technology and any methods or techniques that may be hereafter developed and perfected.

3. *Provision for pain control.*

I ask that medical treatment to alleviate pain, to provide comfort, and to mitigate suffering be provided so that I may be as free of pain and suffering as possible.

4. *Determination of prognosis.*

My Health Care Agent acting pursuant to my duly executed Health Care Proxy shall follow my directions as set out in this Health Care Declaration whenever my Agent has ascertained by applying reasonable medical standards that my condition is as described in Section 1, above. In the absence of the instructions of my Agent, any persons or institutions who are called upon to make decisions affecting my care shall comply with my directions contained herein. In the event of uncertainty or ambiguity as to how my wishes are to be interpreted or applied in any particular situation, any persons or institutions who are treating me shall comply with the interpretations and directions of my Health Care Agent.

5. *Acknowledgement of effects of this Declaration.*

I make and execute this Declaration knowing that, if complied with, my death may occur sooner than it would were all available and appropriate medical treatments considered and used. I accept this as a necessary result of a decision to avoid dependence and pain. And I make the decision now, for myself, after careful consideration, to assure that I will have the level of medical care that I want, and to relieve others of the burden of decision.

Dated:_____, 20__

_____

Statement of Witnesses

I declare that the person who signed this document is person-ally known to me and appears to be of sound mind and acting of his or her own free will. He or she signed (or asked another to sign for him or her) this document in my presence.

_____ Address _____

_____ Address _____

The *Cruzan* court authorized states to establish their own standards of proof concerning a patient's intentions. *A properly executed living will meets those standards in all states.*

How does a living will become effective?

In states with a living will statute, the statute usually contains form and execution requirements. There is usually a requirement that the living will be witnessed by two persons at least 18 years of age who are not relatives by blood or marriage, heirs, health care agents, or otherwise financially responsible for the person's medical care. (Check local laws.) Notarization is not always required, but it can't hurt.

Some states impose additional requirements. For example, Califor-nia requires that a nursing home patient's living will be witnessed by a patient advocate or state-designated representative. Delaware and South Carolina have similar provisions. In Georgia, the living will of a person in a hospital or nursing facility must be witnessed by the medical director or a member of the medical staff not involved in the declarant's care.

Most states with statutes require certain formalities for execution but allow you to use your own words. On the other hand, Oregon's statute mandates use of its statutory form. A few statutes, including those of Virginia, Louisiana, and Texas, specifically authorize oral declarations. Remember that in all states, oral statements can always be used as evidence of the speaker's wishes.

The important thing to remember about a living will is that it is implemented by others. The person who signs a living will is not in a position to enforce it. Someone—a spouse, a child, a friend—will be enforcing it on his or her behalf. Once you have signed your living will, you must communicate its existence to those upon whom you would rely, and either distribute it or leave it where it can easily be found.

An especially important resource to use is Partnership for Caring, a national organization that counsels people facing these issues—and gives them the resources to deal with doctors, hospitals, and others. Partnership for Caring publishes living will forms good for your state and will send you free copies. (See the resources section at the end of this book.)

What kind of living will should be prepared for states without living will statutes or with restrictions on withholding certain treatments?

We recommend the general form (such as the sample form on page 166), especially for states with statutory restrictions on withholding nutrition and hydration. Remember, your constitutional right to refuse treatment overrides any state attempts to restrict it. But you must express your wishes through a living will in order to make sure your rights are respected.

Is a living will valid state to state? Should I prepare separate documents?

It depends. A living will prepared out of state will generally be valid as an alternative to the living will required by the state's law. For example, Arizona recognizes those out-of-state documents that comply with its statute. Other states such as Texas give "full faith and credit" to living wills executed in accordance with the laws of other states.

Even if a state does not honor you out-of-state living will, your living will may be taken as evidence of your intent and used in that respect. A validly signed document offers some proof of your intentions.

It makes no sense to sign 50 documents. If you move to a new residence or buy a vacation home in another state, you should review the validity of your living will in your new state and execute a new one, if needed, in accordance with the requirements of that state.

Where should I keep my living will?

Keep the original in an easily accessible place, and give copies to your primary doctor and close members of your family. Copies should also be given to other doctors and hospitals and attached to your medical record.

Some people carry miniature copies of their living wills with them. In Minnesota, you can note on your driver's license that you have a living will. The Patient Self-Determination Act requires that if you're in the hospital, your living will must be included in your record.

Can I register my living will?

Partnership for Caring maintains a registry of living wills and health care proxies, to which you may subscribe. Louisiana has set up a registry, but it is unpublicized and doctors are not required to consult it. Creation of other registries may be anticipated; one entrepreneur has obtained a patent on a living will data bank.

Who should have copies?

For starters, your family and your doctor. If your doctor is not someone you trust to carry out your wishes even with a copy of your living will, then you should consider changing your doctor. It is important that you agree on appropriate measures.

In some states, the living will must be made a part of your medical records, but *you* have to inform your doctor. This is the rule in Alabama. If you go into a health care facility, the Patient Self-Determination Act requires that you be asked if you have advance directives. If you do, they must be made a part of your permanent medical record.

How do I make sure a living will is current?

Under most state laws, a living will is current if it has not been revoked and no other action is required. There are exceptions; California's Natural Death Act requires that a living will be reexecuted every five years. If you want to make sure that everyone is assured of your intentions, you could reinitial your signed living will and date it on a periodic basis, perhaps yearly.

Can my living will be revoked? How do I revoke it?

Yes. Generally, you can just destroy the old document and execute a new one. You must signify your intent to revoke it, and you should inform anyone who has a copy.

5 WISHES

The *5 Wishes* booklet, a sort of combination living will/health care proxy/relational guide, is a popular newcomer on the advance directive scene. Designed to address some of the issues people deal with and at the same time be more accessible than a dry legal document, the 5 Wishes are spelled out in five separate instruction sections dealing with treatment and proxy choices, as well as comfort, companionship, and relationships.

> Wish #1 The person I want to make decisions for me when I can't make them for myself
> Wish #2 The kind of medical treatment I want or don't want
> Wish #3 How comfortable I want to be
> Wish #4 How I want people to treat me
> Wish #5 What I want my loved ones to know

It claims to meet the legal guidelines in two-thirds of the states. The section on living wills goes into some detail about the types of conditions a person might face: near death, coma, severe brain damage.

5 Wishes was developed by the Commission on Aging with Dignity, a nonprofit private group in Florida, and is distributed with funding from the Robert Wood Johnson Foundation. Copies can be obtained for $5 each ($1 each for 25 or more) from 888/5WISHES.

5 Wishes is not unique in going beyond the four corners of the living will and health agent forms to address the concerns of those making directives. Minnesota's law, for example, incorporates a discussion of beliefs and values, and various scenarios under which the declarant may further describe his or her views. The American Bar Association has also developed a tool kit to help you prepare your instructions, available online at www.abanet.org/elderly.

I have just completed the 5 Wishes. *Do I still need a living will?*
As a general rule, yes. The *5 Wishes* document says to revoke your other documents, but we cannot advise that. *5 Wishes* is not accepted in all states. And even in the states where it is accepted, its language, which is written to cover all bases, may not cover one or more situations in which you could find yourself.

In some cases, it may not address all your needs; in others, it may hamper them. For example, the *5 Wishes* booklet requires two physicians to certify incapacity before your wishes are respected, not necessary in many jurisdictions. Another example: A person named as a health care proxy in New York can authorize withdrawal of hydration and nutrition, but the 5 *Wishes* document does not meet the more stringent requirements of state law in this regard.

HEALTH CARE PROXIES

The living will is a statement of your wishes with regard to your medical treatment, but it does not cover all possibilities. What happens if you're incapacitated and your living will doesn't cover the situation? Or if its language is too general to express what you would want in a given situation and needs interpretation?

You need a person—a health care agent—to act on your behalf when you are unable to speak for yourself. You can appoint a friend or relative to act as your health care agent, in a written document called a *power of attorney for health care* or *durable power of attorney for health care* (also called a *health care proxy* in New York and Massachusetts).

The health care agent tells your doctors what you would have decided if you were able to speak, based on what he or she knows are your wishes (as expressed in your living will or in conversations with you). If it's not clear what you would have decided, your agent may make decisions in accordance with your best interests.

Even if your wishes are clear, physicians may not always honor them. In these cases, your health care agent acts as your spokesperson, advocating to ensure that your wishes are carried out.

Each of the states recognizes some kind of health care power of attorney. The Supreme Court in *Cruzan* suggested that a chosen surrogate would have the same power to refuse treatment as the patient.

Theoretically, the living will is for those with terminal illnesses or long-term persistent mental incapacity from which recovery is not expected. The health care proxy can be used for any incapacity, however temporary. Because health care proxies are governed by state law, requirements as to form and execution vary from state to state.

In some states, the health care proxy is part of the living will statute and may provide for a combined form of living will–health care proxy.

A number of states have authorized unified health care directives or health care instructions. Minnesota law expressly authorizes a single Health Care Directive, appointing a health care agent and a living will. Mississippi and California combine the two into a single Instructions for Health Care, with an expanded list of medical conditions for "qualified patients."

What is the difference between a health care proxy and a power of attorney for health care?

There is no difference. The statutes differ in terminology, so that what is called a "health care proxy" in one state is called a "power of attorney for health care" in another. When we talk about a health care proxy or a power of attorney for health care, we are talking about the same thing.

I have power of attorney over my spouse's financial affairs. Does this cover health care decisions as well?

The answer, in most states, is no. Don't confuse a power of attorney for health care with the power of attorney used in financial affairs. (Alaska and Pennsylvania are exceptions in that they have a durable power of attorney statute that does extend to health care decision making.) The financial power of attorney is explained in Chapter 13.

When does a health care proxy become effective?

A health care power of attorney, like a living will, is used when the declarant is incapable of making and communicating decisions. If you are capable of making and communicating your own decisions, there is no need for your proxy to be invoked.

APPOINTING A HEALTH CARE AGENT

One additional element not present in the living will is the appointment of a person to make decisions for you. This person is usually called the *health care agent.* You are the *principal*; your *agent* is authorized to act on your behalf.

Theoretically, designating a health care agent may be more useful than preparing a living will, because a person rather than a document will be advocating on your behalf. Remember, too, that when you make out your living will you are unable to anticipate every situation that might develop. The health care agent can interpret and apply your wishes as the situation warrants.

Appointment of an agent for health care purposes is regulated by state law. In certain circumstances, this may take on great importance. Some states give additional statutory authority to health care agents. In West Virginia and Wisconsin, for example, an agent may arrange for nursing home placement or home health care. In Massachusetts, an agent can commit the principal to a mental health facility, unless the document states otherwise. A few states that include health care proxies in their living will statutes try to restrict the agent's authority to interpret the patient's living will. A number of states forbid the appointment of a patient's physician or other health care provider as a designated agent.

NEW YORK HEALTH CARE PROXY

(1) I, _____

    hereby appoint _____

                           (name, home address and telephone number)

as my health care agent to make any and all health care decisions for me, except to the extent that I state otherwise. This proxy shall take effect when and if I become unable to make my own health care decisions.

(2) Optional instructions: I direct my proxy to make health care decisions in accord with my wishes and limitations as stated below, or as he or she otherwise knows. (Attach additional pages if necessary.)

_____

(Unless your agent knows your wishes about artificial nutrition and hydration [feeding tubes], your agent will not be allowed to make decisions about artificial nutrition and hydration.)

(3) Name of substitute or fill-in proxy if the person I appoint above is unable, unwilling or unavailable to act as my health care agent.

_____

                      (name, home address and telephone number)

(4) Unless I revoke it, this proxy shall remain in effect indefinitely, or until the date or conditions stated below. This proxy shall expire (specific date or conditions, if desired):

_____

(5) Signature _____

    Address _____

    Date _____

Statement by Witnesses (must be 18 or older)

I declare that the person who signed this document is personally known to me and appears to be of sound mind and acting of his or her own free will. He or she signed (or asked another to sign for him or her) this document in my presence.

Witness 1 _____

Address _____

Witness 2 _____

Address _____

Withdrawal of life-sustaining treatment is also an issue for health care agents. The right of an agent to authorize withholding or withdrawing artificial nutrition and hydration is recognized in more than half the states. However, many states require specificity in granting this authority.

- In Florida, the Life Prolonging Procedure Act, which sets forth comprehensive rights in advance directives, authorizes both a living will with a proxy and a separate health care proxy (called *health care surrogate*). However, the surrogate may order withdrawal only if that power is authorized in a living will.
- Under New York law, an agent may exercise authority over nutrition and hydration only if the agent knows the wishes of the principal in this regard. To provide evidence that this standard has been met, the health care proxy should include language that the principal has discussed his or her wishes in regard to nutrition and hydration with the agent. (See New York's health care proxy form on page 173.)

Who should I appoint as my health care proxy?

Someone you trust to carry out your wishes. And make sure you've asked the person you intend to name. A person can't be compelled to act as your agent—he or she must voluntarily accept the responsibility. More to the point, only someone you've discussed your wishes with can know how to act as your agent. If you don't have someone you trust for these kinds of intimate and painful decisions, don't appoint anyone.

Is it all right to designate more than one person as my agent or my alternate?

The question of how many agents should be named entails both legal and practical considerations. Legally, some states in fact allow only one agent. Usually, an alternate, not a coagent, may be designated.

You are only asking for trouble if you leave your health care up to a committee. You can ask your proxy to consult with people, and you can specify that consultation in your proxy instrument. But the best method is to choose one person.

Pick one and only one as an alternate. Don't be misled by thinking it's "only fair" to designate your two children or your three sisters as coagents. If they argue, you will suffer.

Should I execute both a living will and a health care proxy?

Yes, if possible. If the power of attorney for health care conflicts with the living will, they must be reconciled or chosen one over the other. In Connecticut, for example, the power of an agent must be in accordance with the living will. Contrast Florida, where to authorize withdrawal of life-sustaining treatment, you need express authority in the living will. The rules for resolving conflicts can be similarly varied. A number of states, including Arizona, Rhode Island, South Dakota, Texas, and Vermont, provide that the document signed more recently controls. Partnership for Caring recommends you use the health care proxy only in Wisconsin.

An agent must follow your wishes and is your best defense against unsympathetic medical personnel, with or without a living will. But an agent may die, become disabled, or refuse to act. And not everyone has someone to appoint. In that case, we say don't appoint anyone, but do execute a living will to make sure there is some memorial of your wishes.

PROXY FORMALITIES

State requirements regarding the validity of a document differ in substance and procedure. Usually they require two witnesses or notarization, or both. A statutory form may also be prescribed. For example, Rhode Island requires the specific statutory form and prohibits the use of all others.

There may also be restrictions on who can be a witness. A number of states provide that the witness may not be a health care provider or facility, an heir or a person responsible for health care costs.

Is the health care proxy valid state to state?

States are not obliged to recognize a health care power of attorney from another state. A few states—Kansas, New York, Texas, Utah, and West Virginia—grant statutory recognition to health care powers of attorney from other jurisdictions. This shouldn't deter you from executing a power of attorney for health care in full confidence. Remember that your designated agent may be highly persuasive in expressing your wishes even if his or her status as proxy is not officially sanctioned.

If you move to a new residence or buy a vacation home in another state, you should review the validity of your health care power of attorney or proxy in your new state and execute a new one, if needed, in accordance with the requirements of that state. If you want to execute separate proxy documents for different states, designating the same person as your agent in both documents will avoid conflict later on. If it doesn't make sense to designate a person in a far-off state, make sure each document clearly indicates who is your agent in that jurisdiction.

Where should I keep it?

Keep the original in an accessible place, and give copies to your primary doctor and close members of your family. Copies should also be given to other doctors and hospitals, and attached to your medical record. Remember, federal law provides that you be asked whether you have one and that your health care proxy be made part of your permanent record when you enter the hospital.

Who should have copies?

Don't forget to give a copy to the person who is named as your decision maker. And the alternate.

How do I make sure my proxy is current?

In most states, a health care proxy will remain in effect indefinitely, unless you revoke it. A few states limit its effectiveness to a fixed period of time. For example, a proxy in Ohio remains in effect for seven years (unless you're incapacitated at that time, in which case it will remain in effect until you regain capacity). Also, a divorce or separation may operate to suspend or revoke a proxy designation of a spouse. This rule applies in a number of states, including California, Florida, Massachusetts, and Michigan.

Updating your health care proxy is not required, and no other action is required. If you want to make sure everyone is assured of your intentions, you can reinitial your signed proxy and date it on a periodic basis.

Can my health care proxy be revoked?

Yes. To revoke your health care proxy, or to designate a new health care agent, you can destroy the old document and execute a new one, signifying repeal of all prior documents.

You don't actually have to rip up the old document. But you must signify your intent to revoke it, and you must notify both the agent and any other family members, lawyer, or doctors who have copies of the original document. Some states provide that the signing of a new proxy revokes the old one automatically, and this seems to be the logical meaning of the new proxy.

SURROGATE AND FAMILY CONSENT

What happens when there is no living will, no health care proxy, and no clear evidence of the patient's wishes? In some states, laws set forth a hierarchy of relatives to make medical decisions for an incompetent person, in the absence of instructions to the contrary. This type of surrogacy is commonly used for limited consent in emergency rooms across the country and other instances of mental incapacity.

Family decision-making is invoked when

- The patient lacks capacity to give informed consent
- There is no guardian, or none available
- There is no health care agent designated pursuant to a health care proxy
- There is no living will

Someone must decide. Under a doctrine of "substituted judgment," courts have long recognized the common principle that consent must be obtained from someone, except in cases of emergency. Who is that someone? Usually a family member or relative. Where there is no applicable state law or regulation, institutional policy also may spell out who may give consent by next of kin. As with your health care agent, the choice of surrogate is important. The difference is that in a surrogate situation, the choice is made for you and generally with no flexibility or discretion at all.

Approximately half the states have statutes that specify who can make these decisions for you. The statutory priority is usually: (1) guardian, (2) spouse, (3) adult children, (4) parents, and (5) adult siblings. As a general rule, only one person's consent is needed. Some statutes require unanimous consent from all those within the same category (for example, adult children).

Some states add other people to the statutory list:

- New York's statute adds "close friend" to the list of possible surrogates, as do Arizona, Colorado, Florida, Illinois, and Maryland.
- Idaho allows consent by an attending physician if no one else is available.
- West Virginia authorizes public agencies or public guardians as the choice of last resort.

Surrogate and family consent laws provide a last resort, relying on categories of kinship that may be irrelevant to many people's lives. For this reason alone, you want a proxy you've chosen yourself. If you want to ensure that you do have a choice, the solution is to execute a health care proxy, in which you name your own decision maker.

Is there any difference, from a relative's or other surrogate's point of view, between consenting to treatment and refusing treatment?
Legally, no. From a practical viewpoint, however, refusing recommended treatment is more difficult. The authority of next of kin to con-

sent to medical treatment recommended by physicians almost always goes unquestioned. In cases where consent is refused, physicians and hospitals are more likely to go to court.

In some states, surrogate authority is circumscribed by statute. For example, New York's statute allows surrogate consent for DNR orders only. West Virginia's statute applies only to nursing home and home care decisions.

What if I'm estranged from my family or have different views from them?

You don't want to rely on surrogate and family consent laws if you can't rely on your family. What you do want is a health care power of attorney, which in most states takes precedence over any statutory hierarchy (except yourself or your guardian). In Maine, even if you don't have a person to appoint as a health care proxy, the law provides that you may designate that a particular person *not* serve as a decision maker for you.

What about adults with no relatives to take responsibility?

A court order is usually required before medical treatment can be ordered for incompetent adults without guardians or family members to give consent. In New York, the Surrogate Decision-Making Committee program empowers volunteer committees, or panels, to make these decisions in accordance with the best interests of the patient. The committees are composed of health care practitioners, lawyers, relatives of mentally disabled persons, and mental health advocates.

ORGAN AND TISSUE DONATION

Under laws in effect in every state, a person 18 years or older can donate any or all parts of his or her body for the advancement of medical or dental science, medical or dental research or education, or therapy or transplantation for an individual.

Every state has some version of the Uniform Anatomical Gift Act (a model act), authorizing organ and tissue donation and providing the process for ensuring consent by the donor or by the family. Many states now authorize organ donation instructions in advance directives and allow powers of attorney for health care instruments to be used to make or refuse an anatomical gift. Laws generally limit the authorized recipients to a hospital; a doctor or surgeon; an organization for transplantation; an accredited medical or dental school, college or university; or an individual for needed therapy or transplantation.

A declaration of intent to donate can also be included in your will or set forth on a donor card, available from organ donor programs. A donor card requires that your signature be witnessed by two people. You can make a general donation or specify recipients, impose limitations on how organs may be used, or make other conditions as you may wish to impose. A donor card carried on your person is potentially more useful, because it is more likely to be discovered in the event of sudden illness or accident.

The determination of death plays a critical role in whether or not body organs can be used. Harvesting organs—the plotline for any number of potboilers and horror movies—raises ethical questions about identification of potential donors among the dying.

Donation cannot take place until a person is declared legally dead by a doctor, which is generally based on a medical standard of "brain death." People in a persistent vegetative coma, whether they are on artificial feeding or not, are *not* considered dead. Donors are screened for medical suitability. Organ or tissue donation will not be considered unless a person's death is imminent and the condition irreversible. No one is required to accept organs. Hospitals participating in Medicare and Medicaid must have written protocols to identify potential organ donors, based on causes and conditions of death and age at death, for example, persons recently certified as brain dead.

In addition to the well-known procedures involving solid organs such as the heart, liver, kidney, pancreas, and lungs, transplantation of other body parts such as heart valves, skin, corneas, tendons, bones, and cartilage can also help people hurt by illness or accident.

Despite the benefits, organ donation has been resisted by the vast majority of Americans young and old. Whether out of fear, misunderstanding, or ambivalence, fewer than one out of five have signed donor cards. The liver transplant of Mickey Mantle prior to his death brought much-needed publicity to organ and tissue donation.

If I die without signing a donor card, can my family authorize that my organs be donated?

Yes. In the event a potential donor dies, the family will be asked whether they wish to donate organs. As with other forms of family consent, the order of priority of relatives who can consent is set forth in state statutes. As a practical matter, the family will be consulted regardless of whether you sign a card. It's advisable to make your intentions regarding organ donation known to your family.

If I sign a donor card, does that mean I won't have a burial?

No. After a part or parts of the body are removed, the remains are turned over to the family for burial.

ASSISTED SUICIDE

Your right to die does not mean the right to kill yourself, or to be assisted in your own hastened death. It is *not* the right to suicide, or to assisted suicide. It's important to repeat: *the right to die is the right to determine what treatment you will get and what treatment you may refuse when you are critically ill, in accordance with your wishes and your values.*

For more than 700 years, common law has punished or disapproved of suicide and assisting suicide. In contemporary times, the considerations that underlie those values have been changed by the advent of technology and medical advances, which have kept people alive longer, often to receive unwanted treatment and to suffer needlessly at the end of an otherwise productive life.

While suicide has been decriminalized, assisted suicide continues as a crime in 49 states. Many other states have passed legislation easing restrictions for prescribing pain relief medications to suffering patients, but despite several legislative attempts, only Oregon has succeeded in passing a law allowing physician-assisted suicide.

Whether your right to determine your treatment may extend to a "right" to assisted suicide is currently a matter of national debate.

First, let's define our terms.

- *Suicide.* The taking of one's life by one's own hand.
- *Assisted suicide.* In an assisted suicide, someone helps someone else to their death. Called physician-assisted suicide when it is a doctor who assists.
- *Euthanasia.* Literally, a "good death." Distinguish between *passive euthanasia,* or "letting someone go," and *active euthanasia,* which involves the deliberate termination of someone's life, even if it is at his or her request. Most commonly, the term is used to connote a person's active participation in someone else's death, upon request or on their own initiative. Also called *mercy killing.*

What do these terms have in common? They're all about dying. The differences among them lie in who makes the decision and who carries it out. With suicide, clearly the person taking action has made the decision to do so. But concerns arise with both assisted suicide and euthanasia, for which help is required—and for which the legal and ethical capacity of a suicidal person to request or consent to help is not so certain.

Physician-assisted suicide in the United States. Surveys have revealed a wide disparity among health care practitioners in belief and practice regarding their participation in assisted suicide.

Advocates for physician-assisted suicide cite compelling reasons of humanity and basic principles of patient autonomy, which demand that patients afflicted with unending and unendurable pain and agony be allowed the lethal means to end their suffering. On one end of the spectrum, Dr. Timothy Quill, the Rochester, New York, internist who provided a lethal dose of sleeping pills to a long-suffering leukemia patient, gained widespread sympathy after describing his experience in the *New England Journal of Medicine.* A grand jury failed to indict him and no disciplinary action was taken by the state department of health.

The thoughtful deliberations of Dr. Quill have won many supporters to his position. At the opposite end of the spectrum, the infamous and now jailed Dr. Kevorkian has also mobilized public opinion on the issue of assisted suicide, not always sympathetically. Before his eventual incarceration, the retired pathologist assisted in the suicides of 31 people; he claims to have helped more than 130 people kill themselves.

For many, physician-assisted suicide triggers the specter of doctors playing God, exercising too much power with too few safeguards. Opponents cite the "slippery slope" argument that if assisted suicide were legalized, it would have an immediate effect on the obligations felt toward the elderly, especially those of limited means, who might feel coerced to "choose" suicide to spare loved ones. Then there would be those who want to extend the "option" to people who aren't terminally ill, just chronically ill, such as those suffering from AIDS or Alzheimer's disease.

Is there a consensus in the United States? Thirty-two states have laws prohibiting assisted suicide, most carrying a criminal charge of manslaughter or its equivalent. Some dozen others criminalize assisted suicide through other laws, leaving a handful of states in which the law is unclear. According to one poll, 62 percent of Americans would support a law allowing doctors to end the life of a terminally ill patient in distress who asks to die.

OREGON DEATH WITH DIGNITY ACT

In the fall of 1994, Oregon became the first state in the United States to legalize assisted suicide when voters narrowly approved Ballot Measure

16, an aid-in-dying bill that would allow doctors to provide lethal doses of drugs under the following conditions:

- The patient has six months or less to live, as certified by two doctors.
- The patient makes his or her request on more than one occasion, with at least a 15-day interval, and follows it up with a written request. The written request must be witnessed by two people, one of whom is not a family member.
- The doctor does not perform the procedure. The patient takes his or her own life.

As part of the responsibility of being the first (and thus far only) state to authorize physician-assisted suicide, the Task Force to Improve the Care of Terminally Ill Oregonians was established to deal with the nuts and bolts of implementing the state's Death with Dignity Act. The result: a 91-page document entitled "The Oregon Death with Dignity Act: A Guidebook for Health Care Providers." Guidelines address issues such as

- A doctor's obligation to discuss a patient's concern about dying
- Involvement of the family
- Obtaining medication
- Planning for complications
- Dealing with emergency response personnel
- Reporting requirements
- Financial and insurance issues

Interestingly, many of those who worked on developing the guidelines were among those who opposed the law and the practice.

Federal officials have tried to undermine the law's intent by ordering sanctions against doctors across the country who prescribe lethal drugs. However, in Oregon, the U.S. Attorney General's effort to thwart the law has been ruled unconstitutional. In 2001, a reported 44 terminally ill people asked for prescriptions, and 21 actually took them, according to published reports. All were end-stage cancer patients.

Similar proposals have been considered without success in Alabama, Oregon, California, Washington, and the District of Columbia. In 1994, the New York State Task Force on Life and the Law, a state advisory panel (the same panel that proposed the health care proxy law that was later adopted) unanimously recommended keeping the state ban on physician-assisted suicide, citing the potential for widespread abuse. The U.S. Supreme Court has not yet ruled on state law authorizing physician-assisted suicide, but it has upheld state bans on the practice.

SUPREME COURT RULINGS ON PHYSICIAN-ASSISTED SUICIDE

In 1997, two cases decided by the U.S. Supreme Court changed the landscape of physician-assisted suicide. The twin decisions, from opposite sides of the country (New York and Washington), ruled on the constitutionality of a ban on physician suicide.

Handed down on June 26, 1997, the rulings unanimously upheld the state bans on physician-assisted suicide. The unanimous ruling was:

- There was no constitutional right to physician-assisted suicide.
- There was no constitutional bar to a ban on assisted suicide.

From a legal point of view, the immediate result was to return this issue to the courts and legislatures of the 50 states, which are presumably free to ban or authorize assisted suicide. (So far, only Oregon has done the latter, an act preceding the Supreme Court's decision.)

Perhaps more important, it brought increased attention to the issue of care for the dying. The Court cited legitimate government interests including: prohibiting intentional killing and preserving human life; preventing the serious public health problem of suicide, especially the young, the elderly, and those suffering from untreated pain or from depression or other mental disorders; protecting the medical profession's integrity and ethics and maintaining physicians' role as their patients' healers; protecting the poor, the elderly, disabled persons, the terminally ill, and persons in other vulnerable groups from indifference, prejudice, and psychological and financial pressure to end their lives; and avoiding a possible slide toward voluntary and perhaps even involuntary euthanasia.

It quoted the findings of the New York Task Force on Life and the Law: "While suicide is no longer prohibited or penalized, the ban against assisted suicide and euthanasia shores up the notion of limits in human relationships."

The holding in the New York case was that there did indeed exist a difference between withdrawal/refusal of life-sustaining treatment and assisted suicide and that New York's assisted suicide ban, in treating the two differently, does not violate the U.S. Constitution, specifically the equal protection clause of the 14th Amendment.

Despite the outcome, the Court was very sympathetic to those seeking to overturn assisted-suicide bans, ending with a lofty exhortation to continued public debate. But the decisions offer significant ramifications for right-to-die and end-of-life decision making. The opinion expressly stated that when treatment is withdrawn from a patient, the patient dies from the underlying pathology, in contrast to physician-assisted suicide, where the patient is killed by the medication.

It also authorized the principle of "double effect." In drawing the distinction between withdrawal of life-sustaining treatment and assisted suicide, the Court distinguished assisted suicide from the provision of palliative treatment or other medical care that risks fatal side effects. When the physician's purpose and intent is only to ease a patient's pain, administering painkilling drugs that may hasten the patient's death is far different from a doctor who gives pills to a patient to help him or her die and must necessarily intend that the patient be made dead.

The decision that all the justices agreed upon was that there was no constitutionally protected right to die that included a right to assisted suicide. Nevertheless, the decision did not foreclose the possibility of some sort of right under some as-yet-unspecified circumstances. The concurring opinions revealed profound differences in the scope of a potential right. Justice Sandra Day O'Connor specifically excluded discussion or decision concerning a right to die, for example, suicide. Justice Stephen Breyer's opinion suggested possible support for a "right to die with dignity" (if combined with personal control over manner of death, professional medical assistance, and the avoidance of unnecessary and severe physical suffering combined).

Interestingly, the concurring opinion notes that the physician-assisted suicide bans do not infringe on a "right to die with dignity," and implies that state laws to prevent the provision of palliative care and drugs to avoid pain at the end of life would constitute an infringement of such a right. The decision allowed the possibility that individual circumstances might weigh differently when balanced against state interests, and that terminally ill patients might seek to petition courts for judicial "permission" to receive physician assistance in suicide under more particularized circumstances.

One of the subtexts to the decision was the underlying knowledge of the justices of the inadequacy of pain care. Justice Breyer's opinion pointed out that the number of palliative care centers in the United Kingdom (where physician-assisted suicide is illegal) significantly exceeds that in the Netherlands, where such practices are legal.

What is the experience of the Netherlands, where euthanasia was made legal in 2000?

In 1993, the Dutch adopted euthanasia guidelines that promised immunity to doctors from prosecution while leaving assisted suicide as a crime. Under the guidelines, the request for euthanasia had to be made entirely of the patient's free will; the rules required patients to be experiencing unbearable suffering and have a lasting longing for death. The patient's doctor had to consult with a second doctor who has dealt with euthanasia before.

Even before the guidelines were passed, euthanasia in the Netherlands was tolerated by prosecutors and doctors. Yet studies reported that despite regulation, more than 1,000 people (many mentally incompetent) were killed in a single year without consent. This was termed "nonvoluntary euthanasia."

The Dutch experience received intense scrutiny at home and around the world. New legislation passed in 2000 doesn't change the rules so much as establish strict "due care criteria" that stipulate that when a doctor is ending a life, he or she must

- Be convinced the patient's request was voluntary, well-considered, and lasting
- Be convinced the patient was facing unremitting and unbearable suffering
- Have informed the patient about his or her situation and prospects
- Have reached the firm conclusion with the patient that there was no reasonable alternative solution
- Have consulted at least one other independent physician, who has examined the patient and formed a judgment about the above points
- Terminate the life in a medically appropriate fashion

Under the new law, a patient will be able to make a written request for euthanasia, giving doctors the right to use their own discretion when patients become too physically or mentally ill to decide for themselves. The decision is reviewed by a regional committee that includes a medical expert and a lawyer. One important change in the law eliminates the current practice of reporting to the prosecutor's office, except in cases where criteria are not met.

The legislation expressly recognizes the validity of written requests by a patient for the termination of his or her life, called "euthanasia requests." The Dutch government reports that doctors comply with about one-third of assisted suicide requests each year. In 1999, 2,216 cases were recorded, but there also were believed to be a larger number of unregistered cases.

Other countries that have shown tolerance to euthanasia include Switzerland, Colombia, and Belgium. Switzerland in particular has attracted a growing number of "suicide tourists," the name given to people who travel there to end their lives legally. A 1996 law authorizing voluntary euthanasia in Australia's Northern Territory was later overturned.

What is the legal status of suicide in the United States?

Suicide is no longer a crime anywhere in the United States. Suicide is a real problem among the elderly, and increasing among them at alarming rates. White men have the highest rate of suicide, although the latest studies show the sharpest rate of increase among black men.

What are the consequences to a physician or other person who "assists" a person in a suicide?

Potentially severe. On the criminal side, and depending on the circumstances, he or she could be charged with manslaughter, murder, or a variant in more than half of the states. Despite publicized cases like those of Dr. Quill, who was not prosecuted, and Dr. Kevorkian, who evaded jail for several years, a number of people have been convicted and jailed for helping loved ones. Doctors could also face discipline by state licensing or professional boards, as well as action for malpractice.

On the civil side, there may be other consequences. For example, the law's prohibition on a person's profiting from wrongdoing may operate to disinherit an heir who aids a suicide. In one Pennsylvania case, a woman who aided her sister in suicide was barred from inheriting from her sister's estate.

Oregon law, which authorizes physician-assisted suicide, bars civil or criminal liability or professional disciplinary action for anyone participating in good faith with the state's Death with Dignity Act. This includes being present when a qualified patient takes the prescribed medication to end his or her life in a humane and dignified manner.

PAIN MANAGEMENT STATUTES

The right of patients to palliative care has moved to the forefront of the political end-of-life agenda. The conclusion—long obvious to ethicists and practitioners, but now a conclusion with the imprimatur of the U.S. Supreme Court—is that the aggressive use of pain management is not assisted suicide, even if it hastens death, if the intent is to relieve pain. By clearly upholding the theory of dual, or double, effect, the Court in effect has sanctioned the increased use of appropriate palliative measures for end-of-life care.

Following the Supreme Court decision, several states, including California, Massachusetts, Ohio, Oklahoma, Rhode Island, and West Virginia, adopted laws regarding the management of pain in dying patients and the use of palliative care. Many laws are designed to encourage more aggressive palliative care by doctors by ruling out liability for civil or criminal liability or disciplinary action for justifiable pain management practices. At the same time, a number of states formed study commissions or task forces to review end-of-life care.

Relaxed drug regulations in pain management statutes may be accompanied by a backlash against assisted suicide, ironically making it harder for health care providers, at the same time as federal laws provide funds for research in pain management, palliative care, and access to hospice development. More chillingly, there are real concerns about potential prosecutions, in particular under the federal Controlled Substance Act, which regulates the distribution of scheduled drugs, to prevent trafficking in drugs for unauthorized purposes and drug abuse.

Bills have been considered by both congressional houses to allow the U.S. Food and Drug Administration (FDA) to investigate physicians who write prescriptions for lethal dosages or combinations of drugs. Doctors fear charges for new responsibilities to not underprescribe medication and for the aggressive use of narcotics to alleviate pain. Despite the Supreme Court's deference to the states in this area, assisted suicide threatens to become another highly politicized issue on the national agenda.

Pain management is not the panacea for all the ills of a dying patient. It has been estimated that as much as 10 percent of patient pain is untreatable. We anticipate more legislative action in this area, both allowing the increased use of drugs for pain management and providing lesser and greater regulatory controls; unhappily, we anticipate some administrative and criminal prosecutions as well.

END-OF-LIFE CARE

The Supreme Court has upheld state bans on physician-assisted suicide but has not ruled on state law authorizing the practice. However, concern about the risks attendant to widespread physician-assisted suicide has also led to increased calls for improvements in end-of-life care and legislative remedies in the form of pain management statutes.

A report issued by the Institute of Medicine stated that the assisted suicide debate should not take precedence over those reforms to the health care system that would improve care for dying patients. This report argues that more can be done to relieve suffering, respect personal dignity, and provide opportunities for people to find meaning in life's conclusion. Its recommendations are addressed at strengthening systems through improved measures, tools, and strategies for improving quality of life and holding health care organizations accountable, as well as financing mechanisms to encourage rather than impede good end-of-life care and reform of prescription drug laws and policies.

Other recommendations call for better education for practitioners (to ensure relevant attitudes, knowledge, and skills to care well for dying patients and that palliative care should become, if not a specialty, at least a defined area of expertise, education, and research); research to define and implement priorities for strengthening knowledge in this area; and continuing public discussion essential to a better understanding of the modern experience of dying, support for patients and families, and obligations of communities to those approaching death.

Certainly, the hospice movement was a vanguard in this area, developing a service model to care for dying patients that is now part of Medicare's basic service package. (For more on hospice benefits, see Chapter 3.) A variety of private initiatives are now under way that cover many of the areas of research, training, and model projects to address end-of-life issues. The two most comprehensive are Last Acts, funded by the Robert Wood Johnson Foundation, and Project on Death in America, sponsored by the Open Society Institute, founded by George Soros.

Last Acts aims at raising awareness of the need to improve care of the dying and changing the way health care institutions approach care for the dying. On its agenda are improving provider education on palliative care and developing outcomes and evaluation measures for care. Project on Death in America is a $30 million campaign to transform the culture of dying by supporting projects and fostering changes in the provision of end-of-life care, education, and public policy.

ENFORCING YOUR RIGHTS

Plan ahead. We can't say this often enough. If you utilize the techniques we've discussed in this chapter—living wills and health care proxies—you'll be able to avoid most of the problems encountered in trying to assert your rights against an uncooperative medical establishment.

This is still an evolving area of law. Even with advance planning, you may need outside assistance. There are a number of groups that can advise you on your rights and how to pursue them. We've mentioned Partnership for Caring, which will act as a resource and refer you to others. Other organizations that may be of help are listed in the appendixes at the end of this book.

If none of these measures is successful, get a lawyer. While a legal fight may not be what you want, unfortunately it may be necessary. It is still common to see medical practitioners resisting alternatives to aggressive treatment, such as pain relief at home, for end-of-life patients, even in the face of written instructions to the contrary. The mere hiring of a lawyer will often get doctors and hospitals to take notice of your demands and comply with them. There are any number of lawyers who specialize in this area. There are agencies that can advise you and make referrals to local lawyers. Partnership for Caring, local bar associations, and senior citizens' organizations may also refer you to legal help.

13

Property Management Systems

We've seen how critical a power of attorney can be for health care decisions—designating someone to speak on your behalf in the event that you're unable to do so yourself. By planning ahead and choosing the person best able to act in your interest, you arm yourself against the well-intentioned meddling of others—medical professionals, family members—who might act counter to what you perceive your interest to be.

The same holds true in managing your finances—your property, your assets, your income. And the same type of instrument, the *power of attorney,* is as valuable to ensure your future control over these important areas of your life.

The power of attorney is the single most important document you can use to protect your interests. It's absolutely critical for your future independence in the event of illness or incapacity. Without it, you risk having your affairs being managed by a stranger, under court supervision, and without any input from you. You will lose control.

The power of attorney, along with the living will and the health care proxy, are the cornerstones of your plan to ensure that your wishes will be respected even if you are not able to act for yourself.

POWER OF ATTORNEY

What does it mean when you give someone power of attorney? It means that you've designated someone to act in your place and on your behalf, under certain circumstances. A power of attorney is a written document whereby you appoint someone to manage your financial affairs in the event you are ill or incapacitated and cannot act for yourself.

In a power of attorney, the person executing the power of attorney (called the *principal*) names another (the *attorney-in-fact, proxy,* or *agent*), who then can manage the principal's financial affairs. This can be your spouse or a child, or anyone you want. (The term *power of attorney* is something of a misnomer: the person named does not have to be an attorney nor is he or she required to do any specifically law-related transactions.)

With a power of attorney, the person you designate can pay your bills, make banking transactions on your accounts, even bring a law-suit—all in your name. Generally the power of attorney spells out in detail the specific powers the agent will have.

As with many legal documents, the requirements for a power of attorney vary from state to state. Powers of attorney are governed by state law, which spells out the process required for executing a valid power of attorney, the powers that may be granted under one, and other provisions concerning validity and duration of a power of attorney.

DURABLE POWER OF ATTORNEY

Traditionally, a power of attorney was perceived as a limited tool, useful to delegating authority to someone traveling to another town to transact business on your behalf. It did not survive the death or disability of the principal, thereby making it useless for future planning purposes.

Thus, the *durable power of attorney* evolved, so called because it survives the principal's incapacity. This is doubly important because the use of the durable power of attorney is most important as an easily used and inexpensive alternative to the appointment of a guardian or conservator. (These are discussed in Chapter 14).

The durable power of attorney is now recognized in all 50 states and the District of Columbia. In order to achieve the level of "durable," it must contain words to the effect that

> This power of attorney shall not be affected by subsequent disability or incapacity of the principal.

The specific requirements for the wording differ from state to state. In a few states, such as Georgia, Louisiana, and Maryland, the power of attorney is automatically durable unless the written document provides otherwise.

SPRINGING POWER OF ATTORNEY

As a rule, a power of attorney takes effect immediately. This presents a problem for someone who doesn't want to grant broad powers to someone else who could act now, yet still wishes to provide for the management of his or her financial affairs should it be necessary in the event of a future disability.

The solution is the *springing power of attorney*. The springing power of attorney is a delegation of power that can be exercised only at some specified time in the future or upon the occurrence of a specified event, such as incapacity. Thus the power can be made effective only when it is needed—and only for the duration of the need.

Under the Uniform Probate Code (a model law that states can adopt), for a springing power of attorney to be effective, it must contain language expressly providing that "this power shall become effective upon the disability or incapacity of the principal."

Not all states allow a springing power of attorney. Florida does not, except for documents triggered by the deployment of military personnel. Connecticut only recently sanctioned the springing power of attorney, requiring that the person named as agent must sign an affidavit certifying that the specified contingency has taken place. The springing power of attorney is authorized by statute in Alabama, California, Delaware, Idaho, Illinois, Kansas, Massachusetts, Michigan, Montana, Nebraska, Nevada, New Jersey, New York, North Carolina, Ohio, Oklahoma, Pennsylvania, Tennessee, Utah, Vermont, Virginia, Washington, and Wisconsin. It is presumably sanctioned in states whose laws do not mention it, although a local attorney's advice should be obtained in those states.

One difficulty that occurs in utilizing the springing power of attorney is the determination of the triggering event. How is it determined, and by whom? This is the subject of much debate among lawyers, without any clear-cut answers. But there are some clear guidelines.

- The disability should be clearly defined. (New Jersey's statute in fact defines disability in the law itself.)
- The determining agent or event should be named. Disability may be verified, for example, by a judicial determination or a declaration by two doctors.

As a corollary, it is generally not a good idea to have a determining agent be the same as the agent named as your attorney-in-fact in the instrument.

Remember the great advantage of this technique is that if you don't wish to grant broad powers over your property to another *at the present time,* you don't have to. The springing power of attorney becomes effective when and only when it is needed—upon disability.

APPOINTING AN AGENT

One of the rules of a power of attorney is that you should give it only to a person you trust. Most powers of attorney are not springing, but effective immediately upon signing. Yet even with a person they trust completely, many people are still justifiably wary of about giving someone immediate power to manage their affairs. Obviously, there's a risk of abuse, so it's important that you appoint only someone you trust implicitly.

Be sure that you appoint someone who will be willing to do the job, and lives in your geographic vicinity—so he or she can do it. Nieces and nephews in distant cities may love you dearly but not want the burden of being a long-distant agent.

Of equal importance to *who* you name as your agent is *what* powers you give to your agent. Some states have statutory forms of powers of attorney that enumerate the powers that may be granted an agent and define the extent of those powers, while others limit the power in specific circumstances.

A power of attorney may include the rights to

- Deal with real property
- Make gifts
- Purchase, transfer, sell life insurance
- Handle banking and securities transactions
- Collect and forgive debts
- Disclaim trusts and inheritances
- Deal with retirement plans
- Deal with taxes
- Create and amend trusts
- Make charitable contributions

Depending on the state, it may be necessary for you to expressly include some powers or your agent will not have them. In New York, for example, the power to make gifts, important to tax and Medicaid planning, must be expressly included. Similarly, in states such as Illinois and Mississippi, you must give express authority to amend or revoke a trust.

Is it all right to designate more than one person as my agent?

Opinion differs. If you're unsure about the trustworthiness or ability of your designee, designating people who must act together may be a good idea. They could act as a check on each other. This is not allowed in all states. And it may make the power of attorney ineffective as a practical matter. Another possibility is successive appointments, someone to replace your first choice as agent if he or she fails to act.

Are there any powers an agent can't have?

An agent cannot change your will, make a will on your behalf, or revoke your will. An agent cannot institute a divorce proceeding or consent to a divorce on your behalf. Some states, notably Florida and Georgia, do not allow an agent to delegate his or her authority under the power of attorney to another person.

What is the effect of a guardianship on a durable power of attorney?

In most jurisdictions, the agent becomes accountable to the guardian. In a few states, such as Connecticut, the appointment of a guardian terminates the power of attorney. In others, the court has the power to revoke the power of attorney. States that allow continuation of the power of attorney differ on whether the guardian has the power to revoke a power of attorney.

What kind of document should I draft?

Although it comes in a number of formats, the power of attorney is basically simple; in most states a standard form is available in legal stationery stores and many large general stationery stores. Make sure the form in stock is your state's current one, not an out-of-date form. Be sure to follow the instructions on the form. You can also have your lawyer draw up a durable power of attorney, tailored to your situation and your needs, which is what we recommend. We've included a generic form (see pages 195–197), which you can use as an interim measure, but it's preferable to get one authorized specifically for your state.

A number of powers may or may not appear on the form commonly used in your state. Most states with statutory short forms allow modifications. Among them are Alaska, California, Connecticut, Minnesota, New Mexico, New York, and North Carolina.

Is the power of attorney valid state to state? Should separate documents be prepared?

There is something called *reciprocal recognition,* in which a limited number of states recognize powers of attorney validly executed in other states, according to the laws of that state. However, even then the power may be restricted, especially when dealing with real estate. If you spend a considerable amount of time in another state, it would be wise to have

DURABLE POWER OF ATTORNEY

KNOW ALL MEN BY THESE PRESENTS, that I, _____, residing at
_____, appoint hereby
_____, residing at _____, as my
true and lawful attorney-in-fact, to act, manage and conduct all my affairs
for me and in my name, place and stead, and for my use and benefit as my
act and deed, and for that purpose I give and grant unto my said attorney
full power and authority to do and perform all and every act, deed, matter
and thing whatsoever regarding my property and affairs as fully and effec-
tually to all intents and purposes as I might or could do myself if personally present, the following specially enumerated powers being examples of
the full, complete and general powers granted herein, and not in limitation
or definition thereof:

1. To buy, receive, lease, accept or otherwise acquire; to sell, convey, mortgage, hypothecate, pledge, quit claim or otherwise encumber or dispose
   of, or to contract or agree for the acquisition, disposal or encumbrance of,
   any property whatsoever and wheresoever located, be it real, personal or
   mixed, or any interest or right therein or pertaining thereto, upon such
   terms as my attorney shall think proper;

2. To take, hold, possess, invest, lease or otherwise manage any or all of my
   real, personal or mixed property, or any interest therein or pertaining thereto, to eject, remove or relieve tenants or other persons from, and to maintain, protect, preserve, insure, remove, store, transport, repair, rebuild,
   modify or improve the same or any part thereof;

3. To make, do and transact all and every kind of business of whatever kind or
   nature, including the receipt, recovery, collection, payment, compromise,
   settlement and adjustment of all accounts, legacies, bequests, interests,
   dividends, annuities, rents, claims, demands, debts, taxes and obligations,
   which may now or hereafter be due, owing or payable by me or to me;

4. To make, endorse, accept, receive, sign, seal, execute, acknowledge and
   deliver deeds, bills of sale, mortgages, assignments, agreements, contracts, certificates, hypothecations, checks, notes, bonds, vouchers,
   receipts, releases, documents relating to life or other insurance policies
   and such other instruments in writing of whatever kind and nature, as may
   be necessary, convenient or proper in the premises;

5. To make deposits or investments in, or withdrawals from, any account, holding or interest which I may now or hereafter have, or be entitled to, in any
   banking, trust or, financial investment institution, including postal savings
   depository offices, credit unions, savings and loan associations and similar institutions, to exercise any right, option or privilege pertaining thereto,
   and to open or establish accounts, holdings or interests of whatever kind
   or nature, with any such institution, in my name or in my said attorney's
   name, or in our names jointly, either with or without right of survivorship;

6. To institute, prosecute, defend, compromise, arbitrate and dispose of legal, equitable or administrative hearings, actions, suits, attachments, arrests, distresses or other proceedings, or otherwise engage in litigation in connection with the premises;

7. To act as my attorneys or proxies in respect to any stocks, shares, bonds or other investments, rights or interests, I may now or hereafter hold;

8. To engage and dismiss agents, counsel and employees, and to appoint and remove at pleasure any substitute for, or agent of, my said attorneys, in respect to all or any of the matters or things herein mentioned, and upon such terms as my attorneys shall think fit;

9. To prepare, execute and file gift, income and other tax returns, claims for refund covering all or a portion of any taxes paid and other governmental reports, declarations, applications, requests and documents;

10. To appear for me and represent me before the Treasury Department, or any state taxing agency in connection with any matter involving federal or state gift, income or other taxes for any year to which I am a party, giving my said attorneys full power to do everything whatsoever requisite and necessary to be done in the premises, to receive refund checks, to execute waivers of the statute of limitations and to execute closing agreements as fully as the undersigned might do if personally present, giving my said attorneys authority to appoint attorneys to represent my said attorneys in connection therewith with full power of substitution and revocation at any time; and

11. To enter any safe deposit box or other place of safe keeping or deposit which I may now or hereafter occupy or possess;

12. To disclaim or renounce any property interest pursuant to the Internal Revenue Code of 1986, Section 2518 or any similar provision of any successor law.

13. To waive benefits and/or elect out of survivor annuity payment(s) under Section 417 of the Internal Revenue Code of 1986, or any similar provision of any successor law, and the regulations promulgated thereunder.

I hereby appoint my _____, _____, to serve as successor attorney-in-fact, TO ACT, in the event that _____ shall be unable or unwilling to serve or to continue to serve as my attorney-in-fact, in which case _____ shall be fully authorized to serve hereunder and shall have all of the powers granted originally to _____.

My successor, _____, shall execute an affidavit that _____ is unable or unwilling to serve or to continue to serve, after the occurrence of such event, and such affidavit shall be conclusive evidence insofar as third parties are concerned of the facts set forth therein. Any person acting in reliance upon such affidavit shall incur no liability to my estate because of such reliance.

Notwithstanding any other provision of this instrument, this power of attorney shall not be revoked by my disability through physical or mental incompetence, and any acts done by my attorney or successor pursuant to this power during any such period of disability or incompetence shall have the same effect and be as binding upon me and my heirs, devisees and personal representatives as if I were competent and not disabled.

I hereby ratify all that my said attorney shall lawfully do or cause to be done by virtue of this power of attorney.

I hereby declare that any act or thing lawfully done hereunder by my said attorney shall be binding on me, and my heirs, legal and personal representatives and assigns. To induce any third party to act hereunder, I hereby agree that any third party receiving a duly executed copy or facsimile of this instrument may act hereunder, and that revocation or termination hereof shall be ineffective also to such third party unless and until actual notice or knowledge of such revocation or termination shall have been received by such third party, and I for myself and for my heirs, executors, legal representatives and assigns, hereby agree to indemnify and hold harmless any such third party from and against any and all claims that may arise against such third party by reason of such third party having relied on the provisions of this instrument.

I certify that the following signature is the signature of my attorney-in-fact, _____.

IN WITNESS WHEREOF, I have hereunto set my hand and seal on _____, 20__

_____

Signed in the presence of:

_____ Address _____

_____ Address _____

_____ Address _____

_____

STATE OF   )
                                          :   ss.:
COUNTY OF   )

On _____, 20__, before me personally came _____, to me known, and known to me to be the individual described in and who, by his mark, executed the foregoing instrument, and duly acknowledged to me that he executed the same.

_____
Notary Public

a dual set of documents. Some states, such as Louisiana, expressly authorize a power of attorney to be used by military personnel.

LEGAL CAPACITY AND FORMALITIES

Any document, whether a will or a trust or a power of attorney, is valid only if it is executed by a person with *legal capacity.* A person with legal capacity is one who has the ability to understand the nature and significance of what he or she is doing.

Only a sufficiently competent person possessing the requisite capacity may execute a valid document such as a power of attorney. Does this mean the technique is not available for those severely incapacitated by dementia or other disorder? Generally yes, although an individual who is lucid at intervals may be legally competent to sign a power of attorney during one of those times. In such a case, however, documentation by doctors of the individual's capacity is imperative.

State laws vary on execution requirements, and most are silent as to who must witness a power of attorney, and whether it should be notarized or recorded. In some states, the power of attorney must be witnessed, in some notarized, and in some, both. In a few states, the notarization must be in a special form known as "acknowledgment." Fewer than a dozen states contain specific execution requirements.

Real estate creates special problems in making sure your power of attorney is effective. Often, more formalities in the execution of the durable power of attorney are required to ensure that the agent will in fact have the power to convey or dispose of real estate. In the case of real property, the law of the site of the property controls real estate transactions.

Under the law of some states, a description of the real estate must be in the power of attorney. Others require witnesses (Connecticut and Florida require two) in addition to notarization, recording of the power of attorney as a deed, or execution like a will.

Where do I keep my power of attorney?

One solution is to sign a power of attorney but keep it under your control. However, if you trust a person enough to name him or her as attorney-in-fact, you should trust that person enough to give a copy or tell where it is. If you don't, then that person shouldn't be named. Remember, too, if you've signed a springing power of attorney, it only becomes effective when and only when it is needed, upon disability.

How do I make sure it's current?

Can a power of attorney become stale? Theoretically, it's a legal document, valid on its face, with no time limit. The Uniform Probate Code provides that a power of attorney is not affected by a lapse of time since execution, and remains effective unless it states a time of termination. We know one man whose wife recently tried to use the power of attorney he left with her when he went overseas to fight in the Korean War.

The whole point of the durable power of attorney is that it can be used at an unspecified time in the future, with luck the distant future, without resistance.

The real problem is that although the document may be valid, your agent may have a difficult time using it. Banks, investment firms, and other financial institutions are uncomfortable in the first place with powers of attorney, and often seek to limit their effectiveness through arbitrary policies. An arbitrary rule of one year is a common practice (that is, the power of attorney is accepted only within one year of its signing).

One possible solution is to update it regularly, just changing the date and signature or simply reinitialing it on a yearly basis. Remember, a current document should comply with full notarization and other formal execution requirements of your state.

DEALING WITH BANKS

A common problem with a power of attorney is getting other parties to acknowledge it. Often banks and other institutions are wary of recognizing the authority in a power of attorney. Or they require their own form, displaying misplaced confidence in their own lawyers' ability to protect them from harm. This can be a serious problem when the maker of a power of attorney is no longer well enough to sign the bank's form. In some cases, a bank may refuse a springing power of attorney without a court finding of disability.

Some states have incentives to encourage reliance. New York's statute requires banks and the state pension fund to accept the statutory short form power of attorney. In other states, such as Alaska and Minnesota, parties who refuse to honor powers of attorney may be held liable.

You can always contact your bank and any other financial institution with which you have an account and ask what authorization forms and procedures they require. And don't assume their forms will fulfill your needs. Make sure they have the necessary *durability* language.

REVOKING A POWER OF ATTORNEY

In theory, you can revoke a power of attorney merely by tearing up the document and conducting yourself in a manner inconsistent with the power. Theory, however, is not as reliable as verifiable communication. You want to make sure that institutions, such as banks and investment houses, that may have received your power of attorney receive notice of its termination.

To revoke your power of attorney and make sure your revocation is recognized, you should

- Clearly put the revocation in writing, expressly revoking the powers
- Send copies of the revocation to all parties who have received the original power of attorney, notifying them of the revocation. (You should keep a record of the institutions to which you and your agent give copies)
- Execute the revocation with the same formalities, such as notarization or acknowledgment, as you did the original power of attorney

Send letters certified mail, return receipt requested. (Always send legal documents that way.) And always keep copies. In case there is any question, get a written acknowledgment that your revocation was received.

TRUSTS

A trust works by establishing a fund to be administered under the direction of a trustee or trustees. The creator of the trust makes provision for distribution of the income, usually on a regular basis to the named beneficiary, and eventual disposition of the principal. Assets such as funds or other property are deposited into the trust. The trustee, or trustees, manages the property in accordance with the instructions set forth in the trust instrument.

A number of trust instruments have been developed for financial planning purposes. Today's trusts are designed for a multitude of reasons:

- Tax avoidance on future estates
- Enabling Medicaid eligibility for those in need of long-term and custodial care
- Securing benefits for a disabled child or adult

(See Chapter 9 on Medicaid, Chapter 14 on planning for a disabled child, and Chapter 16 on wills.)

A word of caution. Creating a trust requires the expertise of a lawyer. There are innumerable forms of trusts and hybrids within each category. And in today's world, it requires the expertise of a lawyer versed not only in the traditional world of "trusts and estates" but also in government entitlements. The rules are changing as rapidly as you're reading this page.

Creating the trust. A trust is created by a *settler,* also called a *donor* or *creator.* As with a will, the person setting up a trust must have legal capacity to do so. For the trust to be funded, property must be transferred or deposited into the trust. The trust document or trust instrument establishing the trust does not automatically fund the trust.

Purpose. Trusts are commonly established for a purpose, and contain instructions to the trustees to enable them to carry out their duties.

The purpose of a trust must be carefully crafted. You want to be meaningful enough so the trustees understand your intent. At the same time, if the trust you are establishing is to accomplish a legal function for estate tax or Medicaid qualifying purposes, it must satisfy those other legal requirements as well.

Trustee or trustees. The trustee (or trustees) manages the trust property, administering, investing, and otherwise supervising all the assets of the trust, including cash, real estate, and any other property deposited into the trust.

In performing the job of trustee, the trustee has certain *fiduciary* responsibilities. He or she must undertake the task of managing the trust in accordance with the instructions set forth in the trust instrument. The trust instrument will also spell out the authority of the trustee to act.

Beneficiary. A trust must have a beneficiary, who will receive the income from the trust. In all states but New York, you or your spouse can be both trustee and beneficiary of a trust you have created. Upon a designated event, such as the death of the income beneficiary, the principal then goes to a designated future beneficiary or beneficiaries (or *remaindermen*). These can be children, grandchildren, charity, or any person or institution you choose.

Instructions. The trust instrument must set forth a statement of purpose and instructions. It must also spell out the amount of discretion granted the trustee to distribute funds, invade principal, or otherwise act, as well as any restrictions on distribution of funds or their use.

THE ROLE OF TRUSTS

Trusts can serve a number of purposes. As a general rule, those trusts that are revocable are vulnerable to being counted as available assets for the purpose of determining Medicaid eligibility, while those that are irrevocable are better shielded from being considered as assets. Some forms of trusts stipulate that income should be withheld if the result would be disqualification for government benefits.

Testamentary trusts, created by wills, are used to save considerable estate taxes. Instead of assets passing outright—and taxed—income can be used without incurring estate taxes. Testamentary trusts are also not subject to many of Medicaid's eligibility rules. (See Chapters 9 and 16.)

Living trusts, created by you to take effect during your lifetime, are used to create tax savings in a number of ways. For example, income tax savings may result if principal is sheltered and income directed to someone in a lower tax bracket.

Other types of trusts include

- *Qualified terminable interest property (QTIP) trust,* used when it is anticipated that future care may be needed by a surviving spouse who will be unable to manage the money or be in no position to do so. A "Q-tip" trust qualifies for the marital deduction. (See Chapter 16.)
- *Charitable trust,* which may qualify for estate tax charitable deduction. (See Chapter 16.)
- *Supplemental needs trust,* created for a disabled child or adult. This is a discretionary trust set up to supplement government benefits. (See Chapters 9 and 14.)

JOINT ACCOUNTS

Many people hold bank accounts, real estate, and other forms of property with other people. A common form of joint property is property owned by two or more people, each with a survivor interest.

Joint ownership is extremely common with married persons. Property is also often held jointly with children and grandchildren.

Joint ownership has advantages and disadvantages. Children or grandchildren can easily withdraw funds and use them to pay bills on your behalf; by the same token, they could legally deplete hard-earned assets. There may also be unknown and unwanted gifted tax implications when property is placed in joint ownership. (See Chapter 15.)

Potential problems extend beyond financial ones. If a "convenience account" is set up for the purpose of enabling a child to use the money for the benefit of a parent, it may, when the parent dies, wind up as a windfall for one child to the unintended exclusion of others, engendering bitter family conflict.

Joint property is not a good idea when Medicaid planning may need to be considered. Joint bank accounts in particular can play havoc with your eligibility even before the death of a spouse because either co-owner has access to 100 percent of the account. Stock accounts that permit a co-owner to withdraw the entire amount are also vulnerable. All the money in the account will be treated as belonging to the person applying for Medicaid, unless it can be proven that the nonapplying joint owner contributed to the account.

If you place property you own into joint ownership, you lose control. While in the case of a joint bank account you have the power to withdraw 100 percent of the account funds at any time (as does your co-owner), this is not true with other types of assets. If you place 100 shares of AT&T stock in the names of your son and yourself as joint owners, you will need your son's consent to get it back or to sell it. If it is sold, your son owns half the proceeds.

I have a bank account in trust for my granddaughter. Can she use the money in it to help me pay my bills?

Not unless she also has your power of attorney. Many people commonly put their funds in trust for their children or their grandchildren. This common form of ownership of bank and investment accounts places title and ownership in one person's hands, held in trust for another person or persons.

These kinds of accounts are called *Totten trusts,* named after the owner of a New York bank account at the turn of the 20th century. They are not joint accounts. Until the account owner dies, the person named as beneficiary has no legal rights or interest in the property at all. Upon the owner's death, the money is passed directly to the named beneficiary. In that, it resembles a jointly owned account (described in Chapter 16). Totten trusts are sometimes referred to as "poor men's wills."

A Totten trust provides no estate tax savings. The full amount of the account is included in the account owner's estate.

DESIGNATING A REPRESENTATIVE PAYEE

If you wish, you can designate someone as a representative payee for receiving Social Security or Supplemental Security Income (SSI) checks on your behalf. This a limited form of a power of attorney but a very useful management tool for people who are not able to present checks themselves. Programs offering money management services may also be available in your community.

14

Planning for the Disabled Child

If you are involved in planning for your disabled child or children, you face a series of special challenges. In addition to meeting your child's present needs, you must consider and plan for the long-term needs of a child who may need to have care for a lifetime—in many cases, long after your death. You need to look to the "how" and the "who" of providing such care. You will have to find—or in some cases, create—support networks to provide medical, rehabilitative, and social services as needed.

Financing is a primary concern. Where will the money come from to pay for care? The source may be either your private funds or the government—most likely a combination of both. Planning for a child with disabilities will involve you in decisions concerning future medical care and treatment, your child's place of residence, finances and daily management, and other services that may be available for your child's benefit.

SERVICES AND ENTITLEMENTS

Unless your private funds are plentiful, your major concern is making sure your disabled child will be entitled to necessary government services, such as Supplemental Security Income (SSI) and other entitlements necessary to provide appropriate care.

Before going into the various options, you should understand a bit about the universe of government assistance. Assistance for the disabled has evolved from charity or basic welfare provisions into a range of social programs and benefits. In retrospect, costs made this evolution inevitable; at the same time, the costs of these programs make them a continuing target for budget and service cuts.

In addition to Social Security and SSI for the disabled, there are other programs and benefits, including housing, that you or your child may qualify for. For parents of children with disabilities, the social safety net is more secure by virtue of other available support. (See Chapter 20 and the appendixes at the end of this book.)

One caveat: as a general rule, parents are responsible for their children, unless they are institutionalized. In theory, sound public policy would support maintaining children with disabilities in the home and community. Certainly, the Supreme Court decision in the *Olmstead* case, which we discussed in Chapter 3, pointed to the acknowledged need for community alternatives for all people with a disability or long-term illness. Reform efforts are designed to enable persons of any age who have a disability or long-term illness to live in a community setting, exercise choices about their living environment, and obtain quality services and the support they need. Nevertheless, Medicaid benefits are still easier to obtain for children who are institutionalized than for those who are kept at home.

SUPPLEMENTAL NEEDS TRUST

Since money left for a disabled child must last a lifetime, most experts suggest creating a trust. A trust works by establishing a fund under the direction of a trustee or trustees. A basic trust instrument names a beneficiary, which in this case would be your child, and makes provision for

- Income to your child on a regular basis
- Use of the principal in appropriate cases for your child's benefit
- Eventual disposition of the principal

Income distribution may be subject to the discretion of the trustee. The trustee may also be given discretion to "invade" the principal, sometimes with guidance from the trust document.

The advantage of setting up a trust is that it is a mechanism that will provide continuing support for your child after you have died. At the same time, a trust avoids guardianship for the child and the uncertain outcome and possible delay occasioned by court proceedings. And by setting it up, you can provide for continuity in the provision of income and principal distributions.

Supplemental needs trusts are commonly used to coordinate a financial plan for a disabled child with the child's receipt of public benefits. By using the trust to provide "supplemental needs," combined with public benefits available for your child's other needs, the supplemental needs trust functions as a public-private partnership to ensure your child continues to get the support he or she needs. Commonly, these trusts are used in conjunction with SSI and Medicaid benefits, for which your child will have to establish and maintain eligibility. (See Chapter 20.)

But this has to be done right! The amount your child inherits, directly or through a trust, may cause a number of undesirable results, including reduced benefits, ineligibility, or being charged for benefits.

In a landmark New York case, the court ruled that public assistance was a right, and the trustee could not be compelled to invade an otherwise uninvadable trust to pay for government benefits otherwise available to the beneficiary of the trust. As a general rule, the power given to the trustee must be extremely limited and totally discretionary in order to avoid takeover. That's why the level of discretion a trustee has in invading the principal for use on behalf of the disabled child–beneficiary is important to the courts. The kind of trust you'd set up for a disabled child is akin to the "spendthrift trust" designed to protect wastrel heirs from squandering their family fortunes by limiting the moneys available to creditors.

Don't try this on your own! Trust law is a field strewn with land mines for the innocent; only an experienced practitioner can determine which kind of trust is best for you. You should consult an attorney who specializes in trusts and estates and elder law, preferably one with experience in government entitlements for the disabled.

How will transfers under trusts interfere with my entitlement to any benefit programs?

Transferring assets to an individual child who is blind or permanently and totally disabled does not result in any ineligibility or penalty under Medicaid rules for the transferror. Transfers to a disabled child or to a trust established solely for the benefit of a disabled child, or to a trust for the benefit of a disabled individual under 65, are exempt. However, recent rulings by Medicaid severely limit the kinds of trusts that will be treated as "for the sole benefit" of the disabled child and thus considered exempt. Outright gifts to your child or trusts for his or her benefit that are not properly drawn will make the child ineligible for some government benefits.

What about a court settlement on behalf of a disabled child?

Court settlements are common when dealing with the disabled of any age. Your lawyer should be able to structure the settlement so that it is paid into a trust and not directly to the beneficiary, thereby avoiding jeopardy to any government entitlements.

APPOINTING TRUSTEES

As with any other document designating someone to do your work for you, one of the most important questions is who to pick. The question of who to appoint is almost as difficult as the question of whether to appoint. Your first choice is generally an individual, if there is one who is competent and qualified and willing to do it. The question of whether to impose this burden on a sibling is not an easy one. Professionals can also act as trustees, including banks and trust companies.

Can't I just leave my money to a trusted friend or relative to care for my child?

You can try to create a so-called *constructive trust*, but relying on a close friend or a sibling of a disabled child to take care of the child is not a good idea. Any number of things could happen to derail your intentions, and it's not at all certain there would be anyone to speak up for your child's interests. Your relative could die, divorce, or go bankrupt, and the assets that you have set aside for your child could wind up as a windfall for somebody who knows and cares nothing about your arrangements for your child's future.

Wouldn't a guardianship work just as well?

Maybe. Guardianship covers personal care as well as financial, but may not be necessary. Unless a court is petitioned to have a legal guardian appointed, your child is competent in the eyes of the law at the age of majority. The drawbacks to guardianship include continuing supervision by the courts, added administration costs, and the loss of flexibility in providing for your child's care. Some courts have denied guardians the right to set up supplemental needs trusts on behalf of their wards. (Guardianship is discussed more fully in Chapter 15.)

HOW A TRUST WORKS

A legal document creating a trust usually has a statement of objectives, which serves a number of purposes. Ideally, the trust should have flexibility, providing income and principal in the trustee's discretion. Distributions should not be made for any benefits available through a government program, unless the trustee believes the government services are inadequate or of poor quality. You may make specific provision for what the government will not pay for, such as state-of-the-art systems in communication and transportation and "quality-of-life" purchases. Certain distributions could result in a loss of some SSI benefits, a primary consideration in creating a trust for a child with disabilities.

There is a statutory exception for trusts containing the assets and income of a disabled individual under the age of 65, if the trust is established for the individual's benefit by a parent, grandparent, legal guardian, or the court. Upon the beneficiary's death, the remaining funds must be used to reimburse the state for Medicaid outlays. Any remaining funds would then pass to recipients designated by the trust.

Distinguish between support and discretionary trusts. The former may be available to the trust beneficiary and thus available to Medicaid or creditors. Assets placed in supplemental needs trusts, on the other hand, may be used to pay for "supplemental" needs of the disabled individual, such as nonmedical living expenses (if living in the community) or extra care (if institutionalized). (See Chapter 9.)

What kind of things may be purchased with supplemental needs trust funds?

Whatever the trust beneficiary might need so long as it doesn't include payments for food, clothing, or shelter. Payments for these items will reduce the SSI benefit by up to one-third; in some states, they may affect Medicaid as well. Rules vary state to state, but distributions that will not jeopardize government benefits generally include payments to a third party (not to the beneficiary) for items such as supplemental medical insurance, a customized car or van, a companion, and modifications to a home to make it wheelchair accessible or otherwise adapt it for the individual's particular disability. Be sure to consult with a lawyer familiar with Medicaid rules in your state, to avoid purchases that would result in disqualification or diminution of benefits or any other penalties.

What if my child's disability passes?

If recovery is possible, you should include it in your plans. A trust may include a termination clause, based on a functional assessment of the child's capabilities. It could be structured on a time-release basis, distributing the principal in yearly or other periodic increments to ensure that the disability is ended before the trust terminates.

Pooled trusts. Under recent Medicaid law, assets and income can also be placed in a pooled trust or *master trust* established by a not-for-profit corporation, which could then pay for a disabled person's supplemental needs out of a separate trust account set up for that individual. Choosing an organization that will be able to fulfill the requirements is not necessarily an easy task. In the first place, although nonprofits are often expert in providing social service needs, some may be more skilled than others in meeting the particular needs of your child. Find an organization with a proven track record in the specific area of care needed by your child. Also, the management of a pooled trust requires a different kind of experience to establish and maintain a viable master trust. You want to satisfy yourself that the trust is self-sufficient and able to maintain quality of services.

Different trusts supply different services, for different costs and under different terms. Make sure the agreement spells out the services your child will receive, such as monitoring, social services, medical care, and advocacy services. You can elect different options for the remaining balance after the beneficiary's death. Funds not expended during the beneficiary's lifetime can be left in the trust for the benefit of others after the individual's death, or they may be distributed to others. But remember, those funds that don't remain in the "pool" will first be used to reimburse Medicaid for any outlays to the original trust beneficiary during his or her lifetime.

EDUCATION AND HOUSING

Other major rights of children with disabilities include the right to education, established by the Education for All Handicapped Children Act and its successor, the Individuals with Disabilities Education Act (IDEA), which mandate free appropriate education for children with disabilities.

Under IDEA, your local school district must provide a free appropriate education for your disabled child, in accordance with an evaluation of your child's needs and an individualized education program (IEP) devised expressly for him or her. Related services such as speech and language therapy, counseling, physical therapy, and various other supports may also be required. The law provides that each child be educated in the *least restrictive environment*, although many school districts oppose "inclusion" of children with disabilities as detrimental to children in both "general" and "special" educational programs.

If no appropriate public school setting is available, the school district must educate your child in a private school *at no cost to you.* If this includes residential placement (usually for only the most severely handicapped), the school district will pick up the cost. (The school district is not responsible for all private school costs for the child—only those in cases where it can't locate an appropriate public placement.)

Under federal regulations, you have the right to have an impartial hearing if you contest the evaluation, placement, or services provided for your child. An impartial hearing officer can order modifications in the IEP or make other changes in services and placement. You also have the right to pursue further action in state or federal court. If you are having difficulty with the school district, we suggest contacting an advocacy group or private lawyer familiar with this field.

Although the protections of these laws have traditionally extended to compulsory school-age children (generally five to 21 years of age), recent laws have increased options for children in the three-to-four-year-old age group who are assessed as needing help. Newer laws put the burden on states to identify children at birth to age three in need of services. Preschool children with disabilities may be entitled to related services and programs.

At the other end of the spectrum, older students must be provided with services to ease their transition from school to post-school activities. These may include postsecondary education, vocational training, adult services, or independent living.

As children with disabilities become adults with disabilities, appropriate living arrangements become an important issue. Under a federally financed program, states provide comprehensive living services, including support to help people with disabilities live independently in the community. In recent years, parents have begun to explore more creative options, such as establishing homes in trust for their children, in partnership with licensed nonprofit agencies. By so doing, disabled children may be assured of necessary supervision, services, and support. (For more information, contact the local parent support or advocacy group concerned with your child's particular disability; see also Chapter 22.)

LEGAL PROTECTIONS

There are a number of other laws designed to help people with disabilities, of which you should be aware:

- The Americans with Disabilities Act (ADA) offers a range of legal protections for persons with disabilities seeking jobs as well as transportation services in the community.

These are discussed in Chapters 18 and 22.
- The Fair Housing Act safeguards against discrimination in housing.
- Section 504 of the Rehabilitation Act (commonly called Section 504) forbids discrimination in receiving services.

For more information on these laws, you may also contact agencies listed in the appendixes at the end of this book.

FINDING HELP

As a general rule, local parent support or advocacy groups concerned with particular disabilities are excellent sources of referrals for parents. There are also state protection and advocacy agencies for the disabled in each state, established under federal mandate, which may assist you. (See appendixes in the resources section.)

Some private organizations have begun to help in planning for disabled children. These offer future-care plans on a contract basis, structured to conform with family wishes. Services may include advocacy before public agencies, arranging health care and social service delivery, monitoring living arrangements, and coordinating supplemental services that may be provided through trusts. Lifetime assistance programs are operating in several states.

Private programs designed to function as surrogate families may be of particular help in the future, when children may need an extra voice advocating on their behalf, for instance, arguing for housing services or making a legal claim under the Americans with Disabilities Act. These programs may provide an extra measure of security in your planning. Contact support or advocacy groups or protection agencies for referrals in your area. The National Planned Lifetime Assistance Network and the National Alliance for the Mentally Ill are also sources for information and referrals. (See Appendix I.)

15

Guardians and Protective Services

We've seen that various legal strategies such as powers of attorney and trusts can help manage the affairs of an incapacitated person and maintain him or her in the community when appropriate. When these devices are not in place or not working effectively, the appointment of a guardian or conservator to manage an individual's personal and financial affairs may be necessary.

Guardianship is the judicial appointment of a person with the power and duty to make decisions concerning personal or financial affairs on behalf of another who is considered incapable of doing so for herself or himself. In this it is similar to a power of attorney, except that it is a judge—not you—who decides who is going to serve.

Guardianship was once an all-or-nothing affair in which the incapacitated person relinquished all status and basic rights such as the right to vote, to marry, and to enter into contracts. But an aging society means an increase in the number of functionally disabled older people, a category that includes those with chronic physical disorders as well as the cognitively impaired. There are more than 500,000 adult guardianships in the country today, a number that is expected to rise. An estimated 23 percent of those aged 65 to 74 experience difficulties with specific activities of daily living (ADLs), making it harder for them to remain in the community without help. By age 85, the percentage of those experiencing such difficulties rises to 45 percent. According to surveys, nearly 70 percent of older people seek or receive help with day-to-day tasks such as preparing meals or managing money.

The ability to exercise decisional autonomy can be affected by functional abilities. But decreased abilities as often as not lead to partial or incremental impairment in decision-making ability, not necessarily requiring a total loss of personal autonomy for the affected individual. For those in need of such limited help, guardianship laws may offer new forms of intervention and some additional options, such as conservatorships and limited guardianships. At the same time, the all-or-nothing concept persists in a number of states and in some of the practices of all states, resulting in a significant loss of control.

Protective services agencies provide an array of services, from social support to legal intervention to help maintain the elderly in the community. A variety of demographic and other factors has given rise to a sharp increase in the incidence of personal and financial elder abuse. Intervention by protective services agencies has taken on new significance as the problem of elder abuse has become more prevalent in our society.

THE LAW OF GUARDIANSHIP

Guardianship dates back to ancient Rome and medieval England. Under the doctrine of *parens patriae,* the king as sovereign had an obligation to take care of those under disability. In contemporary times, these royal duties have devolved onto the government. In Europe, guardianships are generally administered by public agencies. In the United States, guardianship proceedings are brought in the state courts—usually a probate court or surrogate's court—seeking the appointment of an individual to act as a guardian.

There are two ways of looking at guardianship:

- Guardianship is a well-intended and benign process designed to afford protections to people in need of them by assigning the power to exercise the rights of an incapacitated person, who is not in a position to do so in his or her own best interests, to someone who can do so on his or her behalf. (According to this view, the guardianship process should be flexible and easy to use so that it is readily available to people in need of its help.)
- Guardianship is the taking away of an individual's rights and freedoms, a deprivation of constitutional magnitude under any circumstances and not necessarily in the best interests of an incapacitated person, who is not always able to protest. (In this view, only the strictest application of due process standards will safeguard against potential abuse and conflicts of interest.)

Which view is right? Both are. Guardianship is an important tool to help manage the affairs of people incapable of doing so themselves. At the same time, transferring control of people's property creates an enormous potential for abuse. And even the most well-intentioned may harbor ageist stereotypes that keep them from recognizing the need for continued autonomy among older people or seeking less drastic alternatives to help them.

Autonomy versus paternalism. Expect to see this dichotomy reflected in your own state guardianship laws—powers and flexibility granted with one hand and restrictions and safeguards imposed with the other in order to achieve a "balanced" approach. Guardianship questions focus on these major stages:

- *Defining the nature of incapacity. What* does incapacity mean?
- *Determining incapacity. When* and under what conditions does a guardianship become effective?
- *The role of the guardian. What is* covered by a guardianship order?
- *Choosing the guardian. Who* is eligible for selection?
- *The hearing process. How* are the issues resolved?
- *Enforcement and monitoring. How* will a guardianship be supervised?

The law of guardianship has its own vocabulary. A person for whom a guardianship is established is called a *ward,* or a *legally incapacitated person.* In some jurisdictions, a guardian is appointed over personal affairs, while a *conservator* or *committee* is used to manage financial affairs. Don't be confused by the terminology, which differs from state to state. What's important is not the jargon, but whether an appointment is validly made and what powers are conferred upon the guardian.

THE NATURE OF INCAPACITY

Who needs a guardian or conservator? Once upon a time, the answer would have been a person who was an "idiot," "insane," or later, "incompetent." Such labels assigned people to vague and generally unhelpful categories.

Today the generally accepted response would be someone who, due to physical or mental incapacity or illness, is incapable of taking care of himself or herself, or someone who is incapable of making or communicating informed or responsible decisions.

The definition of incapacity is an evolving area of law. Reform efforts across the country calling for guardianships tailored to the least restrictive alternative have focused on decision-making and communicating capacity and functional assessment criteria in areas such as personal care, hygiene, nutrition, health care, residence, safety, and daily money management. Depending on the nature of the tasks involved, each area has its own standards of capacity. A person may be incapable of the tasks associated with money management, for example, while continuing to be capable in all others. Colorado, New Hampshire, Rhode Island, and the District of Columbia, among others, require information about a potential ward's functional capacity.

DETERMINING INCAPACITY

The most critical legal issue in guardianship is the assessment of an older person's decision-making capacity, which precedes a determination of the necessity for appointment of a guardian.

Older state statutes still require proof of a particular physical or mental condition as well as a resultant inability to manage one's personal or financial affairs. By contrast, newer laws establish a different measure, requiring an inability to perform and a lack of understanding of the consequences.

This kind of assessment is about specific behavior and limitations. These components should be addressed in any incapacity hearing. With the least restrictive form of guardianship, the ward's decision-making capacity and rights are respected. Nationwide the trend has been to tailor the guardian's powers to the functional limitations of the person. Among the states with comprehensive reform measures are Florida, Michigan, New Mexico, New York, and Washington. For example, New York's guardianship law focuses on functional level and decision-making incapacity.

Is age a "condition" for guardianship purposes?

Although most states have eliminated age or infirmities of age as a statutory condition, seven states still list "advanced age" as a condition upon which a finding of sufficient impairment may be based.

THE ROLE OF THE GUARDIAN

The role of the guardian over a ward's personal affairs is usually spelled out in the court order appointing him or her, in a general statement giving the guardian broad powers over care, custody, and control of the ward.

The power and the responsibility of a guardian vary from state to state. These powers may include the rights to

- Consent to medical treatment
- Decide where to live
- Make a nursing home placement
- Ensure clothing, food, housing, medical care, and personal needs are met
- Initiate divorce or separation proceedings when it is in the ward's best interests
- Make contracts
- Bring and defend lawsuits
- Apply for government benefits

Despite advocates' calls for limited grants of power, guardians continue to be granted broad powers to manage their wards' financial affairs or personal affairs, or both. In the past, guardianship proceedings have commonly resulted in the automatic loss by wards of basic rights such as marrying, voting, working, traveling, and seeking employment and government benefits. In some states, such restrictions are still common. In others, such wholesale forfeiture of rights are no longer the rule. In Massachusetts, for example, express court authority may be needed for placing a ward in a nursing home; similar court sanction is required in New Jersey before consenting to or refusing medical treatment on behalf of a ward. As a general rule, you cannot deprive a ward of the right to have counsel or access to the courts.

The role of the guardian over financial matters is expressed as the power to manage property, finance, and business affairs. In some state laws, it includes a duty to preserve the estate from loss or damage. Powers granted over financial affairs may include the right to

- Enter agreements
- Bring lawsuits
- Manage property
- Invest assets
- Rent or sell an apartment or home
- Control money and determine distribution for food, shelter, and living expenses
- Receive income
- Make gifts or disposition of property

These lists are by no means exhaustive, nor are all guardians granted all these powers in all jurisdictions. The specific powers of a guardian depend on state law and the court's order.

Under what circumstances may a guardian make gifts or dispose of property?

This is an important power. A guardian can make gifts to fulfill support obligations of a ward, for tax planning and Medicaid planning purposes, and to carry out a plan of charitable giving.

What is a limited guardianship? How does it work?

A limited guardianship is a grant of powers of a lesser magnitude than the common broad authority over a ward's person or property. It may even limit powers otherwise authorized by statute. Such an order is allowed in most states. Courts have the inherent power to fashion orders without specific statutory authority, although some states have so provided.

New Mexico's laws allow guardianship only to the extent required by the limitation of the ward, who retains all other rights. Colorado, Florida, Michigan, and New York are among those states that have redrafted their laws authorizing limited guardianship.

While limited guardianships may be appropriate only for some wards, for those individuals it is very important. Wherever possible, ask for a limited guardianship to help preserve the ward's autonomy. The loss of autonomy is keenly felt by all people—no less so by those who've already conceded some.

CHOOSING THE GUARDIAN

A number of state statutes provide an order of priority of persons from whom to choose a guardian. As a general rule, the order is spouse, children, grandchildren, or other next-of-kin.

Often, there is neither friend nor relative available to serve as a guardian. In such cases, courts may appoint lawyers or community agencies (in community and public guardian programs). Banks may also be appointed where substantial assets are involved.

States impose a patchwork quilt of rules and restrictions on the choice of guardian, trying to serve competing interests and policy considerations. Often these rules are an attempt to minimize the potential for abuse, by ensuring that persons are not appointed as guardians who have interests (financial or personal) that conflict with those of the ward. In Florida, for example, a health care provider cannot serve as a guardian except with a specific court finding that there is no such conflict and that the agent is acting in the best interests of the ward. Michigan places a similar restriction on "professional guardians," allowing their appointment only if in the ward's best interests and there is no other suitable person willing to serve. California courts require a statement of whether a petitioner is a creditor of the person over whom conservatorship is sought. In Oregon, professional fiduciaries must undergo criminal records checks. In New York, relatives of judges are ineligible.

These rules vary from state to state. Florida's guardianship law takes a different approach, imposing comprehensive training requirements on guardians. West Virginia law, which specifies a showing of education, ability, and background to perform the duties, also includes mandatory education requirements.

Can someone other than a relative be chosen?

All jurisdictions allow judges to refuse an appointment not in the best interests of the proposed ward. In states without priority statutes, preference may be given to a friend.

Can I choose my own guardian?

A number of states allow a person to name his or her own future guardian, in anticipation of such an appointment becoming necessary. This can be done by making the nomination in a power of attorney or a separate document. Designation works something like a power of attorney. In Florida, a competent person can name his or her future guardian. At the very least, the person designated in advance will be given priority status in consideration by the court.

The person who acts as your guardian should have your best interests at heart; ideally, it would be you who chooses the guardian. Remember, if you have a durable power of attorney, living will, and health care proxy, you will already have made your appointments to manage your future personal and financial affairs—and avoided the need for a guardian.

THE HEARING PROCESS

The process by which a guardianship is imposed on a ward takes place in court. The subject of the hearing is whether the proposed ward has any incapacity, the extent of incapacity, powers needed to manage his or her affairs, and the choice of the guardian. This is usually heard in probate court or surrogate's court, but it may also be before a county court, circuit court, or any other tribunal designated by the state.

A guardianship involves taking away some of a ward's very basic constitutionally protected rights of liberty and property, which are protected under the 14th Amendment of the Constitution. A hearing may be formal or informal, but, at a minimum, the proposed ward is entitled to due process of law, including notice and an opportunity to be heard.

Notice and petition. The court is asked to appoint a guardian in a document that is filed with it called the *petition*. The petition must state the grounds upon which the request for guardianship is based and the statutory basis for that request. There are different requirements in different states. Some require a guardian plan or one for rehabilitation in the petition.

The right to be present. Under most circumstances, the opportunity to be heard means the right of the person to be heard *in person*. Guardianship proceedings often ignore this requirement. Some argue that it is not necessarily in the best interests of the proposed ward, who may be confused and unable to make a good presentation before the court. Sometimes the proposed ward is truly unavailable, in a coma or otherwise incapacitated, incapable of understanding or contributing to the proceeding.

If possible, arrangements can and should be made to facilitate the proposed ward's appearance at the hearing. Scheduling and transportation may need special accommodation. Under appropriate circumstances, there's no reason a hearing can't be held at a hospital or nursing home.

Representation by counsel and appointment of a guardian ad litem. Depending on state law, the guardianship process may require an attorney, a guardian *ad litem*, both, or neither. In many jurisdictions across the country, a guardian *ad litem* (literally, "for the suit") is appointed by the court to protect the interests of the ward. A guardian *ad litem* is a person appointed for the hearing only, usually a lawyer, who functions *both* as an adviser to the court and a representative of the ward. Sometimes a *court evaluator* is appointed as well.

Difficulties arise in the dual role of the guardian *ad litem*. The guardian *ad litem*'s opinion of the proposed ward's best interests may conflict with the proposed ward's own expressed views, but it is the guardian *ad litem*'s responsibility to tell the court his or her own view, rather than advocating the ward's.

This inherent conflict has led to calls for mandatory counsel to represent the ward throughout the guardianship process. Although implemented in a few jurisdictions, including Iowa and Minnesota, this kind of reform has been successfully resisted in most states by opponents who question the need for an adversarial approach to the most common, noncontested situations. These are called "plain vanilla" cases, because no one is questioning the need for the loss of rights by people who have lost some or all of their capacities. In our view, it is this acquiescence that speaks loudest for reform. Who needs legal representation more than people who are unable to speak up for themselves?

What is the difference between a guardian ad litem *and a guardian appointed to manage a ward's personal or financial affairs?*

A guardian *ad litem* represents the ward's interests before the court and advises the court. Except for that narrow purpose, a guardian *ad litem* is not a guardian. Unlike the guardian, the guardian *ad litem* has no powers or responsibilities over a ward's personal affairs or property. If you're dealing with a guardian *ad litem,* or someone functioning in a similar capacity, remember that his or her first loyalty is not to any "client" but to the court.

Can a person file his or her own petition?

Yes. Several states provide for the alleged incompetent or incapacitated person to file.

Can a guardianship be revoked or terminated?

Yes. A guardianship usually lasts the rest of a ward's life but may be ended through a process called a *restoration hearing,* authorized in all states. The ward would have to show that the condition upon which the guardianship was based no longer exists. The guardian would be asked to show cause why the services of a guardian are still needed. If the grounds for which the petition was granted in the first place are gone, then the court may restore the ward's rights.

Can a guardian be removed?

A guardian may always be removed for cause, such as abuse of powers. Most states allow any interested third party to bring an action for removal. Upon the guardian's removal, a substitute guardian will be appointed.

Can a guardian withdraw as guardian and relinquish powers to the ward?

No. A guardian cannot withdraw on his or her own initiative. The guardian has fiduciary responsibility for the ward and is accountable to the court. Even if the ward regains full capacity to manage both personal and financial affairs, application must be made to the court.

MONITORING GUARDIANSHIP

With the exception of a few states, guardianship has been subject only to limited review or oversight. Guardianships over personal affairs have been subject to even less supervision than those over financial affairs.

In recent years, following reported accounts of abuses in a number of states, guardianship accountability has been the goal of substantial reform efforts. Three-quarters of the states require annual or periodic financial accounting. A number of newer guardianship statutes impose on a guardian the requirement to report annually on the ward's personal status, including physical and mental health, social condition, services and treatment, and names of treating physicians, and setting forth the basis for continuing guardianship. Requirements of this nature are in force in Florida, Oklahoma, Michigan, and New Mexico. Most states limit their reviews to investigations of complaints, although some, such as California and Maryland, have attempted to impose more regular review requirements.

A number of programs offer training for guardians. Florida's mandatory course in guardianship must be completed within one year of appointment. The eight-hour training program includes training on guardian duties, rights of wards, local resources, and preparation of annual reports, financial accounts, and guardianship plans. The National Guardianship Association has published standards of practice, as well as a code of ethics, which have been adopted in a number of jurisdictions. And West Virginia is trying a new monitoring scheme, utilizing a citizen guardianship panel to review reports and make recommendations to the court on individual cases.

Who pays for guardianship?

The ward pays the guardian. Usually the fee is either a percentage of the estate or reasonable compensation approved by the court, subject to statutory fee schedules.

What provision is made for those with small estates?

Public guardianship may be available for the incapacitated who are without the funds to pay for a guardianship. These kinds of programs, authorized in the vast majority of states, are often operated by a court or not-for-profit organization. Unfortunately, funding is limited and there are few services available for low-income people without willing guardians. Public guardianship is too often a hodgepodge of services, found in some jurisdictions but not in others, or available in still others in a different form altogether. Florida and Utah have established statewide public guardianship programs, and Oklahoma has recently launched a pilot public guardianship program slated for statewide expansion.

ALTERNATIVES TO GUARDIANSHIP

A number of programs available through local resources may be used as a viable alternative to guardianship. Although unregulated, they may provide help in daily money management and other services with which older people may be having difficulty. Programs of this sort may be found through senior centers, hospitals and social services agencies. (See Chapter 3 and the appendixes in the back of this book.)

Remember, the best alternative to guardianship is advance planning, making use of directives such as power of attorney, a living will, and a health care proxy.

Guardianship and power of attorney. As we discussed in Chapter 12, in most cases a power of attorney should obviate the need for guardianship proceedings. That is not always the case, however, especially in contested matters. Although a court can and will look at a power of attorney for financial matters or one for health care (your health care proxy), there are no uniform rules as to what that review should entail or what weight should be given the preference expressed in the power.

The relationship between advance directives and subsequent guardianship has been addressed by some legislatures in recent years. Some states, such as Georgia, terminate a power of attorney upon institution of a guardianship proceeding. Texas permits the suspension of the power of attorney but doesn't require it.

When it comes to health directives, several states authorize guardian powers to take care of specific needs, such as elective surgery or emergency treatment, without prior court authorization. Few directly address the existence of a health care proxy, although Georgia provides no automatic revocation of a health care power of attorney. Under New York law the appointment of a guardian does not revoke a health care proxy (or a power of attorney) unless the court finds the ward lacked capacity at the time it was signed. By contrast, Michigan law states that the court cannot grant powers to a guardian when there is an existing health care power of attorney, unless that agent is not fulfilling his or her duties.

In circumstances like these, your power of attorney may be even more important! If a guardianship is being sought despite the prior designation by the proposed ward of an agent, the court will generally review the documents in the context of the proposed guardianship. Recent law in North Dakota may take the most practical approach, requiring the court to review any existing health or financial powers of attorney and to consider them in its decision about guardianship.

ELDER ABUSE AND THE LAW

According to national surveys, incidents of abuse, neglect, and exploitation of the elderly rose at a dramatic pace in the 1980s, reaching nearly a half million in 2002. Across the nation, elder abuse has now been estimated to affect upward of 2 million older people annually. According to one congressional report, the rate of abuse among the elderly may be as high as one out of 20 suffering abuse *each year*. Only one out of five cases is ever reported to a public agency.

These are the figures for domestic abuse, occurring outside a nursing home or other health care facility. Revelations of abuse and neglect in nursing homes in the 1970s gave way to discovery of the larger, sub-rosa problem of abuse outside the institutional setting. In fact, elder abuse is more often a family problem. With the rapidly aging population, increasing rates of abuse can be expected.

All 50 states have enacted some type of statute addressing the problem of elder abuse and neglect, most within their already existing adult protective services legislation. Adult protective services commonly provide preventive, supportive, and surrogate services to enable the elderly to maintain independent living in the community and avoid abuse and exploitation.

The contents of state statutes vary, but all include two main components: services for adults at risk, including prevention, support, and treatment services, and the power of the state or local jurisdiction to intervene as needed.

IDENTIFYING ELDER ABUSE

Elder abuse is not easily identified, in part because of misconceptions about just what constitutes mistreatment. Attitudes about aging often ascribe otherwise treatable conditions of frailty and functional decline to the aging process. There is also a notable reluctance among physicians as well as the general public to address family violence. Older adults in institutions are also at risk, vulnerable to mistreatment by facility staff with inadequate training and experience, and without recourse or redress.

Legal definitions of abuse and neglect vary from state to state. The age for defining the "elderly" population varies as well. However, the basic principles may be described by reference to guidelines issued by the American Medical Association, which define elder mistreatment to include

- *Physical abuse.* This includes acts of violence that may result in pain, injury, impairment, or disease.
- *Physical neglect.* This is characterized by a caretaker's failure to provide goods or services necessary for optimal functioning or to

avoid harm. This may include not providing eyeglasses or hearing aids.

- *Psychological abuse.* Psychological abuse involves conduct that causes mental anguish. This includes verbal berating, harassment, or intimidation, threats of punishment or deprivation, treating the older person like an infant, or isolating the older person from family, friends, or activities.
- *Psychological neglect.* Psychological neglect is the failure to provide a dependent elderly person with social stimulation.
- *Financial or material abuse.* This is the misuse of a person's assets or income for the personal gain of another, specifically, the caretaker. This includes stealing money or possessions, either directly or by forcing the older person to sign contracts or assign power of attorney or change a will.
- *Financial or material neglect.* This is failure to use available resources needed to sustain or restore the health and well-being of the older person.
- *Violation of personal rights.* This occurs when caretakers and providers ignore the older person's capacity and desire to make decisions about his or her life, and to otherwise assert autonomy as a human being. This includes denying privacy, denying participation in health care and other personal decisions, and forcible eviction and/or placement in a nursing home.

(Source: Diagnostic and Treatment Guidelines on Elder Abuse and Neglect, American Medical Association, 1992.)

Is there a profile of a typical abused person?

An estimated two-thirds of elder abuse victims in home settings are females. While this statistic may not seem surprising, consider its corollary: one-third of victims of elder abuse are male.

Mistreatment of the elderly occurs throughout all racial, ethnic, and socioeconomic groups. The median age of victims is 78.8. One study reported that those 80 years or older made up more than 40 percent of reported cases.

Who abuses?

Two-thirds of abuse or neglect cases are perpetrated by an adult child or a spouse. Family members are implicated in nine out 10 cases. However, caregivers, paid and otherwise, may also be involved. (Self-neglect is also a major problem among the elderly.)

REPORTING ELDER ABUSE

All states require reporting of elder abuse, although there is variation among states in requirements for identifying and reporting. Forty-two states have passed mandatory reporting laws in recent years, but state officials are skeptical about their effectiveness in combating elder abuse. Illinois joined their ranks in 1999, when it enacted law requiring a wide range of professionals to report elder abuse, but the requirement is only where the older person is unable to self-report. In a survey by the federal government, a majority of officials rated awareness among professionals and the public as the best way to discover abuse. (Prevention of abuse was linked to the provision of home care.)

Categories of people required to report vary from state to state, making comparisons of reporting laws difficult. Mandatory reporting rules in many states cover doctors and other health care providers, professionals and paraprofessionals. Members of more than 50 professional groups are required to report. All states grant some legal immunity for making a complaint or report. Several states, among them California, Florida, and Mississippi, have developed training programs to promote reporting of elder abuse. (See Appendix II for a list of State Adult Protective Service Agencies.)

Elder abuse is underreported for a number of reasons. An abused person is often ashamed to admit victimization by family members, a feeling that is further complicated by guilt as a parent. Add to that dependence on the abuser and apprehension about unknown alternatives, such as removal to a nursing home. To the victimized elderly person, the devil you know is often preferable to the devil you don't know.

INVESTIGATION AND SERVICES

Investigation processes also differ among states. Generally, upon a report, a visit is made and interviews conducted with people having knowledge of the matter under investigation. Some states require on-site investigation; others don't. If a situation merits action under statutory criteria, a range of social services may be offered, from standard casework (including food delivery and preparation, personal care, house cleaning, and visiting nurse services) to special fiscal and legal services.

If the victim does not agree to accept help or lacks the capacity to consent, legal options may include

- Guardianship
- Conservatorship or committee
- Financial management assistance
- Orders of protection

As a general rule, state agencies have insufficient staff with limited experience and training, limited funding, and limited powers.

Local police, sheriff's offices, and district attorneys may investigate and prosecute elder abuse, particularly cases involving sexual abuse, assault, theft, or fraud. In states with statutes making elder abuse a crime, laws generally require suspected abuse to be reported to a law enforcement agency.

ABUSE IN NURSING HOMES

In institutional settings, federal law applies. Under the Nursing Home Reform Act, which provides national standards for care in nursing homes, residents have certain rights, among them the right to be free from verbal, sexual, physical, or mental abuse, corporal punishment, and involuntary seclusion.

Federal guidelines under this law define abuse as "the willful infliction of injury, unreasonable confinement, intimidation, or punishment with resulting physical harm or pain or mental anguish, or deprivation by an individual, including a caretaker, of goods or services that are necessary to attain or maintain physical, mental, and psychological well-being."

Use of physical and chemical restraints is also regulated. Residents have the right to be free from physical restraints or psychoactive drugs administered for purposes of discipline or the convenience of staff (see Chapter 4).

In addition, several states, among them California, Delaware, Florida, Georgia, Maryland, Massachusetts, Missouri, New Mexico, and Oregon, have laws that address abuse in institutional settings. Federal law mandates that the states have long-term care ombudsmen to investigate the quality of care in and complaints about nursing homes, although these positions are often filled on a volunteer basis. However, just the existence of a system for reporting and investigating deters some abuse.

The courts may also provide remedies for institutional abuse for those who file complaints or lawsuits. See Chapter 4 for a discussion of your rights against nursing homes.

16

Wills and Estate Planning

When a person dies without a will, his or her property passes to the closest relatives, as set forth in the laws of the state of residence. If there is no next-of-kin, the property of the deceased will go to the state.

A will allows you to direct how your property will be disposed of after you die. It allows you to divide it the way you choose, to give property to friends and charities as well as relatives, and to set up legal structures to protect your beneficiaries. It also allows you to name the person or persons who will be responsible for carrying out your instructions.

An extra benefit of the will-making process is that it offers you the opportunity to review your financial situation and to plan. This is of considerable importance for another reason—planning for the financing of unanticipated medical expenses or long-term care. In deciding how your estate will be distributed, you will need to consider the possibility that you will need such care, and the best ways to pay for it without dissipating your estate.

UNDERSTANDING THE BASICS

Wills and estate planning involve a number of terms and concepts that require explanation.

Testator. The person making a will is called the *testator* (a woman is sometimes called the *testatrix*). The testator must be an adult and have the mental capacity to make the will in order for it to be a valid instrument. This is called *testamentary capacity.* Physical disability is irrelevant. At the time of the signing, the testator must understand what he or she is doing. That's why wills often contain the phrase "being of sound mind."

Legatees and heirs. The people named to receive bequests in a will are called *legatees.* They are also called *beneficiaries.* An individual's *heirs* are family members who would inherit the estate if there were no will. In some states, these heirs are called *distributees.*

You can divide your money among as many persons as you wish or leave it all to one. It's your call. (There are special protections for children born after a will is made, if they are not mentioned in the will. Spouses also have special rights, which we'll discuss later.)

You can and should state whether the bequest will go to your legatee's heirs or estate if the legatee does not survive you or if the bequest will "lapse." In some states, "antilapse" laws provide that bequests to certain heirs automatically go to *their* heirs if they die before the testator, unless the will provides otherwise. These laws usually protect issue (children or their progeny) or brothers and sisters of the testator. If you want to make an alternative disposition, you need to say so. Making this clear will avoid the need to make a new will every time a legatee dies.

Consider a bequest in your will that provides, "I give $5,000 to my brother Bob Smith." What happens if Bob dies before you? Do you want the bequest to lapse? Go to Bob's wife? His children? In a state that has an antilapse law, it would probably go to Bob's children. You need to spell out your wishes, by stating, for example, "I give $5,000 to my brother Bob Smith if he survives me, but if not, to his wife Sally Smith, if she survives me."

Estate. The estate is the total assets owned at the time of death which will pass to the decedent's survivors either under a will or through intestacy. This is often referred to as the *probate estate.*

Assets in your probate estate include real estate, bank accounts, investment accounts, stocks, bonds, mutual funds, and money owed to you by others. It also includes personal possessions such as jewelry, works of art, furniture, and cars.

Your probate estate does not include property that you own jointly with someone else; bank accounts or United States "E," "EE," or "H" bonds payable on death (POD) to another person; life insurance benefits for which you have designated a policy beneficiary; or pension plan or retirement benefits for which you have designated a beneficiary. These assets will pass "outside" of your estate. They are referred to as *nonprobate assets* and are not affected by the provisions of your will. (They are, however, subject to taxation as part of your *taxable estate.* This is discussed in Chapter 17.)

Bequests can be of specific items of property such as "my antique gold watch" (called *specific bequests*), set amounts or percentages of your estate (called *general bequests*), or the balance of your estate after the specific and general bequests are paid (called *residuary bequests*).

Executor, administrator. The executor (in some states, the *personal representative*) is the person named in the will to dispose of the estate according to your instructions. If there is no will, in most states the person who performs these duties is called the *administrator* (or *administratrix*), although some use the term *personal representative.* This person's responsibilities include arranging for probate if there is a will, gathering the assets, paying debts and expenses, filing the necessary income and estate tax returns and paying any taxes due, investing the estate's assets prudently, and finally distributing the assets as instructed in the will or in accordance with state intestacy laws. (We discuss probate below.)

Being an executor is not an easy job. The selection depends on a number of factors. An executor should be trustworthy and capable of assuming the responsibilities. It may be that the people you are leaving your money to do not have both these characteristics. Other possibilities include your attorney, accountant, a bank, or a trusted friend (some states require additional documents if you name an attorney). Some jurisdictions impose additional requirements for being an executor, such as state residency or being a relative.

Executors receive payment for their work, which comes from your estate. The fee is set by statute, commonly fixed at a percentage of the total estate. You can appoint a person to serve as executor without fee, but no one is obligated to accept appointment. Usually close family members, especially those who are the beneficiaries, will forgo fees, but there may be some cases where taking fees has some tax advantages.

You should always appoint a successor executor in case your first choice is unavailable or declines, is disabled and cannot serve, or dies before you.

Probate. Your executor is charged with the responsibility of gathering and distributing your assets. The first step is probate of your will, to determine whether it is a legal and valid document. Probate means, literally, *proving the will.* This is a court proceeding, done in a probate or surrogate's court. After probate, the executor is authorized to proceed. The court then issues *letters testamentary.*

Domicile. Where you are domiciled affects your will in a number of respects. The states have different will execution requirements and rules governing the rights of family members. Since a few states have inheritance taxes, your place of domicile can affect the taxation of your estate. You may have several residences but only one domicile—the place where your actions and intent demonstrate that you choose to make your primary residence.

If I name my life insurance beneficiary in my will, will it be counted as part of my probate estate?

You cannot change the beneficiary of a life insurance policy by saying in your will who is to get the proceeds of that insurance policy. Nor can you change the designation of who is to get your IRA account. Making changes in beneficiary designation for nonprobate assets must be done in accordance with the insurance policy contract or the rules governing the IRA.

I want to be sure to leave specified property to my nieces and nephews. How can I be sure they will get what I've left them?

Sometimes it's not a good idea to be too specific. Leaving "my 100 shares of Widget, Inc., to my nephew Billy" is not a good idea. If you sell that stock before you die, Billy won't get anything. You'd be better off giving Billy a dollar amount equal to the value of the stock.

I'm concerned that no single member of my family will be in a position to act as executor of my estate. Would it be a good idea to name two or more of them to act as coexecutors?

Naming more than one executor is not always a good idea. Since executors are entitled to payment for their services, having two or more coexecutors can become expensive. And there is always the possibility that the coexecutors may not work well together, leading to disputes that will hinder the smooth administration of an estate. You could name one person as the executor and name another to be the executor if the first person cannot serve as executor, for example, if the first person named does not survive you.

Can I use a do-it-yourself will kit or will forms I find on the Internet?

We don't advise it. No matter how small or simple your financial affairs or how basic your wishes, this area of law is extremely technical and highly specialized. Moreover, the consequences of making an error—both financial or otherwise—may be great. A ready-made set of forms will not point out all the legal considerations or give you answers to any special problems. The cost of a will prepared by a lawyer is generally a good investment. (Don't forget to ask about fees before you engage a lawyer.)

YOUR WILL AND ESTATE TAXES

The federal government imposes a tax on the transfer of wealth from one generation to another, an estate tax when transfer takes place at death and a gift tax when given during one's lifetime. The gift and estate tax is a unified system that allows individuals tax-free transfers of $1 million reflecting a tax credit of $345,800 (2003 figures). Estates above that amount are taxed at a rate starting at 37 percent, subject to certain exceptions.

Under the current federal tax law, the amount of the tax-free transfer will increase over the next few years until, in 2009, it reaches $3.5 million, reflecting a tax credit of $1,455,800. In 2010 the estate tax, but not the gift tax, is repealed. However, the estate tax is reinstated in 2011 with a tax-free transfer of $1 million, reflecting a tax credit of $345,800. Legislation to make the repeal of the estate tax permanent has thus far been defeated, but will no doubt be a recurring political theme over the next few years.

There is no gift or estate tax imposed on gifts or bequests to charities or to spouses who are U.S. citizens. (Noncitizen spouses are not eligible for this *unlimited marital deduction.*)

In drafting your will, there are a number of important estate tax planning tools that you need to consider. The way your will is worded can have a significant effect on the estate tax imposed on your estate. (We discuss estate taxes in more detail in Chapter 15.)

BEQUESTS TO SPOUSES, CHILDREN, AND OTHER FAMILY MEMBERS

Leaving money outright to the people you love is a nice gesture, but it may cost them money. The rules on inheritance are very tight when it comes to family bequests and the tax consequences of uninformed largesse can be appalling.

Bequests to Spouses

Property left to your spouse will not be taxed in your estate so long as he or she is a U.S. citizen. It will be taxed in your spouse's estate later at his or her death, when the unlimited marital deduction will likely no longer apply. For that reason, a simple will leaving everything to your spouse may not be the best approach. It is probably better to set up a trust for your spouse of an amount that will escape estate tax because of the estate tax credit. The funds in this "bypass" trust will be available to him or her, but they will not be taxed either in your estate or your spouse's and will eventually pass estate-tax-free to your other heirs. (See Chapter 17.)

A trust is also a valuable device for providing for a spouse who is ill or incapacitated. Another benefit of a trust is that you can provide for a beneficiary during the beneficiary's lifetime but retain the right to control the ultimate disposition of the trust fund when the beneficiary dies. The trust is particularly useful in second, later-life marriages, allowing you to leave your estate in trust for your spouse but ensuring that your estate will be left to your children by your first marriage if that is your wish.

I have been married three times, a fact my spouse doesn't know. My ex-wives have no legal interest in my estate, so do I have to tell my lawyer or mention them in the will?

By all means, tell your lawyer. Previous marriages may affect both planning and how your will is drafted. For example, your will should always name people, in addition to describing them by relationship, for example leaving money "to my wife Alice Adams" as opposed to just "my wife."

Bequests to Children and Grandchildren

In the language of wills, children and grandchildren descended from you are referred to as your *issue.* Wills commonly leave bequests to unnamed descendants by referring to them as "issue," for example, "I leave everything to Jane Doe, and if she does not survive me, to her issue, *per stirpes.*"

"*Per stirpes*" indicates that if Jane Doe's issue receive an inheritance, it will be divided among them as if all her children were living, and if any are not, the shares of any predeceased children will be passed on to their issue (who, literally, "step into the parent's shoes"). An alternative form of bequest, leaving it to her issue *per capita,* would leave the bequest divided equally among those still living. Another form of bequest is "by representation," a hybrid form that combines elements of *per stirpes* and *per capita* distribution under certain circumstances among the issue of predeceased children in the next generations. (The chart on page 234 illustrates how results may differ among *per stirpes, per capita,* and by-representation bequests.)

Remember that family bequests to "issue" may not necessarily include family members such as adopted children, stepchildren, half siblings, and nontraditional relations. This is vitally important in today's family, when people are living longer and in more complicated family situations than in the past. You have the right to leave your money to anyone you want, but you may have to make special reference to an adopted child or grandchild or a half sibling who may otherwise be excluded. The same applies if you want to exclude someone who would otherwise be included. A lawyer will help sort out who's who and who's legally entitled to a portion of your estate.

BEQUESTS TO CHILDREN AND GRANDCHILDREN
BY REPRESENTATION, *PER STIRPES*, AND *PER CAPITA*

Testator: Jane Doe
Jane Doe's Children: Amy, Bob, and Carl
Jane Doe's Grandchildren: Ann and Bill (Amy's children) Cal and Dan (Bob's children), Ed (Carl's child)

Bequest by representation

I leave everything to Jane Doe and if she does not survive me, to her issue by representation

- If Jane Doe has died and all her children are alive, her children Amy, Bob, and Carl will share equally in the bequest.

- If Jane Doe has died and Bob is also not alive, Amy and Carl will get their 1/3 shares, and Bob's two children Cal and Dan will share Bob's 1/3 share, getting 1/6 each.

- If Jane Doe has died and Bob and Carl are not alive, Amy will get her 1/3 share, the remaining 2/3 will be combined and divided equally among Bob and Carl's children, Cal, Dan, and Ed, that is, each will get 1/3 of the remaining 2/3 (or 2/9) of the estate.

- If Jane Doe has died and all three of her children have also died, her grandchildren, Ann, Bill, Cal, Dan, and Ed, will share equally, each taking a 1/5 share.

Bequest *per stirpes*

I leave everything to Jane Doe and if she does not survive me, to her issue *per stirpes*

- If Jane Doe has died and all her children are alive, her children Amy, Bob, and Carl will share equally in the bequest.

- If Jane Doe has died and Bob is also not alive, Amy and Carl will get their 1/3 shares, and Bob's two children, Cal and Dan, will share Bob's 1/3 share, getting 1/6 each.

- If Jane Doe has died and Bob and Carl are not alive, Amy will get her 1/3 share, Bob's two children, Cal and Dan, will share Bob's 1/3 share, getting 1/6 each, and Carl's child, Ed, will get Carl's 1/3 share.

- If Jane Doe has died and all three of her children have also died, her grand-children Ann and Bill will share the 1/3 share that would have been Amy's, Cal and Dan will share the 1/3 share of Bob, and Ed will take the 1/3 share of Carl.

Bequest *per capita*

I leave everything to Jane Doe and if she does not survive me, to her issue *per capita*

- If Jane Doe has died and all her children are alive, her children Amy, Bob, and Carl will share equally in the bequest.

- If Jane Doe has died and Bob is also not alive, Amy and Carl will get 1/4 shares, and Bob's two children, Cal and Dan, will also get 1/4 shares.

- If Jane Doe has died and all three of her children have also died, all her grandchildren, Ann, Bill, Cal, Dan, and Ed, will share equally, each taking a 1/5 share.

Be careful not to leave money outright to minors. Those bequests to grandchildren may seem like a good idea but in fact may be nothing but trouble. Minors can't own assets, so funds you leave to them can be collected only by a court-appointed guardian who will be severely restricted in using the funds, even for things like college tuition. These guardians, even if they are the parents of the grandchild, will have to go to court to get permission to spend the funds and the court may decline, stating that the funds are to be preserved because the parents have the obligation to pay for college out of their own funds. Bequests to minors should be left in a trust for them, or the will should allow the executor to retain the funds until the minor comes of age, using it for their care in the meantime. The same problem applies to funds your grandchildren may receive from you in ITF ("in trust for") accounts, POD ("paid on death") government bonds, or life insurance.

One method of avoiding these problems is to make a gift under a uniform gifts to minors act or uniform transfers to minors act, which most states have adopted. Under these laws the minor owns the property but it is held by a custodian who manages the property and may use it to take care of the minor. The custodian must preserve the property for the minor and turn it over to him or her when he or she reaches 18 or 21 (depending upon which law applies). These laws protect the gift to the minor while providing for adult management of assets until the minor becomes old enough to take care of the property.

DISPOSING OF YOUR PERSONAL EFFECTS

In legal terminology, your furniture, art, silverware, china and glassware, jewelry, and automobiles, to list just a few things you may own, are called *tangible personal property*. You can specify bequests of these items in your will, but usually this is not necessary. You can give all such property to your spouse or another heir, for example, by simply stating that "I give all of my tangible personal property to my wife, Sally."

If your effects are to be divided among several people, another option is to leave them to one person and "request" that person "distribute the property in accordance with the instructions I will set forth in a letter" to be given to that person. This approach allows you to change your mind without having to redo your will every time. While in most jurisdictions the person you designate is not legally obligated to honor your instructions, you will presumably choose a trustworthy person who will respect your wishes. Some states such as Florida have adopted this kind of procedure in their will laws, making a statement or letter of this nature legally binding.

BURIAL INSTRUCTIONS

Many people choose to include funeral service and burial instructions in their wills. Although there is no reason not to do so, keep in mind that a will may not always be available to the family at the time of death. Technically, your will has no legal effect until it is admitted to probate, so it is important to tell your family or friends of your funeral and burial wishes and set them out in a separate letter of instructions.

I want to donate my organs for use after my death. Can this be included in my will?

Under the Uniform Anatomical Gifts Act, a version of which has been adopted by every state, you can make a "gift" of some or all of your organs upon your death through your will. You can indicate the conditions under which you will donate and further include any burial instructions following donation of organs. Again, just as with burial instructions, the will may not be available at the time of death. With organ donations, time is of the essence, and your family and friends should know your wishes to make an organ donation.

An alternative is to also carry a *uniform donor card,* signed and witnessed, which may be more likely to be found in time to be useful. Many states provide a space on the back of a driver's license for drivers to authorize organ donation. A few states allow your health care agent to consent to organ donation. (Organ and tissue donation is discussed in Chapter 12.)

DISINHERITING YOUR HEIRS

Most states have provisions preventing you from disinheriting your spouse. These laws give surviving spouses a *right of election* to take a share of the deceased spouse's estate, often one-half or one-third. But these laws are often easily avoided in some states because the "estate" of the deceased spouse for the purpose of making a spousal right of election does not always include "nonprobate" property such as assets owned jointly with persons other than the spouse or assets in trust for the benefit of persons other than the spouse. While some states, such as New York, are tightening their laws protecting spouses, many states have a long way to go. (Under federal law, spouses have special rights to pensions, discussed in Chapter 19.)

Spouses can "waive" this right, a common practice in prenuptial agreements signed by couples entering into later-life marriages. Keep in mind that even though you have signed a prenuptial agreement, you can always provide your spouse with more than the agreement calls for.

Disinheriting a child is another matter. Other than a spouse in a state with a "right of election" law, you have no obligation to provide for anyone. In most states, it is not necessary to mention a disinherited child or to leave him or her a nominal sum, although it is required in a few jurisdictions to ensure that a child is not unintentionally omitted. There is no requirement to give a reason, although you can if you like.

An exception to this rule applies when a child is born to you after the date you make your will and not mentioned in it (either by name or as part of an inclusive reference to "children" or "issue"). The new child will be given the equivalent of an intestate share on the premise that you forgot to change your will and provide for him or her. If you wish to disinherit a child in this situation, you need to "republish" your will by making a new one or signing a codicil stating that you do not want to make a provision for that child.

BEQUESTS TO CHARITIES

The common law as adopted in many states had limitations on the percentage of one's estate that could be left to charity when the testator was survived by a spouse or children. The purpose of the limitations was to prevent undue influence from religious bodies. These laws—known as *mortmain statutes*—have been largely superseded by the spousal right of election laws, which have been deemed to protect spouses adequately. But it is a good idea to check your state's law in this regard if you plan to leave substantial amounts to charity.

JOINTLY OWNED PROPERTY

Upon the death of one of the joint owners of property, it becomes the sole property of the surviving *joint tenant*. It does not pass under the deceased person's will or form part of his or her probate estate.

Joint ownership has some advantages. In small estates, property held jointly passes to the surviving spouse quickly without the need for the probate of a will or other administration.

There are disadvantages as well. There may be unexpected gift tax implications when property is placed in joint ownership. For example, parents often set up joint accounts with children. When a parent places stocks in joint ownership with a child, the act may result in a gift of one-half the value of the property. This gift, although probably unintended, may nevertheless result in the imposition of a substantial gift tax. (Other nonestate problems are discussed in Chapter 13. The gift tax is discussed in Chapter 17.)

Moreover, with joint ownership, you lose control. Except for joint bank accounts, you do not retain the power to sell or dispose of 100 percent of the assets at any time (nor does your co-owner). Nor can your will undo joint ownership. If you made your daughter co-owner of a bank account or stock certificate, you can't leave that account or stock to another child.

COMMUNITY PROPERTY STATES

Ten western and southwestern states have community property laws that treat assets acquired during marriage as owned equally by the spouses. These are Alaska, Arizona, California, Idaho, Louisiana, Nevada, New Mexico, Texas, Washington, and Wisconsin. In these states property is deemed either *community property* or *separate property.* While the rules outlined in this chapter generally apply in community property states, there are some differences that may affect you. Make sure to consult your local counsel.

WITNESSES AND OTHER FORMALITIES

The first step in probate of a will is determining whether it is a legal and valid document. A valid will requires compliance with a number of formalities. These execution requirements vary according to the state in which you reside, but there are some general rules.

- *Age.* A will must be completed by an adult. A will executed by a minor is not a valid document and won't be recognized by law. In most states, the *age of majority,* at which time a person ceases to be a minor, is 18.
- *Testamentary capacity.* The testator must be legally capable of making a will. This is called testamentary capacity. Most states define this as knowing you are executing a will, knowing and understanding who your natural heirs are, and knowing the nature and extent of your property.
- *Form.* Most states require wills to be written. Oral wills are recognized in very limited circumstances such as that of a soldier in combat.

- *Signature and date.* Wills must be signed by the testator at the end and dated.
- *Witnesses.* Witnesses are required in all but the most limited circumstances. Witnesses confirm your signature on the will, the voluntariness of your signing your will, your competence to do so, your declaration that it is your will, and each other's signatures as well. States usually require two witnesses, although some require three. Witnesses must generally be adults and competent. Some states have additional requirements concerning who they may be, and, more important, who they may not be. A beneficiary under a will may not be a witness. In some states the signature of a witness who is also a beneficiary may be recognized as valid if the amount received through the will is less than the share he or she would receive if there were no will or if he or she gives up the right to inherit. This penalty may be avoided by not using a beneficiary as a witness.
- *Notarization.* Wills are not notarized. However, many states have adopted a system known as a "self-proving" will, which allows the probate of a will without having to locate witnesses and bring them to court to "prove" the will. In a self-proving will, the witnesses confirm by separate affidavit that the formalities of will execution were followed; the *affidavit* is signed, notarized, and attached to the will.

How many copies do I sign?

Only one! If you execute more than one original and any of the signed copies cannot be found when the time comes to probate the will, the missing copy may be presumed to have been destroyed by you with the intent to revoke it. Never sign more than one copy of a will.

Can my executor be witness to my will?

Yes, unless he or she is also a beneficiary named in your will. Technically, there's no prohibition if the share designated under your will is less than his or her share would be if you had no will. But this is not always possible to determine. The best way to proceed is to select witnesses who are not beneficiaries.

Where can I get witnesses? I don't want people knowing my business.

Your witnesses do not have to be told the contents of your will. All you need to do is declare to them that the document you are asking them to witness is your will (this is called *publication* of your will), that it expresses your wishes, and that you are requesting them to be your witnesses. Anything more is nobody's business but yours. Your attorney will usually provide witnesses, so your family, friends, and neighbors don't even have to know that you're preparing a will.

I want to change a part of my will. Can I do that with a codicil?

A codicil, the technical name for an amendment to a will, is valid if executed with the same formalities required for your will. While a codicil may be simpler than redoing your entire will, it's not always the wisest way to proceed. In most states, if you change your will by a codicil, anyone whose interests are adversely affected will learn of the change and could challenge the codicil. If you incorporate the change in a new will, the earlier provisions are no longer part of the document and it becomes much more difficult to challenge it.

I have a handwritten will stating my intentions. That should be good enough. Why should I give good money to lawyers?

Sorry. While there is no requirement that a will be typed, it is important that a will, whether handwritten or typed, be witnessed and executed following all the usual formalities. A handwritten will, or even a typed one, that is not properly executed would not be valid in most states. In a few states, a handwritten will (called a *holographic* will) is valid under limited circumstances without requiring the usual formalities. This usually applies to wills of military personnel during combat.

When should I update my will?

When your family or financial circumstances change considerably or you change your wishes. Or when tax or other laws affecting your financial plans change, as happens frequently.

Events such as marriage, the marriage of a child, the birth of another child or grandchild, or a significant improvement in your financial situation are the most frequent causes of reviewing wills and estate plans. Or there might be a divorce or other family rift causing you to want to take someone out of your will, or a family member may die or become seriously ill or incapacitated. (We discuss planning for a disabled child in Chapter 14.) You may also want to change the executor (or trustee) if the circumstances of the person or persons you have nominated have changed or if you have lost confidence in them.

Must I change my will when I move to another state?

It's not usually necessary but may be a good idea. All the states will recognize a will drawn in another state if it was properly executed under the laws of that state. But a move to another state is one of the life events that should prompt you to review and update your will.

How do I make the necessary changes? Can I mark up the old one?

No! This could invalidate your will. Your existing will had to be properly witnessed; so must your changes. Either redo the whole will or execute a codicil with the same formalities with which you signed the will itself. It is generally preferable to redo the entire will, one reason being that any persons you may be eliminating from your will do not get to see the earlier provisions.

How do I revoke my will?

You revoke your will by making a new one and stating in the new one that the old will is revoked, or by physically destroying the old will. Be careful if you want to revoke it by tearing it up or burning it. Someone could later allege that it was destroyed accidentally. To revoke a will by destroying it you must destroy it with the *intent* to revoke it, so it is probably a good idea to do this before witnesses and tell them that you mean to revoke it. Remember to execute a new will. (What happens when you die without a will is discussed in the next section.)

Where do I keep it?

The best place to leave the original will is with your lawyer, provided he or she will keep it in a bank vault or a fireproof safe in his or her office. You will get *conformed copies* that you can keep at home and give to your heirs and executor. Other possibilities include keeping the original at home or in your bank safe deposit box.

Keeping it at home has risks—someone could find and destroy it, it could easily be misplaced, or it could be destroyed in a fire. A bank safe deposit box will protect it from accident or mischief, but it may create other problems. In many states safe deposit boxes are sealed upon the death of the owner (or joint owner), and it takes a court order to get into the box even to remove a will.

DYING WITHOUT A WILL

If you die without a will, your property is distributed under your state's laws of intestacy, which prescribe strict orders of distribution. An individual who dies without a will has died *intestate;* the persons who will receive the estate under the intestacy laws are usually called *intestate distributees.* In effect, the state is writing a will for you, and it may not be the will you would have wanted.

Generally, state laws will distribute your property in the following way, although the states do differ.

- If you are survived by your spouse and at least one child, your estate will be divided among them. Depending on the state's law, your spouse may get one-third, one-half, a fixed amount, or some combination, and your children will share the balance. The children of a child who dies before you (a *predeceased child*) will usually take that child's share.

- If you are survived by your spouse but have no children, your spouse will receive your entire estate, although in some states your parents may get a share.
- If you are survived by children but not your spouse, your children will share the entire estate. The children of predeceased children will inherit their parent's share. If all your children have predeceased you, your grandchildren will take the whole estate (depending on the state's law, either by representation, *per stirpes*, or *per capita*).
- If you have neither spouse nor children, your parents will receive your estate. In some states it will be shared with your siblings.
- If you are survived by neither your spouse, descendants, nor parents, your estate will be paid to your siblings and the children of predeceased siblings. If all of your siblings have also died, your nieces and nephews will inherit the estate.

State laws also specify who will be appointed as *administrator* of the estate.

The "will" the state makes for you is probably not going to be the will you would have written for yourself. You might want your entire estate given to or held in trust for your spouse during his or her lifetime and not want to give anything to your children at the time of your death. Or, if you do wish to leave property to your children outright, you may want to make unequal bequests or leave a child's share in trust. Perhaps you want to provide for a parent. Your wishes and the statutory scheme of intestacy may be very different in many ways. But the statutory format will take precedence unless you act.

If the state's intestacy laws make the same provision as I would in a will, why do I need a will?

It's never exactly the same. Without a will, your court-appointed administrator may have to post a bond, a charge on the estate. A will may also ensure that taxes are paid out of your estate and the liability not distributed among your heirs.

RENOUNCING AN INHERITANCE

While it may be hard to imagine, an inheritance is not always what you want. You can't be forced to accept a gift or an inheritance, and you have the right to refuse it. This is called a *disclaimer* or a *renunciation*. Under the tax laws, property you disclaim is treated as never having belonged to you, so you are not liable for gift taxes on the transfer to the person who will get the disclaimed property.

Disclaimers are tricky. The rule is that if a person disclaims, it is treated as if he or she had died immediately before the death of the person whose estate is to be distributed. Under this construct, whether the will makes an alternative disposition takes on critical importance. You don't want to make a disclaimer if the bequest will go to a stranger. Make sure you know who will take the disclaimed property.

There are a number of situations in which, for reasons of family relations or tax planning, a disclaimer may be appropriate. For example, a man may die intestate, with only one-third of his estate going to his widow and the children to inherit the remaining two-thirds. That may not have been what he wanted. The surviving spouse may have limited assets. The children could disclaim their interests and the property would pass to the spouse, *if there are no grandchildren.* But if the children have children, it is those grandchildren of the decedent who would receive the disclaimed property. (If they are minors, the disclaimer won't be valid without court permission. Without that, the children would have to collect their shares and then make gifts to their mother, with possible gift tax consequences.)

A disclaimer might also be a good idea for tax reasons. Remember that assets passing to the spouse are not subject to estate tax, but that property going to children is taxable. It might be better to have the estate unreduced by estate taxes as long as the spouse survives.

A disclaimer is often used by a child with substantial means to have a bequest pass directly to his or her children, thus avoiding having the assets taxed again as part of his or her estate later on. Disclaimers are also quite common in situations where a person leaves the entire estate to the surviving spouse and the estate is greater than the tax-free portion ($1 million in 2003). In this case, it might be wise for the surviving spouse to disclaim assets up to the exclusion amount, having them pass immediately to their children, for tax planning reasons. Of course, this should only be done if the exclusion amount isn't as much as the whole estate and the surviving spouse has adequate resources and income to justify giving up the disclaimed assets.

Caution: Because of recent changes in federal estate tax law, wills that bequeath the "exempt amount" of an estate to children, without naming a specific dollar amount, may inadvertently leave the children more than was intended. A testator who may have wished to give the children $675,000, the maximum "exempt amount" under the old law, may wind up leaving them $1 million (in 2003) or more, as much as $3.5 million by the year 2009. (Estate tax changes are discussed in Chapter 17.)

And the spouse may wind up with nothing, forced to seek the statutory elective share. This may exacerbate an already stressful situation, especially if the children don't get along with the surviving spouse (whether a natural parent or a second spouse).

Specific rules for disclaiming property are contained in the Internal Revenue Code and state laws. Disclaimers must be made within nine months of the creation of the property interest being disclaimed. In the case of a bequest made under a will, the nine-month period begins with the date of the testator's death. If you are disclaiming an asset from a trust, the time period begins at the time of death of the person whose trust interest comes before you.

Disclaimers need to be valid under state law as well. Most jurisdictions require a written document acknowledged by a notary public. Some jurisdictions prescribe a time period during which a disclaimer must be made and filed in court to be effective.

While a person may disclaim an inheritance to avoid creditor problems, disclaimers cannot be used to avoid federal taxes. A disclaimer is ineffective if the person owes federal taxes and the government has a lien for the taxes.

Disclaimers cannot be used to qualify for Medicaid. While disclaimers work fine for tax purposes, keep in mind that for Medicaid planning purposes property disclaimed is considered to be an asset and a disclaimer will be considered as a disqualifying transfer.

THE USE OF TRUSTS

A trust is simply a legal agreement by which a person gives property to a "trust," which is administered by a *trustee* or *trustees*. Assets must actually be deposited into the trust, which becomes the nominal owner by reregistering title to the assets. The principal and the income are administered and applied for the benefit of the *trust beneficiaries* in accordance with the instructions in the trust agreement. (Trusts are a common and useful device for the concerns of older people. Other models are discussed in Chapters 9, 13, and 14.)

A *testamentary trust* is created by a person's will, and takes effect upon his or her death. A testamentary trust may be advisable when

- You think your spouse or child will be unable to manage a large sum of money

- The beneficiary may be ill or incapacitated
- The beneficiary may receive or need Medicaid and you want your bequest to supplement the care provided by Medicaid and not risk disqualification
- You want to control where your property will go after your initial beneficiary dies

Another popular form of trust is the *living trust* (in Latin, an *inter vivos* trust), created by you to take effect during your lifetime. A living trust can accomplish many of the goals of a testamentary trust.

A common method of "avoiding probate" is to create a revocable living trust, name yourself as both trustee and beneficiary, and transfer all your assets into it. Upon death, your assets can then be transferred without the formalities and expense of probate. In a few states, you cannot be the sole trustee of such a trust but must name a cotrustee. The revocable living trust has no tax consequences whatsoever during your lifetime.

Unfortunately, while revocable living trusts have useful purposes and can reduce estate administration expenses to a limited extent, the advantages are greatly overestimated in many situations. A revocable living trust has no tax benefits. You should obtain legal counsel and explore the advantages and disadvantages of revocable trusts fully before you transfer your assets into one.

I have a living trust. My lawyer says I still need a will. Why?

A *pourover will* is a necessary accompaniment to a living trust. Although distribution of your assets is controlled by the living trust, with a pourover will you can have the terms of your trust govern the distribution of any other assets you may own or later receive that weren't put into your living trust during your lifetime.

Part 5

You and Your Taxes

Every decision you make in the context of planning for the future has tax consequences. That makes it critical for your financial planning that you have a basic understanding of how gift, estate, and income taxes may affect you. So important is this point that we've set apart our discussion of taxes for the older citizen for emphasis.

Shifting funds for Medicaid planning, creating trusts to manage your assets or provide for a family member's care, using financial strategies such as reverse mortgages to reap current income or accelerated life insurance benefits to help pay for health care—all of these may have significant tax implications for you.

One word of caution. This chapter provides general guidelines to help you understand the potential impact tax issues may have on your planning; it is *not* intended as advice on your specific financial or tax situation. Before you take any action altering the ownership or distribution of your assets or income, you should seek professional tax counsel.

17

Planning and Tax Implications

Life planning does not take place in the abstract. In all your planning decisions and actions, you must take into account the effect on your taxes. Tax considerations apply to almost all the planning choices available: creating a trust, purchasing or collecting on insurance, planning your estate, purchasing an annuity, purchasing a lifecare contract, moving to another state. Although we cannot offer legal advice on any particular tax situation, here are some general guidelines for understanding the gift, estate, and income tax implications of decisions you may face.

Giving assets away. If you are considering gifts to support or aid family members or make yourself Medicaid eligible, you must consider these questions:

- Will this transfer cause gift tax or future estate tax liability?
- Are the funds free from eventual estate tax?
- Am I liable for taxes on the income on gifted money?
- Are transfers or payments tax-deductible?

Arranging to receive money or assets. If you are using a device that will result in your receiving additional cash payments, such as accelerated life insurance benefits or reverse mortgage, you must consider the following:

- Will payments I receive count as income for income tax purposes?
- Will payments count as income for determining tax liability on my Social Security income?

Medicaid and taxes. Tax considerations are made even more difficult by the question of safeguarding your potential Medicaid eligibility. Whether you are transferring assets or arranging to receive them, you must also ask

- Will giving money away or arranging to receive payments affect Medicaid eligibility?
- Will giving away assets result in taxes that outweigh potential Medicaid benefits?

Often these two considerations can conflict, a fact not readily apparent to people making life decisions under stressful conditions. For example, if you give your home to your children so that it is not available to Medicaid, the tax bill resulting from the gift may be substantially greater than any Medicaid benefits you obtain. In order to avoid this kind of catch-22, you need expert guidance. Remember, both tax rules and benefit eligibility rules are subject to swift change. (We discuss Medicaid eligibility rules in Chapter 9.)

GIFT AND ESTATE TAXES

Death and taxes are inevitable, and inevitably they go together. Whether you have a will or not, upon your death your estate may be subject to taxes.

As a general rule, only estates with assets greater than $1 million are subject to federal estate tax liability. Under the federal system, individuals are allowed a *lifetime exclusion* of $1 million, reflecting a tax credit of $345,800 (roughly equivalent to the tax on $1 million).

The 2001 Tax Act (officially the Economic Growth and Tax Relief Reconciliation Act of 2001) made sweeping changes in the federal estate tax law that gradually eliminate the estate tax by increasing the amount that is exempt from the tax and reducing the top estate tax rate, finally repealing the estate tax for individuals dying in 2010.

Beginning in 2002, the exclusion rate goes up to $1 million, then to $1.5 million in 2004, $2 million in 2006, and $3.5 million in 2009. The tax rate is correspondingly reduced, dropping to 45 percent by 2009. In 2010, there will be no estate tax, and the top gift tax rate will be 35 percent.

The chart on page 250 shows the annual tax credit given to an estate corresponding to the amount excluded from taxes and the highest estate tax rate for each year through 2011. The tax rate for estates over $1 million starts at 37 percent, and tops 49 percent for larger estates.

	FEDERAL ESTATE AND GIFT TAXES		
	Exclusion Amount	**Unified Tax Credit**	**Top Tax Rate**
2002	$1 million	$345,800	50%
2003	$1 million	$345,800	49%
2004	$1.5 million	$555,800	48%
2005	$1.5 million	$555,800	47%
2006	$2 million	$780,800	46%
2007	$2 million	$780,800	45%
2008	$2 million	$780,800	45%
2009	$3.5 million	$1,455,800	45%
2010	taxes repealed	taxes repealed	35% (gift tax only)
2011	$1 million	$345,800	55%

The estate tax is part of a "unified" tax system for gift and estate taxes. Gifts were made part of the system to ensure that people wouldn't escape estate taxes by giving away their money. At the time of death, the computation of the gross estate against which tax will be assessed includes any gifts made over the years (above the annual exclusion, discussed below).

The amount excluded from gift tax rises to $1 million for all years beginning in 2002 and remains at that amount. The gift tax is not being repealed. In 2011, when the estate and gift tax returns, the top estate and gift tax rate reverts to 55 percent.

Several states also have an estate tax. Some of these states impose an *inheritance tax,* which taxes those receiving an inheritance for their share, rather than a tax on the entire estate.

Legislative note: *The 2001 Tax Act contains a "sunset" provision under which the old rules return in 2011. As a result, the estate tax is repealed only for those who die in 2010. Although at this writing, legislation to make the repeal of the estate tax permanent was defeated, we can predict this will be a recurring political theme over the coming decade. One possible outcome: an exclusion for each person of $3.5 million, the top rate reached under the current statute in 2009.*

Federal Estate Taxes

Everything you own is taxable as part of your estate when you die. All the property that you own or control or in which you have an interest at the time of death, whether or not it passes through your will, is part of your *taxable estate*. This includes assets in your name or assets owned jointly with another, POD (payable on death), or ITF (in trust for). Your gross estate will include real estate, stocks, bonds, life insurance, retirement plan funds, IRAs, jointly owned property, and certain transfers made during your lifetime. (This is not the same as your *probate estate,* which is limited to assets passing through your will.) The probate estate is discussed in Chapter 16.

For example, property you have placed in a trust, whether revocable or nonrevocable, will be taxed in your estate if you receive the income from the trust during your lifetime. The basic rule is that if you keep an economic interest or retain control of the use of assets you've placed in a trust, your estate will be taxed on it.

Federal estate tax is due nine months after the decedent's death. Under certain limited circumstances where assets are not liquid, such as a farm or a business, estates may be allowed to pay their taxes in installments (with interest).

Exceptions. The basis for successful estate planning is found in the exceptions. The most common and useful of these techniques to reduce the amount of taxable estate are the annual exclusion and the marital deduction, although there are a number of other techniques you can use. Remember, you don't want to give away more than you can afford (or give up too much control).

Annual exclusion. We explained before that the gift and estate taxes operate as a unified tax system. This means that the *lifetime exclusion of $1 million* applies to gifts made over the course of your lifetime as well as bequests made upon your death. Beginning in 2004, the amount excluded from estate tax rises to $1.5 million, while the amount excluded from gift tax remains at $1 million.

The annual exclusion is the amount you may give to a donee or donees each year without incurring any tax liability. The annual exclusion, which for many years had been $10,000, was made subject to adjustment for inflation. Beginning in 2002, the annual exclusion rose to $11,000. Each year, you can make gifts of up to $11,000 per donee ($22,000 per couple), using the annual exclusion. You can make unlimited gifts up to this amount to any number of people without paying tax.

Annual exclusion gifts do not reduce the $1 million lifetime transfer privilege. Gifts of $11,000 or less are not taxed by virtue of the annual gift tax exclusion. Gifts more than the annual exclusion amount are subject to a gift tax, unless a portion of the lifetime gift tax exclusion is used. The tax advantage of making annual exclusion gifts is that those gifts will not be included in figuring your gross estate, thus reducing your estate and its tax liability.

Education and medical expenses. There is no upper limit on the amount you can pay or education or medical expenses for another person, without tax liability, so long as the amount is paid directly to the provider, that is, the educational or health care institution. For example, if you want to pay for your grandchild's college tuition, you can arrange to make direct payments to the university. And you can still make your grandchild an annual exclusion gift of up to $11,000 (or $22,000 if you're making the gift as a married couple).

Marital deduction. The marital deduction allows gifts and bequests to be made to a spouse without any federal tax liability. All property given or bequeathed to a spouse is free of federal taxes, provided that the spouse receiving the property is a citizen of the United States. If the spouse is not a citizen of the United States, the estate does not get a marital deduction unless the property passes to the noncitizen spouse in a *qualified domestic trust* (QDOT). Some states do tax at least a portion of such gifts or bequests.

Taking advantage of the marital deduction is a two-edged sword. It softens the blow on a surviving spouse when the first spouse dies but leaves that spouse at a disadvantage in planning his or her own estate, now larger and more vulnerable. Under the marital deduction, tax is *deferred,* not eliminated. Planning is needed for the eventual death of the surviving spouse, because that's when the big tax bite will hit.

USING THE LIFETIME EXCLUSION AND MARITAL DEDUCTION

If you and your spouse have, or expect to have, assets worth more than $1 million, you want to make sure your heirs get the maximum benefit of $1 million and don't lose it. If all your assets (including joint assets) are worth more than $1 million and you leave everything outright to your husband or wife, a substantial portion of the excess amount will be lost. Joint property owned by husband and wife may pass to the survivor at the death of the first spouse and will qualify for the estate tax marital deduction, but the benefit of the $1 million estate tax exemption equivalent will be lost. The survivor will wind up with more than $1 million, and subsequent heirs will be taxed for everything above that amount at estate tax rates as high as 49 percent.

The lifetime exclusion can be used to your advantage. Couples should *split their estates* and not have wills leaving everything outright to each other. Each spouse should create a "credit shelter trust" or "bypass trust" of the first $1 million of assets (the exempt amount) of which the surviving spouse can have use but which will pass tax-free to heirs when the surviving spouse dies. By this means, as much as $2 million can be sheltered from estate tax.

For example, if you and your spouse have $2 million in assets, you can divide the total between you, each then leaving up to $1 million in a trust for the benefit of the other. Upon the first spouse's death, the surviving spouse will have $1 million in assets and the use of $1 million in trust. At the latter's death, the $1 million in assets plus the remaining trust principal (including any growth) will pass tax-free to heirs.

Caution: These figures are based on the amounts excluded through 2003. See the chart on page 250 for the exclusion amounts in later years.

SELECTED TRUST STRATEGIES

A variety of strategies exist for minimizing the tax bite on your federal estate, such as the *qualified personal residence trust* (QPRT) or the *family partnership,* in which assets (your home or your business) transferred on a discounted basis during your lifetime can be used to leverage your annual exclusion gift rights and your $1 million lifetime exclusion. Strategies of this level of sophistication require consultation with a lawyer. Other strategies include the following:

Charitable deduction and the charitable remainder trust. There is no gift or estate tax imposed on gifts or bequests to charities. The *charitable remainder trust* is a device that allows you to put your property in trust for a charity while allowing you the income from the trust during your lifetime or that of your spouse or your child. Its chief advantage is that it minimizes estate tax and avoids capital gains tax. One disadvantage is that the principal is not available and cannot be invaded for possible emergency medical needs of the surviving spouse. Another is that your heirs won't receive the property.

The ideal way to use this device is to transfer your appreciated property to the charitable remainder trust now—allowing you to get the benefit of the charitable deduction immediately—have the trust sell the appreciated property, and reinvest the proceeds of the sale—unreduced by capital gains tax—in higher yielding investments so that the trust will pay you a higher return. For example, if you own a property worth $1 million, presently earning 2 percent, or $20,000, yearly and subject to eventual estate taxation, you can transfer the property, getting an annuity from the trust of between $60,000 and $90,000 depending on your age and life expectancy, and use the extra money to purchase a $500,000 life insurance policy. That way, you have the benefit of extra income, a charitable deduction, and when you die, your heirs will receive the same $500,000 inheritance.

Life insurance trust. Although it passes outside of your will and is not part of your probate assets, life insurance is part of your taxable estate. A useful device for removing life insurance from taxation is to assign it to an irrevocable life insurance trust. That way money available to the surviving spouse will not be taxed in his or her estate.

If you already own life insurance and assign it to a trust, you will be subject to a three-year rule during which period it may still be taxable. In that case, it may be possible for the trustee to buy a new policy, which will never have been in your estate. Whether this is desirable depends on the relative costs of your original policy and a new, more expensive one measured against the potential tax savings. You can make gifts to the trust to pay insurance.

QTIP trust. QTIP is an acronym for qualified terminable interest property. This kind of trust allows the testator, who sets it up, to provide for his or her surviving spouse *and* name the beneficiary upon the surviving spouse's death.

The QTIP trust qualifies for the marital deduction if a number of conditions are met, among them:

- The trust must distribute all income to the surviving spouse for life on at least an annual basis.
- The executor must make an irrevocable election to treat it as a QTIP trust.

Use of the QTIP trust is governed by a number of technical rules set forth in the law and IRS regulations. Like any other estate or trust instrument, this requires consultation with a lawyer expert in this area.

I'm happily married and plan on leaving my spouse a marital deduction share outright. Is there any reason I shouldn't?

It depends. A QTIP trust allows you greater control over the disposition of your assets. If you have children from a previous marriage, a QTIP trust is especially desirable for ensuring the eventual receipt of assets by children who might otherwise get nothing if your spouse decides to leave the funds to someone else when he or she dies. It is commonly used to protect the interests of children in the event of subsequent marriage by the surviving spouse.

INCOME TAXES

In the context of elder law, there are a number of income tax issues that may have an effect on your planning. These include

- Income tax on Social Security benefits
- Income tax on reverse mortgages
- Income tax on long-term care insurance benefits, and deduction for premiums
- Income tax on accelerated benefits from a life insurance policy
- Income tax on viatical settlement of a life insurance policy
- Income tax on estates
- Additional standard deduction for individuals over 65 or blind
- Tax credit for the elderly and disabled

Remember, this discussion is not intended as legal advice on your taxes. Only a competent professional familiar with your particular financial situation can counsel you.

Income tax on Social Security benefits. Social Security benefits are not subject to income tax liability except when your income exceeds a certain limit. As a general rule, you are liable for income taxes on a portion of your Social Security benefits if your "combined" income (including part of your Social Security benefits) is more than $25,000 (or $32,000 for a married couple).

The determination of whether you are liable, and if so, for how much, is a two-part calculation:

(1) Am I liable?

    The formula for determining whether your combined income meets the $25,000/$32,000 threshold amount adds together:

- Your regular adjusted gross income, tax-exempt interest, and one-half of your Social Security benefits. For this computation, include in your total Social Security benefits any Medicare premiums withheld from your check and worker's compensation pay.

    If the total exceeds $25,000 for an individual or $32,000 for a married couple, then a portion of your Social Security benefits will be taxable.

(2) How much am I liable for?

- You will be taxed on one-half the amount exceeding $25,000 (or $32,000 for a married couple) or one-half your Social Security benefits, whichever is less.

    If you make more than $34,000 (or $44,000 if you are a married couple), then you will be taxed on 85 percent of the amount exceeding that amount or 85 percent of your benefits, whichever is less.

For example, if a married couple filing jointly receives $17,000 in adjusted gross income, $12,000 in tax-exempt interest income, and $10,000 in Social Security benefits, their gross for determining tax liability for their Social Security benefits is $34,000 ($17,000 plus $ 12,000 plus one half of $10,000), making some portion of their Social Security liable for taxation. That portion is the lesser of the amount exceeding $32,000 ($2,000) or half their benefits ($5,000). Therefore, $2,000 is added to their $17,000 income, for a total of $19,000 that will be subject to federal tax.

Taxes on your Social Security benefits are subject to change, always hard to predict. A few states with income taxes also tax Social Security, usually linked to your federal return, although a smaller number of states treat benefits separately as taxable income. (See Chapter 20 for more on Social Security.)

I purchased annuities precisely because the interest was tax exempt. Now you're saying they can be included in my taxes? Is this legal?

Yes, this indirect taxation of your tax-exempt interest has been upheld by the courts. Technically, it's your Social Security benefits that are being taxed, but you're right that the tax-exempt interest boosts the base upon which your tax liability is calculated. If you have investment shelters, you should discuss with your accountant whether they are subject to this calculation.

Income tax on reverse mortgages. With reverse mortgages, older home owners can use the equity built up in their homes as collateral and receive lump-sum or periodic payments from a bank. As a general rule, these reverse mortgage payments are not taxable. (Nor will they affect your Social Security or your Medicaid benefits.) Make sure you consult a lawyer familiar with your state's regulations before getting a reverse mortgage.

(See Chapter 9, on reverse mortgages, and Chapter 21, on exclusion benefits available upon sale of your home.)

***Income tax on long-term care insurance benefits and deduction
for benefits.*** The cost of premiums for long-term care insurance can be
income tax deductions. Under the law, deductions are based on age:

- $230   for those 40 or less
- $430   age 40–50
- $860   age 50–60
- $2,290   age 60–70
- $2,660   over 70

The hitch is that the deduction is based on the general medical exemption
allowed for expenses that exceed 7.5 percent of adjusted gross income. It is
available only if you itemize expenses, and unless you have many health
expenses in the tax year, the deduction will be of little use to you.

Several states allow deductions, which may be geared to the federal
deduction. A few provide credits, such as New York, which will allow up to
10 percent of the premium paid on qualified plans approved by the state.

Whether or not premiums are deductible is based on whether the
plan under which you are being paid is a "tax-qualified" plan. The rule
is that qualified plan premiums are tax deductible; premiums paid
under unqualified plans are not. Similarly, benefits received under a
qualified long-term care policy are excludable. A tax-qualified policy is
one that bases eligibility for benefits on either the inability to perform
two ADLs or cognitive impairment. It has other requirements as well: It
may not limit or exclude coverage for type of illness, it must be guaranteed renewable, and it must offer nonforfeiture and inflation protection. (A non-tax-qualified policy is one that includes medical necessity
as a benefit trigger.)

Income tax on accelerated benefits and viatical settlements.
Accelerated benefits payments and viatical settlement payments are tax
exempt under present law. In order to qualify for the tax exemption,
your life expectancy must be less than two years. The viatical company
must comply with state laws, licensure, and other requirements. Many
states, such as New York, do not tax proceeds from accelerated benefits—or viatical settlements.

Income tax on estates. This is a tax on income of the estates during that window of time when the estate is being administered and the
assets have not yet been distributed to beneficiaries. Trust income is taxed
as well. The rules that govern the taxation of trusts are extremely complicated. Depending on the facts and the wording of the trust, trust income
may be taxed to the maker of the trust, the beneficiary, or the trust itself.

Additional standard deductions for individuals over 65 or blind. Taxable income is calculated by taking a taxpayer's gross income, making certain deductions to reach an adjusted gross income (AGI), then deducting personal exemptions and standard or itemized deductions.

The standard deduction, available to taxpayers who do not itemize their deductions, may be increased for individuals who are 65 or older and for individuals who are blind. For 2002 returns, the standard deduction allowed a married couple was $7,850 ($3,925 if filing separately). An additional deduction of $900 was allowed each spouse who is 65 or older, and an additional $900 to each spouse who is blind. For these purposes, your eye doctor or optometrist must certify that you cannot see better than 20/200 with corrected lenses, or that your field of vision is 20 degrees or less.

Both partners are entitled to the extra deductions if they meet the qualifications. A single taxpayer, granted a $4,700 standard deduction in 2002, would be entitled to an additional deduction of $1,150 for age and $1,150 if blind. (These amounts are indexed annually for inflation.)

To qualify for the additional deduction, you cannot itemize your deductions. If you are a married taxpayer filing separately and your spouse itemizes deductions, this will also disqualify you. Estates and trusts are not eligible for the standard deduction. (There is also no extra "exemption" for the elderly or the blind.)

Can I deduct payments I make on behalf of my aging parent or disabled child?

Yes, under certain circumstances. If you furnish more than 50 percent of the support of your parent or adult or infant child, you can deduct *all* the unreimbursed medical expenses incurred by that parent or child (to the extent that such expenses exceed 7.5 percent of your AGI). This applies whether or not the person's income exceeds the specified limit to allow you an extra exemption on your return. Remember, you cannot deduct itemized medical expenses and claim the standard deduction or the additional deductions available for individuals over 65 or blind.

Under this rule, you can deduct medical, dental, and prescription drugs expenses for any of the following relatives who qualify as your dependents by virtue of your providing more than one-half of their support:

- Your child, stepchild, adopted child, grandchild, or great-grandchild

- Your son-in-law or daughter-in-law
- Your parent, stepparent, parent-in-law
- Your grandparent or great-grandparent
- Your brother, sister, half sibling, stepsibling, brother-in-law, or sister-in-law
- Your aunt, uncle, nephew, or niece (if related by blood)

Your dependent must be a citizen of the United States or a resident of Canada or Mexico. A married person filing a joint return is generally not eligible to be your dependent.

Tax credit for the elderly and disabled. A tax credit is available to a taxpayer who is

- Sixty-five or older
- Retired on disability and permanently and totally disabled at the time of retirement

The credit is 15 percent of a base that may be as high as $5,000 for a single taxpayer or married taxpayer filing jointly (where only one spouse qualifies), $7,500 for married taxpayers filing jointly (where both spouses qualify), and $3,750 for a married taxpayer filing an individual return. For people qualifying as disabled, this base amount is limited to disability income.

The maximum credit available is $1,125. The credit is not available for single taxpayers with an adjusted gross income of $17,500 ($20,000 if filing jointly but only one spouse claiming eligible). If both spouses claim eligibility, the income limit is $25,000 (for joint returns; $12,500 if filing individually).

There's also no credit if nontaxable income, including Social Security, exceeds $5,000 for an individual, or $7,500 for a couple. In any event, the credit cannot exceed the individual's tax.

STATE TAXES

States often give tax breaks to their older taxpayers, commonly in the form of credits or deductions. These breaks may include a flat-rate income tax credit, a tax credit based on the size of your federal tax bite, a tax credit to older taxpayers, and an exemption for those 65 and older.

Some states also provide tax relief for those who support elderly relatives in their home. A few count only a portion of the income of people in continuing-care or nursing home facilities. Connecticut exempts owners over 65 from state tax on the sale of their homes. Often, too, states have specific tax relief programs for property taxes that allow reduced or deferred payments. (See Chapter 21 for a description of these plans.)

Taxes and tax programs change each year. With each election cycle come promises of greater relief from current tax burdens. It remains to be seen whether these promises will be kept and just who will reap the benefits of such changes.

Part 6

Working and Retirement

Recent years have seen a small revolution in work in the United States. In no small part due to the demographics of our aging population, the linear path from trainee to retiree has been replaced with a new and often bewildering maze of options. With the disappearance of mandatory retirement, many people want to work past traditional retirement age, and many more—in need of income or health benefits—have to work past retirement age. More than 21 million people over 55 are currently in the workforce. It's estimated that 4 million unemployed Americans over the age of 55 are ready and able to work.

These trends have had direct impact on older workers in a variety of ways, from changes in Social Security eligibility and benefits to cutbacks in, and increased cost-sharing for, benefits to employees and retirees to bankrupt companies and lost pensions. At the same time, there are more protections for workers than ever before, more options for retirees, and more safeguards for their families.

This section offers a short course on work and retirement issues that you may face. Chapter 18 explains laws designed to protect you on the job, offering advice on how to identify discrimination and what to do about it. Chapter 19 discusses some of the factors that go into your decision to retire, as well as your legal rights to benefits and pensions, and the protections you have against changes to them. In Chapter 20, we give you the grand tour of Social Security retirement and disability benefits, making sure you understand how to assert your rights in the complicated world of government benefits.

18

Protections in the Workplace

The older worker has long presented a contradictory image to American business. The "early retirement decade" of the 1980s reinforced a view of older workers as unproductive members of the workforce to be "riffed" (from "reduction in force") as soon as possible. At the same time, with 21 million people over 55 in the workforce and another 4 million unemployed and ready to work, public policy and legislation were based on a portrait of the older worker as offering significant benefits to his or her employer and to the nation's economy.

As this stronger, more positive portrait of older worker emerged, there was a noticeable shift in public opinion, in large part brought about by changes in employment practices and employment laws. Some labor-strapped companies showed renewed interest in older workers, offering part-time work, flex-time schedules, and retiree job banks. Laws at the federal, state, and local level recognized the disadvantages faced by older workers in their efforts to obtain and retain employment and sought to promote treatment of older persons based on their abilities rather than age, while prohibiting arbitrary discrimination.

The centerpiece of federal legislation affording older workers protection from age discrimination is the Age Discrimination in Employment Act (ADEA), passed in 1967. More than a quarter-century later, it has been joined by the Americans with Disabilities Act, offering new protections to older workers, and the Family and Medical Leave Act, entitling workers to needed leave for medical or family caretaking purposes. Numerous state and local laws, many patterned on these federal laws, provide different or stronger protections.

AGE DISCRIMINATION IN EMPLOYMENT ACT

Age discrimination? It's as old as Lear, forced out of the family business and into early retirement without a pension. Then as now, older workers were more vulnerable to loss of employment based on age stereotypes and arbitrary age limits unrelated to ability.

The nation's workforce has aged, becoming older (and more experienced) since 1967 when Congress passed the ADEA, thereby extending antidiscrimination protections to people from 40 to 65. Nearly half the country's workforce—70 million over age 40—are covered by the law's provisions. Current projections forecast that the number will increase 50 percent over the next two decades.

What was once revolutionary now passes unremarked. Virtually all states have laws on age discrimination of some sort or another, as do a number of local governments.

New laws on the books, however, do not translate immediately into changes in practice. Age discrimination accounts for more than one out of five complaints—about 16,000—filed against private employers before the Equal Employment Opportunity Commission (EEOC).

As a matter of fact, federal age antidiscrimination efforts get mixed reviews at best, largely due to enforcement problems. To its credit, the law has proven an effective curb on bias in corporate downsizing, but it has been largely ineffective at dealing with discriminatory hiring.

State and local laws often have different rules concerning what constitutes discrimination, to whom they apply, and where and when to complain. Ironically, some states offer greater protection than does the federal government, something that may be important for you.

YOUR RIGHTS UNDER THE ADEA

The ADEA of 1967, as amended, prohibits employment discrimination based on age against persons 40 years of age or older. The ADEA also forbids employers to do any of the following to employees or potential employees over 40:

- Fire or refuse to hire or otherwise discriminate with respect to compensation, terms, conditions, and privileges of employment on the basis of age
- Limit, segregate, or classify employees in any way that would tend to deprive any individual of employment opportunities or adversely affect his or her status, on the basis of age

- Retaliate for opposing an illegal practice or otherwise exercising rights established by the law

Basic cases under ADEA allege unfair treatment based upon age. Such treatment includes not only dismissals based on age but other adverse job decisions, such as demotion, withholding promotions, or not hiring based on age alone. It is illegal to discriminate in any aspect of employment, including hiring and firing; compensation, assignment, or classification of employees; transfer, promotion, layoff, or recall; job advertisements; recruitment; testing; use of company facilities; training and apprenticeship programs; fringe benefits; pay, retirement plans, and disability leave; or other terms and conditions of employment.

Within the basic prohibition, a number of exceptions have been carefully drawn. Examples of employer actions permitted under the ADEA include

- Firing an individual for good cause (for example, incompetence or insubordination). It is legal to discharge or otherwise discipline employees for good cause, regardless of their age. The ADEA offers no extra protections to employees who otherwise deserve to be fired.
- Laying off older workers as part of a wholesale reduction in force (RIF). Reasonable factors other than age may justify a decision that impacts older workers.
- Not hiring or promoting an individual because of failure to meet bona fide occupation qualifications. These are qualifications an employer has established as reasonably necessary to the normal operation of the particular business.

   It is up to the employer to justify an occupational qualification based on age. An employer must show both that the age qualification is reasonably necessary in that those over the given age are unable to perform the job competently or that individual assessments would be impossible or highly impractical. For example, an upper age limit might be justified for hiring or retiring airline pilots or traffic controllers.

How do I show my employer discriminated?

You have the legal burden to show intentional discrimination. To claim you were fired on account of age, you may establish a prima facie case of age discrimination by proving:

- At the time you were fired, you were a member of the class protected by the ADEA
- You were otherwise qualified for the position
- You were fired by the employer and
- The employer hired a younger replacement to fill the vacant position

The burden then shifts to the employer to show that you were rejected, or someone else was preferred, for a legitimate—and nondiscriminatory—reason. But you get another shot to show this is not so. In the recent *Reeves* case, the Supreme Court held that once an employer's reason has been eliminated as not being credible, discrimination may well be the most likely alternative explanation.

I work for a small employer. Does my employer have to comply with the law?

The Age Discrimination in Employment Act applies only to employers with 20 or more employees, working at least 20 or more calendar weeks.

Federal government is subject to the law, regardless of the number of employees. Labor unions and employment agencies are also regulated under the law.

Ironically, the law does not protect state employees from age discrimination. In a 2000 ruling, the U.S. Supreme Court held that Congress did not have the power to tell the states what to do with regard to age discrimination against their own employees. State employees alleging discrimination have to rely on the laws of the state against which they're bringing their claim.

Who qualifies as an employee or prospective employee?

Under the law, employees and potential employees are protected. You are not protected if you are an independent contractor or partner (although what qualifies as a partnership may be subject to interpretation).

Is all age discrimination banned or only discrimination against older people? What age group is protected under the law?

The good news in that there's no longer an upper limit on those covered by the Age Discrimination in Employment Act. The original upper age limit of 65 was first extended (to 70), then removed. Exceptions exist for those not covered by the act. For example, judges and elected state and local officials can be terminated at age 70.

However, there's still a lower limit, and if you're younger than 40, you are *not* protected by the ADEA. Discrimination against people who are 39 or 17 may be wrong, but it is not protected by the federal age discrimination laws. Some states and municipalities have age discrimination laws that cover a greater age range.

Can companies advertise for employees by age?

Employment notices or advertisements indicating any preference, limitations, or specification based upon age are prohibited under the law. Help wanted ads with terms like *girl, boy,* or *recent college grad* discriminate against older workers (and demean younger ones). The prohibitions on help wanted ads apply to employers, employment agencies, and labor organizations.

If a company against which you have a grievance publishes an illegal help wanted ad, hold onto it! In addition to forming the basis for a complaint, it may be of use as evidence should you file a complaint about improper firing or failure to hire.

Can companies ask how old I am?

Not before they hire you. The only preemployment question concerning age that is appropriate and legal is whether you are between 18 and 65. Once you're employed, age becomes an appropriate part of your employment record. (Note that questions asked of prospective employees are even more circumscribed by the Americans with Disabilities Act, discussed later in this chapter.)

Does the law apply to employee benefits?

Yes. A 1989 Supreme Court ruling in *Public Employees' Retirement System of Ohio v. Betts* interpreted the Age Discrimination in Employment Act as applying only to compensation, terms, and conditions of employment, not to so-called nonfringe benefit aspects of employment such as retirement plans. This ruling was overturned by the 1991 Older Workers Benefits Protection Act, which provides that an employer who has a benefit plan must provide equal benefits to older workers or incur the same cost as providing them to younger workers.

Can a company demand that I sign an agreement promising not to sue when I'm hired or when I'm retiring?

A dozen years ago, the answer was, unbelievably, Yes. Although the average employee has a bargaining position about as strong as that of a homeless person challenging the clauses of a standard lease, until 1991 the courts found these waivers and releases to be legal. In one restrictive ruling, the United States Supreme Court upheld a similar clause in an employment contract that mandated compulsory arbitration in lieu of an age discrimination lawsuit.

What's the point of a waiver? Theoretically, your employer confers valuable benefits on you in exchange for your "voluntary" departure. Even if you have a good age discrimination complaint, you've bargained it away.

Under the Older Workers Benefit Protection Act, the answer is still Yes, but only if certain conditions are met. The law sets out minimum criteria that must be satisfied before any waiver of a claim or right under the Age Discrimination and Employment Act will be considered a "knowing and voluntary" waiver:

- The waiver must be part of an agreement that is written in a manner understandable by you (or by the average individual eligible to participate).
- The waiver must specifically refer to rights and claims under the Age Discrimination in Employment Act.
- The waiver does *not* apply to any claims arising after the date you sign.
- The waiver must be in return for "consideration"—you must be getting something in addition to what you would be getting without any waiver.
- You must be advised in writing to consult a lawyer before signing.
- You must be given at least 21 days to consider signing—45 days if it's part of an exit incentive or other employment termination program being offered to a group of employees.
- You must be given a period of at least seven days to revoke your waiver—even after you've signed it.
- If it's an exit incentive or other employment termination program, you must be informed in writing of the class of individuals being covered, eligibility factors, applicable time limits, job titles and ages of everyone in the group, and ages of everyone in the same job classification or organizational unit *not* eligible or selected for the program.

AMERICANS WITH DISABILITIES ACT

A revolutionary event occurred in 1990 when the Americans with Disabilities Act (ADA) was signed into law. The ADA was designed to protect the rights of an estimated 43 million people with disabilities in the United States. This landmark civil rights law contains a sweeping design that mandates a range of protections in public accommodations, commercial facilities, transportation and communication services, and employment. Title I of the ADA sets forth employment protections that may cover older as well as younger persons with disabilities.

The protections of the ADA are not limited to older people. However, as disabilities increase with age in both number and severity, its impact is greater among older workers. According to the Health and Retirement Study conducted by the Institute for Social Research at the University of Michigan and the National Institute for Aging, the four most common reasons for leaving jobs were given as back problems, heart condition, diabetes, and chronic lung disease—all more prevalent among older workers.

One of the trickiest things about the new disability law is that many older people with a disability may not recognize it—or they may not consider themselves to have a disability. As a result, they also may not recognize discrimination when they encounter it.

Don't equate the term *disability* with major impairment. In fact, the law is written to reflect functional abilities, so you may have a limitation that qualifies you for ADA protection without realizing it.

Identifying discrimination. Remember that if you have a disability, you may face discrimination based on disability alone, not age. Or you may encounter discrimination for your disability coupled with age discrimination.

YOUR ADA RIGHTS

Title I of the Americans with Disabilities Act prohibits discrimination against any qualified individual with a disability, because of the disability, in regard to job application procedures, hiring, advancement, discharge, compensation, job training, and other terms, conditions, or privileges of employment. Employers may not discriminate against an individual with a disability in hiring or promotion if the person is otherwise qualified for the job.

The law applies to private employers with 15 or more employees. State government workers have felt the sting of a U.S. Supreme Court ruling holding that the ADA does not protect them, although their own state antidiscrimination laws may. The ADA prohibits discrimination in recruitment, hiring, promotion, compensation, training, assignments, evaluations, termination, layoff and recall, discipline, training, leave, and benefits. It also prohibits employers from limiting, segregating, or classifying an individual in a way that limits or otherwise denies job opportunities because of disability.

In order to be covered by the ADA, you must meet the statutory definition of disability. You are considered an individual with a disability if you

- Have a physical or mental impairment that substantially limits one or more major life activities or
- Have a record of such an impairment or
- Are regarded as having such an impairment

This impairment must cause a *substantial limitation* in one or more major life activities:

- Caring for oneself
- Performing manual tasks
- Walking
- Seeing
- Hearing
- Speaking
- Breathing
- Learning
- Working

This list is not exhaustive. Other examples of major life activities would include sitting, standing, lifting, and reaching.

By substantial, the law factors in the nature and severity of the impairment, its duration or expected duration, and its long-term impact or expected impact.

Under the ADA, an individual claiming disability discrimination must be qualified for the job. This means that you must

- Satisfy the requisite skill, experience, education, and other job-related requirements of the employment position and
- Be able to perform the essential functions of the job, *with or without reasonable accommodation*

This is the crux of the employment provisions of the ADA. The test is whether you can do the job. Once that test is met, if you need "reasonable accommodations" to accomplish that, they must be provided.

What are essential job functions?

These are the basic job duties you as an employee must be able to perform. In analyzing the basic functions and tasks required for your job, factors to consider include

- Whether the reason the position exists is to perform that function
- The number of other employees available to perform the same function or among whom the function is distributed
- The degree of expertise or skill required

What are reasonable accommodations, and when are they required?

If you have a disability, under the law, you are entitled to reasonable accommodations to enable you to enjoy equal employment opportunity:

- In the application process
- In performing the essential functions of the job
- In the benefits and privileges of employment

Reasonable accommodations may include modifications or adjustments such as job restructuring, part-time or modified work schedules, reassignment to a vacant position, buying or modifying equipment or devices, appropriate adjustment or modification of examinations, training materials or policies, and providing qualified readers or interpreters, as well as making facilities accessible to and usable by individuals with disabilities. It is your responsibility to inform your employer of your need for accommodation.

Reasonable accommodations are *not* required if they will cause an employer undue hardship to business operations in the form of significant difficulty or expense. In determining whether there is undue hardship on an employer, the following factors are considered:

- The nature and cost of the needed accommodation
- The overall financial resources of the employer, the number of persons employed, and the effect on expenses and resources

Expense alone does not constitute undue hardship.

What questions are permissible during a job interview? Can an employer question me about my need for reasonable accommodations?

No. Asking a prospective employee about disability is forbidden. Employers are restricted to asking whether the applicant can do the job—with or without a reasonable accommodation. They can ask about your ability to perform the job, but not whether you have a disability. Nor may they use tests that tend to screen out those with disabilities.

An employer's initial offer to you may not be conditioned on whether or not you need accommodation. After an offer is made, the question of whether an accommodation is reasonable may be discussed.

Can I be denied employment because of my spouse's disability?

No. The ADA also prohibits discrimination due to your relationship with a person with a disability. However, your employer is *not* required to provide accommodation for you to care for a disabled relative; it is the *employee* with a disability who is entitled to accommodation under the law. (You may be entitled to leave under the Family and Medical Leave Act, discussed later in this chapter.)

Can I be refused work because of concern about the effect on a company's health care costs?

According to the EEOC, which administers the employment portion of the ADA, the answer is No. Insurance cannot be used as a subterfuge to evade the purposes of the law.

Disabled employees must be given equal access to any health insurance provided to other employees. Distinctions may be made in broad categories, but there may not be a lower level of benefits for a specific illness such as diabetes, deafness, AIDS, kidney disease, or cancer. Exclusions based on experimental drugs and treatments are allowed.

If I have a covered disability, does that mean I have to be hired?

No. An employer is free to select the most qualified applicant available and to make decisions based on reasons unrelated to a disability.

What is an acceptable disability? Does mental illness count? Obesity?

There is no list of "acceptable" disabilities. Federal regulations define physical impairment as any "physiological disorder, or condition, cosmetic disfigurement, or anatomical loss affecting one or more of the following body systems: neurological, musculoskeletal, special sense organs, respiratory (including speech organs), cardiovascular, reproductive, digestive, genito-urinary, hemic and lymphatic, skin, and endocrine." A mental impairment may be any "mental or psychological disorder, such as mental retardation, organic brain syndrome, emotional or mental illness, and specific learning disabilities."

The law includes persons with visual, speech, and hearing impairments, cerebral palsy, epilepsy, muscular dystrophy, multiple sclerosis, diabetes, heart disease, cancer, HIV, or AIDS, as well as individuals with mental retardation, emotional illness, and some learning disabilities. The EEOC has said that under certain conditions, obesity may be a disability as defined by the law; however, it must be an impairment, as defined, and limiting to at least one major life activity.

Physical or emotional characteristics are not disabilities, nor is advanced age by itself, although conditions associated with age such as Alzheimer's, arthritis, cancer, diabetes, osteoporosis, and vision and hearing impairments may be. Alcoholism may also qualify as a disability. However, the ADA does not cover compulsive gamblers, kleptomaniacs, pyromaniacs, or people with sexual disorders.

Is age an impairment?

No. Advanced age, in and of itself, does not constitute an impairment under the ADA. However, various medical conditions commonly associated with age, such as hearing loss, osteoporosis, or arthritis, would constitute impairments within the meaning of the law.

Does the fact that I receive disability benefits qualify me as disabled?

The fact that you may receive disability benefits under any other program, such as Social Security or Supplemental Security Income (SSI), does not mean you are qualified under this law. All laws have their own definitions and eligibility requirements.

ENFORCING YOUR RIGHTS

The Age Discrimination in Employment Act is administered by the Equal Employment Opportunity Commission (EEOC), which also enforces the Americans with Disabilities Act's Title I provisions against employment discrimination on account of disability.

The EEOC is a federal agency, responsible for enforcing a number of equal employment opportunity laws and regulations. EEOC will investigate your charge of employment discrimination (under both the ADEA and ADA) and may litigate those charges, on its own or your behalf. This process also applies to complaints against labor unions and employment agencies, which are regulated under the ADEA.

A number of state laws also proscribe age discrimination. Whether to proceed through the state or federal system with a given complaint should be discussed with a lawyer. (See discussion of state discrimination laws, later in this chapter.)

Bringing a Complaint Before the EEOC

In order to bring a complaint of discrimination, either on the job or in applying for a job, you must file a charge with the EEOC. To do so, you need only allege that some act of discrimination has taken place, and you must specify the act, the date it occurred, and the law that was violated.

Notice and filing. You must file a charge of discrimination with the EEOC within certain time frames. There are strict deadlines that must be observed if you are going to preserve your claim.

Charges may be filed in person, by mail, or by telephone. The EEOC has 50 district and field offices that investigate and resolve charges of employment discrimination filed with it. Call 800/699-4000 to contact the nearest EEOC office.

Filing deadline. For both ADA and ADEA claims, you have the option of filing within the following time periods:

- 180 days after the alleged discriminatory act
- In states or localities with antidiscrimination laws, 300 days after the act, or 30 days after receiving notice that the state or locality (ADA only) has terminated its proceeding, *whichever is earlier*

In order to determine your filing deadline, you must first determine when your case arises (*accrues*). Figuring out when the discriminatory act occurred is not as clear as you may think. As a general rule, the clock starts running when you know (or should know) that you've been discriminated against.

This leaves some room for interpretation. Sometimes the clock doesn't start running until you actually discover you've been discriminated against (which may happen some time after your company acts).

Contents of complaint. The complaint must contain

- Your name, address, and telephone number (or complaining party)
- Name, address, and telephone number of employer
- Names of all persons who committed the act
- A record of specific events

The complaint must be signed and sworn to. It is not necessary to overstate your case. Resist the temptation to be dramatic; be brief and specific.

A charge may be assigned for priority investigation if the initial facts appear to support a violation of law. When the evidence is less strong, the charge may be assigned for follow-up investigation to determine whether it is likely that a violation has occurred.

EEOC Investigation

Upon receipt of your complaint, the EEOC opens a case file and conducts an investigation. (EEOC can seek to settle a charge at any stage of the investigation if the charging party and the employer express an interest in doing so. Some cases are immediately dismissed without investigation.)

As part of its investigation, EEOC staff will

- Interview you
- Notify your employer (or would-be employer) of your charge, and request relevant information
- Interview any other witnesses with direct knowledge of the alleged discrimination

When its investigation is completed, EEOC makes a determination that there either is or is not reasonable cause to believe discrimination occurred.

- If EEOC determines that the evidence shows reasonable cause to believe discrimination occurred, it will attempt to conciliate. Conciliation is a legal process that involves voluntary negotiation with the employer to persuade him or her to remedy the violation. If conciliation fails, EEOC may initiate a court action.
- If EEOC determines that there is no reasonable cause to believe discrimination occurred, it will notify both you and the employer—and issue you a *right-to-sue letter.* This means you may take the employer to court yourself (which is not possible without the right-to-sue letter).

If conciliation fails, must EEOC initiate a court action?
No. EEOC initiates very few court actions. Most charges are conciliated or settled, making further action unnecessary.
Who can file a charge of discrimination?
Any individual who believes that his or her employment rights have been violated may file a charge of discrimination with EEOC. In addition, an individual, organization, or agency may file a charge on behalf of another person in order to protect the aggrieved person's identity. If your case is not settled, and the EEOC, as is likely, does not initiate court action, you will usually be able to bring court action on your own behalf.
How long does it take for EEOC to process a complaint?
You may have to wait several months, perhaps more than a year. That's a long time at any age. Ironically, age discrimination complaints

used to have priority because charging parties had only two years from the time of the alleged discrimination to take offending parties to court. However, the Civil Rights Act of 1991 removed this time limit, and age discrimination cases—up to 16,000 claims annually—are no longer given priority.

The EEOC is also subject to strict budgetary constraints, which limits its effectiveness, and it brings only a limited number of cases to court itself. In response, many employers have established alternative policies for resolving discrimination and other employment complaints. Mediating employment disputes through other processes are discussed later in this chapter.

How long do I have to wait for the EEOC in order to sue?

You are required to go through the process before you can proceed to court on your own. You may, after 180 days have passed since you filed your claim, request that the EEOC issue you a right-to-sue letter. Once you receive a right-to-sue letter, you have 90 days in which to file suit. Under the ADEA, a suit may be filed at any time 60 days after filing a charge with EEOC, but not later than 90 days after EEOC gives notice that it has completed action on the charge.

If the EEOC dismisses my claim, can I still sue?

A charge may be dismissed at any point if, in the agency's best judgment, further investigation will not establish a violation of the law. A charge may be dismissed at the time it is filed if an initial in-depth interview does not produce evidence to support the claim. When a charge is dismissed, a notice is issued in accordance with the law that gives the charging party 90 days in which to file a lawsuit on his or her own behalf.

BACK PAY AND OTHER RELIEF

The available universe of relief that may be sought in an action includes

- Back pay
- Hiring, promotion, reinstatement, benefit restoration, front pay, and other affirmative relief
- Damages for actual pecuniary loss other than back pay (ADA only)
- Liquidated damages (ADEA only)
- Compensatory damages for future monetary losses and mental anguish (ADA)
- Punitive damages (ADA)

- Posting of a notice advising employees of rights under laws and the right to be free from retaliation
- Corrective or preventive actions to cure the source of the identified discrimination and minimize the chance of its recurrence
- Stopping of the specific discriminatory practice
- Remedies also may include payment of attorneys' fees, expert witness fees, and court costs.

In the 1980s, the EEOC collected more than $400 million on behalf of those claiming age discrimination.

Under the Civil Rights Act of 1991, employment discrimination on account of disability under the ADA may entitle you to compensatory damages, *if* it is shown that you were the victim of intentional discrimination. The total amount is limited by the statute and dependent upon the number of employees the company has:

15–100 employees $50,000
101–200 employees $100,000
201–500 employees $200,000
more than 500 employees $300,000

Can I get punitive damages for my ADA claim?
Punitive damages are designed not to compensate you for your injury, but to punish the offending employer. An award of punitive damages is made only in cases of intentional discrimination *and* where the employer's conduct was wanton, willful, or reckless.

The monetary limits of the Civil Rights Act, however, apply to monetary awards, whether they are for compensatory damages alone or for compensatory and punitive damages.

MEDIATING EMPLOYMENT DISPUTES

Many employers have adopted alternative methods for mediating complaints of discrimination and other employment disputes. For reasons including time, cost, and employee relations, both small and large employers use one or more alternative approaches for resolving disputes in order to achieve conciliation between the parties outside the EEOC and court process:

- *Mediation.* A process for resolving disputes in which a neutral trained person (from inside or outside the company) helps negotiate a mutually agreeable solution.

- *Arbitration.* A process similar to a legal challenge, in which the dispute is submitted to a neutral third party for decision, which is usually binding on the parties.
- *Fact finding.* A process in which a neutral person (from inside or outside the company) investigates and develops findings for use in resolving the dispute.
- *Negotiation.* A process in which employee and employer, each with the aid of counsel, discuss the dispute with the goal of coming to settlement.
- *Peer review.* A process in which employees (sometimes including managers) sitting as a panel hear and try to resolve employment complaints.

From an employee point of view, these methods have advantages and drawbacks. Time is the greatest advantage in that most alternative dispute resolution methods will prove faster than going through the EEOC. Very often, employees will have no choice in the matter, being bound to arbitration or another method by a collective bargaining agreement or by a waiver signed as a condition of employment.

Employer policies vary considerably in matters that have great importance, such as selection of the arbitrator or other neutral decision maker. Some call for employee participation in selection, while others provide for unilateral selection by the employer. Although many company policies are silent on the subject, you generally have a right to be represented by counsel or other representative of your choosing.

The ADA encourages the use of alternative means of dispute resolution. In 1995, EEOC established a voluntary program using mediation to handle some workplace discrimination charges as an alternative to a lengthy investigation. Under the program plan, complaining employees and their employers work with a neutral mediator. Participation in the mediation program is confidential, voluntary, and requires consent from both the charging party and the employer. If settlement cannot be reached through this process, the claim is returned to the regular EEOC process.

If I agree to mediation, do I waive my right to seek enforcement under the law?
You may. Many companies use arbitration, peer review courts, and other forms of alternative dispute resolution as "private courts" to allow rapid resolution of employment disputes. These forums do not necessarily apply the same laws or standards as the courts. Your agreement to submit your claim to mediation or arbitration may preclude you from

seeking relief in the courts. Provisions for alternative dispute resolution are becoming more common in collective bargaining agreements and employment contracts.

STATE DISCRIMINATION LAWS

All states have some sort of law banning discrimination on account of age. The specific prohibitions, enforcement mechanisms, and remedies available to the successful complainant vary from state to state.

Forty-six states, 40 localities, and the District of Columbia have established fair employment practices agencies to investigate employment discrimination. Most states have a system that parallels the federal structure. The state agency investigates complaints filed with it, and in appropriate cases will attempt conciliation or bring a court action against the employers. Some states have a dual system, with available forums in both an administrative agency and the state courts. New York has a dual system, as do New Jersey, Pennsylvania, Maine, Minnesota, Oregon, Idaho, West Virginia, and the District of Columbia. A few states allow only for private action.

Some jurisdictions have a work-sharing arrangement, in which case the charge may be processed initially by either EEOC or the state or local agency. The ADA requires that the EEOC defer charges of discrimination to state or local Fair Employment Practice Agencies (FEPAs). State agencies conduct roughly half of current investigations.

Different strategies bring different results. If you choose to go the administrative route before an agency, you may waive your right to pursue the matter in court. You'll want to consult with a lawyer before making any determination about how to proceed.

What do I do if I suspect that I'm the victim of discrimination?

- *Identify.* First of all, recognize it. The first step in combating age discrimination is being able to identify it.
- *Investigate.* You are your own best detective. Who knows better the whys and wherefores of your case? See what you can find out about your company's actions, which may have bearing on your claim, particularly any disparate treatment among you and your colleagues.
- *Document.* Make a paper trail. If at all possible, document your claim with written memoranda sent to you or by you. Keep a log of things said to you. Don't depend on your memory, and don't depend on the memories of witnesses. Although many cases rely

on indirect or circumstantial evidence, often on statistics culled concerning the treatment of other older workers similarly treated, direct evidence is always the best.

- *Get outside help.* Age discrimination is hard to identify, still harder to prove. Your best bet is to contact your local EEOC office or state agency. You may want to file a charge with EEOC or your state's human relations agency.
- *Get a lawyer.* Lawyers who specialize in this field are called employment lawyers. Call your local bar and ask for a referral. If you have a case, your lawyer will tell you. If not, he or she will tell you that, too. These are hard cases to win. Your lawyer will be able to help you determine whether to sue in state court or go to the EEOC, or whether you have a claim at all.

I believe that I've been discriminated against in my job because of my age, which is 30. Do I have any recourse?

Some states and municipalities have laws affording greater protections to a larger age range than the federal laws. For example, people 18 and over are afforded discrimination protection in Iowa, Kansas, Minnesota, New York, Oregon, Vermont, and the District of Columbia. Alaska, Connecticut, Florida, Maryland, Michigan, New Jersey, and New Mexico have no statutory age range. Check with your state human rights agency to see what protections your state offers.

FAMILY AND MEDICAL LEAVE ACT

The Family and Medical Leave Act (FMLA) was passed by Congress in 1993 in recognition of the need for greater balance between work and family life. The demands on American workers have increased steadily in recent years. The growing numbers of elderly dependent on working family members only added to that burden. In many cases older workers, particularly women, have been forced to leave the workforce in order to care for an older relative.

The law gives workers some assurance that they will not have to choose between meeting their obligations at home or on the job. If you qualify under its provisions, you must be granted up to 12 workweeks of unpaid leave during any 12-month period for one or more of these reasons:

- Birth or placement of a child for adoption or foster care
- To care for an immediate family member (spouse, child, or parent) with a serious health condition

- Medical leave when unable to work because of a serious health condition

In order to qualify, you must work for:

- Any public employer
- A private employer, engaged in commerce, with 50 or more employees working at least 20 workweeks in the current or preceding calendar year

And you must meet the following conditions:

- Have worked for a covered employer for a total of at least 12 months
- Have worked at least 1,250 hours over the prior 12 months
- Work at a location where at least 50 employees are employed by the employer within 75 miles.

Under the FMLA, the employee is entitled to this leave, with no loss of health or other benefits, and with job restoration when the leave is concluded. If you take a leave under the FMLA, you must be restored to your original job, or to an equivalent job with equivalent pay, benefits, and other terms and conditions.

The employer's obligation under this law terminates if informed by you that you will not return (although you may still be eligible for health insurance continuation coverage, as described in Chapter 6.)

What happens to my health care coverage when I go on a leave?

If you take a leave under the Family and Medical Leave Act, you must continue to get coverage under the same group plan that would have been provided if you remained at work. If you generally make a contribution to the costs, you would still be required to do so. You can decline coverage during your leave period without jeopardizing your right to be restored to full coverage on your return, but don't give up your health care coverage unless you will be receiving comparable coverage from another source. If you do not return to work at the end of your leave, your right to continuation coverage under federal law would be measured from that date. (See Chapter 6.)

My aunt is sick and needs care. Must I be granted leave to tend to her?

No. The biggest weakness of the act is that it mandates leave only for "an immediate family member." This is defined to mean an employee's spouse, son or daughter, or parents. You are not guaranteed leave to care for your aunt or uncle, or your in-laws, or your grandparents.

The narrow definition of parent and family member ignores the half of the entire problem for which the law was introduced, the working woman upon whom most of these duties invariably fall. If you are a member of the so-called sandwich generation, simultaneously taking care of children and parents, you are guaranteed leave from your job only if you are caring for your own mother and father, not your mother-in-law or father-in-law.

It remains to be seen whether having drafted the law this way will encourage more adult sons to take care of their own parents, with leave available to them. The law provides no relief for those thousands of women—dutiful daughters-in-law—for whom that will not be the case.

Can my employer count my paid vacation and leave time against the unpaid leave time due me under this law?

It's up to your employer and company policy. Remember, the law allows you a full 12 weeks of leave time.

My employer approved my leave for care of my elderly mother, but now keeps pestering me about her recovery. How do I deal with this?

You may be required to submit medical verification of your mother's health condition. However, your employer is not permitted to question you about the details of your family situation.

My mother has a chronic condition that doesn't require medical care. Can my employer deny me leave to care for her?

No. Chronic illness qualifies as a serious health condition under the law. You can space out your leave up to the 12-week limit; you need not take it as consecutive days.

I am a public school teacher. Can I get leave during the school term?

As a general rule, your leave must be taken in blocks of time when the leave is needed intermittently or is required near the end of the school term or semester. These rules apply for teachers and employees of local education agencies.

Enforcing Your Rights

It is unlawful for any employer to interfere with or deny you your rights under the FMLA. It is also unlawful to discriminate or discharge you for attempting to enforce your rights under this law.

The Family and Medical Leave Act is administered by the Department of Labor, Employment Standards Administration, Wage and Hours Division, which has issued regulations to help companies develop leave policies conforming with the law's requirements. For information on the FMLA or to file an FMLA complaint, individuals should contact the nearest office of the Wage and Hour Division, Employment Standards Administration, U.S. Department of Labor. (The Wage and Hour Division is listed in most telephone directories under U.S. Government, Department of Labor, or online at www.dol.gov/esa/public/whd_org.)

The law is relatively new, and thus far compliance has been spotty. Employers' implementation has been characterized by misinformation and disinformation about its requirements. Companies have failed to develop policies and procedures regarding leaves, and training has been nonexistent. In the first year of the law, the Department of Labor investigated 965 complaints, of which 60 percent were deemed violations. Nine out of 10 were settled in the employees' favor.

Case note: *Some federal courts have ruled that state employees are not protected under FMLA, a cruel injustice, similar to the Supreme Court's decisions exempting states from the reach of the ADEA and ADA. At this writing, the status of the FMLA is unclear in 13 states: Arkansas, Delaware, Iowa, Louisiana, Minnesota, Mississippi, Missouri, Nebraska, New Jersey, North Dakota, Pennsylvania, South Dakota, and Texas.*

STATE FAMILY LEAVE LAWS

Two-thirds of the states and the District of Columbia have enacted family leave laws for their residents. The federal Family and Medical Leave Act does not restrict or preempt these laws in any way. If your state's law is more generous than the federal one, then by all means make sure you assert your state rights in this regard. For example, your state's law may provide a greater leave period than the federal law or apply its law to employers with fewer employees. Depending on where you live, you may be able to coordinate your leave under both laws.

In addition, many corporations also have leave policies that are more generous than the federal law. And a number of government agencies allow reduced work schedules for employees under a *leave bank* or *leave pool* program. Check with your employer's human resources division.

19

Pensions, Benefits, and IRAs

Financial planners talk about the "three-legged stool" upon which your retirement income is based: savings and investments, Social Security, and pension.

Your pension is critical to how you will live after you retire. Your right to a pension, how your pension works, what changes may be made by your employer, its very security—all these are governed by laws with acronyms instead of names, such as ERISA, REA, and COBRA. These laws are your protection for your pension and benefits. Antidiscrimination laws also apply to your benefits.

There are many types of retirement plans, including defined benefit, pension, profit sharing, 401(k), multiemployer, ESOPs, 403(b) annuities, 457 plans, SEPs, SIMPLEs, IRAs, and ROTH IRAs. Some are employer provided, some are provided through small businesses, some you may purchase on your own. They are also vehicles that may be used to set aside tax-deferred compensation for use by individuals at their retirement.

Reform proposals offer a potpourri of rights, including a Pension Bill of Rights, guaranteed inclusion and fair treatment, increased funding requirements, portability, and protections against fraud and abuse.

A word about pension law. Your pension plan is a contract. Federal laws provide minimum requirements for pension plans in order to afford you basic protections. You and your employer are also governed by the terms and conditions of the contract, that is, your company's pension plan. This is an important point for you to understand. Your company's plan cannot restrict rights granted you under federal law, but it can be more liberal than the federal law and afford you additional rights that you can enforce.

This chapter focuses primarily on the pension plan rules set out by ERISA. In addition, we provide a quick tour of distribution rules for IRAs and qualified plans. Because of their tax benefits and ultimate tax consequences, it's important to understand how these plans work.

ERISA—THE LAW OF PENSION PLANS

A pension plan is basically a structure for investing money. Funds are paid by a company into a pension fund, which then invests it. Eventually, the invested funds will be used to pay monthly benefits to retirees, under specified conditions.

There are two kinds of pension plans:

- A *defined benefit plan* tells you what benefits the plan will pay out. The final amount may be based upon a percentage of your final year's salary or a flat rate that increases based on the number of years of service. Under this kind of plan, the company is wholly responsible for structuring the plan and funding it; the actual amount of money put into the plan each year can change.
- A *defined contribution plan* sets out how much money your employer will pay into the plan. The company puts a fixed dollar amount, often into a separate account on your behalf. Some plans allow employees to direct investment of their accounts. Defined contribution plans include stock option, profit-sharing, and 401(k) plans. In the typical 401(k) plan, an employer will make matching contributions to an employee's, and the employee decides on investment.

Defined benefit plans, common among the larger, older corporations in the United States, were once the accepted standard for pensions. They also proved to be the most vulnerable to mismanagement, underfunding, bankruptcies, and all the calamities that can affect companies.

Remember the Studebaker? Calls for government backing of pension benefits date back to the car manufacturer's collapse in the early 1960s. Thousands of workers lost their benefits when the Indiana factory closed its doors a few days before Christmas in 1963.

Ten years later, the result was the Employment Retirement Income Security Act of 1974 (ERISA). ERISA was passed by Congress to reform employee pension and welfare benefits programs by providing fiduciary standards for pension funds and some guarantee of benefits. The law requires that minimum standards be met in eligibility, participation, earning benefits, vesting, making claims, and disclosure of information. The Retirement Equity Act (REA) passed in 1984 and the Tax Reform Act (TRA) passed in 1986 amended ERISA rules on participation and vesting and added additional protections for spouses.

My company is setting up a defined contribution plan. How does this affect me?

With a defined contribution plan, you have no idea of what your benefit will be until you actually retire. And that benefit will be a function of the risk you took, not the company. Defined contribution plans are *not* insured by the Pension Benefit Guaranty Corporation.

From a practical point of view, investments in defined contribution plans tend to be conservative, and ultimately less profitable for workers. Since ERISA, companies have tried to reduce their risk by moving from defined benefit plans to defined contribution plans. When ERISA was passed, contributions to defined benefit plans were nearly twice those to defined contribution plans; since then, the balance has shifted in the other direction—payments to defined contribution plans now lead three to one.

YOUR RIGHT TO PARTICIPATE

The first step in establishing your right to a pension is to establish your eligibility and qualify for participation in your company's pension plan. You are a participant when you become a member of the plan. This is an absolute prerequisite for any legal claim to a pension.

A few general comments on your rights to participate in a pension plan:

- There's no legal requirement that your company have a pension plan.
- Even if your company has a pension plan, the law doesn't say that you must be covered. Pension plans usually cover categories of employees and may exclude certain positions. As many as 30 percent of lower-income workers can lawfully be excluded from a plan.
- Your company may have different plans for different employees. Make sure you know under which plan you're covered.
- If you are covered, you may be required to work for your employer for a period of one year before becoming eligible. The one-year

service requirement is usually measured as 1,000 hours during a 12-month period, although you may actually qualify with fewer than 1,000 hours, depending on the terms of your plan. (A two-year requirement may be imposed for plans with full and immediate vesting.)

- Once you are eligible, you must be allowed to become a member of the plan within six months or at the start of the next plan period, whichever is earlier.

The bottom line is, never assume you have pension coverage. Make sure of it. Make sure you know if your company's plan covers you. Make sure you know *which plan* covers you. Remember, there's no law that says you must be covered. And you must put in the time to qualify for participation.

Can my employer impose age requirements on participation in the company's pension plan?

If you're under 21, you may have to wait until six months after your 21st birthday (assuming you've worked for one year prior to that date). If you work for a tax-exempt educational institution that provides a plan with immediate 100 percent vesting, you may be subject to an age requirement of 26 years.

You cannot be denied membership because you're too close to retirement age. That's against the law.

Can I be excluded from coverage under my company's pension plan if other employees in the same job classification are eligible for the plan?

No. Although coverage may lawfully exclude categories of employees, no one person within a single category can be excluded from eligibility. You still have to put in the time to qualify for membership.

Can I waive participation in my company's plan?

Under the law, the company must allow you to participate in its pension plan if you are eligible. But that doesn't prevent a company from asking older workers to waive participation in the company's pension plan before they are hired. You may be caught between a rock and a hard place on this one. If you refuse, you may not get the job—and it would be a difficult age discrimination claim to prove. If you agree to a so-called voluntary waiver that meets the requirements of the Older Workers Benefits Protection Act, it will keep you from collecting benefits later.

Watch out for these one-sided negotiations. Remember, federal law provides that these waivers are revocable for seven days after you sign.

(For more on the Older Workers Benefits Protection Act, see age discrimination in Chapter 18.)

VESTING RULES

Participation in a pension plan does not by itself establish your right to a pension. Your legal right to receive a pension at retirement age becomes effective when the pension vests. Your pension vests after you have met a minimum threshold in length of employment as set forth in your employer's pension plan.

Before ERISA, vesting rules often provided for strict, sometimes onerous requirements before an employee could be eligible for pension. A requirement such as 15 or 20 years of full-time service without a break was not uncommon.

ERISA was passed in part to remedy just such injustices and to promote fairness. Vesting rules now provide for a maximum vesting period of

- *Five years:* 100 percent vested pension to an employee with five years of service or
- *Seven years:* graded vesting at a specified percentage after three years and the remaining percentage proportionately for each subsequent year or
- *Ten years:* 100 percent vested pension after 10 years (for union-negotiated multiemployer pension plans only)

These rules became effective in 1989; workers who retired prior to that date are subject to prior vesting requirements.

These are minimum requirements; plans can be more generous to employees. If the plan is "top-heavy," meaning that managers and owners receive more than 60 percent of benefits, the scheduling of vesting must be even quicker.

All plans must provide for vesting prior to retirement. Once your benefits have vested, they are yours. They cannot be taken away from you. The same is true for benefits due you as a surviving spouse. Once they are vested, they cannot be taken away from you. (We discuss survivor's benefits below.)

My employer says my "break-in-service" (a two-year absence after four years of work) counts against me, and I have lost all credit toward my pension. Have I forfeited my rights?

Probably not. Breaks-in-service are subject to special rules under ERISA. These govern when your pension credits may be reduced (for vesting and benefit accrual) and when your service prior to the break must be recognized by your employer when you return to work.

As a general rule, you can't forfeit vesting or benefit credit unless you've had five consecutive one-year breaks-in-service. Service prior to your break must be recognized unless you've had five consecutive one-year breaks, or consecutive one-year breaks equaling or exceeding the years of service earned before your break, whichever is greater. (If you are talking about a past break-in-service, be aware that some of these laws may have taken effect since the time of your break.)

A break-in-service shorter than one year cannot be counted against you. For most plans, this means the equivalent of 500 hours; if you work less than this amount, you may lose credits toward vesting as well as reducing your benefits later on. (Exceptions may apply for birth, adoption, and caring for a child.)

Protections may vary, depending on the terms of your plan. If you want to protect your pension benefits, make sure you examine your plan's break-in-service provisions, preferably *before* you take a break or reduce your hours. ERISA rules are minimum requirements designed to minimize the likelihood of your exclusion from your pension. Your company's plan may be more liberal.

What happens to my pension when I change jobs?

If you change employers before your pension has vested, you will probably lose all your pension credit, other than your own contributions. Most likely, you will not be entitled to a pension from this job when you retire. However, if you work in an industry that has negotiated an industry-wide pension plan, such as construction or trucking, your participation may continue as you change employers within the same industry.

RECEIVING PENSION BENEFITS

Pension plans generally provide for benefits paid out monthly over the lifetimes of participants and their surviving spouses. In this regard, ERISA requires that two options be offered you:

- *Maximum pension* gives you a life-only payout; the pension ends with your death.
- *Joint-and-survivor* gives you a pension at a fixed percentage (usually 80 percent) of a lifetime pension but pays your spouse from 50 to 75 percent of your pension if you die first.

Some pension plans offer other options. Your plan may give you the option of having it paid out over a fixed number of years or allow you to collect your money in a single lump-sum payment. A lump-sum benefit theoretically lets you invest the principal or shop for annuities to provide you a larger monthly income.

Lump-sum payments are based on actuarial tables that estimate how long you'll live and the anticipated investment earnings of the plan. A few observations about lump-sum payments:

- If your plan doesn't provide for lump-sum payment, your company can't be forced to provide it.
- Under the Retirement Equity Act, your spouse's agreement is necessary to authorize lump-sum withdrawal.
- If your total pension is $3,500 or less, your plan can require that you take in the form of a lump-sum payment.
- You will have to pay taxes on a lump-sum payment unless you roll it over into an IRA (as well as a special penalty tax if you're under 59 and a half). It must be a direct rollover; partial rollovers are also authorized under the law. You may also be able to roll it over to a new employer's pension plan. These should be discussed with your accountant, to avoid incurring unnecessary taxes or penalty.

My company's pension plan provides for "integration" of benefits. How does this affect me?

This is a raw deal. Despite your pension rights, an integrated plan may allow your employer to deduct a substantial portion from its expected payments, based on your anticipated Social Security benefits. By "integrating" with the federal system, many plans deduct as much as half the amount of the Social Security payment from employees' checks!

SURVIVOR PENSIONS

If your spouse has vested rights to a pension, then your rights to a survivor's pension in the event of his or her death are also vested. Under the Retirement Equity Act of 1984, you will collect a survivor's pension unless you have given a written waiver.

The amount of your survivor's pension must be 50 percent of the amount your spouse receives or would have received had he or she lived to retirement age.

I am separated and in the process of getting a divorce from my spouse. Will I have any entitlements to my ex-spouse's pension?

Under federal law, none. But your divorce is governed by state law, your spouse's pension is property, and the terms of your separation and divorce are subject to negotiated agreement and judicial decree. A court order can direct your spouse's pension plan to pay a share of your spouse's pension benefits directly to you. It may also provide for survivor benefits in the event of your spouse's death.

MAKING A CLAIM

Your pension plan has a claims procedure for filing a claim for benefits. It is your responsibility to file a claim in accordance with your plan requirements. According to ERISA, the claims procedure must be included in the plan summary you are given.

ERISA requires that your plan must respond to your written benefits claims. Within 90 days, you must be provided with either notice of a decision or notice of a 90-day extension.

If your claim is approved, you will receive the benefits you claim. If it is denied, the decision must state the reasons and make reference to the provision in the plan upon which the denial is based. If you don't get an answer within the 90-day statutory time frame, you can treat that as a denial also.

If the decision is not in your favor, you will have to take action to enforce your rights by appealing the decision. A process for appeals will also be included in the plan summary you are given. (Plan summaries and appeals are discussed in the next section.)

GETTING INFORMATION ON YOUR PENSION

The first step in enforcing your rights is knowing what they are. ERISA sets forth detailed requirements concerning information and disclosure about pension plans to plan participants.

- *A summary plan description* that outlines requirements for participation, accrual of benefits, vesting, conditions of forfeiture, and procedures for claims and remedies, must be given to you within 90 days after your coverage begins.
- *A summary of any material amendments* will be provided in the year following the year the plan was changed. If there are changes, you'll get an updated summary plan description, supplied every

five years; if there are no changes in the plan, the plan description is due every 10 years.

- *A summary annual report.*
- *A statement of the nature, form, and amount* of deferred vested benefits after your employment has ended, and information on pension plan survivor coverage will be furnished by the plan administrator to each plan participant.
- *A statement of benefits accrued and benefits vested,* if any, or the earliest date on which accrued benefits will become vested must be furnished by your plan administrator on your written request. This statement need only be provided once in a 12-month period. (This requirement doesn't necessarily apply to multiemployer plans.)
- *Additional copies of the latest updated summary plan report, the latest annual report, and documents* under which the plan was established or operated such as plan rules or trust agreement must be supplied by your plan administrator within 30 days of your written request. Be prepared to pay reasonable costs, which the law allows.

Summary plan descriptions, financial reports, and other documents must also be filed with the Department of Labor in Washington, D.C., where they are available for inspection. Copies may be purchased for a per-page charge. Write the Department of Labor, Public Disclosure Room, 200 Constitution Avenue NW, Washington DC 20210, or call 202/523-8771 or a regional office.

Be informed! Read your plan! The summary description will tell you your plan requirements, eligibility rules, and other information that will allow you to be an informed participant and enable you to ensure that you receive the benefits due you.

APPEALING A CLAIM DECISION

If your benefits claim is denied, the denial must state the reasons and make reference to the provision in the plan upon which the denial is based. You can appeal that decision according to the procedures set forth in your plan.

You have 60 days from receiving your notice of denial to appeal the decision. You must appeal in writing, and your appeal should contain your reasons for believing the denial is wrong, along with copies of supporting documents. Pay attention to the reason given for the denial and the provision quoted in the claim decision, and respond to them. Keep copies of anything you send.

This process is called a *fair review*. There is no requirement under ERISA that you be allowed to appear in person, although your plan can grant you that right. Some plans authorize the use of alternative grievance or arbitration procedures for the claims process. If yours is one of them, you may invoke that process, but make sure you don't waive any rights you have to review by the courts.

You are entitled to a decision within 120 days from the plan's receipt of your appeal. (The 120-day time is applicable to most plans). If the appeal decision upholds the denial of your benefits, it must state the reason and make reference to the provision of the plan upon which it is based. This will be important for subsequent legal action.

You may appeal a claim denial in court, if you have first exhausted your remedies through the administrative process. Whether this should be state or federal court likely depends upon the basis for your claim, which may be noncompliance with ERISA provisions or violation of contract provisions in your pension plan.

You will want to consult a lawyer experienced in pensions and benefits. Issues concerning interpretation of ERISA will go to federal court; if you're claiming that legal obligations of the contract are not being met, you will probably sue for compliance in state court. As a federal law, ERISA preempts state rules, and its rules will be applied in either court.

PENSION PLAN TERMINATIONS

Under ERISA, defined-benefit pension plans are required to pay insurance premiums to the federal Pension Benefit Guaranty Corporation. This means that if your employer goes out of business or terminates your pension plan, you may have some benefit protection.

The Pension Benefit Guaranty Corporation insures more than 100,000 pension plans with assets totaling $1 trillion. Whether there will be remedies available for you depends on what kind of pension plan you have and whether your pension has vested.

- Participants in defined-benefit pension plans whose pensions have vested will receive all or some of their pension benefits.
- The protection of the Pension Benefit Guaranty Corporation does not extend to benefits that have not vested.

- Defined-contribution plans are not insured or protected; the account is already in your name and the investment risk is yours.

For pension plans terminating in 2002, the maximum guaranteed amount will cover you up to $3,579.55 a month ($42,954.60 yearly, adjusted for inflation). However, a number of limitations make this less generous than it first appears:

- Benefits are insured for the full amount only if they have been in existence and unchanged for more than five years.
- The maximum monthly payment must be reduced if your benefit is paid or payable to you before age 62, or is paid in a form other than an annuity for your life alone (such as the traditional joint-and-survivor payout).
- Insurance protections are for "basic benefits" only. They do not cover anything else: medical, disability, death, and other benefits are not protected.

ERISA requires that the Pension Benefit Guaranty Corporation be self-financing. However, the corporation, which finances its operations from terminated plans, employer premium payments, and investment, is criticized as being underfunded itself. Under federal law, the United States government is *not* responsible for any obligation or liability incurred by the corporation.

I work as a schoolteacher. How secure is my public sector pension?
An estimated $1 trillion is in public sector pensions ranging from the grossly underfunded to those with large surpluses. These funds are not eligible for insurance by the Pension Benefit Guaranty Corporation. The pensions of public employees must rely on the soundness of their government, whether state, municipal, or other locality.

State governments can't go bankrupt, but cities can. So can school districts. Public pension funds are also vulnerable to invasions for balancing state budgets, as well as questionable investments for public works.

How safe is an underfunded plan?
A pension fund does not actually have to be 100 percent funded to be self-sustaining. After all, not all beneficiaries will draw benefits simultaneously (except in the case of a bankruptcy). At the same time, the average retirement age has dropped to 62 while the average length of retirement—the time retirees will be drawing benefits—has lengthened

294 The Complete Retirement Survival Guide

to 20 years. It's been estimated that fully one-third of companies declared underfinanced are in trouble.

My company switched from its pension plan and bought annuities. Is my pension safe?

Many annuities are bought by pension plans for plan participants; terminating pension plans are *required* to buy annuities for all participants. As a general rule, individuals in pension plans have no say in which insurance company gets the annuity contract. Often, they don't even realize where their checks are coming from. If you're receiving or counting on insurance-backed annuities for retirement, remember that the switch to annuities will cut you off from Pension Benefit Guaranty Corporation protection. Some coverage may still be available under state insurance guaranty funds.

BENEFITS AND WELFARE PLANS

Health benefits, offered after World War II as a way of giving extra benefits to employees restricted by wage freezes, became a common part of employment packages in the 1950s and 1960s as a result of collective bargaining gains. Since that time, benefits have been extended to retirees as well as active employees, in packages as varied as the capitalistic landscape. Benefits offered by employers have included hospitalization and surgery, sickness, accident, death, disability, unemployment, day care, scholarship, legal services, holiday, severance, and training.

At the time ERISA was passed, concern was focused on pensions. Yet ERISA also applied to welfare plans, defined as

> . . . any plan, fund, or program established or maintained by an employer or an employee organization for the purpose of providing medical, surgical, or hospital benefits, or other "fringe benefits" through insurance or otherwise.

Under ERISA, employers who provide welfare benefits are held to these requirements:

- Reporting and disclosure standards, including a mandate that employees be given a summary plan setting forth their rights
- Claims procedures (see description in the preceding section)

However, the protections afforded by ERISA for pension plans were not duplicated for health benefits. Health and welfare benefit packages do not have any legal requirements ensuring minimum capitalization, vesting rules, or guarantees. Benefits are subject to antidiscrimination laws to ensure they are equal for older and younger workers.

CHANGING EMPLOYEE BENEFITS

Employers can change their health benefit plans, so long as they reserve the right to do so in either the benefit plan documents or collective bargaining agreements. Court opinions have upheld the right of companies to alter or amend health care benefits under ERISA. Almost all employers have done so.

What is the net effect for you? Read your plan. The courts have said that the right to change depends on the plain language in the plan. Many plans contain express reservations by the company of its right to change or terminate the plan. Courts have been reluctant to look at other evidence. But if the language in the plan is ambiguous, other evidence may be referred to, such as oral statements and brochures. Under limited circumstances, benefits may "vest" when you retire.

Can my employer cancel health care benefits?

Unless you have a contract or collective bargaining agreement that provides to the contrary, the answer is Yes. With rising health care costs, health and welfare plan modifications are subject to change and more change. Change one year may beget change the next year. Your employer may shift costs by various strategies, such an increasing your contributions toward insurance premiums, eliminating specific benefits such as prescription drugs, or terminating your health benefits entirely (a far less likely possibility).

Am I protected under a self-insuring health benefit plan?

An increasing number of small to medium-sized companies are "self-insuring" their health plans, primarily to avoid taxes on premiums as well as state-mandated coverage. Large firms have generally always been self-insured. Your protection is as good as the soundness of your company. State health care reforms in this area have been largely unsuccessful, ironically because ERISA's authority over employee benefit plans has preempted state regulation.

Can my former employer cancel my health care continuation coverage?

Your continuation coverage can be terminated only if your former employer stops coverage for all active employees. Group health plans are required to provide former employees increased opportunity to have their health care coverage continued, under ERISA amendments contained in the Consolidated Omnibus Budget Reconciliation Act (COBRA).

COBRA applies to medical benefits provided by insurance or any other mechanisms including trusts, self-insured plans, reimbursement, and health maintenance organizations. Medical benefits may include inpatient and outpatient hospital care, physician care, surgery and other major medical, prescription drugs, and other medical benefits such as dental and vision care. COBRA does not apply to life insurance. (For an explanation of continuation coverage, see Chapter 6.)

Can my employer cancel my health care benefits or switch me to continuation coverage when I am on leave under the Family and Medical Leave Act?

No. Under this law, the employer must continue your coverage under the same group plan, as if you were still working. If you notify your employer of your intention not to return to work, then your right to continuation coverage would kick in.

RETIREE BENEFITS

Retiree benefits took a hit with the imposition of a change in accounting standards by the Financial Accounting Standards Board in 1990. Under the new standards, employers were required to accrue and disclose retiree health benefit liabilities in their financial statements. This spurred employers to reduce liabilities and control growth by cutting their retiree health benefit costs.

The standards didn't affect how much employers paid for health care benefits nor did it require them to set aside any given amount or percentage. But health care costs were reflected as a bottom-line liability. And health care costs for early retirees cost as much as four times as much as the same health care provided through Medicare.

Are your benefits secure? Can they be cut back? Under the right circumstances, and within the law, they can be modified or totally eliminated. In a recent survey by the Commonwealth Fund, more than half the employers reported expecting to reduce benefits for future retirees.

I'm a retiree. What happens to my health care coverage if my former employer goes out of business?

As your employer goes, so go your health benefits. If the company goes out of business or ends coverage for its current employees, you are not protected.

What happens if my former employer goes bankrupt?

Under the Retiree Benefits Protection Act of 1988, retirees' health benefits are given priority status in bankruptcy cases. Moreover, a company in bankruptcy cannot change a plan without consent of the retirees' representatives or unless ordered by the court. (This is not as good as it sounds, however. Judges have been more willing to approve change than retirees would like. And this protection does not apply to banks and insurance companies, which are subject to separate state regulation.)

You may still be eligible for COBRA continuation coverage if your former employer is a subsidiary of another company that still provides group health benefits for its employees.

IRA AND RETIREMENT PLAN DISTRIBUTIONS

The basic outline for distributions from IRA and other tax-deferred retirement plans such as 401(k)s, 403(b)s is clear. You can withdraw as much as you like from your plan, as long as you pay the tax, starting at age $59\frac{1}{2}$. You must begin withdrawing money by April 1 of the year following the calendar year in which you turn $70\frac{1}{2}$.

The old rules forced people to make decisions at age $70\frac{1}{2}$ that would bind their finances in future years despite the fact that financial circumstances change. Determinations concerning life expectancy and designated beneficiary determined minimum distribution calculation for individual accounts were complex.

Under the new rules, calculating the amount is simpler, and the pace of withdrawals has slowed considerably. The latest rules, effective January 1, 2003, apply to IRAs and qualified employer-sponsored plans; similar rules are expected for government and nonprofit organizations.

A required distribution will be the amount of the assets divided by the years of the life expectancy. How that life expectancy is calculated decides whether you must pull out all your savings right away, with severe tax consequences, or whether you can wait longer and stay in a lower tax bracket. New tables for account owners and beneficiaries have been issued to more accurately reflect the actuarial realities. Account owners may use the Uniform Lifetime table on page 299, with some exceptions. Owners whose spouses are more than 10 years younger should consult the Joint Life and Last Survivor Expectancy Table, issued in IRS publication 590. The Single Life Expectancy table on pages 300–301 should be used by beneficiaries to determine their required minimum distribution.

If you have a company plan, which is a qualified plan, and you are still working, this date can be delayed until April 1 of the year following the year in which you retire.

Remember that funds in retirement plans may be counted as resources for purposes of Medicaid, while distributions may be considered income. For more, see Chapter 9.

Choosing designated beneficiaries. Once an account owner reaches 70½, minimum distributions of the amount in the plan are determined by consulting a single life expectancy table. Withdrawals are based on an assumption that the eventual beneficiary will be someone at least 10 years younger than the plan owner. With a longer period over which to take distributions, most owners will lower their required minimum distribution amounts.

The rules are even more favorable for spouses. Those who choose their spouse as their designated beneficiary will be allowed to use their actual ages for life expectancy determinations.

The new rules also make it easier for a trust to be named as a designated beneficiary. (Beneficiaries must be identifiable from the trust instrument, which must be a valid trust under applicable state law.) This applies to both living and testamentary trusts; the trust must be irrevocable or become irrevocable upon the death of the employee.

As of the 2003 rules, the final designated beneficiary doesn't have to be selected until September 30 of the year following the plan owner's death. Although estates are not allowed to just name new people as beneficiaries, those who are beneficiaries may opt out in various ways, for tax purposes.

What if my account doesn't have a designated beneficiary? What happens then?

The beneficiaries of your estate will be able to take minimum distributions over the remaining life expectancy of a living individual the same age as the account owner at death. Of course, this only applies to deaths after age 70½. For accounts whose owners die before minimum distributions are required, the "five-year rule" applies.

Spouse rollover. A surviving spouse may elect to treat an inherited IRA as his or her own IRA. The premise is that the surviving spouse could have received a distribution of the entire decedent IRA owner's account and rolled it over to an IRA established in the surviving spouse's own name as IRA owner.

This election is deemed to have been made if the surviving spouse contributes to the IRA or does not take the required minimum distribution for a year. This deemed election is permitted to be made only

UNIFORM LIFETIME
(For Use by Owners)

Age	Distribution period	Age	Distribution period
70	27.4	93	9.6
71	26.5	94	9.1
72	25.6	95	8.6
73	24.7	96	8.1
74	23.8	97	7.6
75	22.9	98	7.1
76	22.0	99	6.7
77	21.2	100	6.3
78	20.3	101	5.9
79	19.5	102	5.5
80	18.7	103	5.2
81	17.9	104	4.9
82	17.1	105	4.5
83	16.3	106	4.2
84	15.5	107	3.9
85	14.8	108	3.7
86	14.1	109	3.4
87	13.4	110	3.1
88	12.7	111	2.9
89	12.0	112	2.6
90	11.4	113	2.4
91	10.8	114	2.1
92	10.2	115 and over	1.9

Source: IRS publication 590

SINGLE LIFE EXPECTANCY
(For Use by Beneficiaries)

Age	Life expectancy	Age	Life expectancy
0	82.4	30	53.3
1	81.6	31	52.4
2	80.6	32	51.4
3	79.7	33	50.4
4	78.7	34	49.4
5	77.7	35	48.5
6	76.7	36	47.5
7	75.8	37	46.5
8	74.8	38	45.6
9	73.8	39	44.6
10	72.8	40	43.6
11	71.8	41	42.7
12	70.8	42	41.7
13	69.9	43	40.7
14	68.9	44	39.8
15	67.9	45	38.8
16	66.9	46	37.9
17	66.0	47	37.0
18	65.0	48	36.0
19	64.0	49	35.1
20	63.0	50	34.2
21	62.1	51	33.3
22	61.1	52	32.3
23	60.1	53	31.4
24	59.1	54	30.5
25	58.2	55	29.6
26	57.2	56	28.7
27	56.2	57	27.9
28	55.3	58	27.0
29	54.3	59	26.1

SINGLE LIFE EXPECTANCY
(For Use by Beneficiaries)

Age	Life expectancy	Age	Life expectancy
60	25.2	86	7.1
61	24.4	87	6.7
62	23.5	88	6.3
63	22.7	89	5.9
64	21.8	90	5.5
65	21.0	91	5.2
66	20.2	92	4.9
67	19.4	93	4.6
68	18.6	94	4.3
69	17.8	95	4.1
70	17.0	96	3.8
71	16.3	97	3.6
72	15.5	98	3.4
73	14.8	99	3.1
74	14.1	100	2.9
75	13.4	101	2.7
76	12.7	102	2.5
77	12.1	103	2.3
78	11.4	104	2.1
79	10.8	105	1.9
80	10.2	106	1.7
81	9.7	107	1.5
82	9.1	108	1.4
83	8.6	109	1.2
84	8.1	110	1.1
85	7.6	111 and over	1.0

Source: IRS publication 590

after the distribution of the required minimum amount for the account, if any, for the year of the individual's death.

Election is permitted only if the spouse is the sole beneficiary of the account and has an unlimited right to withdrawal from the account. This requirement is not satisfied by a trust named as beneficiary of the IRA, even if the spouse is the sole beneficiary of the trust.

Except for the required minimum distribution for the year of the individual's death, the spouse is permitted to roll over the post-death required minimum distribution for a year if the spouse is establishing the IRA rollover account in the name of the spouse as IRA owner. However, if the surviving spouse is age 70$\frac{1}{2}$ or older, the minimum lifetime distribution must be made for the year, and because it is a required minimum distribution, that amount may not be rolled over. The election by a surviving spouse eligible to treat an IRA as the spouse's own may also be accomplished by redesignating the IRA with the name of the surviving spouse as owner rather than beneficiary.

Are distributions being reported to the IRS?

When the new law was first passed, it required IRA trustees to report minimum distributions from accounts to the IRS as well as to the IRA owner. Beginning in 2004, these will not have to be reported to the IRS.

20

Social Security and Disability

The odds are that you're either paying Social Security or getting Social Security. If you're not, someone in your household is. Social Security affects nearly everyone in the United States. In 1999, 44 million people collected Social Security benefits totaling $385 billion.

Is it welfare? Is it insurance? A pension fund? The history of social security dates back to Otto von Bismarck, who as chancellor of imperial Germany in the latter part of the 19th century instituted a state system of "social security" for Germans over 70 years old. Bismarck's adoption of the biblically sanctioned "threescore and ten" as the benchmark for when retirement benefits would begin was later changed by officials to age 65. Social Security was the law in most European nations long before the New Deal made it a reality in the United States in the 1930s.

According to Labor Department reports, 56 percent of the 32 million current retirees 62 and older depend entirely on Social Security for their income. And almost 3.5 million of those receiving Social Security and private pensions get less than $10,000 yearly.

With corporate cutbacks in staff and only half of today's workforce employed by companies with pension plans, and only a quarter of those entitled to future benefits, that three-legged stool of retirement planning is looking a little wobbly. For many lower-income workers, it's already collapsed; an estimated 42 million workers don't have pensions. Social Security represents 100 percent of their retirement plan.

Today's Social Security system is not only a provider of retirement income for the worker. Social Security also provides

- Retirement benefits for spouses of workers
- Disability benefits to disabled workers and their dependents
- Survivor benefits to spouses and children of deceased workers
- Supplemental Security Income (SSI) for low-income people 65 and over, or blind and disabled individuals of any age

Social Security is financed by taxes on employers and employees. (The SSI portion is funded from general revenues.) Problems raised by an aging workforce and a reduced labor pool make the financial structure uncertain. When Social Security was enacted in the 1930s, there were 40 workers for each retiree. By 1950, that figure had dropped to 15 workers. Today, there are just three workers for each retiree; by the year 2030, there will be only two workers for each retiree.

Critics predict that the Social Security disability fund will be in deficit in 2023 and that the pension fund will go broke in 2039. More optimistic estimates forecast that Social Security will continue, relying less on trust fund surpluses and more on pay-as-you-go financing.

Although there have been modifications to Social Security law in recent years (eliminating earning limits for workers over 65, for example), calls for wholesale change in Social Security have been met by resistance on behalf of those across the economic spectrum who feel their financial future threatened. Proposals to impose some form of means testing or include private accounts continue to be debated.

SOCIAL SECURITY ELIGIBILITY AND BENEFITS

Eligibility for Social Security is determined by *credits*. As a worker, you earn Social Security credits up to a maximum of four per year. The general rule is that you need 40 credits, representing 10 years of work, to qualify for benefits.

The amount of money you have to earn to qualify for credits goes up each year. For example, in 2003, one credit is earned for each $890 in earnings. Credits used to be called "quarters," referring to the quarter-year theoretically represented by each. The four credits need not be spread out over four quarters, however, but can be earned any time over the calendar year.

Your benefit is figured to give you an average of 42 percent of your lifetime working income. (This figure is applicable to a worker with average earnings. The earnings-replacement rate is different for low, average, and maximum earners. Because the benefit formula is weighted to favor lower-income workers, with theoretically less opportunity to save and invest, the percentage is higher for them and lower for people in higher-income brackets.)

The formula is very complicated; here is a brief summary. Benefits depend on your average monthly earnings, figured over a number of years. The number of years of earnings is used as a base. That number is figured at 35 for retirement benefits. (For disability and survivor benefits, your actual record is used.) Earnings are adjusted for inflation, and then your average adjusted monthly earnings are determined according to the base number of years. This is then multiplied by a fixed number set forth in the law.

It's difficult to predict exactly what you'll get because of any number of factors, including future benefits adjustments, related congressional action, and your own uncertain future earnings. Social Security will provide you with an estimate of your future benefits, but it will be a rough one at best. As you approach retirement age, the estimate will better approximate the benefits you will actually receive.

Your personalized estimate will include an accounting of

- Earnings history and amount paid in to Social Security
- Estimates of retirement benefits at ages 62, 65, and 70
- Estimates of survivor and disability benefits

To request an estimate, ask for Form SSA-7004, Request for Earnings and Benefits Estimate Statement, from your local Social Security office, or call toll free to 800/973-2000.

Social Security sends annual statements to people over 25 who are not yet collecting benefits.

Make sure you check your records! If there's an error and you're not receiving credit for time you've worked, you want to correct it in time. We recommend checking the record at least once every three years.

How exactly is my benefit calculated?

By a complicated formula. Your earnings since 1951 are adjusted for changes in average wages over the years to make them comparable with current earnings. Earnings are adjusted for each year up to the year you reach age 60. From this list, the 35 highest years of earnings are selected to figure your benefit. The earnings for these years are totaled and divided by 420 (the number of months in 35 years) to get your average monthly earnings.

This is the number used to figure your benefit rate. A three-level formula, readjusted each year for people reaching 62, is applied to your average monthly earnings to arrive at an actual benefit rate. A fixed dollar amount of your monthly earnings (the amount itself changes each year) is multiplied by 90 percent, a larger amount by 32 percent, and any remaining amount by 15 percent. The total is your basic full retirement-age benefit rate. Whether you retire at 62 or later, the formula used is based on the year you turn 62.

RETIREMENT AND EARLY RETIREMENT

The retirement age for Social Security purposes is an artificial construct, chosen by legislators with their eye on the bottom line. When Bismarck picked 70, the average life expectancy in Germany was 45 years. When the Social Security Act was signed into law by President Franklin D. Roosevelt, the average life expectancy in the United States was 61.7. Today's life expectancy exceeds the statutory retirement age by more than a decade.

When are you eligible? It depends on when you were born. You are eligible for your full retirement benefit at age 65, *if* you were born before 1938. For those born after 1938, the full benefit age was increased starting in the year 2000:

Year of birth	Normal retirement age
1937 and prior	65 years
1938	65 and 2 months
1939	65 and 4 months
1940	65 and 6 months
1941	65 and 8 months
1942	65 and 10 months
1943–54	66
1955	66 and 2 months
1956	66 and 4 months
1957	66 and 6 months
1958	66 and 8 months
1959	66 and 10 months
1960 and later	67

You are eligible for reduced benefits at age 62, no matter what year you were born.

If I begin collecting my Social Security benefits when I'm 62, how much less will I receive? Is this a good deal or not?

If you choose the early retirement benefit, your benefits are reduced by a certain percentage for each month prior to your full benefit age. A reduction of 20 percent applies at age 62, prorated for those who retire between 62 and 65. The monthly percentage is five-ninths of 1 percent, or .0055 repeating. For example, if you retire 20 months before your full retirement age, your benefit will be decreased by $20 \times .0055$, or 11.1 percent, making it 88.9 percent of what it would be at age 65.

On the average, you would probably need to collect benefits for 12 years at the full rate to catch up to the amount you're getting starting at 62. Remember, as the full benefit age increases in the coming years, the total amount of the reduction in your benefit amount will reflect the increased number of months between your early retirement and the full retirement age.

In making a decision to retire early, there are a number of factors to take into account, including both your benefits and spousal benefits due your mate. Don't forget to consider pension benefits from your job. These also may be reduced if you leave work before a certain age, especially if they are tied to your Social Security benefits.

APPLYING FOR SOCIAL SECURITY BENEFITS

You can apply for Social Security benefits by telephone or at any Social Security office. The information and documentation needed by Social Security will include

- Your Social Security number and the worker's
- Your birth certificate
- Your marriage certificate if widowed (for survivor's benefits)
- Your divorce papers (if applying as divorced spouse)
- Children's birth certificates and Social Security numbers (if applying for survivor benefits)
- Deceased worker's W-2 forms or self-employment tax return for recent year
- Checkbook or savings passbook for direct deposit

You should file your application a few months before you plan to retire, if possible. Retroactive benefits can be paid for up to six months prior to the date of filing. The timing is more critical if you're retiring before age 65, in which case you can only be paid as of the month you file. Benefits are not retroactive for early retirees.

WORKING PAST RETIREMENT AGE

For many people, the question of early retirement is of purely academic interest. For better or worse, you may be among those thousands of people who continue to work past the "traditional" age—whether out of desire or financial need—at their old jobs, or, often at new careers.

The good news is, you still have a job. Even better, if you're over 65, you can earn any amount without any effect on your benefits. This is the result of the Senior Citizens Freedom to Work Act, which in 2000 eliminated the onerous restrictions imposed on older workers that cut their benefits for earning money.

For those age 62 to 65, the bad news is, Social Security imposes restrictions on the amount you can earn. As a general rule, you can earn up to $10,080 without affecting your benefits. Beyond this maximum amount, the *2-for-1 rule* applies: you'll lose $1 in benefits for every $2 you earn. For those about to turn 65, legislation increases the amount you can earn without adverse effect on your benefits to $17,000 (applicable in the year you attain age 65).

The decision to continue to work may mean having to defer benefits. If you defer collecting till past your retirement age, there are two consequences:

- *Increased average earnings.* Your continued income will probably increase your average earnings and your future benefit, although by a very small amount.
- *Benefit credit.* You will actually be given a credit for the time you continue to work. Your annual benefit will be increased by a certain percentage for each month you work past the full retirement age. For those who turned 65 in 2000, this amounts to 6 percent per year; by 2008, it will be 8 percent.

If you will be working and receiving benefits at the same time, you are required to advise Social Security of your anticipated earnings and verify the year's earnings by April 15 on the following year.

My retirement income comes mainly from my pension and investments. Does this income limit my Social Security benefits?

No. The limitation on earnings for those under age 65 applies only to money you earn at work and after you begin receiving benefits. Investments, pensions, annuities, even Social Security benefits are not counted in determining the amount of your earnings applied to this maximum allowable figure.

Do these earnings limitations apply to my disability or SSI benefits?

No. These limitations apply only to people under 65 collecting Social Security retirement, survivor, or dependent benefits. People who work and collect disability or SSI benefits are subject to different earnings requirements. Keep in mind that if you're working you may not meet the requirements for disability or SSI benefits.

TAXING SOCIAL SECURITY

For decades, Social Security was considered sacrosanct. But with 650,000 millionaires collecting benefits, it was inevitable that the tax collector would come calling. At the present time, people whose incomes exceed a certain specified limit are subject to federal taxation on half or more of their benefits.

Unfortunately, for purposes of determining whether your benefits will be taxed, your "combined income" includes income not otherwise taxed—counting not only your adjusted gross income (AGI) of wages, interest, and dividends but also any tax-exempt interest and half your Social Security benefits. (See Chapter 17 for a description of how tax liability for Social Security is calculated.)

What if I win the lottery? How will that affect my Social Security?

Your check will keep coming—restrictions on your earnings under age 70 apply only to earned income. Depending on the amount of the award, however, it might affect your tax liability, boosting you into another tax bracket *and* subjecting a portion of your Social Security benefits to taxation.

SPOUSAL BENEFITS

If you are 62 or older, you can get Social Security benefits on your own record or on the record of your retired spouse. Generally you will be allowed to take the higher benefit rate.

Your benefits as a spouse may be as much as half of your retired spouse's benefits. There is a limit on the total amount that can be paid to your entire family in so-called derivative benefits. The limit is generally no more than 150 to 180 percent of the benefits of the worker upon whose record these payments are based. In such a case, family members' benefits will be reduced proportionately; the worker's benefits will not be reduced.

When am I eligible for spousal benefits?

When your spouse retires. If you are a married woman, you may get more money through your husband's benefits than through your own. As a married man, you have the same right to derivative benefits from your wife's earnings. If your spouse doesn't want to retire, you can still take retirement based on your own earnings and early retirement at age 62.

What if my spouse retires early?

If you retire along with your spouse (upon whose earnings your benefits will be based), your benefits will also be reduced, up to 25 percent at age 62. If you don't retire but continue to work, and you qualify for spousal benefits (which you may elect as greater than your own benefit), you will receive 50 percent of what your spouse's full benefit would have been had he or she not retired until full retirement age.

My ex and I have been divorced two years. Am I eligible for spousal benefits?

If you are divorced from a person who is at least 62, whether collecting benefits or not, you are eligible for spousal benefits *provided* that the marriage lasted at least 10 years and the divorce was over two years prior to the application. There is no two-year waiting period for divorced spouses whose mates are already collecting benefits. (You're also eligible for survivor benefits.)

SURVIVOR BENEFITS

Social Security is not just a retirement system. A significant part of the Social Security system is survivors insurance, which provides benefits to family members of covered workers. Family members may include widows and widowers, former spouses of deceased workers, children, and dependent parents:

- A widow or widower can get full benefits at age 65 or reduced benefits as early as 60. A disabled widow or widower can get benefits at 50.

  A widow or widower is eligible at any age if he or she is taking care of a child under 16 or a child who is disabled and entitled to or receiving benefits.
- Unmarried children under 18, under 19 if attending elementary or secondary school full-time, are entitled to benefits. Children with disabilities incurred before age 22 may get benefits with no age limit on receipt.
- Dependent parents age 62 or older may be eligible for survivor benefits if they were dependent on the deceased for at least half of their support.

Survivor benefits are payable, depending on the deceased's benefit, at the following rates:

- 100 percent for a widow or widower age 65 or older
- between 71 percent and 94 percent for a widow or widower age 60 to 64
- 75 percent for a widow or widower under 60 with a child under 16
- 75 percent for children

There is an additional one-time death benefit of $255 generally available to a surviving spouse or minor children.

As a divorced spouse, am I entitled to survivor benefits?

Yes, if your marriage lasted at least 10 years. (No time limits apply if you are a divorced spouse taking care of a disabled child.) Benefits paid to a divorced spouse will not affect the benefit rates for others eligible for survivor benefits.

Can I get survivor benefits if I remarry?

Yes, under certain circumstances. If you remarry after age 60, you can still get benefits based on your former spouse's record—or you can choose to receive benefits based on your new spouse's record, whichever affords you higher benefits. If you're disabled and remarried, you can qualify for survivor benefits at age 50.

Which are better, retirement benefits or survivor benefits?

There's no easy answer to that question. You can switch from one form of benefit to another, depending on your individual situation.

If you're already getting benefits on your own record and your spouse dies, you can change to survivor benefits, which may give you more. Or, if you're receiving survivor benefits, you can switch over to your own retirement benefits at a reduced rate as early as age 62. It's also possible to begin one benefit at a reduced rate and switch to the other at an unreduced rate when you reach full retirement age.

These are complicated calculations, and you have to sit down with someone who is familiar with Social Security to figure them out. A Social Security representative will also discuss options with you.

SOCIAL SECURITY OVERPAYMENTS

By law, Social Security must seek repayment of any overpayments it has given. If this occurs in your case, you will receive a notice informing you of the amount overpaid and your right to appeal or request a waiver.

Repayment is usually made by direct refund within 30 days or withholding from future benefits checks.

One possibility is a waiver of repayment. *If* the overpayment wasn't your fault in any way, and *if* you couldn't meet necessary living expenses if you had to pay it back or repayment would cause severe financial hardship, you may not have to pay it back. But you must bear no scintilla of responsibility for the overpayment and could not have known that the amount was not correct. If you didn't report excess earnings, for example, you wouldn't qualify for a waiver. (There is also provision for waiver, rarely invoked, when repayment would be "against equity and good conscience.")

If you disagree with a determination of overpayment, you may challenge it through the appeal process. Unfortunately, notices of overpayment are often inadequate in this respect, not detailing amounts paid or due, or the reasons. An appeal will stay the collection of the overpayment. (Appeals are discussed later in this chapter.)

SOCIAL SECURITY DISABILITY INSURANCE

Disability benefits are available under two programs: the Social Security disability insurance program and the Supplemental Security Income (SSI) program (discussed later in this chapter). The disability insurance program is authorized under Title II of the Social Security Act. Under its provisions, disability benefits are available for people who've worked and qualified.

In 2000, disability insurance provided nearly $91 billion to $10 million disabled workers and their dependents. The disability program, however, is characterized by backlogs and delay. There is an average wait of 75 days for a determination of eligibility—as long as four months in some states! Appeal of an unfavorable decision may drag on for a year.

DISABILITY ELIGIBILITY AND BENEFITS

In order to qualify for Social Security disability insurance, you must have a recent work record of sufficient length. Your work history is determined by your number of credits, earned at the same Social Security rate of four per year, with the minimum requirement dependent on age:

- *Under 24:* You need six credits in the three-year period prior to your disability.

- *24 to 31:* You need credit for working half the time between 21 and the time of your disability (for example, 12 credits—half of six years—if you're disabled at age 27).
- *Over 31:* You need 20 credits from the 10 years immediately preceding your disability, and an additional two credits for each two years of age over 42 up to 62 (for example, 26 credits at age 48, 40 credits at age 62).

In addition to benefits for yourself, disability benefits for your family may be available based on your work record, in much the same way as retirement benefits are available for your family. Members of your family who may be eligible include

- Your husband or wife, if 62 or older (and not collecting a higher Social Security benefit in his or her own name);
- Your husband or wife, if caring for a child under 16 or a child who is disabled and entitled to or receiving benefits; and
- Your children, if unmarried and under 18 (or under 19 but still in public school, or disabled since before age 22).

A disabled widow, widower, or divorced spouse (if the marriage lasted 10 years) may also qualify for benefits, if he or she is over the age of 50.

Benefits start on the sixth full calendar month of your disability. For example, if you become disabled by a stroke on February 15, your benefits will begin as of August, which is the sixth full calendar month you are disabled.

Disability benefits continue until your condition improves or you return to substantial work. You can receive disability benefits at any time. At 65, they become retirement benefits, although the amount remains the same.

Social Security provides a number of work incentives for people receiving disability benefits, including a trial work period of nine months (not necessarily consecutive), in which you can work as much as you can without affecting your benefits.

DETERMINING DISABILITY

Social Security has a very strict definition of disability. It is based entirely on your ability to work and does not cover partial disability. Nor does it cover any short-term disability.

For Social Security purposes, a disability is a physical or mental impairment that is expected to keep you from doing any "substantial" work for at least one year.

These rules apply to the disability insurance program run by Social Security. The rules for qualifying under any other plan, such as your employer's plan or another government agency's, do not necessarily apply.

Applying for Benefits and Determining Disability

There is a five-step evaluation process to determine disability under Social Security law. It requires that you as the applicant give the right answer to each of the following questions *in sequence.*

1. Are you working?
2. Is your condition severe?
3. Is your condition found in the list of disabling impairments?
4. Can you do the work you did previously?
5. Can you do any other type of work?

The Social Security office determines your nonmedical eligibility under Step 1, including whether you are insured or have recently worked. Then your application is forwarded to your state's Disability Determination Services office for an evaluation of whether you are sufficiently disabled to qualify for benefits (Steps 2 through 5). The determination is done by a state Disability Determination Services team, consisting of a physician (or psychologist) and a disability evaluation specialist. Your application will proceed through these last four steps until a determination is made of "disability" or "no disability."

The disability services team is responsible for evaluating your medical records, looking at your condition and treatment, and requesting information about your ability to do work-related activities. You may be asked for an examination, performed by your own or another doctor. Most disability claims focus on this determination. If your claim is denied, you can appeal it.

Step 1. Are you working? More to the point, are you currently working at substantial gainful activity? Disability benefits can be paid only if you are unable to do any substantial work.

What constitutes "substantial" work? The amount of your earnings is the key. In general, if your wages average more than $780 a month (after allowable deductions), you are performing substantial work (2002 amount). If you are self-employed, more consideration will be given to the amount of time you spend in your business than the amount of your income.

Steps 2 and 3. What constitutes sufficient impairment? In Step 2, you are examined to see if you have an impairment that is severe and that will last 12 months (or result in death). A short-term disability, however severe, will not qualify.

Assuming you pass Step 2, Step 3 is a reference to the *Listing of Impairments.* If your condition is on the list, or is similar enough to be medically equivalent to one on the list, you will be allowed disability benefits.

There are 125 impairments defined in the adult listings, descriptive of mental and physical illness and characterized generally by body system, neurological impairment, or mental disorder. Each impairment is defined in terms of specific medical signs, symptoms, or laboratory test results. To match a listing, you must fill *all* the specified criteria. If you display only some of the characteristics, no matter how severe, you will not qualify.

The list is designed to define impairments that would preclude an applicant from any gainful activity. It functions as a presumption of disability, streamlining the process. Under the law, however, the list cannot be the final test.

The law allows disability to someone who is prevented from performing "substantial gainful activity." If your condition is not on the list, the evaluation will proceed to Step 4.

Steps 4 and 5. What constitutes sufficient functional impairment? These steps evaluate your ability to perform work, either work of the kind you have done in the past or generally available work. They measure "residual functional capacity" of what you can still do despite your limitations.

For mental impairments, residual capacity is generally expressed in psychological terms. For physical impairments, it relates to your abilities to perform physical activities, such as walking, lifting, standing, and sitting.

An estimated 25 percent of adult claimants qualify for benefits under Steps 4 and 5.

Step 4 questions whether you can still perform work you have done in the past. According to the Social Security Administration, Step 4 is strictly a denial step. Either you are denied because you have the capacity to perform past work, or the evaluation proceeds to Step 5.

Step 5 evaluates your ability to perform generally available work, subject to some modification. Under the law, your age, work experience, and education must be factored into a determination as to whether you are able to perform any other kind of work. Moreover, the work must "exist" in the national economy.

Step 5 rules for those who cannot do their past work are more lenient for older workers. The rules reflect the belief that age affects significantly a person's ability to adapt to new types of work, assuming the ability to adjust to a significant number of jobs at age 50 and less ability to adjust to any new work at age 55. At age 60, the factor of "skill marketability" is added.

Those aged 55 and over are required to adjust to other work if (1) past work required moderate to heavy levels of physical exertion and (2) the applicant has no skills readily transferrable to lighter work. Moreover, people aged 60 to 64 do not have to adjust to other work if their skills are not highly marketable. Nor do applicants with at least 35 years of arduous, unskilled physical labor and marginal education.

CONTINUING DISABILITY REVIEW

Under the law, Social Security must conduct a review every three years to determine your continuing eligibility for disability benefits. This is required for all but the permanently disabled. Eligibility reviews are viewed as tools to cut ineligible people from the rolls. Over the past several years, however, fewer than half the required reviews have been performed.

The review is performed by the same state Disability Determination Services office that conducts initial application reviews. A full review, much like the application review, includes a face-to-face meeting with a Social Security representative, evaluation by a disability examiner, and frequently a doctor's examination. About 90 percent of such reviews result in a finding of continued eligibility.

If you are denied continued benefits, you may challenge the decision through the appeals process. Forty percent of those denied benefits are successful at the appeals stage, winning back their benefits. (See the discussion of appeals later in this chapter.)

SUPPLEMENTAL SECURITY INCOME

The Supplemental Security Income (SSI) program was enacted by Congress in 1972 to assist individuals over 65, blind, or disabled by setting a guaranteed minimum income level for them. SSI is not funded by the Social Security trust fund or Social Security taxes. Its financing comes from general federal revenues. In effect, the federal government took over public assistance benefits for these categories of people.

The maximum federal SSI payment in 2002 is $545 a month for an individual and $817 a month for a couple. Forty-three states provide an additional state supplement bringing the SSI benefit level up, although it still falls below the poverty level in almost all the states.

In 2000, SSI provided about $24 billion to 6.6 million recipients, 30 percent of whom were over 65. SSI is one of those government programs under attack for eligibility rules that allow benefits to many elderly immigrants as well as the native-born poor. In fact, many elderly people have never heard of SSI or imagined that there is any program other than Social Security to provide them with income. In any year an estimated 1.5 million elderly people potentially eligible for SSI never even apply for it.

Many people who are not eligible for Social Security may be eligible for Supplemental Security Income. In addition, people who receive Social Security retirement or disability benefits that are below SSI allowances may qualify concurrently for benefits under both the Social Security retirement or disability insurance program and SSI.

SSI ELIGIBILITY

To be eligible for SSI, you must

- Be age 65 or older, blind, or disabled (children can also get SSI in some circumstances)
- Have assets and income less than certain amounts

If you are single, you can have no more than $2,000 in assets and be eligible for SSI. The limit for a couple is $3,000. In measuring your assets to determine eligibility for SSI, the following resources will not be included

- Your home and the land it's on
- Your personal and household goods
- Your car (up to $4,500; there is no limit when needed for medical or employment reasons)
- Burial plots for you and members of your immediate family
- Life insurance and burial funds up to $1,500 for you and up to $1,500 for your spouse

The amount of income you can have each month and still get SSI depends partly on where you live. (You can call 800/772-1213 to find out the income limits in your state.)

Social Security does not count the following when deciding SSI eligibility:

- The first $20 of most income received in a month
- The first $65 a month you earn from working and half the amount over $65
- Food stamps
- Most food, clothing, or shelter you get from private nonprofit organizations
- Most home energy assistance

An applicant with resources above the specified limits may be able to "spend down" resources to qualify for SSI. For example, a widow over 65 years old having a savings account of $2,500 would be ineligible for SSI because her assets are above the limit. However, if she takes $750 from her savings and opens a separate burial fund, then her nonexempt assets would be $1,750, under the $2,000 amount.

You must also be a United States citizen, lawfully admitted for permanent residence, or permanently residing in the United States under "color of law." In addition, you must be residing both in the United States *and* in the state where you apply. An individual who leaves the United States for 30 days becomes ineligible for benefits.

NEW TRANSFER RULES FOR SSI

Although SSI applicants were for years shielded from the harsher transfer rules applicable to Medicaid eligibility, new law makes any transfers you make subject to review and possible penalty. (Transfer penalties apply only to transfers since 2000.)

Like Medicaid, SSI uses a three-year look-back period to examine your finances. Any transfers not otherwise permitted within that period will be subject to a penalty period, during which time you will not be eligible for benefits. The penalty period is computed by dividing the amount of the transfer by your monthly benefit amount (including any state supplement).

For example, a transfer of $6,000 in a state where the monthly benefit is $600 would create a period of ineligibility totaling 10 months. The actual period of ineligibility may vary, but unlike Medicaid, there is a maximum period of ineligibility for SSI for up to 36 months.

Exceptions apply for transfers made to

- A spouse (or anyone else for the spouse's benefit)
- A blind or disabled child
- A trust for the sole benefit of a blind or disabled child
- A trust for the sole benefit of a disabled individual under age 65 (even if the trust is for the benefit of the applicant, under certain circumstances)

In addition, special exceptions apply to the transfer of a home. The SSI applicant may freely transfer his or her home to any of the following individuals without incurring a transfer penalty:

- The applicant's spouse
- A child who is under age 21 or who is blind or disabled
- Into a trust for the sole benefit of a disabled individual under age 65 (even if the trust is for the benefit of the applicant, under certain circumstances)
- A sibling who has lived in the home during the year preceding the applicant's institutionalization and who already holds an equity interest in the home
- A child of the applicant who lived in the house for at least two years prior to the applicant's institutionalization and who during that period provided care that allowed the applicant to avoid a nursing home stay.

Does SSI look at transfers to trusts?

In general, SSI rules on transfers to trusts restate the Medicaid trust rules. Starting in 2000, the contents of self-settled trusts (those you create for yourself) will be considered available to you in determining your eligibility for SSI. On the other hand, assets of most trusts that someone else creates naming you as a beneficiary will not be considered to belong to you for purposes of determining your SSI eligibility.

Don't worry about irrevocable trusts created for you before 2000. If properly drawn, these assets will not be considered to belong to you.

Exceptions are "supplemental needs trusts" established by a parent, grandparent, or court solely for the benefit of a disabled person under age 65, and "pooled trusts" established by nonprofit associations. These are described in Chapter 14. The drafting of a valid trust, which is a highly technical document, requires considerable expertise. Make sure you consult an attorney experienced with trusts and SSI matters if you are considering a trust for an individual on SSI.

APPLYING FOR SSI

SSI must be applied for at the Social Security office. If you live in a state that provides a state supplement, you may also have to apply at a state agency.

The law gives states the option of having the federal government administer the state supplement, with the state picking up the administrative costs. In states that choose this option, a single application covers both the federal and state payments.

Some states choose to administer their own supplement. In those states, application for the supplement must be made with the state agency. States that administer their own supplement are Alabama, Alaska, Arizona, Colorado, Connecticut, Florida, Idaho, Illinois, Indiana, Kentucky, Louisiana, Maryland, Minnesota, Missouri, Nebraska, New Hampshire, New Mexico, North Carolina, North Dakota, Ohio, Oklahoma, Oregon, South Carolina, South Dakota, Virginia, and Wyoming.

When filing an SSI application with either Social Security or the state agency, you should bring

- Your Social Security card or number
- Your birth certificate or proof of age
- Information about the home where you live, such as your mortgage or your lease
- Payroll slips, bank books, insurance policies, car registration, burial fund records, and other information about your income and the things you own
- If you're applying for disability, the names, addresses, and telephone numbers of doctors, hospitals, and clinics that have seen you

You can call the Social Security hot line (800/772-1213) to make an appointment at your local Social Security office or to apply over the phone. If you apply over the phone, you will be mailed an application for signature and a notice of what documents you must submit.

SSI BENEFITS

In 2003, the maximum federal SSI payment is $552 a month for an eligible individual living alone and $829 a month for an eligible couple. Benefits are lower for individuals or couples living with others or in another's household. An individual living with others or a disabled person living with parents would be eligible for a maximum of $369.85

monthly (one-third off the maximum benefit rate). Those with other income will also receive less.

For example, a widow over 65 years old receiving $235 a month in Social Security retirement benefits and living alone would have her SSI benefits calculated in the following way. Her $235 income would be reduced by a fixed "noncountable" $20, leaving an income of $215. The $215 income would be deducted from the maximum benefit of $552, giving her an SSI benefit of $337 monthly. (This example does not include any state supplement she might receive.)

The federal benefit will be reduced to $30 if the recipient is institutionalized (unless a doctor certifies that the stay will be for less than three months and the recipient demonstrates a need for the money to maintain the noninstitutional living arrangement).

Supplemental funds are made available in most states. You can call Social Security at 800/772-1213 to find out the amounts for your state. Although the federal amount is increased yearly, the supplement amount may not change, depending on the state.

SSI DISABILITY RULES

The medical requirements for disability payments and the process for determining disability are the same as under the Social Security disability insurance program described in the previous section. The disability determination services teams are the same and subject to the same standards as those concerning medical review for eligibility and continued eligibility determinations.

Other Social Security and SSI rules are different. For example, a disabled person under Social Security's disability insurance program is not paid benefits for five months from the date the disability began. But SSI disability benefits can be paid retroactively to the date the person filed his or her claim. SSI also applies different rules from Social Security's for people with disabilities who want to go back to work.

TICKET TO WORK PROGRAM

The Ticket to Work and Work Incentives Improvement Act of 1999 was designed to give more persons with disabilities the opportunity to participate in the workforce while removing barriers that required them to choose between health care coverage and work.

A Social Security program that provides employment support services for people who want to work, Ticket to Work is for people receiving

SSI or Social Security disability insurance. The program is voluntary. It also includes people receiving benefits as a disabled widow or widower, or an adult who is the disabled child of a wage earner under the Social Security rules. Regulations require ticket recipients to be between the age of 18 and 64.

Social Security and SSI disability beneficiaries will receive a "ticket" they can use to obtain rehabilitation, employment, or other support services (job search assistance, job training, résumé writing, job coaching) from a network of approved providers.

An individual who is "using a ticket" will not be subject to regularly scheduled continuing disability medical reviews, although benefits can still be terminated if earnings are above the limits. Social Security disability beneficiaries who have been receiving benefits for at least 24 months will not be medically reviewed solely because of work activity. Regularly scheduled medical reviews can still be performed and, again, benefits terminated if earnings are too high.

APPEALING A SOCIAL SECURITY DECISION

If you don't agree with a decision about Social Security or SSI regarding your eligibility for benefits, or the amount of benefits awarded you, you can appeal the decision. About 2 million SSI claims are adjudicated each year.

Social Security has a three-part appeal process, after which you may sue in federal court. However, you must proceed in order. The steps in the process are called *reconsideration, hearing,* and *review.* Don't be intimidated by the names of these processes, which have no legal significance other than the convenience of telling them apart.

Step 1: Reconsideration

A reconsideration involves review by a Social Security representative, who will look at all the evidence submitted when the original decision was made. He or she will also look at any new evidence you may wish to submit.

You must request a reconsideration within 60 days of the original decision. The law requires that reconsideration be handled by someone who didn't take part in the initial decision you're challenging. If you're not satisfied with the decision after the reconsideration, you have a right to a hearing.

Step 2: Hearing

A hearing is conducted by an administrative law judge (also called an ALJ) who had nothing to do with any prior decisions made regarding your case. You must request a hearing within 60 days of the reconsideration decision. The hearing will usually be held within 75 miles of your home. If after the hearing you still disagree with the decision, you can ask for a review by the Appeals Council.

Step 3: Review

The Social Security Appeals Council conducts reviews of hearing decisions. You must request a review within 60 days of the hearing decision. The Appeals Council does not review all cases that are appealed. If it does decide to review your case, it will either render a decision or return it to an ALJ for further review. The Appeals Council is located in Falls Church, Virginia.

After Steps 1 through 3, your appeal to Social Security is over. If you're dissatisfied with the result, you have 60 days to file a suit in a federal district court.

Must I be present for Social Security appeals?

It depends. Whether or not you are present for the reconsideration depends upon the kind of decision being considered. Many reconsiderations are strictly "file review," conducted solely by reference to the written documents and without the opportunity for you to meet with a representative. In other circumstances, you will be given the choice. For example, if you've been receiving disability benefits and are going to be cut off, you will be given the opportunity to meet with a disability hearing officer.

For disability claimants, the reconsideration process allows you the option to meet face-to-face with the person who is reconsidering your case to explain why you feel you are still disabled. You can submit new evidence or information and can bring someone who knows about your disability. This special hearing does not replace your right to also have a formal hearing before an ALJ (the second appeal step) if your reconsideration is denied.

At the hearing level, you always have the opportunity to appear in person—and you always should. It is much harder for an ALJ to make a decision against a sympathetic person who has been present than it is when all the judge has seen is the dry-as-dust files. If you don't choose to appear, the ALJ may decide your presence is required. Otherwise, and far more likely, he or she will make a decision based on all the information in your case, including any new information given. You must inform Social Security in writing that you don't wish to attend.

Will I continue to receive payment during the time of my appeal?

Yes, if you want to. You can continue to receive payments if you are appealing a decision that you are no longer eligible for Social Security disability benefits because your condition has improved, that you are no longer eligible for SSI, or that your SSI payment should be reduced. You must inform Social Security of your desire to have payments continue during your appeal within 10 days of the date you receive the notice of the decision about your benefits from Social Security. If you ultimately fail in your appeal, you may have to pay back the money if you were not eligible to receive it.

How does the hearing work?

You will be notified by the ALJ of the time and place of the hearing. You may bring witnesses and a representative to the hearing. The ALJ will question you and any witnesses you choose to bring. You may look at the information in your file and give new information.

The ALJ's decision will be made after the hearing. You will be sent a copy, along with a notice.

Do I need a lawyer? What if I can't afford one?

You are entitled to a lawyer or a nonlawyer "representative" to help you or to appear on your behalf. He or she can act for you in most matters and will receive a copy of any decisions made about your claim. (Your representative must get permission from Social Security to charge you or collect a fee.)

There are groups that can help you find a lawyer or that provide free legal services if you meet certain qualifications. Your local Social Security office should have a list of such groups.

The Social Security Administration determines fees for lawyers, based on regulations setting forth the services performed by the lawyer and the complexity of your case. Your attorney's fee must be approved before he or she may bill you. And you have the right to appeal a determination about the amount of the fee. (So does your lawyer.) At the federal court level, the court has the power to set the fees.

CREDITOR PROTECTION FOR YOUR BENEFITS

Under the law, your Social Security and SSI benefits cannot be attached by a creditor. Even the IRS cannot get them if you owe back taxes. They are "judgment-proof."

YOUR SOCIAL SECURITY NUMBER

About 10 million new numbers are assigned each year. The Social Security Administration has issued an estimated total of 365 million Social Security numbers.

There's actually a law, a little-known section of the Privacy Act of 1974, which governs use of the Social Security number for anything other than the reasons for which it was created. Under the law, you cannot be denied a government benefit for refusing to divulge your Social Security number (unless there is a statute authorizing its use).

Are my Social Security records confidential?

Generally, yes. However, several other government agencies are permitted by law to use Social Security numbers. For example, some state death records are matched to Medicare records using Social Security numbers to uncover Medicare and Social Security fraud.

When do I have to give my Social Security number out?

First, for anything that reflects your income. Or to account for retirement and survivor benefits. For example, banks and other financial institutions use the numbers to report interest earned on accounts to the IRS for income tax purposes.

Federal law does not prohibit the use of Social Security numbers by the private sector (although some states restrict retailers' rights to ask for it). If a business or other enterprise asks you for your Social Security number, you may refuse to give it to them. That may mean doing without the purchase or service for which your number was requested.

Protect yourself against identity theft. Remember, your Social Security number is a "universal identifier," of particular appeal to criminals and con artists as well as advertisers, employers, and bureaucrats. Armed with your number, people can get all sorts of information about you and your credit rating, bank accounts, and finances, without your knowing about it until it's too late.

Part 7

Meeting Your Housing Needs

For older people, living arrangements take on great importance. Most people seek to remain in their own homes, and housing expenses represent a major budget item. On fixed retirement incomes and budgets, they feel the financial pinch. Some may experience difficulties in managing a household or performing chores, but for many, staying in their own homes is worth the extra effort. Witness the vast numbers of those in the over-85 age group who still live in their own homes, often getting care to cope with frailty and ill health.

This section takes a look at legal and financial issues of housing you should consider and discusses the options and opportunities available to you. In Chapter 21, we discuss your status and rights as tenants and homeowners. We give you the tools to help you keep control over your living arrangements, much as you are trying to retain control of your finances, and show you how to deal with discrimination in housing.

For some, circumstance or necessity may compel other choices. In Chapter 22, we turn to the latest trend in retirement living, adult living communities, which have become a $15 billion industry in this country. We tell you what you can expect, what to watch out for, and what your legal rights are in alternative housing arrangements ranging from continuing care facilities to assisted-living communities.

21

Tenants and Homeowners

Surveys indicate that more than 86 percent of older Americans want to stay in their homes. And in fact, according to census data, 75 percent do remain in their homes after retirement. A full 96 percent stay in the same state. For these citizens, housing expenses represent a major budget item. This is true for both renters and homeowners.

TENANTS' RIGHTS

If you are a renter, your landlord-tenant relationship is spelled out in your lease and, to some extent, in state laws and judicial decisions. Tenants have rights in these important areas:

Condition of the premises. Tenants have the right to adequate heat, hot water, and a "habitable" home. Under general principles of law, landlords also have the duty to make repairs and ensure safety.

Occupancy. State and local occupancy laws deal with your right to remain in your home. These laws, generally applicable to public housing and to some private housing, frequently provide that the landlord cannot refuse to renew your lease, so long as you continue to pay the rent. They generally do not apply to housing with fewer than a given number of units. If you live in housing with fewer than the number of units specified in your state's laws, the laws may afford you limited or no protection and allow termination of your lease.

Other rights include the right to form tenant groups, to distribute literature, and to be free from retaliation from your landlord for making complaints.

Your landlord also has rights, including the right to timely payment of rent and the right of access to your apartment in emergencies.

My elderly mother is in the hospital and may be transferred to a nursing home. Is she obligated to continue to pay rent on her apartment?

It depends on the law where she lives. Many jurisdictions provide for termination of the lease in specific cases. For example, in New York, your mother would have the right to terminate her lease upon entering a skilled nursing facility.

HOUSING REGULATION

State laws on the rights of tenants vary from state to state. However, all states have legal rules governing habitability, contained in building codes and warranty-of-habitability laws. These laws and regulations apply to privately owned buildings.

States, counties, and most municipalities have administrative agencies charged with handling complaints governing housing matters such as landlord-tenant disputes, including complaints about heating, services and conditions, and rent overcharge.

In addition some states provide affordable-housing programs, ensuring lower-cost housing by subsidizing renters with modest incomes. There are similar federal programs, as well. Many elderly qualify for these programs but are unaware of their existence.

Some states and municipalities limit rent increases as well and have special programs regulating increases for qualified older tenants. Applying to these programs can lead to substantial rent reductions or smaller rent increases. For example, the Senior Citizens Rent Increase Exemption (SCRIE) program in New York limits rent increases for people over 62 with incomes below $20,000 yearly who spend at least a third of their incomes on rent.

Renters also get some tax relief in the form of rebates, credits, or refunds in a number of states, including California, Michigan, Missouri, Nevada, North Dakota, Oregon, New Mexico, and Pennsylvania. Some states such as Illinois and Connecticut provide direct grants or help with rent. Eligibility for and amount of relief from these programs often depend on income.

RENTAL ASSISTANCE

Elderly renters are particularly affected by high housing costs, the impact of which are made greater by their fixed incomes. As many as half of poor elderly renters spend more than 45 percent of their incomes on housing.

For poorer renters among the elderly, low-cost public housing or federal subsidies are made available under programs dating back to the

1930s and passage of the United States Housing Act in 1937. As a general rule, income must be very low to qualify for these programs. Eligibility criteria vary considerably.

Public housing. Elderly people occupy nearly 45 percent of the country's 1.3 million public housing units. These are federal Housing and Urban Development (HUD) projects, administered by more than 3,300 public housing authorities across the country. Public authorities may be city agencies or independent authorities. (The former provide more safeguards, along with the inevitable red tape.)

Under Section 504 of the Rehabilitative Act of 1973, 5 percent of a public housing authority's units must be made accessible to the disabled. This means accommodations of benefit to the elderly, including exit and entrance ramps and doors equipped for wheelchairs. (Related protections in the Fair Housing Act and the Americans with Disabilities Act are discussed later in this chapter.)

Some of these projects are fairly old, with inadequate insulation, roofing, electric, and plumbing systems. Long-term solutions to sustaining these projects have become mired in partisan politics.

According to government reports, most new public housing projects have been designed exclusively for the elderly. However, the percentage of elderly actually benefiting from public housing is declining as a result of increases in the population of eligible nonelderly people with mental or physical disabilities. And funding for these projects has declined markedly over the past several years.

Section 202 housing. Section 202 housing is designed to give the elderly and handicapped an independent living environment with necessary support services. Residents pay 30 percent of income, and the difference is paid by HUD. Although certain services are required by HUD regulations, they need not be provided on-site. (An assisted living conversion program makes grants to convert existing senior housing to serve the needs of frail elderly through specialized features and support services.) There are waiting lists of one year and longer for this type of housing. Of 138,000 units in 1988, 94 percent were occupied by elderly.

Section 8 subsidies. The federal Section 8 program provides rental assistance to low-income people. "Section 8" refers to Section 8 of the United States Housing Act, enacted in 1937 and amended several times since. The elderly amount to about 44 percent of the 2.5 million participants receiving Section 8 benefits.

- *Certificates and vouchers* provide subsidies for the difference between 30 percent of the renter's income and the "fair market" rent. The difference between a certificate program and a voucher program is that rentals in the certificate program have a fair market rent ceiling established by federal regulations. In the voucher program, participants can live in apartments with higher rents and pay the difference out of pocket. One benefit of vouchers is that they give you more control over where you live. But funding cutbacks and program changes can curtail new tenant-based subsidies and limits to rent increases.

- Section 8 also runs *project-based programs,* which provide assistance for low-income people living in privately owned rental housing. In a project-based program, you and your family must live in designated properties. Again, you are required to pay 30 percent of your income for rent. Your rights are governed by the contract and the regulatory agreement. Unlike the certificate and voucher programs, tenants who move from these Section 8 facilities lose their rental assistance (unless they move to another subsidized property).

HUD has quality standards for safe, decent, and sanitary housing. For HUD-assisted properties, the contract provides for yearly inspection by HUD. Standards require that assisted properties be maintained by owners in good condition. Tenants in Section 8 housing must be provided with

- Properly operating sanitary facilities
- Adequate security
- Properly operating heating and air conditioning
- Ceilings and walls without serious defects

Owners who fail to comply with these standards can be barred or suspended from further participation in Section 8 contracts. In cases of serious physical neglect, payments for individual units can be suspended, the current contract can be ended, and fines may be assessed.

However, this provision is of little help—and may perhaps do harm—to tenants who could be displaced. The threat of a future funding cutoff is effective only against owners who wish to keep participating in HUD programs.

The residents in my housing project were warned of a zero tolerance policy on drugs. My grandson, who stays with me sometimes, unfortunately is a user.

Your grandson is going to have find somewhere else to stay. The U.S. Supreme Court ruled in 2002 that public housing tenants could be evicted if a family member who lives in their unit—or a guest—is arrested for drug-related charges, even if the tenant knew nothing about it. Even elderly tenants in public housing have to worry about the company they keep. Although there has been no nationwide move to evict people wholesale, the authority is there to perform a "no-fault" eviction. As a practical matter, local housing authorities may consent so long as the offending user—relative, worker—is banished from the apartment.

SHARED HOUSING

Homesharing has become increasingly popular over the past two decades, for reasons that include added income, companionship, and a measure of extra security provided by housemates. The number of people sharing homes has reached an estimated 1 million.

No matter how amicable the arrangement, the homesharing relationship is nevertheless a legal one, with concomitant rights and responsibilities that should be codified in a written contract. While the form of the contract can be as simple as a letter or as formal as a lease, the wording should contain basic lease clauses regarding term, notice of termination, and rent amount. The arrangement between the homeowner and the homesharer should be drafted with care. It is more intimate than a regular landlord-tenant relationship, and rights and responsibilities should be spelled out, especially in an arrangement in which an older person is sharing his or her home with a younger one. Expectations concerning the use of the telephone, shared expenses, guests, and other such details should also be made explicit. Remember, too, in figuring the amount, rental income is taxable.

One possible legal obstacle: Local housing ordinances may not allow unrelated parties in a single home. You should check with your local housing authority.

Local agencies may be a source for homesharing candidates, matching compatible older people. One source for information is the National Shared Housing Resource Center (see appendixes).

I am receiving home care services from Medicaid. I have thought about renting out a room in my home in exchange for personal care.

The income might put your Medicaid eligibility in jeopardy, or you could forfeit your extra income. Make sure you consult a lawyer first (See Part 8, Getting Help, and appendixes for a list of organizations that provide lawyer referrals.)

HELP FOR HOMEOWNERS

Housing costs can be a real drain on the limited resources of older homeowners as well as tenants. These problems are compounded by the difficulties owners face as they age. Often homes need to be adapted to changing conditions, to ensure safety as well as comfort, particularly in bathrooms and kitchens. A few federal programs exist to help low-income homeowners repair their homes or make alterations to accommodate their changing needs.

The poorer you are, the worse your problems may be. Although the vast majority of older homeowners own their own houses mortgage-free, as many as half of poor homeowners over 65 report spending more than 45 percent of their income on housing expenses such as real estate taxes, insurance, and utilities.

Assistance for homeowners comes in a number of forms. Among the possibilities of aid for repairs and maintenance are public subsidies and deferral loans as well as tax relief. (Contact your local housing department or Area Agency on Aging.)

Taxes. Tax exemptions, tax abatements, tax credits, and other forms of tax relief based on the value of your home are available in a number of states. Eligibility requirements usually include a minimum age of 65, although some are as low as 55, and specify the value of your home, your income, and the length of your residency. Some states (New Jersey is one) include a provision for residents in adult communities under certain conditions.

Home repair loans and loans for paying property taxes. There are publicly financed loan programs for low- or moderate-income people, including property tax deferral programs and deferred-payment loans. In these kinds of programs, the costs are lower than for private sector loans. Typically the money can be used only for certain purposes, that is, for paying property taxes or for making repairs or improving your home. Acceptable improvements include roof, stair, and floor repairs, plumbing, heating, wiring, and accessibility features such as ramps and rails.

Property taxes deferred under such programs do not have to be paid until you leave your home. You can get a one-time deferral or a new deferral every year. Deferred taxes under these programs are loans. The taxes are not forgiven. Upon your death, payment will be due against the home. Usually the loan is paid off from the proceeds of the sale of your home. (The payment will not come due if a surviving spouse inherits, but the lien continues.)

Programs to defer taxes are available in many states, including California, Colorado, Florida, Georgia, Illinois, Iowa, Maine, Maryland, Michigan, Minnesota, Oregon, Tennessee, Texas, Utah, Virginia, Washington, Wisconsin, and Wyoming. Connecticut, Florida, Iowa, Massachusetts, and New Hampshire also support local programs. Check with your local property tax collector or contact your Area Agency on Aging.

Utility assistance. Some gas and electric companies offer loan programs and deferral loans for insulation and weatherizing. Relief and some help is offered for utility bills in some states, including Connecticut and Wisconsin. Many states offer help for low-income residents through payments from HHS Low Income Home Energy Assistance Program (LIHEAP). Depending on where you live, these may be used for cooling, costs, service shutdowns, or a combination of services. There's also a Weatherization Assistance Program, which may help make your home more energy efficient. Most people don't know about these programs. For information, contact the LIHEAP office. (See Appendix I.)

SALE LEASEBACK

Another way of tapping the equity in your home is the sale leaseback. In a sale leaseback transaction, you sell your home and lease it back from the person who bought it. The buyer of your home is in effect an investor who grants you a life tenancy (or specified term of years), allowing you to remain in your home.

Like a reverse mortgage, the sale leaseback gives you access to the equity tied up in your home without forcing you to move. In the sale leaseback, the homeowner assumes the roles of seller, buyer, and lender:

- *Seller.* As a seller, you receive a lump sum or monthly mortgage payments from the buyer.
- *Buyer (or tenant).* As a buyer, you are purchasing a life tenancy or lease term, for which rental payments are due (and theoretically will be deducted from the amounts you receive).
- *Lender.* As a lender, you're financing the purchase. Payments represent the mortgage due you.

In a sale leaseback, your income is protected by your mortgage and/or annuity purchase. Unlike reverse mortgages, the installment payments in a sale leaseback deal are taxable income and may be subject to both capital gains and income taxes. Tax considerations should dictate the specific arrangement that is best for you. Your lawyer should be familiar with lease, sale, and financing.

SELLING YOUR HOME

Your home is a *capital asset*. If you sell it for more than your purchase cost, including both the original price plus certain improvements, you must pay an income tax on your gains. This is the *capital gains tax*.

For many years, taxes on gains from the sale of your house had tax breaks in the form of a one-time $125,000 exclusion and rollover provisions allowing proceeds to be funneled into a new house.

In 1997, the tax code was revised, eliminating these provisions and replacing them with an exclusion that is potentially available to qualified sellers every two years.

Under the new rules, there is a $250,000 exclusion so long as you pass the "ownership" and "use" tests. These tests require that you must have owned the home for at least two years during the five-year period prior to the date of the sale and lived in it as your primary residence for the same duration (but not necessarily the same two-year period).

The exclusion is $500,000 for married couples on their joint return, if either meets the ownership test, so long as both meet the use test and neither has excluded gain from another sale within the last two years.

Do I have to have lived there for two years straight?

No. The home sale exclusion rules allow you the exclusion so long as it was your principal residence anytime within the five-year period. It doesn't even have to be two years in a row, just 730 days cumulatively.

If I didn't qualify for two years and I sell my house, can my gain be prorated?

Yes, if your failure to qualify is based on a change of place of employment, health, or unforeseen circumstances. The fraction is based on the aggregate period of time of ownership and use. This can be enough, if your gain is smaller. For example, six months would allow you $6/24$ of $250,000, or $62,500, which if your gain is less is all the exclusion you need.

My mother owned her own house for one year and then went into a nursing home. Is her gain prorated?

She can get the full exclusion. A special rule applies for people who go into a licensed facility. However, she'll need a minimum of one year to qualify for the full exclusion.

My mother was widowed this year. Should she sell her house now?

If she sells it the same year as your father's death, she'll be able to shield $500,000 in gain. If she waits, the amount will go back to $250,000.

My future husband and I both own homes from our first marriages. Can we each use the exclusion?

Not after you marry. If two seniors are planning to marry, they should sell their homes first.

Can I use my rollover when I move from my present home into an adult community?

Yes, if you're buying an apartment or other housing unit. If you're merely entering into a lease or contract for services including housing, it may not constitute an ownership interest sufficient to qualify for this tax break, in which case you'll be taxed on any gains from the sale of your home.

Can I use both the rollover and exclusion in selling my home?

Yes, if you meet the requirements for each benefit. Remember, you can only use the $125,000 exclusion one time. Keep in mind that you would only need to use the one-time exclusion if the cost of your new home was less than your previous home.

My house is on the market now. My husband used an exclusion when he sold the residence he and his former wife lived in. Will I still be able to get my one-time exclusion?

No. As long as you're married to your husband, his use of the exclusion precludes you from using it.

MOVING TO ANOTHER STATE

If you are among the 4 percent of retirees who opt to move to another state after retirement, your plans require consideration of additional factors.

In addition to your basic housing costs, you must consider the implications for your tax liability. Investigate the differences in taxes under your new state's laws, including

- Income taxes
- Sales taxes
- Real property taxes
- Tangible or intangible personal property taxes
- Gift and estate taxes

Taken individually or together, these may add considerably to the expenses of your planned move.

The other major area to check is public benefits, particularly if paying for long-term health care costs may present a problem for you. As we discussed in Chapter 9, your potential eligibility for public benefits may change, especially if you are moving to an "income cap" state or one with other restrictive rules. *This is especially important now, with states taking an increasing role in determining how their Medicaid moneys will be spent—and cutting back on expenditures for the elderly in areas such as home care.* If you are unsure, speak to a lawyer or other professional familiar with the Medicaid rules in your new state.

Reminder. If you do move to another state, instruments such as your will, power of attorney, living will, and health care proxy may need to be reviewed and revised to comply with the requirements of your new home state.

ZONING AND AGE DISCRIMINATION

When it comes to housing, older people are doubly disadvantaged. Many are unaware of their housing rights. Many more are unable to represent their own interests because of the very conditions associated with their age—disabilities and frailty.

In addition, older persons are frequently subject to discrimination, which isolates them. Fear of reprisal also keeps some from seeking to enforce their rights.

Federal law provides some legislative tools for addressing these issues. The Fair Housing Act provides for reasonable accommodations, which may allow older tenants to retain their housing, and their independence, as they age.

FAIR HOUSING LAWS

The Fair Housing Act is a federal law that prohibits discrimination in housing on account of race, national origin, religion, sex, familial status, or handicap. It does not have a separate category for age but it does prohibit discrimination on account of handicap—and requires reasonable accommodation be made for them.

As we discussed in Chapter 18, the definition of "handicap" may apply to many people who do not think of themselves as handicapped. You may be protected from housing discrimination if you

- Have a physical or mental disability that substantially limits one or more major life activities, *including* hearing, mobility, and visual impairments, chronic alcoholism, and chronic mental ill-ness or

- Have a record of such disability or
- Are regarded as having such a disability

What that means is that if a potential landlord discriminates against you thinking you are impaired in regard to your mobility, you are in the protected class.

The Fair Housing Act covers most housing, both private and pub-lic, in this country. The only exemptions are for owner-occupied build-ings with no more than four units, single-family housing sold or rented without a broker, and housing operated by organizations and private clubs that limit occupancy to members.

The law's prohibitions relating to the sale and rental of housing are extensive. Under its provisions, no one can take any of the following actions based on race, national origin, religion, sex, familial status, or handicap:

- Refuse to rent or sell you housing
- Refuse to negotiate for housing
- Make housing unavailable
- Set different terms, conditions, or privileges for sale or rental of a dwelling
- Provide different housing services or facilities
- Falsely deny that housing is available for inspection, sale, or rental
- Deny access or membership related to sale or rental of housing

Specific prohibitions related to handicap give you the following additional protections:

- Your landlord must allow you to make *reasonable modifications* necessary for you to use your dwelling (or common use area), *at your expense.*
- Your landlord must make reasonable accommodations in any rules, policies, or services if necessary for you to use the housing.

Elder Community Exemption

Buildings and communities may not discriminate against people based on familial status. That means they can't discriminate against families with one or more children under 18 living with

- A parent
- A person who has legal custody of the child or children
- The designee of a parent or legal custodian, with written permission

Housing for older persons is exempt from this prohibition if

- The HUD secretary determines that it is specifically designed for and occupied by elderly persons under a federal, state, or local government program or
- It is occupied solely by persons who are 62 or older or
- It houses at least one person who is 55 or older in at least 80 percent of the occupied units; it has significant services and facilities for older persons; it adheres to a published policy statement that demonstrates an intent to house persons 55 or older

Making a Discrimination Complaint

If you have a complaint of discrimination, you should write HUD or call the HUD office nearest you or the hot line at 800/669-9777. (See Appendix I for full HUD contact information.)

Conciliation. HUD will try to reach an agreement with the person against whom you've made your complaint. If a conciliation agreement is breached, HUD will recommend the U.S. attorney general file suit.

Complaint referrals. HUD may refer your complaint to a state or local agency with jurisdiction. That agency must begin work on your complaint within 30 days.

Immediate help. HUD may go to court immediately to seek an injunction if necessary.

Administrative hearing. If after its investigation HUD finds reasonable cause to believe discrimination has occurred, your case will be sent for an administrative hearing within 120 days. (Or, alternatively, it may be taken to a federal district court.)

HUD attorneys will represent you before the ALJ, unless you wish to be represented by your own attorney. The ALJ has the power to order a number of penalties:

- Money damages to compensate for your actual damages, as well as for any pain and suffering
- Injunctive relief, if needed

- Civil penalty, between $10,000 and $50,000, payable to the federal government
- Attorneys' fees

SOME HELP FROM THE ADA

The Americans with Disabilities Act (ADA) does not apply to housing, and prohibitions on discrimination in housing are located in the Fair Housing Act and Amendments, described before. However, the ADA does provide protections in other areas that may directly benefit older citizens (as well as younger people with disabilities) to allow them to remain in their homes and their communities.

In this regard, the ADA governs various aspects of

- Public services (including transportation)
- Public accommodations (including hotels, retail stores, restaurants, and other private businesses)
- Telecommunications (including emergency telephone services)

The ADA's protections apply to anyone who has or is regarded as having a physical or mental impairment substantially limiting a major life activity. This broad definition covers many people who do not think of themselves as disabled. (For more on who qualifies, see Chapter 18.

Public services. Individuals with disabilities cannot be excluded from the benefits of public transportation services. Title II of the ADA prohibits discrimination in public transportation and requires that new public transportation equipment be accessible to the disabled. Transportation facilities must also be accessible; those that are not must be made so. This applies to private contractors as well as direct government providers.

The requirements of Title II are designed to increase the mobility of people with disabilities by ensuring access to, around, and in a particular mode of transportation:

- Paratransit and specialized transportation services comparable to those provided the general public
- Lifts and ramps
- Equipment maintenance
- Personnel training
- Information for people with visual, hearing, and cognitive impairments

Eligibility for special transit services may be limited to individuals with temporary or permanent disability who can't access the fixed route services.

Alternative transit services must meet standards relating to hours and days of service, service area, response time, fares, and reservation capability.

My community has a special van service for people using wheelchairs. Can they restrict the number of trips I make?

No. That's not permitted under the law. And no waiting lists limiting service are allowed.

If I use a hotel shuttle, do they have to make any accommodation for me?

Yes. These provisions of the ADA apply to businesses whose primary business is transporting people, whether they are public or private.

Public accommodation. Title III of the ADA prohibits discrimination in any place of public accommodation and requires that such places be made accessible.

ADA regulations focus on eliminating physical, architectural, and communication barriers that may limit access to goods and services offered by these types of facilities. Detailed requirements govern items as diverse as

- Pathways to and from facilities
- Entrances, doors, and gates
- Elevators, stairs, and alternative pathways
- Toilets and rest room stalls
- Drinking fountains
- Parking spaces
- Telephones
- Hotel rooms
- Restaurants and cafeterias
- Location of signs

Private businesses subject to ADA accessibility requirements include hotels, motels, restaurants, bars, theaters, concert halls, museums, libraries, office buildings, banks, doctors' and medical offices, recreation facilities, service establishments such as dry cleaners and beauty shops, and sales establishments such as clothing stores, grocery stores, and shopping centers.

Does the ADA cover private apartments and private homes?

Usually, no. If a place of public accommodation, such as a doctor's office or day care center, is located in a private residence, however, those portions of the residence used for that purpose are subject to the ADA's requirements.

Telecommunications and emergency telephone services. This part of the law requires relay services for nonvoice terminal users and full 24-hour, seven-day-a-week service. Telephone emergency services are operated by many public entities to allow individuals to seek help from police, fire, ambulance, and other emergency services. Direct access to these services is required under the law.

Compliance efforts with ADA requirements have been hampered for a number of reasons, including a statutory exception for financial burdens. The regulatory scheme for the statute is a complicated one, dividing enforcement authority among various agencies. State and local public housing complaints may be made to the housing discrimination hot line at the Department of Housing and Urban Development (800/669-9777). Inquiry and complaints concerning transportation services can be made by phone to the Department of Transportation's Federal Transit Administration (888/446-4511). Questions about architectural barriers may be directed to the Architectural and Transportation Barriers Compliance Board (telephone 800/USA-ABLE; TDD 800/993-2822) or to the Department of Justice (telephone 202/353-1555). (See the appendixes for full listings.)

22

Adult Living Communities

For many older people, staying in their own homes is not an option. Health problems, even relatively minor physical impairment, may make living alone too difficult to manage. A spouse with a similar medical condition may make the situation even more difficult. Unfortunately, home care, community assistance, and financial assistance provided through programs such as Medicare and Medicaid do not offer a solution to everyone's needs. Short of moving into a nursing home, what options are there?

If you are among the growing number of those seeking security or assistance that cannot be provided in your home, the answer may be an *adult living community*. Adult living communities come in different varieties designed to meet a range of needs.

- *Retirement communities,* as they are commonly called, are designed for healthy and frequently younger retirees who seek independent living but with some conveniences and services.
- *Continuing care facilities* provide a place to live, three meals a day, and the availability of a nurse to deal with medical emergencies as needed.
- *Assisted living facilities* provide a broader menu of services for those who need greater nonmedical help and some medical supervision.

In general, an adult living community provides the shelter of a home along with extra services and care, from housekeeping help to a range of personal services and health care comparable to what is provided by a nursing home. Monthly costs range from $1,000 to $4,000—steep but nowhere near comparable costs for a nursing home.

There are an estimated 33,000 assisted living facilities, serving as residence to more than 1 million individuals. High concentrations are in Florida, Pennsylvania, and California. Most are privately rented apartments, independent units or connected to a retirement community or nursing home, with varying levels of services. The average fee nationally surpasses $100 a day, which may cover only some of the services provided. According to a report in *U.S. News & World Report,* an estimated half of the residents in assisted living are believed to have some sort of dementia.

In some states, Medicaid will cover part of costs for some residents, but usually only a small portion of those who need services. California has a demonstration project for providing assisted living to low-income residents.

By any name, these communities have become a billion-dollar industry. The best-known companies include Marriott, Classic Residences by Hyatt, and Sunrise Retirement Homes. An estimated 230,000 people live in 800 continuing care retirement communities nationwide. For retiring people, one-quarter of those moving out of state move to planned adult communities in other states. About 1 million people currently reside in more than 30,000 developments built to provide some form of assisted living.

If you're thinking about an adult community, there are a number of factors for you to consider. After all, you are seeking both a residence *and* medical services in one form or another.

- For the housing part of the equation, the first question is whether you should buy or rent. While the adult living community industry has offered mostly owner-occupied housing, this trend is changing. More and more rental housing, with the same facilities and services, is appearing on the market. Whether you rent or buy, you need to find out just what rights in your apartment you will have—and under what circumstances you could lose the apartment.
- You have to examine the provisions of the "insurance" part of the package you are buying. Consider your future long-term care needs—whether there are limits in the package you are buying, what those limits are, and what the implications are for your ability to finance nursing home care down the road. Depending on your needs, your money might be better spent investing in long-term care insurance.

This chapter explains what to look for in an adult living community. And if you are contemplating a move to an adult community, remember to consult with a knowledgeable professional. Although these facilities are marketed like vacation condos, what you are seeking is both your home and your future medical care. You wouldn't do either of these things without long, hard consideration and professional advice, would you? There is no substitute for such advice when you are considering an adult community.

TYPES OF COMMUNITIES

Although adult living communities are undergoing a radical transformation, coming in almost as many varieties as there are customers, they all derive or borrow features from the traditional continuing care retirement communities. These include structures that provide every level of service:

- *All-inclusive or life-care facilities.* These facilities provide traditional long-term care as part of their package.
- *Modified or continuing care facilities.* These provide similar care but with some limitations as to duration and service.
- *Fee-for-service facilities.* In fee-for-service housing, you pay for additional services provided on an à la carte menu. These are increasingly popular.

(Source: American Association of Homes for the Aging)

As the industry and its market grow, different offerings and service packages have appeared, under a variety of guises. These may be called *adult living communities, assisted living,* or just plain *retirement housing.* What these facilities provide is housing plus a menu of services, whether included in a package fee or on a fee-for-service basis:

- *Medical services,* including dental, ophthalmological, and podiatric services, checkups, and assisted living services such as personal care and help with activities of daily living (ADLs)
- *Hospitality services,* including housecleaning, meals and meal service, laundry, utilities, telephone, and TV
- *Support and social services,* including health club, exercise classes, lectures, library, sports activities, and transportation

Not all of these services are available in all types of facilities, and not all of these services will be available to you. *The services you are eligible to receive—and the services you do receive—depend on the kind of facility you choose and the contract you sign.* State regulations offer limited protections in some areas, but not all facilities are subject to their rules.

For many facilities, you may have to meet extra qualifications to obtain services, particularly medical ones, and you may have to pay additional costs for them as well. This puts the burden on you to examine closely what you are being offered before you sign on the dotted line. Remember, although you may not need those services now, your needs progress as you age.

CONTRACTUAL AGREEMENTS

Buying an interest in an adult community is like buying a combination home and insurance policy. Only you usually don't have an insurance adviser or a lawyer protecting your interests (a mistake, in our opinion). What are the risks? After all, you have a threefold investment at stake: your money, your health, and your home. Each one deserves protection. Any transaction that involves all three deserves your full attention and the advice of any experts you can muster.

The first thing to do is to get a copy of the offering brochure and the contract from the facility. *Then read them.* Reading a contract is always an intimidating experience. Take your time. If you have questions, ask. If you find a clause objectionable and someone tells you "they don't really mean that part," then have it crossed out!

Initially there are two major considerations—the financial soundness of the facility and quality of services. These are discussed in the next section.

I am considering an adult living facility that doesn't offer a contract, just a lease. The facility provides two meals a day. Is this desirable or not?

If you're moving into a rental community, you will usually be given only a lease. A lease is a contract that specifies your rights and your landlord's rights to your apartment. In some cases, the lease will also spell out the other services you will receive. Sometimes, these benefits and services will be set forth in a separate contract, called a *service agreement.* Both lease and service agreement are enforceable in the courts.

Whether you buy or rent, stay away from any community that offers you neither a contract nor a lease and service agreement. If the deal is that you get two meals a day, this must be specified in writing. Don't take an oral promise that "all residents get breakfast and dinner." If breakfast is eliminated the next year, you may have no recourse. If they won't put it in writing, you have no way to enforce your claims.

FINANCIAL SOUNDNESS

If you are shopping for an adult living community, you must investigate the fiscal soundness of any facility you are considering. *This may be the most important part of your search.* Too many community residents have been left high and dry by bankrupt facilities or those with finances so shaky that services are unavailable. Low occupancy and inadequate reserves spell trouble for a number of communities, and state regulation on reserves is often inadequate. While sponsorship by a parent organization may sound nice in a brochure, it may afford you little legal guarantee in the way of protecting your investment. You need to know

Corporation information.

- Who the owners are, that is, the principals and any others with an interest in the facility
- Whether there are any outstanding lawsuits or administrative proceedings against the owners or the parent organization, and if there are any liens or other financial obligations that could affect the financial viability of the development
- Whether there are any license restrictions
- What are the corporate assets, current funds, reserve funds, projected income, and liabilities of the facility

Actuarial and utilization data.

- Market studies, population projections, occupancy rates, and service costs
- Projected and actual data on use of health care services

You're entitled to receive audited financial statements and other certified documentation providing this information. You should have the information reviewed the way you would information about a house before closing, by either an attorney or an accountant. You should also check with local service organizations, consumer groups, and government agencies for information about the project and the owner.

Many states require that you be given this information, although that in itself is no guarantee that it will be given to you. It doesn't matter whether your state requires it or not—don't even bother with a facility that won't give you financial information.

A special note. Make sure the name of the facility on the information you receive matches the name of the facility that appears on the contract. Be wary of facilities that advertise they're sponsored by non-profit groups such as churches. In some cases where ownership is non-profit, the management company calling the shots is for-profit. In others, there may be no legal relationship at all.

What else should I find out?

You should inquire about fees. Current rates are only half the story. You want to know whether they've increased in recent years and by how much, as a gauge of your potential future obligations.

ENTRANCE FEES AND PAYMENTS

The cost of adult living varies by the type of facility and by the level of service you're buying. Other variables to be considered include the size of your residence and the number and age of the people who will be living in it. Cost also varies by geographic area.

Entrance fees. Entrance fees should be detailed in the contract, including whether they are refundable, to what extent, and under what conditions. Often there are limitations on the amount you will be refunded, depending on the payment structure:

- Cash up front. Total fee paid in advance, particularly in lifecare communities
- Entrance fees, with additional monthly fees—by far the most common form of contract
- Rental agreements, with fee-for-service available
- Ownership arrangements, such as cooperative or condominium arrangements, with care services. These are growing in popularity.

Other fees. The contract should also specify

- Monthly payments and increases
- Extra costs, if any, upon your transfer to a nursing facility
- Fee increases
- Spousal fees

The contract should also spell out any other entrance requirements, such as a physical examination of the kind you would have to qualify for insurance, in order to establish your ability to live independently. Your finances may be checked to confirm your ability to meet monthly payments. The contract should also spell out your rights and the facility's rights in regard to termination.

Can I cancel the contract and have my entrance fee refunded?

There should always be some sort of probationary period provided in which you can cancel the contract and get your money back. Many states provide a "free look" period of a week or 30 days, in which the law provides that you can cancel the contract.

Can I cancel after the probationary period and get my entrance fee back?

It depends on the contract. It's not required by law, although a number of facilities are beginning to offer "fully refundable" entrance fees. Some contracts provide for a portion of the entrance fee to be reclaimed, in part, at the end of the residency term. This protects people who don't want to pay a hefty fee that will be forfeited no matter how long they remain in the facility. Nonrefundable fees will probably be lower.

What protections do I have against fee increases?

Very few. Contracts may provide for notice, but rarely do they have limits on the number or rate of fee increases.

See if there is any provision to keep on residents who run out of money. Some nonprofit facilities' contracts provide this.

What if my spouse has to be transferred? What happens to my fees?

It depends on the contract. But couples, who usually pay more in the first place, need to understand the fee implications should either of them require a change in the level of care provided or where that care will be given.

Under what circumstances can my contract be ended?

The contract should include a *termination clause* that spells out both your rights and the facility's rights in regard to termination. Usually you are entitled to a probationary period, during which you may cancel the contract. Facilities protect themselves with clauses allowing them to cancel the contract if you are disruptive or a risk to health or safety of yourself or others. Cancellation is also a possibility if there is fraud on either party's part.

If a facility is threatening to invoke the termination clause in a contract against you, you should consult a lawyer. Some state laws impose limitations on when your contract and residency may be terminated against your will, for example, only for good cause, upon adequate notice to you, and after you have been afforded the opportunity to "cure" the defect.

HOUSING AND RELATED SERVICES

Continuing care facilities have traditionally been akin to rental arrangements, with ownership of the residence remaining in the hands of the facility. More recently, co-ops and condominiums have entered the market.

If you are renting, your accommodations should be clearly defined in the contract. For one thing, make sure the unit that is to be yours is specified, as well as what is provided with it.

You should also know what your rights are in making changes or alterations. Are moves allowed, and under what circumstances? More important, under what circumstances can you be forced to give up your unit or transfer to another? (These determinations are often tied to changes in your or your spouse's need for nursing or medical services. See Assisted Living and Nursing Services, below.)

Other services included in housing and hospitality service packages include food, housekeeping, and laundry. Make sure you know whether your accommodations include kitchen facilities and if there are any restrictions on their use. Are meals provided, and if so, are these in a communal dining room? Fees, schedules, and facilities for housekeeping and laundry services should be clearly indicated.

SOCIAL AND SUPPORT SERVICES

A number of people join retirement communities because their friends are there, or because they want the companionship of people in a certain kind of community. They may also want specific activities to keep them engaged in their lives. To many older people, social and support services are critical to maintain their quality of life as they age, including

- Sports
- Recreation facilities
- Spa and gym facilities
- Entertainment
- Movies
- Transportation
- Beauty salons

A picture in a brochure does not mean a service is available. Social and support services must be spelled out in the contract. Again, fees, schedules, and facilities for services should be clearly indicated. The availability of services and their continuation should *not* be left to the discretion of the facility.

ASSISTED LIVING AND NURSING SERVICES

One of the reasons you enter an adult living community or continuing care facility is the availability of assistance in daily living and nursing care if you need it. This is a very important part of the package you are buying. You don't want any surprises when you need medical attention.

You need to know when you're entitled to care, under what circumstances, and what level of care:

- When you can get assisted living services
- What your rights are to services, including what services will be provided under what conditions
- When you can get nursing care
- Your rights for entry to assisted living or nursing care when you need it
- Where care will be provided (on-site or off-site)
- Whether you will have private accommodations
- What your rights are to a bed, and what provisions are made if one is not available
- What the terms of care are
- What quality guarantees you have concerning care

You also need to know when others may make determinations about the care to which you're entitled, under what circumstances, and what your rights are then.

- When you can be moved to assisted living or nursing care
- Your rights to challenge that move
- Your rights to retain your assigned apartment upon your entry to assisted living or nursing care
- Your rights to remain in your assigned apartment upon your spouse's entry to assisted living or nursing care

Read the contract closely. This is very important. Not all facilities and not all levels of care offered may be licensed or regulated by the state. If it is not in the contract, you may have no protection at all.

What protections do I have against being moved against my will?

This is a key question, as important to you as why you chose this community in the first place. The trigger for a move from an independent unit to an assisted one or a nursing unit should be clearly spelled out in the contract. These provisions are often left vague and undefined.

This is not to your advantage. If you are going to be transferred to assisted living or nursing care, you need to have some say in the matter. At a minimum, a transfer determination should be subject to

- Written criteria for transfer
- Designation of a decision maker
- Your right to involvement in the decision
- An appeal process for challenging the decision

GOVERNMENT BENEFITS

Often people buy into lifecare and continuing care arrangements to avoid Medicare and Medicaid issues. By this method, they intend to purchase care for the rest of their lives.

Depending on the type of contract you have and your facility's participation in Medicare and Medicaid, you may still need or want to apply for Medicaid to meet additional long-term care needs. If your assets are high, you may have to spend down to qualify. Your contract may also be counted as an asset.

Many communities also require residents to maintain certain insurance, either Medicare Part B coverage or supplemental Medigap coverage, as well.

The facility we looked at said we would have to purchase long-term care insurance to enter. Is this a legitimate entrance requirement?

It's a common requirement, but one that should be questioned. If you are already paying them to provide nursing care, why do you need the insurance? If you're getting long-term care coverage, what do you need them for?

RESIDENTS' RIGHTS

Residents' rights should be spelled out in the contract. These may include the rights to

- Appeal transfer decisions
- Participate in residents' councils
- Register grievances through a complaint mechanism
- Participation in or representation before management

In addition, representation of tenants' grievances can be had through residents' councils or mandated participation on boards of directors.

Can my rights be changed?

All rules should be incorporated into the contract. However, policies not included in the contract may be part of a supplemental handbook of rules. Generally, the handbook cannot change rights established by the contract, unless the contract allows it.

My contract says I waive all claims against the retirement facility when I enter it. Can I sue if I fall?

Such "waiver of liability" clauses are common in contracts. They are generally not enforced by the courts.

CHANGES IN YOUR FAMILY

Usually, you purchase an apartment or unit in an adult community as a basic family unit. But what happens if you divorce or your spouse dies? You may want a new roommate or spouse who falls below the facility's age limit.

The eligibility requirements for a new resident, spouse, or roommate should be included in the contract. Additional fees, if any, should be spelled out, as should your options if a new spouse fails to meet eligibility requirements. The contract should also include any restrictions as to number or duration of visits by family and friends.

REGULATING ADULT LIVING COMMUNITIES

Continuing care facilities are regulated in more than 30 states. Of these, fewer than half require anything more than disclosure of financial information. State regulation of mandated reserve funding is generally considered inadequate.

Oregon has been a pioneer in assisted living programs, supported by state policy favoring choice for people outside of nursing homes.

Several states have statutes providing specific resident rights for continuing care residents, similar to their statutory protections of nursing home residents.

One problem of regulation is definition. Although your state may have regulations, the adult living facility you are looking at may not be subject to them, for any number of reasons. The overlapping jurisdictions of insurance, housing, and health authorities leave many gaps. (State authorities are listed in the Resources section.)

Accreditation may be available through the Continuing Care Accreditation Commission for continuing care residential communities. The commission has established standards in finance, health care, and residence, and will send you a list of accredited communities. The Assisted Living Facilities Association is also seeking to establish industry standards of care. (See appendixes for contact information.) Neither are regulators, however. Although their imprimatur may be a good sign, it does not substitute for your own investigation.

At present, there is a great range of regulation among the states, as they grapple with the concerns raised by assisted living facilities. Legislators are trying to balance several factors, including protections for older, frail elderly, individual rights to independence and autonomy, and the need to encourage the development of facilities for those who need them.

Oregon and Washington were early pioneers in licensing assisted living facilities, and although not all states require licensure as a category, several have regulations in place, including Alaska, Illinois, Kentucky, Louisiana, Maryland, Missouri, Nebraska, North Carolina, Rhode Island, Texas, Virginia, and West Virginia. Rhode Island is typical, focusing on residents' needs, and mandating a written individual service plan for residents addressing their health, physical, and social needs, and cognitive needs and preferences.

One issue facing legislators is the extent to which assisted living facilities should provide medical services to frail elderly. Alabama, for example, requires assisted living facilities to discharge any residents who should be in a nursing home or facility with a special unit for dementia. Rules in some states prohibit assisted living facilities from providing full services to clients, in effect banning them from serving people with Alzheimer's disease.

Part 8

Getting Help

This book describes numerous laws and regulations written for your protection and strategies for making sure you can avail yourself of that protection. Federal, state, and local governments have passed countless laws designed to help you make decisions about your health, where you'll live, and how you'll protect your assets and plan for you and your children's future.

But these legal provisions aren't worth the paper they're printed on unless you take action to enforce them. This last, all-important chapter tells you how to go about protecting your rights—what actions you can take on your own, when and how to find and hire a lawyer, and what agencies and organizations to contact for assistance.

23

Protecting Your Rights

Protecting your rights is first and foremost a matter of identifying what those rights are. This book provides the blueprint to do just that. In the preceding chapters, we've laid out the basic areas of elder law and several strategies to deal with problems that you may face in health care, money management, caretaking of others, work and retirement, pensions, and housing. This information will help clarify your position and understand your legal rights and the issues you may be facing.

Once you've identified your rights, the question is what are you going to do about them? We've discussed strategies for action under many different circumstances, but these are not tailored to your individual problem and may not answer your specific questions. Here are some guidelines for where you can turn for help.

ASSERTING YOUR POSITION

Your first line of help is *you.* You are your strongest and best advocate. You know what the problem is, you may have a solution in mind, and you probably know where to complain.

Do it! No matter what your complaint is, it will not be resolved unless you make it known. You must communicate your grievance as effectively as possible to those who can do something about it. Most people are reluctant to pursue their complaints, either because they are too busy or intimidated—and government agencies and private companies rely on that in turning you down.

Don't be intimidated, and don't let bureaucrats give you the runaround. If they tell you it's policy, ask to see the policy. If you're still not satisfied, demand to speak to a supervisor or the manager. Remember, the squeaky wheel gets the grease. Ask for the decision and an explanation in writing.

Put your complaint in writing. You would be surprised how many companies will back down if they get reasonable written objections. If at all possible, type letters. This has two benefits—it gives a businesslike appearance and it makes it easier for people responding to you. Make sure you date and sign all communications, and include your address and daytime phone number. Keep copies of everything you send.

Put *everything* in writing. If you make a telephone call, keep a record of it. Note the date of your call and the name of the person who spoke to you. A log of your communications with an agency or company is essential to keeping track of your actions.

If you can't get any action from a government agency or insurance company or feel you're not being treated fairly, try contacting the director of the agency or the president of the company, by phone or in writing. We guarantee you'll get a response then.

"IN-HOUSE" ASSISTANCE

Often large organizations have individuals designated to assist aggrieved or dissatisfied consumers or clients. There are people in agencies whose job is to help you. For example, the patient advocate in a hospital can help with various problems you may encounter, from informal complaints to formal appeals.

Ask them to tell you whether there is anyone to assist you or with whom you can talk. Remember that persistence pays off.

APPEALING DECISIONS

As a general rule, you have the right to appeal decisions made by government agencies (federal, state, and local) as well as industries regulated by government, such as insurance and nursing homes.

An appeal is simply a challenge to a decision. If you are unhappy with a decision, you can appeal it to a designated forum, usually *not* the original decision maker. Appealing a decision is the same as making an informal complaint, except that the process generally has rules spelling out time and place for filing, time and place of the hearing, whether a complainant has the right to appear in person, whether there is a right to further appeal, and other provisions.

Your rights in these matters will be set forth in policy, regulation, or contract. You may also have additional rights in the law. The process you will have to follow will also be spelled out—and it may be explained as well in written information you are sent about your claim or complaint.

If not, ask for a copy of appeal procedures. Remember, there may be specified time frames for appeal that must be observed. You must always file by the prescribed deadline dates.

Although people are intimidated, it never hurts to appeal an adverse decision. What have you got to lose? Nearly two-thirds of Medicare Part B appeals result in reversed decisions. An estimated 30 percent of insurance company rejections are the result of error.

FEDERAL AND STATE HELP

A government regulatory agency can be of particular help to you in pursuing a complaint within its jurisdiction. At the state level, there are agencies responsible for housing, health, and insurance, among others. The long-term care ombudsman in each state investigates nursing home complaints. Others may provide useful information or referrals.

Additionally, a number of federal agencies have responsibility for matters with direct bearing on your life. A federal agency may be able to direct you for help or listen to your complaint. For example, the Medicare hot line will take complaints of fraud and abuse. Many offer valuable information as well. Those agencies charged with specific duties are noted in the text. A full listing of government agency help is available in the appendixes of this book.

THE OLDER AMERICANS ACT

The Older Americans Act (OAA), a federal law passed in 1965, authorizes grants to the states to provide specific benefits to the elderly. The law was designed to promote the development of programs to help the nation's over-65 population. To its initial mission of community planning, subsequent amendments have added legal assistance and advocacy.

Under the law, states are required to establish a program for ensuring legal and advocacy assistance for elder rights. State and Area Agencies on Aging and other local agencies provide legal assistance along with other programs. Unfortunately, funding has been cut back at all levels of government, affecting many OAA programs. (See Appendix II for a listing of State Agencies on Aging.)

LEGAL PROBLEMS OF THE ELDERLY

Several national organizations specialize in the legal problems of the elderly. These include organizations such as the National Senior Citizens Law Center and the American Bar Association's Commission on Legal Problems of the Elderly. These programs generally provide assistance to lawyers but can also provide helpful information to you or refer you to someone who can.

Other national associations that may be of help include the National Academy of Elder Law Attorneys, which can refer you to a lawyer specializing in elder law. The National Association of Professional Geriatric Care Managers may also be of help.

Depending on your need, there are support and advocacy groups and agencies with specific missions that can help you. For example, Partnership for Caring provides information and assistance in dealing with enforcing treatment decisions, "right-to-die" issues, and advance health care directives. The Medicare Rights Center provides advice about Medicare and how to appeal Medicare decisions. It can also refer you to a lawyer in your area for more help.

HIRING A LAWYER

Lawyers make great punchlines for comics, but the bottom line is, when you need a lawyer, get one! The government has lawyers, insurance companies have lawyers, landlords have lawyers. Why shouldn't you? Don't hesitate to get a lawyer when you need one.

When do you need a lawyer?

- *When planning.* This is when you need a lawyer before you need one—to avert a crisis, to make sure documents are in place and assets structured so that you won't be scrambling for help when it may be too late.
- *When reviewing contracts and documents.* If you're entering a facility, buying an insurance policy, or negotiating retirement with your employer—these all require professional help.
- *When appealing decisions.* Get a lawyer for appeals above a certain level, where expertise in complicated government regulations is needed. And get a lawyer for anything that has big consequences, such as a denial of a Medicaid eligibility claim. (Better yet, get one before—so you can plan when to apply.)
- *When there's a crisis.* Even with planning, you may need a lawyer to help enforce your rights in a crisis.

Having a lawyer on your side expands your team. A letter from your lawyer to an agency or company is often worth the fee by itself because it may avert lengthy future action. Don't try to save money by not hiring a lawyer; it may wind up costing you more. Most problems can be handled for relatively modest costs.

Finding a lawyer. The best lawyer is one who specializes in your problem, whether it is an issue of trusts and estates, Medicaid planning, real estate, or health care. You can get a lawyer through personal recommendations, through the organizations described in this chapter (and others listed in the appendixes of this book), through referrals by other lawyers, or from local bar associations that may have legal referral services or elder law sections or committees. The National Academy of Elder Law Attorneys will provide names of members in your area.

Depending on your problem, you can also get referrals from organizations dedicated to the subject area in which you need assistance, such as the Alzheimer's Association, the Social Security Office, or the National Citizens Coalition for Nursing Home Reform.

On a local level, your Area Agency on Aging may be able to refer you to a lawyer. Good local attorneys may be found through your local city or county bar association, or through people you know.

Interviewing a lawyer. Schedule a consultation—ask in advance what the charge for that will be—and make sure you bring any documents you have pertaining to your problem. The way to avert possible problems is to have an understanding up front of what the cost will be, what work the lawyer will do, and what results may occur.

Make a list of questions and bring the list with you. Your questions should relate to the substance of your problem, the lawyer's background, and costs.

- *The substance of your problem.* Ask what steps he or she proposes to resolve your problem, how long it will take, what may happen, and if there are any other alternatives.
- *Lawyer's background.* Ask about the lawyer's general background, years of practice, education, area of expertise, time devoted to elder law, and particular expertise in the area. Will he or she handle all parts of your problem, including appeals or trials if needed? Who will you be talking to?
- *Cost.* This is the most important consideration. You must ask this question. More and more attorneys are willing to go over your costs with you, explaining their charges and what they will be. Ask if the lawyer can take your case on a *contingent fee* basis, taking as his or her fee a percentage of the money you may eventually be awarded. This arrangement is common in personal

injury suits. If an attorney will not discuss costs with you, find another one who will.

Do not hire anyone who doesn't answer your questions satisfactorily or completely.

AGING ORGANIZATIONS AND AGENCIES

There are numerous agencies in your community that can assist you in legal and nonlegal matters, in finding programs and in enforcing your rights. There are a number of national, state, and local agencies whose missions are just that.

On the national level, there are two kinds of agencies that may be of help to you. The first is national organizations set up to assist the elderly, such as the Gray Panthers, the Older Women's League (OWL), and the American Association of Retired Persons (AARP). They have strong information and assistance programs to aid you in almost any conceivable problem you may have.

A number of organizations exist for help with specific diseases. They may also provide referrals for the services you need. These include organizations such as the Alzheimer's Association and the American Cancer Society. (See Appendix I.)

Don't forget your own backyard. Many communities have programs that provide assistance for local residents. There may be a local chapter of one of the national organizations. You can consult your local Area Agency on Aging for information on these.

The last word. Elder law is a system of tools, built upon strategies to help you with problems you may face. You must pick up the tools to make them work.

Don't be afraid to take action when it is needed. Ask questions. Ask more. When you need help, get it. Remember, you are not alone. You have the information in this book to help you to plan and to deal with problems that you have not anticipated in your planning. Remember, you are your own best planner, your own best advocate, and your own best resource for shaping your future.

Appendix I
Where to Get
Information or Help

PART 1: PLANNING FOR YOUR HEALTH CARE NEEDS

Doctors and Hospitals

American Academy of Family Physicians
11400 Tomahawk Creek Parkway
Leawood, KS 66211-2672
913/906-6000
http://www.aafp.org

American Board of Family Practice, Inc.
2228 Young Drive
Lexington, Kentucky 40505-4294
859/269-5626
888/995-5700
http://www.abfp.org

American Board of Internal Medicine
510 Walnut Street
Suite 1700
Philadelphia, PA 19106
215/446-3500
800/441-ABIM (2246)
http://www.abim.org

American Board of Medical Specialties
1007 Church Street
Suite 404
Evanston, IL 60201-5913
Hot line verification: 866/ASK-ABMS
847/491-9091

American Geriatrics Society
350 Fifth Avenue
Suite 801
New York, NY 10118
212/308-1414
http://www.americangeriatrics.org
http://www.healthinaging.org

American Hospital Association
1 North Franklin Street
Chicago, IL 60606
312/422-3000
http://www.aha.org

American Medical Association
515 North State Street
Chicago, IL 60610
312/464-5000
http://www.ama-assn.org

Association of State and Territorial Health Officials
415 Second Street NE
Washington, DC 20002
202/546-5400

Community Health Assessment Program
800/847-8480

Federation of State Medical Boards
of the United States Inc.
PO Box 619850
Dallas, TX 75261-9850
817/868-4000
http://www.fsmb.org

Joint Commission on the
Accreditation of Healthcare
Organizations
1 Renaissance Boulevard
Oakbrook Terrace, IL 60181
630/792-5000
http://www.jcaho.org

National Practitioner Data Bank
800/767-6732
http://www.npdb-hipdb.com

Public Citizen Health Research
Group
1600 20th Street NW
Washington, DC 20009
202/588-1000
http://www.citizen.org
http://www.questionabledoctors.org

Medical Information

Abramson Cancer Center, University
of Pennsylvania
http://oncolink.upenn.edu

Alzheimer's Association
800/272-3900
http://www.alz.org

American Cancer Society
800/ACS-2345
http://www.cancer.org

American Diabetes Association
800/DIABETES (800/342-2383)
http://www.diabetes.org

Arthritis Foundation
800/283-7800
http://www.arthritis.org

Cancer Information Service
National Cancer Institute
800/4-CANCER

National Parkinson's Foundation
800/327-4545
http://www.parkinson.org

Nutrition Hotline
American Institute for Cancer
Research
800/843-8114
http://www.medem.com
http://my.webmd.com
http://medconnect.com
http://www.rxlist.com
http://www.pharminfo.com
http://www.healthtouch.com
http://www.benefitscheckup.org

Local Referrals, Second Opinions, QMB Program, Information

Long Term Care Ombudsman
Resource Center
1424 16th Street NW
Washington, DC 20036
202/332-2275
http://www.ltcombudsman.org

Medicare hot line
800/MEDICARE

Information on Life-Sustaining Technology, State Laws, and Sample State Forms

5 Wishes
Aging with Dignity
PO Box 1661
Tallahassee, FL 32302
888/5-WISHES (888/594-7437)
http://www.agingwithdignity.org

Partnership for Caring
1035 30th Street NW
Washington, DC 20007
800/939-WILL

Home Care

Community Health Accreditation Program
National League for Nursing
350 Hudson Street
New York, NY 10006
212/480-8828
800/656-9656
http://www.chapinc.org

National Association for Home Care
228 Seventh Street SE
Washington, DC 20003
202/547-7424
http://www.nahc.org

National Council on the Aging
409 Third Avenue SW
Washington, DC 20024
202/479-1200
http://www.ncoa.org

Hospice

Hospice Foundation of America
2001 S Street NW, #300
Washington, DC 20009
800/854-3402
http://www.hospicefoundation.org

Hospiceweb
http://www.hospiceweb.com

Caregiving

Aging Network Services
4400 East-West Highway
Suite 907
Bethesda, MD 20814
301/657-3250
http://www.agingnets.com

Children of Aging Parents
1609 Woodburne Road
Suite 302A
Levittown, PA 19057
800/227-7294

http://www.caps4caregivers.org

Family Caregiver Alliance
690 Market Street
Suite 600
San Francisco, CA 94104
415/434-3388
http://www.caregiver.org

National Alliance for Caregiving
4720 Montgomery Lane
Suite 642
Bethesda, MD 20814
http://www.caregiving.org

National Association of Professional Geriatric Care Managers
1604 North Country Club Road
Tucson, AZ 85716
520/881-8008
http://www.caremanager.org

National Eldercare Locator (sponsored by the Administration on Aging)
800/677-1116
http://www.aoa.gov

Nursing Homes

American Association of Homes for the Aging
2519 Connecticut Avenue NW
Washington, DC 20008
202/738-2242
http://www.aahsa.org

American Health Care Association
1201 L Street NW
Washington, DC 20005
202/842-4444
http://www.ahca.org

Friends and Relatives of the Institutionalized Aged (FRIA)
11 John Street
Suite 601
New York, NY 10038

212/732-4455
http://www.fria.org

National Association of Area Agencies on Aging
927 15th Street
Washington, DC 20005
202/296-8130
http://www.n4a.org

National Association of State Units on Aging (NASUA)
1201 15th Street NW
Suite 350
Washington, DC 20005
202/898-2578
http://www.nasua.org

National Citizens' Coalition for Nursing Home Reform
1424 16th Street NW
Suite 202
Washington, DC 20036
202/332-2275
http://www.nccnhr.org

National Senior Citizen Law Center
http://www.medicare.gov/
NHCompare/Home.asp

Restraint Minimization

Jewish Home & Hospital for the Aged
120 West 106th Street
New York, NY 10025
212/870-5000
800/432-5442
http://www.jewishhome.org

Medigap Counseling

National Association of Area Agencies on Aging
800/677-1116

PART 2: MANAGING AND PAYING FOR HEALTH CARE

Medicare/Medicaid

Center for Medicare Advocacy
203/456-7790
800/262-4414

Centers for Medicare and Medicaid (CMS)
200 Independence Avenue SW
Washington, DC 20201
202/690-6726

Medicare fraud hot line
800/368-5779
800/638-3986 (Maryland)

Medicare-Medicaid Assistance Program
AARP
601 E Street
Washington, DC 20049
800/424-3410
http://www.aarp.org

Medicare Rights Center
1460 Broadway
8th Floor
New York, NY 10036
212/869-3850
800/333-4114

National Council on the Aging
409 Third Street SW
Washington, DC 20024
202/479-1200
http://www.ncoa.org
http://www.benefitscheckup.org

Rating Services

A.M. Best
Ambest Road
Oldwick, NJ 08858
908/439-2200
http://www.ambest.com

Fitch, Inc.
One State Street Plaza
New York, NY 10004
212/908-0500
http://www.fitchratings.com

Moody's Investors Service
99 Church Street
New York, NY 10007
212/553-1658
http://www.moodys.com

Standard & Poor's
55 Water Street
New York, NY 100
212/438-2000
http://www.standardandpoors.com

Weiss Ratings Inc.
4176 Burns Road
Palm Beach Gardens, FL 33410
800/289-9222
http://www.weissratings.com

Accreditation Information

Blue Cross and Blue Shield
Association
676 North St. Clair Street
Chicago, IL 60611
312/440-6000
http://www.bluecares.com

National Commission of Quality
Assurance
2000 L Street NW
Suite 500
Washington, DC 20036
202/955-3500
888/275-7585
http://www.ncqa.org

Insurance Claims, Information, Records, and Referrals

Medical Information Bureau
PO Box 105
Essex Station

Boston, MA 02112
617/426-3660
http://www.mib.com

National Insurance Consumers
Organization (NICO)
121 North Payne Street
Alexandria, VA 22314
703/549-8050

Medicare Supplemental (Medigap) Insurance

Health Insurance Association of
America
1201 F Street NW
Washington, DC 20004
202/824-1600

National Association of Insurance
Commissioners
2301 McGee
Kansas City, MO 64108
816/842-3600
http://www.naic.org

National Insurance Consumer
Helpline
800/942-4242

PART 3: FINANCING LONG-TERM CARE

Long-Term Care Insurance Partnerships

California Partnership for
Long-Term Care
800/CARE445
http://www.dhs.ca.gov/cpltc

Connecticut Partnership
860/418-6318
http://www.ctpartnership.org

Indiana Long-Term Care Insurance
Program
317/233-1470
800/452-4800
http://www.state.in.us/fssa/iltcp

New York State Partnership for
Long-Term Care
800/633-3088
http://www.nyspltc.org

Reverse Mortgages

AARP Home Equity Conversion
Service
1909 K Street NW
Washington, DC 20049
202/434-6030
http://www.aarp.org/revmort

Federal National Mortgage
Association (Fannie Mae)
800/7-FANNIE (800/762-6643)

Federal Trade Commission
Sixth Street and Pennsylvania Avenue
NW
Washington, DC 20580
202/326-2180

National Center for Home Equity
Conversion
360 North Robert, #403
St. Paul, MN 55101
651/222-6775
http://www.reverse.org

Annuities and Life Insurance

American Council on Life Insurance
101 Constitution Avenue NW
Washington, DC 20004
202/624-2000
http://www.acli.com

National Association of People with
AIDS
1413 K Street NW
Washington, DC 20005
202/898-0414
http://www.napwa.org

National Viatical Association
1030 15th Street NW
Suite 870
Washington, DC 20005
800/741-9465

Viatical and Life Settlement
Association of America
800 Mayfair Circle
Orlando, FL 32803
407/894-3797
800/842-9811
http://www.viatical.org

PART 4: LIFE PLANNING FOR YOU AND YOUR FAMILY

Living Wills, Health Care Proxies, and Powers of Attorney for Health Care

Compassion in Dying
Federation
6312 SW Capitol Highway, #415
Portland, OR 97201
503/221-9556
http://www.compassionindying.org

Last Acts
1620 I Street NW
Suite 202
Washington, DC 20006
202/296-8071
http://www.lastacts.org

Disabled Children

Clearinghouse on Disability Information
Office of Special Education and
Rehabilitative Services
Department of Education
330 C Street SW
Room 3132
Washington, DC 20202
202/205-8241

Community Trust for Disabled Adults
Federation of Employment Guidance
Services
315 Hudson Street
New York, NY 10013
212/366-8008

Disability Rights Education and Defense Fund
2212 Sixth Street
Berkeley, CA 94710
510/644-2555 V/TTY
dredf@dredf.org

Disabled and Alone/Life Services for the Handicapped
352 Park Avenue South
Suite 703
New York, NY 10010
212/532-6740
800/995-0066
http://www.disabledandalone.org

Federal Communications Commission
888/225-5322
888/835-5322 (TTY)
http://www.fcc.gov/cib/dro

National Alliance for the Mentally Ill
Colonial Place Three
2107 Wilson Boulevard
Suite 300
Arlington, VA 22201

703/524-7600
800/950-NAMI
http://www.nami.org

National Association of Protection and Advocacy Agencies
900 Second Street NE
Suite 211
Washington, DC 20002
202/408-9514
202/408-9521 (TDD)

National Information Center for Children and Youth with Disabilities
PO Box 1492
Washington, DC 20013
800/695-0285
http://www.nichny.org

National PLAN (Planned Lifetime Assistance Network) Alliance
195 Woodlawn Avenue
Saratoga Springs, NY 12866
518/587-3372
http://www.nami.org

Special Needs Advocates for Parents
1801 Avenue of the Stars
Century City, CA 90067
888/310-9889
http://www.snap.org

Guardianship

American Bar Association
Commission on Legal Problems for
the Elderly
1800 M Street NW
Washington, DC 20036
202/331-2297
202/662-8685
http://www.abanet.org

Clearinghouse on Abuse and Neglect of the Elderly (CANE)
Department of Consumer Studies

University of Delaware
Newark, DE 19716
302/831-3525

**National Association of State Units
on Aging (NASUA)**
1201 15th Street NW
Suite 350
Washington, DC 20005-2800
202/898-2586
http://www.nasua.org

**National Association of Adult
Protective Services
Administrators**
Mental Health and Developmental
Disabilities Services Division
PO Box 14250
2575 Bittern Street NE
Salem, OR 97309-0740
503/945-9491

National Center on Elder Abuse
1201 15th Street NW
Suite 350
Washington, DC 20005-2800
202/898-2586
http://www.elderabusecenter.org

**National Committee for the
Prevention of Elder Abuse**
c/o Institute on Aging
UMass Memorial Health Care
Systems
1101 Vermont Avenue NW
Suite 1001
Washington, DC 20002
202/682-4140
ncpea@erols.com

**San Francisco Consortium for Elder
Abuse Prevention Program**
Institute on Aging
3330 Geary Boulevard
San Francisco, CA 94118
415/447-1989
http://www.ioaging.org

Organ Donation

The Living Bank
PO Box 6725
Houston, TX 77265
800/528-2971
800/GIFT-4-NY (NY office)
http://www.livingbank.org

Organ Donor Hotline
North American Transplant
Coordinator Organization
800/24-DONOR

United Network for Organ Sharing
800/243-6667

PART 6: WORKING AND RETIREMENT

Discrimination Complaints

**Equal Employment Opportunity
Commission**
1801 L Street NW
Washington, DC 20507
202/663-4900
800/669-EEOC (3362)
800/800-3302 (TDD) (and regional
offices)
202/663-4264
For connection to field office: 800/
669-4000
800/669-6820 (TTY)
http://www.eeoc.gov

Americans with Disabilities Act

U.S. Department of Justice
Civil Rights Division
Disability Rights Section
PO Box 66738
Washington, DC 20035-6738
202/514-0301
202/514-0383 (TDD)
http://www.usdoj.gov/crt/ada/
adahom1

Persons with Disabilities

Disability Rights Education and
Defense Fund Inc.
1633 Q Street NW
Suite 220
Washington, DC 20009
202/986-0375 (voice and TDD)
800/466-4232

National Association of Protection
and Advocacy System
900 Second Street NE
Suite 211
Washington, DC 20002
202/408-9514
202/408-9521 (TDD)
http://www.protectionandadvocacy.
com

U.S. Department of Labor
Job Accommodation Network
800/526-7234
http://www.jan.wvu.edu

Family and Medical Leave Act

9 to 5 National Association of
Working Women hot line
800/522-0825

U.S. Department of Labor
Employment Standards
Administration
Wage and Hours Division
200 Constitution Avenue
Washington, DC 20210
202/219-4907
http://www.dol.gov/esa/public/
whd_org

Pensions and Benefits

Pension Benefit Guaranty
Corporation
1200 K Street
Suite 930
Washington, DC 20005

202/326-4000
202/326-4179 (TDD)
http://www.pbgc.gov

Pension Rights Center
1140 19th Street NW
Suite 602
Washington, DC 20036
202/296-3776
http://www.pensionrights.org

U.S. Department of Labor
Pension & Welfare Benefits
Administration
200 Constitution Avenue NW
Washington, DC 20210
202/523-8771

Social Security and Disability

National Organization of Social
Security Claimants'
Representatives (NOSSCR)
6 Prospect Street
Midland Park, NJ 07432
800/431-2804
http://www.nosscr.org

Social Security Administration
hot line
800/772-1213
disability hot line 800/786-6202
earnings estimate 800/973-2000
http://www.ssa.gov

PART 7: MEETING YOUR HOUSING NEEDS

Shared Housing

Shared Housing Resource Center
321 East 25th Street
Baltimore, MD 21218
http://www.nationalsharedhousing.
org

Assistance and Referral

Low-Income Home Energy
  Assistance Program
http://www.acf.dhhs.gov/programs/
  liheap

NASUCA (advocacy utilities)
http://www.nasuca.org

National Energy Assistance Referral
866/674-6327
http://www.ncat.org/neaap/programs

National Housing Law Project
614 Grand Avenue
Suite 320
Oakland, CA 94610
510/251-9400
http://www.nhlp.org
202/347-8775 (DC office)

Weatherization Assistance Program
http://www.eren.doe.gov/buildings/
  weatherization_assistance

Fair Housing and Discrimination Complaints

Department of Transportation
Federal Transit Administration
Office of Chief Counsel
400 Seventh Street SW
Washington, DC 20590
202/366-4011
888/446-4511
http://www.fta.gov/office/civ

HUD User
U.S. Department of Housing and
  Urban Development
PO Box 6091
Rockville, MD 20850
301/251-5154
800/245-2691
http://www.huduser.org

Regional Disability and Business
  Technical Assistance Centers
800/949-4232 (voice/TDD)

U.S. Architectural and
  Transportation Barriers
  Compliance Board (Access Board)
1331 F Street NW
Suite 1000
Washington, DC 20004
800/USA-ABLE (800/872-2253)
800/993-2822 (TTY)
http://www.access-board.gov

U.S. Department of Housing and
  Urban Development
Office of Fair Housing and Equal
  Opportunity
Room 5204
Washington, DC 20410
202/708-0836
202/708-2333
800/669-9777
800/927-9275 (TDD)
800/401-1247 (TTY)
http://www.hud.gov/offices/fheo

U.S. Department of Justice
Civil Rights Division
Coordination and Review Section
PO Box 66118
Washington, DC 20035
202/514-0301
202/514-0381, 0383 (TDD)

Adult Living Communities

American Health Care Association
1201 L Street NW
Washington, DC 20005
202/842-4444

Assisted Living Facilities Association
11200 Waples Mill Road
Fairfax, VA 22030
703/691-8100
http://www.alfa.org

Continuing Care Accreditation
  Commission
2519 Connecticut Avenue NW
Suite 400
Washington, DC 20008
202/783-7286

PART 8: GETTING HELP

Aging Organizations

Administration on Aging
U.S. Department of Health and
  Human Services
Washington, DC 20201
202/619-0724
http://www.aoa.gov

American Society on Aging
833 Market Street
Suite 512
San Francisco, CA 94103
415/974-9600
http://www.asaging.org

Older Women's League
666 11th Street
Suite 700
Washington, DC 20001
202/783-6686
800/825-3695
http://www.owl-national.org

Legal Assistance or Lawyer Referrals

American Bar Association
Commission on Legal Problems for
  the Elderly
740 15th Street NW

Washington, DC 20005
202/662-8692
http://www.abanet.org/elderly

Brookdale Center on Aging,
  Institute on Law
1114 Avenue of the Americas
40th Floor
New York, NY 10036
646/366-1015
http://www.brookdale.org

Center for Social Gerontology
2307 Shelby Avenue
Ann Arbor, MI 48103
734/665-1126
http://www.tcsg.org

Legal Counsel for the Elderly
  AARP
601 E Street NW
Washington, DC 20049
202/833-6720
800/424-3410

National Academy of Elder Law
  Attorneys
1604 North Country Club Road
Tucson, AZ 85716
520/881-4005
http://www.naela.com

National Senior Citizens Law Center
1101 14th Street NW
Suite 400
Washington, DC 20005
202/289-6976
213/639-0930 (Los Angeles office)
510/663-1132 (Oakland office)
http://www.nsclc.org

Appendix II
State Agencies

1. State Agencies on Aging
2. State Long-Term Care Ombudsmen
3. State Elder Abuse Hot Lines
4. State Insurance Departments
5. State Health Departments

1. STATE AGENCIES ON AGING
(Source: Administration on Aging)

Alabama

Melissa M. Galvin, Executive Director
**Alabama Department of Senior
 Services**
RSA Plaza
Suite 470
770 Washington Avenue
Montgomery, AL 36130-1851
334/242-5743
http://www.state.al.us

Alaska

Jane Demmert, Director
Alaska Commission on Aging
Division of Senior Services

Department of Administration
PO Box 110209
Juneau, AK 99811-0209
907/465-3250
http://www.state.ak.us

Arizona

Henry Blanco, Program Director
Aging and Adult Administration
Department of Economic Security
1789 West Jefferson Street, #950A
Phoenix, AZ 85007
602/542-4446

Arkansas

Herb Sanderson, Director

Division of Aging and Adult Services
Arkansas Department of Human
 Services
PO Box 1437
Slot S-530
1417 Donaghey Plaza South
Little Rock, AR 72203-1437
501/682-2441
http://www.state.ar.us

California

Lynda Terry, Director
California Department of Aging
1600 K Street
Sacramento, CA 95814
916/322-5290
http://www.aging.state.ca.us

Colorado

Rita Barreras, Director
Aging and Adult Services
Colorado Department of Human
 Services
1575 Sherman Street
Ground Floor
Denver, CO 80203
303/866-2800
http://www.state.co.us

Connecticut

Christine M. Lewis, Director of Elder
 Services
Division of Elderly Services
25 Sigourney Street
10th Floor
Hartford, CT 06106-5033
860/424-5298
http://www.po.state.ct.us

Delaware

Carolee Kunz, Director
**Delaware Division of Services for
 Aging and Adults with Physical
 Disabilities**

Department of Health and Social
 Services
1901 North DuPont Highway
New Castle, DE 19720
302/577-4791
http://www.state.de.us

District of Columbia

E. Veronica Pace, Executive Director
District of Columbia Office on Aging
One Judiciary Square
9th Floor
441 Fourth Street NW
Washington, DC 20001
202/724-5622
http://www.age.dcgov.org

Florida

Terry White, Secretary
Department of Elder Affairs
Building B
Suite 152
4040 Esplanade Way
Tallahassee, FL 32399-7000
850/414-2000
http://www.elderaffairs.org

Georgia

Maria Green, Director
Division of Aging Services
Department of Human Resources
2 Peachtree Street NE
9th Floor
Atlanta, GA 30303-3142
404/657-5258
http://www.dhr.state.ga.us

Hawaii

Marilyn Seely, Director
Hawaii Executive Office on Aging
250 South Hotel Street
Suite 109
Honolulu, HI 96813-2831

808/586-0100
http://www.health.state.hi.us

Idaho

Lois Bauer, Administrator
Idaho Commission on Aging
PO Box 83720
Boise, ID 83720-0007
208/334-3833

Illinois

Margo E. Schreiber, Director
Illinois Department on Aging
421 East Capitol Avenue
Suite 100
Springfield, IL 62701-1789
217/785-3356
312/814-2630 (Chicago office)
800/252-8966 (in-state Senior
  HelpLine)
http://www.aging.state.il.us

Indiana

Bob Hornyak, Acting Deputy
  Director
**Bureau of Aging and In-Home
  Services**
Division of Disability, Aging and
  Rehabilitative Services
Family and Social Services
  Administration
402 West Washington Street, #W454
PO Box 7083
Indianapolis, IN 46207-7083
317/232-7020
http://www.fssa.state.in.us

Iowa

Mark Haverland, Interim Director
Iowa Department of Elder Affairs
Clemens Building
3rd Floor
200 Tenth Street

Des Moines, IA 50309-3609
515/242-3333
http://www.dea.state.ia.us

Kansas

Connie L. Hubbell, Secretary
Department on Aging
New England Building
503 South Kansas Avenue
Topeka, KS 66603-3404
785/296-4986
http://www.aging.state.ks.us

Kentucky

Jerry Whitley, Director
Office of Aging Services
Cabinet for Families and Children
Commonwealth of Kentucky
275 East Main Street
Frankfort, KY 40621
502/564-6930

Louisiana

Paul "Pete" F. Arcineaux, Jr., Director
Governor's Office of Elderly Affairs
PO Box 80374
Baton Rouge, LA 70898-0374
225/342-7100
http://www.goea.state.la.us

Maine

Christine Gianopoulos, Director
Bureau of Elder and Adult Services
Department of Human Services
35 Anthony Avenue
State House, Station #11
Augusta, ME 04333
207/624-5335
http://www.state.me.us

Maryland

Sue Fryer Ward, Secretary
Maryland Department of Aging
State Office Building

Room 1007
301 West Preston Street
Baltimore, MD 21201-2374
410/767-1100
http://www.ooa.state.md.us

Massachusetts

Lillian Glickman, Secretary
**Massachusetts Executive Office of
  Elder Affairs**
One Ashburton Place
5th Floor
Boston, MA 02108
617/727-7750
http://www.state.ma.us/elder

Michigan

Lynn Alexander, Director
**Michigan Office of Services to the
  Aging**
611 West Ottawa
North Ottawa Tower
3rd Floor
PO Box 30676
Lansing, MI 48909
517/373-8230

Minnesota

James G. Varpness, Executive
  Secretary
Minnesota Board on Aging
444 Lafayette Road
St. Paul, MN 55155-3843
651/296-2770
800/627-3529 (TTY)

Mississippi

Edna Caston, Acting Director
Division of Aging and Adult Services
750 North State Street
Jackson, MS 39202
601/359-4925
http://www.mdhs.state.ms.us

Missouri

Richard Dunn, Director
Division of Senior Services
Department of Health and Senior
  Services
PO Box 1337
615 Howerton Court
Jefferson City, MO 65102-1337
573/751-3082
http://www.state.mo.us

Montana

Charles Rehbein, State Aging
  Coordinator
Senior and Long Term Care Division
Department of Public Health and
  Human Services
PO Box 4210
111 Sanders
Room 211
Helena, MT 59620
406/444-4077
http://www.dphhs.state.mt.us/sltc

Nebraska

Department of Health and Human
  Services
Division on Aging
PO Box 95044
1343 M Street
Lincoln, NE 68509-5044
402/471-2307
http://www.hhss.state.ne.us

Nevada

Mary Liveratti, Administrator
Nevada Division for Aging Services
Department of Human Resources
State Mail Room Complex
3416 Goni Road
Building D-132
Carson City, NV 89706
775/687-4210
http://www.state.nv.us

New Hampshire

Catherine A. Keane, Director
Division of Elderly and Adult Services
State Office Park South
129 Pleasant Street
Brown Building #1
Concord, NH 03301
603/271-4680

New Jersey

Department of Health and Senior
    Services
New Jersey Division of Senior Affairs
PO Box 807
Trenton, NJ 08625-0807
609/943-3436
800/792-8820
http://www.doh.state.nj.us

New Mexico

Michelle Lujan Grisham, Director
State Agency on Aging
La Villa Rivera Building
228 East Palace Avenue
Ground Floor
Santa Fe, NM 87501
505/827-7640
http://www.state.nm.us

New York

Patricia P. Pine, Director
New York State Office for the Aging
Two Empire State Plaza
Albany, NY 12223-1251
800/342-9871
518/474-5731
http://www.ofa.state.ny.us

North Carolina

Karen E. Gottovi, Director
Department of Health and Human
    Services

Division of Aging
2101 Mail Service Center
Raleigh, NC 27699-2101
919/733-3983

North Dakota

Linda Wright, Director
Department of Human Services
Aging Services Division
600 South Second Street
Suite 1C
Bismarck, ND 58504
701/328-8910
800/451-8693
701/328-8968 (TDD)
http://www.state.nd.us

Ohio

Joan W. Lawrence, Director
Ohio Department of Aging
50 West Broad Street
9th Floor
Columbus, OH 43215-5928
614/466-5500

Oklahoma

Roy R. Keen, Division Administrator
Aging Services Division
Department of Human Services
PO Box 25352
312 Northeast 28th Street
Oklahoma City, OK 73125
405/521-2281 or 2327
http://www.okdhs.org

Oregon

Lydia Lissman, Acting Administrator
Seniors and People with Disabilities
500 Summer Street NE
3rd Floor
Salem, OR 97301-1073
503/945-5811
http://www.state.or.us

Pennsylvania

Lori Gerhard, Acting Secretary
Pennsylvania Department of Aging
Commonwealth of Pennsylvania
Forum Place
555 Walnut Street
5th Floor
Harrisburg, PA 17101-1919
717/783-1550
http://www.state.pa.us

Rhode Island

Barbara A. Rayner, Director
Department of Elderly Affairs
160 Pine Street
Providence, RI 02903-3708
401/222-2858
http://www.dea.state.ri.us

South Carolina

Elizabeth Fuller, Deputy Director
**Office of Senior and Long Term Care
Services**
Department of Health and Human
Services
PO Box 8206
Columbia, SC 29202-8206
803/898-2501
http://www.dhhs.state.sc.us

South Dakota

Gail Ferris, Administrator
Office of Adult Services and Aging
Richard F. Kneip Building
700 Governors Drive
Pierre, SD 57501-2291
605/773-3656
http://www.dss.state.sd.us

Tennessee

James S. Whaley, Executive Director
Commission on Aging and Disability
Andrew Jackson Building
9th Floor
500 Deaderick Street
Nashville, Tennessee 37243-0860
615/741-2056

Texas

Mary Sapp, Executive Director
Texas Department on Aging
4900 North Lamar
4th Floor
Austin, TX 78751-2316
512/424-6840
http://www.tdoa.state.tx.us

Utah

Helen Goddard, Director
Division of Aging and Adult Services
Box 45500
120 North 200 West
Salt Lake City, UT 84145-0500
801/538-3910
http://www.hs.state.ut.us

Vermont

Patrick Flood, Commissioner
**Vermont Department of Aging and
Disabilities**
Waterbury Complex
103 South Main Street
Waterbury, VT 05671-2301
802/241-2400
http://www.dad.state.vt.us

Virginia

Jay W. DeBoer, Commissioner
Virginia Department for the Aging
1600 Forest Avenue
Suite 102
Richmond, VA 23229
804/662-9333
http://www.vdh.state.va.us

Washington

Kathy Leitch, Assistant Secretary
**Aging and Adult Services
   Administration**
Department of Social and Health
   Services
PO Box 45050
Olympia, WA 98504-5050
360/725-2310
800/422-3263 (in-state)
http://www.dshs.wa.gov

West Virginia

Ann Stottlemyer, Commissioner
**West Virginia Bureau of Senior
   Services**
Holly Grove, Building 10
1900 Kanawha Boulevard East
Charleston, WV 25305
304/558-3317
http://www.boss.state.wv.us

Wisconsin

Donna McDowell, Director
Bureau of Aging and Long Term Care
   Resources
**Department of Health and Family
   Services**
One West Wilson Street
Room 450
Madison, WI 53707-7850
608/266-2536
http://www.dhfs.state.wi.us

Wyoming

Dan Stackis, Administrator
Division on Aging
Wyoming Department of Health
6101 Yellowstone Road
Suite 259B
Cheyenne, WY 82002-0710
307/777-7986
http://www.state.wy.us

2. STATE LONG-TERM CARE OMBUDSMEN
(Source: National Long-Term Care Ombudsman Resource Center)

Alabama

Marie Tomlin, State LTC
   Ombudsman
**Alabama Department of Senior
   Services**
770 Washington Avenue
RSA Plaza
Suite 470
Montgomery, AL 36104
334/242-5743

Alaska

Ron Cowan, State LTC Ombudsman
Office of the State Ombudsman
Alaska Mental Health Trust Authority
550 West Seventh Avenue
Suite 1830
Anchorage, AK 99501
907/334-4480

Arizona

Bob Nixon, State LTC Ombudsman
**Arizona Aging and Adult
   Administration**
1789 West Jefferson 2SW 950A
Phoenix, AZ 85007
602/542-6454

Arkansas

Alice Ahart, State LTC Ombudsman
**Arkansas Division of Aging and
   Adult Services**
PO Box 1437

Slot 1412
Little Rock, AR 72201-1437
501/682-8952

California

Gordon Migliore, Interim State LTC
Ombudsman
California Department on Aging
1600 K Street
Sacramento, CA 95814
916/323-6679
http://www.aging.state.ca.us

Colorado

Pat Tunnell, State LTC Ombudsman
The Legal Center
455 Sherman Street
Suite 130
Denver, CO 80203
800/288-1376
http://www.thelegalcenter.org/
services_older.html

Connecticut

Teresa Cusano, State LTC
Ombudsman
State LTC Ombudsman Office
**Connecticut Department of Social
Services**
25 Sigourney Street
10th Floor
Hartford, CT 06106-5033
860/424-5200

Delaware

Tim Hoyle, State LTC Ombudsman
**Division of Services for Aging and
Adults**
1901 North Dupont Highway
Main Administration Building Annex
New Castle, DE 19720
302/577-4791

District of Columbia

Jerry Kasunic, State LTC
Ombudsman
Legal Counsel for the Elderly
601 E Street NW
Suite A4-315
Washington, DC 20049
202/434-2140

Florida

Martie Daemy, Acting State LTC
Ombudsman
**Florida State LTC Ombudsman
Council**
600 South Calhoun Street
Suite 270
Tallahassee, FL 32301
888/831-0404
http://www.myflorida.com/
ombudsman

Georgia

Becky Kurtz, State LTC Ombudsman
**Office of the State Long-Term Care
Ombudsman**
Two Peachtree Street NW
9th Floor
Atlanta, GA 30303-3142
888/454-5826
http://www2.state.ga.us/departments/
dhr/aging.html

Hawaii

John McDermott, State LTC
Ombudsman
Executive Office on Aging
250 South Hotel Street
Suite 406
Honolulu, HI 96813-2831
808/586-0100

Idaho

Cathy Hart, State LTC Ombudsman
Idaho Commission on Aging
3380 Americana Terrace
Suite 120
PO Box 83720
Boise, ID 83720-0007
208/334-2220

Illinois

Beverly Rowley, State LTC
  Ombudsman
Illinois Department on Aging
421 East Capitol Avenue
Suite 100
Springfield, IL 62701-1789
217/785-3143

Indiana

Arlene Franklin, State LTC
  Ombudsman
Indiana Division Disabilities/Rehab
  Services
402 West Washington Street
Room W 454
PO Box 7083
Indianapolis, IN 46207-7083
800/545-7763

Iowa

Debi Meyers, State LTC Ombudsman
Iowa Department of Elder Affairs
Clemens Building
200 10th Street
Des Moines, IA 50309-3609
515/242-3327

Kansas

Matthew Hickam, State LTC
  Ombudsman

Kansas Office of the State LTC
  Ombudsman
610 Southwest 10th Street
2nd Floor
Topeka, KS 66612-1616
785/296-3017

Kentucky

John Sammons, State LTC
  Ombudsman
Office of Aging Services
5C-D
275 East Main Street
Frankfort, KY 40621
502/564-6930
http://www.chs.state.ky.us/aging

Louisiana

Linda Sadden, State LTC
  Ombudsman
Office of Elderly Affairs
412 North Fourth Street
3rd Floor
PO Box 80374
Baton Rogue, LA 70898-0374
225/342-7100

Maine

Brenda Gallant, State LTC
  Ombudsman
Maine Long-Term Care Ombudsman
  Program
One Weston Court
PO Box 128
Augusta, ME 04332
207/621-1079
http://www.maineombudsman.org

Maryland

Patricia Bayliss, State LTC
  Ombudsman
Maryland Department of Aging

301 West Preston Street
Room 1007
Baltimore, MD 21201
401/767-1100

Massachusetts

Mary McKenna, State LTC
  Ombudsman
**Massachusetts Executive Office of
  Elder Affairs**
One Ashburton Place
5th Floor
Boston, MA 02108-1518
617/727-7750

Michigan

Brenda Roberts, State LTC
  Ombudsman
Elderlaw of Michigan
221 North Pine
Lansing, MI 48933
866/485-9393

Minnesota

Sharon Zoesch, State LTC
  Ombudsman
**Office of Ombudsman for Older
  Minnesotans**
121 East Seventh Place
Suite 410
St. Paul, MN 55101
800/657-3591

Mississippi

Anniece McLemore, State LTC
  Ombudsman
**Mississippi Department of Human
  Services**
Division of Aging
750 North State Street
Jackson, MS 39202
601/359-4927

Missouri

Carol Scott, State LTC Ombudsman
**Department of Health and Senior
  Services**
PO Box 570
615 Howerton Court
Jefferson City, MO 65102
800/309-3282
http://www.dss.state.mo.us/da/
  ombud.htm

Montana

Robin Homan, State LTC
  Ombudsman
**Montana Department of Health and
  Human Services**
PO Box 4210
111 North Sanders
Helena, MT 59604-4210
406/444-4676

Nebraska

Cindy Kadavy. State LTC Ombudsman
Division of Aging Services
PO Box 95044
Lincoln, NE 68509-5044
402/471-2307
http://www.hhs.state.ne.us/ags/
  ltcombud.htm

Nevada

Gilda Johnstone, State LTC
  Ombudsman
Nevada Division for Aging Services
445 Apple Street, #104
Reno, NV 89502
775/688-2964

New Hampshire

Ronald Adcock, Acting State LTC
  Ombudsman

New Hampshire Long-Term Care
　Ombudsman Program
129 Pleasant Street
Concord, NH 03301-3857
603/271-4375

New Jersey

William Isele, State LTC Ombudsman
Office of Ombudsman for
　Institutional Elderly
PO Box 807
Trenton, NJ 08625-0807
609/943-4026

Ohio

Beverley Laubert, State LTC
　Ombudsman
Ohio Department of Aging
50 West Broad Street
9th Floor
Columbus, OH 43215-3363
614/466-1221

Oklahoma

Esther Houser, State LTC
　Ombudsman
Aging Services Division Oklahoma
　Department
312 Northeast 28th Street
Oklahoma City, OK 73105
405/521-6734

Oregon

Meredith Cote, State LTC
　Ombudsman
Oregon Office of the Long-Term
　Care Ombudsman
3855 Wolverine NE
Suite 6
Salem, OR 97305-1251
503/378-6533
http://www.teleport.com/~ombud/

Pennsylvania

Cynthia Boyne, State LTC
　Ombudsman
Pennsylvania Department of Aging
555 Walnut Street
5th Floor
PO Box 1089
Harrisburg, PA 17101
717/783-7247

Rhode Island

Roberta Hawkins, State LTC
　Ombudsman
Alliance for Better Long Term Care
422 Post Road
Suite 204
Warwick, RI 02888
401/785-3340

South Carolina

Jon Cook, State LTC Ombudsman
South Carolina Department of
　Health and Human Services
Office of Aging
PO Box 8206
Columbia, SC 29202-8206
803/898-2850

South Dakota

Jeff Askew, State LTC Ombudsman
Department of Social Services
South Dakota Office of Adult
　Services and Aging
700 Governors Drive
Pierre, SD 57501-2291
605/773-3656

Tennessee

Adrian Wheeler, State LTC
　Ombudsman
Tennessee Commission on Aging
　and Disability

Andrew Jackson Building
500 Deaderick Street
9th Floor
Nashville, TN 37243
615/741-2056

Texas

John Willis, State LTC Ombudsman
Texas Department on Aging
4900 North Lamar Boulevard
Fourth Floor
PO Box 12786
Austin, TX 78711
512/424-6875
http://www.tdoa.state.tx.us

Utah

Chad McNiven, State LTC
 Ombudsman
Department of Human Services
**Utah Division of Aging and Adult
 Services**
120 North 200 West
Room 401
Salt Lake City, UT 84103
801/538-3924

Vermont

Jacqueline Majoros, State LTC
 Ombudsman
Vermont Legal Aid, Inc.
264 North Winooski
PO Box 1367
Burlington, VT 05402
802/863-5620

Virginia

Joani Latimer, State LTC
 Ombudsman
**Virginia Association Area Agencies
 on Aging**
530 East Main Street
Suite 800

Richmond, VA 23219
804/644-2804
http://www.vaaaa.org

Washington

Kary Hyre, State LTC Ombudsman
**South King County Multi-Service
 Center**
1200 South 336th Street
PO Box 23699
Federal Way, WA 98093
253/838-6810
http://www.ltcop.org/index.htm

West Virginia

Larry Medley, State LTC
 Ombudsman
**West Virginia Bureau of Senior
 Services**
1900 Kanawha Boulevard East
Holly Grove Building, #10
Charleston, WV 25302
304/558-3317

Wisconsin

George Potaracke, State LTC
 Ombudsman
**Wisconsin Board on Aging and Long
 Term Care**
214 North Hamilton Street
Madison, WI 53703
608/266-8945

Wyoming

Deborah Alden, State LTC
 Ombudsman
Wyoming Senior Citizens, Inc.
756 Gilchrist
PO Box 94
Wheatland, WY 82201
307/322-5553

3. STATE ELDER ABUSE HOT LINES

Many states have instituted 24-hour toll-free numbers for receiving reports of abuse. Calls are confidential.

State	Domestic Elder Abuse	Institutional Elder Abuse
Alabama	800/458-7214	None available
Alaska	800/478-9996	800/730-6393
	907/269-3666	907/334-4483
Arizona	877/767-2385	877/767-2385
Arkansas	800/482-8049	800/582-4887
California	None available	800/231-4024
Colorado	800/773-1366	800/238-1376
Connecticut	888/385-4225	860/424-5241
Delaware	800/223-9074	800/223-9074
District of Columbia	202/727-2345	202/434-2140
Florida	800/962-2873	800/962-2873
Georgia	800/677-1116	404/657-5726
		404/657-4076
Hawaii	808/832-5115	Same
	808/243-5151	
	808/241-3432	
	808/933-8820	
	808/327-6280	
Idaho	208/334-2220	None available
Illinois	800/252-8966	800/252-4343
Indiana	800/992-6978	800/992-6978
Iowa	800/362-2178	515/281-4115
Kansas	800/922-5330	800/842-0078
	785/296-0044	
Kentucky	800/752-6200	800/752-6200
		800/372-2991
Louisiana	800/259-4990	800/259-4990
Maine	800/624-8404	800/624-8404
Maryland	800/91-PREVENT	Same
	(800/917-7383)	

State	Domestic Elder Abuse	Institutional Elder Abuse
Massachusetts	800/922-2275	800/462-5540
Michigan	800/996-6228	800/882-6006
Minnesota	800/333-2433	800/333-2433
Mississippi	800/222-8000	800/227-7308
Missouri	800/392-0210	800/392-0210
Montana	800/332-2272	None available
Nebraska	800/652-1999	800/652-1999
Nevada	800/992-5757	800/992-5757
New Hampshire	800/949-0470	800/442-5640
	603/271-4386	603/271-4396
New Jersey	800/792-8820	800/792-8820
New Mexico	800/797-3260	800/797-3260
	505/841-6100	505/841-6100
New York	800/342-9871	800/220-7184
		800/425-0314
		800/837-9018
		800/425-0319
		800/425-0316
		800/425-0320
		800/425-0323
North Carolina	800/662-7030	Same
North Dakota	800/451-8693	800/451-8693
Ohio	None available	800/282-1206
Oklahoma	800/522-3511	Same
Oregon	800/232-3020	Same
Pennsylvania	800/490-8505	800/254-5164
Rhode Island	401/222-2858 × 321	Same
South Carolina	800/868-9095	Same
South Dakota	605/773-3656	Same
Tennessee	888/277-8366	Same
Texas	512/834-3784	512/438-2633
	800/252-5400	800/458-9858
Utah	801/264-7669	Same
	800/371-7897	

State	Domestic Elder Abuse	Institutional Elder Abuse
Vermont	800/564-1612	
Virginia	888/832-3858	Same
	804/371-0896	Same
Washington	800/422-3263	800/562-6078
West Virginia	800/352-6513	Same
Wisconsin	608/266-2536	800/815-0015
		608/266-8944
Wyoming	307/777-6137	307/777-7123

Source: Elder Abuse Center.

4. STATE INSURANCE DEPARTMENTS
(Source: U.S. Department of Labor)

Alabama Department of Insurance
200 Monroe Street
Suite 1700
Montgomery, AL 36104
334/269-3550

Alaska Division of Insurance
Department of Community and
    Economic Development
PO Box 110805
Juneau, AK 99811-0805
907/465-2515

Arizona Department of Insurance
2910 North 44th Street
Suite 210
Phoenix, AZ 85018-7256
602/912-8444

Arkansas Department of Insurance
1200 West Third Street
Little Rock, AK 72201-1904
501/371-2600

California Department of Insurance
300 Capitol Mall

Suite 1500
Sacramento, CA 95814
213/897-8921

Colorado Division of Insurance
1560 Broadway
Suite 850
Denver, CO 80202
303/894-7499

Connecticut Department of Insurance
PO Box 816
Hartford, CT 06142-0816
860/297-3800

Delaware Department of Insurance
Rodney Building
841 Silver Lake Boulevard
PO Box 7007
Dover, DE 19903
302/739-4251

Insurance Administration District of Columbia Government
441 Fourth Street NW

8th Floor North
Washington, DC 20001
202/442-7817

Florida Department of Insurance
200 East Gaines Street
Tallahassee, FL 32399-0322
850/922-3131

Georgia Department of Insurance
Two Martin L. King, Jr.
Dr. Floyd Memorial Building
604 West Tower
Atlanta, GA 30334
404/656-2070

Hawaii Insurance Division
Department of Commerce and
    Consumer Affairs
250 South King Street
5th Floor
Honolulu, HI 96813
808/586-2790

Idaho Department of Insurance
700 West State Street
3rd Floor
Boise, ID 83720-0043
208/334-4250

Illinois Department of Insurance
320 West Washington Street
4th Floor
Springfield, IL 62767
217/785-5044

Indiana Department of Insurance
311 West Washington Street
Suite 300
Indianapolis, IN 46204-2787
317/232-2395

Iowa Division of Insurance
Lucas State Office Building
6th Floor
Des Moines, IA 50319
515/281-4241

Kansas Department of Insurance
420 Southwest Ninth Street
Topeka, KS 66612-1678
800/432-2484

**Kentucky Department of
    Insurance**
PO Box 517
215 West Main Street
Frankfort, KY 40602-0517
502/564-6027

**Louisiana Department of
    Insurance**
950 North Fifth Street
Baton Rouge, LA 70804-9214
225/342-4717

Maine Bureau of Insurance
Department of Professional and
    Financial Regulation
34 State House Station
Augusta, ME 04333-0034
207/624-8475

**Maryland Insurance
    Administration**
501 St. Paul Plaza
Stanbalt Building
7th Floor South
Baltimore, MD 21202-2272
410/468-2244

Commonwealth of Massachusetts
Division of Insurance
470 Atlantic Avenue
6th Floor
Boston, MA 02210-2223
617/521-7794

Michigan Insurance Bureau
Department of Consumer and
    Industry Services
611 West Ottawa Street
2nd Floor North
Lansing, MI 48933-1020
517/373-9273

Minnesota Department of
Commerce
133 East Seventh Street
St. Paul, MN 55101
651/296-4026

Mississippi Department of Insurance
1804 Walter Sillers Building
Jackson, MS 39205
601/359-2453

Missouri Department of Insurance
301 West High Street
Room 630
Jefferson City, MO 65102-0690
573/751-4126

Montana Department of Insurance
126 North Sanders
270 Mitchell Building
Helena, MT 59601
406/444-2997

Nebraska Department of Insurance
Terminal Building
941 O Street
Suite 400
Lincoln, NE 68508
402/471-2201

Nevada Division of Insurance
1665 Hot Springs Road
Suite 152
Carson City, NV 89710
702/687-4270

New Hampshire Department of
Insurance
169 Manchester Street
Concord, NH 03301
603/271-2261

New Jersey Department of Insurance
20 West State Street
CN325
Trenton, NJ 08625
609/292-5316

New Mexico Department of
Insurance
PO Drawer 1269
Santa Fe, NM 87504-1269
505/827-4601

New York Department of Insurance
160 West Broadway
New York, NY 10013
212/480-6400

North Carolina Department of
Insurance
4140 Dobbs Building
PO Box 26387
Raleigh, NC 27611
919/733-7349

North Dakota Department of
Insurance
600 East Boulevard
Bismarck, ND 58505-0320
701/328-2440

Ohio Department of Insurance
2100 Stella Street
Columbus, OH 43215
614/644-2658

Oklahoma Department of Insurance
3814 North Santa Fe
Oklahoma City, OK 73118
405/521-2828

Oregon Division of Insurance
Department of Consumer and
Business Services
350 Winter Street NE
Room 200
Salem, OR 97310-0700
503/947-7226

Pennsylvania Insurance Department
1326 Strawberry Square
13th Floor
Harrisburg, PA 17120
717/787-2317

Rhode Island Insurance Division
Department of Business Regulation
233 Richmond Street
Suite 233
Providence, RI 02903-4233
401/222-2223

South Carolina Department of
Insurance
1612 Marion Street
PO Box 100105
Columbia, SC 29202-3105
803/737-6160

South Dakota Division of Insurance
Department of Commerce and
Regulation
500 East Capitol
Pierre, SD 57501-3940
605/773-3563

Tennessee Department of Commerce
and Insurance
Fourth Floor
Davy Crockett Tower
500 James Robertson Parkway
Nashville, TN 37243-0586
615/741-2218

Texas Department of Insurance
333 Guadalupe Street
PO Box 149104
Austin, TX 78714-9104
512/463-6464

Utah Department of Insurance
3110 State Office Building
Salt Lake City, UT 84114-1201
801/538-3800

Vermont Division of Insurance
Department of Banking, Insurance
and Securities
89 Main Street
Drawer 20
Montpelier, VT 05620-3601
802/828-2900

Virginia Bureau of Insurance
State Corporation Commission
PO Box 1157
Richmond, VA 23219
804/371-9741

Washington Office of the Insurance
Commissioner
14th Avenue and Water Street
PO Box 40255
Olympia, WA 98504-0255
360/753-7301

West Virginia Department of
Insurance
PO Box 50540
Charleston, WV 25305-0540
304/558-3386

State of Wisconsin
Office of the Commissioner of
Insurance
121 East Wilson
Madison, WI 53707-7873
608/266-0102

Wyoming Department of Insurance
Herschler Building
122 West 25th Street
3rd East
Cheyenne, WY 82002-0440
307/777-7401

5. STATE HEALTH DEPARTMENTS

Alabama Department of Public Health
Epidemiology Division
PO Box 303017
Montgomery, AL 36104
334/206-5347
http://www.alapubhealth.org

Alaska Division of Health
3601 C Street
Suite 540
Anchorage, AK 99503
907/465-3090
http://www.hss.state.ak.us/dph

Arizona Department of Health
1740 West Adams
Phoenix, AZ 85007
602/542-1000
http://www.hs.state.az.us

Arkansas Department of Health
4815 West Markham Street
Slot # 39
Little Rock, AR 72205
501/661-2882
501/661-2357
http://www.healthyarkansas.com

California Department of Health Services
PO Box 942732
MS-486
Sacramento, CA 94234-7320
916/327-6989
http://www.dhs.cahwnet.gov/index.htm

Colorado Department of Public Health and Environment
4300 Cherry Creek Drive South
Denver, CO 80246-1530
303/692-2035
http://www.cdphe.state.co.us/cdphehom.asp

Connecticut Department of Public Health
410 Capitol Avenue
PO Box 340308
Hartford, CT 06134-0308
860/509-8000
http://www.state.ct.us/dph/index.html

Delaware Division of Public Health
PO Box 637
Dover, DE 19903
302/739-4701
http://www.state.de.us/dhss/dph/index.htm

Florida Department of Health
4052 Bald Cypress Way
Tallahassee, FL 32399
850/245-4444
http://www.doh.state.fl.us

Georgia Department of Community Health
Two Peachtree Street NW
Atlanta, GA 30303
404/656-4507
http://www.communityhealth.state.ga.us

Hawaii Department of Health
1250 Punchbowl Street
Honolulu, HI 96813
808/586-4400
http://www.state.hi.us/health/index.html

Public Health Districts of Idaho
Central Board
500 West Idaho
Suite 202
Boise, ID 83702-6001
208/334-3566
http://www2.state.id.us/phd/hdcopage.htm

Illinois Department of Public Health
535 West Jefferson Street
Springfield, IL 62761
217/782-4977
http://www.idph.state.il.us

Indiana Department of Health
Two North Meridian Street
Indianapolis, IN 46204
317/233-1325
http://www.in.gov/isdh

Iowa Department of Public Health
Lucas State Office Building
Des Moines, IA 50319-0075
515/281-5787
http://www.idph.state.ia.us

Kansas Division of Health
900 Southwest Jackson
6th Floor
Topeka, KS 66612
785/296-1343
785/296-1562
http://www.kdhe.state.ks.us/health

Kentucky Department for Public Health
275 East Main Street
Frankfort, KY 40621
502/564-3970
502/564-2556
http://publichealth.state.ky.us

Louisiana Department of Health
1201 Capitol Access Road
PO Box 629
Baton Rouge, LA 70821-0629
225/342-9500
225/342-5568
http://www.dhh.state.la.us

Maine Bureau of Health
11 State House Station
157 Capitol Street
Augusta, ME 04333
207/287-8016
http://www.state.me.us/dhs

Maryland Department of Health and Mental Hygiene
201 West Preston Street
3rd Floor
Baltimore, MD 21201
410/767-5300
http://mdpublichealth.org

Massachusetts Department of Public Health
250 Washington Street
Boston, MA 02108-4619
617/624-6000
http://www.state.ma.us/dph/dphhome.htm

Michigan Department of Community Health
320 South Walnut Street
Lansing, MI 48913
517/373-3500
http://www.mdch.state.mi.us

Minnesota Department of Health
PO Box 64975
St. Paul, MN 55164-0975
651/296-9619
http://www.health.state.mn.us/index.html

Mississippi Department of Health
PO Box 1700
Jackson, MS 39215-1700
601/576-7725
http://www.msdh.state.ms.us

Missouri Department of Health
PO Box 570
Jefferson City, MO 65102
573/751-6400
http://www.health.state.mo.us

Montana Department of Public Health
PO Box 4210
Helena, MT 59604-4210

406/444-5622
http://www.dphhs.state.mt.us

Nebraska Department of Health
PO Box 95044
Lincoln, NE 68509-5044
402/471-2306
http://www.hhs.state.ne.us

Nevada Health Division
505 East King Street
Room 201
Carson City, NV 89701
775/684-4200
http://www.state.nv.us/health

New Hampshire Department of Health
129 Pleasant Street
Concord, NH 03301
800/852-3345
603/271-4685
http://www.dhhs.state.nh.us

New Jersey Department of Health
PO Box 360
Trenton, NJ 08625-0360
609/984-0157
http://www.state.nj.us/health

New Mexico Department of Health
PO Box 26110
Santa Fe, NM 87502-6110
505/827-2613
http://www.health.state.nm.us

New York State Health Department
Empire State Plaza
Albany, NY 12237
518/473-4959
http://www.health.state.ny.us

North Carolina Division of Public Health
1916 Mail Service Center
Raleigh, NC 27699-1916

919/733-3816
http://www.dhhs.state.nc.us/dph

North Dakota Department of Health
600 East Boulevard Avenue
Bismarck, ND 58505-0200
701/328-2372
http://www.health.state.nd.us/ndhd/default.asp

Ohio Department of Health
246 North High Street
Columbus, OH 43216-0118
614/466-3543
http://www.odh.state.oh.us

Oklahoma Department of Health
1000 Northeast Tenth
Oklahoma City, OK 73117
405/271-5600
800/522-0203
http://www.oklaosf.state.ok.us

Oregon Health Division
800 Northeast Oregon Street
Portland, OR 97232
503/731-4000
http://www.ohd.hr.state.or.us/cgi/contact.cgi

Pennsylvania Department of Health
PO Box 900
Harrisburg, PA 17108
877/724-3858
http://www.health.state.pa.us

Rhode Island Department of Health
3 Capitol Hill
Providence, RI 02908
401/222-2231
http://www.health.state.ri.us/default.htm

South Carolina Department of Health and Human Services
PO Box 8206
Columbia, SC 29202-8206

803/898-2500
http://www.dhhs.state.sc.us

South Dakota Department of Health
600 East Capitol
Pierre, SD 57501-2536
800/738-2301
http://www.state.sd.us/doh

Tennessee Department of Health
425 Fifth Avenue North
Nashville, TN 37247
615/741-3111
http://www.state.tn.us/health

Texas Department of Health
1100 West 49th Street
Austin, TX 78756-3199
512/458-7111
http://www.tdh.state.tx.us

Utah Department of Health
PO Box 1010
Salt Lake City, UT 84114-1010
801/538-6101
http://www.health.state.ut.us

Vermont Department of Health
108 Cherry Street
Burlington, VT 05402-0070
800/464-4343
http://www.state.vt.us/health

Virginia Department of Health
1500 East Main Street
Room 123
Richmond, VA 23219
804/786-6261
http://www.vdh.state.va.us

Washington Department of Health
PO Box 47890
Olympia, WA 98504-7890
360/236-4010
http://www.doh.wa.gov

West Virginia Department of Health
350 Capitol Street
Charleston, WV 25301-3712
304/558-2971
http://www.wvdhhr.org

Wisconsin Department of Health
One West Wilson Street
Madison, WI 53702
608/266-1865
http://www.dhfs.state.wi.us

Wyoming Department of Health
117 Hathaway Building
Cheyenne, WY 82002
307/777-7656
http://wdhfs.state.wy.us/WDH/index.htm

Index

A

abuse of elderly. *See* elder abuse and neglect
accelerated death benefits 152–153
 tax issues 248, 257
access requirements, in Americans with Disabilities Act
 complaint process for 342
 to public accommodations 341–342
 to public services 340–341
 to telecommunications 342
accreditation
 of continuing care facilities 353–354
 of home care agencies 37
 of hospitals 10–11
 of managed care 111
Accreditation Commission for Health Care 37
activities of daily living (ADLs) 30–31, 213
 as long-term care insurance standard 140
ADA. *See* Americans with Disabilities Act
ADLs. *See* activities of daily living
Administration on Aging
 Eldercare Locator 36, 42, 365

administrative hearings, in appealing denial of coverage 80, 82–83
administrator, of will 230
 appointed 242
ADS. *See* adult day service
adult day care 32–33
adult day services (ADS) 32–33, 39
adult living communities 343–354
 contract 346, 348–349
 cost of 343
 entrance fees 348
 refund of 349
 evaluation of 344–353
 contract 346
 fees and payments 348–349
 if spouse departs 349
 increases in 349
 financial soundness 347–348
 housing and services 349–350
 medical care options 351–352
 rights 352–353
 if spouse is transferred 349, 350, 351
 to retain apartment 350, 351–352
 to sue 353

visitors, roommates, and new spouses 353
 social and support services 350
 types of services 345–346
 fair housing exemptions 338–339
 licensing and regulation of 353–354
 Medicaid and Medicare in 344, 352
 rental 344, 346 (*See also* renters)
 service agreements 346
 services provided in 345–346
 types of 343, 345–346
advance directives. *See* health care proxies; living wills; power of attorney
advertising for employees, discrimination in 266
age discrimination
 Age Discrimination in Employment Act (ADEA) 262–267
 ages covered under 265–266
 complaint process 272–275, 278–279
 exempt employers 265
 hiring and benefits 266

legal remedies under
275–276
mediation 276–278
prohibited actions
under 263–264
proving discrimina-
tion under 264–265
right to sue under
275, 277–278
waivers and releases
266–267
Americans with Disabil-
ities Act 211–212,
267–272
complaint process
272–275, 278–279
definition of disabil-
ity in 269, 271–272
exempt employers
268
hiring process and
270–271
legal remedies under
275–276
mediation 276–278
older workers cover-
age under 268, 272
prohibited activities
under 268–270
reasonable accom-
modations under
269–271
right to sue under
275, 277–278
in housing
complaint process
339–340
protections against
337–339
pension plans and 286
state protections 278
Supreme Court on 265,
266
aging organizations 361
Alzheimer's Association 69,
360, 361
Alzheimer's disease
adult living communi-
ties and 354
Medicare and 69–70

A.M. Best 92, 111, 139
ambulatory care. See outpa-
tient (ambulatory) care
American Academy of Fam-
ily Practice 3
American Association of
Retired Persons (AARP)
Medicare/Medicaid as-
sistance programs 84
programs and services
of 361
reverse mortgage infor-
mation 150
American Bar Association
170
Commission on Legal
Problems of the
Elderly 359–360
American Board of Family
Practice 4
American Board of Internal
Medicine 3–4
American Board of Medical
Specialties 4
certification hot line 4
American Cancer Society
361
American Geriatrics Society
physician referral service
3
American Homeowner and
Economic Opportunity
Act (2000) 147
American Hospital Association
Patient's Bill of Rights
13–16, 21, 24
American Medical Associa-
tion 224–225
Americans with Disabilities
Act (ADA)
access requirements in
complaint process
for 342
to public accommo-
dations 341–342
to public services
340–341
to telecommunica-
tions 342

age discrimination pro-
visions 211–212,
267–272
complaint process
272–275, 278–279
definition of disabil-
ity in 269,
271–272
exempt employers
268
hiring process and
270–271
legal remedies under
275–276
mediation 276–278
older workers cover-
age under 268, 272
prohibited activities
under 268–270
reasonable accom-
modations under
269–271
right to sue under
275, 277–278
community-based treat-
ment and 35
complaint process under
272–275, 278–279, 342
enforcement of 342
annual exclusion 251–252
annuities
community spouse
resource allowance
and 151–152
for funding long-term
care 151–152
of 151
pension plan use of 294
and taxes 256
antidumping laws 11, 26
antilapse laws 229
appeals from decisions
357–358
ERISA 291–595
health insurance deter-
minations 89, 94–95
home care determina-
tions 118
HMO determinations
109–110

insurance company
determinations 95
M+C decisions
110–111
pensions 290–292
Medicaid decisions
135–136
Medicare determina-
tions 79–84
arbitration, definition of
277
Architectural and Trans-
portation Barriers Com-
pliance Board 342
architectural barriers, complaint process for 342
Area Agencies on Aging 36,
360
asset(s)
probate and nonprobate
229
protection under Med-
icaid
annuities for
151–152
exempt assets
124–125
public-private part-
nership policies
142–144
reverse mortgages
for 150
spousal protections
125–129
transfers of assets
to child with disabil-
ities 130, 207
to individuals
127–128, 129–131
long-term care
insurance and
138, 141
to spouses 130
to trusts 131–134
assisted living facilities. *See
also* adult living commu-
nities
accreditation of 354
characteristics of 343,
344
cost of 344

Assisted Living Facilities
Association 354
assisted suicide 180–186
definition of 180
ethics of 180–181, 182,
183–185
nations tolerating 186
in Netherlands 184–186
Oregon Death with Dig-
nity Act 181–183
state law on 181
Supreme Court on
183–185, 187
vs. end-of-life care
187–188
vs. right to die 27, 180
attending physicians 4–5,
12–13
in nursing homes 49
attorney-in-fact 191
autonomy, guardianships
and 214–215
Avicenna 23

B

balance billing 74
Balanced Budget Act
(1997), impact of 118
beneficiaries
of will, definition of
228–229
as witnesses 239
Beneficiaries Improvement
and Protection Act (BIPA)
79
benefit period, in Medicare
72
benefits
employee (*See also* Em-
ployment Retirement
Income Security Act of
1974, Social Security)
age discrimination
and 266
benefit plans
283–296
family leave
279–282
health care 294–297
from bankrupt
or out-of-

business firms
296, 297
changes in
295–296
COBRA 91,
96–98
continuation of
91, 96–98,
295–296
Family and Med-
ical Leave Act
and 279–282,
296
history of 294
for retirees
296–297
self-insuring 295
government (*See also
specific programs*)
for persons with dis-
abilities 205–206,
207, 208
reverse mortgages
and 150
benefits
Older Workers Benefits
Protections Act
266–267
pension benefits
283–296
retiree benefits 296
state laws 282
waivers 266–267
bequest(s). *See* will(s)
billing, balance 74
Bill of Rights
Patient's Bill of Rights
13–16
Pension Bill of Rights
283
resident rights, adult living communities
352–353
Resident's Bill of Rights,
in nursing homes
53–55
BIPA. *See* Beneficiaries
Improvement and Protec-
tion Act
Bismarck, Otto von 303,
306

blindness
SSI income and 316
standard deductions for
258
Blumer case 128–129
board certification, of doctors 3–4
bonds, POD (paid on death)
estate taxes and 251
minors and 235
Breyer, Stephen 184
Brookdale Foundation 33
Browning, Estelle 159
Browning case 159
burial instructions, in wills
236
burial trusts 124, 125
bypass trusts 232, 253
"by representation"
bequests 233–234

C

capacity. *See also* incapacity
legal, definition of 198
testamentary 228, 238
capital gains tax, home sale
and 335–336
capitation 10
Cardozo, Benjamin 19
caregiving xxii
and Family and Medical
Leave Act 279–281
family caregivers 34–35
private care managers
38–39
support programs
34–35
care managers
in long-term care insurance 140
private care managers
38–39
carriers, Medicare 64
case management, in health
insurance 88–89
categorical needy program
(Medicaid) 123
Center for Health Dispute
Resolution (CHDR)
110

Centers for Medicare and
Medicaid Services (CMS)
36, 69, 79
managed care standards
111
Medicare intermediaries
and carriers and 64
certificates, in Section 8
program 330–331
certification
of doctor 3–4
of home care agencies
37
charitable bequests 237
charitable donations, taxes
and 253–254
charitable remainder trusts
253–254
charitable trusts 202
CHDR. *See* Center for
Health Dispute Resolution
children
with disabilities
contesting placement/evaluation of
211
court settlements
208
government benefits
205–207
older children, services for 211
parent's responsibility for 206
planning for
205–212
pooled trusts
209–210
preschool 211
Social Security disability for 313
survivor benefits and
310
trusts 204–210. *See
also* supplemental
needs trusts
trusts *vs.* guardianships 208
discrimination against
families with 338–339

from previous marriage,
protecting inheritance
of 254–255
survivor benefits and
310
tax deductions for
258–259
wills and bequests to
children 233–235
children born after
writing of will 237
disinheriting 237
Civil Rights Act (1991), discrimination claims and
275, 276
claims
ERISA 290
health insurance 93–95
pension 290
CMS. *See* Centers for Medicare and Medicaid Services
COBRA 91, 96–98
continuation rights
under 295–296
codicils 239–240
Commission on Aging with
Dignity 170–171
Commonwealth Fund
296–297
Community Health Accreditation Program 37
community health care. *See*
home and community
health care
community property states,
wills in 238
community services, Medicaid coverage for 130
community spouse resource
allowance (CSRA)
125–128
annuities and 151–152
court-ordered increases
in 126
competitive medical plans
105
complaints. *See also* appeals
about access 342
about age discrimination 272–275,
278–279

about Family and Medical Leave Act 282
about home and community health care 40
about housing discrimination 339–340
about insurance 95
about medical treatment 17
about mortgages 150
about nursing homes 54, 57–58
about public housing 342
about transportation 342
appealing decisions about 357–358
asserting your position 356–357
against health care system 17
help with contact information 373
government agencies 358
in-house sources 357
lawyers 360–361
organizations 358–359, 361
comprehensive/major medical insurance 86–87
conditionally renewable policy 91
confidentiality. *See* privacy
consent 20–23. *See also* informed consent
family consent 24, 176, 178
conservator, definition of 215
Consolidated Omnibus Budget Reconciliation Act. *See* COBRA
constructive trusts 208
consumer rights, in reverse mortgages 149
continuation coverage 91, 96–98
right to 295–296

continuing care facilities 345. *See also* adult living communities
accreditation of 353–354
characteristics of 343, 349–350
numbers in 344
vs. nursing homes 46
Controlled Substance Act, palliative care and 187
conversion coverage 91, 97–98
co-op apartments, reverse mortgages and 147
copayments 10
in health insurance 88
in Medicare 72–73
court evaluators 220
credit shelter trust 253
Cruzan, Nancy 19, 156, 165
Cruzan decision (1990) 19, 24, 156–157, 159, 165, 167, 171
CSRA. *See* community spouse resource allowance
customary and reasonable charges
in health insurance 87–88, 93–95
in Medicare 73–74

D

death and dying
accelerated death benefits 152–153
tax issues 248, 257
advance directives on, *See* health care proxies; living wills; power of attorney
care during, efforts to improve 187–188
hospice services 33
history of 188
Medicare coverage of 119
legal standards for 161, 179
pain management in educating doctors in 188

law regarding 186–187
rights during, enforcement of 188–189
death benefit 311
and right to die 26–27
deductible(s)
definition of 72
in health insurance 88
in long-term care insurance 140–141
in Medicare 72
defined benefits plans 284, 292
defined contribution plans 284, 285, 293
dental services, in nursing homes 50
Departmental Appeals Board 83
Department of Health and Human Services 25
on nursing homes 41
utility bill assistance 334
Department of Housing and Urban Development (HUD) 146
complaint process for 339–340
hot line 342
public housing administration 330, 331
Department of Labor 281–282, 291
Department of Transportation
complaint process 342
dependents, tax deductions for 258–259
Diagnosis Related Groups (DRG) system 75–76
hospital length of stay and 77
diet and nutrition, discussing with doctor 7
dietary services, in nursing homes 50
dignity, right to die with 184

disabilities, persons with
  access requirements for
    to public accommo-
      dations 341–342
    to public services
      340–341
    to telecommunica-
      tions 342
  children
    contesting place-
      ment/evaluation of
      211
    court settlement 208
    government benefits
      205–207
    older children, ser-
      vices for 211
    parent's responsibil-
      ity for 206
    planning for
      205–212
    pooled trusts
      209–210
    preschool 211
    Social Security dis-
      ability for 313
    survivor benefits and
      310
    trusts 204–210. See
      also supplemental
      needs trusts
    trusts vs. guardian-
      ships 208
  community-based treat-
    ment for 35, 206
  court settlements 208
  employment support
    programs 321–322
  government services and
    entitlements for
    205–206, 207, 208
  help for 212
  housing discrimination
    protections 337–339
      complaint process
        339–340
  legal protections for
    211–212
  Medicaid and 130, 206,
    207, 209, 210
  Medicare and 63

Medigap insurance and
  101–102
public housing and 330
rights of
  to education
    210–211
  to housing 211
  to public accommo-
    dations 341–342
  to public services
    340–341
  to telecommunica-
    tions 342
SSI income and 316
supplemental needs
  trusts for 132, 134,
  202, 206–210
    allowable purchases
      209
    alternatives to 208
    operation of
      208–210
    trustee selections
      208
  tax credits for 259
  transition to adult life,
    help with 211
Disability Determination
  Services 314, 316
disability insurance. See
  under Social Security benefits
discharge from hospital
  appeal of 76, 77–78
  discharge planning pro-
    grams 10
  discharge planning
    rights 76–77
  nursing homes and
    51–52, 77
disciplinary action, against
  doctors 5–6
disclaiming of inheritance
  244
discretionary trusts 132
discrimination. See age discrimination protections,
  Age Discrimination
  Employment Act, Ameri-
  cans with Disabilities Act,
  Equal Employment

Opportunities Commis-
  sion, Fair Housing Act
disease. See illness
distributees 229
  intestate 241–242
divorce
  pensions and 290
  Social Security benefits
    and 310, 311, 313
DNR ("do not resuscitate")
  orders 162–164
    enforcement of 163,
      164
    vs. "do not treat" 164
DNT ("do not treat")
  orders 164
doctor(s). See also physi-
  cian(s)
  background checks on
    5–6
  board certification 3–4
  communicating with
    6–7
  conflicts of interest and
    17, 118
  continuing education
    requirements 4
  disciplinary actions
    against 16–17
  and dying patients, edu-
    cation in caring for
    188
  education of 3, 188
  ethics
    conflict of interest 118
    of refusing futile care
      161
      exemption from
        treatment contrary
        to religious beliefs
        161
      investigations of
        drug prescriptions
        187
  fee structures of 9–10
    Medicare and 73–75
  hospital affiliation 4–5,
    10
  and living wills, respon-
    sibility and liability
    164–165

Medicare and 73–75
and pain management,
liability 187
participating 73–74
referral services 3, 7,
364
regulation of 16–17
second opinions and
7, 21, 364
doctrine of substituted
judgment 24, 177
domestic abuse, of elderly
35
domicile, wills and 230
donor cards 178–180, 236
"do not resuscitate"
(DNR) orders. See DNR
("do not resuscitate")
orders
"do not treat" (DNT)
orders 164
double effect principle
184, 186–187
dread disease insurance 87
DRG. See Diagnosis
Related Groups (DRG)
system
drugs
illegal, public housing
and 331–332
prescription, See pre-
scription drugs
drugstores, and medical
records privacy 9
durable power of attorney.
See also power of attor-
ney
definition of 191
for health care. See
health care proxies
sample form 195–197

E

early retirement, Social
Security benefits and
307, 310
Economic Growth and Tax
Relief Reconciliation Act
(2001) 249–250
sunset provision of
250

education
expenses, taxes and
252
rights to for persons
with disabilities
210–211
Education for All Handi-
capped Children Act
210
EEOC. See Equal Employ-
ment Opportunities
Commission
Elbaum, Jean 164–165
elder abuse and neglect
223–227
definition of 224–225
investigation of 226
in nursing homes 56,
227
perpetrators 225
remedies for 226–227
reporting of 226
rise in 214, 223–224
Eldercare Locator (Admin-
istration on Aging) 36,
42, 365
elder law
areas covered by xxiii
history of xvii–xx
role of xxii–xxiii
eligible expenses, in health
insurance 87–88
elimination period, in
long-term care insurance
140–141
emergencies
home care agencies
and 38
medical, informed con-
sent and 22
emergency rooms
requirement to have
11
requirement to treat
11–12, 27
emergency telephone ser-
vices, persons with dis-
abilities right to 342
Emergency Treatment and
Active Labor Act
(EMTALA) 11

employee benefits. See
benefits
employer(s)
bankrupt, retiree
health coverage and
297
information sources on
370–371
and medical records
privacy 9
out-of-business, retiree
health coverage and
296
employment. See also older
workers; pension plans
reasons for leaving 268
support programs for
persons with disabili-
ties 321–322
Employment Retirement
Income Security Act of
1974. See ERISA
employment support pro-
grams for persons with
disabilities 321–322
EMTALA. See Emergency
Treatment and Active
Labor Act
end-of-life care. See death
and dying
Equal Employment Op-
portunities Commission
(EEOC) 263, 272–275
ADA 271–272
filing complaint with
272–273, 279
investigation process of
273–275
laws enforced by 272
phone number of 273
ERISA
amendments of 285
benefits plans require-
ments 294–297
benefit changes
295–296
claims
appeal of 290,
291–292
filing procedure
290

history of 284–285
HMOs and 109–110
information and disclo-
sure requirements
290–291
payout options in
288–289
rights of participation
285–287
service breaks and
287–288
termination of plans
292–294
vesting rules in 287–288
errors, medical, prevention
of 20–21
estate(s)
definition of 229
income tax on 257, 258
probate 251
taxable 250–251
estate planning. *See* trust(s);
will(s)
estate taxes 249–252
annual exclusion
251–252
changes in 249–250
lifetime exclusion
251–253
marital deduction 252
recent changes in
243–244
state 250
taxable estate 250–251
wills and 231–232
ethics
of assisted suicide
180–181, 182, 183–185
doctor's conflict of
interest 118
of Medicaid planning
127, 137
of refusal of treatment
177–178
of requiring doctors to
treat 161
withdrawing *vs.* with-
holding of life support
162
euthanasia
definition of 180

ethics of 180–181, 182,
183–185
nations tolerating 186
in Netherlands 184–186
Oregon Death with Dig-
nity Act 181–183
state law on 181
Supreme Court on
183–185, 187
vs. end-of-life care
187–188
vs. right to die 27, 180
excess shelter allowance
128
executor, of will 230
as witness 239
experimental procedures
15, 19, 23

F

fact finding, definition of
277
Fair Employment Practice
Agencies (FEPAs) 278
Fair Hearing, in appealing
denial of coverage 80, 82,
136
Fair Housing Act 212
complaint process under
339–340
protections under
337–339
Family and Medical Leave
Act (FMLA) 35, 279–282
eligible occasions for
leave 279–280,
280–281
eligible workers 280–281
enforcement of
281–282
filing complaints under
282
health care benefits and
280, 296
information sources on
371
teachers and 281
family caregiving *xxii,*
34–35
support programs for
34–35

family consent laws 24,
176–178
organ donation and
179
family partnership 253
family status, discrimination based on 338–339
Fannie Mae (Federal
National Mortgage Asso-
ciation) 150
federal court, Medicare
appeals and 80, 83–84
federal government
assisted suicide and 182
help with complaints
from 358
Nursing Home Com-
pare website 45
regulation of doctors
and hospitals 17
services and entitle-
ments for persons
with disabilities
205–206, 207, 208
spending, for home and
community health
care 29, 30
Federal Housing Adminis-
tration (FHA) 146
federal law. *See also* law
insurance regulation
86, 93, 95, 96–98
patient's bill of rights
13
Federal National Mortgage
Association (Fannie Mae)
150
Federal Trade Commission
150
fee-for-service coverage 86
fee-for-service facilities 345
FEPAs. *See* Fair Employ-
ment Practice Agencies
FHA. *See* Federal Housing
Administration
financial abuse and neglect
of elderly 225
financing. *See* paying
Fitch Ratings 92, 139
5 Wishes 170–171
flexible plans 99

FMLA. *See* Family and Medical Leave Act
401(k) plans
  defined contribution plans 284
  distributions from 297–298
403(b) plans, distributions from 297–298

G

general bequests 229
geriatric care management 38–39
gift taxes 231–232, 249–252
  annual exclusion 251–252
  changes in 249–250
  lifetime exclusion 251–253
  marital deduction 252
  Medicaid eligibility and 248
  purpose of 250
government. *See* federal government; state(s)
grandchildren
  bequests to 233–235
  education expenses of 252
  medical expenses of 252
Gray Panthers 361
guaranteed renewal policy 91
guarantees of payment, nursing homes and 47–48
guardianships 213–223
  adult, numbers of 213
  alternatives to 222–223
  dangers of 214–215
  guardians
    ad litem 220–221
    oversight of 221–222
    payment of 222
    powers assumed by 214–215, 217–218
    removal/withdrawal of 221
    role of 216–218

selection of 218–219
  training for 222
  health care proxies and 223
  hearing process for 219–221
  history of 214
  incapacity determination and 215–216
  issues in 214–215
  limited guardianships 218
  oversight of 221–222
  paternalism *vs.* autonomy in 214–215
  power of attorney and 194, 223
  property disposal and gifts in 218
  state regulation of 218–219, 223
  termination/revocation 221
  terminology of 215
  uses of 213
  vs. trusts 208

H

handicapped. *See* persons with disabilities, children with disabilities
health care
  decisions about, as basic right 18–19
  planning, help with 363–367
health care agent, appointment of 172–174
health care benefits, employee 294–297. *See also* health insurance
  changes in 295–296
  continuation of 91, 96–98, 295–296
  Family and Medical Leave Act and 280, 296
  history of 294
  for retirees 296–297
    from bankrupt firms 297

from out-of-business firms 296
  self-insuring 295
health care costs
  acceleration of 61
  efforts to control *xxii*
  for home and community health care 29
health care directives. *See* living wills
Health Care Financing Administration 64. *See also* Centers for Medicare and Medicaid Services
health care planning, help with 363–367
health care proxies 171–176
  appointing an agent in 172–174
  copies storage and distribution 176
  definition of 157
  5 Wishes and 170–171
  guardianships and 223
  legal formalities of 175–176
  with living will 171, 174–175
  nutrition/hydration and 174
  revocation of 176
  sample form 173
  state law on 172–174
  state-to-state validity of 175
  triggering of 172
health care spending, for home and community health care 29, 30
health care system 2–17. *See also* doctor(s); hospital(s)
  complaints against 17
  patient's bill of rights 13–16
health insurance 85–103. *See also* health care benefits, employee; Medicaid;

Medicare; Medicare sup-
plemental insurance
ADA requirements 271
benefits
  factors in 85
  laws governing 86
case management 88–89
claims 93–95
  denial of 94
    appeal of 89,
      94–95
continuation coverage
  91, 96–98
  right to 295–296
conversion coverage 91,
  97–98
copayments 88
customary and reason-
  able charges in 87–88,
  93–95
deductibles 88
denial of claims 94
  appeal of 89,
    94–95
eligible expenses in
  87–88
Family and Medical
  Leave Act and 280,
  296
flexible plans 99
job change and 91,
  96–98
medical savings
  accounts 98–99
policy terms and condi-
  tions 87–89
preexisting conditions
  and 86, 89–91
premiums
  increases in 91–92,
    95
  state subsidies for
    95
preventive care and 90
records, obtaining copy
  of 90–91
regulation of 86, 93, 95,
  96–98
renewability of 86,
  91–92
self-insured plans 93

soundness of insurance
  company 92–93
types of 85, 86–87
utilization review 88–89
waiting periods and
  89–91
Health Insurance Portability and Accountability Act
  (1997) [HIPAA] 8–9, 86,
  89–90, 91, 96
health maintenance organizations. *See* HMOs
Hebrew Home for the Aged
  (New York) 55
heir(s)
  definition of 228–229
  disinheriting 236–237
help
  with complaints
    from government
      agencies 358
    from in-house
      sources 357
    from lawyers
      cost of 360–361
      finding 360
      interviewing
        360–361
      need for 359
      value of 359–360
    from organizations
      358–359, 361
  with health care plan-
    ning 363–367
help-wanted ads, age dis-
  crimination and 266
Hill-Burton Act (1946) 12
HIPAA. *See* Health Insurance Portability and
  Accountability Act (1997)
hiring
  age discrimination and
    266
  Americans with Disabil-
    ities Act and 270–271
HMOs (health maintenance
  organizations)
  accountability of 13
  accreditation of 111
  appealing denial of cov-
    erage 109–110

businesses required to
  offer 108
coverage in 105
definition of 104–105
denial of coverage,
  appealing 109–110
doctor choice in 3
evaluating 111
fee structures of 9–10
impact of 105
lawsuits against 110
patient rights under
  109–110
purpose of 105
regulation of 105,
  109–110
utilization reviews 106
Hollywood codes 163
home and community
  health care 29–40
activities of daily living
  in 30–31
agencies and associa-
  tions for 365
complaints against 40
cost of 29, 30
doctor conflict of inter-
  est and 118
evaluation of 37–38
finding 36
funding cutbacks in 118
long-term care insur-
  ance and 140
Medicaid coverage for
  130
Medicare coverage for
  30, 39–40
  covered services
    116–117, 118
  denial of coverage,
    appeal of 118
  eligibility 116–117
need for 30–31
paying for 39–40
private care managers
  38–39
respite services 34
state and local assistance
  services 117
support programs for
  34–35

types of programs
31–36
home equity conversion
mortgages. *See* reverse
mortgages
home repair assistance 334,
372
homeowners. *See* housing
hospice services 33
history of 188
Medicare coverage of
119
hospital(s). *See also* emergency rooms
accreditation of 10–11
discharge from
appeal of 76, 77–78
discharge planning
programs 10
discharge planning
rights 76–77
nursing homes and
51–52, 77
doctor's affiliation with
4–5, 10
information sources on
10–11
legal responsibility for
doctors' actions 5
Medicare and, *See*
Medicare, Part A
nursing home slots and
51–52, 77
organization of 12–13
patient's bill of rights
13–16
post-release care,
Medicare coverage of
114–116
regulation of 16–17
requiring treatment
contrary to religious
beliefs 161
right to leave 25–26
right to remain in 26
right to treatment in
75, 76–77
selection of 10
types of 12
hospital-indemnity policies
87

hospital-surgical insurance
86
housing. *See also* adult living communities
age discrimination pro-
tections 337–342
ADA and 340–342
fair housing laws
complaint
process in
339–340
protections
under 337–339
interstate moves
336–337
owners
assistance programs
333–334
home repair assistance
334, 372
remaining in home 327,
328
sale leaseback
334–335
sale of home
335–336
tax relief for
333–334
utility bill assistance
334, 372
public housing 329–330
complaint process 342
no-fault evictions 332
persons with disabil-
ities and 330
right to remain in
328
Section 8 housing
330–332
Section 202 housing
330
standards for 331
zero tolerance drug
policy in 331–332
renters
lease cancellation
rights 328–329
rent increase limits
329
rental assistance pro-
grams 329–332

public housing
329–330
Section 8 hous-
ing 330–332
Section 202
housing 330
tax relief for 329
tenants' rights
328–329
state laws on 329
rights of persons with
disabilities to 211
sale leaseback 334–335
shared 332, 371
HUD. *See* Department of
Housing and Urban
Development
Hyatt Corporation 344
hydration and nutrition
instructions
health care proxies and
174
in living wills 162

I

IADLs. *See* instrumental
activities of daily living
IDEA. *See* Individuals with
Disabilities Education
Act
identity theft, protection
against 325
illness
catastrophic, patient
wishes and 7
chronic, home health
care and 29
information sources on
7–8
terminal, *See* death and
dying
immigrants, Medicaid eligibility 124
incapacity
definition of 215–216
determination of inca-
pacity 216
guardianships for, *See*
guardianships
informed consent and
22, 24

legal documents and 198
spouses, providing for 232
income caps, in Medicaid 124
income limits, in Social Security 308–309
income of spouse, Medicaid protections for 128–129
income tax 255–259
  accelerated benefits and 248, 257
  credits for elderly and persons with disabilities 259
  deductions
    for dependent support 258–259
    standard 258
  on estates 257, 258
  long-term care insurance and 257
  on Social Security benefits 255–256
  on trusts 257, 258
  viatical settlements and 257
individualized education programs (IEPs) 210, 211
individual retirement accounts. See IRA accounts
Individuals with Disabilities Education Act (IDEA) 210
inflation protection, in long-term care insurance 141
informed consent 20–23
  adequate information for 20–21
  emergencies and 22
  incapacitated persons and 22, 24
  legal requirements for 21–23
  notification requirements for 25
  and Patient Self-Determination Act 24–26

research studies and 15, 19, 23
inheritance, renouncing of 242–244
inheritance taxes, state 230, 250
Institute for Social Research 268
Institute of Medicine 21, 188
institutional review boards (IRBs) 23
instructional directives. See living wills
instrumental activities of daily living (IADLs) 30–31
insurance. See health insurance; life insurance
insurance companies
  complaints against, filing 95
  doctor's fees limits of 10
  evaluating soundness of 92–93, 139
  information sources on 367
  medical underwriting by 90
  second opinions and 7, 21
integration of benefits 289
intermediaries, Medicare 64
Internet, and personal information security 9
inter vivos trust. See living trusts
intestacy, distributees in 241–242
in trust for (ITF) accounts
  estate taxes and 251
  minors and 235
investment shelters, and taxes on Social Security 256
IRA accounts 297–302
  beneficiary designation 231, 298

distributions
  distribution period, table 299
  IRS reporting of 302
  life expectancy, table 300
  required minimum 297–298
  spouse rollover of 298–302
IRBs. See institutional review boards
irrevocable trusts 132–133, 202
  SSI benefits and 319
ITF ("in trust for") accounts
  estate taxes and 251
  minors and 235

J

Jewish Home and Hospital for the Aged (JHHA) 51, 366
job change, health insurance and 91, 96–98
Johnson, Lyndon 62, 120
joint accounts 202–203
joint-and-survivor pensions 287, 288, 289–290
  benefits protection for 293
  divorce and 290
Joint Commission on Accreditation of Healthcare Organizations 10–11, 37, 111
Joint Life and Last Survivor Expectancy Table 297
joint ownership, pros and cons of 237–238

K

Kevorkian, Jack 181, 186

L

Last Acts 188
lawyer(s)
  cost of 360–361
  finding 360
  interviewing 360–361

legal assistance sources 358–361

need for 359

in adult living community selection 346, 347, 349

in discrimination complaint 278, 279

in end-of-life rights enforcement 28, 189

in Medicaid disputes 136

in Medicaid planning 16, 332, 337

in pension claim appeals 292

for reverse mortgages 256

in tax planning 247

in trust creation 207, 253, 254, 319

in will preparation 231, 240

value of 359–360

lease cancellation rights 328–329

least restrictive environment 210

legal capacity, legal documents and 198

legatee(s)

deceased 229

definition of 228–229

letters testamentary 230

licensing

of adult living communities 354

of home care agencies 37

of nursing homes 43

life-care facilities 345

life estates, Medicaid and 135

life expectancy, calculation of 297–298

life insurance

accelerated death benefits 152–153

tax issues 248, 257

beneficiaries

designation of 231

minors as 235

for funding long-term care 152–153

purchased from charitable remainder trust 254

taxes and 254

life insurance trusts 254

life planning

importance of 155

information sources on 368–370

life-sustaining technology, information on 364

lifetime exclusion 251–253

LIHEAP. See Low Income Home Energy Assistance Program

limited guardianships 218

living benefits 152–153

living trusts 202

pros and cons of 245

wills with 245

living wills 157–169

definition of 157

demands for treatment in 160–161

5 Wishes and 170–171

guardianships and 223

with health care proxy 171, 174–175

help with preparing 168, 170

instructions in 160

legal formalities of 167–168

nutrition and hydration instructions 162

oral statements as 165, 168

physician responsibility and liability 164–165

pregnant women and 161

purpose of 157–158

religion and 161

revocation of 169

right to 14

sample form 166–167

state laws on 158–159, 161, 165–169

triggering of 158–159, 167–168

LM. v. Olmstead 35, 206

long-term care. See also home and community health care; nursing home(s)

cost of 113

financing of

annuities 151–152

life insurance 152–153

long-term care insurance 138–144

Medicaid and 120–137

Medicare and 113–119

reverse mortgages 145–150

need for, projected xxii

long-term care insurance 138–144

as adult community entrance requirement 352

benefits level 140–141

benefits period 138, 141

conditions covered in 140

cost of 139, 141

deductible period 140–141

evaluating 139–142

group policies 141–142

home care benefits in 140

income tax and 257

inflation protection in 141

level of care in 139–140

major sellers of 139

post-claim underwriting in 140

premium waiver feature 141

public-private partnership policies 142–144

future of 143–144

purchasing additional
coverage 141
purpose and uses of 138
renewability of 141
restrictions on coverage
140
state partnerships
367–368
triggering event 140
long-term care ombudsman
42, 56–57, 58, 227
look-back period
for Medicaid
individuals 129–131
trusts 133
for SSI 318
lottery winnings, Social
Security and 309
Low Income Home Energy
Assistance Program
(LIHEAP) 334

M

Maimonides 23
malpractice claims
data on 5
determining validity of
17
for informed consent
breech 21
managed care. *See also*
HMOs; Medicare +
Choice
numbers enrolled in
104
standards and accredita-
tion 111
success of 104
types of 104–105
managed medical systems
105
M+C. *See* Medicare +
Choice (MAC)
Mantle, Mickey 179
marital deduction 252
TIP trusts and 254
marriage(s). *See also*
spouse(s)
multiple, wills and 233
prenuptial agreements
237

master trusts, for persons
with disabilities 209–210
Matter of Shah 137
maximum pension 288
mediation
definition of 276
of discrimination com-
plaints, right to sue
and 277
Medicaid
adult living communi-
ties and 344, 352
appealing decisions by
135–136
applying for 123
claims for recovery by
134–135
cost control efforts *xxii*
coverage under
121–122
appealing decisions
about 135–136
eligibility 123–124
annuities and
151–152
categorical needy
program 123
community spouse
resource allowance
125–128
disabilities and 130,
206, 207, 209, 210
exempt assets
124–125
for home care and
community ser-
vices 130
income caps 124
legal advice and 16,
332, 337
look-back period
129–131
for trusts 133
medically needy pro-
gram 124
renouncing of inher-
itance and 244
rental income and
332
reverse mortgages
and 150

spending down 122
spousal asset protec-
tions 125–128
spousal income pro-
tections 128–129
spousal right of
refusal and 127
taxes and 248–249
transfer of assets
to children with dis-
abilities 130
to individuals
127–128, 129–131
long-term care
insurance and
138, 141
to spouses 130
to trusts
131–134
trusts and 131–134,
202
future of 136–137
home care certification
program 37
home/community
health care and 30,
39–40
life estates and 135
long-term care under
120–137
need for 120, 122
and nursing homes
certification of 43
cost of 120
discrimination by
45, 46–47
waiving rights under
48
planning 122, 127, 137
public-private partner-
ship policies
142–144
recovery from estates
134–135
unskilled care and 120
Medicaid qualifying trusts
132–133
medical directives. *See* living wills
medical equipment copay-
ments 116

medical errors, prevention of 20–21

medical expenses, taxes and 252, 258–259

medical information
gaining access to 6–8

Medical Information Bureau 90–91

medically needy program (Medicaid) 124

medical records
access to 8
privacy and 8–9, 14–15, 54

medical savings accounts 98–99

medical treatment, complaints 17

medical underwriting, definition of 90

Medicare 62–84
adult living communities and 352
Alzheimer's disease and 69–70
appealing denial of coverage 77–84, 118
deadlines for 77–78, 80, 83–84
help with 84
benefit period 72
Buy-in Program 66–67
carriers 64
continuation coverage and 98
copayments 72–73
cost control efforts xxii
covered services 67–68
deductibles 72
doctor referrals from 7
doctor's fees limits 10, 73–75
eligibility for 63
enrollment
Part A 64–65
Part B 65–66
exclusions 68–69
financing of 62–63
help with 84
history of 62

home care certification 37

home/community health care under 30, 39–40
covered services 116–117, 118
denial of coverage, appeal of 118
eligibility 116–117
hospice services under 119
hospital costs and 75–77
appealing denial of coverage 77–84
deadlines for 77–78, 80, 83–84
help with 84
hot line 7, 56, 67, 358, 364
for fraud 366
intermediaries 64
long-term care and 113–119
medical equipment copayments 116
and nursing homes
certification of 43
eligibility 48, 68, 72
outpatient (ambulatory) care and 72–73

Part A
appealing denial of coverage 79–84
deadlines for 77–78, 80, 81, 83–84
help with 84
copayments 72
covered services 67
deductibles 72
enrollment in 64–65
hospital costs and 75–77
appealing denial of coverage 77–84
intermediaries for 64
premiums for 65

retroactive benefits 65

Part B
appealing denial of coverage 79–84
deadlines for 80, 81, 83–84
help with 84
carriers for 64
copayments 72
covered services 67–68
deductibles 72
doctor's fees and 73–75
enrollment 65–66
optional nature of 66
premium penalty in 66
premiums for 65, 66
prescription drugs and 70
retroactive benefits 66
participating doctors 73–74
finding 74–75
post-hospital care under covered services 114–115
eligibility 115–116
notices of noncoverage 115–116
prescription drugs and 70
private purchase of 65
reform proposals for 71
retroactive benefits
Part A 65
Part B 66
returning to 108
as secondary insurance 103
self-referral and 17
unskilled care and 63
website 68

Medicare + Choice (MAC)
appealing denial of coverage 110–111

assessing success of
111–112

coverage in 107, 108

definition of 106

denial of coverage,
appealing 110–111

enrolling in 106–107

leaving 108–109

rights of patients in
107–108

Medicare Appeals Council
80, 83

Medicare Buy-in Program
66–67

Medicare patients, requirement to treat 75

Medicare supplemental
insurance 99–103

guaranteed availability
of 100

help with 103

Medicare + Choice and
108

plans and plan options,
table 102

premiums 101

purpose of 87, 99–100

renewability of
102–103

required basic benefits
100–102

returning to 103

transferability of 103

value of 75

Medicare Survey Report 37

Medigap Hotline 103

Medigap insurance. See
Medicare supplemental
insurance

mental illness, and
informed consent 22

mercy killing. See euthanasia

MetLife 34

Miller trusts 124

minimum monthly mainte-
nance needs allowance
128–129

minor(s), bequests to 235

monthly income allowances
128–129

Moody's Investors Service
92, 139

mortmain statutes 237

N

National Academy of Elder
Law Attorneys 360

National Alliance for the
Mentally Ill 212

National Association of
Adult Day Services 37

National Association of
Insurance Commissioners
(NAIC) 95, 98, 139

National Association of
Professional Geriatric
Care Managers 39

National Center for Home
Equity Conversion 150

contact information
368

National Center on Elder
Abuse, contact informa-
tion 370

National Citizens' Coalition
for Nursing Home
Reform 45, 360

National Committee for
Quality Assurance (NCI)
111

National Council on the
Aging (NCO) 71

National Eldercare Locator
36, 42, 365

National Family Caregiver
Support Program 34–35

National Guardianship
Association 222

National Homecoming
Council 37, 38

National Institute for Aging
268

National Institute of Medicine 29

National Planned Lifetime
Assistance Network
212

National Practitioners Data
Bank 6

National Senior Citizen Law
Center 359

Natural Death Act (California) 169

neglect of elderly. See elder
abuse and neglect

negotiation, definition of
277

Netherlands, euthanasia in
184–186

New Deal 303

New York State Task Force
on Life and the Law 182

Nixon, Richard 158

No codes 163

nonparticipating doctors
73–74

notice of noncoverage

appealing 77–84

deadlines for 77–78,
83–84

help with 84

from hospital 77–78

from skilled nursing
facility 116

failure to receive 78,
115

nursing care, skilled,
Medicare eligibility and
114–116

nursing home(s) 41–59. See
also long-term care;
skilled nursing facility

admission to 46–47

alternatives to 42

autonomy and self-
determination in
53–55

bed holding and reser-
vations 51–52

complaints and griev-
ances 54, 57–58

cost of 61, 113

dental services in 50

deposit requirements
47–48

dietary services in 50

discrimination in
admission 45, 46–47

disruptive residents
52–53

elder abuse and neglect
in 56, 227

evaluation of 42, 43–45
extra service fees 48
finding 42, 44
hospital discharges and
  51–52, 77
lawsuits against 58–59
leave, right to 54
licensing and regulation
  of 43, 50, 56–57
likelihood of needing
  41
Medicaid and
  certification of 43
  cost of 120
  discrimination by
    45, 46–47
  waiving rights under
    48
Medicare and 43, 48,
  68, 72
payments and deposits
  47–48, 53
pharmacy services in 50
physical environment
  requirements 43–44,
  50
plan of care in 49
privacy rights in 53–54
quality of care in 41, 43,
  48–50
Reform Act of 1987
  45–46
restraints, physical and
  chemical 44, 50–51,
  227, 366
rights of residents 49,
  53–55, 227
  enforcement of
    57–59
screenings and assess-
  ments 49
services provided 42, 43
sex in 44, 55–56
staff requirements 50
therapy and rehabilita-
  tion services in 50
transfers and discharges
  52–53
visitors, right to 54
waiting lists 47

Nursing Home Compare
  website 45
Nursing Home Reform Act
  of 1987 45–46, 227
nutrition and hydration
  instructions
  health care proxies and
    174
  in living wills 162

O

obesity, under ADA
  271–272
O'Connor, Sandra Day 184
Older Americans Act of
  1965 (OAA)
  and community-based
    care 32
  grants from 36, 39
  legal and advocacy assis-
    tance provisions 358
  long-term care ombuds-
    man in 42, 58
Older Women's League
  (OWL) 361
older workers. *See* age discrimination, employment,
  Social Security
  Older Workers Benefits
    Protection Act (1991)
    266–267
Olmstead case 35, 206
ombudsman. *See* long-term
  care ombudsman; patient
  advocates
Onassis, Jacqueline 158
Open Society Institute 188
OPPS. *See* Outpatient Prospective Payment System
optionally renewable policy
  91
oral statements, as living
  wills 165, 168
ORBA '87. *See* Nursing
  Home Reform Act of 1987
Oregon Death with Dignity
  Act 181–183
organ and tissue donation
  178–180
  burial and 180
  family consent and 179

information sources on
  370
wills and 236
outpatient (ambulatory)
  care, Medicare and 72–73
Outpatient Prospective Payment System (OPPS)
  72–73

P

paid on death (POD) bonds
  estate taxes and 251
  minors and 235
pain management
  educating doctors in
    188
  law regarding 186–187
palliative care
  educating doctors in
    188
  law regarding 186–187
participating doctors
  73–74
  finding 74–75
Partnership for Caring
  26–27, 168, 169, 175, 189
patient(s)
  attitudes toward 2
  bill of rights for 13–15
    enforcement of 16
  ignoring wishes of 28
  rights of (*See also*
    informed consent)
    as basic right 18
    bill of rights 13–15
      enforcement of
        16
    to continue treat-
      ment 26–27, 75,
      76–77, 160–161
    to discharge plan-
      ning 76–77
    enforcement of 16,
      27–28
    history of 19
    under HMOs
      109–110
    to leave hospital
      25–26
    in Medicare +
      Choice 107–108

to refuse treatment
24, 54–55, 161 (*See
also Cruzan* deci-
sion)
to remain in hospital
26
right to die 26–27
wishes of, communicat-
ing to doctor 7
patient advocates 16, 28, 78
patient representatives 16,
78
Patient Self-Determination
Act (PSDA) 24–26, 161,
169
paying. *See also* health
insurance, Medicaid,
Medicare
for home and commu-
nity health care 39–40
for long-term care
annuities 151–152
life insurance
152–153
long-term care
insurance 138–144
Medicaid and
120–137
Medicare and
114–119
reverse mortgages
145–150
for prescription drugs
70–71
for unwanted treatment
165
Peer Review Organizations
(PROs). *See* Quality
Improvement Organiza-
tions
peer review process, definition of 277
penalty period 129–131
testamentary trusts and
133
Pension Benefit Guaranty
Corporation 285,
292–293, 294
pension plans
annuities bought by
294

benefits protection for
292–293
claims
appeal of 290,
291–292
filing procedure 290
as contractual obligation
283
defined benefits plans
284, 292
defined contribution
plans 284, 285, 293
early retirement and
307
information and disclo-
sure requirements
290–291
integration of benefits
289
job change and 288
payout options 288–289
public-sector 293
regulation of. *See*
Employment Retire-
ment Income Security
Act of 1974 (ERISA)
requirement to have
285
right to participate in
285–287
service breaks and
287–288
safety of 293–294
surviving spouses
divorce and 290
rights of 287,
289–290, 293
termination of
292–294, 294
underfunded 293–294
vesting rules 287–288
waiving right to 286
per capita bequests
233–234
per stirpes bequests
233–234
personal effects, in wills
235–236
personal representative, in
estate administration
230

pharmacy services, in nursing homes 50
physician(s). *See also* doc-
tor(s)
attending (voluntary)
4–5, 12–13
nursing home resi-
dents and 49
physician-assisted suicide
definition of 180
ethics of 180–181, 182,
183–185
nations tolerating 186
in Netherlands 184–186
Oregon Death with Dig-
nity Act 181–183
state law on 181
Supreme Court on
183–185, 187
vs. end-of-life care
187–188
vs. right to die 27, 180
planning
of health care, help with
363–367
life planning
importance of 155
information sources
on 368–370
for Medicaid
ethics of 127, 137
importance of 122
plan of care
for home care agencies
38
in nursing homes 49
POD (paid on death) bonds
estate taxes and 251
minors and 235
pooled trust 134
for persons with disabil-
ities 209–210
SSI benefits and 319
post-claim underwriting,
long-term care insurance
and 140
power of attorney 190–204
acknowledgment of,
assuring 199
agents, whom to
appoint 193, 194

copies and storage of
198
currency of 199
definition of 190–191
document for
requirements for
194
sample template of
195–197
durable
definition of 191
sample form
195–197
guardianships and 194,
223
for health care. *See*
health care proxies
importance of 190
legal capacity and 198
powers given by 193,
194
representative payees
204
revocation of 200
springing 192–193
state-to-state validity of
194–198
vs. health care proxies
172
PPOs. *See* preferred
provider organizations
preexisting conditions
definition of 89, 90
and health insurance
86, 89–91
long-term care insur-
ance and 140
preferred provider organizations (PPOs) 105
pregnant women, living
wills and 161
premium waiver feature, in
long-term care insurance
141
prenuptial agreements 237
preschool children with disabilities 211
prescription drugs
discounts for seniors 71
knowledge about,
importance of 7

Medicare and 70
medigap insurance and
101
out-of-pocket costs 70
palliative care law and
187
paying for 70–71
preventive care, health
insurance and 90
primary care providers, in
HMOs 105
primary care specialties 3
Privacy Act of 1974 325
privacy rights
medical records and
8–9, 14–15, 54
in nursing homes 53–54
right to 14
Social Security number
and 324–325
private care managers
38–39
probate 230
avoiding 245
probate estate 251
definition of 229
Project on Death in Amer-
ica 188
property management sys-
tems. *See also* power of
attorney; trust(s)
joint accounts 202–203
representative payee
204
property taxes
deferral of 333–334
reverse mortgages and
149
PROs (Peer Review Organi-
zations). *See* Quality
Improvement Organiza-
tions
protective services agencies
214
PSDA. *See* Patient Self-
Determination Act
psychological abuse and
neglect of elderly 225
publication, of will 239
Public Citizen's Health
Research Group 6, 17

contact information
364
*Public Employees' Retire-
ment System of Ohio* v.
Betts (1989) 266
public housing 329–330
complaint process 342
persons with disabilities
persons and 330
right to remain in 328
Section 8 housing
330–332
Section 202 housing
330
standards for 331
zero tolerance drug pol-
icy in 331–332
public-private partnership
long-term care policies
142–144
future of 143–144
public sector pensions 293
public services and accommodations, access for persons with disabilities
340–342

Q

QDOT. *See* qualified
domestic trust
QIOs. *See* Quality Improvement Organizations
QMB (Qualified Medicare
Beneficiary Program). *See*
Medicare Buy-in Pro-
gram
QPRTs. *See* qualified personal residence trusts
QTIP (qualified terminable
interest property) trusts
202, 254–255
qualified domestic trust
(QDOT) 252
Qualified Independent
Contractors (QICs) 79
Qualified Medicare Beneficiary Program (QMB).
See Medicare Buy-in Program
qualified personal residence
trusts (QPRTs) 253

qualified terminable interest property (QTIP) trusts 202, 254–255
Quality Improvement Organizations (QIOs) 76, 77–78, 81
Questionable Doctors databank 6
Quill, Timothy 181, 186

R

REA. *See* Retirement Equity Act
real estate transactions, power of attorney and 198
reciprocal recognition, power of attorney and 194–198
reconsideration of Medicare Part A claims 79–84
Reeves case 265
referrals, medical 3, 7, 364
refusal of treatment
  ethics of 177–178
  right to 24, 54–55, 161
  (*See also Cruzan* decision)
regulation. *See also* accreditation
  of adult living communities 353–354
  of doctors and hospitals 16–17
  of guardianships 218–219, 223
  of HMOs 105, 109–110
  of home care agencies 37
  of insurance industry 86, 93, 95, 96–98
  of nursing homes 43, 50, 56–57
  of pension plans, *See* Employment Retirement Income Security Act of 1974 (ERISA)
Rehabilitation Accreditation Commission 37
Rehabilitation Act of 1973 212, 330

religion
  living wills and 161
  right to die and 161
renouncing of inheritance 242–244
rental income, taxes and 332
renters
  lease cancellation rights 328–329
  rental assistance programs 329–332
    public housing 329–330
    Section 8 housing 330–332
    Section 202 housing 330
  rent increase limits 329
  tax relief for 329
  tenants' rights 328–329
    state laws on 329
representative payees 204
required minimum distributions, for retirement plans 297–298
research studies, informed consent and 15, 19, 23
residuary bequests 229
respite services 34
restraints, physical and chemical, in nursing homes 44, 50–51, 227, 366
retirement age
  for Social Security benefits 306
  working beyond. *See* older workers
retirement communities 343. *See also* adult living communities
Retirement Equity Act (REA) 284, 289
retirement funds, Medicaid eligibility and 126
retirement plans. *See* 401(k) plans; 403(b) plans; IRA accounts; pension plans
reverse mortgages
  absences from property and 149

  amount due on 148
  benefits and 150
  complaints about 150
  consumer rights 149
  co-op apartments and 147
  counseling on 148, 150
  finding 150
  for funding long-term care 145–150
  information sources on 368
  loan amounts 147
  payment options 148
  property taxes and 149
  qualifying for 147
  risks of 148–149, 150
  tax issues 248, 256
  types of 146–147
  uses and benefits of 145–146
review of Medicare Part B claims 79–84
revocable trusts 132, 202
rights
  of consumer, in reverse mortgages 149
  to die 26–27
    religion and 161
    vs. assisted suicide 27, 180
  to die with dignity 184
  of dying persons, enforcing 188–189
  of elderly, abuse of 225
  of election 236–237
  of nursing home residents 49, 53–55, 227
    enforcement of 57–59
  of patients (*See also* informed consent)
    as basic right 18
    bill of rights 13–15
    to continue treatment 26–27, 75, 76–77, 160–161
    to discharge planning 76–77
    enforcement of 16, 27–28

history of 19
under HMOs
109–110
to leave hospital
25–26
in Medicare +
Choice 107–108
to refuse treatment
24, 54–55, 161 (*See
also Cruzan* deci-
sion)
to remain in hospital
26
resistance to 19
right to die 26–27
of persons with disabil-
ities
to education
210–211
to housing 211
to public accommo-
dations 341–342
to public services
340–341
to telecommunications
342
to privacy
medical records and
8–9, 14–15, 54
in nursing homes
53–54
right to 14
Social Security num-
ber and 324–325
protection of 356–361
appeals 357–358
assertiveness in
356–357, 361
help with
from govern-
ment agencies
358
from in-house
sources 357
from lawyers
359–361
from organiza-
tions 358–359,
361
of refusal (in spousal
support) 127

to refuse treatment 24,
54–55, 161 (*See also
Cruzan* decision)
to rescission of reverse
mortgage 149
of tenants 328–329
of wards 217, 218, 220
Robert Wood Johnson
Foundation 33, 170, 188
Roosevelt, Franklin D. 306

S

safe deposit boxes, wills in
241
sale leaseback 334–335
sale of home 335–336
SCRIE. *See* Senior Citizens
Rent Increase Exemption
second opinions 7, 364
importance of 21
Section 8 housing 330–332
Section 504 (of Rehabilitation Act) 212, 330
Section 202 housing 330
self-insured health insurance 93
self-insuring benefits funds
295
self-referrals 17
self-settled trusts 132
senior centers, in commu-
nity-based care 32
Senior Citizens Freedom to
Work Act (2000) 308
Senior Citizens Rent
Increase Exemption
(SCRIE) 329
settlements, for persons
with disabilities, government entitlements and
208
sex, in nursing homes 44,
55–56
shared housing 332
Shared Housing Resource
Center, contact informa-
tion 371
Single Life Expectancy
Table 297, 298, 300–301
skilled nursing care
definition of 115

Medicare eligibility and
114–116
skilled nursing facility
(SNF), Medicare eligibility
and 115–116
Social Security
appealing decision by
322–324
confidentiality and 325
hot line for 320
legal referrals from 360
Social Security Appeals
Council 322–324
Social Security benefits
appealing decision on
322–324
creditor immunity of
324
disability insurance
312–316
application process
314–316
benefits 313
disability determina-
tion 313–316
appeal of 314, 316
disability reviews
316–317
eligibility 312–313
for family members
313
information sources
on 371
programs offering
312
future of 304
overpayments 311–312
representative payees for
204
retirement benefits
304–312
applying for 307
calculation of
304–306
deferring collection
of 308
divorce and 310
early retirement and
307, 310
eligibility 304

income limits and
308–309
income taxes on
255–256
investment income
and 308
overpayments
311–312
pension income and
308
for persons with dis-
abilities 206
prediction/estima-
tion of 305
retirement age for
306
retirement planning
and 283
spousal benefits
309–310
survivor benefits
310–311
vs. retirement
benefits 311
working past retire-
ment age and
308–309
spousal benefits
309–310
Supplemental Security
Income (SSI) 316–322
applying for 320
benefits under
316–317, 320–321
creditor immunity of
324
disability determina-
tion under 321
disability insurance
under 312
eligibility 317–318
transfer rules
318–319
for persons with dis-
abilities 205–206,
207, 209
purpose of 304
representative payees
for 204
state supplements to
320

Ticket to Work pro-
gram and 321–322
survivor benefits
310–311
switching between types
of 304–306
taxing of 309
Ticket to Work program
321–322
types of 304
Soros, George 188
Social Security number
324–325
specific bequests 229
spending down, for Medic-
aid eligibility 122
spouse(s)
in adult living commu-
nities
new spouse 353
transfer of spouse
349, 350, 351
bequests to 232–233
disabilities
ADA and 271
providing for 232
Social Security dis-
ability for 313
disinheriting 236–237
estate taxes and 232
gift taxes and 232
incapacitated, providing
for 232
as IRA beneficiary
minimum with-
drawals and 298
rollover 298–302
and Medicaid
asset protections
125–128
community spouse
resource allowance
125–128
annuities and
151–152
court-ordered
increases in
126
income protections
128–129
right of refusal 127

transfer of assets
130
pension plan rights of
287, 289–290, 293
divorce and 290
right of inheritance
236–237
Social Security benefits
for 309–310
springing power of attorney
192–193
SSI. *See* Supplemental Security Income
Standard and Poor's 92, 139
standard deductions, on
income tax 258
state(s)
affordable housing pro-
grams 329
Age Discrimination in
Employment Act and
265
Americans with Disabil-
ities Act and 268
doctor's fee restrictions
74
elder abuse and neglect
hot lines 386–388
estate taxes 250
Family and Medical
Leave Act and 282
help with complaints
from 358
home care assistance
services 117
inheritance taxes 230,
250
Medicaid and
application process
123
income allowances
and 128
restrictions 121–122
spending by 120
prescription drugs sub-
sidy programs 70
SSI supplementation by
320
state law
on adult living commu-
nities 353

age discrimination
protections 278
on assisted suicide
181–183, 187
doctor's fees limits 10
on elder abuse
223–224, 226
on emergency rooms
11–12
on family consent 177
on guardianships
218–219, 223
on health care proxies
172–174
on inheritance 229,
237, 238
on living wills 158–159,
161, 165–169
on nursing homes 47,
57, 58
on organ and tissue
donation 178
patient's bill of rights
13
on power of attorney
191, 198
on renouncing of
inheritance 244
on tenants' rights 329
state regulation
of doctors and hospi-
tals 16–17
of HMOs 105, 109
of insurance 93, 95,
96–97, 97–98
state taxes 259–260
on accelerated benefits
257
deduction for long-
term care insurance
premiums 257
homeowner tax relief
333–334
inheritance taxes 230,
250
renters relief programs
329
on viatical settlements
257
stop loss 88
substituted consent 22

substituted judgment doc-
trine 24, 177
suicide
assisted. *See* assisted
suicide
definition of 180
legal status of 186
supplemental needs trusts
132, 134, 202, 206–210
allowable purchases
209
alternatives to 208
operation of 208–210
SSI benefits and 319
trustee selections 208
Supplemental Security
Income (SSI) 316–322
applying for 320
benefits under
316–317, 320–321
creditor immunity of
324
disability determina-
tion under 321
disability insurance
under 312
eligibility 317–318
transfer rules
318–319
for persons with dis-
abilities 205–206,
207, 209
purpose of 304
representative payees
for 204
state supplements to
320
ticket to work program
and 321–322
Supreme Court, U.S.
on ADA 268
on age discrimination
265, 266
on Americans with Dis-
abilities Act 35, 206
on assisted suicide
183–185, 187
on HMO regulation
13, 109–110
on Medicaid income
allowances 128–129

on pain management
laws 184, 186–187
on right to refuse life
support 19, 24,
156–157, 159, 165,
167, 171
on zero tolerance drug
policies 332
surgery, second opinions
and 7, 364
surrogates. *See* family consent laws; health care
proxies
survivor benefits 310–311
Switzerland, euthanasia in
18

T

Task Force to Improve the
Care of Terminally Ill
Oregonians 182
taxable estate 250–251
Tax Act of 2001 249–250
sunset provision of
250
taxes. *See also* estate taxes;
gift taxes; income tax;
inheritance taxes; state
taxes
charitable donations
and 253–254
education expenses
252
homeowners and
333–334
home sale and
335–336
importance of under-
standing 247, 248
interstate moves and
336–337
joint ownership and
237–238
life insurance and 248,
254
living trusts and 245
Medicaid eligibility
and 248–249
medical expenses 252,
258–259

renouncing of inheritance and 242–244
rental income and 332
reverse mortgages and 248, 256
on Social Security benefits 309
tax-qualified long-term care plans 257
Tax Reform Act of 1986 (TRA) 285
telecommunications, access for persons with disabilities 342
tenants
    lease cancellation rights 328–329
    rent increase limits 329
    rental assistance programs 329–332
        public housing 329–330
        Section 8 housing 330–332
        Section 202 housing 330
    tax relief for 329
    tenants' rights 328–329
    state laws on 329
tenure plans 148
terminal illness. See death and dying
testamentary capacity 228, 238
testamentary trusts 244–245
    penalty period and 133
    uses of 202
testator(s) 228
therapeutic privilege 22
therapy and rehabilitation services, in nursing homes 50
third-party trusts 132
Ticket to Work program 321–322
tissue and organ donation 178–180
    burial and 180
    family consent and 179
    wills and 236

Totten trusts 203
TRA. See Tax Reform Act of 1986
transfer of assets, and Medicaid eligibility
    to child with disabilities 130
    to individuals 127–128, 129–131
    to spouses 130
    to trusts 131–134
transfer of spouse, in adult living communities 349, 350, 351
transfer to another hospital, rights regarding 11, 15, 26
transportation
    complaint process for 342
    persons with disabilities, rights to 340–341
treatment, unwanted, paying for 165
trust(s) 200–202
    beneficiaries of 201
    bypass 232, 253
    charitable 202
    charitable remainder 253–254
    constructive 208
    creation of 201
    credit shelter 253
    definition of 200, 244
    discretionary 132
    elements of 201
    income tax on 257, 258
    irrevocable 132–133, 202, 319
    lawyer needed for 207, 253, 254, 319
    life insurance 254
    living 202
        pros and cons of 245
        wills with 245
    master 209–210
    Medicaid eligibility and 131–134, 202
    Miller 124
    pooled 134

    for persons with disabilities 209–210
    SSI benefits and 319
    QDOT (qualified domestic) 252
    QPRTs (qualified personal residence) 253
    QTIP (qualified terminable interest property) 202, 254–255
    as retirement plan beneficiary 298, 302
    revocable 132, 202
    self-settled 132
    SSI eligibility and 319
    strategies for 253–255
    supplemental needs trusts 132, 134, 202, 206–210
        allowable purchases 209
        alternatives to 208
        operation of 208–210
        SSI benefits and 319
        trustee selections 208
    taxes and 245
    testamentary 244–245
        penalty period and 133
        uses of 202
    third-party 132
    Totten 203
    types of 131–133, 202, 244–245
    uses of 200–201, 202
    vs. guardianships 208
Truth in Lending Act, reverse mortgages and 149
2-for-1 rule 308

U

Uniform Anatomical Gift Act 178
uniform donor cards 178–180, 236
Uniform Gift to Minors Act 235

Uniform Lifetime Table 297, 299
Uniform Probate Code 192
Uniform Transfers to Minors Act 235
United Hospital Fund 34
United States Housing Act of 1937 329–330, 330
unskilled care
  Medicaid and 120
  Medicare and 63
unwanted treatment, paying for 165
utility bill assistance 334, 372
utilization reviews
  in health insurance 88–89
  in HMOs 106

V

vesting rules for pension plans 287–288
viatical settlements 152–153
  tax issues 257
voluntary physicians. *See* attending physicians
vouchers, in Section 8 program 330–331

W

waiting lists, in nursing homes 47
waiting periods, and health insurance 89–91
waiver of liability clauses 353
waiver programs 130
ward(s)
  definition of 215
  rights retained by 217, 218, 220
Weiss Ratings 92, 111, 139

welfare plans
  definition of 294
  ERISA requirements for 294–297
will(s) 228–244. *See also* living wills; testamentary trusts
  antilapse laws and 229
  benefits of 228
  bequests
    to charity 237
    to children and grandchildren 233–235
    general 229
    to minors 235
    per capita 233–234
      table 234
    per stirpes 233–234
      table 234
    by representation 233–234
      table 234
    residuary 229
    specific 229
    to spouses 232–233
  burial instructions in 236
  changes to 239–240
  children born after 237
  codicils 239–240
  community property states and 238
  copies of 239, 241
  deceased legatees 229
  disinheriting heirs 236–237
  domicile and 230
  dying without 241–242
  estate taxes and 231–232

executor of 230
  coexecutors 231
formal requirements 238–239
joint ownership and 237–238
legal advice for 231, 240
with living trusts 245
multiple marriages and 233
oral 238
personal effects in 235–236
power of attorney and 194
publication of 239
revocation of 241
storage of 241
terms and concepts 228–231
testamentary capacity 228, 238
witnesses 239
Winter, Edward 164
withdrawing *vs.* withholding of life support 162
witness(es), of wills 239
women
  burden of caretaking and *xxii,* 34
  and doctors, communicating with 6
  and nursing homes, likelihood of needing 41
  pregnant, living wills and 161

Z

zero tolerance drug policy, public housing and 331–332